MONETARY POLICY IN THE CONTEXT OF THE FINANCIAL CRISIS: NEW CHALLENGES AND LESSONS

International Symposia in Economic Theory and Econometrics

Series Editor: ***William A. Barnett***

Volume 15: *Modelling Our Future: Population Ageing, Social Security and Taxation*
Edited by Ann Harding and Anil Gupta

Volume 16: *Modelling Our Future: Population Ageing, Health and Aged Care*
Edited by Anil Gupta and Ann Harding

Volume 17: *Topics in Analytical Political Economy*
Edited by Melvin Hinich and William A. Barnett

Volume 18: *Functional Structure Inference*
Edited by William A. Barnett and Apostolos Serletis

Volume 19: *Challenges of the Muslim World: Present, Future and Past*
Edited by William W. Cooper and Piyu Yue

Volume 20: *Nonlinear Modeling of Economic and Financial Time-Series*
Edited by Fredj Jawadi and William A. Barnett

Volume 21: *The Collected Scientific Works of David Cass – Parts A–C*
Edited by Stephen Spear

Volume 22: *Recent Developments in Alternative Finance: Empirical Assessments and Economic Implications*
Edited by William A. Barnett and Fredj Jawadi

Volume 23: *Macroeconomic Analysis and International Finance*
Edited by Georgios P. Kouretas and Athanasios P. Papadopoulos

International Symposia in Economic Theory and Econometrics
Volume 24

MONETARY POLICY IN THE CONTEXT OF THE FINANCIAL CRISIS: NEW CHALLENGES AND LESSONS

EDITED BY

WILLIAM A. BARNETT
University of Kansas, Lawrence, KS, USA; Center for Financial Stability, New York, NY, USA

FREDJ JAWADI
University of Evry, Evry, France

Emerald

United Kingdom – North America – Japan
India – Malaysia – China

Emerald Group Publishing Limited
Howard House, Wagon Lane, Bingley BD16 1WA, UK

First edition 2015

British Library Cataloguing in Publication Data
A catalogue record for this book is available from the British Library

ISBN: 978-1-78441-780-2
ISSN: 1571-0386 (Series)

Contents

List of Contributors

Marcel Aloy, *Aix-Marseille Université and Aix-Marseille School of Economics (GREQAM & CNRS & EHESS), Aix-en-Provence Les Milles, France* (Ch. 12)

Tiziana Assenza, *Department of Economics and Finance, CLE, Università Cattolica del Sacro Cuore, Milano, Italy; Amsterdam School of Economics, CeNDEF, University of Amsterdam, Amsterdam, The Netherlands* (Ch. 13)

Mohamed Safouane Ben Aissa, *LAREQUAD & FSEGT, University of Tunis El Manar, Tunis, Tunisia* (Ch. 1)

Nidhaleddine Ben Cheikh, *ESSCA School of Management, Angers, France* (Ch. 5)

Michele Berardi, *School of Social Sciences, The University of Manchester, Manchester, UK* (Ch. 13)

Gilles Dufrénot, *Aix-Marseille Université and Aix-Marseille School of Economics (GREQAM & CNRS & EHESS), Banque de France, CEPII, Aix-en-Provence Les Milles, France* (Ch. 12)

Domenico Delli Gatti, *Department of Economics and Finance, CLE, Università Cattolica del Sacro Cuore, Milano, Italy* (Ch. 13)

Qiheng Han, *Department of Securities and Futures, Shanghai University of Finance and Economics, Shanghai, PR China* (Ch. 9)

Mohamed Kadria, *LAREQUAD & FSEGT, University of Tunis El Manar, Tunis, Tunisia* (Ch. 1)

Junqing Li, *Department of Economics, Nankai University, Tianjin, PR China* (Ch. 9)

Waël Louhichi, *ESSCA School of Management, Angers, France* (Ch. 5)

Nikolay Markov, *Pictet Asset Management, Geneva, Switzerland* (Chs. 7, 8)

Enrique Martínez-García, *Research Department, Federal Reserve Bank of Dallas, Dallas, TX, USA; Economics Department, Southern Methodist University, Dallas, TX, USA* (Ch. 4)

Iuliana Matei, *IESEG Paris and University Paris 1, Paris, France* (Ch. 3)

J. Huston McCulloch, *Department of Economics (Emeritus), Ohio State University, Columbus, OH, USA; FAS Economics Department (Adjunct), New York University, New York, NY, USA* (Ch. 11)

Nicolò Pecora, *Department of Economics and Social Science, Catholic University, Piacenza, Italy* (Ch. 14)

Christian R. Proaño, *Department of Economics, The New School for Social Research, New York, NY, USA; Macroeconomic Policy Institute (IMK), Düsseldorf, Germany* (Ch. 6)

Michel Roux, *Honorary Dean of the Faculty of Economic and Management Sciences, Université Paris 13 – Sorbonne Paris Cité, Paris, France* (Ch. 15)

Willi Semmler, *Department of Economics, The New School of Social Research, New York, NY, USA; Zentrum für Europäische Wirtschaftsforschung (ZEW), Mannheim, Germany* (Ch. 6)

Alessandro Spelta, *Department of Economics and Finance, Catholic University, Milano, Italy* (Ch. 14)

George A. Waters, *Department of Economics, Illinois State University, Normal, IL, USA* (Ch. 2)

Marcin Wolski, *European Investment Bank, Luxembourg; The Institute of Economic Sciences at the Polish Academy of Sciences, Warsaw, Poland* (Ch. 10)

Jianbo Zhang, *Department of Economics, University of Kansas, Lawrence, KS, USA* (Ch. 9)

Editorial Advisory Board Members

Introduction

For several decades, monetary policy has been one of the key economic policy tools used to stimulate economic activity and ensure its efficiency. However, its effectiveness has been at the center of economic debate for many years, with economists from competing schools of thought and paradigms remaining divided on the issue. Indeed, while, in the 19th century, the eminent economist, Ricardo (1817), argued for the centralized control of money creation in accordance with gold reserves, Tooke (1844) advocated more flexibility for money creation based on householders' needs. After the First World War, Germany and the United Kingdom, as a consequence of the Versailles Agreement, were marked by hyperinflations, generating severe challenges for monetary policy. During the post-Second World War period (1945–1970), an International Monetary System was created based on the Bretton-Woods agreement producing fixed exchange rates relative to the US dollar. Since the first oil shock of 1973, there was an explosion in the international financial and monetary systems, leading several central banks to conduct monetary policy with an implicit or explicit inflation target. Accordingly, central banks have controlled money supply via different policy instruments, such as reserve requirements, a central bank interest rate, credit controls, exchange rate interventions, and open market operations. Indeed, activation of any such instrument by the central bank is liable to affect interest rates and credit conditions, and thereby induce a change in banking behavior.

Monetary policy is conducted in most countries by central banks. Their main role is to regulate the money supply in order to achieve three objectives: (i) control inflation, (ii) promote economic growth, and (iii) attain full employment. Thus, central bank interventions enable the economic system to pursue standard aims associated with economic growth, full employment, and market equilibria.

In recent decades, most monetary policies have fallen into four categories: (i) policies that keeps the exchange rate unchanged (as often used by China), (ii) policies that target monetary aggregates, often indirectly through interest rates, (iii) policies that target inflation, and (iv) policies that target a linear combination individual targets, such as through the Taylor rule. The third has been widely used in the last decade with certain intended objectives, such as to help fix householders' expectations influencing inflation stable in the long run, while improving central bank transparency.

Since the 1980s, the inflation-targeting monetary policy has been widely advocated by policymakers and economists. The policy was adopted by several central banks and proved relatively successful during the well-known Great Moderation period. The Great Moderation was marked by a significant reduction in the volatility of macroeconomic variables, not only in the United States but in all the developed countries. This period was also marked by business cycle stabilization and crisis stabilization, resulting in an improved and stabilized economic structure.

But the Great Moderation induced firms to decrease capital holding and take greater private risk. Accordingly debt levels increased rapidly and substantially, while the risk premia required by investors was considerably reduced, reflecting over-confidence in the economy. This optimism was expressed in Lucas' (2003) affirmation in his 2003 presidential address to the American Economic Association, when he declared that the "*central problem of depression-prevention has been solved, for all practical purposes.*" The resulting risk excess induced a significant level of volatility excess for equites and real estate prices. However, as the asset prices were not explicitly targeted, the bubbles in financial and real estate markets escaped standard and conventional monetary policy rules.

The Great Moderation along with the associated excess risk taking came to an end in 2007 with the appearance of the subprime crisis. With the global financial crisis in 2008–2009 and the European debt crisis in 2010, major central banks cut their interest rates repeatedly to attenuate the effects of the crisis, to stimulate liquidity, and to minimize the risk of recession. Despite the activist policies and low-level interest rates, the year 2008 was market by a major credit crunch and a severe banking crisis.

Since 2007, with the effectiveness of conventional monetary policies being in question, several economists and policymakers have begun devising new tools and instruments for central banks, enabling them to switch to non-conventional monetary policies marked by new monetary instruments such as quantitative easing, credit easing, qualitative easing, and twisting of the interest rate yield curve. However, these changes have been complicated for at least three reasons. First, the coordination between central banks and national treasuries compromises the principle of central bank independence. Second, as the mandate differs among central banks, they have sequentially adopted uncoordinated non-conventional monetary policies, often following different programs at different times. Third, the lack of synchronization among central banks complicates the management of non-conventional monetary policy in an international framework. For example, the Fed began adopting non-conventional monetary policies in 2008, but the Bank of England and the ECB did not officially followed suit until 2011.

Furthermore, an analysis of the experience of non-conventional monetary policies generates at least two troublesome findings. On the one hand, analysis of the effects of non-conventional instruments shows that the resulting decreases in interest rates have not necessarily stimulate the credit markets, with the purchase of credit remaining weak. On the other hand, there is a major question about the appropriate date at which the non-conventional monetary policies should end with a return to normalcy. Furthermore, while non-conventional monetary policies may appear to be appropriate for developed countries, those policies might not be appropriate for emerging countries, such as China and Brazil, since such policies in those countries could promote high inflation and thereby generate risk of a currency war. These concerns have led some policymakers and governments to introduce new forms of capital taxes to control capital mobility between countries.

This volume presents a collection of chapters analyzing monetary policies and central bank actions in the context of the recent global financial crisis. The first part discusses standard monetary policies and inflation-targeting rules. Such approaches were useful in achieving two main objectives during the Great Moderation: namely, controlling inflation and accommodating economic growth. However, the end of the Great Moderation revealed the inadequacy of such monetary policies, which were compromised during the rapid rise of financial and credit markets. Speculative bubbles, revealing financial instability, led to a credit crunch, a global financial crisis, and deep economic recession for all the major economies. The second part of the book focuses on the non-conventional monetary policies recently introduced by several central banks. In particular, new monetary rules and variations on standard monetary rules are documented. Besides the well-known monetary policy targets of inflation, unemployment, and economic growth, these new rules often direct their focus on asset prices to moderate the development of financial markets and financial cycle volatility. The second part of the book also investigates the effects of non-conventional monetary policies on developed and emerging economies as well as issues concerning alternative finance.

The volume contains 15 chapters. The first four chapters focus on inflation-targeting policies and price/inflation dynamics. The book's first chapter, entitled "Adoption of Inflation Targeting and Economic Policies Performance in Emerging Countries: A Dynamic Treatment Effect Evaluation," co-authored by Mohamed Kadria (University of Tunis El Manar) and Mohamed Safouane Ben Aissa (University of Tunis El Manar), evaluates the effects of conventional monetary policy in emerging countries. In particular, it investigates the interactions between the well-known inflation-targeting monetary policy and the performance of other common economic policies, such as fiscal and exchange rate policies. The authors assess the effects of these policies on the budget deficit and exchange rate volatility. To this end, they use panel data for a sample of 34 economies over the period 1990–2010. The authors show that the inflation-targeting policy had a significant impact on reducing the budget deficit in the emerging countries that adopted that monetary policy tool. Its impact appears less convincing on exchange rate volatility.

Chapter 2, George A. Waters (Illinois State University) authored a chapter entitled "Careful Price Level Targeting," which also focuses on inflation targeting. In particular, the author examines a class of interest rate rules that respond to public expectations and several lagged variables. Using impulse response functions, he investigates the effects of interest rate change on outcome and price and discusses the sensitivity of optimal level commitment to the method of expectation formation. He concludes that policymakers should adjust price levels toward a target, but complete adjustment is neither necessary nor desirable.

Chapter 3 entitled "Are Price Dynamics Homogenous across Emerging Europe? Empirical Evidence from Panel Data" by Iuliana Matei (IESEG Paris), the author checks whether price dynamics are homogenous in 11 emerging European countries. Using dynamic panel estimation techniques over the period 2003–2013, she defines Germany as the benchmark reference to evaluate price convergence. Accordingly, she points to further evidence of heterogeneity across the emerging European members in terms of price speed convergence. This finding gives further insights into the difficulties associated with the conduct of monetary policy by the European Central Bank (ECB).

Chapter 4 entitled "The Global Component of Local Inflation: Revisiting the Empirical Content of the Global Slack Hypothesis with Bayesian Methods" by Enrique Martínez-García (Federal Reserve Bank of Dallas and Federal Reserve Bank of Dallas, Dallas, TX, USA and Southern Methodist University), focuses on the local inflation issue. Using the orthogonalization method developed by Aoki (1981) and Fukuda (1993) in a new open economy macro (NOEM) model, the author breaks down local inflation into a global component and an inflation differential component. Through the estimation of a full NOEM model, using the Bayesian method with data for the United States and an aggregate of its 38 largest trading partners over the period 1980–2011, the author shows that the strength of international spillovers through trade is reflected in the response of global inflation and its local inflation dynamics.

Chapter 5 features the study by Nidhaleddine Ben Cheikh (ESSCA School of Management) and Waël Louhichi (ESSCA School of

Management) entitled "Pass-Through of Exchange Rate Shocks to Prices in the Euro Area: Evidence from Pricing Chain Model," which focuses on the currency market in the context of active monetary policy. The authors analyze exchange rate pass-through shocks with different prices for 12 Euro area countries. Using vector error correction models and impulse response functions, they show that inflation level, inflation volatility, and exchange rate persistence are the main macroeconomic factors to influence pass-through. They also point to the considerable impact of exchange rate and import price shocks on inflation.

Financial risk and the conduct of monetary policy by the ECB are central issues in the next three chapters. Indeed, Chapter 6, entitled "Escape Routes from Sovereign Default Risk in the Euro Area" by Willi Semmler (The New School of Social Research) and Christian R. Proaño (The New School of Social Research), focuses on Sovereign default risk and its escape routes. Accordingly, the authors propose a theoretical model to evaluate endogenously the macroeconomic effects of a rise in the sovereign default risk and financial market stress. Their empirical investigation points to the usefulness of such a model to understand default and non-default environments, as well as recent financial turmoil episodes such as the US financial crisis and the EU sovereign debt crisis.

Chapter 7 entitled "Actual versus Perceived Taylor Rules: How Predictable Is the European Central Bank?" authored by Nikolay Markov (Picet Asset Management). This chapter investigates the predictability of the European monetary policy according to professional forecasters from a large investment bank. To analyze the forward-looking actual and perceived Taylor Rules for the European Central Bank, the author uses a newly constructed database for the period April 2000–November 2009. He provides evidence of efficient forecasting by professionals and suggests that there has been an increase in the ECB response to macroeconomic fundamentals through the long forecast. However, this responsiveness seems to have decreased, since the bankruptcy of Lehman Brothers.

Chapter 8 entitled "A Regime Switching Model for the European Central Bank" and is authored by Nikolay Markov (Picet Asset Management). The chapter studies the Taylor Rule for the European Central Bank using a switching model to investigate nonlinearities in the forward-looking policy reaction function. Interestingly, the author shows that the Taylor Rule is characterized through two regimes. While the Taylor Principle is satisfied in the first regime during which the ECB stabilized the economic outlook, the ECB made more aggressive cuts and put greater emphasis on stabilizing real output growth expectations in the second regime. The author also suggests that the ECB switched to a crisis regime after 2008 as the ECB focused on preventing a further decline in economic activity and securing the financial stability of the system.

After analyzing the context, conduct, and effects of well-known conventional monetary policy and inflation target rules in the first part of the book, the second part looks at new and recently implemented monetary rules. In particular, it is designed to: (i) compare recent monetary policies and their effects across regions, (ii) discuss the dimensions of non-conventional monetary policy, and (iii) debate the initial consequences of these new rules.

"International Trade Imbalance: The Amplification of Monetary Policy Effects through Financial Markets" is the subject of Chapter 9, authored by Qiheng Han (Shanghai University of Finance and Economics), Junqing Li (Nankai University), and Jianbo Zhang (University of Kansas). Using an uncertainty model with an infinite horizon based on a DSGE model, this chapter analyzes how financial development and monetary policy can affect international trade, capital flows, individual behavior, and welfare in two major countries: China and the United States. Accordingly, the author shows that heterogeneous monetary policies in capital markets have had a significant impact on trade imbalances between China and the United States. Indeed, differences in capital market development are the major contributing factors for trade and investment imbalance between countries. Furthermore, monetary policy seems to have a significant effect on trade balance, consumption, and investment. More explicitly, the United States adopts a policy of stabilizing nominal GDP, while China pegs the dollar. Thus, to restore the trade balance between these two countries, China and the United States need to coordinate their monetary policies. This is a difficult challenge in our turbulent times, however, and the Fed relies far more than China on non-conventional monetary policy.

In Chapter 10, Marcin Wolski (European Investment Bank) provides an interesting chapter entitled "Modern Monetary Rules: Any Role for Financial Targeting?" In a new-Keynesian model with the presence of banking activities, the author tests the properties of the standard and financial sector augmented Taylor Rule. In particular, he proposes an extension of the basic fully rational environment to take heterogeneous expectations into account. Accordingly, the author shows that the presence of the banking sector could change the determinacy structure of the equilibrium. However, benefits from extra financial targeting seem to be limited, perhaps as financial variables raise a number of possible measurement imperfections.

Chapter 11, entitled "The Taylor Rule, the Zero Lower Bound, and the Term Structure of Interest Rates" by J. Huston McCulloch (Ohio State University), also focuses on Taylor Rules. The author shows that the Taylor Rule zero lower bound can be solved by pegging interest rates on longer maturity bonds. Furthermore, the elimination of interest on excess reserves would help to restore the effectiveness of monetary policy.

In Chapter 12, entitled "A Comparison of the Fed's and ECB's Strategies during the Subprime Crisis," Marcel Aloy (Aix-Marseille University) and Gilles Dufrénot (Aix-Marseille University) offer an interesting comparative analysis of the monetary policies followed by the Fed and the European Central Bank (ECB) after the subprime crisis. Through a comprehensive comparative approach, the authors note a specific difference between the United States and Euro Area monetary policies associated with a structural problem of balance of payment disequilibria for the Eurozone countries. This difference justifies the intervention of the Fed but not the ECB in tackling the illiquidity challenges for the banking sector. Furthermore, while quantitative easing (QE) programs have been used in the United States since 2008 to exert downward pressure on the long-term interest rate, QE policies only began to be used by the ECB in 2013. In their study, the authors conducted a new survey on monetary policies following the subprime crisis in two major regions: the United States and the Euro Area.

"Was Bernanke Right? Targeting Asset Prices May Not Be a Good Idea After All" is the title of Chapter 13, co-authored by Tiziana Assenza (Catholic University of Milan), Michele Berardi (University of Manchester), and Domenico Delli Gatti (Catholic University of Milan). This chapter investigates whether asset price targeting is required and whether central banks should limit their rules to target price, or should instead extend them to ensure financial stability. Pursuing a specific modeling strategy that differs from Bernanke and Gertler, Gali, and Clarida's (1999) model, the authors point to the fact that inflation volatility is higher in asset price targeting and conclude that targeting asset prices may not be advantageous.

Nicolò Pecora (Catholic University of Piacenza) and Alessandro Spelta (Catholic University of Milano) co-authored Chapter 14 entitled "Shareholding Relationships and Financial Crisis: A Network Analysis." This chapter also focuses on the banking system in the context of the recent global financial crisis. In particular, the authors analyze the properties of the network structure underlying the shareholding relationships of the banking sector in the Euro area. Their analysis highlights the presence and the importance of banks in the financial system. Accordingly, while such a network structure is seemingly strong and robust during good times, the risk of bank distress during crises implies a degree of fragility for the whole financial system, making the intervention of the Central Bank necessary. Furthermore, in a bid to evaluate such a structure, the authors examine whether the single supervisory mechanism based on banks total assets, which was introduced by the ECB, is a good proxy to measure their systemic importance. Accordingly, they show that not all financial institutions with a high total asset value are systemically important. Such findings indicate ways to proceed towards a possible reform of the current global financial architecture to protect the interbank market from further risk of contagion.

Finally, the last chapter, entitled "Finance Otherwise: The End of Banks?" by Michel Roux (University of Paris 13), also focuses on the banking system following the global financial crisis. The author suggests revising banking systems to make them more responsible, to better control banking risk, and to improve the management of their operations, making it possible to attenuate losses and bankruptcies during turbulent times.

The book's chapters explore the properties of conventional and non-conventional monetary policies, the effects of the financial crisis, and the consequences of its main outcomes. The empirical findings provide evidence of a number of limitations of standard conventional monetary tools and policies. While alternative non-conventional monetary policies cover various types and forms of monetary tools, all of the chapters share a common emphasis on moderating risk and on the direct and indirect effects induced by these policies.

Overall, the research topics discussed in these chapters give a rapid overview of major areas of monetary policy controversies and open up areas for further research.

William A. Barnett
Fredj Jawadi
Editors

References

Aoki, M. (1981). *Dynamic analysis of open economies*. New York, NY: Academic Press.

Fukuda, S. (1993). Informational advantage, exogenous variability, and economic welfare: Can the informational advantage of the policymaker reduce welfare? *Journal of Macroeconomics*, *15*, 349–363.

Gertler, M., Gali, J., & Clarida, R. (1999). The science of monetary policy: A new Keynesian perspective. *Journal of Economic Literature,* American Economic Association, *37*(4), 1661–1707.

Lucas, R. E. (2003). Macroeconomic priorities. *The American Economic Review*, *93*(1), 1–14.

Ricardo, D. (1817). *On the principle of political economy and taxation* (1st ed.). London: John Murray.

Tooke, T. (1844). *An inquiry into the currency principle: The connection of the currency with prices and the expediency of a separation of issue from banking* (2nd ed.). London: Longman, Brown, Green, Longmans.

Acknowledgment

The editors would also like to thank the editorial advisory board members and the scientific committee members of the third International Symposium in Computational Economics and Finance (www.iscef.com, Paris, April, 10–12, 2014) for the quality of their feedback and their reports on these book chapters.

Chapter 1

Adoption of Inflation Targeting and Economic Policies Performance in Emerging Countries: A Dynamic Treatment Effect Evaluation

Mohamed Kadria and Mohamed Safouane Ben Aissa

LAREQUAD & FSEGT, University of Tunis El Manar, Tunis, Tunisia, e-mail: mohamed.kadria@gmail.com; safouane.benaissa@univmed.fr

Abstract

This chapter attempts to analyze mainly the interactions between the implementation of inflation targeting (IT) policy and performance in the conduct of economic policies (fiscal and exchange rate) in emerging countries. More precisely, empirical studies conducted in this chapter aim to apprehend the feedback effect of this strategy of monetary policy on the budget deficit and volatility of exchange rate performance. This said, we consider the institutional framework as endogenous to IT and analyze the response of authorities to the adoption of this monetary regime. To do this, the retained methodological path in this chapter is an empirical way, based on the econometrics of panel data. First, our contribution to the existing literature is to evaluate the time-varying treatment effect of IT's adoption on the budget deficit of emerging inflation targeters, using the propensity score matching approach. Our empirical analysis, conducted on a sample of 34 economies (13 IT and 21 non-IT economies) for the period from 1990 to 2010, show a significant impact of IT on the reduction of budget deficit in emerging countries having adopted this monetary policy framework. Therefore, we can say that the emerging government can benefit ex post and gradually from a decline in their public deficits. Retaining the same econometric approach and sample, we tried secondly to empirically examine whether the adoption of IT in emerging inflation targeters has been effectively translated by an increase in the nominal effective exchange rate volatility compared to non-IT countries. Our results show that this effect is

International Symposia in Economic Theory and Econometrics, Vol. 24
William A. Barnett and Fredj Jawadi (Editors)

ISSN: 1571-0386/doi: 10.1108/S1571-038620150000024002

decreasing and that this volatility is becoming less important after the shift to this monetary regime. We might suggest that this indirect and occasional intervention in the foreign exchange market can be made by fear of inflation rather than by fear of floating hence in most emerging countries that have adopted the IT strategy. Finally, we can say that our conclusions corroborate the literature of disciplining effects of IT regime on fiscal policy performance as well as the two controversial effects of IT on the nominal effective exchange rate volatility.

Keywords: inflation targeting, budget deficit, nominal effective exchange rate volatility, propensity score matching, time-varying treatment effect evaluation, emerging countries

JEL Classifications: C5, E4, E5, E6, F3, F4, H6

1. Introduction

Following in the footsteps of New Zealand that initiated the establishment of inflation targeting (IT) policy in 1990 and with reference to the macroeconomic performance realized under this monetary policy framework by industrialized countries, many emerging and development economies have chosen to explicitly target inflation over the medium term. Indeed, valuable theoretical studies (see, e.g., Bernanke, Laubach, Mishkin, & Posen, 1999; Bernanke & Mishkin, 1997; Svensson, 1997) were motivated by the common finding in many empirical studies (see, e.g., Gonçalves & Salles, 2008; Lin & Ye, 2009), for, the IT policy has helped emerging inflation targeters (thereafter ITers) to have a significant improvement in macroeconomic performance which is mainly measured through the behavior of inflation, output, and interest rates. It must be noted that the success of these countries toward the conduct of their forward IT policy must be accompanied by a pro-active management of institutional (the independence and transparency of the central bank), structural, and techniques dimensions.[1]

But by achieving relatively good performances under a climate of a non-total compliance of the preconditions for IT adoption, the first emerging countries that have implemented this strategy have led many economists, Carare, Schaechter, and et Stone (2002), to validate that the IT monetary

[1] Roger and Stone (2005), Batini and Laxton (2006), and others were more interested in the study of these factors in the successful application of the IT rule.

policy would be a good option for such countries since that they can quickly catch up their standard institutional efficiencies through the establishment of rigorous reforms. Then the question that arises from this observation is to know, at what extent the adoption of IT can be performed in respect for these prerequisites, especially those of fiscal discipline and flexibility of the exchange rate regime, even under the effect of the adoption of this monetary policy strategy. Precisely, the central point of this chapter was to study the "feedback" effect of the IT policy on institutional strengthening in emerging countries. Despite the relatively sufficient hindsight that we have henceforth in order to meet this goal, this field of institutional roles in post-adoption and the feedback effect of IT seems until today to mark a vacuum in the literature mainly attributed to the relative success of the IT policy. Hence it seemed essential to fill this empty little.

In recent decades, an extensive literature has focused on further analyzing the interactions that may exist between monetary and fiscal policies, mainly through the focus on the link between public deficit and inflation phenomenon. Amato and Gerlach (2002), Fischer, Sahay, and Vegh (2002), Vu (2004), Catao and Terrones (2005), Wimanda, Turner, and Hall (2011) argue that the high rate of inflation, observed especially in many developing countries, is associated with important deficits, mainly financed by seigniorage revenue. Alesina and Tabellini (1987), Obstfeld (1991), Jensen (1994), Van der Ploeg (1995), Van Aarle, Bonvenberg, and Raith (1995) and Minea, Tapsoba, and Villieu (2012) agree on the fact that if the central bank decides to grant significant weight in its loss function to the price stability objective, it will reduce seigniorage revenue and compel the State to increase tax revenues through tax mobilization effort.

But this monetary strategy requires (at least) theoretically the transition to a flexible exchange rate regime. This is one of the preconditions that is considered for some authors such as Masson, Savastano, and Sharma (1997) as essential to the adoption of IT. The importance of this prerequisite has been widely argued in the literature. Indeed, as suggested by the now famous Tinbergen Rule (1952), "economic policy with goals set must have at least as many instruments as targets." So when targeting simultaneously an official inflation and an implicit exchange rate target using the same instrument, the interest rate, a central bank may be facing what is common to call a conflict of objectives. Thus, if a central bank is led to focus on the external objective of the exchange rate at the expense of internal inflation target, and with no justification in terms of price stability cannot be advanced, this can eventually undermine the credibility of monetary policy and its ability to anchor inflation expectations (Lucotte, 2012). So we can expect that the emerging economies that have adopted IT are characterized by relatively greater exchange rate volatility than those pursuing an alternative monetary policy strategy of monetary aggregates targeting or others. However, we can notice, from the classification of the de facto flexibility degree of exchange of Reinhart and Rogoff (2004) as well as for Ghosh, Ostry, and Tsangarides (2011),[2] that few emerging countries met the precondition of exchange rate flexibility to their respective dates of IT's adoption. That being said these two classifications show that a lot of central banks seem to lead a policy of managed floating. So what reason(s) will explain the reluctance of these emerging ITers to let their currencies float freely? One of the main reasons which is usually advanced in the academic literature is the "fear of floating" of Calvo and Reinhart (2002). Indeed, most emerging countries are certainly characterized by a high level of debt in foreign currency and a relatively high degree of pass-through, hence their fear of currency depreciation (exchange rate depreciation). On the empirical front, a range of recent studies (see e.g., Aizenman, Hutchinson, & Noy, 2011; Ostry, Ghosh, & Chamon, 2012; Stone et al., 2009) have tried to emphasize on this "fear of floating" of emerging ITers. Therefore, we can situate the problem of this chapter at the intersection of the two fields of the empirical literature on IT previously explained: the literature on the role of economic and institutional prerequisites in the choice of monetary authorities to adopt IT (see e.g., Batini & Laxton, 2006; Levya, 2008; Lucotte, 2010; Samaryna & De Haan, 2011; Truman, 2003) and the literature related to the conduct of exchange rate policy in emerging ITers. This chapter therefore seeks to empirically test whether the adoption of IT in emerging ITers has effectively resulted in an increased volatility in the exchange rate, specifically nominal effective, compared to non-ITers.

The remainder of the chapter is organized as follows: Section 2 presents a brief literature review. Sections 3 and 4 describe, respectively, the data and the methodology. Section 5 discusses our econometric results. Section 6 concludes by highlighting the main policy implications of our empirical findings.

2. Literature Review

Recently, some empirical studies had an intense interest in verifying the theoretical link above-mentioned between the adoption of IT and the performance of fiscal policy indicators in emerging and developing countries. Indeed, works like that of Miles (2007), Tapsoba (2010) have sought to test whether the IT policy, as a monetary policy framework aimed at stabilizing the inflation especially in emerging countries, could act positively on fiscal

[2] These authors classify exchange regimes of 1–14, (of) more fixed to flexible.

discipline. First, Minea and Villieu (2008) and Minea et al. (2012) show that IT does produce an incentive for governments to improve institutional quality and this monetary strategy should encourage the government to reinforce its tax collection system and rationalize its public expenditures. Lucotte (2012) conducted an empirical analysis of 59 countries (40 non-ITers and 19 are ITers) over the period 1980–2009 via the method of propensity score matching. He concluded that on average, the adoption of IT, which involves strengthening the independence of the central bank and maintaining a low level of inflation, had a large and significant effect on the effort of tax revenue mobilization or collection. Second, few empirical works have sought to investigate the effect of the adoption of IT on budgetary discipline in terms of the budget deficit performance. Abo-Zaid and Tuzemen (2011), using data from developed and developing countries covering the period from 1980 to 2007, with an econometric specification inspired by Ball and Sheridan (2005) and by adopting the strategy of "Diff in-Diff," have come to the conclusion that the developed ITers were leading a more disciplined manner of their fiscal policy after the adoption of IT. Furthermore, improvements in budgetary imbalances in some developing ITers may be partly due to attempts of achieving the inflation target. They conclude that these imbalances are significantly improved when countries, especially developed, explicitly target inflation. Thus, the non-ITers will greatly benefit from adopting the IT policy. More recently, Kadria and Ben Aissa (2014) tried to examine whether the implementation of IT monetary policy and its discipline character allow reducing the budget deficit in emerging countries. To do this, they used the propensity score matching methodology to evaluate the treatment effect of IT on fiscal discipline, in terms of budget deficit performance, in emerging countries that have adopted this monetary policy framework. Their empirical analysis, conducted on a sample of 41 economies (20 IT and 21 non-IT economies) for the period from 1990 to 2010, shows that on average IT adoption has had a considerable and significant effect in reducing the budget deficit. The results are confirmed by the robustness tests and corroborate the literature of the disciplining effects of IT regime on the fiscal policy performance.

It must be noted, based on Brun, Chambas, and Guerineau (2008), that the fiscal effort is indirectly influenced by monetary policy. More precisely and to the extent that there exists for many taxes a time lag between the date of taxation and the date of tax collection by the state, the real value of tax revenue collected is eroded by inflation (Keynes–Tanzi–Oliveira effect). When inflation reaches high levels, this effect constitutes a constraint for the mobilization of fiscal resources. The contemporary fiscal policy can be constrained by the monetary policy of previous years. Moreover, the lag in effect of monetary policy contains vital information for the policy evaluation (Fang & Miller, 2011). Time lags, thus, play an important role in evaluating this policy and its interaction with the other policies. Hence, our contribution to the previous literature is then to evaluate the time-varying effect of the IT's adoption by emerging countries on their budgetary discipline in terms of reducing or mastering the budget deficit (*1st interaction*), using the dynamic PSM used by Fang and Miller (2011)[3] to take account of "the lag effect" and the time-varying effect of the IT's adoption on budget deficit performance in emerging countries and to stand out from the existing empirical literature while providing additional responses elements of economic policy.

In addition to solve the problem mentioned above in this chapter which consists of testing whether the adoption of IT in emerging economies has led to an increase in the volatility of the nominal effective exchange rate, we try to emphasize and refer to the earlier empirical studies that have examined this relationship. However, the theoretical debate on the issue remains open and ambiguous. In the following, we will do a sweep on some investigations and academic studies that have revealed a paradoxical or even negative relationship between the implementation of the IT policy and the volatility of the nominal (and/or real) effective exchange rate (see e.g., Ball & Reyes, 2008; Edwards, 2006; Pétursson, 2009; Pontines, 2013; Rose, 2007) among others, whom advanced the contrary (see e.g., Berganza & Broto, 2012; Gali & Monacelli, 2005).

Indeed, Edwards (2006) conducted a study in the context of developing and emerging countries in order to appreciate the impact of the adoption of IT and the floating exchange regime on conditional volatility of the nominal effective exchange rate, and this using the GARCH model. The results show that the conditional volatility of the exchange rate decreases with the transition to the IT regime while this volatility increases with the switching to a floating exchange rate regime, since the author discusses the flexible exchange condition preliminary to the adoption of IT in evaluating the effect of such monetary strategy. In addition, Edwards (2006) explains the found result, despite the coexistence of the two regimes, that IT positively affects the credibility of the central bank and makes the monetary policy more transparent and predictable thereby mitigating the unanticipated effects of external shocks. This does not eliminate the other explanations in this direction namely the "fear of floating" of Calvo and Reinhart (2002) or the fear of inflation of Nogueira and Leon-Ledesma (2009). In addition, Rose (2007), in the lineage of many economists, defends the idea that the management of exchange by some emerging economies is done in order to

[3] These authors have sought, through the PSM method but takes into account the duration (in terms of years), to assess the impact of the IT's adoption on inflation performance but assuming that this effect is not immediate.

achieve the inflation target and not in the purposes of maintaining the fixed parity of their currency. Indeed, Rose (2007) conducted a study on 45 industrial and developing countries for the period 1990M1–2005M12, and this by regressing the volatility of the exchange rate (nominal and real) to a dummy variable that reflects the adoption (or not) of IT and a set of control variables. The results arising from this study show essentially that the IT has a negative but not a significant (non-significant) impact on the nominal and real effective exchange rate volatility. In addition, the author argues that the occasional intervention in the FOREX under an IT regime is done in the context of inflation mastery. For their part, Ball and Reyes (2008) share the view above mentioned, considering that central banks in open economies must take into account, in addition to inflation, the exchange rate and this by fear of inflation. Indeed and while following, mostly, methodological traces of Calvo and Reinhart (2002), it appears from their study that the variability of the exchange rate is lower in the IT regime compared to floating exchange rate regimes, and the IT can be considered as an intermediate regime between fixed and floating regimes. In addition, Pétursson (2009) analyzed in his paper whether the adoption of IT affects the excessive volatility of the exchange rate, that is, the share of the exchange rate fluctuations not related to the fundamentals of the economy. To do this, Pétursson (2009) used an approach of "signal-extraction" within 44 countries. The empirical results show non-systematic relationship between IT and excessive volatility of the exchange rate. More precisely, the author tried to deepen its analysis by examining the effect of the IT policy in the member countries of the European Monetary Union (EMU). However, the results show that an economy member of the MU sees this excessive volatility reduced. At the same time, the results suggest that the adoption of IT does not by itself contribute to the excessive volatility of the exchange rate. Recently, Pontines (2013) examined empirically whether ITers have systematically an experience marked by high volatility of the exchange rate. Based on models of the treatment effect via the propensity score matching method (PSM) used in the same context by Lin (2010),[4] his analysis shows that the volatility of the nominal effective exchange rate and those real are lower in ITers than those that doesn't target inflation. More precisely, results suggest that developing ITers have lower nominal and real effective exchange rate volatility than non-ITers. However, industrialized IT countries are characterized by high volatility.

[4] In this lineage, Lin (2010), trying to empirically study "the international effects" of IT and using a variety of PSM methods, he could detect a strong relationship which shows that IT significantly increases the stability of the real and nominal exchange rate in developing countries.

But contrary to the results from previous work, Gali and Monacelli (2005) have argued that the IT regime, primarily aimed at stabilizing inflation, has an increased effect on the nominal exchange rate volatility compared to the fixed exchange rate regime, and this in the context of small open economies characterized by a certain rigidity of prices' adjustment. In turn, Berganza and Broto (2012) have empirically shown, based on a sample of panel data composed of 37 developing and emerging countries, that the implementation of IT has a positive impact on the exchange rate volatility given that exchange rate flexibility constitutes a prerequisite for the adoption of such monetary policy. Even more interesting, these authors showed that in order to reduce the volatility of exchange rates, the interventions of central bank on the Forex market are effective in ITers than non-ITers. This is due mainly, according to Berganza and Broto (2012), to the strengthening of the credibility of countries that have adopted IT as a new framework for conducting its monetary policy.

Our contribution to the previous literature is then to evaluate the effect of the adoption of IT in emerging countries on the performance of the conduct of their exchange rate policy in terms of the exchange rate volatility (*2nd interaction*), by using also the dynamic PSM used by Fang and Miller (2011) to take into account in this case the "lag effect" and the effect throughout the time of the IT's adoption on the nominal effective exchange rate volatility in emerging countries and stand out of the existing empirical literature (including recently Pontines, 2013) while providing elements of additional responses of economic policy. We have had the idea that the "switching" of emerging ITers toward a flexible exchange rate regime is not statistically instantaneous,[5] and build on the "time varying treatment effect" approach of Fang and Miller (2011) would highlight this gradualism.

3. Data and Stylized Facts

We start from a set of annual data, a heterogeneous sample of 34 emerging countries, 13 are ITers (treatment group) and 21 non-ITers (control group), covering the period between 1990 and 2010. We retain here all emerging countries that have pursued an IT regime in the treatment group except (to) the new targeters such as Ghana, Guatemala, Romania, Slovakia, Serbia, and Turkey that have adopted IT after 2005. In addition, our

[5] As already indicated above, few emerging ITers respect the precondition of exchange rate flexibility to their respective dates of IT adoption, and this from the classification of the de facto flexibility exchange degree of Reinhart and Rogoff (2004) and that of Ghosh et al. (2011).

Table 1: List of the Sample Countries with Dates of IT Adoption

IT countries	Full-fledged adoption	Non-IT countries	
Brazil	1999	Algeria	Pakistan
Chile	2000	Angola	Russia
Colombia	2000	Argentina	Senegal
Czech Republic	1998	Bulgaria	Singapore
Hungary	2001	China	Tunisia
Israel	1997	Côte d'Ivoire	Uruguay
Mexico	2001	Dominican Republic Egypt	Venezuela
Peru	2002	El Salvador	
Philippines	2002	Ecuador	
Poland	1999	India	
South Africa	2000	Malaysia	
South Korea	1998	Morocco	
Thailand	2000	Nigeria	

Source: Lin and Ye (2009) and Internet sites of central banks. Note that Slovakia abandoned the IT in 2009 and joined the euro area.

control group was selected relying on the criteria defined by Lin and Ye (2009), which is based on the level of economic development and the size of the country.[6] Table 1 shows the full sample of countries selected for this study, as well as the respective adoption dates for the ITers.

To examine in a preliminary manner whether the adoption of the IT policy has reduced the public deficit or allowed to increase (or not) the nominal effective exchange rate volatility in the emerging ITers, we identified two key variables namely the budget deficit or budgetary imbalance (% of GDP) which corresponds to a negative public sector balance. It must be noted that the fiscal balance is calculated as follows: the state revenue (including grants) minus expense, minus net acquisition of non-financial assets and the nominal effective exchange rate volatility, which refers to the work of Rose (2007) and others, as an indicator of unconditional volatility of the exchange rate. It is constructed by calculating the annual standard deviation of monthly variations' rates of nominal effective exchange rate. The data were obtained through various sources. The other variables so called "conditional" will be presented in the fourth subsection, after the explanation of the methodology of the work, noting that the definitions/sources of all variables and the descriptive statistics are in the appendices.

[6] Given these two criteria, the authors do not include in the control group that countries with a GDP/capita at least as high as the poorest targeting country and having a population at least as important as the least populated targeting country.

On one hand, Figures A.1a and A.1b provide, respectively, the average public deficit in emerging ITers before and after the adoption of IT as well as the time-varying of their average budget deficit, since the date of IT's adoption[7] (PD0) and for four consecutive years (either PD1, …, 4) as well as the level at the end (date) of the study period (PD2010). Two results emerge from these figures. Firstly, we note that the average budget deficit (% of GDP) was reduced at the emerging ITers after the application of IT, below 0.37%. Secondly and more interesting, we find that there has been no improvement in the fiscal balance in emerging countries after one year of its adoption and, more specifically, there have been an average slight deterioration of 0.6 percentage points. But from the second year following their adoption, we note that the level of the average budget deficit gets better over time attenuating low levels that can go up to (−1.56%) and (−1.82%), respectively, in the fourth year of adoption and the last year 2010. Therefore, we can appreciate, statistically, the effect of the IT adoption on reducing the public deficit in emerging countries which have adopted this monetary policy framework and that this feedback effect is not immediate but rather comes with a delay of two years from the date of adoption. At this stage we cannot confirm whether this is the disciplining effect of IT on the performance of the budget deficit and/or the efficiency in the coordination between monetary and fiscal policy.

On the other hand, Figures A.2a and A.2b provide respectively the average nominal effective exchange rate volatility in emerging ITers and non-ITers as well as this average volatility in emerging ITers before and after the adoption of IT. Even more interesting, Figure A.2c gives us an idea about the time-varying of the average nominal effective exchange rate volatility only in emerging ITers, since the date of IT's adoption ($NEERV_0$) and for four consecutive years (either $NEERV_1, \ldots, {}_4$) as well as the level at the end date of the study period ($NEERV_{2010}$). These figures emerge three preliminary results. Firstly (see Figure A.2a), we observe that on average, the volatility of the nominal effective exchange rate is lower in emerging ITers than non-ITers, either 2.3% against 2.38%. An against-intuitive result since it is expected a priori that the followers of IT exhibit a higher average volatility of the exchange rate than non-ITers based on the fact that the adoption of IT requires, at least theoretically, a floating exchange rate regime. Secondly and more specifically (Figure A.2b), the average volatility of the nominal effective exchange rate was reduced at the level of emerging ITers after the application of IT, either 0.12%. This result gives

[7] The date of 1999 is taken as a period of demarcation and more specifically, it is about the average dates of IT's adoption in emerging economies (see, e.g., Coulibaly & Kempf, 2010).

us an idea that "may be" emerging ITers are managing their exchange rate and do not respect the pre-condition of strict floating exchange rate mentioned above, because of the fear of floating and/or inflation. Finally, Figure A.2c shows that the nominal effective exchange rate volatility has decreased during the first year of the adoption of IT but it increased, with a delay of two years from the date of adoption (i.e., a peak of 2.864), after moving to this monetary policy framework. But we are witnessing in the third period a continuous decrease with a low volatility point at the year 2010 (either 1.73) compared to year 1999 (either 2.598). We can then draw a preliminary result that the increased volatility of the nominal effective exchange rate in emerging countries following their adoption of IT strategy, that passes through the relative strengthening of the independence and credibility of central banks as well as the satisfaction of the exchange flexibility condition, is not immediate but happens with a delay. This effect looks natural and will take place after a twinning between the conduct of IT monetary policy and an occasional management of the exchange rate.

4. Methodology

In this section, indeed, we will try to define the econometric methodology (mentioned above) to be used in order to empirically test the impact of the adoption of the IT policy on the conduct of fiscal and exchange policies in emerging economies that have adopted this monetary policy framework, respectively, in terms of budget deficit performance and the nominal effective exchange rate volatility.

4.1. The Propensity Score Matching Method[8]

The principle of the PSM method consists of matching a treated observation with an untreated observation whose observable characteristics are comparable (and) considering the result Y_{i0} of the latter as the counterfactual of the treated observation. In other words, it accomplishes the matching of the ITers with the non-ITers that have the same observed

[8] This approach is initiated by Rubin (1977) and recently developed by Heckman, Ichimura, and Todd (1998) in the aim to solve the problem of selection on observables. That may be mentioned recent macroeconomic studies using this method such as Vega and Winkelried (2005), Lin and Ye (2007, 2009), Walsh (2009), De Mendonça and DeGuimarães eSouza (2012), etc. Note that this approach is widely used in micro-econometrics as well as in different areas such as health, education, etc.

characteristics, so that the difference between the result of a targeter and the matching counterfactual can be attributed to the treatment (the adoption of IT). In addition, the empirical validity of the PSM is based on two fundamental assumptions. The first is *the conditional independence* assumption which implies that conditional on a set of observable characteristics X_{it}, the results variables Y_0 and Y_1 are independent from the treatment variable IT_{it}. This assumption is expressed as follows:

$$(Y_0, Y_1 \perp \mathrm{IT}_{it} | X_{it}). \qquad (1)$$

We may thus write the Equation of the average treatment effect on the treated (ATT) as follows:

$$\mathrm{ATT} = E(Y_{i1} | \mathrm{IT}_i = 1, X_i) - E(Y_{i0} | \mathrm{IT}_i = 0, X_i). \qquad (2)$$

However, as shown by the theorem of Rosenbaum and Rubin (1983), compliance with the conditional independence assumption is essential because it allows to match the treated and untreated observations on the basis of their propensity score $P(X_{it})$, and not on all the conditioning variables as was the case with the matching method previously developed by Rubin (1977), in order to overcome the difficulty of matching X_{it} in the practical case, that the number of covariates in these variables tends to increase. This therefore means that

$$(Y_0, Y_1 \perp \mathrm{IT}_{it} | P(X_{it})) \text{ or else } (Y_0 \perp \mathrm{IT}_{it} | P(X_{it})). \qquad (3)$$

Thus, the propensity score, which in our study elucidate the probability for an emerging country i to adopt in year t an IT policy conditionally to the observable covariates X_{it}, and it can be noted:

$$P(X_i) = E[\mathrm{IT}_i | X_i] = \Pr(\mathrm{IT}_i = 1 | X_i). \qquad (4)$$

The second hypothesis is the *common support* condition of propensity scores, whose importance for the application of PSM was emphasized by Heckman, Ichimura, and Todd (1998). This condition ensures the existence of some control countries comparable to each of the treated countries. Formally, the condition of common support can be written as

$$0 < p(X_{it}) < 1. \qquad (5)$$

Therefore, the ATT can be estimated as follows:

$$\mathrm{ATT} = E[Y_{i1} | \mathrm{IT}_i = 1, P(X_i)] - E[Y_{i0} | \mathrm{IT}_i = 0, P(X_i)]. \qquad (6)$$

4.2. The Time-Varying Treatment Effect

Using propensity score matching approach, the intertemporal average treatment effect on the treated (ATT_t) of every period at and after the adoption year of IT depends on the following equation:

$$ATT_t = 1/N_t * \Sigma_{i \in T \cap S_p}[Y_{it} - \Sigma_{j \in C} w(P_i, P_j)\, Y_{jt}], \quad (7)$$

where Y_i and Y_j equal the values of the public deficit or the nominal effective exchange rate volatility for countries i in the targeting group T and j in the control group C, respectively. P_i and P_j equal the predicted probabilities of adopting IT for countries i and j. N_t equals the number of treated units. The match for each treated unit $i \in T \cap S_p$ equals a weighted average of the outcomes of non-treated countries, S_p is the region of common support, and $w(P_i, P_j)$ equals the weight function.

In this study, t equals 0, 1, 2, 3, 4, denoting the adopting year[9] ($t=0$) and four years after ($t=1 \ldots 4$). We are also interested in the final year of our study period, $t = 2010$.

Moreover, the process of estimating the average treatment effect on the treated includes four steps referring in particular to Caliendo and Kopeinig (2008) and Khandker, Koolwal, and Samad (2010). Indeed, the first step consists of estimating the propensity scores[10] relying on the conditioning variables X_{it} retained (and) which will be described in the next section. Once the estimated propensity scores, we proceed to the determination of the area of the common support densities of the two groups of countries propensity scores (ITers and non-ITers) inside which will be calculated the ATT, (and) relying on the "Min-Max" technique developed by Dehejia and Wahba (1999) and detailed by Smith and Todd (2005). The third step is to estimate the ATT, specifically the average effect of the IT's adoption on the budget deficit (as a percentage of GDP) of economies that have adopted this monetary policy framework. To do this, we have chosen to retain three among four propensity score matching methods knowing that there are four types.[11] First, it refers to the estimator of N nearest neighbor (Nearest-neighbor matching) paired with replacement and consists of matching each treated or treatment observation with N control units (or the N non-treated observations) having the scores of the nearest propensity (we consider

[9] Recall that the average date of IT's adoption in emerging economies is 1999.

[10] According to Caliendo and Kopeinig (2008), the use of probit/logit models, where the treatment variable is a dichotomous variable, provides almost the same results.

[11] Nearest-neighbor matching, radius matching, local linear regression matching and kernel matching.

$N = 1$, $N = 2$, and $N = 3$). The second method is the Local linear regression matching (LLRM) developed by Heckman et al. (1998). Finally, we use the method of Kernel matching (Tricube[12]) which consists to retain all untreated units (non-ITers) (of retaining all the untreated units) belonging to the common support for the construction of the counterfactual; that is, where each observation being weighted untreated so decreasing in function of its distance to the considered treated observation. In other words, this method proposed by Heckman et al. (1998) allows matching a treatment unit (an ITer) to all control units (non-ITers) proportionally weighted in function of their proximity (in terms of propensity scores) to the treated unit. The last step is to calculate the standard deviation which allows the assessment of the statistical significance of the ATT using the bootstrap technique proposed by Lechner (2002) and detailed by Brownstone and Valletta (2001); noting that the retained number of replications is 1000 (see details in the note of Tables 4 and 5).

4.3. Treatment, Result, and Conditioning Variables

4.3.1. Treatment versus Outcome Variables

In our study, the treatment variable as it was already described above is the IT (IT_{it}). It is considered as a dummy variable, taking the value 1 if a country led an IT strategy during the considered year, and 0 if not. In addition, we have chosen to study the treatment variable (IT_FF) for "accomplished" adoption (fully fledged adoption), counter to the works of Levya (2008) and others who have considered two dates corresponding to a "partial" adoption and another "accomplished." These two dates may differ if a country does not meet all the criteria or prerequisites characterizing an IT policy. Concerning the outcome variables, we have retained for the first link the budget deficit (B_DEFICIT) as % of GDP and the nominal effective exchange rate volatility (NEERv) for the second link presented in the previous section.

4.3.2. The Conditioning Variables

Finally, the departure conditioning variables applied in our study to estimate the propensity scores and expected to affect both the outcome indicator and the treatment variable are seven or eight in number, thereby satisfying the conditional independence hypothesis developed in the methodology section. In fact, four of these variables refer to the institutional and

[12] There are others types of functions aside from tricube namely Gaussian, Epanechnikov, biweight, uniform.

economic preconditions theoretically required for the adoption of IT (see e.g., Batini & Laxton, 2006). These variables are the lagged inflation rate of one period[13] (INF_1), the rotation rate of Governors at the head of the central bank calculated by sub-periods of five years (TOR_5) as a reverse proxy of the monetary authority independence, the degree of de facto flexibility of the exchange rate (EXCH), and the domestic credit for the private sector to GDP ratio (CRED) measuring the level of financial development. We expect, on the basis of the literature results, a negative correlation between the probability of IT adoption and inflation, the rate of rotation variables, while the two other variables are supposed to act positively on this probability. In addition, following Lin and Ye (2007, 2009), we consider the degree of trade openness (OPEN) as a conditioning variable that reflects the "fear of floating,"[14] and which is measured by the sum of exports and imports as a percentage of GDP. We can therefore theoretically expect a negative effect of this variable on the probability of IT adoption. The sixth conditioning variable, according to Truman (2003), is the rate of real GDP per capita growth (GDPpc_G). We expect a negative effect for this variable on the probability of the IT adoption (Samaryna & De Haan, 2011; Truman, 2003), knowing that a high rate of real GDP per capita growth can be considered as the result of the macro-economic policies success, which does not necessarily imply an alternative framework of IT. The other conditioning variable that theoretically affect both IT_FF and B_DEFICIT or NEERv variables and whose objective is to satisfy the conditional independence assumption is the democracy indicator of polity IV (POLITY2). We expect that the democracy indicator has a positive effect on the probability of IT adoption. Finally, we add the total public debt as a percentage of GDP (PUB_DEBT) which affects both only IT_FF and B_DEFICIT variables. We expect that the public debt has a negative effect on the probability of IT adoption.

5. Results

5.1. Intertemporal Estimation of Propensity Scores

We estimate the propensity scores using a probit model[15] and the results of the probit estimates with time varying are presented in Tables 2 and 3

[13] The variable measuring the inflation rate is lagged one period in order to take account a possible endogeneity bias.
[14] See Calvo and Reinhart (2002).
[15] Logit model does not change the results significantly.

Table 2: Time-Varying Probit Estimates of Propensity Scores (1st Interaction)

IT_FF (1)	(t_0)	(t_1)	(t_2)	(t_3)	(t_4)	(t_{2010})
GDPpc_G	−0.012	0.374**	0.333**	0.292***	0.292***	0.292***
	(0.262)	(0.179)	(0.134)	(0.104)	(0.104)	(0.104)
INF_1	−0.478	−0.340**	−0.357***	−0.382***	−0.382***	−0.382***
	(0.350)	(0.159)	(0.108)	(0.099)	(0.099)	(0.099)
TOR_5	−5.606	1.881	0.492	0.830	0.830	0.830
	(6.376)	(3.235)	(2.016)	(1.984)	(1.984)	(1.984)
EXCH	1.985*	0.955***	0.880***	0.911***	0.911***	0.911***
	(1.193)	(0.376)	(0.255)	(0.240)	(0.240)	(0.240)
CRED	−0.166	−0.009	−0.008	−0.009	−0.009	−0.009
	(0.142)	(0.019)	(0.012)	(0.013)	(0.013)	(0.013)
OPEN	−0.029	−0.012	−0.009*	−0.010*	−0.010*	−0.010*
	(0.026)	(0.011)	(0.008)	(0.007)	(0.007)	(0.007)
PUB_DEBT	0.042	−0.008	−0.010	−0.017**	−0.017**	−0.017**
	(0.041)	(0.015)	(0.010)	(0.008)	(0.008)	(0.008)
POLITY2	3.927	0.853*	0.766***	0.885***	0.885***	0.885***
	(2.976)	(0.443)	(0.289)	(0.320)	(0.320)	(0.320)
No. of obs.	122	141	164	189	189	189
Pseudo-R^2	0.825	0.764	0.782	0.795	0.795	0.795

Note: Values in parentheses are standard deviations.
***, **, * represent, respectively, the statistical significance at threshold of 1%, 5%, and 10%.

Table 3: Time-Varying Probit Estimates of Propensity Scores (2nd Interaction)

IT_FF (1)	(t_0)	(t_1)	(t_2)	(t_3)	(t_4)	(t_{2010})
GDPpc_G	−0.011	0.092	0.063	0.147***	0.158***	0.163***
	(0.091)	(0.088)	(0.072)	(0.066)	(0.062)	(0.056)
INF_1	−0.157	−0.199***	−0.171***	−0.183***	−0.208***	−0.215***
	(0.099)	(0.077)	(0.057)	(0.051)	(0.049)	(0.044)
TOR_5	0.080	−2.195	−1.799	−1.584	−2.043***	−1.915**
	(1.809)	(1.522)	(1.135)	(1.009)	(0.924)	(0.882)
EXCH	0.120	0.286***	0.289***	0.329***	0.350***	0.375***
	(0.110)	(0.094)	(0.077)	(0.077)	(0.073)	(0.071)
CRED	0.000	0.011	0.002	0.000	0.000	−0.0003
	(0.011)	(0.009)	(0.007)	(0.006)	(0.006)	(0.006)
OPEN	−0.005	−0.015	−0.006	−0.005	−0.006***	−0.006
	(0.013)	(0.010)	(0.006)	(0.005)	(0.005)	(0.004)
POLITY2	0.995*	0.431*	0.406***	0.421***	0.453***	0.473*
	(0.541)	(0.229)	(0.161)	(0.142)	(0.134)	(0.124)
No. of obs.	213	241	270	299	328	357
Pseudo-R^2	0.469	0.555	0.558	0.590	0.627	0.650

Note: Values in parentheses are standard deviations.
***, **, * represent, respectively, the statistical significance at threshold of 1%, 5%, and 10%.

(where the considered endogenous variable is the accomplished adoption (IT_FF)). Table 2 shows that apart from the turnover rate of central bank governors and the domestic credit, the intertemporal estimated coefficients associated with the other retained conditioning variables such as GDPpc_G, INF_1, EXCH, OPEN, PUB_DEBT, and POLITY2 are statistically significant at 1%, 5%, and 10% especially from the second year of adoption and have the expected sign, except for the real GDP per capita growth. This result is nonetheless consistent with those found by Lin and Ye (2009). In addition, the explanatory power of the model is high, with an average pseudo-R^2 of McFadden equal to 79%.

Otherwise, Table 3 shows the intertemporal significance of POLITY2 at the 1% and 10% threshold and that of INF_1 and EXCH variables at the 1% threshold, except for the adoption year. In addition, the real GDP per capita growth rate is statistically significant at t_3, t_4, and t_{2010} (dates) and the OPEN variable is significant only in the fourth year of the IT adoption, at the threshold of 1%. From the fourth year and the year 2010, the TOR_5 variable becomes significant at the thresholds of 1% and 5%, respectively. We also note that apart from the domestic credit for the private sector to GDP ratio, the intertemporal estimated coefficients associated with the other retained conditioning variables are statistically significant at different periods and different thresholds and have the expected sign, except for the real GDP per capita growth. This result is nonetheless consistent with those found by Lin and Ye (2009). In addition, the explanatory power of the model is high, with an average pseudo-R^2 of McFadden equal to 57.5% (i.e., that continuously grow starting from the year of IT's adoption to attain 65% in the last period of our study).

5.2. The Results of Matching

Concerning the first link, the time-varying estimation results in different matching methods (which are shown in Table 4) are generally satisfactory and considerable enough to observe a significant impact of the IT adoption on reducing the budget deficits of economies having implemented this monetary policy framework. More precisely, we observe since the adoption year a significant yet a low impact of IT's adoption on reducing the budget deficit of these economies. This impact is on the order of 0.285 percentage points. But in the years following the adoption, we observe the same effect but on a larger scale that stabilizes in the medium term around 2.7% (in absolute value). This result emanating from the treatment effect study which is done in a dynamic mode seems very interesting. Indeed, the low performance in terms of reducing the public deficit in emerging economies during the early years following the adoption of IT is due in large part to a non-full compliance prerequisites considered as essential to the viability of

Table 4: Intertemporal Matching Estimates of Treatment Effect on the Budget Deficit (in % of GDP)

	Algorithms of matching				
	Nearest-neighbor matching			LLRM (Tricube)	Kernel matching (Tricube)
	$N=1$	$N=2$	$N=3$		
	IT_FF				
(2) ATT$_0$	**−0.285*****	**−0.658**	**–**	**−4.505**	**−0.337**
	(0.785)	(0.474)	(–)	(0.608)	(1.857)
(3) ATT$_1$	**−1.131**	**−1.593**	**−1.74****	**−2.063**	**−0.908**
	(1.145)	(1.398)	(1.504)	(84.243)	(1.194)
(4) ATT$_2$	**−1.691**	**−1.771**	**−1.947****	**−1.745**	**−1.794**
	(1.153)	(1.081)	(0.935)	(19.945)	(1.587)
(5) ATT$_3$	**−2.691****	**−2.345****	**−2.659*****	**−2.861**	**−3.035*****
	(1.178)	(1.043)	(0.929)	(3.045)	(1.138)
(6) ATT$_4$	**−2.691****	**−2.345****	**−2.659*****	**−2.861**	**−3.035****
	(1.155)	(0.940)	(0.974)	(2.763)	(1.475)
(7) ATT$_{2010}$	**−2.691*****	**−2.345****	**−2.659*****	**−2.861**	**−3.035*****
	(1.004)	(1.073)	(1.004)	(6.804)	(1.197)

Note: Bootstrapped standard errors on the basis of 1000 replications are in parentheses. Noting that one or more parameters could not be estimated in several bootstrap replicates. So standard-error estimates include only complete replications.
***, **, * represent, respectively, the statistical significance at threshold of 1%, 5%, and 10%.

IT, but this situation is changing over time with the strengthening of the economic and institutional conditions, it will have a significant effect in reducing the budget deficit. This result proves that emerging ITers are becoming more disciplined after the implementation of the IT strategy, which has been intensifying their efforts to collect tax revenue and/or expenditure rationalization, allowing the reduction of their budget deficits. This corroborates the theoretical and empirical literature review that puts in evidence the disciplining effect of the IT on the tax policy.

Concerning the second interaction between IT and the conduct of exchange policy and based on the time-varying estimation results for different matching methods (which are shown in Table 5), we observe starting from the adoption year a significant and positive impact of IT's adoption on the nominal effective exchange rate volatility in emerging economies having implemented this monetary policy framework. On average, this impact is on the order of 2.497 percentage points. After two years of the adoption, we observe the same effect but to a much less magnitude around 0.643%. But in the fourth year of the adoption and the last year 2010, we

Table 5: Intertemporal Matching Estimates of Treatment Effect on the Nominal Effective Exchange Rate Volatility

	Algorithms of matching				
	Nearest-neighbor matching			LLRM (Tricube)	Kernel matching (Tricube)
	$N=1$	$N=2$	$N=3$		
	IT_FF				
(2) ATT_0	**3.014**	**2.808*****	**2.403**	**2.187***	**2.089**
	(2.511)	(1.298)	(1.583)	(1.252)	(1.902)
(3) ATT_1	**−0.421**	**0.481**	**0.757**	**0.515**	**0.291**
	(1.273)	(1.308)	(1.071)	(0.920)	(1.049)
(4) ATT_2	**1.102**	**0.741**	**0.643***	**0.742**	**0.912**
	(0.952)	(0.702)	(0.763)	(0.639)	(0.823)
(5) ATT_3	**0.690**	**1.014**	**0.962**	**0.691**	**1.333**
	(1.245)	(1.101)	(1.042)	(0.779)	(1.068)
(6) ATT_4	**0.107**	**−1.049**	**−0.349***	**0.006**	**0.498**
	(0.988)	(0.936)	(1.239)	(0.801)	(0.654)
(7) ATT_{2010}	**0.022**	**−1.048**	**−0.343***	**0.018**	**0.462**
	(0.947)	(0.740)	(0.835)	(0.757)	(0.839)

Note: Bootstrapped standard errors on the basis of 1000 replications are in parentheses. Noting that one or more parameters could not be estimated in several bootstrap replicates. So standard-error estimates include only complete replications.
***, **, * represent, respectively, the statistical significance at threshold of 1%, 5%, and 10%.

notice a negative and significant effect around 0.35% of the IT's implementation on the nominal exchange rate volatility.

6. Conclusion and Policy Implications

In this chapter, we studied the dynamic interaction that may exist between the adoption of IT monetary policy and the conduct of fiscal and exchange policies, in terms of the public deficit the exchange rate volatility performance, in the case of emerging economies.

Taking inspiration from previous works having studied the disciplining effect of the IT on tax policy performance and using the propensity score matching approach, we could evaluate the time-varying treatment effect (the adoption of IT) on the budget deficit of ITers. Our estimation results show a low performance in terms of reducing the public deficit in emerging countries during the early years following the adoption of IT. Nevertheless, that situation is changing over time with the consolidation of the institutional and economic conditions; it will have a significant effect on reducing the budget deficit. This impact is on average in the order of 2.7 percentage points. In sum, the lag in effect of IT on public deficit performance proves shorter for emerging countries having adopted this monetary policy framework. As a result, we can say that the emerging government can benefit ex-post and gradually from a decline in their public deficits, and our conclusions corroborate the literature disciplining effect of IT on fiscal policy.

Furthermore, we tried to empirically examine whether the adoption of IT in emerging ITers has effectively translated by an increase in the nominal effective exchange rate volatility compared to non-IT countries. Inspired by the previous works having studied this link, while distinguishing itself in particular from those whose recent including Pontines (2013), and using the time-varying treatment effect approach used by Fang and Miller (2011), we were able to evaluate the intertemporal treatment effect of IT's adoption on the nominal effective exchange rate volatility of ITers. Our empirical analysis, show that this effect is decreasing and that this volatility is becoming less important after the switch to this monetary regime. More precisely, we can say that the first years following the adoption of IT are marked by a relatively increased nominal effective exchange rate volatility. But this situation is changing in the fourth year since it is clear that this effect is negative and significant. Having said that we could appreciate simultaneously the two controversial effects in the literature. So with the results emanating from this non-parametric approach that takes into account the effect of the treatment over the years, there has been a partial exchange management on the part of emerging ITers and therefore a downward volatility of their nominal effective exchange rate. Therefore, we can say that the emerging economies are convinced that the condition to achieve satisfying exchange rate flexibility may be fulfilled after the adoption of IT, and it is not considered as an indispensable prerequisite for the adoption of such monetary strategy. In other words, the combination of a disinflationary monetary policy and an occasional exchange rate management may not be cons-productive. To conclude, we might suggest, like Nogueira and Leon-Ledesma (2009), that the indirect and occasional interventions in the foreign exchange market are made by fear of inflation rather than by fear of floating in most emerging countries that have adopted the IT strategy.

The policy implications can manifest at three points. On one hand, the adoption of IT renders monetary authorities more independent toward the public authorities and does produce an incentive for governments to improve institutional quality, prompting the latter to reform their tax systems and therefore to perform their budget deficits. On the other hand, the adoption of IT renders monetary authorities more credible, thereby reducing the effects of unanticipated external shocks and therefore benefits a posteriori of less volatility in their exchange rates. Even more, it is true that having a flexible exchange regime is a precondition for the adoption of IT, but given the economic constraints of emerging countries, these economies can benefit from high flexibility of their exchange rates under the IT regime, with "softer" and occasional interventions in the foreign exchange market and when using the interest rate instrument rather than international reserves, and/or the establishment of new measures proposed in 2011 by the IMF called "macro-prudential" aiming to replace the traditional instruments of capital controls and prudential measures.

Acknowledgments

We are grateful to Jean-Paul Pollin (Laboratoire d'Economie d'Orléans -LEO-, France), Patrick Villieu (LEO), and Yannick Lucotte (LEO) for their helpful comments on an earlier draft of this chapter. Also, we thank the anonymous reviewers for improving this version.

References

Abbas, S. A., Belhocine, N., ElGanainy, A., & Horton, M. (2010). *A historical public debt database*. IMF Working Paper No. 10/245. Washington, DC.

Abo-Zaid, S., & Tuzemen, D. (2011). Inflation targeting: A three-decade perspective. *Journal of Policy Modeling*, *5940*(20), 621–645.

Aizenman, J., Hutchinson, M., & Noy, I. (2011). Inflation targeting and real exchange rates in emerging markets. *World Development*, *39*(5), 712–724.

Alesina, A., & Tabellini, G. (1987). Rules and discretion with noncoordinated monetary and fiscal policies. *Economic Inquiry*, *25*(4), 619–630.

Amato, J. D., & Gerlach, S. (2002). Inflation targeting in emerging market and transition economies: Lessons after a decade. *European Economic Review*, *46*, 781–790.

Ball, C., & Reyes, J. (2008). Inflation targeting or fear of floating in disguise: A broader perspective. *Journal of Macroeconomics*, *30*, 308–326.

Ball, L., & Sheridan, N. (2005). Does inflation targeting matter? In B. Bernanke & M. Woodford (Eds.), *The inflation targeting debate* (pp. 249–276). Chicago, IL: The University of Chicago Press.

Batini, N., & Laxton, D. (2006). *Under what conditions can inflation targeting be adopted? The experience of emerging markets*. Working Paper No. 406. Central Bank of Chile, Santiago.

Berganza, J. C., & Broto, C. (2012). Flexible inflation targets, forex interventions and exchange rate volatility in emerging countries. *Journal of International Money and Finance*, *31*, 428–444.

Bernanke, B., & Mishkin, F. (1997). Inflation targeting: A new framework of monetary policy? *Journal of Economic Perspectives*, *11*, 97–116.

Bernanke, B. S., Laubach, T., Mishkin, F. S., & Posen, A. S. (1999). *Inflation targeting: lessons from the international experience*. Princeton, NJ: Princeton University Press.

Brownstone, D., & Valletta, R. (2001). The bootstrap and multiple imputations: Harnessing increased computing power for improved statistical tests. *Journal of Economic Perspectives*, *15*(4), 129–141.

Brun, J.-F., Chambas, G., & Guerineau, S. (2008). *Aide et mobilisation fiscale dans les pays en développement*. CERDI, Etudes et Documents, E, 2008.12, p. 76.

Caliendo, M., & Kopeinig, S. (2008). Some practical guidance for the implementation of propensity score matching. *Journal of Economic Surveys*, *22*, 31–72.

Calvo, G., & Reinhart, C. (2002). Fear of floating. *The Quarterly Journal of Economics*, *117*(2), 379–408.

Carare, A., Schaechter, A., & Stone, M. (2002). *Establishing initial conditions in support of inflation targeting*. IMF Working Papers 02/102. International Monetary Fund, Washington, DC.

Catao, L. A. V., & Terrones, M. E. (2005). Fiscal deficits and inflation. *Journal of Monetary Economics*, *52*(3), 529–554.

Coulibaly, D., & Kempf, H. (2010). *Does inflation targeting decrease exchange rate pass through in emerging countries*? Document de travail No. 303, Banque de France.

Darvas, Z. (2012). *Real effective exchange for 178 countries: A new database*. Bruegel Working Paper No. 2012/06.

Dehejia, R., & Wahba, S. (1999). Causal effects in non-experimental studies: Re-evaluating the evaluation of training programs. *Journal of the American Statistical Association*, *94*, 1053–1062.

De Mendonça, H. F., & DeGuimarães eSouza, G. J. (2012). Is inflation targeting a good remedy to control inflation? *Journal of Development Economics*, *98*(2), 178–191.

Dreher, A., Sturm, J. E., & De Haan, J. (2008). Does high inflation cause central bankers to lose their job? Evidence based on a new dataset. *European Journal of Political Economy*, *24*, 778–787.

Edwards, S. (2006). *The relationship between exchanges rates and inflation targeters revisited*. NBER Working Paper No. 12163. National Bureau of Economic Research, Cambridge.

Fang, W., & Miller, S. (2011). The lag in effect of inflation targeting and policy evaluation. *Applied Economics Letters*, *18*(14), 1371–1375.

Fischer, S., Sahay, R., & Vegh, C. A. (2002). Modern hyper- and high inflations. *Journal of Economic Literature*, *40*(3), 837–880.

Gali, J., & Monacelli, T. (2005). Monetary policy and exchange rate volatility in a small open economy. *The Review of Economic Studies*, *72*(3), 707–734.

Ghosh, A., Ostry, J., & Tsangarides, G. (2011). *Exchange rate regimes and the stability of the International Monetary System*. IMF Occasional Paper No. 270, International Monetary Fund, Washington, DC.

Gonçalves, C., & Salles, J. (2008). Inflation targeting in emerging economies: What do the data say? *Journal of Development Economics*, *85*, 312–318.

Heckman, J. J., Ichimura, H., & Todd, P. (1998). Matching as an econometric evaluation estimator. *Review of Economic Studies*, *65*, 261–294.

Jensen, H. (1994). Loss of monetary discretion in a simple monetary policy game. *Journal of Economic Dynamics and control*, *18*(3–4), 763–779.

Kadria, M., & Ben Aissa, M. S. (2014). Implementation of inflation targeting and budget deficit performance in emerging countries: A treatment effect evaluation. *Journal of Applied Business Research*, *30*(4), 1077–1090.

Khandker, S. R., Koolwal, G. B., & Samad, H. A. (2010). *Handbook on impact evaluation: Quantitative methods and practices*. Washington, DC: The World Bank.

Lechner, M. (2002). Some practical issues in the evaluation of heterogenous labour market programmes by matching methods. *Journal of the Royal Statistical Society*, *165*(1), 59–82.

Levya, G. (2008). *The choice of inflation targeting*. Working Paper No. 475. Central Bank of Chile, Santiago.

Lin, S. (2010). On the international effects of inflation targeting. *Review of Economics and Statistics*, *92*(1), 195–199.

Lin, S., & Ye, H. (2007). Does inflation targeting really make a difference? Evaluating the treatment effect of inflation targeting in seven industrial countries. *Journal of Monetary Economics*, *54*, 2521–2533.

Lin, S., & Ye, H. (2009). Does inflation targeting make a difference in developing countries? *Journal of Development Economics*, *89*, 118–123, In: Brito, R.D. & Bystedt, B. (2010). Inflation targeting in emerging economies: Panel evidence. *Journal of Development Economics*, *91*, 200–201.

Lucotte, Y. (2010). The choice of adopting inflation targeting in emerging economies: Do domestic institutions matter? Document de recherche du LEO, No. 2010-29, Laboratoire d'Economie d'Orléans.

Lucotte, Y. (2012). Adoption of inflation targeting and tax revenue performance in emerging market economies: An empirical investigation. Economic Systems, *387*(20), 609–628.

Masson, P., Savastano, M. A., & Sharma, S. (1997). *The scope for inflation targeting in developing countries*. IMF Working Paper Nos. 97/130. International Monetary Fund, Washington, DC.

Miles, W. (2007). Do inflation targeting handcuffs restrain leviathan? Hard pegs vs. Inflation targets for fiscal discipline in emerging markets. *Applied Economics Letters*, *14*(9), 647–651.

Minea, A., Tapsoba, R., & Villieu, P. (2012). *Can inflation targeting promote institutional quality in developing countries?* Mimeo.

Minea, A., & Villieu, P. (2008). *Financial development, institutional quality and inflation targeting*. Unpublished paper.

Nogueira, R. P., & Leon-Ledesma, M. (2009). Fear of floating in Brazil: Did inflation targeting matter? *The North American Journal of Economics and Finance*, *20*(3), 255–266.

Obstfeld, M. (1991). *Dynamic seigniorage theory: An exploration*. Discussion Paper No. 519. Center for Economic Policy Research, London.

Ostry, J. D., Ghosh, A., & Chamon, M. (2012). *Two targets, two instruments: Monetary and exchange rate policies in emerging market economies*. IMF Staff Discussion Note 12/01. International Monetary Fund.

Pétursson, T. (2009). *Does inflation targeting lead to excessive exchange rate volatility?* Working Paper No. 43. Central Bank of Iceland.

Pontines, V. (2013). Inflation targeting and exchange rate volatility: A treatment effect regression approach. *International Economic Journal*, *27*(1), 25–39.

Reinhart, C. S., & Rogoff, K. S. (2004). The modern history of exchange rate arrangements: A reinterpretation. *The Quarterly Journal of Economics*, *119*, 1–48.

Roger, S., & Stone, M. (2005). *On target? The international experience with achieving inflation targets*. IMF Working Paper No. 05/163. Monetary and Financial Systems Department.

Rose, A. (2007). A stable international monetary system emerges: Inflation targeting is Bretton Woods, reversed. *Journal of International Money and Finance*, *26*, 663–681.

Rosenbaum, P., & Rubin, D. (1983). The central role of the propensity score in observational studies for causal effects. *Biometrika*, *70*, 41–55.

Rubin, D. (1977). Assignment to treatment group on the basis of a covariate. *Journal of Educational Statistics*, *2*, 1–26.

Samaryna, H., & De Haan, J. (2011). Right on target: Exploring the determinants of inflation targeting adoption. De Nederlandsche Bank. WP number 321.

Smith, J. A., & Todd, P. (2005). Does matching overcome LaLonde's critique of nonexperimental estimators. *Journal of Econometrics*, *125*(1–2), 303–353.

Stone, M., Roger, S., Shimizu, S., Nordstrom, A., Kisinbay, T., & Restrepo, J. (2009). *The role of the exchange rate in inflation-targeting emerging economies*. IMF Occasional Paper No. 267. International Monetary Fund, Washington, DC.

Svensson, L. (1997). Inflation forecast targeting: Implementing and monitoring inflation targets. *European Economic Review*, *41*, 1111–1146.

Tapsoba, R. (2010). *Does inflation targeting improve fiscal discipline? An empirical investigation*. CERDI, Etudes et Documents, E 2010, 20.

Tinbergen, J. (1952). *On the theory of economic policy*. Amsterdam: North-Holland.

Truman, E. M. (2003). *Inflation targeting in the world economy*. Washington, DC: Institute for International Economics.

Van Aarle, B., Bonvenberg, L., & Raith, M. (1995). Monetary and fiscal policy interaction and government debt stabilization. *Journal of Economics*, *62*(2), 111–140.

Van der Ploeg, F. (1995). Political economy of monetary and budgetary policy. *International Economic Review*, *36*(2), 427–439.

Vega, M., & Winkelried, D. (2005). Inflation targeting and inflation behavior: A successful story? *International Journal of Central Banking*, *1*, 153–175.

Vu, U. (2004). Inflation dynamics and monetary policy strategy: Some prospects for the Turkish economy. *Journal of Policy Modeling*, *26*(8–9), 1003–1013.

Walsh, C. (2009). Inflation targeting: What have we learned? *International Finance*, *12*(2), 195–233.

Wimanda, E. R., Turner, P. M., & Hall, M. J. B. (2011). Expectations and the inertia of inflation: The case of Indonesia. *Journal of Policy Modeling*, *33*(3), 426–438.

Appendix A: Stylized Facts

Figure A.1

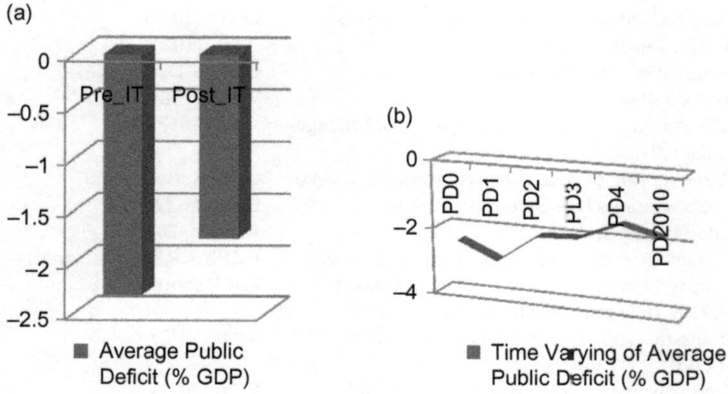

Figure A.2

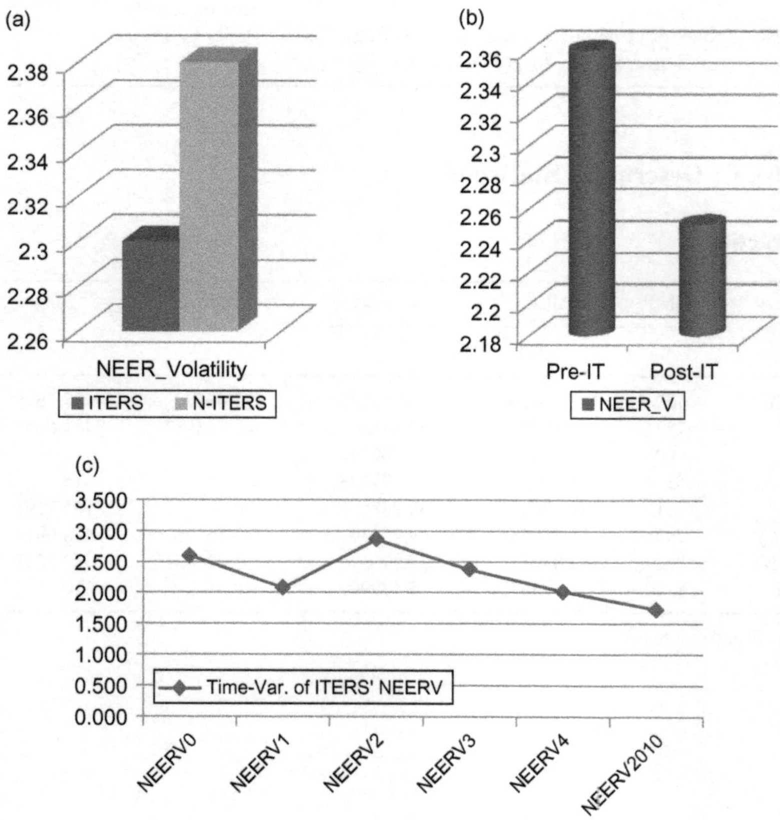

Appendix B: Variables Definitions and Sources

Variables	Definitions	Sources
IT_FF	Fully fledged adoption of inflation targeting.	Levya (2008)
B_DEFICIT	Budget deficit as % of GDP.	WDI (2012)
NEERv	Nominal effective exchange rate volatility.	Bruegel/Darvas (2012)
GDPpc_G	Real GDP per capita growth.	WDI (2012)
INF_1	One-year lagged inflation rate (as annual change of the CPI).	WDI (2012)
TOR_5	Turnover rate of central bank governors based on 5-year averages (De facto central bank independence indicator).	Dreher, Sturm, and De Haan (2008); Lucotte (2012)
EXCH	De facto flexibility indicator of exchange rate, comprised between 1 and 14 from the least to more flexible exchange rate regime.	IMF's AREAR; Reinhart and Rogoff (2004)
CRED	Domestic credit to private sector ratio in % of GDP.	WDI (2012)
OPEN	Trade openness (as the sum of exports and imports of goods and services as a share of GDP).	WDI (2012)
PUB_DEBT	Total public debt as a share of GDP.	Abbas, Belhocine, ElGanainy, and Horton (2010)
POLITY2	Indicator of democracy taking values from −10 (very autocratic) to +10 (very democratic).	Polity IV Project

Appendix C: Descriptive Statistics

1st Interaction

Variables	Obs.	Mean	Std. dev.	Min	Max
		(1990–2010)			
GDPpc_G	820	2.366194	4.816255	−37.08575	17.76985
INF_1	782	56.17121	370.8253	−1.753557	7481.664
TOR_5	800	.22375	.2091426	0	1
EXCH	535	8.770093	3.897738	1	15
CRED	791	39.72655	30.9886	0	165.7191
OPEN	799	73.38848	49.47239	13.75305	438.0917
PUB_DEBT	762	55.0335	32.97057	1.026661	289.5542
POLITY2	837	4.574671	5.479909	−8	10

Source: Authors' calculations.

2nd Interaction

Variables	Obs.	Mean	Std. dev.	Min	Max
	Inflation targeters (1990–2010)				
GDPpc_G	260	2.344233	3.44739	−12.65506	10.22163
INF_1	236	80.38261	556.5233	−.8457161	7481.664
TOR_5	260	.2192308	.2013837	0	1
EXCH	165	10.1697	2.853377	4	15
CRED	256	48.30981	30.94118	9.259671	165.7191
OPEN	259	69.193	34.29145	14.93284	161.6729
POLITY2	270	7.937037	2.421964	−5	10
	Non-inflation targeters (1990–2010)				
GDPpc_G	420	2.583429	4.878795	−31.78159	17.76985
INF_1	416	50.63732	286.8235	−1.753557	4145.107
TOR_5	410	.2268293	.2206064	0	1
EXCH	283	7.208481	4.036491	1	15
CRED	410	38.91996	32.85404	0	158.5054
OPEN	407	76.52378	60.49379	13.75305	438.0917
POLITY2	439	2.148064	5.886556	−8	10

Source: Authors' calculations.

Chapter 2
Careful Price Level Targeting

George A. Waters

Department of Economics, Campus Box 4200, Illinois State University, Normal, IL 61761-4200, USA, e-mail: gawater@gmail.edu

Abstract

This chapter examines a class of interest rate rules that respond to public expectations and to lagged variables. Varying levels of commitment correspond to varying degrees of response to lagged output and targeting of the price level. If the response rises (unintentionally) above the optimal level, the outcome deteriorates severely. Hence, the optimal level of commitment is sensitive to the method of expectations formation and partial commitment is the robust, optimal policy. The policymaker should adjust the price level toward a target, but complete adjustment is neither necessary nor desirable.

Keywords: learning, monetary policy, interest rate rules, commitment, price level targeting

JEL Classifications: E52, E31, D84

1. Introduction

Under rational expectations, commitment by a monetary policymaker to an interest rate rule that targets the level of an aggregate price index can lead public expectations to respond to shocks in a desirable way (Woodford, 1999, 2003). However, such rules must be history dependent, and the proper degree of response to lagged variables is sensitive to the underlying modeling assumptions, in particular, the method the public uses to form expectations.

International Symposia in Economic Theory and Econometrics, Vol. 24
William A. Barnett and Fredj Jawadi (Editors)

ISSN: 1571-0386/doi: 10.1108/S1571-038620150000024014

Evans and Honkapohja (2003, 2006) study a class of interest rate rules that respond to public expectations and lagged output and shows that they have the desirable properties of determinacy and expectational stability for a wide range of parameter values under both commitment and discretion. The present work examines a broader class of such rules to include a range of levels of commitment, which corresponds to the degree of the response to lagged output, and their performance under varying assumptions about expectations formation.

The optimality of a high degree of commitment, as advocated by Blake (2001) and Jensen and McCallum (2002), obtains when public expectations are formed with least squares learning, but this result is fragile. Outcomes across varying levels of commitment are asymmetric in that over-commitment can lead to large fluctuations in inflation and output. Hence, unless the policymaker has precise information about the underlying model, high degrees of commitment are problematic. With the inclusion of errors in the policy rule, the policymaker should adopt a lesser degree of commitment, corresponding to a smaller magnitude of response to lagged output in the interest rate rule. If expectations are formed adaptively, a la Cagan (1956), the case for any level of commitment is weakened considerably.

Such commitment implies that the policymaker is acting to affect the price level, not just inflation. In Woodford's (1999, 2003) baseline model, commitment is equivalent to targeting a fixed price level. Under an intermediate level of commitment, referred to as partial commitment here, the policymaker acts to adjust the price level, but does not make an effort to return it all the way to a predetermined target. A comparison is made both analytically and using impulse response functions for one calibration of the model.

The importance of considering nonrational expectations formation has been well established, see Andrade and Le Bihan (2013) for a detailed empirical study of forecast survey data. Though there are a number of models of expectations formation under learning, see Evans and Honkapohja (2013) for an overview, the focus here is on expectational stability. Expectational stability is related to a number of expectations formation mechanisms besides least square learning, and there is an established literature connecting it to monetary policy.

2. The Model

The core of the model is the standard New Keynesian, expectations augmented IS and Phillips Curve relations including a cost-push (supply) shock u_t.

$$x_t = -\varphi(i_t - E_t^* \pi_{t+1}) + E_t^* x_{t+1} + g_t \tag{1}$$

$$\pi_t = \lambda x_t + \beta E_t^* \pi_{t+1} + u_t \tag{2}$$

The variables x_t and π_t are the deviations of output and inflation from their target values. The notation E_t^* indicates private sector expectations formed in time t where the (*) is used to show that expectations might not be rational. The parameters φ, λ, β are all positive and the discount rate β is such that $\beta < 1$.

The policymaker sets the nominal interest rate to stabilize the endogenous variables. A positive demand shock g_t will increase both output and inflation. In contrast, output and inflation move in opposite directions in response to the supply shock u_t, so the policymaker faces must balance competing goals. In the language of Blanchard and Gali (2007), the *divine coincidence* is broken. While there are many potential sources of uncertainty, supply shocks are particularly difficult for the monetary policymaker and are deserving of special attention.

Formally the task is to set i_t to minimize the loss function

$$L = E_t \sum_{s=0}^{\infty} \beta^s \left(\pi_{t+s}^2 + \alpha x_{t+s}^2\right), \tag{3}$$

The parameter α indicates the relative importance of inflation and output stabilization. Minimizing the loss function at time t constrained by the Phillips Curve (2), while taking expectations to be fixed, yields the following:

$$\lambda \pi_t + \alpha x_t = 0. \tag{4}$$

Such *discretionary* policy does not consider the effect on future expectations and so is not optimal under rational expectations. The optimal *commitment* policy, which does account for the reaction of the public, takes the form

$$\lambda \pi_t + \alpha(x_t - x_{t-1}) = 0. \tag{5}$$

Policy under commitment is not time consistent as, in a given period, discretionary policy produces superior inflation and output outcomes. Thus, a policymaker under commitment is said to have a *timeless perspective*.

The following condition allows for a study of a range of commitment:

$$\lambda \pi_t + \alpha(x_t - \kappa x_{t-1}) = 0 \tag{6}$$

where discretion is a special case of Equation (6) where $\kappa = 0$, and full commitment is equivalent to setting $\kappa = 1$. Here, the level of commitment corresponds to the degree that the policymaker takes lagged information into account. Policies that satisfy the condition (6) at an intermediate level of κ, where $0 < \kappa < 1$, are particularly interesting in an environment where public agents do not have fully rational expectations. The gains to commitment depend on the effect on expectations so different assumptions about the formation of expectations could lead to different conclusions. Also, Blake (2001) and Jensen and McCallum (2002) advocate for the value $\kappa = \beta$ based on a loss function without discounting on the grounds that such an approach better represents the timeless perspective. This policy is called *modified commitment*, and a policy using any value of κ below, $0 < \kappa < \beta$, is called *partial commitment*.

The resulting interest rate rule is determined by the general condition (6) and the IS relation (1). As in Evans and Honkapohja (2006) and Woodford (2003), the interest rate responds directly to observed public expectations. The alternative is to impose rational expectations and express expected inflation and output in terms of current variables. Evans and Honkapohja (2006) refer to such rules as "fundamentals based" and show that for a range of parameter values they lead to model specifications that are neither determinate nor learnable. The expectations based interest rate rule is

$$i_t = \delta_L x_{t-1} + \delta_\pi E_t^* \pi_{t+1} + \delta_x E_t^* x_{t+1} + \delta_g g_t + \delta_u u_t \tag{7}$$

where the coefficient on the lagged output term is

$$\delta_L = \frac{-\kappa\alpha}{\varphi(\lambda^2 + \alpha)}.$$

The parameter δ_L is the only one in Equation (7) that depends on the commitment parameter κ, so the level of commitment corresponds to the magnitude of the response to the interest rate to x_{t-1}. Again, under discretion ($\kappa = 0$), there is no response, while full commitment ($\kappa = 1$) represents the greatest response a policymaker would knowingly make.

I say "knowingly," since the possibility that the policymaker over-responds is a serious concern. To have precise knowledge of the correct value of δ_L requires that policymaker understands connection between the policy rate and the economy and knows the values of the output gap and the parameters. Waters (2009) shows that setting δ_L corresponding to a value $\kappa > 1$ (inadvertently) could create indeterminacy and explosive solutions.

Proposition 1. (Waters, 2009) *Under rational expectations, there exists a non-explosive and determinate solution to the model defined by Equations (1), (2), and (7) if* $0 < \kappa < 1 + \frac{\lambda^2}{\alpha(1-\beta)}$.

The solution is learnable for any $\kappa \geq 0$.

In one sense, the above result is positive, since it ensures unique, stable, and learnable[1] solutions for the present class of interest rate rules. For a conservative central bank, meaning α is small, the bound above may not be a major concern, but for a policymaker who does place significant emphasis on output stabilization, the bound is only slightly above 1.

To analyze the quantitative importance of potentially over-reaction of the interest rate to lagged output, Waters (2009) simulates the model where public expectations are formed using least squares learning. For the model given by the IS (1) and Phillips Curve (2), the minimum state variables solution has the following form:

$$\begin{aligned} x_t &= b_x x_{t-1} + c_x u_t \\ \pi_t &= b_\pi x_{t-1} + c_\pi u_t \end{aligned} \tag{8}$$

Agents use a model with the same for structure as above for forecasting output and inflation and update their estimates of the coefficients (b_x, b_π, c_x, c_π) of the model using OLS on a rolling window of past data, that is, constant gain learning. Figure 1 shows the mean losses[2] for a range of values of κ representing commitment and α representing the conservatism of the policymaker.

The gains to commitment are clear in the figure. For any α, the loss is minimized near the full commitment level of $\kappa = 1$ and the discretionary outcome ($\kappa = 0$) is at least 50% worse as measured by the loss. Close examination of the results shows that the modified commitment setting $\kappa = \beta = 0.99$ is best for any α. However, in the neighborhood of this loss-minimizing policy, there is notable asymmetry across the levels of commitment. As the commitment level rises above the loss-minimizing level, the deterioration of the loss is much greater than if the level falls, particularly for larger values of α, in line with Proposition 1. While the results shown in Figure 1 confirm the optimality of commitment, they do not ameliorate concerns about the necessary precision of knowledge about the model.

A natural next step to examine the issue of the knowledge of the policymaker is to include an error term in the interest rate rule (7). Such shocks arise due to measurement error of the public expectations or the output gap. Furthermore, there is uncertainty about the impact of changes in the policy rate on the broader economy. Figure 2 reports policy outcomes across varying levels of commitment where half the volatility from demand

[1] Here, learnable means expectationally stable as defined by Evans and Honkapohja (2006).

[2] The mean is over 10,000 runs of 200 periods each. The parameter values are taken from McCallum and Nelson (2004).

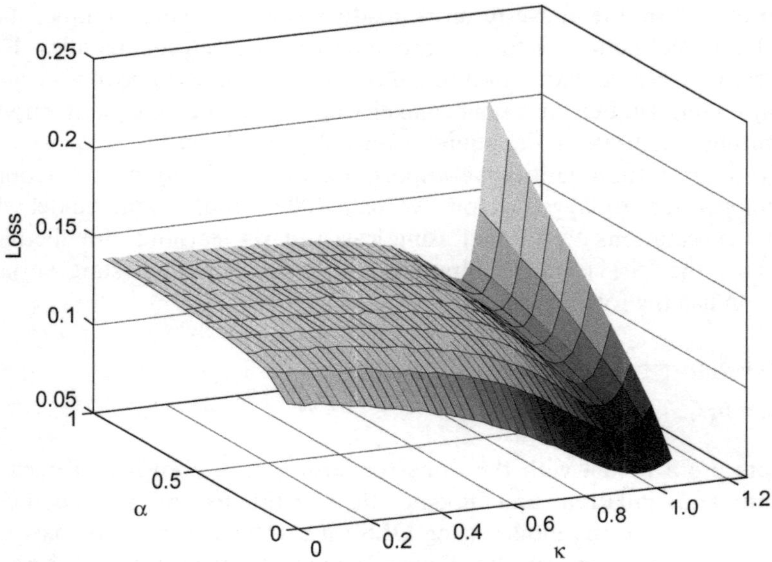

Figure 1: Policy Outcomes under Least Squares Learning.

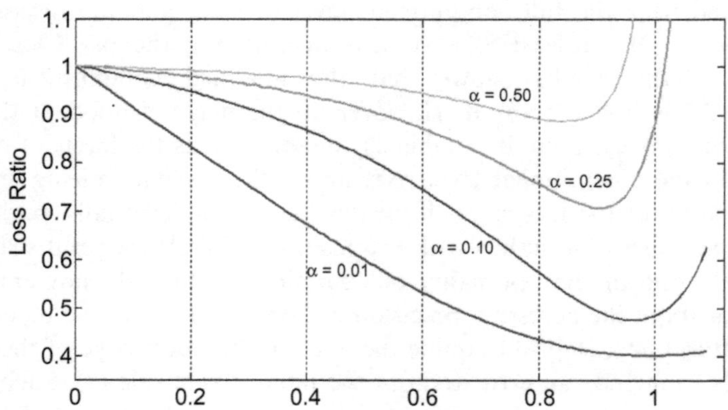

Figure 2: Policy Outcomes under Least Squares Learning with Policy Rule Shocks.

shocks comes from the policy rule errors. For ease of comparison, for each choice of κ, the outcome is reported as the ratio of the loss with its value under discretion, $\kappa = 0$. While modified commitment ($\kappa = 0.99$) is still best for lower levels of α, when the policymaker places significant emphasis on output stabilization a lower level of commitment is optimal. For example, when the parameter α is set to an intermediate value $\alpha = 0.25$, the optimal level of commitment falls to the partial commitment value $\kappa = 0.91$, and the improvement over discretion is comparatively modest. Summarizing results reported in Figure 2 and Waters (2007), larger shocks to the policy rule and a less conservative central banker imply a lower optimal level of commitment.

Furthermore, the optimal level of commitment depends on the information and methods used by the public to form expectations. In simulations with least squares learning, the gain parameter is a key value that determines the emphasis the policymaker places on recent information. One can interpret the gain parameter as a measure of credibility, low gain meaning that the public trusts the policymaker's ability and desire to respond to shocks so recent information has a limited effect on forecasting procedures. The value of 0.15 in the simulations discussed in Figures 1 and 2 is one of the higher values found in the literature, but, in the presence of policy rule errors, some degree of partial commitment is still optimal for the lower value of 0.025, even with a conservative central banker ($\alpha = 0.01$). Results with the high gain parameter are important considering the potential for external factors, such as a financial crisis, to affect the credibility of the policymaker. A potentially fruitful extension would be to make the gain parameter endogenous, as in Marcet and Nicolini (2004), where the gain falls over time unless there is a large forecast error in a given period, when the gain reverts to a higher level. Such an approach captures the idea that credibility builds slowly over time, but can be lost quickly.

Broadening the discussion to other approaches to expectations formation, under rational expectations, modified commitment is best even with policy rule errors. However, the asymmetry shown in Figure 1 still exists and partial commitment may be optimal in the presence of policymaker uncertainty about model parameter values, as shown in Waters (2011). Under adaptive expectations, as introduced by Cagan (1956) where the expectation of a variable is a weighted average of the realization and expectation from the previous period, the case for modified or full commitment is weaker. Compared to least squares learning, as used to generate the simulation results in Figures 1 and 2, under adaptive expectations agents are less sophisticated in their use of information when forming expectations and the case for partial commitment becomes stronger. For the case discussed above ($\alpha = 0.25$), the optimal level of commitment is much lower at $\kappa = 0.6$ and the loss under discretion is typically less that 12% worse than the optimal partial commitment outcome, even though there are no policy rule errors in the simulations with adaptive expectations. The case for full or modified commitment depends on a public being sophisticated in their method of expectations formation and the policymaker having a high degree of confidence in their model.

Note that determinacy is not an issue in any of these simulation results. The model that agents use to make forecasts (the "perceived law of motion") does not allow for extraneous variables that could introduce alternative solutions. Consideration of such solutions would further weaken the case for full commitment. For the results in Figures 1 and 2, modified commitment is not optimal for some parameter values due to the interaction of the learning mechanism and the policy rule errors.

3. Partial Commitment in Practice

The difference between discretion and commitment of the type analyzed here is often characterized by the resulting response of the price level to supply shocks under these policies. Under full commitment ($\kappa = 1$), the policymaker acts to completely undo the effect of the supply shock and return the price level to its former value. Under discretion, the policymaker is unconcerned about the price level and the impact of a supply shock is permanent. The policymaker using partial commitment does act to counter the change in the price level, but target value is in between the original target and the value under discretion.

To illustrate policies under varying degrees of commitment, Figure 3 shows impulse responses,[3] assuming rational expectations, to an unforecastable, single period supply shock $u_0 = 1$ under discretion, partial commitment and full commitment, the parameter $\kappa = 0.0, 0.8$, and 1.0, respectively. The starting target level for all variables is zero, and the immediate effect of the shock is to increase inflation and the price level and to decrease output. The result of the discretionary policy is to immediately return inflation to zero, so the policymaker makes no effort to counter the change in the price level, which remains constant past period 1. In contrast, under full and partial commitment, the policymaker does act to lower the price level, meaning inflation falls below zero beyond the first period. The benefit of commitment is apparent in all three graphs. Since public expectations take the policymaker's commitment into account, the effect of the shock to each variable in period 0 is mitigated compared to the outcome under discretion. The primary difference between full and partial commitment is apparent in the response of the price level. Considering the inflation and output graphs,

[3] This exercise follows Woodford (1999b, 2003). Note that partial commitment is different than the "hybrid" policy in the former paper.

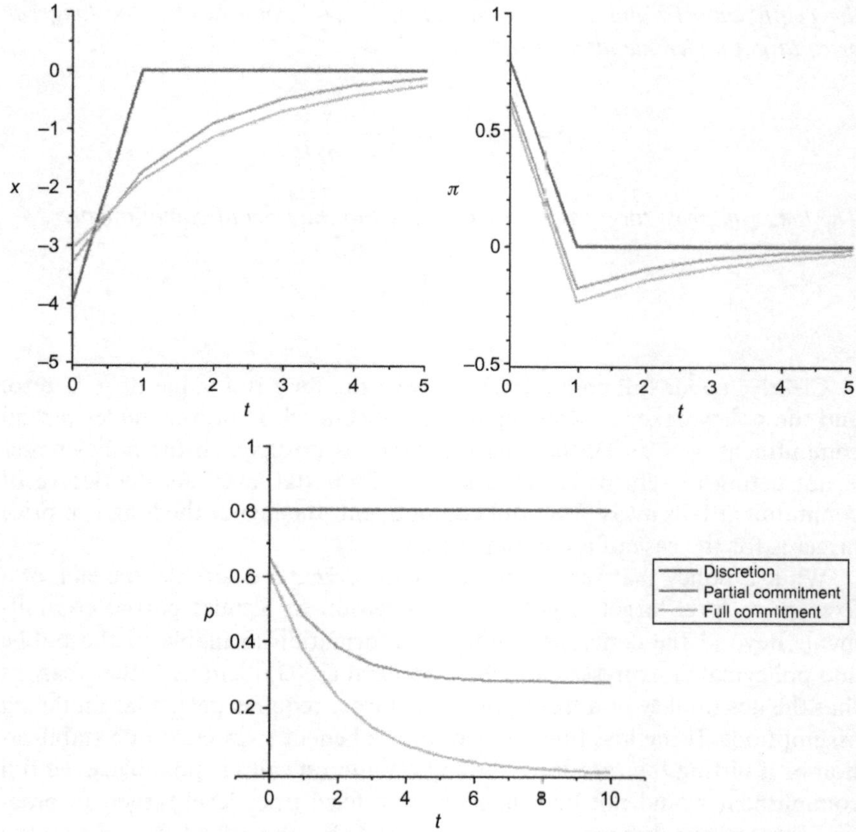

Figure 3: Impulse Responses to a Supply Shock.

the contrast between partial and full commitment appears to be modest. The initial effects of the shock are larger under partial commitment, compared to full commitment, but the difference is slight compared to the outcome under discretion. There is a fundamental difference in the response of the price level under partial commitment in that it does not return all the way to zero. While the policymaker does respond to the price level under partial commitment, the policy cannot be characterized as having a fixed price level target.

One can derive the asymptotic value of the price level for any level of commitment κ.

Proposition 2. *For the model given by Equations (1) and (2) with the minimum state variables solution (8) under rational expectations, if the initial price level is zero,* $p_{-1}=0$*, and the shocks* u_t *are serially independent,* *the coefficients b_x and c_π are such that $0 < b_x < 1$, and $c_\pi > 0$. The long run price target under the interest rate rule (7) is*

$$\bar{p} = \lim_{t \to \infty} p_t = c_\pi \left(\frac{1-\kappa}{1-b_x} \right).$$

The long run price target is inversely related to the level of commitment.

$$\frac{d\bar{p}}{d\kappa} < 0$$

Clearly, under full commitment ($\kappa = 1$), the long run value of p_t is zero, and the policymaker is targeting a fixed price level. However, under partial commitment ($0 < \kappa < 1$), the long run target is positive, so the policymaker is not acting to return the price level to its initial level. As the degree of commitment falls away from full commitment, the higher the long run price target is for the case of a one-time shock.

While a policy that can be simply characterized is desirable, the lack of a fixed price level target is not a serious reason to dismiss partial commitment. Beyond the concerns about the information available to the public and policymaker expressed above, Woodford (2003) identifies other reasons that the desirability of a fixed price level target requires particular modeling assumptions. If the loss function captures a benefit to interest rate stabilization or if hitting the zero lower bound on interest rates is possible, even full commitment would not be equivalent to a fixed price level target. In practice, the policymaker would publish forecasts for the price level, as does the Bank of England and Norges Bank (Norway), that allow for the target to vary.

4. Conclusion

There are clear gains to commitment to an interest rate rule that responds to lagged output in a way that constrains public expectations. Such rules differ from discretion in that they respond to changes in the price level. Nevertheless, these gains and the optimal degree of commitment are sensitive to assumptions about expectations formation and the policymaker's estimates of those expectations, as well as the structure and parameter values of the model being used. The potential for very poor outcomes if the response to lagged variables is excessive, that is, over-commitment means that it is essential for the policymaker to know that such a policy is robust to a variety of modeling assumptions.

The present work focuses on some different ways the public can form expectations, though the list is hardly exhaustive, and there are other modeling choices to be considered. One could extend the analysis to include heterogeneous expectations or Bayesian updating when the correct model specification is uncertain. There are alterative versions of the underlying model that include capital in production or interest rate smoothing, to note two examples.

These concerns about commitment are arguments concerning the long-run strategy for monetary policy. Given special circumstances, such as concern about deflation or the zero lower bound on interest rates, a policymaker could announce a short run price level target if the usual rule-based procedures do not apply. The primary message is that, while countering price level movements is a potentially important tool for monetary policymakers, there is a real danger to overdoing it, and the policymaker should be confident that the gains to such a policy exist under all reasonable modeling assumptions, particularly those related to expectations.

References

Andrade, P., & Le Bihan, H. (2013). Inattentive professional forecasters. *Journal of Monetary Economics*, *60*(8), 967–982.

Blake, A. P. (2001). *A "Timeless Perspective" on optimality in forward-looking rational expectations models*. Working Paper. National Institute for Economic and Social Research. Retrieve at http://repec.org/res2002/Blake.pdf

Blanchard, O., & Gali, J. (2007). Real wage rigidities and the New Keynesian model. *Journal of Money, Credit and Banking*, *39*(1), 35–65.

Cagan, P. (1956). The monetary dynamics of hyperinflation. In M. Friedman (Ed.), *Studies in the quantity theory of money*. Chicago, IL: University of Chicago Press.

Evans, G., & Honkapohja, S. (2003). Expectations and the stability problem for optimal monetary policies. *Review of Economic Studies*, *70*, 807–824.

Evans, G., & Honkapohja, S. (2006). Monetary policy, expectations and commitment. *Scandinavian Journal of Economics*, *108*, 15–38.

Evans, G., & Honkapohja, S. (2013). Learning as a rational foundation for macroeconomics and finances. In R. Frydman & E. S. Phelps (Eds.), *Rethinking expectations: The way forward for macroeconomics*. Princeton, NJ: Princeton University Press.

Evans, G., & McGough, B. (2004). Monetary policy, indeterminacy and learning. *Journal of Economic Dynamics and Control*, *29*, 1809–1840.

Jensen, C., & McCallum, B. (2002). The non-optimality of proposed monetary policy rules under timeless-perspective commitment. *Economics Letters*, *77*(2), 163–168.

Marcet, A., & Nicolini, J. (2004). Recurrent hyperinflations and learning. *American Economic Review*, *93*(5), 1476–1498.

McCallum, B. T., & Nelson, E. (2004). Timeless perspective vs. discretionary monetary policy in forward looking models. *Federal Reserve Bank of St. Louis Review*, *86*(2), 43–56.

Waters, G. (2007). Regime changes, learning and monetary policy. *Journal of Macroeconomics*, *29*(2), 255–282.

Waters, G. (2011). Dangers of commitment under rational expectations. *Journal of Economics and Finance*, *35*(4), 371–381.

Waters, G. A. (2009). Learning, commitment and monetary policy. *Macroeconomic Dynamics*, *13*(4), 421–449.

Woodford, M. (1999). Commentary: How should monetary policy be conducted in an era of price stability? In *New challenges for monetary policy* (pp. 277–316). Federal Reserve Bank of Kansas City. Retrieved at http://www.kc.frb.org/publications/research/escp/escp-1999.cfm

Woodford, M. (2003). *Interest and prices*. Princeton, NJ: Princeton University Press.

Chapter 3

Are Price Dynamics Homogenous across Emerging Europe? Empirical Evidence from Panel Data

Iuliana Matei

IESEG Paris and University Paris 1, France, e-mail: i.matei@ieseg.fr

Abstract

The aim of this chapter is to explore whether price dynamics is homogenous across Emerging Europe. We employ dynamic panel estimation techniques (including the Pooled Mean Group estimator of Pesaran, Smith, and Shin) over the 2003–2013 period and use Germany, and respectively, the European Union (EU) as the references. Results highlight some heterogeneity across the Emerging Europe members in terms of price convergence speed. Findings are robust across different specifications.

Keywords: price convergence, Emerging Europe, panel unit root tests, half-life

JEL Classifications: C23, E31, F15, F41

1. Introduction

This chapter investigates the price convergence through the PPP concept for 11 Emerging European countries over the 2003–2013 period. After joining the EU as a result of their progress during a still unfinished transition and convergence process, the new European member countries had as objective to join the euro area for some reasons: this entry could guarantee

International Symposia in Economic Theory and Econometrics, Vol. 24
William A. Barnett and Fredj Jawadi (Editors)

ISSN: 1571-0386/doi: 10.1108/S1571-038620150000024015

them lower interest rate, a certain monetary stability and a more easily access to foreign funds. As shown in the Maastricht Treaty, the accession to Eurozone requires the achievement of five criteria including inflation convergence and nominal exchange rate stability within member states. Among these criteria, the nominal exchange rates and price convergence process are essential for a future integration of these states into Eurozone.

The most frequent way in investigating the price convergence process is to study the validity of absolute purchasing power parity (PPP). A large body of literature has analyzed in great detail, in the last decade, the long-run PPP relationship using different econometric methods and sample periods. Despite them, the speed of convergence documented in international markets still remains a puzzle. Possible explanations of these conflicting results are related to the insufficiently longer time span to overcome the problem of "small sample distortions," the low power of unit root tests, the degree of cross correlation and heterogeneity of the series in the panel, the appropriate price indices and the potential structural breaks because data could cover both the fixed and floating exchange rate regimes. Exploring the PPP relationship in the empirical literature usually consists in searching unit roots in the real exchange rates. If the unit root is rejected in favor of stationarity in level, then deviations from parity are temporary and the PPP hold in the long run. The speeds of adjustment of prices are also evaluated in the literature with time series or panel-data techniques.

This chapter aims to explore the absolute price convergence hypothesis using panel data for 11 new EU countries over the 2003–2013 period. Results show evidence in favor of a heterogeneous price dynamic process across countries.

The rest of the chapter is structured as follows. The next section describes the empirical specification and reviews the employed data. In Section 3, we present and interpret the results. The last section summarizes the main findings and conclusions.

2. Empirical Specification and Data

2.1. Theoretical Aspects

The strict form of PPP highlights that the nominal exchange rate is proportional to the relative price ratio so that the real exchange rate is constant over time. We consider e_t the nominal exchange rate (expressed as the number of domestic currency units per foreign currency unit), and p and p^* are, respectively, the domestic price level, and the foreign prices level, all measured in natural logarithms. If the real exchange rate is defined as follows:

$q_t = e_t - p_t + p_t^*$ a stationary process then, the deviations from parity are temporary and disappear with time, and PPP is said to hold in the long run. On the contrary, if q_t contains a unit root then, the deviations from the equilibrium will not be eliminated over time and PPP fails in the long run.

The literature distinguishes two main approaches regarding the PPP relationship: the absolute PPP and the relative PPP. Accordingly, the absolute PPP states that $e_t = p_t - p_t^*$ meaning that the adjustment toward absolute PPP is realized only through the goods market and that the monetary union is highly integrated. A potential violation of absolute PPP implies imbalances in the goods market, and consequently, trade deficits and imbalances of the balance of payments (Juselius, 2003). The relative PPP shows that $\Delta e_t = \Delta p_t - \Delta p_t^*$ where Δe_t is the variation of the log of exchange rate and Δp_t and Δp_t^* are the inflation rates of domestic and respectively, foreign country (Germany).

Since our panel countries don't form a monetary union with a single currency on the whole period, we cannot assume that $\Delta e_t = 0$ and therefore, that convergence in inflation rates would be equivalent with the similarity of price levels across EU countries (Guerreiro, Joets, & Mignon, 2012). If the price levels differ inside Emerging Europe, the viability of the monetary union is challenged on the long run. Countries characterized by lower price levels are expected to catch up their delay (Balassa Samuelson effect[1]) which involves higher inflation rates going against relative PPP inside the Eurozone.

2.2. Econometric Specification

Our empirical analysis aims to investigate the homogeneity of price dynamics process inside Emerging Europe over the 2003–2013 period. For this purpose, we apply panel unit root tests and the Pooled Mean Group estimator of Pesaran, Shin, and Smith (1999) (PMG). By using the PMG estimator, our analysis overcomes two drawbacks of the traditional dynamic panel-data literature: a single intercept and the homogeneity of slope parameters. The main advantage of this approach is that it estimates a different slope parameter for each country, and allows for the non-stationarity of variables; and therefore, for the estimation of half-live deviations from PPP for each country of the panel.

The long-run relationship between the price levels (in natural logarithms) is given in Equation (1):

$$e_{it} = \alpha_i + \beta_i \left(p_{it} - p_{jt}^* \right) + \varepsilon_{it}, \tag{1}$$

[1] Please see for a review Balassa (1961).

i, j, and t are subscripts and represent, respectively, countries and time periods, α_i are country-specific intercepts, and ε_{it} are the error terms. The subscript i corresponds to each country of Emerging Europe whilst the subscript j stands for Germany or EU which are taken as the benchmark. The dependent variable e_{it} indicates the spot exchange rate. Before turning to estimations, we check for the stationarity of our variables, using several panel unit root tests. If the panel contains non-stationary data, this leaves us the option to assess the PPP hypothesis with an error-correction framework.

2.3. Variables and Data

To study the absolute/relative PPP, we consider both time and cross-country variation in the data. Our data sample covers 12 European Union (EU) countries (Bulgaria, Croatia, Czech Republic, Estonia, Latvia, Lithuania, Hungary, Poland, Romania, Slovenia, Slovakia, and Germany) and the period from 2003 until 2013. In all our estimations, we consider Germany as the reference country given its key role inside the Euro area and EU, which reduces our panel to 11 Emerging countries. For robustness purpose, the EU aggregates are taken also as reference region. For all variables (the nominal exchange rate/euro and the comparative price levels) we employ yearly data provided by the Eurostat and estimate our models using the variables in logarithms. Table 1 displays the main descriptive statistics of these variables.

In order to explore the absolute PPP, we need price levels of new EU countries rather than CPIs that only depict the evolution of the prices. To this end, we use the Comparative Price Levels (CPL) for the Emerging European countries provided by Eurostat in yearly frequency only starting with 2003. The CPLs are defined as the ratios of PPPs for private final consumption expenditure to exchange rates and measure differences in price levels between countries.

Table 1: Descriptive Statistics of Explained and Explanatory Variables (Log Values)

Variable	Observations	Mean	Std. dev.	Min	Max
CPL	121	4.149	0.167	3.709	4.476
CPL Germany	121	4.639	0.018	4.616	4.673
NER	121	1.888	1.831	−0.397	5.693
CPL UE27	121	4.607	0.001	4.606	4.607

Note: CPL – the comparative price level; NER – the nominal exchange rate.

3. Results and Discussion

3.1. Exploring Cross-Sectional Dependence and Panel Stationarity

There are two types of panel unit root tests developed by the literature on panel data: first-generation tests, constructed on the assumption of cross-sectional independence, and second-generation tests focusing on cross-sectional dependence. Thus, before investigating the stationarity of our variables, it is necessary to account for the dependence between countries in the panel. Strong interdependencies between cross-sectional units arise generally because of the presence of globally common global shocks with heterogeneous impacts across countries (e.g., financial, monetary, oil shocks, and wars), spatial spillover effects, and other unobserved components (coming from the economic and financial integration experienced in the last decade by EU countries).

We assess the presence of cross-sectional dependence in our data using the Pesaran (2004a, 2004b) test, based on the pair-wise correlation of coefficients, and report results in Table 1. The test strongly rejects the null hypothesis of no cross-sectional dependence at the 1% level of significance for variables in levels. Next, we check for the stationarity of our variables by applying second-generation panel unit root tests (PURT) developed by Pesaran (2007) and Choi (2002) that allow for dependence between countries. We use also a first generation test, the Hadri (2002) test, which allows for stationarity in heterogeneous panels as is our case. The Pesaran (2007) and Choi (2002) tests assume that the dependent variable can be represented by unobserved common factors and that countries can respond differently to unobserved common factors. However, the Choi's test uses the orthogonalization procedure to deal with cross-section dependence while the CIPS test of Pesaran (2007) employs augmented cross-section average which does not eliminate the individual and time effects. Furthermore, the Hadri (2002) LM tests the null hypothesis that data are stationary versus the alternative that at least one panel contains a unit root. The series are stationary around a deterministic level, specific to the unit (i.e., a fixed effect), or around a deterministic trend; the error process may be homoskedastic across the panel, or heteroskedastic across countries (see Table 2).

If the Pesaran (2007) results are somewhat sensible to the number of lags of each variable, the Hadri (2002) benchmark strongly reject the null hypothesis that all panel series are stationary in levels (indicating that variables are integrated of order 1). We observe also that CIPS and Choi's test leads to somewhat different results. Choi's results show evidence that all three statistics strongly reject the null hypothesis that all the panels contain unit roots (at 1% and 5% significance level). Overall, the Choi's approach

Table 2: Results of Pesaran (CD), Pesaran CIPS (2007), Choi's (2002), and Hadri LM (2002) Tests

	Pesaran (CD): levels				Pesaran CIPS (2007)		Hadri LM (2002)	
	Avg ρ	Avg $\|\rho\|$	CD	p-Value	CIPS	p-Value	LM	p-Value
Price differential	0.75	0.76	18.72[a]	0.00	0.19[a]	(0.58)	11.53[a]	(0.00)
Exchange rate	−0.01	0.44	−0.24	0.81	0.46[a]	(0.68)	8.24[a]	(0.00)

PURT tests	Choi (2002)		Madalla and Wu (1999)	
	Price differential	Exchange rate	Price differential	Exchange rate
P_m	47.94[a] (0.00)	29.33 (0.14)	50.82[a] (0.00)	11.42 (0.97)
Z	−3.448[a] (0.00)	−1.999[b] (0.02)		
L^*	−3.508[a] (0.00)	−1.830[b] (0.04)		

Notes: (i) *a* significant at the 1% level; *b* at the 5% level; *c* at the 10% level; (ii) the PURT (with 1 lag) includes only the constant, we do not retain the trend in models; (iii) the values in brackets are the associated probabilities.

shows that absolute PPP relative to Germany is validated for Emerging European countries. Regarding the models including trends, there is strong evidence that the PPP form is violated.

3.2. Pooled Mean Group Results

Table 3 summarizes the findings using the PMG model of Pesaran et al. (1999). This approach assumes the heterogeneity in the short-run dynamics and in the error-correction coefficients (column 2) and the homogeneity of parameters for the long-run relationship. It also allows estimating the half-life of deviations from PPP for each country of the panel (column 3). The half-lives of deviations from the equilibrium, computed as $(\ln(0.5)/\ln(1+\varphi))$, indicate the number of periods needed to halve the distance from the mean. Table 3 considers the case where the selected countries do not form a monetary union (i.e., where the logarithm of the nominal exchange rate is different to one). Results show evidence of heterogeneity across countries. Croatia and Poland exhibit the greatest price convergence process because the half-live coefficients are smaller than one year. These countries are followed by the half-lives of Romania (4.18 years), Estonia (7.80 years), Lithuania (14.03 years) and lastly, by Bulgaria which exhibits the highest half-life (about 62 years). These results could be partially related to the respect of the nominal convergence criteria that are needed to integrate

Table 3: PMG Estimates of Error-Correction Coefficient (φ) and Estimated Half-Lives

Countries	Error-correction term (φ)	Half-lives (in years)
Bulgaria	−0.011*** (0.002)	62.10
Croatia	−0.754*** (0.306)	0.49
Czech Republic	−0.213 (0.267)	–
Estonia	0.085*** (0.043)	7.80
Latvia	−0.001 (0.001)	–
Lithuania	−0.048*** (0.121)	14.03
Hungary	−0.111 (0.085)	–
Poland	−0.883*** (0.247)	0.32
Romania	−0.153*** (0.041)	4.18
Slovenia	−0.442 (0.263)	–
Slovakia	−0.103 (0.216)	–

Note: Half-lives are expressed in years; models with the exchange rate.
*$p<0.10$, **$p<0.05$, ***$p<0.01$.

Table 4: PMG Estimates of Error-Correction Coefficient (φ) and Estimated Half-Lives

Countries	Error-correction term (φ)	Half-lives (in years)
Bulgaria	−0.166** (0.075)	3.82
Croatia	−0.081 (0.141)	–
Czech Republic	−0.300** (0.151)	1.94
Estonia	−0.276*** (0.050)	2.15
Latvia	−0.312*** (0.074)	1.85
Lithuania	−0.269*** (0.061)	2.21
Hungary	−0.246 (0.202)	–
Poland	−0.496* (0.274)	1.01
Romania	−0.464*** (0.182)	1.11
Slovenia	−0.280 (0.63)	–
Slovakia	−0.235*** (0.062)	2.59

Note: Half-lives are in years; models without the exchange rate.
*$p<0.10$, **$p<0.05$, ***$p<0.01$.

the euro area. Surprisingly, the half-lives of Czech Republic, Hungary, Slovenia, and Slovakia indicate that these countries are not on the cointegration path because their speeds of adjustment coefficients are not statistically significant. Although the economic integration increased over time, it is possible that some idiosyncratic features (related to the institutional environment, to the economic policies in place, to the financial shocks) remain, which can impede the price convergence process.

Table 4 considers the case where the nominal exchange rate is equal to one meaning that countries have the same currency on the selected period (i.e., they are members of a currency union). Mean-reversion speeds (i.e., the half-lives) are different across Emerging European countries. More precisely, Romania and Poland exhibit a fast price convergence process because the half-live coefficients are equal to one year. They are relatively closely followed by the half-lives of Czech Republic (1.94 years) and the Baltic States (Latvia – 1.85 years, Lituania – 2.21 years, and Estonia – 2.15 years). These results could be also linked to the necessity to respect of the nominal convergence criteria to join Eurozone. Bulgaria and Slovakia have a relatively lower price convergence process – with half-lives larger than 2.5 years (3.82 years, and respectively, 2.59 years) which goes against the PPP on the short-run.

Although the adoption of the euro is expected to contribute to the price convergence process, little effects in terms of price convergence can be observed in the cases of Slovakia and Slovenia. This result could be explained by weaker adjustment mechanisms within the currency union. One of the most disturbing results is the half-lives of Hungary and Croatia, which indicates that these countries are running out the cointegration path, may be, because of some idiosyncratic shocks.

3.3. Robustness Checks

Even though Germany is a natural choice for a reference country to study the relative price adjustment process, this may create a bias related to the geographic proximity. The previous section pointed out that the price adjustment process is the shortest for Poland and the longest for Bulgaria. To checks for the robustness of the previous results, it will be useful to perform the estimations by taking the European Union aggregates (27 countries) as the reference region. Tables 5 and 6 display the results of these estimations.

In the case where countries do not form a currency union, only three of them are on the cointegration path with the half-lives varying from about 0.4 years for Hungary to 2.94 years for Romania (see Table 5). Table 6 shows the results where countries are considered to be integrated into euro area (this imply that the log of the nominal exchange rate equals zero).

The results of these estimations show evidence in favor of a price convergence process within euro area. This may also highlight the positive effects of integration into a monetary union (Frankel & Rose, 1996). Regarding the individual countries, the heterogeneity across countries is less marked. Furthermore, one of the surprising results is the speed of adjustment of Estonia, which is negative but, statistically irrelevant. Overall, the results presented in Table 5 are better and in line with the existing literature on the optimal currency area arguing that the adoption of a common currency

Table 5: PMG Estimates of Error-Correction Coefficient (φ) and Estimated Half-Lives

Countries	Error-correction term (φ)	Half-lives (in years)
Bulgaria	−0.617*** (0.056)	0.72
Croatia	−0.239 (0.188)	–
Czech Republic	−0.186 (0.258)	–
Estonia	−0.345 (0.249)	–
Latvia	−0.036 (0.046)	–
Lithuania	−0.276 (0.309)	–
Hungary	−0.826*** (0.173)	0.40
Poland	−0.181 (0.128)	–
Romania	−0.210** (0.088)	2.94
Slovenia	−0.442 (0.263)	–
Slovakia	−0.156 (0.180)	–

Note: Half-lives are expressed in years; models with the exchange rate.
$^{*}p<0.10$, $^{**}p<0.05$, $^{***}p<0.01$.

Table 6: PMG Estimates of Error-Correction Coefficient (φ) and Estimated Half-Lives

Countries	Error-correction term (φ)	Half-lives (in years)
Bulgaria	−0. 331*** (0.131)	1.72
Croatia	−0.697*** (0.209)	0.58
Czech Republic	−0.358*** (0.209)	1.56
Estonia	−0.117 (0.125)	–
Latvia	−0.321** (0.144)	1.79
Lithuania	−0.290** (0.140)	2.03
Hungary	−0.838** (0.349)	0.38
Poland	−1.289*** (0.353)	−0.87
Romania	−0.505*** (0.204)	0.99
Slovenia	−0.338** (0.146)	1.68
Slovakia	−0.288*** (0.097)	2.04

Note: Half-lives are in years; models without the exchange rate.
$^{*}p<0.10$, $^{**}p<0.05$, $^{***}p<0.01$.

contribute to remove the existing trade barriers, to lower trade costs and to diminish the uncertainty.

4. Conclusion

This chapter aims to explore the price dynamics of some Emerging European countries from an ex-post perspective. We use a data panel of

11 new EU member states from 2002 to 2013 and estimate an empirical model in which Germany and EU are taken as benchmarks. The yearly data suggests the use of panel unit root tests and of a pooled mean estimator to test the absolute PPP assumption. Results favor the heterogeneity of the price dynamics inside Emerging European countries. In the case where countries become euro area members, the PPP hypothesis is not validated for countries such as Hungary, Croatia, and Slovenia. Furthermore, the results are statistically and economically significant where the EU aggregates are taken as reference (except for Estonia). This finding points out also the positive effects of the integration into a monetary union (Frankel & Rose, 1996). In the case where countries are not euro area members, the heterogeneity across members is more marked.

References

Balassa, B. (1961). Towards a theory of economic integration. *Kyklos*, *14*, 1–17.

Choi, I. (2002). *Combination unit root tests for cross-sectionally correlated panels*. Mimeo, Hong Kong University of Science and Technology.

Guerreiro, D., Joets, M., & Mignon, V. (2012). *Is price dynamics homogeneous across Eurozone countries?* EconomiX Working Paper 2012-04. University of Paris Ouest, France.

Frankel, J. A., & Rose, A. K. (1996). *The endogeneity of Optimum Currency Area Criteria*. NBER Working Papers 5700, National Bureau of Economic Research, Inc.

Hadri, K. (2002). Testing for stationarity in heterogeneous panel data. *The Econometrics Journal*, *3*(2), 148–161.

Juselius, K. (2003). *Wage, price, and unemployment dynamics in the convergence to PPP in the Euro area*. Discussion Paper no. 03-01, Institute of Economics, University of Copenhagen.

Maddala, G. S., & Wu, S. (1999). A comparative study of unit root tests with panel data and new simple test. *Oxford Bulletin of Economics and Statistics*, *61*, 631–652.

Pesaran, M. H. (2004a). A simple panel unit root test in the presence of cross-section dependence. *Journal of Applied Econometrics*, *22*(2), 265–312.

Pesaran, M. H. (2004b). *General Diagnosis Tests for cross-section dependence in Panels*. IZA Discussion Papers 1240, Institute for the Study of Labor (IZA).

Pesaran, M. H. (2007). A simple panel unit root test in the presence of cross-section dependence. *Journal of Econometrics*, *22*, 265–312.

Pesaran, M. H., Shin, Y., & Smith, R. P. (1999). Pooled mean group estimation of dynamic heterogeneous panels. *Journal of the American Statistical Association*, *94*, 621–634.

Chapter 4

The Global Component of Local Inflation: Revisiting the Empirical Content of the Global Slack Hypothesis with Bayesian Methods

Enrique Martínez-García[a,b]

[a] *Research Department, Federal Reserve Bank of Dallas, Dallas, TX, USA*
[b] *Economics Department, Southern Methodist University, Dallas, TX, USA*
e-mail: enrique.martinez-garcia@dal.frb.org

Abstract

The global slack hypothesis is central to the discussion of the trade-offs that monetary policy faces in an increasingly more integrated world. The workhorse New Open Economy Macro (NOEM) model of Martínez-García and Wynne (2010), which fleshes out this hypothesis, shows how expected future local inflation and global slack affect current local inflation. In this chapter, I propose the use of the orthogonalization method of Aoki (1981) and Fukuda (1993) on the workhorse NOEM model to further decompose local inflation into a global component and an inflation differential component. I find that the log-linearized rational expectations model of Martínez-García and Wynne (2010) can be solved with two separate subsystems to describe each of these two components of inflation.

I estimate the full NOEM model with Bayesian techniques using data for the United States and an aggregate of its 38 largest trading partners from 1980Q1 until 2011Q4. The Bayesian estimation recognizes the parameter uncertainty surrounding the model and calls on the data (inflation and output) to discipline the parameterization. My findings show that the strength of the international spillovers through trade – even in the absence of common shocks – is reflected in the response of global inflation and is incorporated into local inflation dynamics. Furthermore, I find that key features of the economy can have different impacts on global and local inflation – in particular, I show that the parameters that determine the import share and

International Symposia in Economic Theory and Econometrics, Vol. 24
William A. Barnett and Fredj Jawadi (Editors)

ISSN: 1571-0386/doi: 10.1108/S1571-038620150000024016

the price-elasticity of trade matter in explaining the inflation differential component but not the global component of inflation.

Keywords: global slack hypothesis, new open economy macroeconomics, open-economy Phillips curves, Bayesian estimation

JEL Classifications: C11, C13, F41

1. Introduction

Martínez-García (2008) and Martínez-García and Wynne (2010) build on the New Open Economy Macro (NOEM) literature (see, e.g., the related work of Clarida, Galí, & Gertler, 2002) to develop a tractable theory of the relationship between the cyclical component of local inflation and developments in global economic activity as measured by global slack – the so-called "global slack hypothesis." As the economy becomes more integrated with the rest of the world through trade, the direct contribution of inflation on imported goods to local inflation naturally rises. However, as explained in Martínez-García and Wynne (2013), the "global slack hypothesis" suggests that the changing dynamics of local inflation may be the result of increased international competition and reflect the fact that increasingly local producers can charge more for their goods in their domestic market when they face increases in world demand even when domestic demand remains unchanged.

A closer inspection of the empirical evidence on both the role that trade openness plays on the dynamics of inflation and on the support that the data provides for the global slack hypothesis is warranted. There are well-known drawbacks and mixed evidence found with reduced-form estimates of the empirical relationship between cyclical inflation and global slack (see, e.g., Borio-Filardo, 2007; Ihrig, Kamin, Lindner, & Marquez, 2007 and Martínez-García & Wynne, 2013 for further discussion). Therefore, a structural approach for estimation and empirical inference has been suggested instead.

However, a fully structural approach to the estimation of the "global slack hypothesis" requires a general-equilibrium model that incorporates the many factors and diverse channels that are influencing the global economy which can then be taken to the data for validation. The NOEM model of Martínez-García and Wynne (2010) is an important step in the direction of building such a model, but bringing it to the data is not without its challenges (as shown in Martínez-García, Vilán, & Wynne, 2012; Martínez-García & Wynne, 2014).

In order to explore further the dynamics of local inflation through the lens of the NOEM model, I propose an alternative approach with less ambitious scope but with concrete results. On the one hand, I propose to use the orthogonalization method advocated by Aoki (1981) and Fukuda (1993) to re-express the workhorse model of Martínez-García and Wynne (2010) into two separate subsystems which describe global inflation and the inflation differentials across countries. The decomposition is arguably model-specific, but it illustrates that when open to trade the dynamics of local inflation fluctuate around the path of global inflation (whereby global inflation helps explain and even predict future local inflation). Local inflation has a common component through those trade linkages measured by global inflation) even when all shocks driving business cycle fluctuations are country-specific – that is, even when there are no common shocks driving the global cycle.

On the other hand, beyond theory, I argue that data is needed to assess the empirical significance of the global component of local inflation. In order to better understand the strength of the international transmission mechanism of shocks embedded in the model of Martínez-García and Wynne (2010), I estimate a standard version of it for the United States and for an aggregate of its 38 largest trading partners – using data from 1980Q1 until 2011Q4 on PPP-adjusted real GDP and CPI inflation.

The Bayesian estimation and forecasting methods that I use have a long history in econometrics – one of the seminal works cited in this field is Zellner (1971). Adolfson, Laséen, Lindé, and Villani (2005), and Adolfson, Laséen, Lindé, and Villani (2007), and Adolfson, Laséen, Lindé, and Villani (2008) are among the recent papers that have attempted a more structural approach to open-economy estimation using Bayesian techniques.

In contrast to classical methods, the main advantages of Bayesian techniques for evaluating open-economy models are: (a) they treat unobserved variables (such as measures of slack) and parameters as jointly distributed random variables implying that the Bayesian estimates of each more appropriately reflect the uncertainty about the others; and (b) they take advantage of subjective and/or out-of-sample prior information for inference. I follow this route and estimate the NOEM model with Bayesian techniques. However, given that this workhorse model remains quite stylized, I interpret my estimation results from a more limited perspective. Simply put, I estimate the NOEM model to discipline its parameterization and to ensure that its predictions – on which I base my assessment – are not out of line with the actual data that I seek to better understand.

The model presented in this chapter can be used to evaluate how global inflation and inflation differentials are incorporated into the dynamics of local inflation. More specifically, it shows that the nature of shocks and the structure of the economy matter when investigating how local inflation responds to shocks – but that those features work differently on the global component of local inflation than on the inflation differential component. Even without common (or strongly correlated) shocks, I show empirically that spillovers from shocks occurring in one country get incorporated into the inflation process of other economies so long as those countries are intertwined through trade. These spillovers go above and beyond the effects that may arise from the exogenous comovement between country-specific shocks. However, changes in global inflation which affect all economies are not the only factor to consider. The features of the economy that affect the differential responses in inflation in reaction to a direct impact from shocks can also play a crucial role in how the local inflation response unfolds.

Thus, with the additional insights and evidence presented here to help understand how local inflation is influenced by foreign developments, the contribution of the global component of inflation may be better delineated. My hope is that these ideas will contribute to a deeper understanding of foreign influences on local inflation and that they can be used to develop better tests of the "global slack hypothesis" but also better tools/indicators for forecasting inflation and for policymaking.

The remainder of the chapter proceeds as follows: Section 2 outlines the building blocks of the workhorse NOEM model of Martínez-García and Wynne (2010) and discusses the log-linearized equilibrium conditions that I use to approximate its solution. In Section 3, I discuss the data and priors used to estimate the model with Bayesian methods. Section 4 applies the Aoki (1981) and Fukuda (1993) decomposition to the model illustrating the theoretical role that global inflation can play on the dynamics of local inflation. Then, it proceeds to discuss the Bayesian estimation of the model and its predictions for both global and local inflation. Section 5 provides a recap of the insights gained from this exercise and concludes. A brief appendix with the relevant proofs is also provided.

2. A Model of Inflation Determination in the Global Economy

In this chapter, I investigate how global inflation arises from country-specific shocks in an open-economy setting, what drives global and local inflation, and the contribution of the global component to local inflation. I build my analysis on the workhorse NOEM model laid out in Martínez-García and Wynne (2010).[1] The two-country dynamic stochastic general

[1] A seminal contribution in the development of the workhorse NOEM framework of Martínez-García and Wynne (2010) is the model of Clarida et al. (2002).

equilibrium model of Martínez-García and Wynne (2010) provides a very tractable environment under monetary non-neutrality to more deeply explore the dynamics of global and local inflation and the international propagation mechanism for country-specific shocks.

The model features nominal rigidities modeled with two standard distortions in the markets for goods: monopolistic competition in production and price-setting behavior constrained by contracts à la Calvo (1983). Monopolistic competition distorts labor allocation which can be undone with a labor subsidy for local firms funded with non-distortionary, lump-sum taxes raised from local households. Short-run monetary non-neutrality – the implication that monetary shocks can have real effects – hinges on the assumption of price stickiness. However, the introduction of price stickiness à la Calvo (1983) does not overturn long-run monetary neutrality in the model.

As in Martínez-García and Wynne (2010), only country-specific shocks are considered explicitly in the model. Hence, the response of global inflation to shocks and its influence on local inflation must arise entirely through the effect of cross-border spillovers arising through trade. In the model I retain the conventional distinction between aggregate supply-side drivers of the business cycle (aggregate productivity shocks) and aggregate demand-side drivers (monetary policy shocks) in order to identify the international transmission of country-specific shocks and its impact on local inflation, conditional upon different sources of business cycle movements.

I adopt the standard cashless economy specification where money only plays the role of unit of account – for further discussion on this, see chapter 2 in Woodford (2003). I assume pass-through is complete (even with price stickiness) and that the law of one price holds at the variety level because prices are set domestically and in the export markets in the producer's own currency.[2] Deviations from purchasing power parity (PPP) still arise in the aggregate whenever households put a higher weight on domestic varieties in their consumption basket than the share that domestically produced varieties represent of the world production of differentiated varieties (local-consumption bias).

For simplicity, I abstract from capital accumulation – considering only linear-in-labor technologies – and I assume complete domestic and international asset markets. The model can be augmented with capital accumulation and the assumption of complete international asset markets can also be relaxed, but the added complexity that comes from including those features does not seem warranted for the general goals of this chapter.

---

[2] For details on the role of international price-setting in the conduct of optimal monetary policy and the international propagation mechanism see Engel (2009).

As shown extensively in the work of Martínez-García and Søndergaard (2009), Martínez-García (2011), and Martínez-García and Søndergaard (2013), those features do not necessarily change qualitatively – even though they may change quantitatively – the implication that international spillovers through trade play a key role in explaining the dynamics of global inflation and its contribution to local inflation.

2.1. Building Blocks of the NOEM Model

2.1.1. Households

The lifetime utility for the representative household in the Home country is additively separable into consumption, C_t, and labor, L_t, that is,

$$\sum_{\tau=0}^{+\infty} \beta^{\tau} \mathbb{E}_t \left[\frac{1}{1-\gamma} (C_{t+\tau})^{1-\gamma} - \frac{\kappa}{1+\varphi} (L_{t+\tau})^{1+\varphi} \right], \tag{1}$$

where $0 < \beta < 1$ is the subjective intertemporal discount factor, $\gamma > 0$ is the inverse of the intertemporal elasticity of substitution, and $\varphi > 0$ is the inverse of the Frisch elasticity of labor supply. The scaling factor $\kappa > 0$ determines the steady-state labor. The Home household maximizes its lifetime utility subject to the sequence of budget constraints,

$$P_t C_t + \int_{\omega_{t+1} \in \Omega} Q_t(\omega_{t+1}) B_t(\omega_{t+1}) \leq B_{t-1}(\omega_t) + W_t L_t + \mathrm{Pr}_t - T_t, \tag{2}$$

where W_t is the nominal wage in the Home country, P_t is the Home consumption price index (CPI), T_t is a nominal lump-sum tax (or transfer) from the Home government, and Pr_t are (per-period) nominal profits from all firms producing the Home varieties. The budget constraint includes a portfolio of one-period Arrow–Debreu securities (contingent bonds) traded internationally and in zero-net supply, $B_t(\omega_{t+1})$. For simplicity, these contingent bonds are quoted in the unit of account of the Home country. The Home price of the contingent bonds is denoted $Q_t(\omega_{t+1})$, while S_t is the nominal exchange rate and the Foreign price of the contingent bonds is simply $Q_t^*(\omega_{t+1}) = \left((1/S_t) Q_t(\omega_{t+1})\right)$. Similarly, for the representative household in the Foreign country.

Access to a full set of internationally traded, one-period Arrow–Debreu securities completes the local and international asset markets recursively. Under complete asset markets, households can perfectly share risks domestically and internationally. Hence, the intertemporal marginal rate of substitution is equalized across countries in every state of nature,

$$\beta\left(\frac{C_{t+1}}{C_t}\right)^{-\gamma}\frac{P_t}{P_{t+1}}=\beta\left(\frac{C^*_{t+1}}{C^*_t}\right)^{-\gamma}\frac{P^*_t S_t}{P^*_{t+1}S_{t+1}}, \tag{3}$$

where P^*_t is the Foreign CPI and C^*_t stands for Foreign consumption. I define the real exchange rate as $\mathrm{RS}_t\equiv(S_tP^*_t)/(P_t)$, so by backward recursion the *perfect international risk-sharing condition* in Equation (3) becomes,

$$\mathrm{RS}_t=\upsilon\left(\frac{C^*_t}{C_t}\right)^{-\gamma}, \tag{4}$$

where $\upsilon\equiv(S_0P^*_0/P_0)(C^*_0/C_0)^{\gamma}$ is a constant that depends on initial conditions. If the initial conditions correspond to the symmetric steady state, then the constant υ is equal to one. From the price of the contingent Arrow–Debreu securities, I obtain a standard pair of stochastic Euler equations for both countries,

$$\frac{1}{1+i_t}=\beta\mathbb{E}_t\left[\left(\frac{C_{t+1}}{C_t}\right)^{-\gamma}\frac{P_t}{P_{t+1}}\right], \tag{5}$$

$$\frac{1}{1+i^*_t}=\beta\mathbb{E}_t\left[\left(\frac{C^*_{t+1}}{C^*_t}\right)^{-\gamma}\frac{P^*_t}{P^*_{t+1}}\right], \tag{6}$$

where i_t is the riskless, nominal interest rate in the Home country and i^*_t is its Foreign country counterpart. The households' optimization problem also results in a pair of labor supply equations,

$$\frac{W_t}{P_t}=\kappa(C_t)^{\gamma}(L_t)^{\varphi}, \tag{7}$$

$$\frac{W^*_t}{P^*_t}=\kappa(C^*_t)^{\gamma}(L^*_t)^{\varphi}, \tag{8}$$

plus the appropriate (no-Ponzi games) transversality conditions and the budget constraints of both representative households.

C_t is a CES aggregator of Home and Foreign goods for the representative Home household defined as,[3]

[3] Unlike in Martínez-García and Wynne (2010), I assume an equal population size of households in both countries and an even split of the total varieties to be produced in each country (i.e., 1/2 of the population and the varieties is located in each country). Moreover, I also adopt symmetric local-product bias in preferences as reflected in the composition of each country's consumption basket (i.e., the share of imported goods for both countries is set at $(1-\xi)$).

$$C_t = \left[(\xi)^{\frac{1}{\sigma}} \left(C_t^{\mathrm{H}} \right)^{\frac{\sigma-1}{\sigma}} + (1-\xi)^{\frac{1}{\sigma}} \left(C_t^{\mathrm{F}} \right)^{\frac{\sigma-1}{\sigma}} \right], \tag{9}$$

where $\sigma > 0$ is the elasticity of substitution between the Home-produced consumption bundle C_t^{H} and the Foreign-produced consumption bundle C_t^{F}. Analogous preferences are assumed for the Foreign representative household, except that C_t^* is defined as a CES aggregator of Home and Foreign goods in the following terms:

$$C_t^* = \left[(1-\xi)^{\frac{1}{\sigma}} \left(C_t^{\mathrm{H}*} \right)^{\frac{\sigma-1}{\sigma}} + (\xi)^{\frac{1}{\sigma}} \left(C_t^{\mathrm{F}*} \right)^{\frac{\sigma-1}{\sigma}} \right]. \tag{10}$$

The share of Home-produced goods in the Home consumption basket and Foreign-produced goods in the Foreign basket must satisfy that $\frac{1}{2} \leq \xi < 1$.

The sub-indexes C_t^{H} and $C_t^{\mathrm{H}*}$ indicate, respectively, Home and Foreign consumption of the bundle of differentiated varieties produced in the Home country. Similarly, C_t^{F} and $C_t^{\mathrm{F}*}$ denote Home and Foreign consumption of the bundle of differentiated varieties produced in the Foreign country. These sub-indexes are defined as follows:

$$C_t^{\mathrm{H}} = \left[\left(\frac{1}{2} \right)^{-\frac{1}{\theta}} \int_0^{\frac{1}{2}} C_t(h)^{\frac{\theta-1}{\theta}} \mathrm{d}h \right]^{\frac{\theta}{\theta-1}}, C_t^{\mathrm{F}} = \left[\left(\frac{1}{2} \right)^{-\frac{1}{\theta}} \int_{\frac{1}{2}}^1 C_t(f)^{\frac{\theta-1}{\theta}} \mathrm{d}f \right]^{\frac{\theta}{\theta-1}}, \tag{11}$$

$$C_t^{\mathrm{H}*} = \left[\left(\frac{1}{2} \right)^{-\frac{1}{\theta}} \int_0^{\frac{1}{2}} C_t^*(h)^{\frac{\theta-1}{\theta}} \mathrm{d}h \right]^{\frac{\theta}{\theta-1}}, C_t^{\mathrm{F}*} = \left[\left(\frac{1}{2} \right)^{-\frac{1}{\theta}} \int_{\frac{1}{2}}^1 C_t^*(f)^{\frac{\theta-1}{\theta}} \mathrm{d}f \right]^{\frac{\theta}{\theta-1}}, \tag{12}$$

where $\theta > 1$ is the elasticity of substitution across differentiated varieties within a country. Similarly, total output and labor are expressed as,

$$\frac{1}{2} Y_t = \left[\left(\frac{1}{2} \right)^{-\frac{1}{\theta}} \int_0^{\frac{1}{2}} Y_t(h)^{\frac{\theta-1}{\theta}} \mathrm{d}h \right]^{\frac{\theta}{\theta-1}}, \frac{1}{2} Y_t^* = \left[\left(\frac{1}{2} \right)^{-\frac{1}{\theta}} \int_{\frac{1}{2}}^1 Y_t^*(f)^{\frac{\theta-1}{\theta}} \mathrm{d}f \right]^{\frac{\theta}{\theta-1}}, \tag{13}$$

$$\frac{1}{2} L_t = \left[\left(\frac{1}{2} \right)^{-\frac{1}{\theta}} \int_0^{\frac{1}{2}} L_t(h)^{\frac{\theta-1}{\theta}} \mathrm{d}h \right]^{\frac{\theta}{\theta-1}}, \frac{1}{2} L_t^* = \left[\left(\frac{1}{2} \right)^{-\frac{1}{\theta}} \int_{\frac{1}{2}}^1 L_t^*(f)^{\frac{\theta-1}{\theta}} \mathrm{d}f \right]^{\frac{\theta}{\theta-1}}, \tag{14}$$

where Y_t and Y_t^* denote the total output per household produced by firms in the Home and Foreign countries, respectively, while L_t and L_t^* refer to the per household total labor employed. The CPIs that correspond to this specification of consumption preferences are,

$$P_t = \left[\xi \left(P_t^{\mathrm{H}}\right)^{1-\sigma} + (1-\xi)\left(P_t^{\mathrm{F}}\right)^{1-\sigma}\right]^{\frac{1}{1-\sigma}}, \tag{15}$$

$$P_t^* = \left[(1-\xi)\left(P_t^{\mathrm{H}*}\right)^{1-\sigma} + \xi\left(P_t^{\mathrm{F}*}\right)^{1-\sigma}\right]^{\frac{1}{1-\sigma}}, \tag{16}$$

and,

$$P_t^{\mathrm{H}} = \left[2\int_0^{\frac{1}{2}} P_t(h)^{1-\theta}\mathrm{d}h\right]^{\frac{1}{1-\theta}}, P_t^{\mathrm{F}} = \left[2\int_{\frac{1}{2}}^{1} P_t(f)^{1-\theta}\mathrm{d}f\right]^{\frac{1}{1-\theta}}, \tag{17}$$

$$P_t^{\mathrm{H}*} = \left[2\int_0^{\frac{1}{2}} P_t^*(h)^{1-\theta}\mathrm{d}h\right]^{\frac{1}{1-\theta}}, P_t^{\mathrm{F}*} = \left[2\int_{\frac{1}{2}}^{1} P_t^*(f)^{1-\theta}\mathrm{d}f\right]^{\frac{1}{1-\theta}}, \tag{18}$$

where P_t^{H} and P_t^{F} are the price sub-indexes for the Home-produced and Foreign-produced bundles of varieties in the Home market. The Home and Foreign price of the Home-produced variety h is given by $P_t(h)$ and $P_t^*(h)$, respectively. Similarly, for the sub-indexes $P_t^{\mathrm{H}*}$ and $P_t^{\mathrm{F}*}$ in the Foreign market and for the prices $P_t(f)$ and $P_t^*(f)$ of the Foreign-produced variety f.

2.1.2. Firms

Each firm supplies the Home and Foreign markets with its own differentiated variety under monopolistic competition. I assume producer currency pricing (PCP), so firms set Home and Foreign prices by invoicing local sales and exports in their local currency. The PCP assumption implies that the law of one price (LOOP) holds at the variety level (i.e., $P_t(h) = S_t P_t^*(h)$ and $P_t(f) = S_t P_t^*(f)$), so it follows that $P_t^{\mathrm{H}} = S_t P_t^{\mathrm{H}*}$ and $P_t^{\mathrm{F}} = S_t P_t^{\mathrm{F}*}$. However, $\xi \neq 1/2$ leads to deviations from purchasing power parity (PPP) (i.e., $P_t \neq S_t P_t^*$) and so the real exchange rate deviates from one (i.e., $\mathrm{RS}_t \equiv ((S_t P_t^*)/(P_t)) \neq 1$).

Given households' preferences, I can derive the demand for any Home variety h and for any Foreign variety f as,

$$\begin{aligned} Y_t(h) &= \frac{1}{2}C_t(h) + \frac{1}{2}C_t^*(h) \\ &= \left(\frac{P_t(h)}{P_t^{\mathrm{H}}}\right)^{-\theta}\left\{\left(\frac{P_t^{\mathrm{H}}}{P_t}\right)^{-\sigma}\left[\xi C_t + (1-\xi)\left(\frac{1}{\mathrm{RS}_t}\right)^{-\sigma} C_t^*\right]\right\}, \text{if } h \in \left[0, \frac{1}{2}\right], \end{aligned} \tag{19}$$

$$Y_t^*(f) = \frac{1}{2}C_t(f) + \frac{1}{2}C_t^*(f)$$
$$= \left(\frac{P_t(f)}{P_t^{\mathrm{F}}}\right)^{-\theta}\left\{\left(\frac{P_t^{\mathrm{F}}}{P_t}\right)^{-\sigma}\left[(1-\xi)C_t + \xi\left(\frac{1}{\mathrm{RS}_t}\right)^{-\sigma}C_t^*\right]\right\}, \text{if } f \in \left(\frac{1}{2}, 1\right]. \quad (20)$$

Firms maximize profits subject to a partial adjustment rule à la Calvo (1983) on nominal prices at the variety level. In each period, every firm receives, with probability $0 < \alpha < 1$, a signal to maintain their prices and, with probability $1 - \alpha$, a signal to re-optimize. The re-optimizing Home firms in any given period choose a price $\tilde{P}_t(h)$ optimally to maximize the expected discounted value of their profits, that is,

$$\sum_{\tau=0}^{+\infty} \mathbb{E}_t\left\{(\alpha\beta)^{\tau}\left(\frac{C_{t+\tau}}{C_t}\right)^{-\gamma}\frac{P_t}{P_{t+\tau}}\left[\tilde{Y}_{t,t+\tau}(h)\left(\tilde{P}_t(h) - (1-\phi)\mathrm{MC}_{t+\tau}\right)\right]\right\}, \quad (21)$$

subject to the constraint of always satisfying demand given by Equation (19) at the chosen price $\tilde{P}_t(h)$ for as long as those prices remain unchanged. $\tilde{Y}_{t,t+\tau}(h)$ indicates the total consumption demand of variety h at time $t+\tau$ whenever the prevailing prices are unchanged since time t, that is, whenever $P_{t+\tau}(h) = \tilde{P}_t(h)$. Similarly, I describe the problem of the re-optimizing Foreign firms and define their optimal price $\tilde{P}_t^*(f)$ and their corresponding demand schedule $\tilde{Y}_{t,t+\tau}^*(f)$.

Local governments raise lump-sum taxes from households in order to subsidize labor employment. I introduce the labor subsidy ϕ as proportional to the nominal marginal cost and assume it to be time-invariant. Firms produce their own varieties subject to a linear-in-labor technology. Moreover, I impose competitive local labor markets and homogeneity of the labor input (although labor is immobile across countries) ensuring that wages equalize within a country (but not across countries). Hence, the (before-subsidy) nominal marginal cost is given by,

$$\mathrm{MC}_t \equiv \left(\frac{W_t}{A_t}\right), \quad \mathrm{MC}_t^* \equiv \left(\frac{W_t^*}{A_t^*}\right), \quad (22)$$

where MC_t and MC_t^* are the Home and Foreign (before-subsidy) nominal marginal cost, respectively. Home and Foreign nominal wages are denoted by W_t and W_t^*, while Home and Foreign productivity shocks are A_t and A_t^*.

The stochastic process for aggregate productivity in each country evolves according to the following bivariate autoregressive process:

$$\begin{pmatrix} \ln A_t \\ \ln A_t^* \end{pmatrix} = \begin{pmatrix} \delta_a & \delta_{a,a^*} \\ \delta_{a,a^*} & \delta_a \end{pmatrix}\begin{pmatrix} \ln A_{t-1} \\ \ln A_{t-1}^* \end{pmatrix} + \begin{pmatrix} \varepsilon_t^a \\ \varepsilon_t^{a*} \end{pmatrix}, \quad (23)$$

$$\begin{pmatrix} \varepsilon_t^a \\ \varepsilon_t^{a*} \end{pmatrix} \sim N\left(\begin{pmatrix} 0 \\ 0 \end{pmatrix}, \begin{pmatrix} \sigma_a^2 & \rho_{a,a^*}\sigma_a^2 \\ \rho_{a,a^*}\sigma_a^2 & \sigma_a^2 \end{pmatrix}\right). \tag{24}$$

The Home and Foreign productivity shock innovations are labeled ε_t^a and ε_t^{a*}, respectively. I assume a common volatility $\sigma_a^2 > 0$, a common autoregressive parameter δ_a and a spillover parameter δ_{a,a^*} such that the corresponding eigenvalues are within the unit circle and the VAR(1) system remains stationary, and allow the cross-correlation of innovations between the two countries to be $-1 < \rho_{a,a^*} < 1$.

The optimal pricing rule of the re-optimizing Home firms at time t is given by,

$$\tilde{P}_t(h) = \left(\frac{\theta}{\theta-1}(1-\phi)\right) \frac{\sum_{\tau=0}^{+\infty} (\alpha\beta)^\tau \mathbb{E}_t\left[\left(\frac{C_{t+\tau}^{-\gamma}}{P_{t+\tau}}\right) \tilde{Y}_{t,t+\tau}(h) \mathrm{MC}_{t+\tau}\right]}{\sum_{\tau=0}^{+\infty} (\alpha\beta)^\tau \mathbb{E}_t\left[\left(\frac{C_{t+\tau}^{-\gamma}}{P_{t+\tau}}\right) \tilde{Y}_{t,t+\tau}(h)\right]}, \tag{25}$$

and the optimal pricing rule of the re-optimizing Foreign firms is,

$$\tilde{P}_t^*(f) = \left(\frac{\theta}{\theta-1}(1-\phi)\right) \frac{\sum_{\tau=0}^{+\infty} (\alpha\beta)^\tau \mathbb{E}_t\left[\left(\frac{C_{t+\tau}^{*-\gamma}}{P_{t+\tau}^*}\right) \tilde{Y}_{t,t+\tau}^*(f) \mathrm{MC}_{t+\tau}^*\right]}{\sum_{\tau=0}^{+\infty} (\alpha\beta)^\tau \mathbb{E}_t\left[\left(\frac{C_{t+\tau}^{*-\gamma}}{P_{t+\tau}^*}\right) \tilde{Y}_{t,t+\tau}^*(f)\right]}. \tag{26}$$

Monopolistic competition in production introduces a mark-up between prices and marginal costs, $\theta/(\theta-1)$, which is a function of the elasticity of substitution across varieties within a country $\theta > 1$. I choose an optimal labor subsidy $\phi = 1/\theta$ in both countries to neutralize this mark-up wedge.

Given the inherent symmetry of the Calvo-type pricing scheme, the price sub-indexes P_t^{H} and $P_t^{\mathrm{F}*}$ evolve according to the following pair of equations:

$$\left(P_t^{\mathrm{H}}\right)^{1-\theta} = \alpha\left(P_{t-1}^{\mathrm{H}}\right)^{1-\theta} + (1-\alpha)\left(\tilde{P}_t(h)\right)^{1-\theta} = \left(S_t P_t^{\mathrm{H}*}\right)^{1-\theta}, \tag{27}$$

$$\left(P_t^{\mathrm{F}*}\right)^{1-\theta} = \alpha\left(P_{t-1}^{\mathrm{F}*}\right)^{1-\theta} + (1-\alpha)\left(\tilde{P}_t^*(f)\right)^{1-\theta} = \left(\frac{P_t^{\mathrm{F}}}{S_t}\right)^{1-\theta}. \tag{28}$$

The price sub-indexes, $P_t^{\mathrm{H}*}$ and P_t^{F}, follow from the LOOP condition.

2.1.3. Monetary Policy

I model monetary policy in the Home and Foreign countries according to Taylor (1993)-type rules on the short-term nominal interest rates, i_t and i_t^*, that is,

$$1+i_t=\left(1+\bar{i}\right)\frac{M_t}{M}\left[\left(\frac{\Pi_t}{\overline{\Pi}}\right)^{\psi_\pi}\left(\frac{Y_t}{\overline{Y}_t}\right)^{\psi_x}\right], \tag{29}$$

$$1+i_t^*=\left(1+\bar{i}^*\right)\frac{M_t^*}{M^*}\left[\left(\frac{\Pi_t^*}{\overline{\Pi}^*}\right)^{\psi_\pi}\left(\frac{Y_t^*}{\overline{Y}_t^*}\right)^{\psi_x}\right], \tag{30}$$

where M_t and M_t^* are the Home and Foreign monetary policy shocks, and $\psi_\pi>1$ and $\psi_x>0$ represent the sensitivity of the monetary policy rule to changes in inflation and the output gap, respectively. $\bar{i}$ and $\bar{i}^*$ are the steady-state Home and Foreign nominal interest rates, and $M=M^*$ is the unconditional mean of the Home and Foreign monetary shocks. $\Pi_t\equiv P_t/P_{t-1}$ and $\Pi_t^*\equiv P_t^*/P_{t-1}^*$ are the (gross) CPI inflation rates, while $\overline{\Pi}$ and $\overline{\Pi}^*$ are the corresponding steady-state inflation rates. The ratios $Y_t/\overline{Y}_t$ and $Y_t^*/\overline{Y}_t^*$ define the output gap in levels for the Home and Foreign country, where Y_t and Y_t^* define the per household output levels and $\overline{Y}_t$ and $\overline{Y}_t^*$ are the potential per household output levels – potential output being defined as the output level that would prevail if nominal rigidities could be eliminated, that is, in a frictionless economy with competitive firms and flexible prices.

The stochastic process for the monetary policy shocks in each country evolves according to the following bivariate autoregressive process:

$$\begin{pmatrix}\ln M_t\\ \ln M_t^*\end{pmatrix}=\begin{pmatrix}\delta_m & 0\\ 0 & \delta_m\end{pmatrix}\begin{pmatrix}\ln M_{t-1}\\ \ln M_{t-1}^*\end{pmatrix}+\begin{pmatrix}\varepsilon_t^m\\ \varepsilon_t^{m*}\end{pmatrix}, \tag{31}$$

$$\begin{pmatrix}\varepsilon_t^m\\ \varepsilon_t^{m*}\end{pmatrix}\sim N\left(\begin{pmatrix}0\\0\end{pmatrix},\begin{pmatrix}\sigma_m^2 & \rho_{m,m^*}\sigma_m^2\\ \rho_{m,m^*}\sigma_m^2 & \sigma_m^2\end{pmatrix}\right). \tag{32}$$

The Home and Foreign monetary policy shock innovations are labeled ε_t^m and ε_t^{m*}, respectively. I assume a common volatility $\sigma_m^2>0$, a common autoregressive parameter $-1<\delta_m<1$, and allow the cross-correlation of innovations between the two countries to be $-1<\rho_{m,m^*}<1$.

2.2. The Workhorse NOEM Model

I derive a deterministic, zero-inflation steady state for the model and log-linearize the equilibrium conditions around that steady state. I denote $\widehat{g}_t\equiv\ln G_t-\ln\overline{G}$ as the deviation of a variable in logs from its steady state, where G_t is the corresponding model variable in levels and $\overline{G}$ is the steady state in levels. In the NOEM model, price stickiness preserves monetary policy neutrality in the long run while allowing a break from it in the short run. The NOEM dynamics are summarized in Tables 1 and 2. Assuming

Table 1: New Open Economy Macro (NOEM) Model: Core Equations

	Home economy
Phillips curve	$\hat{\pi}_t \approx \beta \mathbb{E}_t(\hat{\pi}_{t+1}) + \left(\frac{(1-\alpha)(1-\beta\alpha)}{\alpha}\right)\left[(\xi\varphi + \Theta\gamma)\hat{x}_t + ((1-\xi)\varphi + (1-\Theta)\gamma)\hat{x}_t^*\right]$
Output gap	$\gamma(2\xi-1)(\mathbb{E}_t[\hat{x}_{t+1}] - \hat{x}_t) \approx ((2\xi-1)+\Gamma)\left[\hat{r}_t - \hat{\bar{r}}_t\right] - \Gamma\left[\hat{r}_t^* - \hat{\bar{r}}_t^*\right]$
Monetary policy	$\hat{i}_t \approx \left[\psi_\pi \hat{\pi}_t + \psi_x \hat{x}_t\right] + \hat{m}_t$
Fisher equation	$\hat{r}_t \equiv \hat{i}_t - \mathbb{E}_t[\hat{\pi}_{t+1}]$
Natural interest rate	$\hat{\bar{r}}_t \approx \gamma\left[\Theta\left(\mathbb{E}_t\left[\hat{\bar{y}}_{t+1}\right] - \hat{\bar{y}}_t\right) + (1-\Theta)\left(\mathbb{E}_t\left[\hat{\bar{y}}_{t+1}^*\right] - \hat{\bar{y}}_t^*\right)\right]$
Potential output	$\hat{\bar{y}}_t \approx \left(\frac{1+\varphi}{\gamma+\varphi}\right)\left[\Lambda\hat{a}_t + (1-\Lambda)\hat{a}_t^*\right]$
	Foreign economy
Phillips curve	$\hat{\pi}_t^* \approx \beta \mathbb{E}_t(\hat{\pi}_{t+1}^*) + \left(\frac{(1-\alpha)(1-\beta\alpha)}{\alpha}\right)\left[((1-\xi)\varphi + (1-\Theta)\gamma)\hat{x}_t + (\xi\varphi + \Theta\gamma)\hat{x}_t^*\right]$
Output gap	$\gamma(2\xi-1)\left(\mathbb{E}_t\left[\hat{x}_{t+1}^*\right] - \hat{x}_t^*\right) \approx -\Gamma\left[\hat{r}_t - \hat{\bar{r}}_t\right] + ((2\xi-1)+\Gamma)\left[\hat{r}_t^* - \hat{\bar{r}}_t^*\right]$
Monetary policy	$\hat{i}_t^* \approx \left[\psi_\pi \hat{\pi}_t^* + \psi_x \hat{x}_t^*\right] + \hat{m}_t^*$
Fisher equation	$\hat{r}_t^* \equiv \hat{i}_t^* - \mathbb{E}_t\left[\hat{\pi}_{t+1}^*\right]$
Natural interest rate	$\hat{\bar{r}}_t^* \approx \gamma\left[(1-\Theta)\left(\mathbb{E}_t\left[\hat{\bar{y}}_{t+1}\right] - \hat{\bar{y}}_t\right) + \Theta\left(\mathbb{E}_t\left[\hat{\bar{y}}_{t+1}^*\right] - \hat{\bar{y}}_t^*\right)\right]$
Potential output	$\hat{\bar{y}}_t^* \approx \left(\frac{1+\varphi}{\gamma+\varphi}\right)\left[(1-\Lambda)\hat{a}_t + \Lambda\hat{a}_t^*\right]$
	Exogenous, country-specific shocks
Productivity shock	$\begin{pmatrix}\hat{a}_t \\ \hat{a}_t^*\end{pmatrix} \approx \begin{pmatrix}\delta_a & \delta_{a,a^*} \\ \delta_{a,a^*} & \delta_a\end{pmatrix}\begin{pmatrix}\hat{a}_{t-1} \\ \hat{a}_{t-1}^*\end{pmatrix} + \begin{pmatrix}\hat{\varepsilon}_t^a \\ \hat{\varepsilon}_t^{a*}\end{pmatrix}$ $\begin{pmatrix}\hat{\varepsilon}_t^a \\ \hat{\varepsilon}_t^{a*}\end{pmatrix} \sim N\left(\begin{pmatrix}0 \\ 0\end{pmatrix}, \begin{pmatrix}\sigma_a^2 & \rho_{a,a^*}\sigma_a^2 \\ \rho_{a,a^*}\sigma_a^2 & \sigma_a^2\end{pmatrix}\right)$
Monetary shock	$\begin{pmatrix}\hat{m}_t \\ \hat{m}_t^*\end{pmatrix} \approx \begin{pmatrix}\delta_m & 0 \\ 0 & \delta_m\end{pmatrix}\begin{pmatrix}\hat{m}_{t-1} \\ \hat{m}_{t-1}^*\end{pmatrix} + \begin{pmatrix}\hat{\varepsilon}_t^m \\ \hat{\varepsilon}_t^{m*}\end{pmatrix}$ $\begin{pmatrix}\hat{\varepsilon}_t^m \\ \hat{\varepsilon}_t^{m*}\end{pmatrix} \sim N\left(\begin{pmatrix}0 \\ 0\end{pmatrix}, \begin{pmatrix}\sigma_m^2 & \rho_{m,m^*}\sigma_m^2 \\ \rho_{m,m^*}\sigma_m^2 & \sigma_m^2\end{pmatrix}\right)$
	Composite parameters
	$\Theta \equiv \xi\left[\frac{\sigma\gamma - (\sigma\gamma-1)(2\xi-1)}{\sigma\gamma - (\sigma\gamma-1)(2\xi-1)^2}\right]$
	$\Lambda \equiv 1 + (\sigma\gamma-1)\left[\frac{\gamma(1-\xi)(2\xi)}{\varphi\left(\sigma\gamma - (\sigma\gamma-1)(2\xi-1)^2\right)+\gamma}\right]$
	$\Gamma \equiv (1-\xi)[\sigma\gamma + (\sigma\gamma-1)(2\xi-1)]$

Table 2: NOEM Model: Non-Core Equations

	Home economy
Output	$\hat{y}_t = \hat{\overline{y}}_t + \hat{x}_t$
Consumption	$\hat{c}_t \approx \Theta \hat{y}_t + (1-\Theta)\hat{y}_t^*$
Employment	$\widehat{l}_t \approx \hat{y}_t - \hat{a}_t$
Real wages	$\left(\hat{w}_t - \hat{p}_t\right) \approx \gamma \hat{c}_t + \varphi \hat{l}_t \approx (\varphi + \gamma\Theta)\hat{y}_t + \gamma(1-\Theta)\hat{y}_t^* - \varphi \hat{a}_t$
	Foreign economy
Output	$\hat{y}_t^* = \hat{\overline{y}}_t^* + \hat{x}_t^*$
Consumption	$\hat{c}_t^* \approx (1-\Theta)\hat{y}_t + \Theta \hat{y}_t^*$
Employment	$\widehat{l}_t^* \approx \hat{y}_t^* - \hat{a}_t^*$
Real wages	$\left(\hat{w}_t^* - \hat{p}_t^*\right) \approx \gamma \hat{c}_t^* + \varphi \widehat{l}_t^* \approx \gamma(1-\Theta)\hat{y}_t + (\varphi + \gamma\Theta)\hat{y}_t^* - \varphi \hat{a}_t^*$
	International relative prices and trade
Real exchange rate	$\widehat{rs}_t \approx (2\xi - 1)\widehat{tot}_t$
Terms of trade	$\widehat{tot}_t \approx \left[\frac{\gamma}{\sigma\gamma - (\sigma\gamma - 1)(2\xi - 1)^2}\right]\left(\hat{y}_t - \hat{y}_t^*\right)$
Home real exports	$\widehat{exp}_t \approx \Xi \hat{y}_t + (1-\Xi)\hat{y}_t^*$
Home real imports	$\widehat{imp}_t \approx -(1-\Xi)\hat{y}_t - \Xi \hat{y}_t^*$
Home real trade balance	$\widehat{tb}_t \equiv \hat{y}_t - \hat{c}_t = (1-\xi)\left(\widehat{exp}_t - \widehat{imp}_t\right) \approx (1-\Theta)\left(\hat{y}_t - \hat{y}_t^*\right)$
	Composite parameters
	$\Theta \equiv \xi \left[\frac{\sigma\gamma - (\sigma\gamma - 1)(2\xi - 1)}{\sigma\gamma - (\sigma\gamma - 1)(2\xi - 1)^2}\right]$
	$\Xi \equiv \left[\frac{\sigma\gamma + (\sigma\gamma - 1)(2\xi - 1)(1-\xi)}{\sigma\gamma - (\sigma\gamma - 1)(2\xi - 1)^2}\right]$

Table 3: Flexible Price (IRBC) Model: Core and Non-Core Equations

	Home economy
Inflation	$\mathbb{E}_t\left[\hat{\overline{\pi}}_{t+1}\right] \approx \psi_\pi \hat{\overline{\pi}}_t + \hat{m}_t - \hat{\overline{r}}_t$
Output (potential)	$\hat{\overline{y}}_t \approx \left(\frac{1+\varphi}{\gamma+\varphi}\right)\left[\Lambda \hat{a}_t + (1-\Lambda)\hat{a}_t^*\right]$
Monetary policy	$\hat{\overline{i}}_t \approx \psi_\pi \hat{\overline{\pi}}_t + \hat{m}_t$
Fisher equation	$\hat{\overline{r}}_t \equiv \hat{\overline{i}}_t - \mathbb{E}_t\left[\hat{\overline{\pi}}_{t+1}\right]$
Natural interest rate	$\hat{\overline{r}}_t \approx \gamma\left[\Theta\left(\mathbb{E}_t\left[\hat{\overline{y}}_{t+1}\right] - \hat{\overline{y}}_t\right) + (1-\Theta)\left(\mathbb{E}_t\left[\hat{\overline{y}}_{t+1}^*\right] - \hat{\overline{y}}_t^*\right)\right]$
Consumption	$\hat{\overline{c}}_t \approx \Theta \hat{\overline{y}}_t + (1-\Theta)\hat{\overline{y}}_t^*$
Employment	$\hat{\overline{l}}_t \approx \hat{\overline{y}}_t - \hat{a}_t$
Real wages	$\left(\hat{\overline{w}}_t - \hat{\overline{p}}_t\right) \approx \gamma \hat{\overline{c}}_t + \varphi \hat{\overline{l}}_t \approx (\varphi + \gamma\Theta)\hat{\overline{y}}_t + \gamma(1-\Theta)\hat{\overline{y}}_t^* - \varphi \hat{a}_t$

Table 3: (*Continued*)

	Foreign economy
Inflation	$\mathbb{E}_t\left[\hat{\bar{\pi}}^*_{t+1}\right] \approx \psi_\pi \hat{\bar{\pi}}^*_t + \hat{m}^*_t - \hat{\bar{r}}^*_t$
Output (potential)	$\hat{\bar{y}}^*_t \approx \left(\frac{1+\varphi}{\gamma+\varphi}\right)\left[(1-\Lambda)\hat{a}_t + \Lambda\hat{a}^*_t\right]$
Monetary policy	$\hat{\bar{i}}^*_t \approx \psi_\pi \hat{\bar{\pi}}^*_t + \hat{m}^*_t$
Fisher equation	$\hat{\bar{r}}^*_t \equiv \hat{\bar{i}}^*_t - \mathbb{E}_t\left[\hat{\bar{\pi}}^*_{t+1}\right]$
Natural interest rate	$\hat{\bar{r}}^*_t \approx \gamma\left[(1-\Theta)\left(\mathbb{E}_t\left[\hat{\bar{y}}_{t+1}\right] - \hat{\bar{y}}_t\right) + \Theta\left(\mathbb{E}_t\left[\hat{\bar{y}}^*_{t+1}\right] - \hat{\bar{y}}^*_t\right)\right]$
Consumption	$\hat{\bar{c}}^*_t \approx (1-\Theta)\hat{\bar{y}}_t + \Theta\hat{\bar{y}}^*_t$
Employment	$\hat{\bar{l}}^*_t \approx \hat{\bar{y}}^*_t - \hat{a}^*_t$
Real wages	$\left(\hat{\bar{w}}^*_t - \hat{\bar{p}}^*_t\right) \approx \gamma\hat{\bar{c}}^*_t - \varphi\hat{\bar{l}}^*_t \approx \gamma(1-\Theta)\hat{\bar{y}}_t + (\varphi+\gamma\Theta)\hat{\bar{y}}^*_t - \varphi\hat{a}^*_t$
	International relative prices and trade
Real exchange rate	$\widehat{\overline{rs}}_t \approx (2\xi-1)\widehat{\overline{tot}}_t$
Terms of trade	$\widehat{\overline{tot}}_t \approx \left[\frac{\gamma}{\sigma\gamma-(\sigma\gamma-1)(2\xi-1)^2}\right]\left(\hat{\bar{y}}_t - \hat{\bar{y}}^*_t\right)$
Home real exports	$\widehat{\overline{exp}}_t \approx \Xi\hat{\bar{y}}_t + (1-\Xi)\hat{\bar{y}}^*_t$
Home real imports	$\widehat{\overline{imp}}_t \approx -(1-\Xi)\hat{\bar{y}}_t - \Xi\hat{\bar{y}}^*_t$
Home real trade balance	$\widehat{\overline{tb}}_t \equiv \hat{\bar{y}}_t - \hat{\bar{c}}_t = (1-\xi)\left(\widehat{\overline{exp}}_t - \widehat{\overline{imp}}_t\right) \approx (1-\Theta)\left(\hat{\bar{y}}_t - \hat{\bar{y}}^*_t\right)$
	Exogenous, country-specific shocks
Productivity shock	$\begin{pmatrix}\hat{a}_t \\ \hat{a}^*_t\end{pmatrix} \approx \begin{pmatrix}\delta_a & \delta_{a,a^*} \\ \delta_{a,a^*} & \delta_a\end{pmatrix}\begin{pmatrix}\hat{a}_{t-1} \\ \hat{a}^*_{t-1}\end{pmatrix} + \begin{pmatrix}\hat{\varepsilon}^a_t \\ \hat{\varepsilon}^{a*}_t\end{pmatrix}$ $\begin{pmatrix}\hat{\varepsilon}^a_t \\ \hat{\varepsilon}^{a*}_t\end{pmatrix} \sim N\left(\begin{pmatrix}0 \\ 0\end{pmatrix}, \begin{pmatrix}\sigma^2_a & \rho_{a,a^*}\sigma^2_a \\ \rho_{a,a^*}\sigma^2_a & \sigma^2_a\end{pmatrix}\right)$
Monetary shock	$\begin{pmatrix}\hat{m}_t \\ \hat{m}^*_t\end{pmatrix} \approx \begin{pmatrix}\delta_m & 0 \\ 0 & \delta_m\end{pmatrix}\begin{pmatrix}\hat{m}_{t-1} \\ \hat{m}^*_{t-1}\end{pmatrix} + \begin{pmatrix}\hat{\varepsilon}^m_t \\ \hat{\varepsilon}^{m*}_t\end{pmatrix}$ $\begin{pmatrix}\hat{\varepsilon}^m_t \\ \hat{\varepsilon}^{m*}_t\end{pmatrix} \sim N\left(\begin{pmatrix}0 \\ 0\end{pmatrix}, \begin{pmatrix}\sigma^2_m & \rho_{m,m^*}\sigma^2_m \\ \rho_{m,m^*}\sigma^2_m & \sigma^2_m\end{pmatrix}\right)$
	Composite parameters
	$\Theta \equiv \xi\left[\frac{\sigma\gamma-(\sigma\gamma-1)(2\xi-1)}{\sigma\gamma-(\sigma\gamma-1)(2\xi-1)^2}\right]$
	$\Lambda \equiv 1 + (\sigma\gamma-1)\left[\frac{\gamma(1-\xi)(2\xi)}{\varphi\left(\sigma\gamma-(\sigma\gamma-1)(2\xi-1)^2\right)+\gamma}\right]$
	$\Xi \equiv \left[\frac{\sigma\gamma+(\sigma\gamma-1)(2\xi-1)(1-\xi)}{\sigma\gamma-(\sigma\gamma-1)(2\xi-1)^2}\right]$

Table 4: NOEM and Flexible Price (IRBC) Models: Steady State

	Home economy
Output	$\overline{Y}=\overline{Y}(h)=\overline{C}$
Consumption	$\overline{C}=\left(\frac{1}{\kappa}\right)^{\frac{1}{\gamma+\varphi}}(A)^{\frac{1+\varphi}{\gamma+\varphi}}$
	$\overline{C}(h)=2\overline{C}^{\mathrm{H}},\overline{C}(f)=2\overline{C}^{\mathrm{F}},\overline{C}^{\mathrm{H}}=\xi\overline{C},\overline{C}^{\mathrm{F}}=(1-\xi)\overline{C}^{*}$
Employment	$\overline{L}=\overline{L}(h)=\frac{\overline{Y}}{A}$
Real wages	$\frac{\overline{W}}{\overline{P}}=A$
Prices	$\overline{P}=\overline{P}^{\mathrm{H}}=\overline{\tilde{P}}(h)$
Interest rates	$1+\overline{i}=1+\overline{r}=\frac{1}{\beta}$
	Foreign economy
Output	$\overline{Y}^{*}=\overline{Y}^{*}(f)=\overline{C}^{*}$
Consumption	$\overline{C}^{*}=\overline{C}$
	$\overline{C}^{*}(h)=2\overline{C}^{\mathrm{H}*},\overline{C}^{*}(f)=2\overline{C}^{\mathrm{F}*},\overline{C}^{H*}=(1-\xi)\overline{C}^{*},\overline{C}^{\mathrm{F}*}=\xi\overline{C}^{*}$
Employment	$\overline{L}^{*}=\overline{L}^{*}(f)=\frac{\overline{Y}^{*}}{A}$
Real wages	$\frac{\overline{W}^{*}}{\overline{P}^{*}}=A$
Prices	$\overline{P}^{*}=\overline{P}^{\mathrm{F}*}=\overline{\tilde{P}}^{*}(f)$
Interest rates	$1+\overline{i}^{*}=1+\overline{r}^{*}=\frac{1}{\beta}$
	International relative prices and trade
Real exchange rate	$\overline{\mathrm{RS}}\equiv\frac{\overline{SP}^{*}}{\overline{P}}=1$
Terms of trade	$\overline{ToT}\equiv\frac{\overline{P}^{\mathrm{F}}}{\overline{SP}^{\mathrm{H}*}}=\frac{\overline{P}^{\mathrm{F}}}{\overline{P}^{\mathrm{H}}}=\frac{\overline{P}^{\mathrm{F}*}}{\overline{P}^{\mathrm{H}*}}=1$
Home real exports	$\overline{EXP}=\overline{C}^{\mathrm{H}*}=(1-\xi)\overline{C}^{*}=(1-\xi)\overline{C}$
Home real imports	$\overline{IMP}=\overline{C}^{\mathrm{F}}=(1-\xi)\overline{C}$
Home real trade balance	$\overline{TB}=\overline{EXP}-\overline{IMP}=0$

flexible prices and competitive firms, monetary policy has no real effects in the long run (steady state) or the short run (dynamics). The dynamics absent nominal rigidities are described in Table 3. The steady state with or without price stickiness in the model is the same, as indicated in Table 4. In this chapter, I solve and estimate the resulting linear rational expectations model in Tables 1–4.

As shown in Table 1, the log-linearized core equilibrium conditions can be summarized with an open-economy Phillips curve, an open-economy investment-savings (IS) equation, and a Taylor rule for monetary policy in each country.[4] The core (or state) endogenous variables $\hat{\pi}_t$ and $\hat{\pi}_t^*$ denote Home and Foreign inflation (quarter-over-quarter changes in the consumption-based price index), $\hat{x}_t$ and $\hat{x}_t^*$ define the Home and Foreign output gaps (deviations of output from its potential in the frictionless environment), while $\hat{i}_t$ and $\hat{i}_t^*$ are the short-term nominal interest rates instrumented by the monetary policymakers. The Fisherian equation for real interest rates in the Home and Foreign country defines them as $\hat{r}_t \equiv \hat{i}_t - \mathbb{E}_t[\hat{\pi}_{t+1}]$ and $\hat{r}_t^* \equiv \hat{i}_t^* - \mathbb{E}_t\left[\hat{\pi}_{t+1}^*\right]$, respectively, while the natural (real) rates of interest that would prevail in the frictionless model are denoted $\hat{\bar{r}}_t$ for the Home country and $\hat{\bar{r}}_t^*$ for the Foreign country. Potential output in the Home and Foreign countries is denoted as $\hat{\bar{y}}_t$ and $\hat{\bar{y}}_t^*$.

The open-economy Phillips curve fleshes out the global slack hypothesis – that is, the idea that in a world open to trade under short-run monetary non-neutrality, the relevant trade-off for monetary policy is between domestic inflation and global (rather than local) slack. Martínez-García and Wynne (2010) provide some further discussion of the open-economy Phillips curve and describe other extensions. Nominal rigidities are fundamental in explaining the dynamics of the model; therefore, the open-economy Phillips curve is crucial for the propagation of shocks (monetary shocks in particular).

The open-economy IS equation illustrates how output deviations from potential are tied to both Home and Foreign demand forces, where potential output is defined as the output that would prevail in a frictionless environment with the same shock realizations. Nominal rigidities à la Calvo (1983) introduce an intertemporal wedge between the actual real interest rate (the opportunity cost of consumption today versus consumption tomorrow) and the natural rate of interest that would prevail in the same

[4] The core of the model refers to a (minimal) set of equations that uniquely determines the path of a subset of endogenous variables (the core or state variables) by their initial conditions and the path of the exogenous shocks specified. In turn, all noncore (or non-state) variables can be expressed as functions of the core endogenous variables and the specified exogenous shocks. The core system of the model, therefore, suffices to uniquely determine the future paths of all the core and noncore endogenous variables. Often there is no unique way of characterizing the core and solving the model through the orthogonalization technique pioneered by Aoki (1981) – the work of Fukuda (1993) provides a practical example of that. Moreover, for Bayesian estimation purposes the number of observables – and, therefore, the number of estimating equations (core or noncore) – is tied to the number of shocks to be estimated from the data. Hence, the core equations may need to be complemented with noncore equations for estimation purposes (e.g., if exogenous labor supply and government consumption shocks in each country were added to our model).

economy without frictions yet subject to the same shocks. Demand itself responds to deviations of each country's real interest rate from its natural real rate as those deviations shift consumption across time, but the open-economy IS equation recognizes that local aggregate production will be driven by global (not just local) aggregate demand.

Whenever the real interest rate is above its natural real rate, more consumption today is postponed for consumption tomorrow than would be in the frictionless environment. Ceteris paribus, this implies a demand shortfall today and an expected decline in the output gap. Analogously, when the real interest rate is below the natural rate, the resulting boost in consumption today (at the expense of future consumption) leads to an expected increase in the output gap. The open-economy IS equation illustrates that demand for local goods can be either domestic or foreign (in the form of exports), so real interest rate deviations in both countries matter.

The natural real interest rate does not equalize across countries despite the symmetry of the model because the assumption of Home-production bias in consumption translates (except in a knife-edge case where $\xi = 1/2$) into different consumption baskets for the Home and Foreign countries. Differences in the consumption baskets across countries, in turn, imply that each country's consumption demand responds differently to domestic and foreign demand forces (resulting in differences among the natural rates of interest in the Home and Foreign countries). The model derivations indicate that the natural real rates can be expressed as a function of expected changes in Home and Foreign potential output. Potential output for each country is a function of the Home and Foreign productivity shocks, since monetary shocks (the only other shock in the model) have no real effects absent nominal rigidities.

The Home and Foreign monetary policy rules close the model, reflecting the standard view on the prevailing monetary policy regime and playing a crucial role in the international transmission of shocks. The conventional approach that I follow here is that monetary policy pursues the goal of domestic stabilization (even in a fully integrated world) and, hence, solely responds to changes in domestic economic conditions. Monetary policy is modeled with a Taylor (1993)-type rule and is assumed to react to local conditions as determined by each country's inflation and output gap alone. I assume that the persistence in policy rates reflects inertia that is *extrinsic* or exogenous to the policymaking process and out of the policymakers' control.

There are two types of country-specific, exogenous shocks in the model: productivity shocks, $\hat{a}_t$ and $\hat{a}_t^*$, and monetary shocks, $\hat{m}_t$ and $\hat{m}_t^*$. Productivity and monetary policy shocks follow VAR(1) stochastic processes each, but I have only incorporated spillovers in the stochastic process for productivity shocks (and not for monetary shocks). Productivity and monetary policy innovations can be correlated across countries but not with each other.

An observation equation for each country relating the output gap to other observables (to current output) and a model-consistent specification of the output potential must be added to the core model in Table 1 for estimation purposes. Table 2 summarizes the standard observation equation relating output (i.e., $\hat{y}_t$ and $\hat{y}^*_t$) to output potential and the output gap as well as other endogenous (noncore) variables of the model. Those (noncore) endogenous variables in Table 2 provide theoretical constraints on the data that can also be exploited to estimate the model.

Consistent with the structure of the model, Table 2 characterizes aggregate consumption, $\hat{c}_t$ and $\hat{c}^*_t$, aggregate employment, $\hat{l}_t$ and $\hat{l}^*_t$, and real wages, $\hat{w}_t - \hat{p}_t$ and $\hat{w}^*_t - \hat{p}^*_t$, in both countries. I also derive expressions for the terms of trade, $\widehat{tot}_t$, the real exchange rate, $\widehat{rs}_t$, and the real exports and real imports, $\widehat{exp}_t$ and $\widehat{imp}_t$. Finally, I define the real trade balance, $\widehat{tb}_t$, as $\widehat{tb}_t \equiv (\overline{EXP}/\overline{Y})\widehat{exp}_t - (\overline{IMP}/\overline{Y})\widehat{imp}_t$ where $\overline{EXP}/\overline{Y} = \overline{IMP}/\overline{Y} = (1-\xi)$ refer to the steady-state export and import shares and are tied to the parameter ξ that regulates the degree of openness in the model.

2.3. The Frictionless Model

Table 3 describes the full dynamics of the economy in the frictionless environment with flexible prices and perfect competition. I distinguish variables from the frictionless equilibrium by marking them with an upper bar but still maintain a caret above to indicate that those variables are expressed in log deviations from steady state. The exogenous monetary and productivity shocks are invariant to the specification of the model – they are the same for both the frictionless and the NOEM models.

The complete system of log-linearized equations that describes the frictionless equilibrium can be found in Table 3. I characterize the frictionless model reported in Table 3 as a special case of the NOEM model discussed before where nominal rigidities are completely removed, assuming that prices are flexible and that markets for goods are perfectly competitive. All endogenous variables described in Section 2.2 have a natural counterpart in the frictionless model except for the output gaps because, by construction, current and potential output are the same in a model without any frictions.

The main change in the frictionless setting occurs on the supply-side and is reflected in the pricing behavior of firms. In the frictionless model, the decisions of firms can simply be described with a standard rule whereby prices must equate marginal costs. Home and Foreign inflation, $\hat{\bar{\pi}}_t$ and $\hat{\bar{\pi}}^*_t$, are still determined by monetary policy and are sensitive to both productivity and monetary shocks. However, it follows from the characterization of the dynamics of the frictionless model that neither the monetary policy rule nor monetary shocks have an impact on any real variables (i.e., monetary policy has no effect on potential output, consumption, employment, real wages, or the natural interest rates), as monetary neutrality holds in the short run as well as in the long run absent any nominal rigidities.

For the purposes of this chapter, the frictionless equilibrium matters only in so far as it determines the potential output and the natural rates of interest for the Home and Foreign countries that serve as the benchmark targets for monetary policymaking in the NOEM model. In that spirit, the following proposition gives a precise characterization of the potential output and the natural rates of interest for both countries derived from the properties of the stochastic VAR(1) for productivity shocks in the following terms:

Proposition 1. *Given the VAR*(1) *structure assumed for the productivity shocks, the vector of Home and Foreign potential output,* $\hat{\bar{y}}_t$ *and* $\hat{\bar{y}}_t^*$*, respectively, follows a VAR*(1) *stochastic process,*

$$\begin{pmatrix} \bar{y}_t^* \\ \hat{\bar{y}}_t \end{pmatrix} \approx \begin{pmatrix} \delta_a & \delta_{a,a^*} \\ \delta_{a,a^*} & \delta_a \end{pmatrix} \begin{pmatrix} \hat{\bar{y}}_{t-1} \\ \hat{\bar{y}}_{t-1}^* \end{pmatrix} + \begin{pmatrix} \hat{\varepsilon}_t^y \\ \hat{\varepsilon}_t^{y*} \end{pmatrix}, \tag{33}$$

$$\begin{pmatrix} \hat{\varepsilon}_t^y \\ \hat{\varepsilon}_t^{y*} \end{pmatrix} \sim N\left(\begin{pmatrix} 0 \\ 0 \end{pmatrix}, \sigma_y^2 \begin{pmatrix} 1 & \rho_{y,y^*} \\ \rho_{y,y^*} & 1 \end{pmatrix} \right), \tag{34}$$

where

$$\sigma_y^2 = \sigma_a^2 \left(\frac{1+\varphi}{\gamma+\varphi} \right)^2 \left((\Lambda)^2 + 2\rho_{a,a^*}\Lambda(1-\Lambda) + (1-\Lambda)^2 \right), \tag{35}$$

$$\rho_{y,y^*} = \frac{\rho_{a,a^*}(\Lambda)^2 + 2\Lambda(1-\Lambda) + \rho_{a,a^*}(1-\Lambda)^2}{(\Lambda)^2 + 2\rho_{a,a^*}\Lambda(1-\Lambda) + (1-\Lambda)^2}. \tag{36}$$

Similarly, the vector of Home and Foreign natural rates of interest, $\hat{\bar{r}}_t$ *and* $\hat{\bar{r}}_t^*$*, respectively, follows a VAR*(1) *stochastic process,*

$$\begin{pmatrix} \hat{\bar{r}}_t \\ \hat{\bar{r}}_t^* \end{pmatrix} \approx \begin{pmatrix} \delta_a & \delta_{a,a^*} \\ \delta_{a,a^*} & \delta_a \end{pmatrix} \begin{pmatrix} \hat{\bar{r}}_{t-1} \\ \hat{\bar{r}}_{t-1}^* \end{pmatrix} + \begin{pmatrix} \hat{\varepsilon}_t^r \\ \hat{\varepsilon}_t^{r*} \end{pmatrix}, \tag{37}$$

$$\begin{pmatrix} \hat{\varepsilon}_t^r \\ \hat{\varepsilon}_t^{r*} \end{pmatrix} \sim N\left(\begin{pmatrix} 0 \\ 0 \end{pmatrix}, \sigma_r^2 \begin{pmatrix} 1 & \rho_{r,r^*} \\ \rho_{r,r^*} & 1 \end{pmatrix} \right), \tag{38}$$

where

$$\sigma_r^2 = \sigma_a^2 \gamma^2 \left(\frac{1+\varphi}{\gamma+\varphi} \right)^2 \left((\Pi_1)^2 + 2\rho_{a,a^*} \Pi_1 \Pi_2 + (\Pi_2)^2 \right),$$

$$\rho_{r,r^*} = \frac{\rho_{a,a^*} (\Pi_1)^2 + 2\Pi_1 \Pi_2 + \rho_{a,a^*} (\Pi_2)^2}{(\Pi_1)^2 + 2\rho_{a,a^*} \Pi_1 \Pi_2 + (\Pi_2)^2},$$

$$\Pi_1 \equiv \delta_{a,a^*} - \xi \left(\frac{\varphi(\sigma\gamma - (\sigma\gamma - 1)(2\xi - 1)) + \gamma}{\varphi(\sigma\gamma - (\sigma\gamma - 1)(2\xi - 1)^2) + \gamma} \right) (1 + \delta_{a,a^*} - \delta_a),$$

$$\Pi_2 \equiv (\delta_a - 1) + \xi \left(\frac{\varphi(\sigma\gamma - (\sigma\gamma - 1)(2\xi - 1)) + \gamma}{\varphi(\sigma\gamma - (\sigma\gamma - 1)(2\xi - 1)^2) + \gamma} \right) (1 + \delta_{a,a^*} - \delta_a).$$

Home and Foreign potential output – as well as the Home and Foreign natural rates – inherit the VAR(1) stochastic structure of the productivity shocks and, moreover, some of the basic features of the underlying productivity shocks – in particular, their persistence δ_a and spillovers δ_{a,a^*}. In turn, Proposition 1 also indicates that the variance-covariance matrix (both the volatility and the correlation) of the potential output and natural rate processes is different from the one posited for the exogenous productivity shocks. Other structural parameters of the model apart from the parameters on the variance-covariance matrix for the exogenous productivity shocks modify the variance-covariance matrix of the endogenous potential output and natural rates.

Productivity shocks enter into the dynamics of the NOEM model described in Table 1 only through their impact on the natural real rates, $\hat{\bar{r}}_t$ and $\hat{\bar{r}}_t^*$. Having established the solution to the natural rates in Proposition 1 simplifies the specification of the NOEM model because the stochastic processes for the natural rates and the monetary shocks suffice to describe its stochastic forcing processes. The Home and Foreign monetary shock processes $\hat{m}_t$ and $\hat{m}_t^*$ enter directly into the model through the Taylor rule for monetary policy in each country.

2.4. The Deterministic Steady State

The deterministic steady state of the model is presented in Table 4. With an optimal labor subsidy to neutralize the distortionary effect of monopolistic competition, the resulting steady state for the NOEM model of Martínez-García and Wynne (2010) with nominal rigidities is the same as that of the frictionless model. Monetary policy has no direct impact on the real variables in steady state, so long-run neutrality is preserved even when the nominal rigidities in the NOEM model introduce a verifiable trade-off between local inflation and the global output gap in the short-run dynamics.

3. Bayesian Estimation: Bringing Data to Discipline the Theory

The theoretical model of Martínez-García and Wynne (2010) synthesized in Section 2 provides the backbone of the NOEM literature's understanding of the channels through which foreign factors determine local inflation, which arguably has been the hallmark of international macro over the past 15 years. There remains uncertainty, however, regarding the specification of certain features of the model – such as the monetary policy rules – and also about how to parameterize the NOEM model.

The parameterization choices, in particular, have consequences for the sensitivity of local inflation to foreign developments implied by the model, so I adopt Bayesian estimation methods to discipline those parameterization choices with the data. While the difficulties associated with Bayesian estimation and identification are well-known (see, e.g., An & Schorfheide, 2007; Martínez-García et al., 2012; Ríos-Rull, Schorfheide, Fuentes-Albero, Kryshko, & Santaeulália-Llopis, 2012), these methods are still useful – for instance, being able to recognize and account for the parameter uncertainty discussed in the literature in addition to also being able to incorporate additional information from the observable data into the parameter estimates that I use to investigate the implications of the NOEM model.

In this section, I describe the data that disciplines the estimation, and the mapping between the observable variables and the endogenous variables of the model. I also give a brief overview of the selection of priors for the structural parameters of the model, and I explain how extraneous information factors into my choice of priors for the estimation.

3.1. Variables and Data

The NOEM model presented in Tables 1–3 is estimated using quarterly data from 1980Q1 until 2011Q4 for the United States and an aggregate of its 38 largest trading partners. In my estimation, I take the NOEM model specification as given and choose the priors so that they reflect the uncertainty surrounding the structural parameters. In this section, I discuss the data to inform both the choice of priors and the Bayesian estimation of the model.

As in Martínez-García and Wynne (2010), the NOEM model built for this chapter is a stationary model that only describes the behavior of the two-country economy around its balanced growth path (BGP). Given that the NOEM model does not explicitly specify the underlying trend process for the data and defines only stationary variables, the detrending of the observable variables used for the estimation must be done outside the model. In this section, therefore, I discuss the detrending of the data and how to specify the mapping between the detrended observable data and the stationary model variables needed for the estimation of the model.

3.1.1. *Observables for Estimation*

The estimation of any model requires the specification of a set of observables. There are no precise guidelines, however, on how to choose observables for estimation. The research on data selection is still rather limited, but a set of guidelines on the matter can be inferred from the recent contributions of Guerrón-Quintana (2010), Martínez-García et al. (2012), and Martínez-García and Wynne (2014).

(a) Use observables that facilitate the identification of the parameters of interest, since even structural parameters that are theoretically identified may not always be identifiable given the chosen observables; the structural parameters of interest are those that determine the behavior of the model along the dimensions that are novel to the specification or that relate to the particular model features that are being tested.
(b) Be aware of poorly measured data that introduce noise and error into the estimation; if precisely measured data are hard to come by, modeling measurement error in the mapping between the observable data and the model variables is warranted.

The NOEM model posits monetary non-neutrality and allows the international propagation of shocks through the trade channel. Hence, given the emphasis of the model on the international transmission of monetary shocks and monetary non-neutrality, it seems natural under the set of best practices described before to include both real and nominal variables in the set of observables in order to detect any real effects from monetary shocks in the data.

In order to avoid stochastic singularity in Bayesian estimation, the same number of observable variables as structural shocks is necessary in the model. Since I have monetary and productivity shocks that are country-specific, I have four structural shocks; accordingly, I should have four observable variables. I take the observable variables to be Home and Foreign output as well as Home and Foreign inflation.

The underlying data that I use to define the output and inflation observables is quarterly real GDP in PPP-adjusted terms and headline CPI data for the United States and 38 of its largest trading partners – including

Argentina, Australia, Austria, Belgium, Brazil, Canada, China, Czech Republic, Denmark, Finland, France, Germany, Greece, Hong Kong, Hungary, India, Indonesia, Ireland, Italy, Japan, Korea, Luxembourg, Malaysia, Mexico, The Netherlands, New Zealand, Norway, Peru, Poland, Singapore, South Africa, Spain, Sweden, Switzerland, Taiwan, Thailand, Turkey, and the United Kingdom.[5]

The GDP and headline CPI data covers the period from 1980Q1 to 2011Q4 at quarterly frequency, although a few countries have shorter time series. The GDP data comes from the OECD and from various national statistics offices, while headline CPI is from the OECD, the IMF International Financial Statistics (IFS), and various national statistics offices.

To construct the real GDP series in PPP-adjusted terms, I start with the nominal GDP in local currency for each country from 2005Q1 to 2005Q4, adjusted by the IMF's purchasing power parity (PPP) conversion rates for 2005 to facilitate international comparisons. The 2005 data is then extended using the quarterly growth rates of real GDP in local currency (with 2005 as its base year) backwards and forwards. Gross inflation is defined as the ratio of the headline CPI in two subsequent quarters. For the NOEM model, however, it is useful to work with the net inflation rate (in percent terms) instead as the observable. Net inflation is computed as gross inflation minus one, but I approximate it for each country with the log of gross inflation times 100 – that is, with the log-difference of the quarterly headline CPI in two subsequent quarters times 100 (where the quarterly CPI is the average of the reported monthly CPI).

The individual country series for PPP-adjusted real GDP and headline CPI inflation are combined, excluding the United States, to compute a foreign aggregate for output and inflation with fixed weights based on the PPP-adjusted GDP shares for 2005 from the IMF corresponding to the 38 countries in the sample. Countries with missing observations are excluded for the time period for which they have no observations and the aggregate is re-weighted accordingly.[6]

[5] Separately, I have also used an alternative dataset covering a different selection of 39 advanced and emerging economies obtained from the database of global economic indicators of the Federal Reserve Bank of Dallas (see, e.g., Grossman, Mack, & Martínez-García, 2014). The empirical findings with this data were very similar, so I do not report them in the chapter.

[6] The GDP series can be reconstructed back to 1980Q1 for most countries (except Czech Republic and Poland which start in 1990Q1, and Taiwan in 1981Q1). Similarly, the headline CPI series can be reconstructed back to 1980Q1 for most countries (except Brazil which starts in 1992Q4, Czech Republic in 1991Q2, China in 1984Q2, and Argentina and Peru in 1982Q4).

The NOEM model is not built to capture variations at seasonal frequency. Accordingly, all data I use is seasonally adjusted by the source or has been seasonally adjusted with the Census X-12 procedure whenever reported not seasonally adjusted. For countries that have experienced periods of high inflation (Argentina, Brazil, and Peru), the seasonal-adjustment is performed by parts rather than on the whole time series.

3.1.2. Mapping the Observable Data to Model Variables

The core of the NOEM model described in Table 1 suggests that the tradeoff between nominal and real variables can be articulated in terms of inflation and the output gaps (more precisely, between local inflation and a combination of Home and Foreign output gaps). However, output gaps are not directly measured in the available macro data. In order to map the observable data into model variables, I have to complete the estimation model with a measurement equation that relates actual observed output to the output gap and its output potential (from Table 2). This requires that I take a stand on what potential output is in the context of this model (which is given in Table 3). Hence, I must jointly estimate a model for the natural rates of interest and potential output – as synthesized in Proposition 1 – together with the fully fledged NOEM model of Table 1.

The observed series for U.S. output and for Foreign output grow over time, so a mapping between the non-stationary data and the corresponding output variables in the NOEM model is needed. Typically, the trend is ascribed to long-term growth in the labor force and to technological progress (i.e., to the long-term growth in aggregate productivity). There are different ways of removing the trend from output – irrespective of what the ultimate sources of long-term growth are. Since the NOEM model itself does not specify a trend, I simply follow Stock and Watson (1999) and use the one-sided Hodrick–Prescott (HP) filter to retain only the fluctuations of the time series at business cycle frequencies.[7]

I impose a standard penalty parameter of $\lambda = 1600$ on the one-sided HP-filter and apply it to the log of observed output multiplied by 100. Taking the log of output makes the resulting series scale invariant. Then, multiplying the logged series by 100 means that the cyclical component extracted by the one-sided HP-filter can be interpreted as the percent deviation from trend. Different filters may lead to different characteristics of the implied business cycles – for example, the one-sided HP-filter is likely to generate less persistent deviations from trend than a deterministic polynomial trend

[7] For a recent discussion on pre-filtering the data versus estimating the trend jointly with the rest of the model, see Ferroni (2011).

would. The one-sided HP-filtered series also has (approximately) zero mean, so there is no mismatch in this regard with the corresponding model variable which has zero mean in population terms.

In contrast to output data, nontrending observable variables like net CPI inflation (in percent terms) have more direct counterparts in the stationary variables of the NOEM model. The corresponding model variables are defined as the percentage deviation of net inflation from a zero-inflation steady state. Hence, I need to remove the steady state inflation term from the data to accurately match the observable data on net CPI inflation to the inflation variables in the model. One common approach to deal with this issue is to simply use demeaned net inflation rates – which, by construction, results in a zero-mean observable series. However, I would argue that using a filter that removes a time-varying trend component from net inflation is more appropriate for the series that I investigate here. For that reason, I use the same detrending procedure – the one-sided HP-filter with penalty parameter $\lambda = 1600$ – used for output, so the filtered series still has (approximately) zero mean.

3.2. Eliciting Priors

All priors are summarized in Table 5 and Figure 1. I only consider prior densities of the Beta, Gamma, Inverse Gamma, Normal, Uniform, and the degenerate distribution that puts mass one on a single value of the parameter space since they are the distributions most commonly used in Bayesian estimation. While a case can be made for defining the prior distribution jointly on all structural parameters, I follow the standard practice in the empirical literature of assigning independent prior distributions to each parameter.

There is no uniquely agreed upon way of eliciting priors, so there is scope for disagreement. Other researchers may push for a different selection of prior distributions based on other sources of information or based on weighting differently the ones discussed here. I select priors that reflect my ex ante views and beliefs about the structural parameters of the NOEM model, incorporating both my current understanding of what are plausible values for the parameterization/calibration of the model and my own perceptions of how uncertain each one of those parameter values is.

For all parameters, I impose that the mean of the prior distribution must be equal to the conventional calibration of the parameter in the literature in order to be consistent and comparable. Then, I choose the prior distribution for each parameter – as well as its dispersion – to reflect the degree of uncertainty that exists around the prior mean of the parameters. While I discuss the basic aspects of my choice of priors and my selection strategy here, I refer the interested reader to Martínez-García et al. (2012)

Table 5: Structural and Shock Parameters: Prior Distributions

		Prior distributions			
		Domain	Density	Mean	Std. Dev.
Structural Parameters					
Non-policy parameters					
β	Intertemporal discount factor	(0,1)	Fixed	0.99	–
γ	Inverse intertemporal elasticity of substitution	$\mathbb{R}^+$	Gamma	5	1
φ	Inverse Frisch elasticity of labor supply	$\mathbb{R}^+$	Gamma	$\varphi=\gamma$	–
σ	Elasticity of substitution between Home and Foreign varieties	$\mathbb{R}^+$	Gamma	1.5	1
$2\xi-1$	(Transformed) share of local goods in consumption basket	(0,1)	Beta	0.88	0.01
α	Calvo (1983) price stickiness parameter	(0,1)	Beta	0.75	0.02
Policy parameters					
$\psi_\pi-1$	(Transformed) policy response to inflation	$\mathbb{R}^+$	InvGamma	0.24	2
ψ_x	Policy response to the output gap	$\mathbb{R}^+$	InvGamma	0.33	2
Shock Parameters					
δ_a	Persistence parameter in productivity	(0,1)	Beta	0.97	0.02
$\frac{1}{2}+\frac{1}{2}\frac{\delta_{a,a^*}}{0.03}$	(Transformed) spillover parameter in productivity	(0,1)	Beta	0.91667	0.05
σ_a	Std. deviation of productivity innovations	$\mathbb{R}^+$	InvGamma	0.73	3
ρ_{a,a^*}	Cross-correlation of productivity innovations	(0,1)	Beta	0.29	0.18
δ_m	Persistence parameter in the monetary shock	(0,1)	Beta	0.92	0.09
σ_m	Std. deviation of monetary shock innovations	$\mathbb{R}^+$	InvGamma	0.36	5
ρ_{m,m^*}	Cross-correlation of monetary shock innovations	(0,1)	Beta	0.50	0.2

Notes: The share of locally produced goods ξ and the spillovers between Home and Foreign productivity shocks δ_{a,a^*} are transformed to adjust their range to the domain of the Beta distribution. I also transform the sensitivity of monetary policy to deviations from the inflation target ψ_π to adjust its range (set above one to satisfy the Taylor principle) to the domain of the Gamma distribution. The existence and uniqueness of a solution for the NOEM model requires the policy parameter ψ_π to be slightly above 1 for very low values of the policy parameter ψ_x but is consistent with a threshold slightly below 1 at high values of ψ_x. Hence, restricting the policy parameter ψ_π to satisfy the Taylor principle for the NOEM model is neither necessary nor sufficient to ensure determinacy but is a conventional practice that ensures most draws from these prior distributions will fall in a region of the parameter space for which a unique solution exists. Similarly, the priors on the parameters of the shock processes are chosen to ensure that both productivity and monetary shocks are well-behaved and stationary processes under almost any draw generated by them.

This table reports only the prior mean and prior standard deviation for each model parameter. Each one of the prior distributions considered can be fully characterized with two parameters υ and s. For any plausible choice of the prior mean and the prior standard deviation there is a one-to-one mapping that uniquely determines parameters υ and s and fully characterizes the prior distribution. For the Normal distribution, the mean is $\mu=\upsilon$ and the variance is $\sigma^2=s^2$. For the Beta distribution, the mean is $\mu=\upsilon/(\upsilon+s)$ and the variance is $\sigma^2=\upsilon s/\left((\upsilon+s)^2(\upsilon+s+1)\right)$. For the Gamma distribution, the mean is $\mu=\upsilon s$ and the variance is $\sigma^2=\upsilon s^2$. For the Uniform distribution, the upper and lower bound of the support are υ and s, respectively, while the mean is $\mu=(\upsilon+s)/2$ and the variance is $\sigma^2=(\upsilon-s)^2/12$. For the Inverse Gamma distribution, the mean is $\mu=s/(\upsilon-1)$ and the variance is $\sigma^2=s^2/\left((\upsilon-1)^2(\upsilon-2)\right)$.

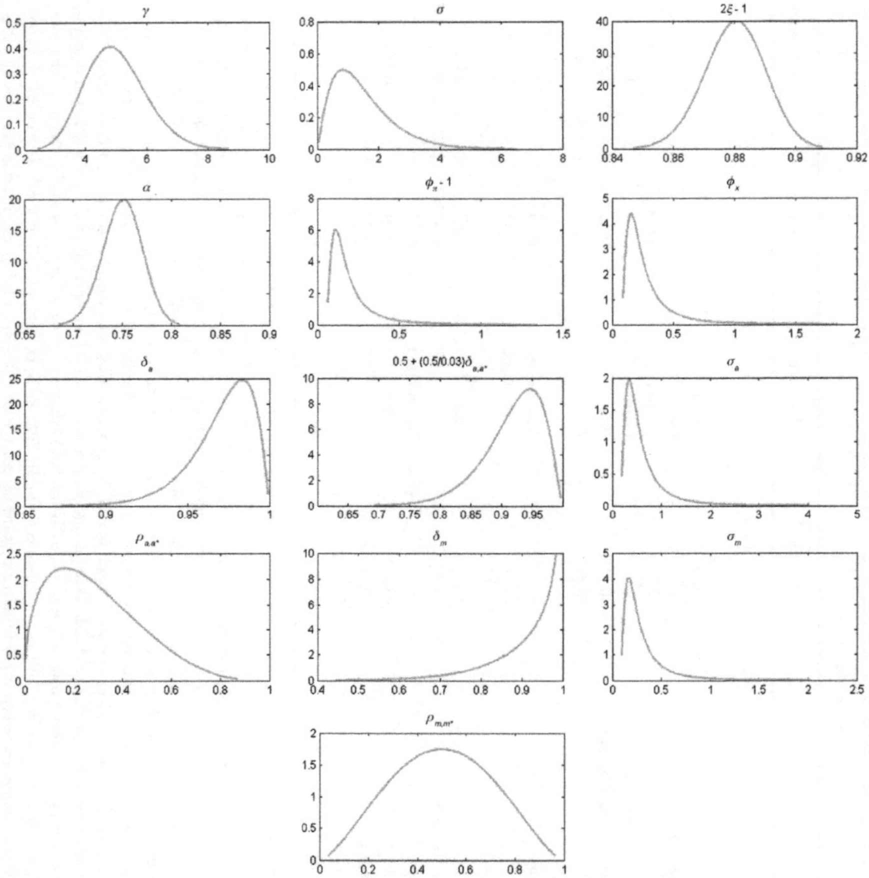

Figure 1: Prior Distributions. Notes: The code is written for Matlab version 8.3.0.532 and Dynare version 4.3.2. This figure plots the prior distributions of all 13 structural (policy and non-policy) and shock parameters that do not receive a degenerate prior distribution. The code for this figure is available upon request from the author.

for a more in-depth discussion of the choice of priors and the sources of information most often cited to set the priors on the structural parameters of the NOEM model.[8]

[8] Martínez-García et al. (2012) also provides suggested guidelines on the selection of priors and on using data sources to set economically relevant values for the parameter values that characterize the prior distribution.

The characterization of the priors may involve imposing restrictions on the feasible range on which the structural parameters are defined so as to minimize the number of draws from the prior distributions coming from regions of the parameter space that produce multiple solutions or no solution for the NOEM model. Moreover, for some parameters I also restrict their feasible range because certain parts of the parameter space may be feasible in theory but in practice are deemed *unrealistic* to match the observed data.

Furthermore, I rely on transformations of a few relevant parameters in order to ensure that the range of values for the parameter conforms with the range of values on which the preferred prior distribution function is defined. In cases where a transformation of the parameter range is pertinent, a linear transformation suffices to match the ranges of the prior distribution with those implied by theory.

3.2.1. Structural Parameters

I extract the business cycle component from the observable output and CPI inflation data using the one-sided HP-filter recommended by Stock and Watson (1999), as indicated in Section 3.1. Hence, all the filtered series used for estimation have (approximately) zero mean. Both the steady-state gross inflation rate $\Pi = \overline{\Pi}$ and the discount factor β represent two well-known examples of structural parameters for whose estimation I would need stationary variables (output and inflation) that preserve their respective means (see, e.g., Fernández-Villaverde, 2010). Using the demeaned data that I described before, therefore, implies the loss of the mean and makes it difficult to estimate either one of those two parameters.

The NOEM model is log-linearized around a zero-net inflation steady state, so that demeaned inflation data would not be an issue in my application. The parameter β could be estimated with stationary data on short-term interest rates that preserve the mean. Taking as given a zero-inflation steady state, an observation equation would have to be added that links the observed interest rates to $\hat{i}_t - \ln \beta$ and $\hat{i}_t^* - \ln \beta$ for the Home and Foreign countries, where $-\ln \beta$ is the log of the steady-state real interest rate.

Since I use demeaned data and do not include short-term interest rates among the observables for estimation, I forego any further attempts to estimate β. Instead, I use a degenerate prior for the intertemporal discount factor β and fix it at 0.99. I impose this degenerate prior on β targeting an average yearly interest rate of 4% which is standard in the literature. This parameter value is based on the long-run historical average of the real interest rate (nominal rate minus realized inflation) which, as indicated before, does not enter into the set of observables that I use for the estimation of the model.[9]

I choose a tight prior for the share of locally produced goods in the consumption basket ξ to recognize that this parameter is tied to the import share through the steady state and hence cannot deviate too much from the import share's historical average. I use a Beta distribution for the prior and transform the parameter to $2\xi-1$ in order to ensure that the range of possible values of the transformed parameter corresponds with the domain of the Beta distribution. Accordingly, I center the prior of the transformed parameter around 0.88, which implies a prior mean for ξ that is equal to 0.94 consistent with a long-run import share of just 6%. I impose a small standard deviation of 0.01, which implies that the prior Beta is single-peaked and puts most of its mass within a small neighborhood around the prior mean. This prior specification acknowledges that one should not expect ex ante the structural parameter $1-\xi$ – which defines the degree of trade openness – to be too large when the import shares observed for the United States have been rather low during most of the sample period under consideration.

The remaining (non-policy) structural parameters are also key for monetary non-neutrality and to determine the strength of the propagation mechanism through the trade channel in the NOEM model – those structural parameters are the inverse of the intertemporal elasticity of substitution, γ, the inverse of the Frisch elasticity of labor supply, φ, the elasticity of substitution between Home and Foreign bundles, σ, and the Calvo price stickiness parameter, α. The different information sources that can be brought to bear in calibrating them are sometimes hard to reconcile with each other or give a wide range of possible values for these parameters. Those concerns will be subsumed into a wide-enough prior distribution, letting the data ultimately be the deciding factor to pick the value that attains the best fit in the estimation.

Given the specification of preferences underlying the NOEM model, I impose $\varphi=\gamma$ to be more consistent with the notion of a balanced growth path (BGP). Then, I adopt the Gamma distribution centered around 5 for γ with a wide standard deviation of 1 in order to encompass a broad range of values considered as plausible in the macro literature for both parameters.

[9] The parameter β illustrates how important the selection of observables is for the estimation. Guerrón-Quintana (2010), Martínez-García et al. (2012), and Martínez-García and Wynne (2014) argue that the observables one chooses matter for how well identified the parameter estimates are. Here I show with the parameter β that the selection of observables may determine whether a parameter can be estimated at all or not. This case also highlights that first-order moments contain useful information for identification that cannot be disregarded without loss of generality.

I adopt the Gamma distribution centered around 1.5 for σ. I recognize the importance of this parameter for the international transmission of shocks through the trade channel, but I impose a wide standard deviation of 1 to capture the uncertainty surrounding its true value. This prior specification results in a wide range of plausible values for the intratemporal elasticity of substitution between Home and Foreign bundles, with a unimodal distribution skewed towards the left.

I adopt the Beta distribution centered around 0.75 for the Calvo parameter, α.[10] For α, I pick a prior Beta distribution with a standard deviation of 0.02 which is not too tight. The Calvo parameter α indicates the fraction of firms that are unable to re-optimize in any given period, so I favor a unimodal Beta prior that internalizes the empirical evidence – mostly micro evidence – suggesting that an average duration of four quarters for each price spell ($\alpha = 0.75$) is plausible for the United States. This prior distribution puts little mass on values of the parameter range above 0.85 (which implies expected durations of more than six quarters) and below 0.65 (which implies expected durations of less than three quarters).

Finally, I must consider the policy parameters ψ_π and ψ_x for both their impact on the distortionary effects of nominal rigidities and the strength of the propagation mechanism of the NOEM model. I center the policy parameters around their standard values, but I impose an Inverse Gamma distribution for both of them and select fairly wide priors. The parameter for the policy response to deviations from the inflation target needs to be transformed in order to be consistent with the domain of the Inverse Gamma distribution and to rule out violations of the Taylor principle where monetary policy is likely not aggressive *enough* to rule out indeterminacy or no equilibrium. Hence, I estimate $\psi_\pi - 1$ with a prior centered at 0.24 that implies a prior mean of 1.24 for the corresponding policy parameter. The prior mean on the sensitivity to the output gap ψ_x is set at 0.33. While these prior means are plausible based on the existing literature (see, e.g., Rudebusch, 2006), I still select a prior standard deviation of 2 for both parameters that puts positive mass over a reasonably wide range of values between 0 and 2.

---

[10] The Calvo parameter α regulates the impact of monetary non-neutrality in the short-run dynamics of the NOEM model. However, β and α are difficult to identify simultaneously through the Phillips curve relationship. This is where being able to relate the mean of the observable data on interest rates to the steady state interest rate would be important not just to identify β itself, but to help identify α separately as well. The Calvo parameter α relates to the nominal friction of the model (the degree of nominal rigidity) that breaks with monetary neutrality in the short run, but is generally regarded as more uncertain than the intertemporal discount factor β. Hence, imposing a degenerate prior on β is meant (at least in part) to facilitate a more precise identification in the estimation of the Calvo parameter α.

3.2.2. Parameters of the Shock Processes

The prior distributions for the partial autocorrelations of both shocks are restricted to lie in the (0,1)-interval, so as to rule out negative values for δ_a and δ_m which would imply dynamics for the endogenous variables of the model that are difficult to reconcile with the actual observable data. However, that does not suffice to ensure the stationarity of the productivity VAR(1) process because in that case I also need to consider the possible values of the spillover parameter δ_{a,a^*}.

For the prior mean on the parameters of the productivity shock process, I match the calibration used in Heathcote and Perri (2002). For the parameters of the monetary shock process I primarily rely on the estimates provided by Rudebusch (2006) to set their prior means. I adopt a Beta distribution for the persistence of the productivity shock δ_a to match the value of 0.97. Since there seems to be broad agreement that Solow residuals tend to be quite persistent, I set the standard deviation of the prior to be 0.02 so the mass is concentrated at high values but somewhat skewed to the left.

Adopting a prior mean of 0.97 for δ_a, I choose to impose a tight prior on the key spillover parameter δ_{a,a^*} while still guaranteeing the stationarity of the stochastic process for productivity around the prior mean. For δ_a arbitrarily close to 0.97, δ_{a,a^*} needs to be between −0.03 and 0.03 in order for the VAR(1) process of the productivity shocks to maintain stationarity (with both its eigenvalues inside the unit circle). I transform the spillover parameter to become

$$\frac{1}{2}+\frac{1}{2}\frac{\delta_{a,a^*}}{0.03}$$

so that its range can be defined over the (0,1)-interval. I select the Beta distribution as the prior, and I center it around 0.91667 to be consistent with a value of δ_{a,a^*} equal to 0.025. Moreover, I set the prior standard deviation at 0.05 resulting in a unimodal distribution that is skewed to the left.

Having imposed *extrinsic* inertia on monetary policy, the first-order autocorrelation of the monetary shocks δ_m ought to be highly positive in order to match the parsimonious interest rate movements seen in the data. I reflect this in the prior for δ_m by restricting the parameter space to the interval (0,1). I select a Beta distribution centered around 0.92 with a prior standard deviation equal to 0.09. This implies that the prior Beta for δ_m is unimodal, and it recognizes that the empirical evidence seems to favor values consistent with high persistence of the monetary shock. The prior means of the productivity shock and monetary shock volatilities, σ_a and σ_m, are set at 0.73 and 0.36, respectively. I then pick an Inverse Gamma distribution to represent the prior distribution of both volatility parameters. However, I impose a large standard deviation of 3 and 5 respectively, leaving it up the data to determine the contribution of each shock to explain the endogenous business cycle volatility.

Finally, I restrict the range of the parameter space for the cross-country correlation of innovations ρ_{a,a^*} and ρ_{m,m^*} to lie in the (0,1)-interval. I select the Beta distribution for both parameters. I choose rather diffuse priors for these cross-country correlations because these parameters can be important for propagation, but their values are often debated in calibrated and estimated models. I center ρ_{a,a^*} at 0.29 with a standard deviation of 0.18, and ρ_{m,m^*} at 0.5 with a standard deviation of 0.2. As a result, the prior Beta distribution for the cross-correlation of the productivity innovations is skewed toward the right while the Beta distribution for the cross-correlation of the monetary shock innovations is more symmetric around the prior mean. In choosing these disperse priors, I am recognizing that the proper value for these correlations is not well-established in the literature yet.

4. Understanding Local Inflation in an Open-Economy Setting

In order to understand the inflation dynamics through the lens of the NOEM model of Martínez-García and Wynne (2010), I establish a number of analytical results first. I discuss how inflation can be decomposed into one global component that is common to all countries and another term that accounts for the inflation differential across countries. Furthermore, I show that this decomposition leads to two separate sub-systems for global inflation and inflation differentials that can be solved independently. Finally, I also argue that some key features – structural parameters – of the model matter for the determination of local inflation only through their impact on the dynamics of one of these two components. Similarly, the nature of the shocks also matters for how these two components of local inflation behave.

Then, equipped with these insights about the NOEM model, I report the empirical findings from the Bayesian estimation of the full NOEM model. I use the data to discipline the parameterization of the model and illustrate the strength of the transmission mechanism for the determination of both global and local inflation with the empirical evidence that follows from the estimated model.

4.1. The Global Component of Local Inflation

In order to clarify the dynamics of the two-country model in Martínez-García and Wynne (2010), I rely on the decomposition method into aggregates and differences postulated by Aoki (1981) and Fukuda (1993) to re-express the core linear rational expectations system described in Table 1 into two separate sub-systems with half the number of equations. Productivity shocks enter into the dynamics described in Table 1 only through their impact on the dynamics of the natural real rates in this economy, $\hat{\bar{r}}_t$ and $\hat{\bar{r}}_t^*$, established in Proposition 1. The Home and Foreign monetary shock processes, $\hat{m}_t$ and $\hat{m}_t^*$, enter through the specification of the monetary policy rule of each country.

The two countries are assumed to be symmetric in every respect, except on their consumption baskets due to the assumption of Home-product bias in consumption. Even so, this bias is inherently symmetric as the share of local goods in the local-consumption basket is the same in both countries and determined by the parameter ξ. Hence, the Aoki (1981)–Fukuda (1993) decomposition approach is applicable to the NOEM model that I have developed in this chapter.

I define the world aggregate and the difference variables $\hat{g}_t^{\text{W}}$ and $\hat{g}_t^{\text{R}}$ as,

$$\hat{g}_t^{\text{W}} \equiv \frac{1}{2}\hat{g}_t + \frac{1}{2}\hat{g}_t^*, \tag{39}$$

$$\hat{g}_t^{\text{R}} \equiv \hat{g}_t - \hat{g}_t^*, \tag{40}$$

which implicitly establishes that both countries are identical in size (with the same share of the household population and varieties located in each country). I re-write the country variables $\hat{g}_t$ and $\hat{g}_t^*$ as,

$$\hat{g}_t = \hat{g}_t^{\text{W}} + \frac{1}{2}\hat{g}_t^{\text{R}}, \tag{41}$$

$$\hat{g}_t^* = \hat{g}_t^{\text{W}} - \frac{1}{2}\hat{g}_t^{\text{R}}. \tag{42}$$

Then, if I can characterize the dynamics for $\hat{g}_t^{\text{W}}$ and $\hat{g}_t^{\text{R}}$, the transformation above backs out the corresponding variables for each country $\hat{g}_t$ and $\hat{g}_t^*$. Naturally, these transformations can be applied to any of the endogenous and exogenous variables of the NOEM model.

Hence, I can orthogonalize the original two-country economic model presented in Table 1 into one aggregate (or world) economic system and one difference system that can be studied independently. Notice that the weights on the world aggregate variables $\hat{g}_t^{\text{W}}$ implied by this orthogonalization are given by the economic size of these two countries, and not by the long-term (steady state) trade linkages between them. I have implicitly used this idea already in Section 3 when constructing a foreign aggregate with GDP-weighted data for 38 of the largest trading partners of the United States.

However, it is important to emphasize this point here as well in order to correctly interpret my subsequent findings. The way these world aggregates – and global inflation in particular – are constructed is not affected by the degree of openness of the economy as measured by the parameter ξ in the model. Therefore, even a fairly closed economy such as the United States is expected to move along the global economy's path. The implication from this is that foreign developments have a larger impact on this global component than what trade alone can explain.[11]

In turn, I argue that differential variables – and inflation differentials in particular – $\hat{g}_t^{\mathrm{R}}$ do respond to key features of the economy related to trade (including to trade openness ξ and the elasticity of substitution between Home and Foreign varieties σ) and are critical to determine whether the movements in global variables get either amplified or dampened in the local variables (i.e., in $\hat{g}_t$ and $\hat{g}_t^*$).

4.1.1. The World or Global Economy System

The global system describes the world economy as if it were that of a closed economy based on the following system of three equations:

$$\hat{\pi}_t^{\mathrm{W}} \approx \beta \mathbb{E}_t\left[\hat{\pi}_{t+1}^{\mathrm{W}}\right] + \left(\frac{(1-\alpha)(1-\beta\alpha)}{\alpha}\right)(\varphi+\gamma)\hat{x}_t^{\mathrm{W}}, \tag{43}$$

$$\gamma\left(\mathbb{E}_t\left[\hat{x}_{t+1}^{\mathrm{W}}\right] - \hat{x}_t^{\mathrm{W}}\right) \approx \left(\hat{i}_t^{\mathrm{W}} - \mathbb{E}_t\left[\hat{\pi}_{t+1}^{\mathrm{W}}\right]\right) - \hat{\bar{r}}_t^{\mathrm{W}}, \tag{44}$$

$$\hat{i}_t^{\mathrm{W}} \approx \left[\psi_\pi \hat{\pi}_t^{\mathrm{W}} + \psi_x \hat{x}_t^{\mathrm{W}}\right] + \hat{m}_t^{\mathrm{W}}. \tag{45}$$

To close the global economy system, I derive the world forcing processes $\hat{\bar{r}}_t^{\mathrm{W}}$ and $\hat{m}_t^{\mathrm{W}}$ as follows:

Proposition 2. *Given the derivation of the natural rates for each country in Proposition 1 and the maintained assumptions on the monetary shocks, the world forcing processes for $\hat{\bar{r}}_t^{\mathrm{W}}$ and $\hat{m}_t^{\mathrm{W}}$ can be described as follows:*

$$\begin{pmatrix} \hat{\bar{r}}_t^{\mathrm{W}} \\ \hat{m}_t^{\mathrm{W}} \end{pmatrix} = \begin{pmatrix} \delta_a + \delta_{a,a^*} & 0 \\ 0 & \delta_m \end{pmatrix} \begin{pmatrix} \hat{\bar{r}}_{t-1}^{\mathrm{W}} \\ \hat{m}_{t-1}^{\mathrm{W}} \end{pmatrix} + \begin{pmatrix} \hat{\varepsilon}_t^{r\mathrm{W}} \\ \hat{\varepsilon}_t^{m\mathrm{W}} \end{pmatrix}, \tag{46}$$

[11] In fact, although the model is not set-up to capture this explicitly, one can expect the effect to increase over time as the share of economic activity attributed to the Home country declines.

$$\begin{pmatrix} \hat{\varepsilon}_t^{rW} \\ \hat{\varepsilon}_t^{mW} \end{pmatrix} \sim N\left(\begin{pmatrix} 0 \\ 0 \end{pmatrix}, \begin{pmatrix} \sigma_r^2\left(\frac{1+\rho_{r,r^*}}{2}\right) & 0 \\ 0 & \sigma_m^2\left(\frac{1+\rho_{m,m^*}}{2}\right) \end{pmatrix}\right), \tag{47}$$

where the volatility term for the world natural rates can be tied to parameters of the productivity shock and other structural parameters of the model as follows:

$$\sigma_r^2\left(\frac{1+\rho_{r,r^*}}{2}\right) = \sigma_a^2\left(\frac{1+\rho_{a,a^*}}{2}\right)\left[\gamma\left(\frac{1+\varphi}{\gamma+\varphi}\right)(\delta_a+\delta_{a,a^*}-1)\right]^2. \tag{48}$$

The degree of openness ξ does not factor into the world system or the world forcing processes and neither does the intratemporal elasticity of substitution between Home and Foreign consumption bundles σ. The parameter σ regulates the price-elasticity of trade in the NOEM model, while ξ helps pin down the steady-state import shares. Therefore, neither the composition of the consumption basket nor the sensitivity of the trade balance to movements in the terms of trade (that support risk-sharing across countries) matter for the dynamics of the world economy – and, in particular, for the dynamics of global inflation. The only structural parameters that affect the world dynamics are the Calvo parameter α, the intertemporal discount factor β, the inverse of the intertemporal elasticity of substitution γ, the inverse of the Frisch elasticity of labor supply φ, and the policy parameters ψ_π and ψ_x.[12]

This is an important implication of the decomposition method, as it reveals that the structural parameters that affect the world dynamics are not related to the trade channel. In fact, as it will be soon apparent, the features of the economy that matter for the global component of inflation are not the same ones that affect the local inflation dynamics. In the full linear rational expectations model presented in Table 1 the proper identification of ξ and σ appears to be crucial to understanding the dynamics of inflation and the international transmission mechanism of shocks. The world system discussed here, in turn, shows that the strength of these trade linkages is

[12] The estimation of the world system does not suffice to identify the parameters of the exogenous shock processes in general. I am only able to precisely estimate $\sigma_a^2(1+\rho_{a,a^*})$, $(\delta_a+\delta_{a,a^*})$, and $\sigma_m^2(1+\rho_{m,m^*})$. In other words, I can only identify the reduced-form representation of the world shocks and not the underlying features of the Home and Foreign shocks.

netted out when it comes to describing the global dynamics. This indicates that the global component of local inflation and its response to shocks is unconnected to the sensitivity and extent of trade on which the Home and Foreign countries are engaged.

As I mentioned earlier when describing the world aggregates for the decomposition, the contribution of each country to the aggregate is determined not by the extent of the trade linkages between these countries either but by their respective economic sizes. Even countries with traditionally low import shares (such as the United States) incorporate a large contribution of inflation from the rest of the world through the global component of local inflation. Local inflation would, of course, also incorporate a differential component too. Understanding the cross-difference system that characterizes the differential path between the Home and Foreign economies is, therefore, important to determine whether the effects operating through global inflation will be amplified or diluted in the resulting dynamics of local inflation.

4.1.2. The Cross-Country Difference System

The world as a whole is completely unaffected by how open its constituent economies might be or how sensitive trade is to movements in the terms of trade. In fact, greater openness or increased international risk-sharing through terms of trade have an economic impact on the economy of each country; however, this is not because they influence the dynamics of the global economy, but because these features of the economy affect how divergent the economic performance of the Home and Foreign countries can become. In other words, the world economy behaves as a closed economy but key features of the model related to trade patterns affect the differences that arise across these two countries.

The cross-country difference system defines how far apart a country is from the rest of the world. Then, the difference system can be characterized as follows:

$$\hat{\pi}_t^{R} \approx \beta \mathbb{E}_t\left[\hat{\pi}_{t+1}^{R}\right] + \left(\frac{(1-\alpha)(1-\beta\alpha)}{\alpha}\right)((2\xi-1)\varphi + (2\Theta-1)\gamma)\hat{x}_t^{R}, \tag{49}$$

$$\gamma(2\xi-1)\left(\mathbb{E}_t\left[\hat{x}_{t+1}^{R}\right] - \hat{x}_t^{R}\right) \approx ((2\xi-1)+2\Gamma)\left[\left(\hat{i}_t^{R} - \mathbb{E}_t\left[\hat{\pi}_{t+1}^{R}\right]\right) - \hat{\bar{r}}_t^{R}\right], \tag{50}$$

$$\hat{i}_t^{R} \approx \left[\psi_\pi \hat{\pi}_t^{R} + \psi_x \hat{x}_t^{R}\right] + \hat{m}_t^{R}. \tag{51}$$

Here, the degree of openness ξ plays an important role in the differential system and so does the elasticity of substitution between Home and Foreign consumption bundles σ (through the composite parameters Θ and Γ).

To close the difference economy system, I derive the difference forcing processes $\hat{\bar{r}}_t^{\mathrm{R}}$ and $\hat{m}_t^{\mathrm{R}}$ as follows:

Proposition 3. *Given the derivation of the natural rates for each country in Proposition 1 and the maintained assumptions on the monetary shocks, the difference forcing processes for* $\hat{\bar{r}}_t^{\mathrm{R}}$ *and* $\hat{m}_t^{\mathrm{R}}$ *can be described as follows:*

$$\begin{pmatrix} \hat{\bar{r}}_t^{\mathrm{R}} \\ \hat{m}_t^{\mathrm{R}} \end{pmatrix} = \begin{pmatrix} \delta_a - \delta_{a,a^*} & 0 \\ 0 & \delta_m \end{pmatrix} \begin{pmatrix} \hat{\bar{r}}_{t-1}^{\mathrm{R}} \\ \hat{m}_{t-1}^{\mathrm{R}} \end{pmatrix} + \begin{pmatrix} \hat{\varepsilon}_t^{r\mathrm{R}} \\ \hat{\varepsilon}_t^{m\mathrm{R}} \end{pmatrix}, \tag{52}$$

$$\begin{pmatrix} \hat{\varepsilon}_t^{r\mathrm{R}} \\ \hat{\varepsilon}_t^{m\mathrm{R}} \end{pmatrix} \sim N\left(\begin{pmatrix} 0 \\ 0 \end{pmatrix}, \begin{pmatrix} 2\sigma_r^2(1-\rho_{r,r^*}) & 0 \\ 0 & 2\sigma_m^2(1-\rho_{m,m^*}) \end{pmatrix} \right), \tag{53}$$

where the volatility term for the difference natural rate can be tied to parameters of the productivity shock and other structural parameters of the model as follows:

$$2\sigma_r^2(1-\rho_{r,r^*}) = 2\sigma_a^2(1-\rho_{a,a^*}) \left[\gamma \left(\frac{1+\varphi}{\gamma+\varphi} \right) (2\Theta - 1)(2\Lambda - 1)(\delta_a - \delta_{a,a^*} - 1) \right]^2. \tag{54}$$

These findings indicate that the degree of openness ξ and the elasticity of substitution between Home and Foreign consumption bundles σ (through the composite parameters Θ and Λ) affect the dynamics of the difference system as well as the volatility of the forcing processes (the volatility of the difference natural rate), unlike what I showed for the world economy system. This is one important insight that needs to be recognized – the structural parameters that are most connected to the specification of the trade channel have an effect on the differential behavior of the economy (and in particular on the inflation differential component of local inflation), but not on global dynamics and global inflation.

Global inflation dynamics can be driven by common or correlated shocks. However, global inflation also reflects the spillover effects of country-specific shocks that are transmitted to the rest of the world through the trade channel and complete international asset markets. In the specification of the NOEM model used in this chapter, I abstract entirely from common shocks to emphasize the importance of these cross-country spillovers. In turn, inflation differentials across countries can only be the result of asymmetric shocks across countries – but not common or symmetric (perfectly correlated) shocks. The impact the differential component of inflation has on local inflation characterized by this difference system will depend not just on the specification of the trade channel implied by the model but on the nature of the shocks themselves.

To explore how global inflation and inflation differentials actually feed into local inflation, I will now rely on the posterior Bayesian estimates of the full NOEM model to both take parameter uncertainty explicitly into account and bring the observed data on output and CPI inflation to bear in the parameterization of the model dynamics.

4.2. Empirical Findings: What Matters Most for Local Inflation?

I estimate the full NOEM model developed in Section 2 using Bayesian techniques to quantify the importance of spillovers arising through trade linkages in the dynamics of local inflation and its global and differential components. I draw on the experience of the United States and its 38 largest trading partners between 1980Q1 and 2011Q4 to investigate the propagation of shocks and their effects on local inflation with an emphasis on the role of global inflation. I also explore how global inflation can help with other relevant tasks such as the identification of the type and origin of shocks or the forecasting of inflation.

The main empirical findings from the Bayesian estimation of the NOEM model are illustrated by the posterior Bayesian estimates, the Bayesian impulse response functions (IRFs) and the Bayesian forecasts – all of which I review in the remainder of this section.

4.2.1. Posterior Distributions

Conventional beliefs about the structural parameters of the NOEM model are represented through the prior distributions I have discussed in Section 3.2. Bayesian estimation aims to extract all useful information from the available observations of macro aggregates – that is, from observations on Home and Foreign output and Home and Foreign inflation – to modify those prior beliefs about the model parameters whenever the data calls for it. The posterior and prior distributions of each parameter can be compared to each other in Table 6 and Figure 2. With few exceptions, the estimated posterior means appear to be very close to the corresponding prior means chosen for each of the structural parameters of the model.

The exceptions where a gap between the posterior and prior means is more noticeable, interestingly, correspond to the two policy parameters that describe the Taylor rule and to parameters related to the specification of the monetary policy shock process. The evidence reported in Table 6, in particular, suggests that the posterior estimates of the sensitivity of the

Table 6: Structural and Shock Parameters: Posterior Distributions

		Prior	Posterior	
			Mean	90%-CI
Structural Parameters				
Non-policy parameters				
β	Intertemporal discount factor	0.99	0.99	–
γ	Inverse intertemporal elasticity of substitution	5	4.9332	[4.2680, 5.5490]
φ	Inverse Frisch elasticity of labor supply	$\varphi=\gamma$	$\varphi=\gamma$	–
σ	Elasticity of substitution between Home and Foreign varieties	1.5	1.6137	[0.0942, 3.2349]
$2\xi-1$	(Transformed) share of local goods in consumption basket	0.88	0.8810	[0.8640, 0.8974]
α	Calvo (1983) price stickiness parameter	0.75	0.7450	[0.7161, 0.7732]
Policy parameters				
$\psi_\pi-1$	(Transformed) policy response to inflation	0.24	0.1640	[0.0667, 0.2685]
ψ_x	Policy response to the output gap	0.33	0.1554	[0.0794, 0.2315]
Shock Parameters				
δ_a	Persistence parameter in productivity	0.97	0.9659	[0.9588, 0.9732]
$\frac{1}{2}+\frac{1}{2}\frac{\delta_{a,a^*}}{0.03}$	(Transformed) spillover parameter in productivity	0.91667	0.9069	[0.8198, 0.9894]
σ_a	Std. deviation of productivity innovations	0.73	0.6991	[0.1997, 1.2853]
ρ_{a,a^*}	Cross-correlation of productivity innovations	0.29	0.2806	[0.0093, 0.5401]
δ_m	Persistence parameter in the monetary shock	0.92	0.7941	[0.7667, 0.8225]
σ_m	Std. deviation of monetary shock innovations	0.36	0.2816	[0.0940, 0.4799]
ρ_{m,m^*}	Cross-correlation of monetary shock innovations	0.50	0.5027	[0.1823, 0.8242]

Notes: This table reports the prior mean, and the posterior point estimates and 90% confidence intervals for each one of the 13 structural (policy and non-policy) and shock parameters of the NOEM model that do not receive a degenerate prior distribution. The table reports the Bayesian estimates after pre-filtering the data using the one-sided Hodrick–Prescott Filter with parameter set at 1600. I estimate the NOEM model for a time series of 128 observations from 1980Q1 until 2011Q4 for the United States and a foreign aggregate composed of the 38 largest trading partners of the United States. The estimation is based on four observables: Home and Foreign output, Home and Foreign CPI inflation. The code for the Bayesian estimation is written for Matlab version 8.3.0.532 and Dynare version 4.3.2, and it is available upon request from the author.

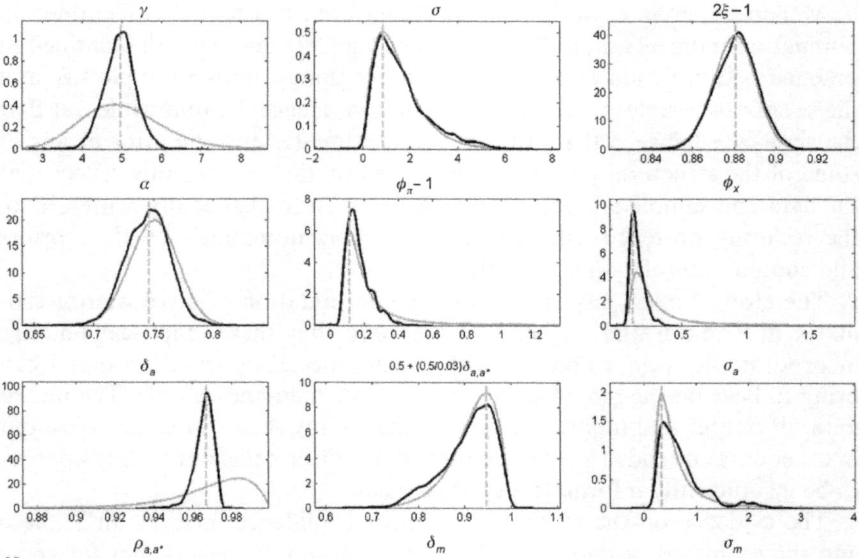

Figure 2: Priors and Posteriors. Notes: The code is written for Matlab version 8.3.0.532 and Dynare version 4.3.2. This figure plots the prior distributions of all 13 structural (policy and non-policy) and shock parameters that do not receive a degenerate prior distribution. It also includes the posterior distribution estimated from the sample of 128 quarterly observations for the United States and a foreign aggregate composed of the 38 largest trading partners of the United States. The estimation is based on four observables: Home and Foreign output, Home and Foreign CPI inflation. The code for this figure is available upon request from the author.

policy rule to inflation and the output gap (ψ_π and ψ_x respectively) are somewhat lower than indicated by the prior means. Both the volatility and the persistence of the monetary shock process (σ_m and δ_m respectively) are also lower than under the prior means.

Martínez-García et al. (2012) show that even if a model is identified in population moments, not all structural parameters may be well identified in practice – that would depend, among other things, on the sample size and the set of observables used for the estimation. Hence, I cannot rule out that the similarity between the posterior mean estimates and the prior means of some of the structural parameters in my estimation may simply reflect that the data and sample are not informative enough to change my priors. If so, the resulting posterior estimates end up being dominated by their priors and should naturally align with them.

Therefore, I must provide a cautious interpretation of my posterior estimates in Table 6 and Figure 2. I say only that these empirical findings incorporate my priors updated with the additional information that I can bring to bear on the model given my available data and sample. The macro data on output and inflation serves to change my priors in some cases, but in other cases it tends to either confirm those prior beliefs or simply appears to be insufficiently informative to alter them.

The evidence on the estimated posterior confidence intervals in Table 6 and the estimated posterior distributions in Figure 2 suggest that for some structural parameters the data and sample available results in posterior distributions that are dominated by their priors. This may be because the prior distribution for a given parameter reasonably approximates not just its mean, but also other higher moments of the distribution such as its dispersion or skewness. It can also be because the data and sample are neither informative enough to change the prior mean nor to change the prior perceptions on the uncertainty surrounding the true value of the parameter (or other relevant features of the parameter distribution such as the skewness). Hence, the same cautious interpretation applies more generally to my reading of the posterior distributions and to my inferences on parameter uncertainty.

In other words, the information that can be extracted from output and inflation data through Bayesian estimation is simply insufficient to modify my initial priors on a number of the structural parameters of the NOEM model. Among those structural parameters for which I get fairly similar prior and posterior distributions, I find shock parameters like ρ_{a,a^*} and ρ_{m,m^*} in addition to the two main structural parameters related to the strength of the trade channel ξ and σ. The shock parameters ρ_{a,a^*} and ρ_{m,m^*} describe the correlation across countries in the innovations to both productivity and monetary policy shocks and are crucial to understanding the exogenous component of the international propagation of shocks. The findings reported show that it is quite difficult to infer the exogenous propagation of shocks from data on output and inflation.

In regards to the structural parameters ξ (which determines the openness to trade) and σ (which defines the elasticity of substitution between Home and Foreign varieties), my findings are consistent with those of

Martínez-García et al. (2012). These two trade-related parameters tend to be difficult to pin down with the data that I use here, but they are central to describing the trade channel and the endogenous propagation of shocks. Martínez-García et al. (2012) recommend the use of trade data among the observables in order to help more tightly identify these trade parameters.[13]

A corollary of the decomposition presented in Section 4.1 is that an alternative strategy can be worked out to estimate the model using its two constituent sub-systems (the world economy system and the differential economy system) to more tightly pin down the estimation of parameters like ξ and σ. The decomposition of the model allows us, for instance, to consider using aggregate output and inflation to estimate the world economy system and trade and real exchange rate (or terms of trade) data in order to estimate the differential economy system. Given that the trade parameters ξ and σ only enter into the differential economy system, estimating this block of the model separately but incorporating the posteriors estimated from the world system as priors for the rest of the parameters may help identify the trade channel while keeping the two blocks chained in the estimation.

I do not pursue this alternative strategy here formally, but I want to draw attention to the fact that the orthogonalization approach does not only provide insight to interpret the theory but it can also be a useful technique to facilitate the estimation by blocks of the NOEM model and other medium- to large-scale general equilibrium models. I see this as a potential added advantage of the methodology. In any event, I do not pursue in the chapter the recommendation of Martínez-García et al. (2012) to include some trade data among the observables either. Hence, the uncertainty about the endogenous international propagation of shocks through the trade channel remains essentially the same one I incorporated in my priors before.

Without further work on the estimation – which is left for future research – the additional economic insight gained from the Bayesian estimation on the exogenous and endogenous international propagation mechanism is rather limited. Those parameters are, in fact, important for the questions posited by this chapter because they affect the dynamic response of inflation differentials – so Bayesian estimation in its current

[13] To be more precise, what Martínez-García et al. (2012) show is that trade data can be useful to better pin down σ and less so for ξ. One must also take into account that the trade balance and the real exchange rate (or terms of trade) are exactly related to each other through the observation equations in Table 2. Using trade data as an observable, in turn, requires an additional shock to be added or one of the current observables to be replaced to avoid the stochastic singularity in Bayesian estimation. Either that, or the parameter σ in particular should be parameterized with extraneous information not used in the estimation of the model.

implementation is not significantly shifting my initial views on them or the uncertainty surrounding them. This, in turn, has implications for the responses of differential inflation and the uncertainty about them that I get from the estimated NOEM model.

The structural (policy and non-policy) parameters with fairly different prior and posterior distributions are $\gamma = \varphi$ (which enter into the slope of the Phillips curve), α (which indicates the degree of price stickiness), ψ_π (which describes the policy response to inflation), and ψ_x (which describes the policy response to the output gap). Most shock parameters appear to report differences between their priors and posteriors too, including the volatility of the productivity and monetary policy shocks, σ_a and σ_m, as well as the persistence and spillover parameters of the productivity and monetary policy shocks, δ_a, δ_{a,a^*}, and δ_m. The posterior distributions appear particularly tight for the preference parameter, $\gamma = \varphi$, as well as for the productivity and monetary policy parameters, δ_a and δ_m.

Figure 3 plots the filtered observable data used in the Bayesian estimation of the NOEM model. Another relevant aspect of the model estimation is illustrated through the recovered innovations to the productivity shocks

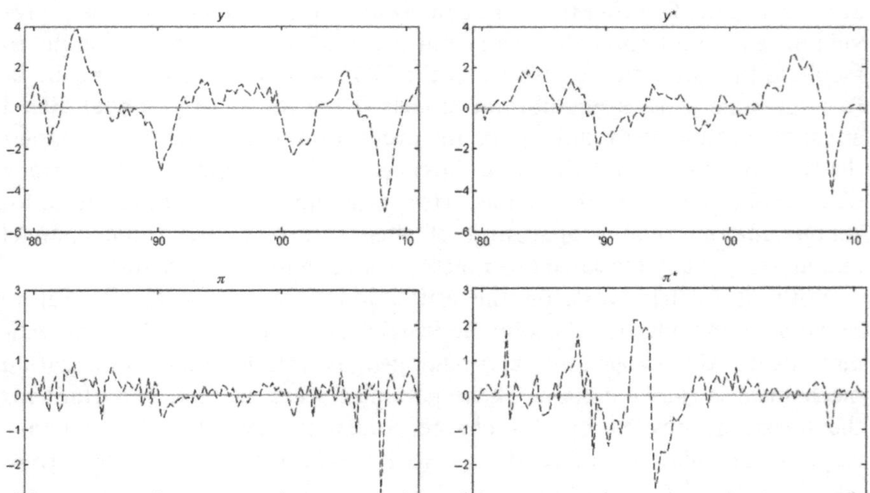

Figure 3: Time Series of Observable Variables. Notes: The code is written for Matlab version 8.3.0.532 and Dynare version 4.3.2. This figure plots the time series for the observables used to estimate the NOEM model: Home and Foreign output, Home and Foreign CPI inflation. The observable data distinguishes between the United States and a foreign aggregate composed of the 38 largest trading partners of the United States. The estimation sample includes 128 quarterly observations from 1980Q1 until 2011Q4. The code for this figure is available upon request from the author.

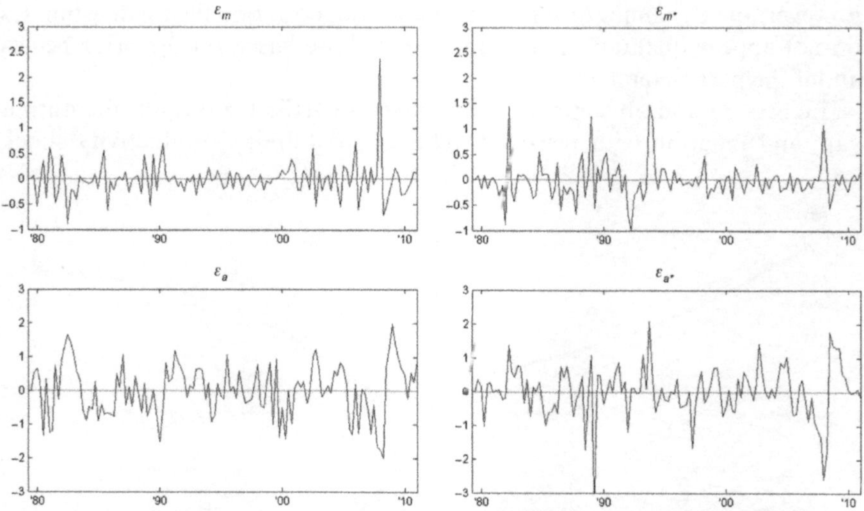

Figure 4: Smoothed Shock Innovations. Notes: The code is written for Matlab version 8.3.0.532 and Dynare version 4.3.2. This figure plots the smoothed innovations of the monetary and productivity shocks inferred from the estimated NOEM model for the United States and a foreign aggregate composed of the 38 largest trading partners of the United States. The estimation sample includes 128 quarterly observations and is based on four observables: Home and Foreign output, Home and Foreign CPI inflation. The code for this figure is available upon request from the author.

($\hat{\varepsilon}_t^a$ and $\hat{\varepsilon}_t^{a*}$) and monetary policy shocks ($\hat{\varepsilon}_t^m$ and $\hat{\varepsilon}_t^{m*}$), shown in Figure 4. Another way of looking at the empirical evidence plotted in Figure 3 is through the lens of these smoothed shocks obtained from the estimated NOEM model (Figure 4). Interestingly, the 2008 global recession is accounted for in the estimated NOEM model with a combination of both negative domestic and foreign productivity shock innovations and a significant tightening through monetary policy shock innovations (unexpected increases in the monetary policy shock) affecting primarily the U.S. economy.

4.2.2. Bayesian IRFs

Other than through posterior distributions, one can look at the Bayesian impulse response functions (IRFs) of the estimated NOEM model to assess the economic insight attained through Bayesian estimation. The structural parameters of the model should have a direct effect on the endogenous business cycle fluctuations generated by the country-specific productivity and monetary policy shocks driving the NOEM model. In practice, however, the dynamics of the model under the posterior Bayesian estimates do not appear qualitatively different from those based on the prior beliefs about the parameters.

Figures 5a and 5b summarize the Bayesian IRFs for output, the output gap, and inflation with respect to Home and Foreign productivity shock

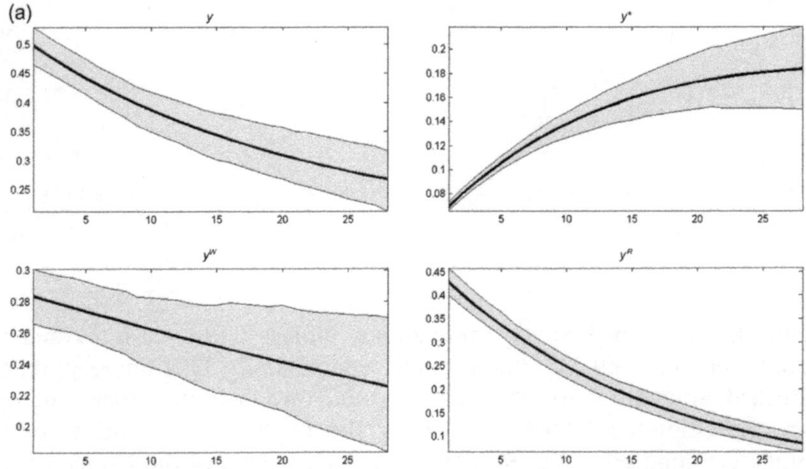

Figure 5: Bayesian IRFs in Response to: (a) Home Productivity Shock; (b) Foreign Productivity Shock. Notes: (a) The code is written for Matlab version 8.3.0.532 and Dynare version 4.3.2. This figure plots the Bayesian impulse response functions (IRFs) for output, the output gap and inflation distinguishing between the United States (H), the foreign aggregate (F), global (W) and the United States differential with respect to the foreign aggregate (R) in response to United States productivity shock innovations. The Bayesian IRFs are estimated from a sample of 128 quarterly observations using data for the United States and an aggregate of 38 of the largest trading partners of the United States on four observables: Home and Foreign output, Home and Foreign inflation. The code for this figure is available upon request from the author. (b) The code is written for Matlab version 8.3.0.532 and Dynare version 4.3.2. This figure plots the Bayesian impulse response functions (IRFs) for output, the output gap and inflation distinguishing between the United States (H), the foreign aggregate (F), global (W) and the United States differential with respect to the foreign aggregate (R) in response to Foreign productivity shock innovations. The Bayesian IRFs are estimated from a sample of 128 quarterly observations using data for the United States and an aggregate of 38 of the largest trading partners of the United States on four observables: Home and Foreign output, Home and Foreign inflation. The code for this figure is available upon request from the author.

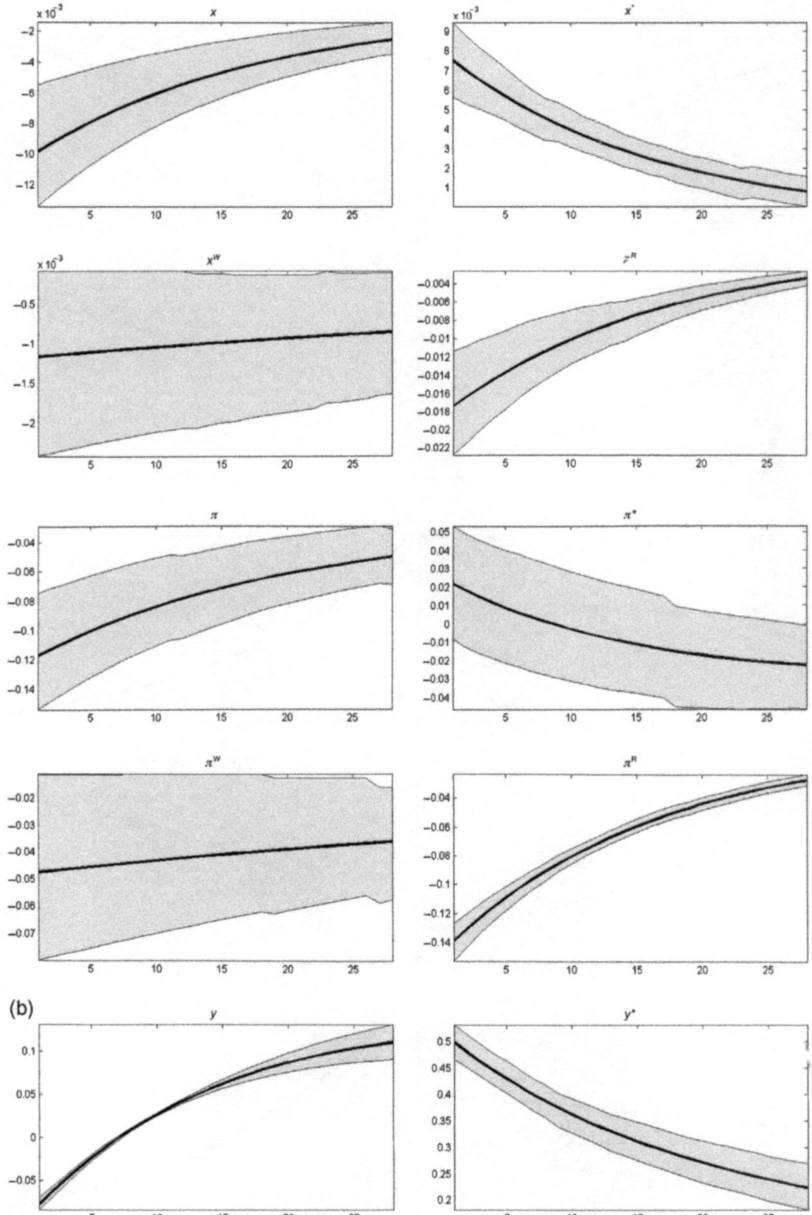

Figure 5: Continued.

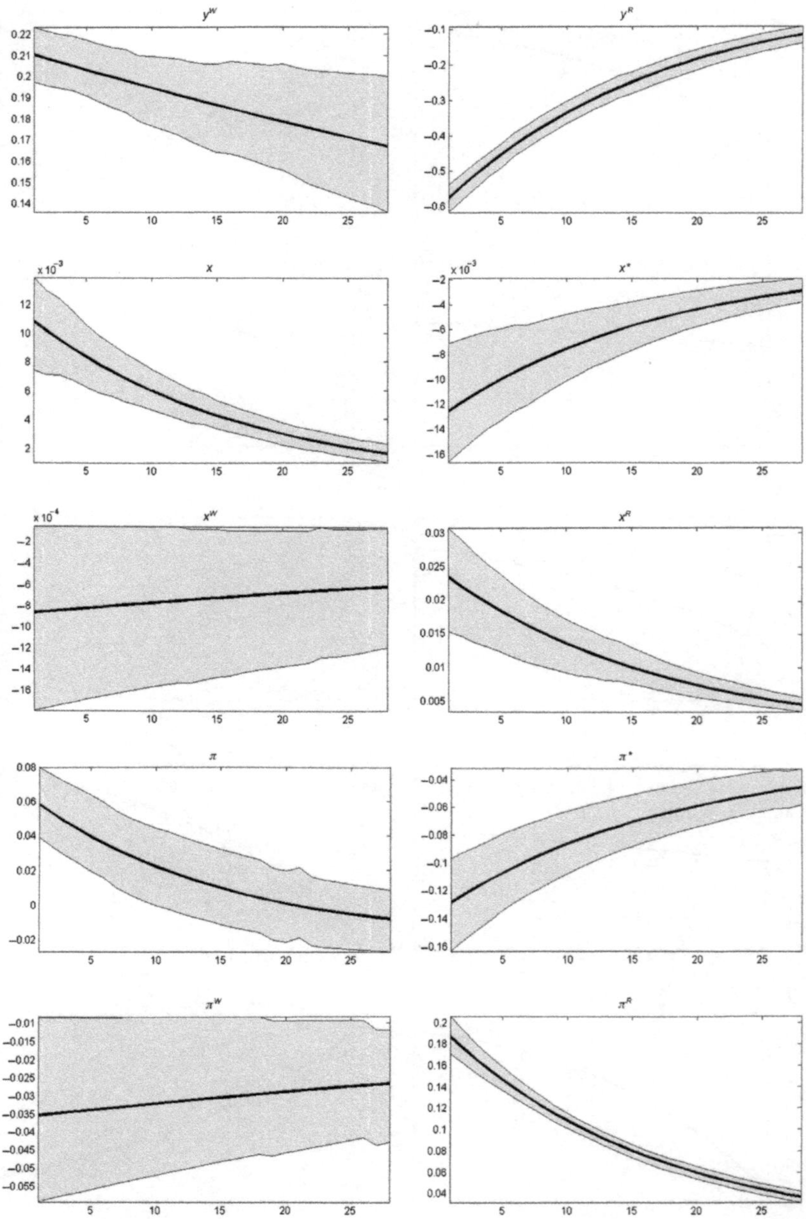

Figure 5: Continued.

innovations based on the estimated NOEM model that uses Home and Foreign output as well as Home and Foreign inflation as its observables. Each one of the endogenous variables whose response is plotted here is represented in four different perspectives: I include the Home (the United States) and Foreign (an aggregate of the 38 largest trading partners of the United States) variables for each, but also a global or world aggregate and a differential variable that illustrates the gap between the Home and Foreign economies. Similarly, Figures 6a and 6b summarize the exact same information on the endogenous variables with the Bayesian IRFs for output, the output gap, and inflation with respect to Home and Foreign monetary policy shock innovations.

The Bayesian IRFs suggest that the endogenous response to monetary policy shock innovations tends to be more tightly estimated than for productivity shock innovations. In other words, the precision by which the model estimation recovers the Bayesian IRFs is dependent upon both the type of shock and the endogenous variable that is being shocked. The international transmission of shocks implied by the model, however, is qualitatively plausible and quantitatively significant.

The dynamics of the NOEM model reported through Figures 5 and 6 are cast in a different light when I take into account the decomposition of local variables proposed in the chapter. Positive productivity shock innovations in the Home or the Foreign economies tend to increase global output and lead to modest declines in the global output gap and in global inflation. The typical pattern of a supply-side shock appears at the aggregate level. An unexpected tightening in the form of a positive innovation to the monetary policy shock in the Home or the Foreign economies results in a noticeable decline of global output, the global output gap, and global inflation. Hence, the typical pattern of a monetary policy shock hitting the aggregate demand appears at the aggregate level as well.

What the dynamics of the Bayesian IRFs reveal, then, is that these global dynamics are a significant part of the dynamics of output, the output gap, and inflation at the country level. Differences between the two countries emerge that reflect the strength of the trade channel and its spillovers – those differences will reflect to a great extent how the different countries absorb the effects of these country-specific shocks. The intensity of those effects will depend on the structural features of the economy, of course. However, the evidence illustrated by the Bayesian IRFs shows plainly that the global component of inflation in particular is more than a theoretical result that is qualitatively interesting but one that has quantitative bite.

Finally, I want to make note of an important point on the origin and type of shocks. From the perspective of the Home country, the tightening of monetary policy in the Foreign country (a positive innovation to the Foreign monetary policy shock) looks qualitatively like a loosening of

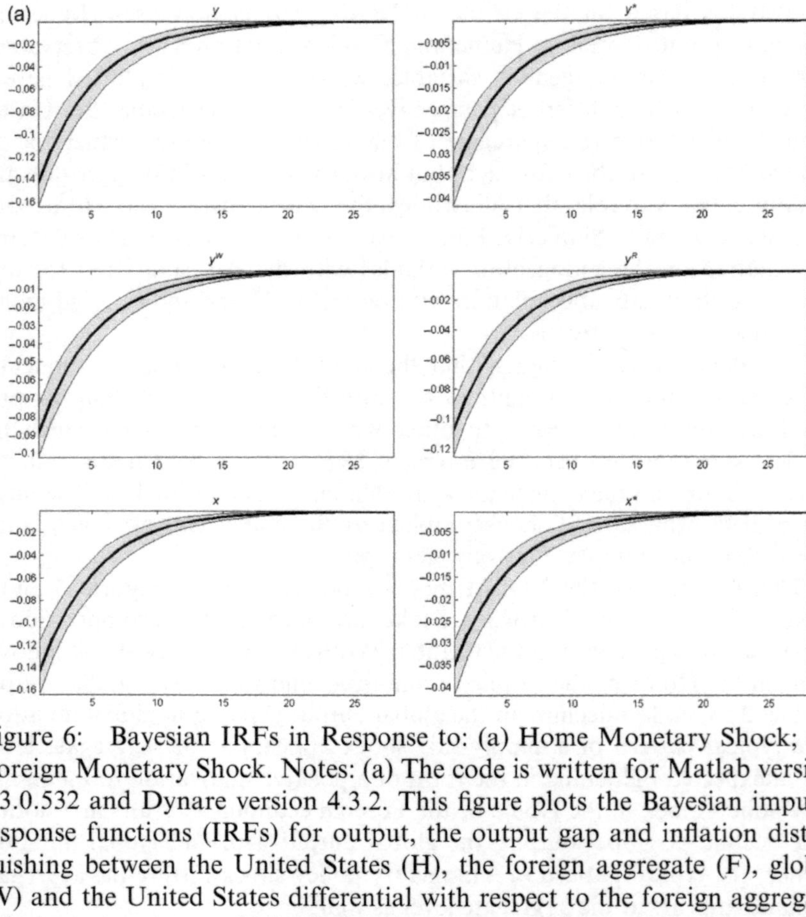

Figure 6: Bayesian IRFs in Response to: (a) Home Monetary Shock; (b) Foreign Monetary Shock. Notes: (a) The code is written for Matlab version 8.3.0.532 and Dynare version 4.3.2. This figure plots the Bayesian impulse response functions (IRFs) for output, the output gap and inflation distinguishing between the United States (H), the foreign aggregate (F), global (W) and the United States differential with respect to the foreign aggregate (R) in response to United States monetary shock innovations. The Bayesian IRFs are estimated from a sample of 128 quarterly observations using data for the United States and an aggregate of 38 of the largest trading partners of the United States on four observables: Home and Foreign output, Home and Foreign inflation. The code for this figure is available upon request from the author. (b) The code is written for Matlab version 8.3.0.532 and Dynare version 4.3.2. This figure plots the Bayesian impulse response functions (IRFs) for output, the output gap and inflation distinguishing between the United States (H), the foreign aggregate (F), global (W) and the United States differential with respect to the foreign aggregate (R) in response to Foreign monetary shock innovations. The Bayesian IRFs are estimated from a sample of 128 quarterly observations using data for the United States and an aggregate of 38 of the largest trading partners of the United States on four observables: Home and Foreign output, Home and Foreign inflation. The code for this figure is available upon request from the author.

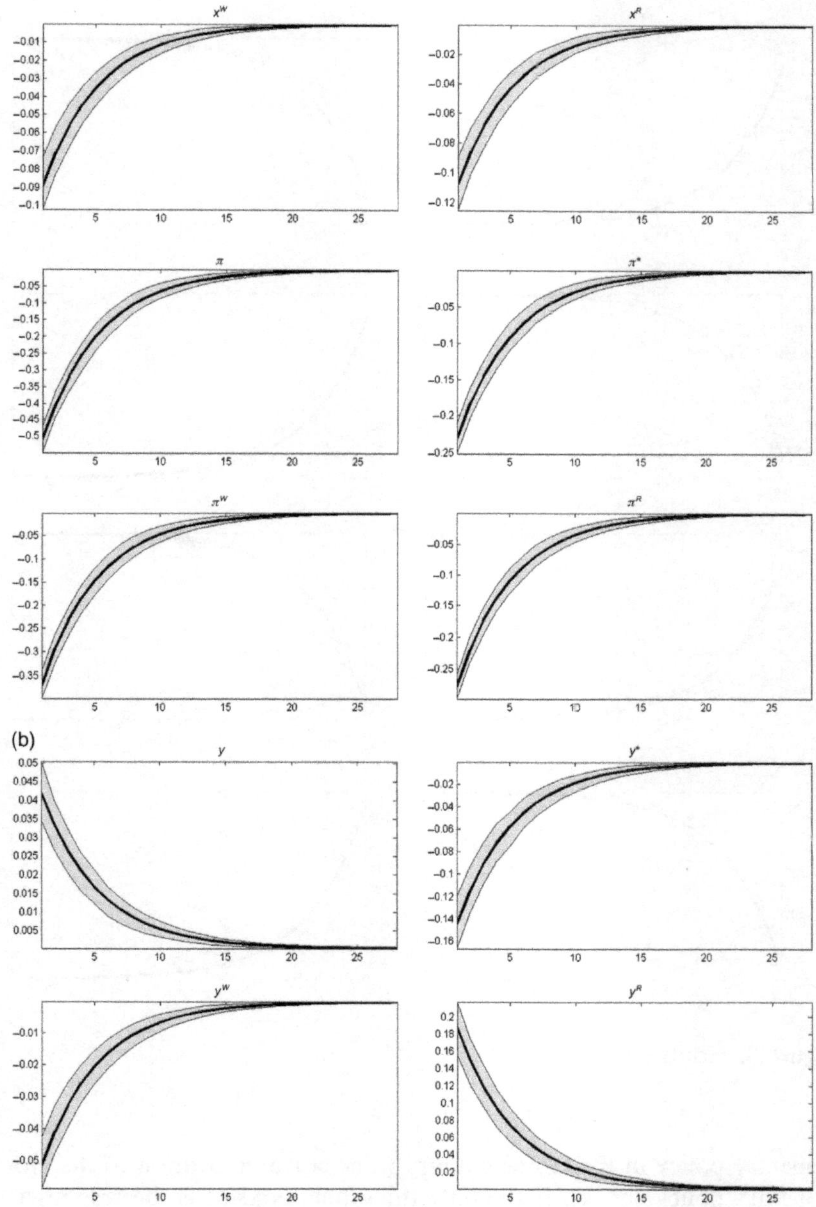

Figure 6: Continued.

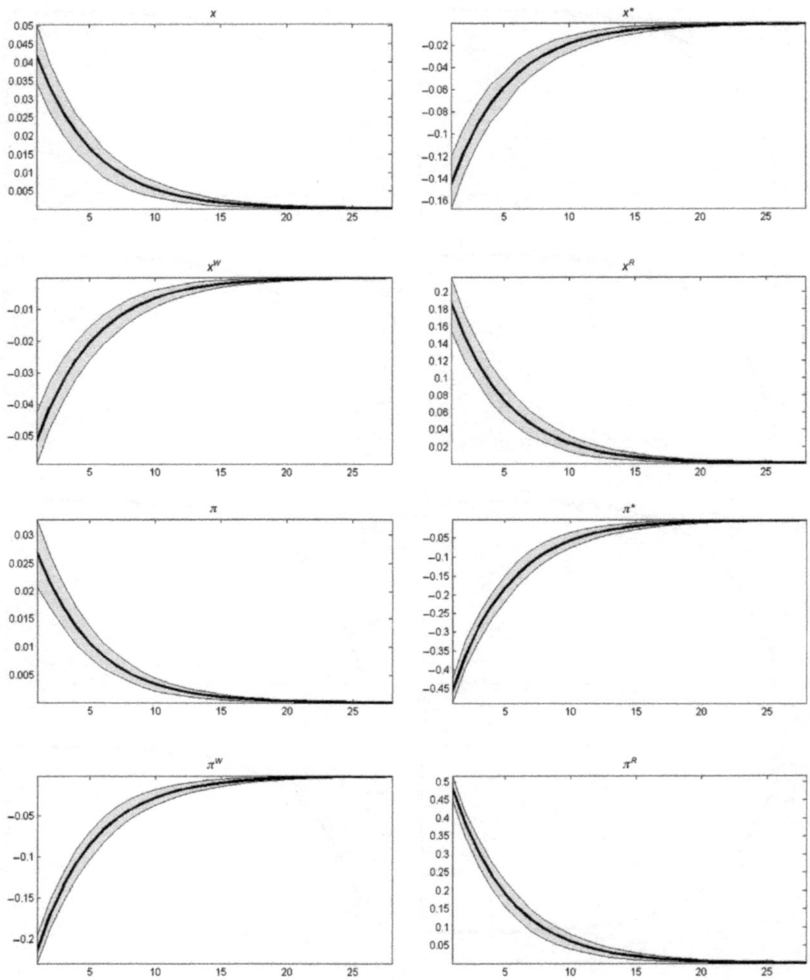

Figure 6: Continued.

monetary policy in the Home country (a negative innovation to the Home monetary policy shock). If the only thing one looks at is the responses of Home output and inflation to monetary shocks, then Home and Foreign monetary policy shock innovations would be confounded, leading to potentially erroneous empirical inferences. Naturally, looser monetary policy at

Home is not the same as tighter monetary policy in the Foreign economy. A similar argument can be made about confounding Home and Foreign productivity shock innovations.

The way to distinguish between Home and Foreign shocks is to look at the impact of each type of shock through the inflation differential and the output differential. A related way would be to look at how the gaps between Home output and inflation relative to their respective global counterparts respond to shocks. In any event, looking at the rest of the world seems very important to avoid the type of confusion on the origin of shocks to which I allude here. While a simpler model that ignores the international dimension would still be able to distinguish between monetary policy and productivity shocks driving Home and Foreign inflation, in general it will not be enough to distinguish shocks that originate at Home from those that originate in the rest of the world. This, in turn, biases the measurement of the contribution of each type of shock to account for the observed business cycle fluctuations. It can also result in inaccurate interpretations of the forces driving the business cycle and even justify sub-optimal policies.

4.2.3. Bayesian Forecasts

Other than through posterior distributions and Bayesian IRFs, Bayesian forecasts can provide signs of empirical validation out-of-sample on which to evaluate the economic insight gained through the estimated NOEM model. Figure 7 summarizes the mean trajectory (black line) and the forecast deciles around the mean forecasts (grey lines). The evidence of fairly broad confidence bands around the mean forecasts suggests that the estimated NOEM model cannot constrain the endogenous dynamics sufficiently in order to give tighter forecasts. This could be seen as evidence that the NOEM model is not rich enough (and possibly even misspecified), but could also be indicative of the fact that the transmission of shocks across countries through the trade channel remains quite uncertain even after estimation – as noted earlier.

The forecasts, however, suggest again that the global component of inflation is an important factor on the forecasts of local inflation. While the workhorse NOEM model was not meant for forecasting, it can indicate whether the theory has some predictive content out-of-sample. Interestingly, the forecasts appear broadly consistent with a period of low inflation in the United States and for the world aggregate including the United States (below their respective time-varying means) over the period 2012Q1–2014Q1 which I would regard as consistent with the path of cyclical inflation for those years.

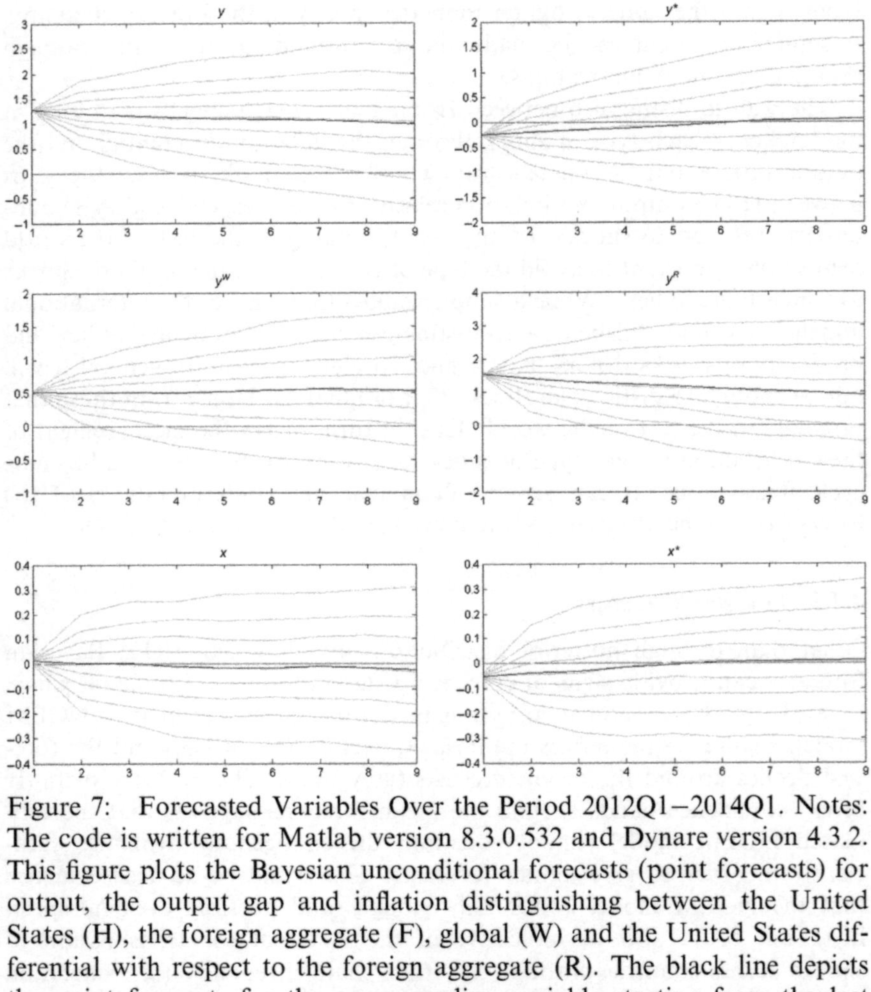

Figure 7: Forecasted Variables Over the Period 2012Q1–2014Q1. Notes: The code is written for Matlab version 8.3.0.532 and Dynare version 4.3.2. This figure plots the Bayesian unconditional forecasts (point forecasts) for output, the output gap and inflation distinguishing between the United States (H), the foreign aggregate (F), global (W) and the United States differential with respect to the foreign aggregate (R). The black line depicts the point forecasts for the corresponding variable starting from the last observation of the sample (2011Q4). The grey lines depict the point forecast deciles taking into account both the parameter uncertainty as well as the uncertainty about future shocks. The Bayesian forecasts are inferred from a sample of 128 quarterly observations using data for the United States and an aggregate of 38 of the largest trading partners of the United States on four observables: Home and Foreign output, Home and Foreign inflation. The code for this figure is available upon request from the author.

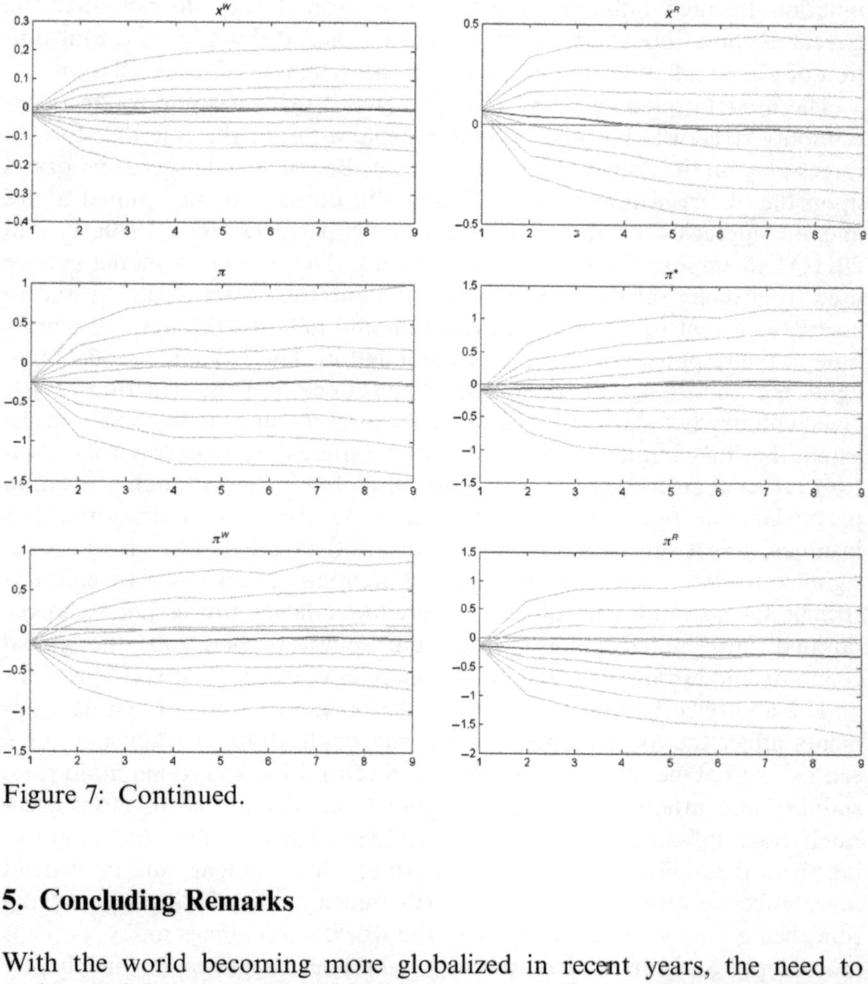

Figure 7: Continued.

5. Concluding Remarks

With the world becoming more globalized in recent years, the need to understand how countries are intertwined is ever increasing. Martínez-García and Wynne (2010) and Martínez-García and Wynne (2013) explain the connection between global factors and domestic inflation. The model in this chapter adds to the NOEM workhorse model of Martínez-García and Wynne (2010) by redefining the dynamics of inflation using the orthogonalization method of Aoki (1981) and Fukuda (1993). This approach conveys a novel perspective on how global factors can affect domestic inflation. Notably, it explains how international spillovers cause shocks that originate in one economy affect global inflation, and how these shocks are incorporated into local inflation in other countries. The model also explains why the structure of an economy and, in particular, features such as the degree of openness, matter when analyzing the impact of foreign shocks on local inflation through inflation differentials – even if they do not alter the effects of these shocks on global inflation – and it describes the contribution of global inflation that accounts for the dynamics of local inflation.

The model presented relies on a framework that incorporates an open-economy structure that allows for the exploration of the role that foreign forces play on the domestic economy. It uses Bayesian techniques and draws upon the observed time series (inflation and output) for the United States and an aggregate of its 38 largest trading partners since 1980Q1 until 2011Q4 to impose discipline on the theory. The estimated model can be used to evaluate the dynamic responses to different types of shocks and to assess the extent to which global inflation and inflation differentials contribute to the responses observed on local inflation. The estimated model highlights the importance of the nature of the shock and the structure of any given country but shows that certain structural features matter solely to the extent that they influence how the inflation differentials behave across countries rather than through a direct role on global inflation (among them, in particular, the openness to trade and trade elasticity parameters). For instance, a relatively closed economy, such as the United States, may not see significant effects through inflation differentials in response to country-specific shocks but it will still incorporate the spillover effects that are incorporated into global inflation (i.e., the spillovers permeate the global economy and eventually reach even economies that are "relatively closed").

The ability to build a better model that examines how foreign developments affect the local economy has many implications, particularly for a central bank. One of the major goals of a central bank is to maintain price stability and attain a sustainable output level. Being able to more accurately track inflation may help the central banks achieve this goal by granting them the ability to monitor international developments and implement more effective monetary policies. Furthermore, with inflation (even deflation) being a major issue in many of the world's economies today, perhaps more depth and further research along the lines suggested in this chapter on the relationship between foreign factors and local inflation will provide a more stable and predictable economic environment for the future.

Acknowledgments

I would like to thank Yamin Ahmad, Roberto Duncan, María Teresa Martínez-García and many others for helpful suggestions and comments. I also acknowledge the excellent research assistance provided by Bradley Graves and Valerie Grossman. All remaining errors are mine alone. The views expressed in this chapter are those of the author and do not necessarily reflect the views of the Federal Reserve Bank of Dallas, or the Federal Reserve System.

References

Adolfson, M., Laséen, S., Lindé, J., & Villani, M. (2005). The role of sticky prices in an open economy DSGE model: A Bayesian investigation. *Journal of the European Economic Association*, *3*(2–3), 444–457.

Adolfson, M., Laséen, S., Lindé, J., & Villani, M. (2007). Bayesian estimation of an open economy DSGE model with incomplete pass-through. *Journal of International Economics*, *72*(2), 481–511.

Adolfson, M., Laséen, S., Lindé, J., & Villani, M. (2008). Evaluating an estimated new Keynesian small open economy model. *Journal of Economic Dynamics and Control*, *32*(8), 2690–2721.

An, S., & Schorfheide, F. (2007). Bayesian analysis of DSGE models. *Econometric Reviews*, *26*(2–4), 113–172.

Aoki, M. (1981). *Dynamic analysis of open economies*. New York, NY: Academic Press.

Borio, C. E. V., & Filardo, A. (2007). *Globalisation and inflation: New cross-country evidence on the global determinants of domestic inflation*. BIS Working Paper No. 227. Basel, SUI, Bank for International Settlements.

Calvo, G. A. (1983). Staggered prices in a utility-maximizing framework. *Journal of Monetary Economics*, *12*(3), 383–398.

Clarida, R., Galí, J., & Gertler, M. (2002). A simple framework for international monetary policy analysis. *Journal of Monetary Economics*, *49*(5), 879–904.

Engel, C. (2009). *Currency misalignments and optimal monetary policy: A reexamination*. NBER Working Paper No. 14829. National Bureau of Economic Research, Cambridge, MA.

Fernández-Villaverde, J. (2010). The econometrics of DSGE models. *SERIEs*, *1*(1–2), 3–49.

Ferroni, F. (2011). Trend agnostic one-step estimation of DSGE models. *B.E. Journal of Macroeconomics, Advances*, *11*(1), 25.

Fukuda, S.-I. (1993). International transmission of monetary and fiscal policy. A symmetric N-country analysis with union. *Journal of Economic Dynamics and Control*, *17*(4), 589–620.

Grossman, V., Mack, A., & Martínez-García, E. (2014). A new database of global economic indicators. *The Journal of Economic and Social Measurement*, *39*(3), 163–197.

Guerrón-Quintana, P. A. (2010). What you match does matter: The effects of data on DSGE estimation. *Journal of Applied Econometrics*, *25*(5), 774–804.

Heathcote, J., & Perri, F. (2002). Financial autarky and international business cycles. *Journal of Monetary Economics*, *49*(3), 601–627.

Ihrig, J., Kamin, S. B., Lindner, D., & Marquez, J. (2007). *Some simple tests of the globalization and inflation hypothesis*. International Finance Discussion Paper No. 891. Federal Reserve Board, Washington, DC.

Martínez-García, E. (2008). *Globalization and monetary policy: An introduction*. Globalization and Monetary Policy Institute Working Paper No. 11. Federal Reserve Bank of Dallas.

Martínez-García, E. (2011). *A redux of the workhorse NOEM model with capital accumulation and incomplete asset markets*. Globalization and Monetary Policy Institute Working Paper No. 74. Federal Reserve Bank of Dallas.

Martínez-García, E., & Søndergaard, J. (2009). Investment and trade patterns in a sticky-price, open-economy model. In G. Calcagnini & E. Saltari (Eds.), *The economics of imperfect markets. The effect of market imperfections on economic decision-making*. Contributions to Economics. Heidelberg: Springer (Physica-Verlag).

Martínez-García, E., & Søndergaard, J. (2013). Investment and real exchange rates in sticky price models. *Macroeconomic Dynamics*, *17*(2), 195–234.

Martínez-García, E., Vilán, D., & Wynne, M. A. (2012). Bayesian estimation of NOEM models: Identification and inference in small samples. *Advances in Econometrics*, *28*, 137–199.

Martínez-García, E., & Wynne, M. A. (2010). *The global slack hypothesis. Federal Reserve Bank of Dallas*. Staff Papers, No. 10.

Martínez-García, E., & Wynne, M. A. (2013). Global slack as a determinant of U.S. inflation. In A. Filardo & A. Mehrotra (Eds.), *Globalisation and inflation dynamics in Asia and the Pacific* (pp. 93–98). Volume BIS Papers No. 70. Basel, Switzerland: Bank for International Settlements.

Martínez-García, E., & Wynne, M. A. (2014). Assessing Bayesian model comparison in small samples. *Advances in Econometrics*, *34*, 71–115.

Ríos-Rull, J.-V., Schorfheide, F., Fuentes-Albero, C., Kryshko, M., & Santaeulàlia-Llopis, R. (2012). Methods versus substance: Measuring the effects of technology shocks. *Journal of Monetary Economics*, *59*(8), 826–846.

Rudebusch, G. D. (2006). Monetary policy inertia: Fact or fiction? *International Journal of Central Banking*, *2*(4), 85–135.

Stock, J. H., & Watson, M. W. (1999). Forecasting inflation. *Journal of Monetary Economics*, *44*(2), 293–335.

Taylor, J. B. (1993). Discretion versus policy rules in practice. *Carnegie-Rochester Conference Series on Public Policy*, *39*, 195–214.

Woodford, M. (2003). *Interest and prices. Foundations of a theory of monetary policy*. Princeton, NJ: Princeton University Press.

Zellner, A. (1971). *An introduction to Bayesian inference in econometrics*. New York: Wiley.

Appendix: Proofs

Proof of Proposition 1.

The potential output of both countries can be expressed as a linear transformation of the productivity shocks as,

$$\begin{pmatrix} \hat{\bar{y}}_t \\ \hat{\bar{y}}_t^* \end{pmatrix} \approx \left(\frac{1+\varphi}{\gamma+\varphi}\right) \begin{pmatrix} \Lambda & 1-\Lambda \\ 1-\Lambda & \Lambda \end{pmatrix} \begin{pmatrix} \hat{a}_t \\ \hat{a}_t^* \end{pmatrix}.$$

Assuming invertibility, the vector of potential output inherits the VAR(1) stochastic structure of the productivity shocks. Accordingly, the potential output process takes the following stochastic form,

$$\begin{pmatrix} \hat{\bar{y}}_t \\ \hat{\bar{y}}_t^* \end{pmatrix} \approx \begin{pmatrix} \Lambda & 1-\Lambda \\ 1-\Lambda & \Lambda \end{pmatrix} \begin{pmatrix} \delta_a & \delta_{a,a^*} \\ \delta_{a,a^*} & \delta_a \end{pmatrix} \begin{pmatrix} \Lambda & 1-\Lambda \\ 1-\Lambda & \Lambda \end{pmatrix}^{-1} \begin{pmatrix} \hat{\bar{y}}_{t-1} \\ \hat{\bar{y}}_{t-1}^* \end{pmatrix}$$
$$+ \left(\frac{1+\varphi}{\gamma+\varphi}\right) \begin{pmatrix} \Lambda & 1-\Lambda \\ 1-\Lambda & \Lambda \end{pmatrix} \begin{pmatrix} \hat{\varepsilon}_t^a \\ \hat{\varepsilon}_t^{a*} \end{pmatrix},$$

$$\begin{pmatrix} \hat{\varepsilon}_t^a \\ \hat{\varepsilon}_t^{a*} \end{pmatrix} \sim N\left(\begin{pmatrix} 0 \\ 0 \end{pmatrix}, \begin{pmatrix} \sigma_a^2 & \rho_{a,a^*}\sigma_a^2 \\ \rho_{a,a^*}\sigma_a^2 & \sigma_a^2 \end{pmatrix} \right),$$

where

$$\begin{pmatrix} \Lambda & 1-\Lambda \\ 1-\Lambda & \Lambda \end{pmatrix} \begin{pmatrix} \delta_a & \delta_{a,a^*} \\ \delta_{a,a^*} & \delta_a \end{pmatrix} \begin{pmatrix} \Lambda & 1-\Lambda \\ 1-\Lambda & \Lambda \end{pmatrix}^{-1} = \begin{pmatrix} \delta_a & \delta_{a,a^*} \\ \delta_{a,a^*} & \delta_a \end{pmatrix}.$$

This implies that the VAR(1) for potential output inherits the persistence structure of the underlying productivity shocks. Moreover, the innovations to the output potential process are related to the innovations of the underlying productivity shocks as follows:

$$\begin{pmatrix} \hat{\varepsilon}_t^r \\ \hat{\varepsilon}_t^{r*} \end{pmatrix} \equiv \left(\frac{1+\varphi}{\gamma+\varphi}\right) \begin{pmatrix} \Lambda & 1-\Lambda \\ 1-\Lambda & \Lambda \end{pmatrix} \begin{pmatrix} \hat{\varepsilon}_t^a \\ \hat{\varepsilon}_t^{a*} \end{pmatrix},$$

$$\begin{pmatrix} \hat{\varepsilon}_t^r \\ \hat{\varepsilon}_t^{r*} \end{pmatrix} \sim N\left(\begin{pmatrix} 0 \\ 0 \end{pmatrix}, \left(\frac{1+\varphi}{\gamma+\varphi}\right)^2 \begin{pmatrix} \Lambda & 1-\Lambda \\ 1-\Lambda & \Lambda \end{pmatrix} \begin{pmatrix} \sigma_a^2 & \rho_{a,a^*}\sigma_a^2 \\ \rho_{a,a^*}\sigma_a^2 & \sigma_a^2 \end{pmatrix} \begin{pmatrix} \Lambda & 1-\Lambda \\ 1-\Lambda & \Lambda \end{pmatrix}^T \right),$$

where

$$\left(\frac{1+\varphi}{\gamma+\varphi}\right)^2 \begin{pmatrix} \Lambda & 1-\Lambda \\ 1-\Lambda & \Lambda \end{pmatrix} \begin{pmatrix} \sigma_a^2 & \rho_{a,a^*}\sigma_a^2 \\ \rho_{a,a^*}\sigma_a^2 & \sigma_a^2 \end{pmatrix} \begin{pmatrix} \Lambda & 1-\Lambda \\ 1-\Lambda & \Lambda \end{pmatrix}^T$$

$$= \sigma_a^2 \left(\frac{1+\varphi}{\gamma+\varphi}\right)^2 \left((\Lambda)^2 + 2\rho_{a,a^*}\Lambda(1-\Lambda) + (1-\Lambda)^2\right)$$

$$\times \begin{pmatrix} 1 & \dfrac{\rho_{a,a^*}(\Lambda)^2 + 2\Lambda(1-\Lambda) + \rho_{a,a^*}(1-\Lambda)^2}{(\Lambda)^2 + 2\rho_{a,a^*}\Lambda(1-\Lambda) + (1-\Lambda)^2} \\ \dfrac{\rho_{a,a^*}(\Lambda)^2 + 2\Lambda(1-\Lambda) + \rho_{a,a^*}(1-\Lambda)^2}{(\Lambda)^2 + 2\rho_{a,a^*}\Lambda(1-\Lambda) + (1-\Lambda)^2} & 1 \end{pmatrix}.$$

The natural rates of both countries can be expressed as a linear transformation of the productivity shocks as,

$$\begin{pmatrix} \hat{\bar{r}}_t \\ \hat{\bar{r}}_t^* \end{pmatrix} \approx \gamma \left(\frac{1+\varphi}{\gamma+\varphi}\right) \begin{pmatrix} \Theta\Lambda + (1-\Theta)(1-\Lambda) & 1 - (\Theta\Lambda + (1-\Theta)(1-\Lambda)) \\ 1 - (\Theta\Lambda + (1-\Theta)(1-\Lambda)) & \Theta\Lambda + (1-\Theta)(1-\Lambda) \end{pmatrix}$$

$$\times \begin{pmatrix} \mathbb{E}_t[\Delta\hat{a}_{t+1}] \\ \mathbb{E}_t\left[\Delta\hat{a}_{t+1}^*\right] \end{pmatrix} \approx \gamma \left(\frac{1+\varphi}{\gamma+\varphi}\right) \begin{pmatrix} \Pi_1 & \Pi_2 \\ \Pi_2 & \Pi_1 \end{pmatrix} \begin{pmatrix} \hat{a}_t \\ \hat{a}_t^* \end{pmatrix},$$

where

$$\Theta\Lambda + (1-\Theta)(1-\Lambda) = \xi \left(\frac{\varphi(\sigma\gamma - (\sigma\gamma - 1)(2\xi - 1)) + \gamma}{\varphi\left(\sigma\gamma - (\sigma\gamma - 1)(2\xi - 1)^2\right) + \gamma}\right),$$

$$\Pi_1 \equiv \delta_{a,a^*} - \xi \left(\frac{\varphi(\sigma\gamma - (\sigma\gamma - 1)(2\xi - 1)) + \gamma}{\varphi\left(\sigma\gamma - (\sigma\gamma - 1)(2\xi - 1)^2\right) + \gamma}\right) \left(1 + \delta_{a,a^*} - \delta_a\right),$$

$$\Pi_2 \equiv (\delta_a - 1) + \xi \left(\frac{\varphi(\sigma\gamma - (\sigma\gamma - 1)(2\xi - 1)) + \gamma}{\varphi\left(\sigma\gamma - (\sigma\gamma - 1)(2\xi - 1)^2\right) + \gamma}\right) \left(1 + \delta_{a,a^*} - \delta_a\right).$$

Assuming invertibility, the natural interest rates inherit the VAR(1) stochastic structure of the productivity shocks. Accordingly, the natural rates take the following stochastic form,

$$\begin{pmatrix} \hat{\bar{r}}_t \\ \hat{\bar{r}}_t^* \end{pmatrix} \approx \begin{pmatrix} \Pi_1 & \Pi_2 \\ \Pi_2 & \Pi_1 \end{pmatrix} \begin{pmatrix} \delta_a & \delta_{a,a^*} \\ \delta_{a,a^*} & \delta_a \end{pmatrix} \begin{pmatrix} \Pi_1 & \Pi_2 \\ \Pi_2 & \Pi_1 \end{pmatrix}^{-1} \begin{pmatrix} \hat{\bar{r}}_{t-1} \\ \hat{\bar{r}}_{t-1}^* \end{pmatrix}$$
$$+ \gamma \left(\frac{1+\varphi}{\gamma+\varphi} \right) \begin{pmatrix} \Pi_1 & \Pi_2 \\ \Pi_2 & \Pi_1 \end{pmatrix} \begin{pmatrix} \hat{\varepsilon}_t^a \\ \hat{\varepsilon}_t^{a*} \end{pmatrix},$$

$$\begin{pmatrix} \hat{\varepsilon}_t^a \\ \hat{\varepsilon}_t^{a*} \end{pmatrix} \sim N \left(\begin{pmatrix} 0 \\ 0 \end{pmatrix}, \begin{pmatrix} \sigma_a^2 & \rho_{a,a^*}\sigma_a^2 \\ \rho_{a,a^*}\sigma_a^2 & \sigma_a^2 \end{pmatrix} \right),$$

where

$$\begin{pmatrix} \Pi_1 & \Pi_2 \\ \Pi_2 & \Pi_1 \end{pmatrix} \begin{pmatrix} \delta_a & \delta_{a,a^*} \\ \delta_{a,a^*} & \delta_a \end{pmatrix} \begin{pmatrix} \Pi_1 & \Pi_2 \\ \Pi_2 & \Pi_1 \end{pmatrix}^{-1} = \begin{pmatrix} \delta_a & \delta_{a,a^*} \\ \delta_{a,a^*} & \delta_a \end{pmatrix}.$$

This implies that the VAR(1) for the natural interest rates inherits the persistence structure of the underlying productivity shocks, just as it happened for potential output. Moreover, the innovations to the natural interest rate process can be related to the innovations of the productivity shocks as follows:

$$\begin{pmatrix} \hat{\varepsilon}_t^r \\ \hat{\varepsilon}_t^{r*} \end{pmatrix} \equiv \gamma \left(\frac{1+\varphi}{\gamma+\varphi} \right) \begin{pmatrix} \Pi_1 & \Pi_2 \\ \Pi_2 & \Pi_1 \end{pmatrix} \begin{pmatrix} \hat{\varepsilon}_t^a \\ \hat{\varepsilon}_t^{a*} \end{pmatrix},$$

$$\begin{pmatrix} \hat{\varepsilon}_t^r \\ \hat{\varepsilon}_t^{r*} \end{pmatrix} \sim N \left(\begin{pmatrix} 0 \\ 0 \end{pmatrix}, \gamma^2 \left(\frac{1+\varphi}{\gamma+\varphi} \right)^2 \begin{pmatrix} \Pi_1 & \Pi_2 \\ \Pi_2 & \Pi_1 \end{pmatrix} \begin{pmatrix} \sigma_a^2 & \rho_{a,a^*}\sigma_a^2 \\ \rho_{a,a^*}\sigma_a^2 & \sigma_a^2 \end{pmatrix} \begin{pmatrix} \Pi_1 & \Pi_2 \\ \Pi_2 & \Pi_1 \end{pmatrix}^T \right),$$

where

$$\gamma^2 \left(\frac{1+\varphi}{\gamma+\varphi} \right)^2 \begin{pmatrix} \Pi_1 & \Pi_2 \\ \Pi_2 & \Pi_1 \end{pmatrix} \begin{pmatrix} \sigma_a^2 & \rho_{a,a^*}\sigma_a^2 \\ \rho_{a,a^*}\sigma_a^2 & \sigma_a^2 \end{pmatrix} \begin{pmatrix} \Pi_1 & \Pi_2 \\ \Pi_2 & \Pi_1 \end{pmatrix}^T$$
$$= \sigma_a^2 \gamma^2 \left(\tfrac{1+\varphi}{\gamma+\varphi} \right)^2 ((\Pi_1)^2 + 2\rho_{a,a^*}\Pi_1\Pi_2 + (\Pi_2)^2)$$
$$\times \begin{pmatrix} 1 & \dfrac{\rho_{a,a^*}(\Pi_1)^2 + 2\Pi_1\Pi_2 + \rho_{a,a^*}(\Pi_2)^2}{(\Pi_1)^2 + 2\rho_{a,a^*}\Pi_1\Pi_2 + (\Pi_2)^2} \\ \dfrac{\rho_{a,a^*}(\Pi_1)^2 + 2\Pi_1\Pi_2 + \rho_{a,a^*}(\Pi_2)^2}{(\Pi_1)^2 + 2\rho_{a,a^*}\Pi_1\Pi_2 + (\Pi_2)^2} & 1 \end{pmatrix}.$$

Proof of Propositions 2 and 3.

Given Proposition 1 and the maintained assumptions on the productivity and monetary shocks, it is straightforward to derive these world and difference forcing processes from the definition of the world and difference variables in equations (39) and (40).

Chapter 5

Pass-Through of Exchange Rate Shocks to Prices in the Euro Area: Evidence from Pricing Chain Model

Nidhaleddine Ben Cheikh and Waël Louhichi

ESSCA School of Management, 1 Rue Lakanal, 49000 Angers, France, e-mail: nbcheikh@gmail.com

Abstract

This chapter analyzes the exchange rate pass-through (ERPT) into different prices for 12 euro area (EA) countries. We provide new up-to-date estimates of ERPT by paying attention to either the time-series properties of data and variables endogeneity. Using VECM framework, we examine the pass-through at different stages along the distribution chain, that is, import prices, producer prices, and consumer prices. When carrying out impulse response functions analysis, we find a higher pass-through to import prices with a complete pass-through (after one year) detected for roughly half of EA countries. These estimates are relatively large compared to single-equation literature. We denote that the magnitude of the pass-through of exchange rate shocks declines along the distribution chain of pricing, with the modest effect recorded for consumer prices. When assessing for the determinant of cross-country differences in the ERPT, we find that inflation level, inflation volatility, and exchange rate persistence are the main macroeconomic factors influencing the pass-through almost along the pricing chain. Thereafter, we have tested for the decline of the response of consumer prices across EA countries. According to multivariate time-series Chow test, the stability of ERPT coefficients was rejected, and the impulse responses of consumer prices over 1990–2010 provide an evidence of general decline in rates of pass-through in most of the EA countries. Finally, using the historical decompositions, our results reveal that external factors,

International Symposia in Economic Theory and Econometrics, Vol. 24
William A. Barnett and Fredj Jawadi (Editors)

ISSN: 1571-0386/doi: 10.1108/S1571-038620150000024017

that is, exchange rate and import prices shocks, have had important inflationary impacts on inflation since 1999 compared to the pre-EMU period.

Keywords: exchange rate pass-through, prices, vector error correction models

JEL Classifications: C32, E31, F31

1. Introduction

Movements in the exchange rate can have a significant influence on inflation dynamics, both in terms of their direct effect on prices and their indirect effect through changes in aggregate demand and wages. Thorough knowledge of the underlying behavior behind exchange rate pass-through is a key input to determine the appropriate monetary policy responses. Policymakers must be able to prevent changes in relative prices – such as those stemming from exchange rate movements – which may fuel a continuous inflationary process. As is well known, the Exchange Rate Pass-Through (ERPT) to consumer prices involves both first and second-stage pass-through at once, that is, the transmission of exchange rate changes to import prices, and in turn, the transmission of import prices changes to consumer prices. Thereby, estimating the ERPT to consumer prices would include the effect of exchange rate movements on both import prices and on other prices in the consumer basket, such as those of domestically produced goods, services, and other non-tradable prices.

In order to provide reliable estimates, we need to build a framework that includes different kinds of price indices as well as the nominal exchange rate, allowing us to measure the extent of pass-through at different levels. To achieve this, McCarthy (2007) propose a VAR analysis that include different stages of the distribution chain – import prices, producer prices, and consumer prices – to analyze how exchange rate fluctuations "pass-through" the production process from the import of products to the consumer level. Contrary to the *single-equation* method, this framework allows for underlying dynamic interrelations among prices at different stages of distribution and other variables of interest. The advantage of simultaneous equation approach allows for potential and highly likely endogeneity between the variables of interest; ignoring such simultaneity would result in simultaneous equation bias. In a single-equation pass-through regression, for example, the fact that domestic inflation may affect the exchange rate is ignored.

Recently, many empirical studies have adopted the modeling strategy of McCarthy (2007) to estimate the ERPT along the distribution chain (see e.g., Ca'Zorzi, Kahn, & Sánchez, 2007; Choudhri, Faruquee, & Hakura, 2005; Faruqee, 2006; Ito & Sato, 2008; Parker & Wong, 2014, to name but a few). However, an important drawback regarding this literature, including McCarthy (2007), is that the time-series properties of the data, particularly non-stationarity and cointegration issues, were neglected. Very few studies, such as Hüfner and Schröder (2002), estimated a Vector Error Correction Model (VECM) incorporating the long-run relationships among the variables. Deriving impulse response functions from the VECM, Hüfner and Schröder (2002) examine how external shocks are propagated from one price stage to the next. As a matter of fact, the main drawback of Hüfner and Schröder (2002) study is that they do not take into consideration the post-European Monetary Union (post-EMU) era. Consequently, the aim of our chapter is to fill this gap by providing recent estimates of pass-through for 12 euro area (EA) countries using a longer time period and more observations covering the pre- and post-euro episodes. This consideration is very useful in assessing the effectiveness of the EMU in reducing disparities between EA countries. Consequently, in our empirical work, we propose a VECM model as it allows us to take proper account of the non-stationarity of the data, that is, look for cointegration properties in the data, and at the same time disentangle short- and long-run dynamics. Then, different techniques and tools of VAR models – impulse response functions, variance decompositions, and historical decompositions – are implemented in order to provide reliable estimates of ERPT.

The objective of our study is twofold: on one hand, we seek to remedy some of the shortcomings of the previous studies, by taking into account the non-stationarity and the endogeneity of the variables within a VECM framework. On the other hand, in the spirit of McCarthy (2007), we propose a VECM model that permits to track pass-through from exchange rate fluctuations to each stage of the distribution chain. The methodology of McCarthy (2007) is applied here with some modifications. After considering the long-run proprieties of the data, a measure of foreign costs is included in the system as an exogenous variable which is considered as a primary variable throughout ERPT literature. We pretend that the introduction of this variable provides a more accurate estimates of pass-through.[1] After estimating our *VECM pricing model*, several analytical tools are used to explore the impact of exchange rate shocks: first, impulse responses are computed to analyze the size and speed of the pass-through

[1] The relevance of incorporating such variable is discussed in detail when describing data in Section 4.

of external shocks along the distribution chain; second, variance decompositions are provided to capture the relative importance of external shocks in explaining fluctuations in the different price indices; next, the existence of a decline in the response of consumer prices is checked; and finally, historical decompositions are used to assess how the external factors – exchange rate and import prices shocks – have contributed to the consumer inflation in the pre- and post-EMU episodes.

The rest of the chapter is organized as follows: Section 2 provides an overview of some ERPT VAR studies with a focus on EA countries. Section 3 outlines the VECM system used for the empirical analysis. In Section 4, the data set and their properties are discussed. In Section 5, the empirical results are presented and discussed. Section 6 concludes.

2. ERPT in EA Countries: Overview of VAR Studies

There has been a growing interest in examining the extent of pass-through in EA countries during the last decade, although the number of studies is still relatively limited compared to empirical literature on the US economy.[2] In this section, we intend to give some insight on the empirical literature that used VAR models to measure the degree of ERPT in EA countries. In Table 1, we provide an overview of VAR studies that cover EA countries. Mainly, we emphasize on three points regarding this literature. First, the data frequency and variables employed in the VAR system. Second, the type of VAR model (level, first-difference, cointegrated), techniques and tools of VAR models (impulse response functions, variance decompositions, historical decompositions), and identification schemes of the structural shocks (short-run Choleski decompositions, long-run Blanchard-Quah restrictions, both short- and long-run identifying restrictions as in Gali, 1992). Finally, the size as well as the speed of the response of consumer prices to exchange rate shock – that is, a 1% currency depreciation shocks.

Among the most cited VAR study is the influential paper of McCarthy (2007) who investigates the pass-through on the aggregate level for selected industrialized countries, including four EA countries, namely Belgium, Germany, France, and the Netherlands. The author estimates a first-difference VAR model at different stages along the distribution chain, that is, import prices, producer prices, and consumer prices. In this study,

[2] European ERPT studies have been scarce given that the time horizon since the introduction of the euro is rather short.

Table 1: Main VAR Studies on EA Countries

Study	Data and variables	Methodology	Response of consumer prices to 1% currency depreciation
Hüfner and Schröder (2002)	Monthly data from 1982:1 to 2001:1 for five large EA countries (France, Germany, Italy, the Netherlands, and Spain) *Endogenous variables:* Oil price, NEER, output gap, interest rate, and 3 price indices (import prices, producer prices, and consumer prices)	Cointegration analysis using Johansen procedure Impulse responses and variance decompositions derived from the VECM Identification of shocks by Cholesky decomposition	France: 0.01 (6 months), 0.07 (12 months), 0.12 (18 months), 0.16 (24 months) Germany: 0.07 (6 months), 0.08 (12 months), 0.09 (18 months), 0.10 (24 months) Italy: 0.06 (6 months), 0.12 (12 months), 0.16 (18 months), 0.18 (24 months) The Netherlands: 0.12 (6 months), 0.11 (12 months), 0.11 (18 months), 0.11 (24 months) Spain: 0.09 (6 months), 0.08 (12 months), 0.08 (18 months), 0.08 (24 months)
Hahn (2003)	Quarterly data from 1970:2 to 2002:2 for the euro area *Endogenous variables:* Oil prices, interest rate, output gap, exchange rate, non-oil import prices, producer prices, and HICP	Impulse responses, variance and historical decompositions derived from a first-difference VAR model Identification of shocks by Cholesky decomposition	1st quarter: 0.025 1st year: 0.08 3 years: 0.16
Choudhri et al. (2005)	Quarterly series at annual rates 1979:1 to 2001:3 for non-US G-7 countries 7 *endogenous variables:* Interest rate, exchange rate, import price, export price, producer price, consumer price, and wage rate 2 *exogenous variables:* Foreign interest and foreign consumer price	Impulse responses derived from restricted VAR model Identification of shocks using structural short-run restrictions	Germany: 0.15 (1 quarter), 0.20 (4 quarters), 0.36 (10 quarters) France: 0.00 (1 quarters), 0.10 (4 quarters), 0.09 (10 quarters) Italy: 0.02 (1 quarter), 0.14 (4 quarters), 0.26 (10 quarters)

Table 1: (*Continued*)

Study	Data and variables	Methodology	Response of consumer prices to 1% currency depreciation
Faruqee (2006)	Monthly data from 1990 to 2002 for the euro area wide data	Impulse responses derived from VAR in first differences	0.00 after 1 month 0.01 after 6 months 0.02 after 12 months
	Endogenous variables: Nominal effective exchange rate, wages, import prices, export prices, producer prices, consumer prices	Identification of shocks by Cholesky decomposition	0.02 after 18 months
McCarthy (2007)	Quarterly data from 1976:1 to 1998:4 for 9 developed countries among them 4 EA members (Germany, France, Belgium, and the Netherlands) *Endogenous variables:* Oil price, NEER, output gap, import prices, producer prices, consumer prices, interest rate, and monetary aggregate	Impulse responses, variance, and historical decompositions derived from a first-difference VAR model Identification of shocks by Cholesky decomposition	ERPT is particularly large in Belgium and the Netherlands Wrong (negative) sign for France By the end of two years the response is imprecisely estimated
Shambaugh (2008)	Quarterly data from 1973:1 to 1999:4 for 16 countries among them 4 EA members (Austria, Finland, Germany, and Greece)	Impulse responses and variance decompositions derived from a first-difference VAR model	*ERPT ratio following external shock:* Austria: 0.83 (1 quarter), 0.55 (4 quarters) Finland: 0.71 (1 quarter), 0.79 (4 quarters) Germany: 0.32 (1 quarter), 0.37 (4 quarters)
	Endogenous variables: Industrial production, real exchange rate, CPI, nominal exchange rate, import price	Blanchard-Quah long-run restrictions methodology	Greece: 0.25 (1 quarter), 0.70 (4 quarters)

ERPT to consumer prices is found to be modest in most of the analyzed countries, with the exception of Belgium and the Netherlands. Also, the results show that import share of a country and the persistence of exchange rate changes are found to be positively correlated with the extent of pass-through to consumer prices, while exchange rate volatility is found to be negatively correlated. A similar pricing chain model was estimated for the EA by Hahn (2003). In spite of the weakness of the ERPT, the author argued that external shocks – oil prices and exchange rate shocks together – seem to have contributed largely to inflation in the euro area since the start of the monetary union.[3]

Main criticism addressed to these studies is that they neglect the time-series properties of the data, particularly non-stationarity and cointegration issues. Hüfner and Schröder (2002) found that the endogenous variables in their VAR system are cointegrated using the Johansen procedure.[4] Thereby, they propose to analyze the ERPT to consumer prices in the five largest countries of the EA by applying a Vector Error Correction Model (VECM) that retains information attained from any cointegrating relationships found. After aggregating the national results, the authors found a rather modest pass-through for the whole EA: 4% after one year, which rises to its long-run level of 8% after about three years.[5] Those results are obtained from the impulse responses functions which are derived from the VECM.

Besides, most VAR studies on ERPT have adopted standard recursive identifying restrictions. This implies that the identified shocks contemporaneously affect their corresponding variables and those variables that are ordered at a later stage, but have no impact on those that are ordered before. It is well known that the results derived from VAR models may strongly depend on the ordering of the variables.[6] Hahn (2003) has carried out different identification schemes to check the robustness of

[3] The euro had depreciated by roughly 25% against the US dollar in the first two years of his existence.

[4] Using panel cointegration techniques within a single-equation, Ben Cheikh and Cheik (2013) give support to the presence of a long-run equilibrium relationship between variables entering the ERPT equation.

[5] Approximations for the euro area data are derived using the relative weights of each country's inflation rate in the Harmonized Index of Consumer Prices (HICP). In Table 1, we provide the individual pass-through estimates for the five EA countries.

[6] Faust and Leeper (2003) provide a strong rejection of recursive ordering procedures that assume some variables can or cannot respond to other variables in the first period of a shock. They show that if one tests a wide variety of reasonable restrictions on the relationships between the variables, the responses to shocks can vary a great deal.

the pass-through estimates. Different plausible orderings of the variables in the Choleski decomposition as well as an identification scheme that includes both short- and long-run restrictions were used. The author argued that these had minimal effects on the results. Alternatively, Shambaugh (2008) proposes to use the Blanchard and Quah (1989) methodology imposing the restriction that certain shocks cannot affect the level of certain variables in the long run. This leaves the short-run reactions free and enforce the long-run assumptions to identify the shocks. Finally, Mihailov (2008) proposes generalized impulse response analysis, in the spirit of Pesaran and Shin (1998), as an alternative to the traditional orthogonalized recursive one. This does not require orthogonalization of shocks and, thus, it is invariant to the ordering of variables. For this reason, we use this approach as a complementary check of robustness in our empirical work.

3. Empirical Methodology

As our analysis aims at estimating the effect of nominal exchange rate changes on different prices, we implement a model that incorporates features of pricing chain in the spirit of McCarthy (2007) and Hüfner and Schröder (2002). We call this *VECM pricing chain system*, which enables us to examine the pass-through at different stages along the distribution chain, that is, import prices, producer prices, and consumer prices. This exercise is of great interest for EA price analysis as it reveals how exchange rate shocks are propagated from one price stage to the next. Therefore, in a cointegrated framework, we consider the following system of endogenous variables relating the pricing chain – import prices (mpi_t), producer prices (ppi_t) and consumer prices (cpi_t) – to measures of oil price (oil_t), aggregate income (y_t), the nominal exchange rate (e_t), and interest rates (r_t):[7]

$$x_t = (\text{oil}_t, y_t, e_t,\ \text{mpi}_t, \text{ppi}_t,\ \text{cpi}_t, r_t)'. \tag{1}$$

Having first tested the stationarity of the variables, we apply cointegration tests for each country to check whether long-term relationships exist between the variables. The Johansen test is used to assess whether or not cointegration exists in the system of variables. To this end, we begin by considering the following system of seven-equation VAR (k) model:

$$x_t = A_1 x_{t-1} + \cdots + A_k x_{t-k} + \mu + \psi D_t + \varepsilon_t, \qquad t = 1, 2, \ldots, T. \tag{2}$$

[7] A further discussion of the variables selection is presented in Section 4.

Equation (2) can be expressed as an error or vector equilibrium correction model (VECM) which is formulated in terms of differences as follows:

$$\Delta x_t = \Gamma_1 \Delta x_{t-1} + \cdots + \Gamma_{k-1} \Delta x_{t-k+1} + \Pi x_{t-1} + \mu + \psi D_t + \varepsilon_t, \tag{3}$$

where x_t is a (7×1) vector of $I(1)$ endogenous variables as given in Equation (1), k is the lag length, μ is a constant term, D_t is a vector including deterministic variables (centered seasonal dummies and intervention dummies) and weakly exogenous variables, ε_t is a (7×1) vector of errors which is assumed identically and independently distributed and follows a Gaussian distribution $\varepsilon_t \sim \text{iid } N_p(0,\Omega)$, where Ω denotes the variance-covariance matrix of the disturbances. The VECM representation encompasses both short- and long-run information of the data. The matrix Π assembles the long-run information and the Γ_i's contain the short-run properties. $\Pi = \alpha\beta'$ has reduced rank r, where α depicts the speed of adjustment and β represents the cointegrating vectors. The Johansen procedure estimates Equation (3) subject to the hypothesis that Π has a reduced rank $r < 7$. This hypothesis can be written as

$$\text{H}(r) = \alpha\beta'. \tag{4}$$

To determine the number of cointegrating vectors (r) in the system, that is, the cointegration rank, we employ the widely used trace test statistics:

$$\text{Trace} = -N \sum_{i=r+1}^{7} \ln(1 - \hat{\lambda}_i), \tag{5}$$

where N is the number of observations and $\hat{\lambda}_i$ is the estimated eigenvalue. When the appropriate model has been identified for the system in terms of lag length and cointegration rank, the coefficients on the α matrix reveal the long-run dynamic while the coefficients on the β matrix reveal the drivers toward the long-run equilibrium.[8]

After checking for the possible existence of long-run equilibrium relationships among our key variables, we carry out an impulse response function analysis on the VECM that includes the distribution chain of pricing. To this end, structural shocks in our *VECM pricing chain system* must be identified. In our study, we follow the recursive identification scheme adopted by McCarthy (2007). According to this structure, inflation at each stage of distribution chain – import, producer, and consumer – in period t is assumed to comprise several components. The first component is

[8] Results of Johansen trace tests is discussed in Section 4 with full results reported in Table A.3.

the expected inflation at that stage based on the available information at the end of period $t-1$. The second and third components are the effects of period t domestic supply and demand shocks on inflation at that stage, respectively. The fourth component is the effect of exchange rate shocks on inflation at a particular stage. Next components are the effects of shocks at the previous stages of the chain. Finally, there is that stage's shock.

The inflation shocks at each stage are simply that portion of that stage's inflation which cannot be explained using information from period $t-1$ plus information about domestic supply and demand variables, exchange rates, and period t inflation at previous stages of the distribution chain. These shocks can thus be thought of as changes in the pricing power and markups of firms at these stages. Two other features of the model are worthy of note. First, the model allows import inflation shocks to affect domestic consumer inflation both directly and indirectly through their effects on producer inflation. Second, there is no contemporaneous feedback in the model; for example, consumer inflation shocks affect inflation at the import and producer stages only through their effect on expected inflation in future periods.

Under these assumptions, the inflation rates of country i in period t at each of the three stages – import prices (mpi_t), producer prices (ppi_t), and consumer prices (cpi_t) – can be written as

$$\Delta\text{mpi}_t = E_{t-1}(\Delta\text{mpi}_t) + \delta_{1i}\varepsilon_{it}^s + \delta_{2i}\varepsilon_{it}^d + \delta_{3i}\varepsilon_{it}^e + \varepsilon_{it}^{\text{mpi}} \tag{6}$$

$$\Delta\text{ppi}_t = E_{t-1}(\Delta\text{ppi}_t) + \varphi_{1i}\varepsilon_{it}^s + \varphi_{2i}\varepsilon_{it}^d + \varphi_{3i}\varepsilon_{it}^e + \varphi_{4i}\varepsilon_{it}^{\text{mpi}} + \varepsilon_{it}^{\text{ppi}} \tag{7}$$

$$\Delta\text{cpi}_t = E_{t-1}(\Delta\text{cpi}_t) + \eta_{1i}\varepsilon_{it}^s + \eta_{2i}\varepsilon_{it}^d + \eta_{3i}\varepsilon_{it}^e + \eta_{4i}\varepsilon_{it}^{\text{mpi}} + \eta_{5i}\varepsilon_{it}^{\text{ppi}} + \varepsilon_{it}^{\text{cpi}}, \tag{8}$$

where ε_{it}^s, ε_{it}^d, and ε_{it}^e are the supply, demand, and exchange rate shocks, respectively; $\varepsilon_{it}^{\text{mpi}}$, $\varepsilon_{it}^{\text{ppi}}$, and $\varepsilon_{it}^{\text{cpi}}$ are the import price, producer price, and consumer price inflation shocks, respectively; and $E_{t-1}(.)$ is the expectation of a variable based on the information set at the end of period $t-1$. The shocks are assumed to be serially uncorrelated as well as uncorrelated with one another within a period.

The structure of the models (6)–(8) is a part of a recursive VAR framework. Thus, to complete the empirical model, the following assumptions are added. First, supply shocks (ε_{it}^s) are identified from the dynamics of oil price inflation (Δoil_t) denominated in the local currency. Second, demand shocks (ε_{it}^d) are identified from the dynamics of the GDP growth (Δy_t) in the country after taking into account the contemporaneous effect of the supply shock. Finally, exchange rate shocks (ε_{it}^e) are identified from the dynamics of exchange rate depreciation (Δe_t) after taking into account the contemporaneous effects of the supply and demand shocks.

$$\Delta \text{oil}_{it} = E_{t-1}(\Delta \text{oil}_t) + \varepsilon^s_{it} \tag{9}$$

$$\Delta y_{it} = E_{t-1}(\Delta y_t) + \beta_{1i}\varepsilon^s_{it} + \varepsilon^d_{it} \tag{10}$$

$$\Delta e_{it} = E_{t-1}(\Delta e_t) + \gamma_{1i}\varepsilon^s_{it} + \gamma_{2i}\varepsilon^d_{it} + \varepsilon^e_{it}. \tag{11}$$

Furthermore, short-term interest rates are used to incorporate central bank policy in the system. Monetary policy may react to exchange rate fluctuations and then policy may affect exchange rates and domestic inflation. That way, the observed relationship between prices and exchange rates would take into account the central bank behavior rather than the direct influence of exchange rates on prices. As discussed by Parsley and Popper (1998), taking into account monetary policy significantly improves the estimation results of ERPT. In fact, central banks are concerned with keeping domestic inflation within its target range which may insulate prices from exchange rate movements. Thus, neglecting the effects of monetary policy may result in a commonly omitted variables problem. Given this view, the last portion of the model consists of a central bank reaction function. The reaction function relates short-term nominal interest rates (r_t) to the previously cited variables in the model as central banks use the short-term rate as their monetary policy instrument.

$$\Delta r_{it} = E_{t-1}(\Delta r_{it}) + \lambda_{1i}\varepsilon^s_{it} + \lambda_{2i}\varepsilon^d_{it} + \lambda_{3i}\varepsilon^e_{it} + \lambda_{4i}\varepsilon^{\text{mpi}}_{it} + \lambda_{5i}\varepsilon^{\text{ppi}}_{it} + \lambda_{6i}\varepsilon^{\text{cpi}}_{it} + \varepsilon^r_{it}. \tag{12}$$

Finally, the conditional expectations, $E_{t-1}(.)$, in Equations (6)–(12) are assumed to be replaced by linear projections on lags of the seven variables in the system. In such framework, the model can be expressed and estimated as a VECM using a Cholesky decomposition to identify the shocks.[9] As is well known, this identification technique can be sensitive to the ordering of variables. As explained above, within McCarthy (2007) framework, the use of a recursive identification scheme implies that the identified shocks contemporaneously affect their corresponding variables and those variables that are ordered at a later stage but have no impact on those that

[9] Note that even though the data in this study have both cross-sectional and time-series aspects, the model will be estimated for each country separately. We think that the persistent heterogeneity across EA may lead to different responses in terms of pass-through.

are ordered before. As a matter of fact, when the reduced-form residuals from the system do not display high cross correlations, the order of factorization makes little difference. However, according to the variance-covariance matrix, we find that the correlations between residuals are less than 0.3, with the notable exceptions of the exchange rate and import prices and between oil prices and producer prices. Nevertheless, given that we are aware of the possible sensitivity of the Cholesky approach to the ordering of the variables, we conduct a sensitivity analysis by computing the generalized impulse response functions, as introduced by Pesaran and Shin (1998), where ordering of the variables does not matter (see Appendix C).

It is worth highlighting that our model differs from that of McCarthy (2007). The author estimates a first-difference VAR model ignoring the possibility of cointegration among the levels of the variables. However, if the levels of a time series are non-stationary, non-sense results may occur if the non-stationarity is ignored. Thus, we feel that it is more appropriate to retain the information contained in the levels of the variables and then derive impulse responses from the VECM, which incorporates the long-run relationships among the variables. Moreover, throughout the *single-equation* literature of ERPT, a proxy for foreign producers' costs was considered as a primary control variable. Along with this literature, we propose to include a measure of foreign costs as exogenous variables in our VECM. Doing so, we think that this gives more reliable estimates of pass-through.

4. Data Selection and Their Properties

In order to measure the effects of exchange rate changes along the pricing chain, we consider a vector of seven endogenous variables as in Equation (1). In addition to our key variables – exchange rate, import prices, producer prices, and consumer prices – we have included three macroeconomic variables which may directly affect the domestic prices. The choice of the variables is based on the following considerations: first, oil prices enter the VECM to control for the impact of supply shocks; second, to balance the model with respect to the demand side, a measure of national income is entered in the system; and finally, we include a short-run interest rate to allow for the effects of monetary policy.[10] We focus our analysis on 12 EA countries (Austria, Belgium, Germany, Spain, Finland, France, Greece,

[10] With the exception of interest rates, all variables are in logs.

Ireland, Italy, Luxembourg, the Netherlands, and Portugal). For each country, a set of quarterly data was collected covering the time period 1980:1–2010:4. The consumer price (cpi_t) is the overall consumer price index to provide the broadest measure of inflation at the consumer level. We did not use the Harmonized Index of Consumer Prices (HICP) due to the short data availability of this variable. We include the non-oil import prices as a measure of import prices (mpi_t) (to avoid double-counting with oil prices index) and the producer prices index (ppi_t) in manufacturing. Exchange rate data are effective nominal exchange rates of the national currencies which use the trade weights of each country.[11] The oil price (oil_t) is represented by a crude oil price index denominated in US dollar in order to avoid multicollinearity issues with the exchange rate.[12] The national income (y_t) is proxied by the real GDP. The three-month interest rate is used to model monetary policy. As mentioned above, ERPT equation must contain a proxy for foreign costs as recommended by the bulk of empirical literature (see Goldberg & Knetter, 1997). Given that foreign costs are exogenously determined variables across our EA countries, we propose to include a proxy for costs of a country's trading partners as an exogenous variable in our basic VECM. Therefore, to capture changes in foreign costs, we construct a typical export partners' cost proxy (W_{it}^*) that is used throughout the ERPT literature (see inter alia Bailliu & Fujii, 2004; Campa & Goldberg, 2005): $W_{it}^* = Q_{it} \times \frac{W_{it}}{E_{it}}$, where Q_{it} is the unit labor cost-based real effective exchange rate, W_{it} is the domestic unit labor cost, and E_t is the nominal effective exchange rate. Taking the logarithm, we obtain the following expression: $w_t^* \equiv q_t + w_t - e_t$. Since the nominal and real effective exchange rate series are trade weighted, we obtain a measure of foreign firms' costs with each partner weighted by its importance in the domestic country's trade.[13] Furthermore, in our VECM system Equation (3), in addition to seasonal dummy variables, we introduce a shift dummy in 1990:07 (D_{90}) and kicks in until the end of the sample. We conducted Chow tests for multivariate models, as introduced by Candelon and Lutkepohl (2001), which denotes the presence of structural break in

[11] The nominal effective exchange rate is defined as domestic currency units per unit of foreign currencies, which implies that an increase represents a depreciation for domestic country.

[12] McCarthy uses local price of oil to identify supply shocks, but this will include the exchange rate effect. Thus, much of the exchange rate effect may be mixed into the supply shock.

[13] To measure the extent of pass-through in the non-US G-7 countries, Choudhri et al. (2005) enter two foreign exogenous variables – foreign interest rate and the foreign consumer price index – in their first-difference VAR model.

the vicinity of 1990 (see Table B.1).[14] It is worth noting that centered seasonal dummies, shift dummy, and exogenous foreign costs enter the vector D_t in Equation (3). To collect data, we have followed a cascade order, choosing when possible only one institutional source, that is, IMF's *International Financial Statistics,* and OECD's *Main Economic Indicators* and *Economic Outlook*, in that order.

Next, we check the non-stationarity of the data. All variables are tested for unit roots using the traditional ADF test which tests the null hypothesis of non-stationarity. To ensure the robustness of the order of integration of the variables, ADF test is supplemented by two stationarity tests. First, the Kwiatkowski–Phillips–Schmidt–Shin (KPSS) test which is structured under the opposite null hypothesis that of stationarity against a unit root alternative. Second, the DF-GLS test, proposed by Elliott, Rothenberg, and Stock (1996), which is an augmented Dickey–Fuller test where the time series is transformed via a generalized least squares (GLS) regression before performing the test. Elliott et al. (1996) have shown that this test has significantly greater power than the previous versions of the augmented Dickey–Fuller test. In constructing the unit root tests, the variables in levels were tested in the presence of both an intercept and a trend. The subsequent tests of first differences included only an intercept given the lack of trending behavior in the first-differences series.

Results of the unit root tests of the variables reveal that the majority of the variables to have been generated via an integrated order one $I(1)$ process (see Table A.1). First-differences variables are found to be stationarity in at least two of the three tests undertaken for most cases. We can summarize the results of the three unit root tests as follows: According to ADF tests, all variables are stationary in first differences with exception of consumer prices in Ireland; for the KPSS test, the null hypothesis of stationarity is accepted for most of the variables in first differences except for consumer prices in the Netherlands and Portugal, while import prices are stationary in level for Luxembourg. Finally, we find that all variables $I(1)$ within DF-GLS test, with the exception of: consumer prices for Luxembourg and Portugal; nominal effective exchange rate for Portugal; and producer prices for Ireland.

Building on these results, the Johansen cointegration tests were undertaken to assess the existence of long-run equilibrium relationships among

[14] One can think that May 1998 – the month in which the parities among European currencies replaced by the euro were announced – should be considered as a date for structural break. However, most of empirical studies reported that the date of creation of the euro does not represent a regime shifts in ERPT relationship for EA countries (see Campa & Goldberg, 2002, 2005, among others).

the variables. Given that the choice of the rank of Π should be made on the basis of a well-specified model, it is important to include the appropriate number of lags before rank tests are undertaken. The lag structure for each VECM was based on the assessment of the AIC compatible with well-behaved residuals (see Table A.2). When we conduct trace test, as reported in Table A.3, results indicate the presence of one cointegrating vector at least for each EA country (as in Austria and the Netherlands). The null hypothesis of no cointegration was rejected for all our EA countries, with a cointegration rank identified between one and three. Regarding the specification of VECM of each of our 12 EA countries, in most of cases the most appropriate model appears to be that including a trend in the cointegrating equation and permits the intercept to enter both the cointegration space and the VAR, that is, unrestricted intercept and restricted trend. The only exceptions are Spain, Ireland, and Luxembourg where we include only a constant in the cointegrating equations and in the short-term part of the VECM, that is, unrestricted intercept.[15] A summary of the number of cointegrating equations (CE) identified across each country as well as the optimal lag length are reported in Table 2.

Table 2: Summary of VECM Models

Country	VAR lags	Number of CE	Type of model
Austria	2	1	Restricted trend
Belgium	2	2	Restricted trend
Germany	2	3	Restricted trend
Spain	3	2	Unrestricted intercept
Finland	1	2	Restricted trend
France	2	3	Restricted trend
Greece	5	2	Restricted trend
Ireland	3	3	Unrestricted intercept
Italy	2	3	Restricted trend
Luxembourg	3	2	Unrestricted intercept
The Netherlands	2	1	Restricted trend
Portugal	2	3	Restricted trend

Note: The optimal number of lags in the VECM was determined using the AIC criterion. The number of cointegrating equations is equal to the number of cointegration equations found by the Johansen trace test.

[15] The use of unrestricted intercepts and restricted trends is consistent with data that exhibit some form of trending behavior. When we expect some of the data to be trend stationary, a good idea is to start with a restricted linear trend and then test the significance of the trends.

5. Empirical Results

In order to explore the impact of exchange rate shocks in the EA countries, different techniques and tools of VAR models are used to first, the impulse responses functions are derived from a system of seven-equation VECM that incorporates the long-run relationships among the variables. This framework allows for underlying dynamic interrelations among prices at different stages of distribution and the rest of variables. It furthermore enables us to trace the dynamic responses of prices to external shocks, that is, exchange rate and import prices shocks, by capturing both the size as well as the speed of the pass-through. In addition to impulse responses, variance decompositions are computed to capture the relative importance of the different shocks in explaining fluctuations across price indices. Finally, we use historical decompositions to examine the influence and the contribution of exchange rate and import prices shocks to consumer prices variation during two sub-sample periods: on one hand, during the first and second stage of EMU (1990:1−1998:4), on the other hand, since the creation of the euro till the end of our time sample (1999:1−2010:4).

5.1. Responses to Exchange Rate Shocks

In this sub-section, we report the impulse responses of all stages of the distribution chain, that is, import prices (mpi_t), producer prices (ppi_t), and consumer prices (cpi_t), to exchange rate shocks. This gives us the opportunity to analyze how exchange rate fluctuations are propagated from one price stage to the next. Although the model is estimated in first differences, it is then transformed into levels so that cumulative price level responses are displayed over a time horizon of 12 quarters.[16] All shocks are standardized to a 1% shock to allow a comparison of the sensitivity to currency shocks across countries. The horizontal axis measures the time horizon in terms of quarters after the shock; the vertical axis measures the deviation in (log) prices from their baseline levels indicating the approximate percentage point change in the respective price index due to a 1% shock in the exchange rate (which corresponds to 1% depreciation); that is, the percentage of the ERPT. In the second part of this sub-section, we discuss some macroeconomic determinants that may affect the degree of ERPT.

[16] This is the most relevant time period for our analysis since the effects thereafter in most cases are not significant.

5.1.1. Impulse Responses Analysis

Figures 1–3 display, respectively, the responses of the import price, the producer prices, and the consumer prices to a 1% exchange rate shock in each of the EA countries.[17] Also, in Table 3, we report the response of each price index at various horizons, that is, after 0, 1, 4, and 8 quarters. As mentioned before, the robustness of the identification scheme adopted in our study is checked using generalized impulse response functions (Pesaran & Shin, 1998). According to the response of consumer prices reported in Appendix C, our ERPT estimates are broadly robust, using generalized impulse responses, instead of the *orthogonalized* recursive ones, do not change the broad pattern and magnitude of the transmission of exchange rate shocks to consumer prices.

We begin with the impact of an exchange rate depreciation on import prices which is displayed in Figure 1. As expected, the response is positive following 1% of currency depreciation with a considerable cross-country variation in our EA sample. The highest immediate response, namely 0 quarter in Table 3, is recorded in Italy roughly 0.62%, while the lowest is in Austria equal to 0.29%. Also, Italy has the fastest import prices reaction, with a complete ERPT after a single quarter. Interestingly, we notice that, by the end of the first year, a complete pass-through was detected in 7 out of 12 EA countries.

Comparing our results with previous studies, our estimates of pass-through seem to be higher. We think that differences in the results are owing to different econometric methods used to estimate pass-though. In a single-equation context, Anderton (2003) found that 0.50–0.70% of changes in the euro are passed-through to import prices (in the long-run) over 1989–2001. As is well known, contrary to the single-equation method, a VECM model allows for system estimation where the endogenous variables are simultaneously determined. Simply ignoring such simultaneity, as is often done in single-equation approaches, would result in simultaneous equation bias. Furthermore, in a pricing chain model, VECM model permits for underlying dynamic interrelations among prices at different stages of distribution and other variables which cannot be done within single-equation method. Thus, it is not surprising that import price pass-through in our VECM analysis lies somewhat above those single-equation estimates. We pretend that VECM models would provide more relevant measure of the extent of ERPT since it gives us the opportunity to analyze how

[17] Confidence intervals for the impulse response functions are estimated using the Bayesian Monte Carlo method employed by RATS with 1000 replications.

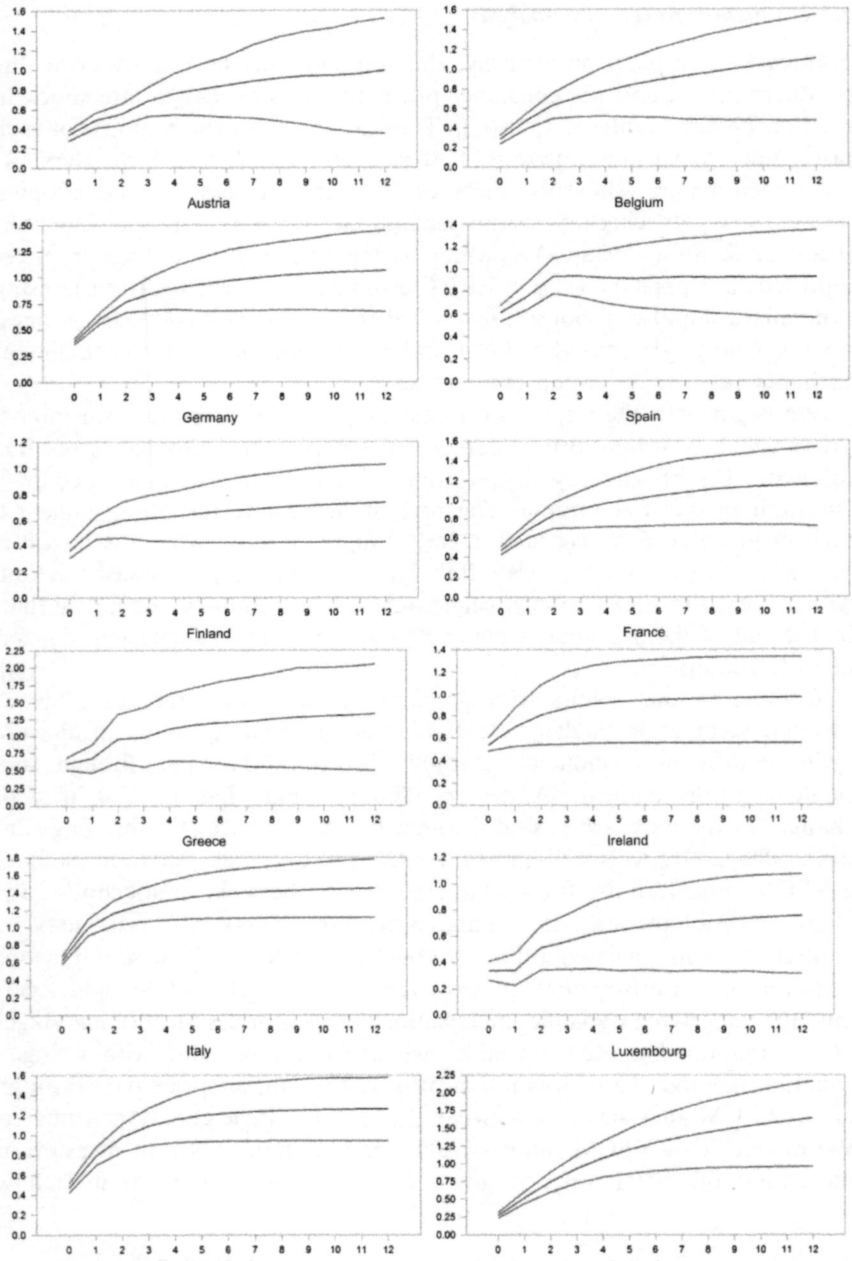

Figure 1: Response of Import Prices to 1% Exchange Rate Shock.

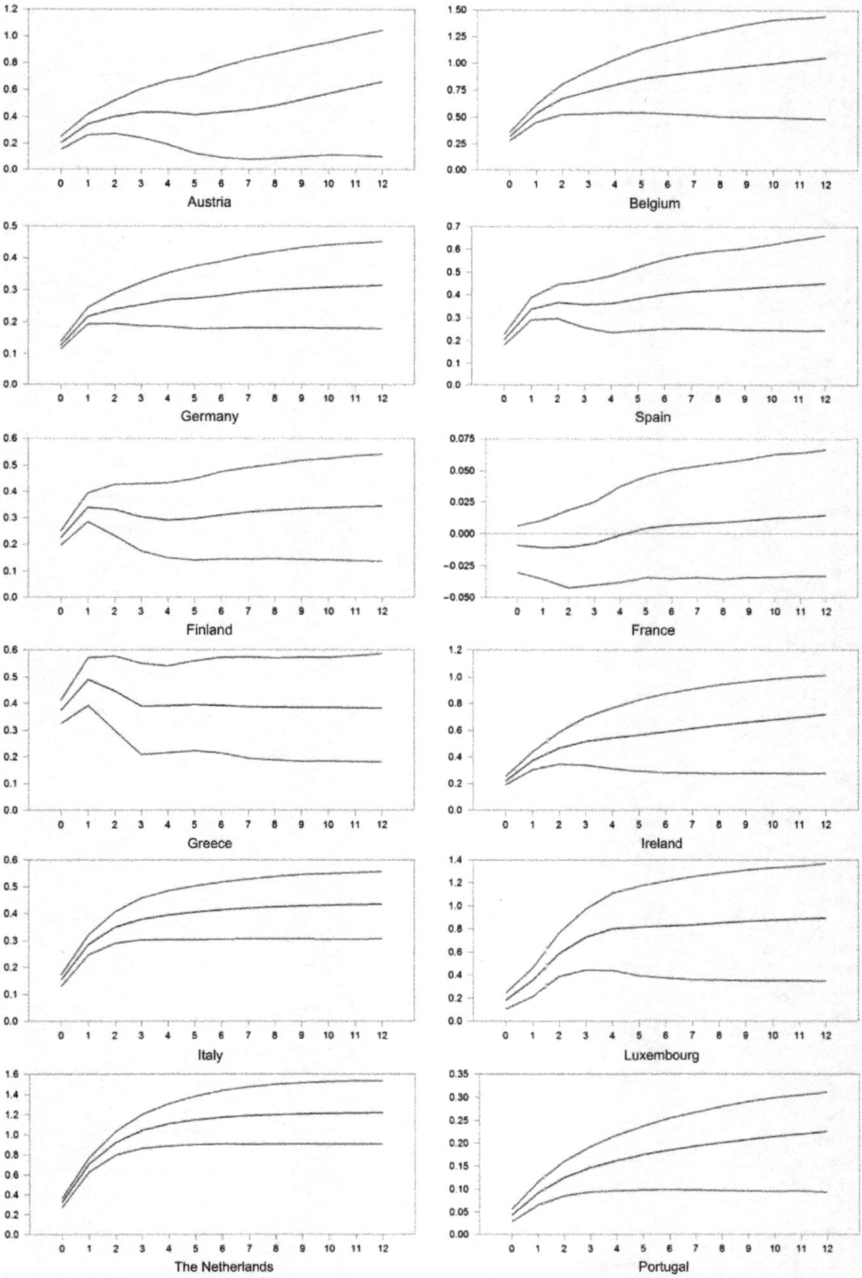

Figure 2: Response of Producer Prices to 1% Exchange Rate Shock.

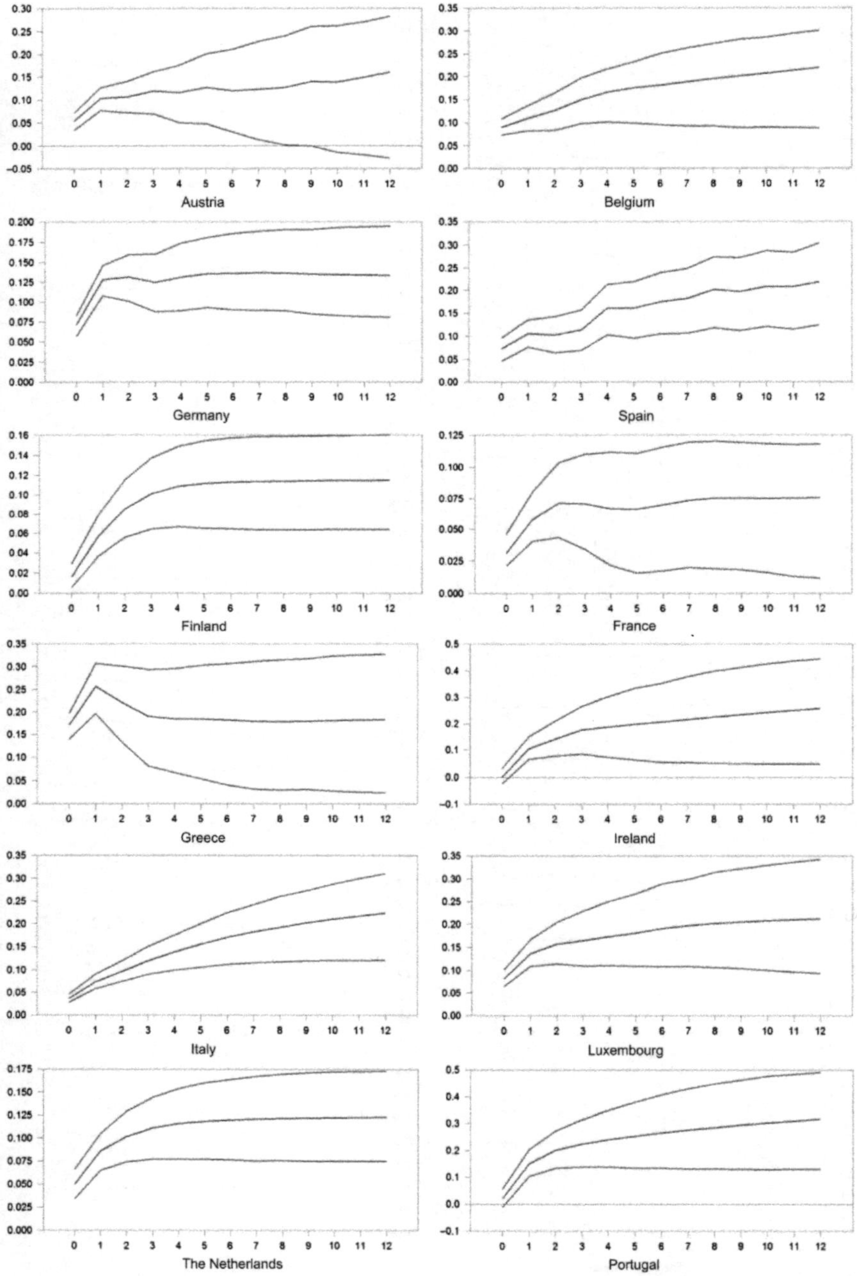

Figure 3: Response of Consumer Prices to 1% Exchange Rate Shock.

Table 3: Impulse Response along the Distribution Chain of Pricing

Accumulated response of import prices to 1% exchange rate shock

Response horizon	Austria	Belgium	Germany	Spain	Finland	France
0	0.289	0.297	0.359	0.653	0.411	0.481
1	0.442	0.486	0.614	0.819	0.591	0.697
4	0.710	0.775	0.871	0.981	0.654	0.946
8	0.835	0.865	0.955	0.959	0.694	1.033

Response horizon	Greece	Ireland	Italy	Luxembourg	The Netherlands	Portugal
0	0.508	0.555	0.615	0.342	0.478	0.360
1	0.587	0.732	1.016	0.344	0.810	0.616
4	1.015	0.913	1.297	0.570	1.172	1.051
8	1.067	0.927	1.373	0.633	1.229	1.216

Accumulated response of producer prices to 1% exchange rate shock

Response horizon	Austria	Belgium	Germany	Spain	Finland	France
0	0.197	0.318	0.119	0.244	0.229	0.004
1	0.340	0.549	0.205	0.390	0.346	0.001
4	0.405	0.795	0.253	0.425	0.290	0.016
8	0.401	0.867	0.270	0.486	0.315	0.026

Response horizon	Greece	Ireland	Italy	Luxembourg	The Netherlands	Portugal
0	0.459	0.270	0.176	0.155	0.279	0.052
1	0.646	0.432	0.309	0.318	0.654	0.105
4	0.518	0.571	0.418	0.721	1.048	0.171
8	0.421	0.570	0.440	0.728	1.113	0.194

Accumulated response of consumer prices to 1% exchange rate shock

Response horizon	Austria	Belgium	Germany	Spain	Finland	France
0	0.056	0.105	0.062	0.080	0.014	0.046
1	0.103	0.126	0.125	0.111	0.054	0.079
4	0.113	0.179	0.123	0.164	0.103	0.075
8	0.106	0.192	0.134	0.199	0.105	0.077

Response horizon	Greece	Ireland	Italy	Luxembourg	The Netherlands	Portugal
0	0.180	0.009	0.049	0.087	0.073	0.058
1	0.263	0.107	0.090	0.141	0.111	0.184
4	0.203	0.182	0.152	0.172	0.140	0.251
8	0.191	0.200	0.195	0.177	0.143	0.278

Note: Response horizon 0, 1, 4, and 8 correspond, respectively, to immediate, one quarter, one year, and two years response after the initial shock.

exchange rate fluctuations pass-through the production process from the import of products to the consumer level.

Besides, Hahn (2003) found that pass-through amounts to about 0.50% after three quarters for the whole euro area. However, the author estimated a VAR in first differences which does not incorporate the long-run relationship. We think that the neglect of time-series properties of the data – non-stationarity and cointegration relationship – would explain the relative weakness of ERPT estimates in comparison to our study.

As regards to the response of producer prices, Figure 2 points out a more pronounced cross-country difference, which is an expected phenomenon. We find that ERPT is surprisingly not significant (slightly negative) in France, very weak in Portugal (not exceeding 0.2% within two years), and complete in the Netherlands within only one year. The higher responsiveness of producer prices in the Netherlands was confirmed by McCarthy (2007). The authors found pass-through to be particularly large in Belgium and the Netherlands in comparison to the rest of his sample of nine industrialized countries. For the euro area, Hahn (2003) reports that 1% exchange rate shock is passed-through on producer prices by 0.10% after one quarter, by 0.28% after one year, and amounts to about 0.30% after three years. These estimates are close to those found for Germany in our study.

Finally, we focus on the pass-through of a 1% depreciation of exchange rate to consumer prices. Our results reveal a weak response in most of the EA countries with as usual a wide dispersion of rates of pass-through. The highest immediate effect can be observed in Greece with a consumer price index increase of 0.12%, which increases to 0.20% after one year. While the lowest estimated pass-through is found in France, the response of consumer prices does not exceed 0.08% across the different time horizons. For France, this result is not surprising since the response in the previous stage of distribution, that is, producer price, was not significant. Moreover, we can say that results from impulse response functions corroborate with what we find in the cointegration analysis. According to this latter, the highest long-run ERPT was found in Greece and Portugal, while the lowest was recorded in France and Finland. In fact, the weakness of consumer prices responsiveness was confirmed throughout VAR literature (see summary of VAR literature in Table 1). In their study, Hüfner and Schröder (2002) found that the highest effect is observed in the Netherlands which is equal to 0.12% within one year. Also, for France, Hüfner and Schröder (2002) report ERPT estimates as low as those found in our study. The pass-through of 1% depreciation on the consumer prices in the first year is roughly 0.07%.

For the non-US G7 countries, Choudhri et al. (2005) estimate a first-difference VAR model that contained exogenously determined foreign variables, namely foreign consumer price index and foreign interest rate. In a very similar framework without including foreign exogenous variables, Faruqee (2006) reports a quite weak pass-through to consumer prices (see Table 1). Thus, we pretend that is a sensible way to enter foreign exogenous variables – such as foreign prices or costs – when estimating the extent of pass-through within VAR framework.

Otherwise, the response of the consumer prices to the exchange rate shock is found to be weaker than that of the producer prices. Imports as intermediate goods need to go through production or distribution processes before they are consumed by households. The production or distribution channels can dampen the effect of exchange rate changes and can account for a low pass-through to consumer prices. Also, our results point out that pass-through declines along the distribution chain with the largest effect occurring in import prices. This decline is due to a smaller fraction of goods affected by external factors in the price indices at later stages of the distribution chain. In other words, the fraction of goods that is affected by exchange rate shocks seems to decrease along the distribution chain, pointing to a declining pass-through. For example, the share of tradables that are likely to be more prone to external shocks than non-tradables (services), tends to decrease in price indices along the distribution chain.

Furthermore, assuming that shocks are, at least partially, passed-through via previous stages, thus, accumulation over different stages basically implies a decline in the pass-through along the distribution chain. Another line of argumentation used in pass-through literature to explain the observed smaller pass-through to consumer prices compared to import prices: the presence of local distribution costs, the extent of imported inputs being used for domestic production (see Burstein, Eichenbaum, & Rebelo, 2005), or the optimal pricing strategies of foreign producers and domestic wholesalers/retailers (see Bacchetta & van Wincoop, 2002).

5.1.2. Factors Influencing ERPT

In order to explain the cross-country differences detected from impulse responses along distribution chain, we introduce some macroeconomic determinants which can explain the differences in pass-through estimates in our 12 EA countries. To this end, we examine the Spearman rank correlation statistic between the impulse responses for different prices (import prices, producer prices, and consumer prices) at various horizons and some factors expected to influence pass-through. There are various theoretical arguments have been made for cross-country differences in exchange rate pass-through rates. In our study, we analyze the differences in the degree of pass-through into import prices across the five following determinants: (1) mean of import share or degree of openness (imports as a percentage of domestic demand) over the sample period 1980–2010; (2) exchange rate persistence measured as the impulse response at the eight-quarter horizon of the exchange rate to its own standardized shock;[18] (3) exchange rate volatility measured by the standard deviation of quarterly percentage changes in the exchange rate $\sigma_{\Delta e}$;[19] (4) inflation level as the mean of the year-on-year quarterly inflation rate over sample period; (5) inflation volatility as the standard deviation of the year-on-year quarterly inflation rate over sample period. Results of rank correlation are reported in Table 4.

Concerning imports prices, as expected, the extent of pass-through is positively correlated with the persistence of exchange rate, inflation level, and inflation volatility with a significant relationship. This latter result is in line with Taylor (2000) who has put forward the hypothesis that the responsiveness of prices to exchange rate fluctuations depends positively

Table 4: Rank Correlation between ERPT and Selected Variables

	Response horizon			
	0	1	4	8
(a) Impulse response of import prices				
Import share	−0.286	−0.153	−0.118	−0.132
Exchange rate persistence	0.629**	0.769***	0.657**	0.643**
Exchange rate volatility	−0.655**	−0.566*	−0.325	−0.398
Inflation	0.622**	0.3147	0.601**	0.538*
Inflation volatility	0.594**	0.3287	0.531*	0.538*
(b) Impulse response of PPI				
Import share	0.587**	0.748***	0.769***	0.748***
Exchange rate persistence	−0.384	−0.370	−0.244	−0.153
Exchange rate volatility	−0.655**	−0.566*	−0.384	−0.398
Inflation	0.511*	0.517*	0.2081	0.1617
Inflation volatility	0.1307	−0.1818	−0.2657	−0.3077
(c) Impulse response of CPI				
Import share	0.132	0.062	0.335	0.475
Exchange rate persistence	−0.138	0.161	0.554*	0.676**
Exchange rate volatility	−0.655**	−0.566*	−0.384	−0.398
Inflation	0.675**	0.861***	0.506*	0.392
Inflation volatility	0.269	0.613**	0.581**	0.527*

Note: *, **, and *** denote significance level at 10%, 5%, and 1%, respectively.

[18] As defined by McCarthy (2007).
[19] We adopt the same exchange rate volatility proxy employed by Barhoumi (2006).

on inflation environment. Also, Taylor (2000) explained that a higher perceived persistence of exchange rate shocks would entail a larger extent of pass-through. However, Table 4 reports a significant negative correlation between imports prices response and exchange rate volatility. In fact, ERPT literature is not conclusive with respect to the relationship between the volatility of exchange and the degree of pass-through. On one hand, there is a strand of literature supporting the presence of a negative correlation. Greater exchange rate volatility may make importers more wary of changing prices and more willing to adjust profit margins, thereby reducing measured pass-through (see Mann, 1986). This hypothesis was confirmed by some empirical studies (see Barhoumi, 2006; Webber, 1999, among others). On the other hand, it is expected that import prices responsiveness would be higher when volatility of exchange rate is larger. As pointed by Devereux and Engel (2002), the relative stability of importing country's currency plays a substantial role in determining pass-through. Countries with low relative exchange rate variability would have their currencies chosen for transaction invoicing (LCP strategy). Campa and Goldberg (2005) found that exchange rate volatility affects the degree of pass-through in a statistically significant way. We see that our results are rather in line with the first hypothesis. As for import share, the relationship with ERPT is very weak with a wrong negative sign. This is not surprising since the greater openness of a country may be an indicative of increased foreign competitive pressures limiting exchange rate transmission. Empirically, this was confirmed by Ca'Zorzi et al. (2007) and McCarthy (2007) using first-difference VAR model.

As regards producer prices, the results are quite different in comparison to import prices. We point out a positive relationship with the degree of openness, which is statistically significant throughout different time horizons. Imported goods as intermediate goods have to go through production or distribution processes before they reach consumers. Thus, higher import shares could be correlated with a greater producer price response. Inflation environment has the expected correlation and it is statistically significant in shorter horizons. For exchange rate volatility, the relationship is rather negative as in the case of import prices. However, exchange rate persistence and inflation volatility display no strong correlation with the producer price response. Finally, regarding consumer prices response, the results are quite similar to those for import prices. The exception is the degree of openness, which is found to be positively correlated with the ERPT to consumer prices, although the relationship is not statistically significant. These results are consistent with the empirical literature dealing with the so-called "second-stage pass-through." In a panel of 71 countries, Choudhri and Hakura (2006) show that ERPT is positively correlated to the average of inflation rate and the inflation and exchange rate volatility, but no significant role for the degree of openness was founded.[20]

To sum up, our results show a higher pass-through to import prices with a complete pass-through detected in roughly half EA countries after one year. These results are relatively large compared to single-equation literature. The magnitude of the pass-through of exchange rate shocks declines along the distribution chain of pricing with the modest effect recorded with consumer prices. Also, referring to the magnitude of the pass-through, we can say that results from impulse response functions corroborate in some extent to what we find in the cointegration analysis. The highest ERPT estimates were found in Greece and Portugal, while the lowest was recorded in France and Finland. When assessing possible reasons for cross-country differences in the ERPT, inflation level, inflation volatility, and exchange rate persistence are the main macroeconomic factors that influence the degree of pass-through almost along the distribution pricing chain. The exchange rate volatility is surprisingly negatively correlated with response of different prices index.

5.2. Responses to Import Price Shocks

In this sub-section, we focus on the responses of domestic prices; that is, producer prices and consumer prices, to 1% shock in import prices. This analysis is of great interest since it provides insights on how shocks are propagated from one price stage to the next. We have seen in the identification scheme that the import price shock is estimated given past values of all the variables plus the current value of oil prices, the real GDP, and the exchange rate. Results of pass-through of import prices to domestic prices are reported in Figures 4, 5, and in Table 5.

Beginning with producer prices, as expected the pass-through is positive in most of EA countries but not significant for some countries, namely Spain, France, Greece, and Ireland. The highest response is identified in Belgium and the Netherlands; this may explain why ERPT to producer prices is found to be higher in these EA countries. Especially, for Belgium, the pass-through of 1% increase in import prices raises producer prices more than 1% within one year. Similarly, McCarthy (2007) reports responses particularly large in Belgium, with the pass-through eventually

[20] It is noteworthy that a regime dependence of ERPT to inflation environment was pointed out in a more recent literature using nonlinear regime-switching models (see inter alia Ben Cheikh & Louhichi, 2014; Shintani, Terada-Hagiwara, & Tomoyoshi, 2013).

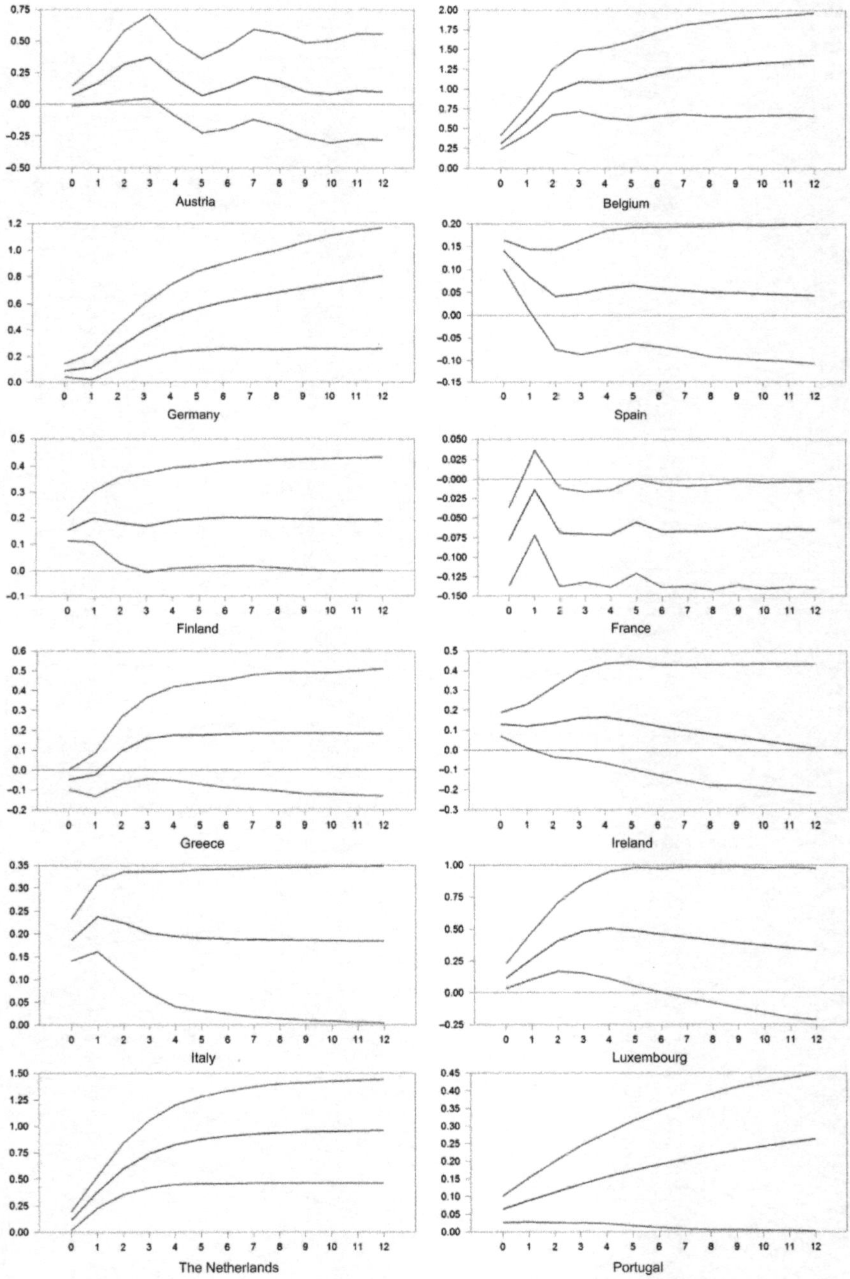

Figure 4: Response of Producer Prices to 1% Increase in Import Prices.

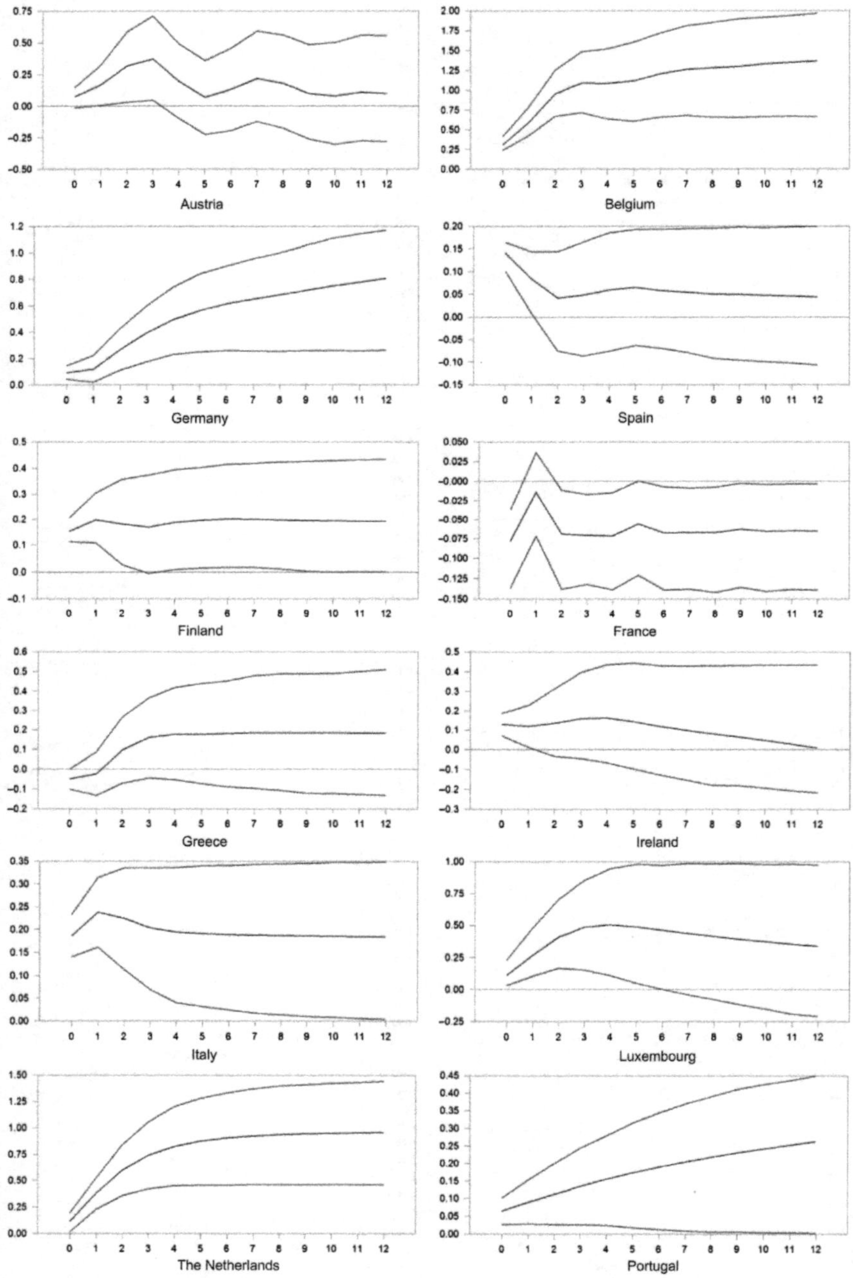

Figure 5: Response of Consumer Prices to 1% Increase in Import Prices.

Table 5: Impulse Response along the Distribution Chain of Pricing

Accumulated response of producer prices to 1% increase in import prices						
Response horizon	Austria	Belgium	Germany	Spain	Finland	France
0	0.160	0.342	0.042	0.114	0.159	−0.092
1	0.174	0.671	0.043	0.072	0.221	−0.042
4	0.341	1.157	0.402	0.088	0.224	−0.093
8	0.229	1.287	0.486	0.090	0.225	−0.091
Response horizon	Greece	Ireland	Italy	Luxembourg	The Netherlands	Portugal
0	0.176	0.227	0.124	0.232	0.114	0.085
1	0.166	0.257	0.172	0.437	0.378	0.118
4	0.153	0.335	0.130	0.639	0.819	0.184
8	0.476	0.305	0.120	0.500	0.893	0.223
Accumulated response of consumer prices to 1% increase in import prices						
Response horizon	Austria	Belgium	Germany	Spain	Finland	France
0	−0.031	0.070	0.073	0.014	−0.001	0.134
1	0.031	0.174	0.017	−0.090	0.012	0.191
4	0.024	0.353	0.120	−0.070	0.006	0.217
8	0.034	0.373	0.121	−0.077	0.001	0.239
Response horizon	Greece	Ireland	Italy	Luxembourg	The Netherlands	Portugal
0	0.263	−0.100	0.031	0.013	0.013	0.206
1	0.379	−0.150	0.064	0.050	0.047	0.250
4	0.540	−0.232	0.047	0.079	0.065	0.431
8	0.631	−0.256	0.048	0.045	0.066	0.514

Note: Response horizon 0, 1, 4, and 8 correspond, respectively, to immediate, one quarter, one year, and two years response after the initial shock.

exceeding 1%. For the whole EA, Hahn (2003) found that the impact of a 1% increase in non-oil import prices on producer prices is extremely large. In the first quarter, the pass-through amounts to 0.22%, increasing to 0.61% after one year. Also, we note that the effect of import prices is broadly weak compared to exchange rate shocks with the exception of Germany (see previous Section 5.1). Nevertheless, Hahn (2003) points out that pass-through of oil prices and exchange rate to producer prices are smaller than impact of import prices. According to the author, this may be due to a higher perceived persistence of the import price shocks. While exchange rate and oil price shocks are known to be pretty volatile, import price shocks are likely to contain the more persistent external sources of variation. Besides, according to our results, the response of producer prices has insignificantly the wrong (negative) sign in France. These negative coefficients consolidate what we found in the previous section, namely the insignificant (negative) ERPT to producer prices. In fact, when domestic currency is depreciating, domestic producer and wholesalers may stop stocking foreign products (as intermediate goods) since their price becomes too high. Thus, a substitution effect occurs and producer prices will be more insulated from import price changes. This may explain why the response of producer prices is not significant in some EA countries such as France.

The response of consumer prices to import price shocks is also positive for most EA countries but statistically significant only for the half of our sample (with negative sign for Spain and Ireland). This outcome would explain the weakness of ERPT to consumer prices in our sample. The highest effect is detected in Greece and Portugal which is a natural result as these countries have the highest degree of pass-through of exchange rate. This latter result may be considered as an evidence of weak pricing-to-market behavior in the domestic markets of Portugal and Greece in comparison to the rest of EA members. Furthermore, we note that for 8 out of 12 EA countries the effect of import prices on consumer prices is smaller than exchange shocks.

As is well known, exchange rate changes may be transmitted directly to prices of consumer through the price of imports. In the case of depreciation, domestic currency price of the imported good will rise in proportion. This change in import prices is then likely to translate into changes in the producer and consumer prices if producers raise their prices in line with the increase in import prices. On the other hand, currency depreciation may affect consumer prices indirectly through changes in the composition of demand or in the levels of aggregate demand and wages. A depreciation of the exchange rate makes domestic products relatively cheaper for foreign buyers, and as a consequence exports and aggregate demand will rise and induce an increase in the domestic price level. At the same time, the increase of domestic demand also leads to a higher demand for labor and, potentially, to rising wages, which will in turn be reflected in higher prices. Consequently, it is expected that exchange shocks would have a higher effect than import prices shocks as showed by our results.

5.3. Variance Decompositions

It is known that impulse responses trace the effects of a shock to one endogenous variable on to the other variables in the VECM system, allowing us to estimate the effect of exchange rate and import price shocks on domestic producer and consumer prices. However, impulse responses do not enable us to determine the importance of these "external" shocks for domestic price fluctuations over the sample period. To get additional insights on this, we examine the variance decompositions of the different price indices, that is, import prices, producer prices, and consumer prices. Variance decompositions separate the variation in an endogenous variable into the component shocks to the VECM system. Thus, the variance decomposition provides information about the relative importance of each random innovation in affecting the variables in the system. In other words, variance decompositions indicate the percentage contribution of the different shocks to the variance of the h-step ahead forecast errors of the variables. Hence, the relative importance of the different external shocks for the development of the price indices could be assessed.

From Tables 6–8, we summarize the results on the variance decompositions of import, producer, and consumer prices over a forecast horizon of zero, one, four, and eight quarters. For import prices, we report only the contribution exchange rate shocks, while for producer and consumer prices, the contribution of "external shocks," that is, of exchange rate shocks, and import price shocks is displayed. Also, in the lower part of different tables, we set out the rank correlations between the percentage of one price index

Table 6: Percentage of Import Price Forecast Variance Attributed to Exchange Rate Shocks

Country	Forecast horizon			
	0	1	4	8
Austria	1.84	9.80	10.75	10.61
Belgium	13.26	10.10	11.19	11.74
Germany	16.09	16.51	16.52	16.53
Spain	26.97	19.60	19.23	19.18
Finland	14.98	14.03	12.97	12.88
France	25.37	27.76	31.72	32.26
Greece	65.22	59.03	52.83	52.73
Ireland	60.02	55.40	54.85	54.85
Italy	41.79	43.95	43.30	43.12
Luxembourg	0.00	0.94	5.01	4.99
The Netherlands	21.64	24.54	25.80	25.79
Portugal	39.65	42.17	46.75	47.38
Spearman rank correlation coefficient with:				
Import share	−0.636**	−0.629**	−0.573*	−0.575*
Exchange rate persistence	0.587*	0.545*	0.587**	0.587**
Exchange rate volatility	−0.439	−0.474	−0.460	−0.461
Inflation	0.671**	0.587*	0.573*	0.584*
Inflation volatility	0.804***	0.776***	0.790***	0.785***

Note: *, **, and *** denote significance level at 10%, 5%, and 1%, respectively.

Table 7: Percentage of Producer Prices Forecast Variance Attributed to External Shocks

Country	Forecast horizon			
	0	1	4	8
Austria	1.64	1.97	3.66	5.22
Belgium	5.51	9.02	10.57	10.61
Germany	15.89	17.17	15.63	15.70
Spain	15.99	13.28	12.22	12.85
Finland	14.14	12.19	12.41	12.43
France	7.36	9.35	10.01	10.04
Greece	17.07	20.78	25.85	25.95
Ireland	42.02	47.60	48.78	48.77
Italy	11.69	13.89	16.52	16.66
Luxembourg	4.79	6.44	8.84	8.96
The Netherlands	4.87	10.08	10.82	20.89
Portugal	12.86	12.89	13.29	13.33
Spearman rank correlation coefficient with:				
Import share	0.364	0.396	0.398	0.537*
Exchange rate persistence	0.132	0.174	0.132	0.104
Exchange rate volatility	−0.206	−0.206	−0.255	−0.263
Inflation	0.559*	0.468	0.510*	0.426
Inflation volatility	0.342	0.363	0.447	0.272

Note: External shocks denote exchange rate and import shocks together. *, **, and *** denote significance level at 10%, 5%, and 1%, respectively.

variance attributed to exchange rate shocks and the different macroeconomic determinants listed in Sub-section 5.1.

Beginning by examining the variance decomposition of import price reported in Table 6. Again, results differ across countries. It can be seen that exchange rate shocks explain a fairly large part of the fluctuation of import prices especially in Greece, Ireland, Italy, and Portugal. In these countries, the shares range from over 40% to 60%. While for other countries like Austria, Belgium, Finland, and Luxembourg, the importance of exchange rate does not exceed 15%. We point out that the percentage of contribution exchange rate shocks increases for most countries as the forecast horizon increases, as a proof of gradual adjustment of import prices; it takes time until changes in exchange rate are reflected in the import prices.

Thereafter, we look at the correlation between the percentage of import price variance attributed to exchange rate and factors influencing ERPT. Our results reveal the same conclusion when using impulse responses: the contribution of exchange rate to import prices fluctuations is negatively correlated with the degree of openness and exchange rate volatility (albeit

Table 8: Percentage of Consumer Prices Forecast Variance Attributed to Exchange Rate and Import Price Shocks

Country	Forecast horizon			
	0	1	4	8
Austria	5.42	5.44	8.61	8.93
Belgium	4.08	3.86	3.87	3.87
Germany	3.60	4.23	6.56	6.58
Spain	12.11	10.56	10.36	10.24
Finland	2.12	2.81	4.19	4.17
France	0.70	2.75	9.80	10.04
Greece	9.52	10.60	15.98	16.51
Ireland	2.84	3.37	3.55	3.55
Italy	8.76	8.40	8.77	8.77
Luxembourg	5.88	6.73	9.56	9.44
The Netherlands	0.22	3.79	4.21	4.22
Portugal	15.14	16.53	16.93	17.06
Spearman rank correlation coefficient with:				
Import share	−0.342	−0.335	−0.615**	−0.573*
Exchange rate persistence	0.646**	0.705**	0.499*	0.479
Exchange rate volatility	0.133	0.201	0.397	0.412
Inflation	0.650**	0.538*	0.573*	0.531*
Inflation volatility	0.647**	0.710***	0.709***	0.710***

Note: External shocks denote exchange rate and import shocks together. *, **, and *** denote significance level at 10%, 5%, and 1%, respectively.

not significant), while the relationship is strongly significant (with a positive sign) with exchange rate persistence, inflation level, and inflation volatility.

With regard to the variance of producer prices, the contribution of external factors – exchange rates and import prices – is still high for the same group of countries, namely Greece, Ireland, Italy, and Portugal (see Table 7). It should be noted that these countries have the highest long-run ERPT according to the cointegration analysis. Results reveals that external factors explain from 40% to 65% of producer prices forecast variance in the mentioned countries, which is a quite high contribution compared to the other shocks that may heat the economy (such as supply or demand shocks). The contribution in the other countries is more modest, especially for Austria and Luxembourg. For the whole euro area, Hahn (2003) found that between 5% and 20% of the variance of producer prices is accounted for exchange rate and import price shocks, respectively. This result masks the wide dispersion between EA countries in terms of the importance of exchange rate and import prices shocks. Besides, we find that the percentage of producer prices variance attributed to external factors tends to be higher for countries with higher exchange rate persistence, inflation level, and inflation volatility. The relationship with import share is still having the wrong negative sign.

Finally, we focus on the importance of external shocks for consumer prices fluctuations. In contrast to producer prices, the influence of external factors on consumer prices variance is weak. In most of EA countries, exchange rate and import prices shocks explain less than 18% of the variance of the consumer prices. This percentage tends to increase as the forecast horizon increases since it takes time until changes in the external factors are reflected in the consumer prices. Again, Greece and Portugal have the largest contribution of external shocks to consumer prices fluctuations. This may explain once again why ERPT to consumer prices are higher in the two countries compared to the rest of EA members. Otherwise, as usual, the differences across EA countries appear to be positively related with inflation level, inflation volatility, and exchange rate persistence throughout time horizons.

For the degree of openness, the relationship is as usual negative. In fact, it is expected that the more country is open, the more exchange rate changes affect domestic prices. In a more open economy, with larger presence of imports and exports, a given depreciation would have a larger effect on prices. Thus, the most immediate connection between the two variables is positive. However, Romer (1993) provided a theoretical explanation why inflation could be negatively correlated with openness, showing how openness puts a check on inflationary pressure. In this sense, inflation could be negatively correlated with openness.

As explained by Ca'Zorzi et al. (2007), the existence of two mechanisms going in opposite directions may lead to a puzzling result and the overall sign of the correlation between pass-through and openness can thus be either positive or negative. In summary, the variance decompositions indicate that external factors explain only a modest proportion of the forecast variance of domestic consumer prices over 1980–2010, while this contribution is to some extent high in Portugal and Greece. For the latter countries, this would explain why ERPT to consumer is relatively large compared to the other EA members. Mainly, three macroeconomic factors – inflation level, inflation volatility, and exchange rate persistence – are found to be crucial in explaining the cross-country differences regarding the influence of external shocks. The degree of openness is surprisingly negatively correlated with the contribution of external shocks.

5.4. Testing for the Recent Decline in ERPT

In this sub-section, we investigate, whether the ERPT to consumer prices has changed over our sample period 1980–2010. Empirical literature has put forth the decline of rates of pass-through in major of industrialized countries (see inter alia Gagnon & Ihrig, 2004). Given the different developments experienced by the EA members, such as institutional arrangements (the introduction of the single currency in 1999), convergence of inflation rates, monetary and financial shocks (1992/1993 ERM crises), we examine the possible existence of structural shift in response of consumer prices to exchange rate shocks.

When assessing the stability of ERPT to consumer prices, we can speculate that the introduction of the euro, as a major economic event, would entail a change in the behavior of the exchange rate transmission. The literature raised a number of reasons why the rate of pass-through may have changed for the EA members as a result of entering the monetary union. Namely, the introduction of the single European currency has changed the competitive conditions by decreasing the share of trade exposed to exchange rate fluctuations. Also, the advent of the euro as well established currency in the 2000s, creating a single market for exporters, has favored an expansion of the euro as the currency of denomination of its external trade. Referring to these factors, one can think that ERPT has declined in monetary union members following that date. As a matter of fact, empirical literature does not provide a strong evidence of structural break in pass-through coefficients since the creation of the euro area. In a set of studies, Campa and Goldberg (2002, 2005), Campa, Goldberg, and González-Mínguez (2005), and Campa and Gonzàlez (2006) have tested the presence of structural break in the vicinity of the introduction of the common currency. Their results do not support the view that ERPT has declined around the date of the creation of the euro.

We have seen in the previous section that inflation environment (inflation level and inflation volatility) is an important macroeconomic factor influencing the ERPT. As argued by Taylor (2000), the transition to the low inflation environment in many industrialized countries has successfully reduced the degree of pass-through to domestic prices.

For the EA countries, the inflation convergence process has started before the adoption of the single currency, and more exactly, after the implementation of the Maastricht treaty.[21] Since higher inflation levels and volatility contribute to higher degree of pass-through, countries that have experienced reduction in inflation and nominal volatility may have seen a significant lowering in pass-through elasticities. Thus, for EA countries, we assume that a break exists and it would take place in the vicinity of the first

[21] Among the Maastricht criteria for joining the EMU, each country's inflation in 1997 had to be less than 1.5 percentage points above the average rate of the three European countries with the lowest inflation over the previous year.

stage of the EMU (in July 1990). To address this issue, we perform Chow test for structural change designed for multiple time series, as introduced by Candelon and Lutkepohl (2001), assuming an exogenously imposed break point around the third quarter of 1990.[22] According to the test results reported in Table B.1, there is a strong evidence of structural break around the starting of the first stage of the EMU for all EA countries.[23]

To provide further insights on the changing behavior of ERPT, we use a simple strategy of re-estimating our VECM pricing chain model over a shorter sample period that does not include the 1980s, that is, during 1990–2010. After deriving the impulse response of consumer prices to exchange rate shocks, this allows us to check the differences between the responses estimated over the whole sample (1980–2010) and those estimated over the shorter sub-sample (1990–2010) as in Figure 6. Almost all of EA countries (with few exceptions) show that exchange rate seems to have a less inflationary effect during the last 20 years. According to impulse responses, there is an evidence of a general decline in rates of pass-through in most of euro zone countries. These findings confirm the presence of structural break as shown by chow tests. Given that inflation environment is an important determinant of ERPT, it is an expected result that the decline in response of consumer prices coincided with the steady reduction of inflation rates during the 1990s. This result is more apparent for the "peripheral" EA countries, namely Greece, Ireland, Portugal, and Spain.[24]

5.5. Historical Decompositions

In this sub-section, we use historical decompositions to examine the role played by the external shocks in the development of the consumer prices during two sub-sample periods: during the first and second stage of EMU (1990:1–1998:4) and since the creation of the euro till the end of our time sample (1999:1–2010:4). This VAR technique provides an indication of how unusual development in the consumer prices inflation was during a given period, and how the contribution of different shocks was over at that time period.[25]

[22] More details on Candelon and Lutkepohl (2001) chow tests in Appendix B.

[23] For some countries, the structural shift does not happen exactly in 1990:3, but in the vicinity of that date.

[24] Since the European sovereign debt crisis, the term "GIPS" is used to refer to this group of countries as a label for heavily indebted economies.

[25] We talk about "inflation" of consumer prices since our VECM system is estimated in log differences.

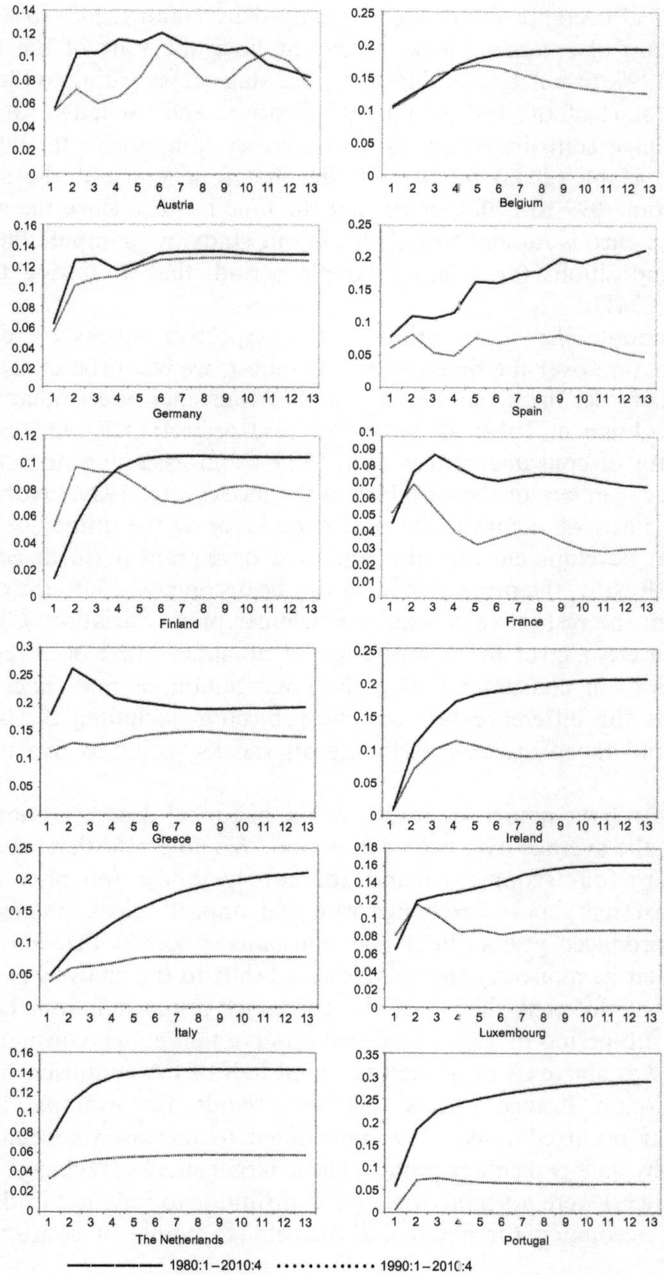

Figure 6: Comparison of Response of Consumer Prices.

Historical decompositions were employed by Hahn (2003) to assess the contribution of external shocks, occurred since the start of the EMU in January 1999, to inflation at different price stages. According to the author, since the start of the EMU in 1999, oil prices and exchange rate shocks seem to have contributed strongly to increase inflation in the euro area. However, Hahn (2003) focused on the first four years of the monetary union (from 1999 to 2002), given that the time horizon since the introduction of the euro is rather short. Thus, in our study, we compute the historical decompositions for a larger sample period, that is, during the three stages of EMU.

To compute the contribution of the respective shocks on consumer prices inflation over the time period of interest, we will proceed as follows: first, we consider the actual development of consumer prices inflation series (second column in Table 9); second, a base projection is made using the actual data of consumer prices until 1989:4 and assuming no subsequent shocks occur in any of the variables of the model after 1989:4 (column 3 in Table 9); next, we compute the projection error as the difference between the actual development and the projected development (forth column in Table 9). Finally, the projection error can be decomposed into the contributions from the respective shocks to consumer prices variation. Given that projection error gives the contribution of all shocks that occurred over a time period on consumer prices, the contribution of one shock is then derived as the difference between the projection including this shock of interest and the projection excluding all shocks (columns five to last in Table 9).

In Table 9, we report the results of the historical decompositions which represent the average over each sub-period. We note also that we combine shocks into four groups: demand and supply shocks (oil price and real GDP), external shocks (exchange rate and import price), domestic price shocks (producer prices (PPI) and consumer prices (CPI), and interest shocks, that is, monetary shocks. Now, we shift to the analysis of the contribution of different shocks of the consumer prices inflation. Beginning with the sub-period of 1990–1998, we observe that actual consumer prices inflation was above its projection in about half of EA countries, namely in Austria, Spain, France, Greece, the Netherlands. For example, in Spain, the shocks occurred since 1989 contributed to increased consumer price inflation by 0.08 percentage points. The external shocks (exchange rate and import prices) were a slightly positive contributor to inflation in this country; they accounted for about 0.01 percentage points of consumer price inflation.

Concerning the other shocks, the most inflationary impacts are due to domestic prices shocks (producer and consumer prices together), accounting for 0.06 percentage points. On the other hand, for the rest of EA

Table 9: Historical Decomposition of Consumer Prices

Country	Actual	Forecast	Projection error	Contribution of shocks			Interest rate
				Oil price and GDP	External factors	PPI & CPI	
Austria							
1990–1998	0.63%	0.55%	0.08%	0.00%	–0.01%	0.07%	0.01%
1999–2010	0.47%	0.50%	–0.03%	–0.01%	0.02%	–0.03%	0.00%
Belgium							
1990–1998	0.52%	0.53%	–0.01%	–0.03%	0.00%	0.03%	–0.02%
1999–2010	0.56%	0.51%	0.05%	0.03%	0.02%	0.01%	0.00%
Germany							
1990–1998	0.73%	0.77%	–0.04%	–0.01%	–0.01%	–0.01%	–0.01%
1999–2010	0.40%	0.37%	0.03%	–0.01%	0.03%	0.01%	–0.01%
Spain							
1990–1998	1.11%	1.03%	0.08%	0.01%	0.01%	0.06%	0.01%
1999–2010	0.74%	0.73%	0.02%	–0.01%	0.01%	0.01%	0.00%
Finland							
1990–1998	0.53%	0.54%	–0.01%	–0.01%	–0.02%	0.02%	0.01%
1999–2010	0.45%	0.42%	0.03%	0.00%	0.03%	0.00%	0.00%
France							
1990–1998	0.44%	0.43%	0.01%	–0.01%	–0.02%	0.04%	–0.01%
1999–2010	0.43%	0.44%	–0.01%	–0.01%	0.00%	0.00%	0.00%
Greece							
1990–1998	2.12%	2.07%	0.05%	0.00%	0.01%	0.01%	0.03%
1999–2010	0.78%	0.84%	–0.06%	0.01%	–0.02%	–0.04%	–0.01%
Ireland							
1990–1998	0.55%	0.55%	0.00%	0.00%	–0.01%	0.00%	0.01%
1999–2010	0.78%	0.70%	0.08%	0.01%	0.00%	0.07%	0.00%
Italy							
1990–1998	0.96%	1.02%	–0.06%	–0.01%	0.00%	–0.03%	–0.02%
1999–2010	0.57%	0.56%	0.01%	0.00%	0.01%	0.00%	–0.01%
Luxembourg							
1990–1998	0.53%	0.67%	–0.14%	0.01%	0.01%	–0.03%	–0.13%
1999–2010	0.57%	0.58%	0.00%	–0.02%	0.01%	–0.01%	0.01%
The Netherlands							
1990–1998	0.61%	0.57%	0.04%	0.01%	–0.07%	0.10%	0.00%
1999–2010	0.54%	0.54%	0.01%	0.00%	0.03%	–0.01%	–0.01%
Portugal							
1990–1998	1.54%	1.82%	–0.28%	–0.02%	–0.17%	0.00%	–0.09%
1999–2010	0.65%	0.67%	–0.02%	0.00%	0.04%	–0.04%	–0.02%

Note: Numbers are the average over each sub-period (expressed in percentage). Actual corresponds to the actual development of the consumer prices. Projected is made using the actual data of consumer prices up to 1989:4 and assuming no subsequent shocks occur in any of the variables of the model after 1998:4. The projection error is defined as the difference between the actual development and the projected development. The contribution of the shock is defined as the difference between the projection including the respective of interest and the projection excluding all shocks.

countries (except Ireland), consumer price inflation was exceptionally low during 1990–1998, as inflation rates were below the base projection, namely in Belgium, Germany, Finland, Italy, Luxembourg, and Portugal. For the latter country, actual consumer prices inflation was 0.28 percentage points below its projection on average during 1990–1998. The external shocks contributed strongly to lowering consumer prices inflation by having a disinflationary impact of –0.17%. In addition, monetary shocks were also an important negative contributor to inflation reduction (–0.09 percentage points), suggesting that Portugal may have conducted a tighter monetary policy in anticipation of the creation of the euro.

As regards the sub-sample of 1999–2010, it is interesting to note that for countries where the inflation was low during 1990–1998, now, the actual consumer prices inflation is above the model's base projection. This is true for more than half of our EA sample. This may be due to the inflationary effects of large depreciation of the euro in the first three years of his existence. In Belgium, for example, the actual consumer price inflation was (negatively) close to its projection before 1999, while during the third stage of EMU, the actual inflation is higher than projected by 0.05 percentage points, with an inflationary effect of external shocks by 0.02%. Also, it is worth stressing that, contrary to the sub-period 1990–1998, the external shocks were important contributors to consumer prices inflation in most of EA members during 1999–2010. Especially, in four EA countries, namely Germany, Finland, and the Netherlands, external factors have the relative higher inflationary effect compared to the other shocks (accounted for about 0.03% of consumer prices inflation).

As mentioned before, the euro zone has experienced a large depreciation of the single currency since its creation in 1999. Between the end of 1998 to the last quarter of 2001, the euro depreciated by nearly 20% in nominal effective terms. Thereby, this decline in the value of the euro may explain the rise of inflationary pressure since 1999. To sum up, compared to the period of 1990–1998, external factors had important inflationary impacts on inflation since the starting of the third stage of EMU. This finding is in line with Hahn (2003) who found that exchange rate shocks are an important contributor to inflation increase during the first three years of the euro zone.

6. Concluding Remarks

In this chapter, the pass-through of exchange rate into different prices is analyzed for 12 EA countries within a VECM framework. Using quarterly data ranging from 1980:1 to 2010:4, our study provides new up-to-date estimates of ERPT with paying attention to either the time-series properties of data and variables endogeneity. Using the Johansen cointegration procedure, our results indicate the existence of one cointegrating vector at least for each EA country of our sample. Thereafter, we carried out impulse response functions analysis. This exercise is done using a VECM system that incorporates features of a distribution chain pricing framework in the spirit of McCarthy (2007) and Hüfner and Schröder (2002). This VECM pricing chain model enables us to examine the pass-through at different stages along the distribution chain, that is, import prices, producer prices, and consumer prices. Our results show a higher pass-through to import prices with a complete pass-through (after one year) detected for roughly half of EA countries. These estimates are relatively large compared to single-equation literature. We denote that the magnitude of the pass-through of exchange rate shocks declines along the distribution chain of pricing, with the modest effect recorded with consumer prices. Our results reveal a wide dispersion of rates of pass-through. For example, the highest ERPT to consumer prices were found in Greece and Portugal, while the lowest was recorded in France and Finland. When assessing for the determinant of cross-country differences in the ERPT, we find that inflation level, inflation volatility, and exchange rate persistence are the main macroeconomic factors influencing the pass-through almost along the pricing chain. Next, we have investigated the contribution of external shocks (exchange rate and import prices shocks together) using the variance decompositions. Results show that external factors explain only a modest proportion of the forecast variance of domestic consumer prices over 1980–2010, while this contribution is significantly higher in Portugal and Greece. This would explain why ERPT to consumer is relatively larger compared to the rest of EA members. We also point out that mainly three macroeconomic factors – inflation level, inflation volatility, and exchange rate persistence – are found to be crucial in explaining the cross-country differences regarding the influence of external shocks. The degree of openness is surprisingly negatively correlated with the contribution of external shocks (in line with findings of Romer, 1993). Thereafter, we have tested for the decline of the response of consumer prices across EA countries. According to multivariate time-series Chow test, the stability of ERPT coefficients was rejected, and the impulse responses of consumer prices over 1990–2010 provide an evidence of general decline in rates of pass-through in most of EA countries. Finally, using the historical decompositions, our results reveal that external factors had important inflationary impacts on inflation since 1999, compared to the pre-EMU period. This finding is in line with Hahn (2003) who found that exchange rate shocks are an important contributor to inflation increase during the first three years of the monetary union.

References

Anderton, B. (2003). *Extra-euro area manufacturing import prices and exchange rate pass-through*. European Central Bank Working Paper No. 219.

Bacchetta, P., & van Wincoop, E. (2002). *Why do consumer prices react less than import prices to exchange rates?* Working Paper No. 9352. NBER.

Bailliu, J., & Fujii, E. (2004). *Exchange rate pass-through and the inflation environment in industrialized countries: An empirical investigation*. Working Paper No. 2004-21. Bank of Canada.

Barhoumi, K. (2006). Differences in long run exchange rate pass-through into import prices in developing countries: An empirical investigation. *Economic Modeling*, *23*(6), 926–951.

Ben Cheikh, N., & Cheik, H. M. (2013). A panel cointegration analysis of the exchange rate pass-through. *Economics Bulletin*, *33*(4), 2778–2790.

Ben Cheikh, N., & Louhichi, W. (2014). Revisiting the role of inflation environment in exchange rate pass-through: A panel threshold approach. *Economic Modeling*. doi: 10.1016/j.econmod.2014.11.004

Blanchard, O., & Quah, D. (1989). The dynamic effects of aggregate demand and supply disturbances. *American Economic Review*, *79*(4), 655–673.

Burstein, A., Eichenbaum, M., & Rebelo, S. (2005). Large devaluation and the real exchange rate. *Journal of Political Economy*, *113*, 742–784.

Campa, J., & Goldberg, L. (2002). *Exchange rate pass-through into import prices: A macro or micro phenomenon*? Working Paper No. 8934. NBER.

Campa, J., & Goldberg, L. (2005). Exchange rate pass-through into import prices. *The Review of Economics and Statistics*, *87*(4), 679–690.

Campa, J., Goldberg, L., & González-Mínguez, J. (2005). *Exchange rate pass-through to import prices in the euro area*. Discussion paper. Working Paper No. 11632. National Bureau of Economic Research, Cambridge, MA.

Campa, J., & Gonzàlez, J. (2006). Difference in exchange rate pass-through in the euros areas. *European Economic Review*, *50*, 121–145.

Candelon, B., & Lutkepohl, H. (2001). On the reliability of Chow-type tests for parameter constancy in multivariate dynamic models. *Economics Letters*, *73*, 155–160.

Ca'Zorzi, M., Kahn, E., & Sánchez, M. (2007). *Exchange rate pass-through in emerging markets*. ECB Working Papers Series No. 739.

Choudhri, E., Faruquee, H., & Hakura, D. (2005). Explaining the exchange rate pass-through in different prices. *Journal of International Economics*, *65*, 349–374.

Choudhri, E., & Hakura, D. (2006). Exchange rate pass through to domestic prices: Does the inflationary environment matter? *Journal of International Money and Finance*, *25*, 614–639.

Devereux, M., & Engel, C. (2002). Exchange rate pass-through, exchange rate volatility, and exchange rate disconnect. *Journal of Monetary Economics*, *49*, 913–940.

Elliott, G., Rothenberg, T., & Stock, J. (1996). Efficient tests for an autoregressive unit root. *Econometrica*, *64*(4), 813–836.

Faruqee, H. (2006). Exchange rate pass-through in the euro area. *IMF Staff Papers*, *53*, 63–88.

Faust, J., & Leeper, E. (2003). Monetary policy's role in exchange rate behavior. *Journal of Monetary Economics*, *50*(7), 1403–1424.

Gagnon, J., & Ihrig, J. (2004). Monetary policy and exchange rate pass-through. *International Journal of Finance and Economics*, *9*(4), 315–338.

Gali, J. (1992). How well does the IS-LM model fit postwar U.S. data? *Quarterly Journal of Economics*, *107*, 709–738.

Goldberg, P., & Knetter, M. (1997). Goods prices and exchange rates: What have we learned? *Journal of Economic Literature*, *35*, 1243–1272.

Hahn, E. (2003). *Pass-through of external shocks to euro area inflation*. Working Paper No. 243. European Central Bank.

Hüfner, F., & Schröder, M. (2002). *Exchange rate pass-through to consumer prices: A European perspective*. Discussion Paper No. 02-20. ZEW Centre for European Economic Research.

Ito, T., & Sato, K. (2008). Exchange rate changes and inflation in post-crisis Asian economies: Vector autoregression analysis of the exchange rate pass-through. *Journal of Money, Credit and Banking*, *40*(7), 1407–1438.

Mann, C. L. (1986). Prices, profits margins, and exchange rates. *Federal Reserve Bulletin*, 366–379.

McCarthy, J. (2007). Pass-through of exchange rates and import prices to domestic inflation in some industrialized economies. *Eastern Economic Journal*, *33*(4), 511–537.

Mihailov, A. (2008). Exchange rate pass-through to prices in macrodata: A comparative sensitivity analysis. *International Journal of Finance and Economics*, *14*(4), 346–377.

Parker, M., & Wong, B. (2014). *Exchange rate and commodity price pass-through in New Zealand*. Analytical Note Series N_2014/01. Reserve Bank of New Zealand.

Parsley, D., & Popper, H. (1998). Exchange rates, domestic prices, and central bank actions: Recent U.S. experience. *Southern Economic Journal*, *64*(4), 957–972.

Pesaran, M. H., & Shin, Y. (1998). Generalized impulse response analysis in linear multivariate models. *Economics Letters*, *58*, 17–29.

Romer, D. (1993). Openness and inflation: Theory and evidence. *Quarterly Journal of Economics*, *4*, 869–903.

Shambaugh, J. (2008). A new look at pass-through. *Journal of International Money and Finance*, *27*, 560–591.

Shintani, M., Terada-Hagiwara, A., & Tomoyoshi, Y (2013). Exchange rate pass-through and inflation: A nonlinear time series analysis. *Journal of International Money and Finance*, *32*, 512–527.

Taylor, J. (2000). Low inflation, pass-through and the pricing power of firms. *European Economic Review*, *44*, 1389–1408.

Webber, A. (1999). Dynamic and long run responses of import prices to the exchange rate in the Asia-Pacific. *Asian Economic Journal*, *13*(3), 303–320.

Appendix A: Specification Tests

Table A.1: Results of the Unit Root Tests

Country	ADF		KPSS		DF-GLS	
	Level	1st diff.	Level	1st diff.	Level	1st diff.
CPI						
Austria	−2.512	−3.0937*	0.518243**	1.039	−1.154	−3.011*
Belgium	−0.972	−4.1361**	0.414952**	0.120	−1.246	−2.820*
Germany	−1.372	−3.1581*	0.267249**	0.085	−1.843	−3.616**
Spain	−1.667	−4.5183**	0.255063**	0.104	−0.996	−2.757*
Finland	−0.923	−3.4638**	0.556912**	0.069	−1.165	−3.239*
France	−2.084	−5.0115**	0.474786**	0.298	−1.619	−2.038*
Greece	−1.515	−3.051*	0.631763**	0.124	−1.445	−2.894*
Ireland	−0.949	−3.9255**	0.306229**	0.166	−1.070	−2.126*
Italy	−2.125	−3.1928*	0.547267**	0.086	−1.565	−2.864**
Luxembourg	−1.062	−4.9549**	0.329039**	0.160	−1.693	−1.404
The Netherlands	0.192	−4.5356**	0.251542**	0.491894*	−1.436	−2.966*
Portugal	−1.796	−4.6488**	0.304176**	0.558627*	−1.505	−2.245
Nominal effective exchange rate						
Austria	−0.951	−8.5404**	0.561378**	0.373	−1.244	−4.692**
Belgium	−2.931	−7.0648**	0.187107*	0.175	−1.700	−2.953**
Germany	−2.129	−8.4702**	0.393234**	0.086	−2.535	−4.784**
Spain	−3.296	−7.4751**	0.200878*	0.384	−1.121	−3.282**
Finland	−2.243	−7.7206**	0.326954**	0.066	−2.829	−4.158**
France	−1.953	−8.9225**	0.210352*	0.337	−1.466	−3.296**
Greece	−0.771	−8.3779**	0.619331**	0.207	−0.529	−2.045*
Ireland	−2.027	−8.3887**	0.214021*	0.203	−1.400	−2.801**
Italy	−1.904	−7.5047**	0.349329**	0.102	−1.266	−4.457**
Luxembourg	−1.763	−7.2815**	0.289906**	0.113	−1.683	−3.355**
The Netherlands	−1.916	−8.0551**	0.227835**	0.120	−2.459	−4.964**
Portugal	−1.942	−5.8794**	0.352049**	0.143	−1.383	−2.469
GDP						
Austria	−2.913	−7.9166**	1.810626**	0.121	−2.158	−2.816**
Belgium	−0.334	−5.0765**	2.499921**	0.130	−1.930	−3.671**
Germany	−1.198	−7.6517**	2.139009**	0.082	−2.602	−4.124**
Spain	−0.979	−2.9660*	2.401370**	0.154	−2.238	−2.844**
Finland	−0.418	−8.5876**	2.276504**	0.098	−2.557	−2.466*
France	−1.215	−4.8021**	2.410361**	0.163	−2.090	−2.495*
Greece	0.108	−3.9337**	2.262626**	0.368	−0.792	−4.126**
Ireland	−0.717	−3.1905*	2.405650**	0.419	−1.583	−2.658**
Italy	−1.873	−6.9938**	2.355765**	0.305	−0.941	−3.794**
Luxembourg	−0.723	−10.6741**	2.409973**	0.166	−1.799	−3.460**
The Netherlands	−0.199	−10.0595**	2.427777**	0.288	−1.507	−2.720**
Portugal	−1.194	−3.7643**	2.376592**	0.395	−1.911	−2.143*
Interest rate						
Austria	−3.129	−6.3400**	1.574195**	0.084	−1.568	−2.144*
Belgium	−2.081	−6.2442**	0.223654**	0.054	0.271	−3.309**

Table A.1: (*Continued*)

Country	ADF		KPSS		DF-GLS	
	Level	1st diff.	Level	1st diff.	Level	1st diff.
Germany	−1.957	−5.3625**	1.476766**	0.096	−1.513	−4.384**
Spain	−1.405	−5.7984**	2.354212**	0.092	−0.032	−4.463**
Finland	−0.988	−7.4761**	2.146838**	0.091	−0.770	−4.944**
France	−1.054	−6.3973**	2.201712**	0.067	−0.100	−4.562**
Greece	0.321	−4.7748**	2.246433**	0.227	−0.166	−4.951**
Ireland	−1.857	−7.7125**	2.214257**	0.051	0.002	−4.256**
Italy	−0.957	−5.6865**	2.371547**	0.115	0.082	−2.107*
Luxembourg	−2.081	−6.2442**	2.156896**	0.054	0.271	−3.309**
The Netherlands	−2.028	−6.1353**	1.681538**	0.054	−0.222	−5.270**
Portugal	−1.054	−5.6402**	2.262505**	0.109	−0.616	−4.737**
Import prices						
Austria	−1.740	−5.2184**	0.293895**	0.089	−2.050	−4.303**
Belgium	−2.976	−4.9145**	0.171710*	0.293	−1.370	−3.852**
Germany	−2.448	−6.7764**	0.157448*	0.155	−2.178	−2.000*
Spain	−0.596	−5.9655**	0.181320*	0.459	−1.552	−3.384**
Finland	−2.475	−8.9163**	0.316630**	0.416	−1.271	−4.284**
France	−1.908	−5.7997**	0.169495*	0.193	−1.480	−3.553**
Greece	−0.600	−9.2081**	0.188599*	0.152	−1.870	−4.641**
Ireland	−1.404	−9.2233**	0.162430*	0.078	−2.019	−2.045*
Italy	−0.821	−6.2556**	2.070254**	0.393	−1.560	−2.495*
Luxembourg	−0.360	−9.0961**	0.095	0.039	−1.811	−3.822**
The Netherlands	−0.180	−6.6482**	0.318671**	0.167	−2.118	−4.411**
Portugal	−0.983	−3.3908*	0.478687**	0.052	−0.501	−3.020*
PPI						
Austria	−1.482	−4.6157**	0.385971**	0.126	−2.207	−4.501**
Belgium	−2.677	−5.8743**	0.294241**	0.259	−1.799	−4.331**
Germany	−3.003	−6.6539**	0.156822*	0.054	−1.578	−4.004**
Spain	−2.049	−3.5715**	0.322361**	0.049	−1.150	−3.064*
Finland	−2.657	−5.5032**	0.265933**	0.067	−1.177	−4.338**
France	−2.886	−3.3363**	0.561824**	0.420	−1.932	−3.530**
Greece	−3.086	−6.3399**	0.295182**	0.059	−2.648	−3.482**
Ireland	−3.056	−5.5857**	0.344062**	0.227	−0.610	−0.812
Italy	−2.400	−3.3184*	0.533521**	0.101	−2.281	−3.842**
Luxembourg	−3.060	−6.0600**	0.350788**	0.125	−1.232	−4.713**
The Netherlands	−2.017	−5.4149**	0.289999**	0.114	−1.690	−4.385**
Portugal	−3.126	−6.3424**	0.338455**	0.400	−1.083	−1.338
Foreign costs						
Austria	−1.902	−8.9765**	0.431481**	0.090	−1.871	−5.005**
Belgium	−3.247	−7.3116**	0.118	0.087	−1.582	−3.085**
Germany	−1.917	−9.2879**	0.348081**	0.072	−2.476	−4.254**
Spain	−2.518	−7.1836**	0.140	0.253	−1.681	−3.368**
Finland	−1.950	−8.0770**	0.321281**	0.302	−2.398	−3.713**
France	−3.376	−8.0228**	0.128	0.095	−1.466	−3.866**
Greece	−0.771	−9.1764**	0.632549**	1.177470**	−0.382	−2.045*
Ireland	−2.377	−9.2779**	0.383129**	0.306	−1.089	−4.729**

Table A.1: (*Continued*)

Country	ADF		KPSS		DF-GLS	
	Level	1st diff.	Level	1st diff.	Level	1st diff.
Italy	−1.873	−7.9844**	0.465492**	0.430	−0.922	−4.490**
Luxembourg	−3.060	−8.0464**	0.113	0.076	−2.093	−3.279**
The Netherlands	−1.645	−8.9249**	1.443464**	0.090	−2.606	−4.025**
Portugal	−2.045	−6.4277**	0.540070**	0.251	−1.332	−2.501
Oil price index	−1.778	−9.4680**	0.545785**	0.200	−1.111	−3.199**

Note: The tests were performed on the logs of the series (except interest rates) for levels including an intercept and trend. The critical values at 1% and 5% levels, respectively are ADF: −3.99, −3.43; KPSS: 0.216, 0.146; DF-GLS: −3.48, −2.89. For the first differences, the tests included only an intercept and were based on the following critical values at the 1%, 5%, and 10% levels, respectively: ADF: −3.46, −2.88; KPSS: 0.739, 0.463; DF-GLS: −2.58, −1.95. ** and *, respectively, refer to significance at the 1% and 5%.

Table A.2: Lag Selection for Pricing Chain VECM

	Austria	Belgium	Germany	Spain	Finland	France
0	−707.649	−1719.496	−1802.515	−981.602	−91.776	−1116.134
1	−3116.696	−4064.421	−4674.068	−3685.959	**−2301.892**	−3608.798
2	**−3167.887**	**−4098.574**	**−4704.113**	−3721.812	−2297.081	**−3643.728**
3	−3140.334	−4050.572	−4697.863	**−3741.014**	−2294.245	−3627.965
4	−3119.215	−3937.324	−4654.755	−3684.688	−2294.572	−3603.182
5	−3159.858	−3818.671	−4575.063	−3637.260	−2288.652	−3587.996
6	−3142.221	−3660.384	−4455.447	−3543.071	−2237.942	−3532.887
7	−3095.840	−3463.321	−4295.768	−3401.457	−2179.878	−3483.165
8	−3047.109	−3224.676	−4112.951	−3182.100	−2126.362	−3414.625
	Greece	Ireland	Italy	Luxembourg	The Netherlands	Portugal
0	45.165	−74.602	−328.235	−338.479	−555.000	52.303
1	−1992.475	−2052.221	−2647.038	−2441.852	−2654.382	−2381.231
2	−2035.218	−2076.474	**−2683.614**	−2445.347	**−2681.073**	**−2424.304**
3	−2081.116	**−2085.094**	−2676.574	**−2457.898**	−2657.344	−2417.389
4	−2055.176	−2053.489	−2653.193	−2419.032	−2631.082	−2387.883
5	**−2088.453**	−1996.437	−2614.111	−2372.169	−2624.315	−2327.063
6	−2052.830	−1937.264	−2570.460	−2321.386	−2584.743	−2275.389
7	−2002.637	−1866.812	−2521.844	−2264.651	−2537.194	−2213.436
8	−1926.744	−1840.338	−2471.435	−2205.522	−2469.914	−2171.147

Note: The minimum of the AIC values are in bold.

Table A.3: Johansen Trace Test

H_0: *rank* = *r*	Austria	Belgium	Germany	Spain	Finland	France
0	98.540	126.785	150.707	211.569	217.555	165.362
	(0.000)	(0.000)	(0.000)	(0.000)	(0.000)	(0.000)
1	41.959	59.014	76.514	108.246	50.993	96.584
	(0.160)	(0.003)	(0.002)	(0.000)	(0.023)	(0.000)
2	13.324	23.376	43.402	24.111	19.720	51.757
	(0.875)	(0.236)	(0.043)	(0.460)	(0.453)	(0.006)
3	3.048	6.922	13.679	12.779	6.436	21.500
	(0.957)	(0.593)	(0.688)	(0.390)	(0.649)	(0.173)
4	0.411	2.339	2.708	3.425	0.061	7.596
	(0.521)	(0.126)	(0.896)	(0.515)	(0.805)	(0.306)
H_0: *rank* = *r*	Greece	Ireland	Italy	Luxembourg	The Netherlands	Portugal
0	135.823	114.898	125.457	81.370	113.458	164.218
	(0.000)	(0.000)	(0.000)	(0.004)	(0.001)	(0.000)
1	85.627	62.078	74.453	47.904	57.245	93.617
	(0.007)	(0.001)	(0.004)	(0.048)	(0.314)	(0.000)
2	47.398	28.905	43.141	21.175	26.916	50.983
	(0.125)	(0.064)	(0.046)	(0.357)	(0.794)	(0.005)
3	25.689	5.763	22.141	4.666	12.708	19.253
	(0.236)	(0.725)	(0.137)	(0.840)	(0.784)	(0.272)
4	12.220	0.073	4.760	1.932	0.060	2.990
	(0.172)	(0.787)	(0.636)	(0.165)	(1.000)	(0.867)

Note: *p*-values are in parentheses.

Appendix B: Chow Tests For Multiple Time-series Systems

Table B.1: Chow Test for the VECM Pricing Chain Model

Chow test	Austria	Belgium	Germany	Spain	Finland	France
Break point test	741.118	1038.114	590.512	783.370	550.273	928.758
Bootstrapped *p*-value	(0.000)	(0.020)	(0.000)	(0.000)	(0.000)	(0.070)
Sample split test	481.848	460.226	419.039	495.692	402.790	639.689
Bootstrapped *p*-value	(0.000)	(0.010)	(0.020)	(0.000)	(0.010)	(0.000)
Chow test	**Greece**	**Ireland**	**Italy**	**Luxembourg**	**The Netherlands**	**Portugal**
Break point test	896.897	663.445	414.849	1079.036	755.095	759.694
Bootstrapped *p*-value	(0.100)	(0.000)	(0.470)	(0.030)	(0.000)	(0.000)
Sample split test	576.060	367.118	224.312	456.455	467.483	448.913
Bootstrapped *p*-value	(0.000)	(0.320)	(0.490)	(0.040)	(0.000)	(0.000)

Note: Candelon and Lutkepohl (2001) consider two versions of Chow tests, sample split (SS) tests, and break point (BP) tests. They have proposed using bootstrap versions of the Chow tests to improve their small sample properties. Bootstrapped *p*-values are obtained from 1000 bootstrap replications.

Appendix C: Generalized Impulse Response For Consumer Prices

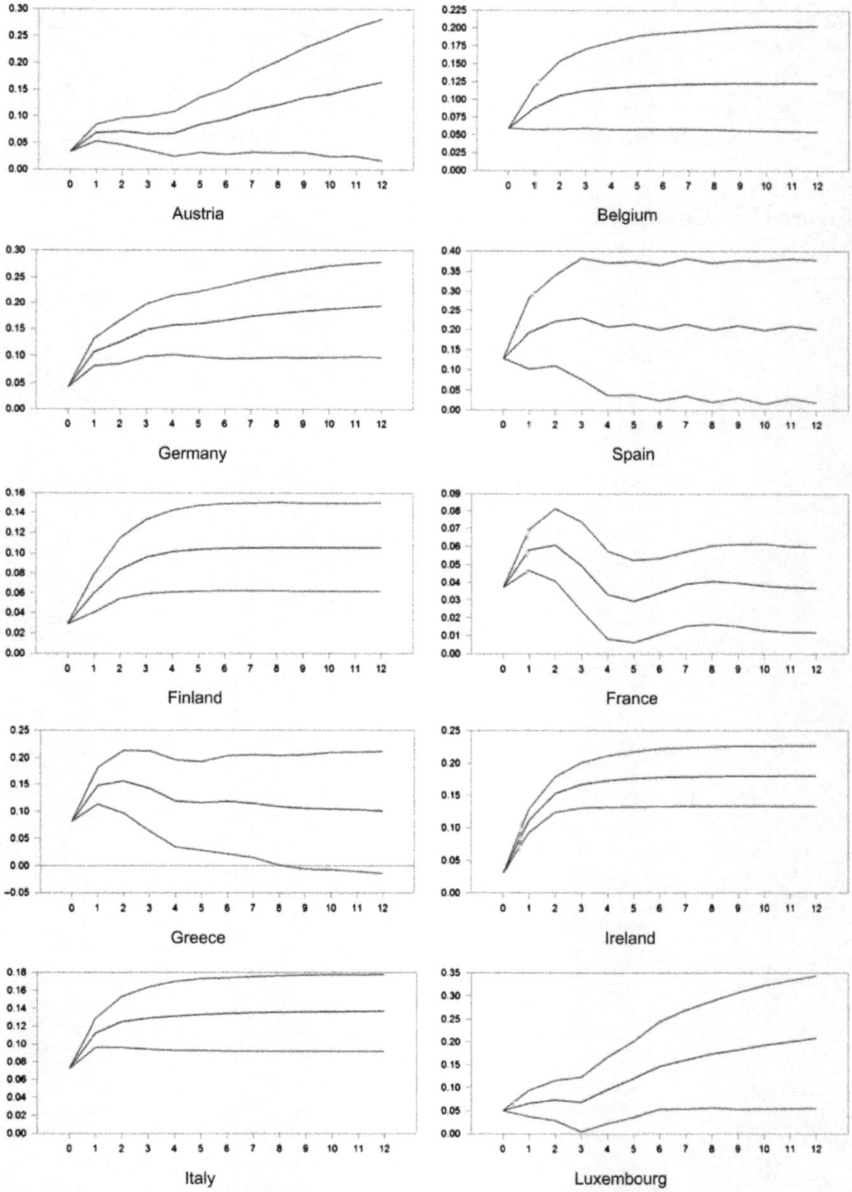

Figure C.1: Response of Consumer Prices to 1% Exchange Rate Shock.

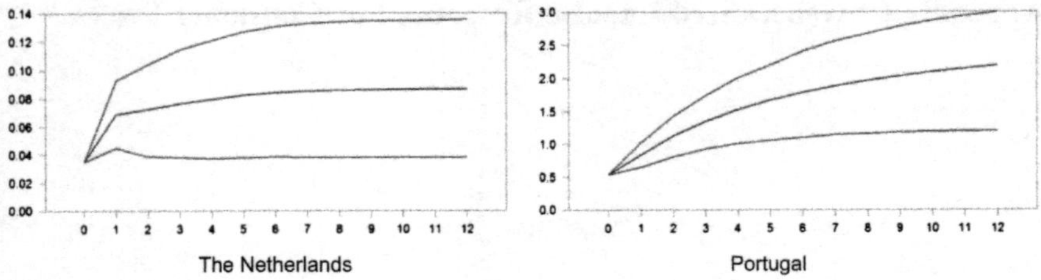

Figure C.1: Continued.

Chapter 6

Escape Routes from Sovereign Default Risk in the Euro Area

Willi Semmler[a,b] and Christian R. Proaño[c]

[a]*Department of Economics, The New School of Social Research, New York, NY, USA*
[b]*Zentrum für Europäische Wirtschaftsforschung (ZEW), Mannheim, Germany, e-mail: semmlerw@newschool.edu*
[c]*Economics Department, University of Bamberg, Germany; Macroeconomic Policy Institute (IMK), Düsseldorf, Germany*

Abstract

The recent financial and sovereign debt crises around the world have sparked a growing literature on models and empirical estimates of defaultable debt. Frequently households and firms come under default threat, local governments can default, and recently sovereign default threats were eminent for Greece and Spain in 2012–2013. Moreover, Argentina experienced an actual default in 2001. What causes sovereign default risk, and what are the escape routes from default risk? Previous studies such as Arellano (2008), Roch and Uhlig (2013), and Arellano et al. (2014) have provided theoretical models to explore the main dynamics of sovereign defaults. These models can be characterized as threshold models in which there is a convergence toward a good no-default equilibrium below the threshold and a default equilibrium above the threshold. However, in these models aggregate output is exogenous, so that important macroeconomic feedback effects are not taken into account. In this chapter, we (1) propose alternative model variants suitable for certain types of countries in the EU where aggregate output is endogenously determined and where financial stress plays a key role, (2) show how these model variants can be solved through the Nonlinear Model Predictive Control numerical technique, and (3) present some empirical evidence on the nonlinear dynamics of output,

International Symposia in Economic Theory and Econometrics, Vol. 24
William A. Barnett and Fredj Jawadi (Editors)

ISSN: 1571-0386/doi: 10.1108/S1571-038620150000024018

sovereign debt, and financial stress in some euro areas and other industrialized countries.

Keywords: sovereign default risk, financial stress, macroeconomic dynamics, euro crisis

JEL Classifications: E44, E62, H63

1. Introduction

As it is well-known, the sharp increase in sovereign default risk premia of several euro-area countries (in particular Greece, Portugal, Spain, and Ireland) since 2008 deteriorated significantly the debt-refinancing conditions of the central governments. These developments were magnified by two main forces which led to the outbreak of a full-fledged sovereign debt crisis that threatened the macroeconomic stability of the euro area, and the European unification project as a whole. First, the surge of the yields of sovereign bonds led also to an increase in the borrowing costs of the corporate and the household sector in the euro area, affecting in a direct manner the private sector's consumption and investment decisions. And second, once the break-up of the euro area began to be considered as an actual possibility by the financial markets, this risk was also incorporated in the sovereign default risk premia of several euro-area countries (see for instance Coimbra, 2014; Semmler & Gevorkyan, 2014), leading to even higher sovereign yields. All these developments let aggregate output and income decrease even further, generating less sovereign revenues and increasing primary fiscal deficits.

The historical experience of previous sovereign debt crises suggests that successful strategies implemented in these crises around the world, such as debt relief, a change in the debt maturity structure, the announcement of credit guarantees not only have reduced the sovereign debt servicing burdens, but also have managed to lower the credit costs for private borrowers and the overall financial stress as well, thereby increasing nominal production and income.[1] For instance, Reinhart and Trebesch (2014) show that debt relief accounts historically for roughly 20% of recovery and macroeconomic improvement. They attribute improved ratings and reduced debt service to this improvement. If successful these measures are likely to increase

[1] For an early study on the escape routes, see Tobin (1963, 1987).

economic activity, aggregate income, and tax revenues, and to reduce sovereign deficit and fiscal debt levels – all this lowering sovereign default risk and aiding to escape a default threat environment. Yet, the debt reduction may mean that there is a balance sheet effect on the side of the creditors, for example, in the banks' asset position. This could trigger, as the EU crisis has shown, some threat of banking insolvency, possibly entailing further financial stress, as discussed by Brunnermeier and Oehmke (2012) and Coimbra (2014).[2]

At the theoretical level, the occurrence of euro-area sovereign crisis and the related surge in perceived sovereign default risk of many European Economic and Monetary Union (EMU) countries triggered a new generation of theoretical studies which investigate how such a high default risk regime can emerge in the first place, as well as how policies should be designed to reverse eminent defaults in the second place.[3] In particular, Arellano (2008), Roch and Uhlig (2013), and Arellano, Maliar, Maliar, and Tsyrennikov (2014) analyze consumption-based models on sovereign debt and default risk with optimal choice of sovereign bonds, where aggregate income fluctuations are exogenously determined. The main escape routes suggested by such theoretical frameworks are consumption reduction (see also Uhlig, 2014), or bailouts with "fair bond pricing" (see Gavin, Keen, Richter, & Throckmorton, 2013).

Yet, as we will argue, the insight from these types of models needs to be complemented with a study of further macroeconomic feedback channels in order to investigate what important routes are available to escape from a regime of high sovereign default risk. In this chapter we thus propose a broader macroeconomic model which also includes economic production and capital investment. We make production and income fluctuations endogenous, include capital stock as state variable and investment as a decision variable. Since there can be a pass-through of sovereign risk to the private sector, and the reverse, the main route is likely to be to reduce

[2] In contrast, historical experience with partial and full default episodes has shown that interest rates and credit costs are likely to rise rapidly immediately after the default, leading to a reduction of aggregate consumption and investment. This effect depends however on the reaction of output: With a falling output, credit spreads can surge, deteriorating the macroeconomic performance even more (see Arellano, 2008).

[3] While in early models of fiscal sustainability (see, e.g., Bohn, 1998) the transmission mechanisms from sovereign debt to economic activity and vice versa were mostly linear, recent studies such as Mittnik and Semmler (2012), Baum, Poplawski-Ribeiro, and Weber (2012), De Grauwe (2012), Blanchard and Leigh (2013), Blanchard, Dell'Ariccia, and Mauro (2013), among others, have highlighted the fact that the multiplier might be state dependent and fiscal consolidation could be strongly contractionary when implemented in the midst of a recession.

default threat through reducing financial market stress and credit spreads, using exceptional monetary policy tools. Because the sovereign risk is passed-through to the private sector borrowing cost, the transition out of this debt crisis regime to a better regime also works through those channels, namely through a reduction of financial stress and interest cost, not only for sovereign bonds but also for private borrowing.[4,5]

Accordingly, we propose here a small scale macro model which, in contrast to the above mentioned previous literature, includes economic production and capital investment. We make production and income fluctuations endogenous, including capital stock as state variable and investment as a decision variable. Because the sovereign risk is allowed to be passed-through to the private sector borrowing cost, the transiting out of this regime to a better regime, also works through those channels, namely through a reduction of financial stress and interest cost, not only for sovereign bonds but also for private borrowing. In this context exceptional monetary policy becomes particularly important, since there are often strong adverse macroeconomic feedback loops.

In contrast to the standard approach where eventually destabilizing feedback loops tend to be smoothed out due to the infinite horizon underlying the agent's economic decisions, or are only captured in some adverse shocks,[6] we propose here an alternative framework with a finite planning horizon that allows for endogenous destabilizing feedback loops. To solve this model variant we use the Nonlinear Model Predictive Control (NMPC) algorithm proposed by Grüne and Pannek (2011) (see also Grüne, Semmler, & Stieler, 2013 and the appendix of this chapter). We build a regime change model variant with high sovereign debt, high financial stress, and strong macro feedback loops. On the other hand, what maybe typical is a regime with moderate sovereign debt, but low financial stress and low credit spreads and also more favorable macroeconomic feedback loops.

The remainder is organized as follows. In Section 2 we set up a model along the lines of Arellano (2008) and Arellano et al. (2014) and modify it to analyze default risk and non-default risk countries. In Section 3 we study

---

[4] See also Lorenzoni and Werning (2013) who distinguish between a good equilibrium with no default and a bad equilibrium associated with a slowly emerging debt crisis.

[5] Note that in the subsequent discussion we leave aside the issue of generating sustainable sovereign debt through fiscal policy such as fiscal consolidations, through an increase in taxes or a cut in public spending, strategies which have not been particularly successful in a regime of economic and financial stress as discussed by Buiter (2010) (see also Mittnik & Semmler, 2012).

[6] Note that there are also now models of regime change available that move away from those smoothness properties (see Farmer, Waggoner, & Zha, 2009).

empirically the nonlinear relationship between output growth, sovereign debt, and financial stress in the main euro-area countries and other industrialized economies. Finally, we draw some concluding remarks from this study in Section 4. The appendix outlines the numerical procedure (called Nonlinear Model Predictive Control or NMPC) used for the solution of our model.

2. Theoretical Analysis

As mentioned, recent studies such as Arellano (2008), Roch and Uhlig (2013), Lorenzoni and Werning (2013), and Arellano et al. (2014) have elaborated on the dynamics of sovereign default risk. We here briefly discuss their standard default risk model and then introduce our extension with production and investment.

2.1. The Infinite Horizon Standard Model on Sovereign Default Risk

The standard theoretical framework can be summarized in a generic way as follows:

$$V(b,y) = \max_{c_t, b_{t+1}} E_t \sum_{t=0}^{\infty} \beta^t (U(c_t) - \chi d) \tag{1}$$

subject to

$$c_t + (1-\theta)b_t = y_t + q(b_{t+1}, y_t)(b_{t+1} - \theta b_t), \tag{2}$$

where $V(b,y)$ is the expected present discounted value of the agent's utility out of consumption c_t (either private or by the government), with y_t being aggregate income (or government revenues), b_t outstanding (private or government) debt, and χd the cost of default when a default event d occurs. Agents maximize thus the expected present value of intertemporal utility – with $U(\cdot)$ being the period utility function – by choosing c_t and b_{t+1} subject to a period budget constraint given by Equation (2), where θ denotes the fraction of bonds repaid in a given period. Aggregate income y_t is assumed to be given by an exogenous stochastic process, and $q(b_{t+1}, y_t)$ is the bond price given the choice of issued bonds b_{t+1} and the income stream y_t.[7]

---

[7] Arellano (2008) and for most part of their analysis also Roch and Uhlig (2013) assume $\theta = 0$.

Since for the bond yield we have $R_t = 1/q(b_{t+1}, y_t)$, and $r_t = R_t - 1$, we can write for $\theta = 0$ a state equation in continuous time such as[8]

$$db_t = (r_t b_t - (1 + r_t)(y_t - c_t))dt. \tag{3}$$

According to Equation (3) the increase in sovereign debt from t to $t+1$ is driven by the bond price – or the bond yield respectively – the current sovereign debt level and the current surplus, the latter given by the exogenous income fluctuations and the endogenously chosen consumption stream.[9] As it should be clear, as income is driven by an exogenous process macroeconomic feedback loops from output to sovereign debt – for instance, through their impact on income and credit spreads – are not endogenized in such frameworks.

The above literature studies a high-stress regime with high debt, and low-income stream resulting in low bond prices and high yields, and a low-stress regime with low debt, low yields, and higher bond prices. An extreme case is given when the sovereign chooses to default, with an appropriate effect on consumption and welfare. In this case it is assumed that the country actually chooses defaults when the welfare of non-defaulting $V(b,k)$ becomes lower than that the welfare associated with a default $V^{\text{def}}(k)$, thus when $V(b,k) < V^{\text{def}}(k)$. This means that welfare is smaller with borrowing than for default and autarky. This is an interesting case to be considered – as done, for example, in Arellano et al. (2014) – though such an event has not yet occurred in the euro area (this issue will be further discussed below).

What is a limitation of those models is that since output and income are stochastic, macroeconomic feedback loops of stabilizing or destabilizing nature which affect growth rates, the default risk, and the macroeconomic performance as a whole are by and large neglected. Nonetheless, such macroeconomic feedback loops between sovereign debt, bonds yields, and output can bring the economy into a downward spiral of low growth, high sovereign risk, and increasing sovereign debt. Yet the reverse, more stabilizing spiral, may also hold. Therefore, it is key to acknowledge that these macroeconomic feedback effects may be state dependent, and that their overall effect may switch from destabilizing to stabilizing.

[8] While in discrete time b_{t+l} is a choice variable to be decided in time period t, in a continuous time variant of this model one can write this expression as in Equation (3).

[9] As mentioned, in the context of sovereign debt the exogenous income fluctuation is interpreted in Roch and Uhlig (2013) as tax revenues, and c as public consumption.

2.2. A Model Variant 1: Weak Macroeconomic Feedback Effects

Building on the just discussed modeling approach we first present a model variant based on a finite decision horizon and with weak macro feedbacks. We do so to characterize short-run behavior in a more realistic manner, as the infinite horizon framework implies a pronounced smoothness in the evolution of the choice variables by construction, as discussed by Grüne et al. (2013). We also introduce production and investment. Accordingly, Equations (1) and (2) in our modified framework read[10]

$$V(k,d) = \max_{c_t, i_t} E \int_0^T e^{-\rho t}\left(\ln(c_t) - \chi\left(\mu_t - \mu^*\right)^2\right)\mathrm{d}t \tag{4}$$

subject to

$$\mathrm{d}k_t = (i_t - \delta k_t)\mathrm{d}t, \tag{5}$$

$$\mathrm{d}b_t = (r(\cdot)b_t - (1 + r(\cdot))(y_t - c_t - i_t - \varphi(i_t)))\mathrm{d}t. \tag{6}$$

In Equation (4) there are preferences over log utility, now penalized by some excess with $\mu_t = b_t/k_t$ and μ^* being steady state debt-to-capital ratio.[11] The decision variables are consumption, c_t, and investment i_t.[12] Equation (5) represents the evolution of capital stock, which increases due to investment but declines due to the capital depreciation δk_t. Equation (6) represents the dynamics of sovereign debt, with $y = Af(k) = Ak^{\alpha}$ being the production function, and $A > 0$. The interest payment on debt $r(\cdot)b_t$ is state dependent, with the interest rate r_t being an increasing function of the issued bonds and a decreasing function in the capital stock, in a similar way as in Arellano (2008).[13] Moreover, debt decreases with the surplus $y_t - c_t - i_t - \varphi(i_t)$ – the excess of income over spending, and rises with

[10] For details of how such type of short decision horizon model can approximate models with longer time horizons well on the basis of much less information, see Grüne et al. (2013).

[11] Roch and Uhlig (2013) allow for a one-time cost of default. We stretch this default cost out over time, making it depending on the excess leveraging. A similar approach as ours has been proposed by Blanchard.

[12] Since we mainly want to focus on endogenous credit spreads arising from sovereign risk, with pass-through of public default risk to private borrowing cost, we interpret consumption and investment spending as private as well as public spending, and income y_t as GDP, a fraction of it be used as tax revenue. Accordingly, neither public spending nor tax revenues will be explicitly modeled, but they are simply endogenized through movements of the aggregates.

[13] There the bond yield is a function of the size of bond issuing and the stochastic income shock.

a deficit. Moreover, $\varphi(i_t)$ is the adjustment cost for investment, which is presumed to be quadratic. We thus introduce production and a capital stock dynamics, as well as the evolution of sovereign debt by defining debt now as state variable.

Note that the model has now two decision variables and two state variables,[14] and that we make a distinction between the discount rate ρ and the interest rate r_t, the latter being affected by the credit spread. In more advanced settings (see, e.g., Brunnermeier & Sannikov, 2014), the capital stock is shared by households and financial intermediaries, but in our setting it remains relatively passive in this respect.

As previously mentioned, a key mechanism in the dynamics of sovereign default risk discussed by Arellano (2008) and Lorenzoni and Werning (2013) is the endogenous reaction of the bond yield to the perceived sovereign risk. In the following we also make the yield on bonds a nonlinear function of the sovereign leveraging. Yet it is reasonable to assume the function to be bounded, so we define it by a function such as

$$r(s_t|\gamma, c^*) = [1 + \exp(-\gamma(s_t - c^*))]^{-1}, \ \gamma > 0, c^* > 0. \tag{7}$$

This function makes now the sovereign credit cost depending, in a nonlinear way, on a state variable s_t (here μ_t, the debt-to-capital ratio), a threshold variable, c^* (here equal to μ^*), and a slope parameter, γ.[15] Note that this logistic function is roughly the nonlinear function that has been estimated empirically in De Grauwe and Ji (2012) in their analysis of EU debt and bond yield data (see also Corsetti, Meier, & Müller, 2012).[16]

When there are state-dependent risk premia and credit cost, but the macro feedback loops are weak, interest rates can still stay low. Credit risk and financial stress do not build up and there are little adverse macro feedback loops. Figure 1 illustrates this case, with initially low stress and with

[14] We could have formulated the second state equation in terms of net worth and leveraging, the latter as a decision variable as in Brunnermeier and Sannikov (2014). We prefer leveraging here as a state variable where then debt can only sluggishly be redeemed and issued again.

[15] The above represents the logistic function often used in regime change models such as the STAR and STVAR models (see Schleer & Semmler, 2013).

[16] In Arellano (2008) and Roch and Uhlig (2013) the sovereign risk and credit spreads are driven by exogenous shocks in income and bond issuing. Arellano (2008) justifies an increasing interest rate (discount rate) with the high negative correlation of risk perception of lenders with the output shock. In more standard DSGE models the rise of risk premia and its persistence on a high level is often simply modeled through large shocks with some strong persistent (see also Gilchrist & Zakrajsek, 2012).

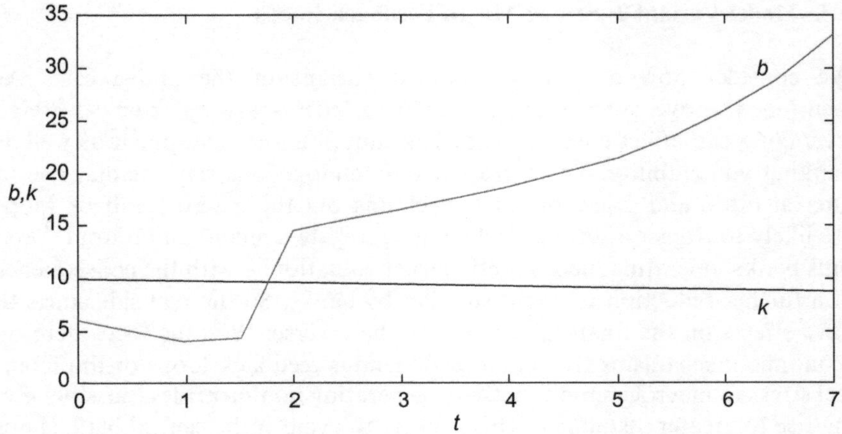

Figure 1: Dynamics for Capital Stock k and Debt b under Borrowing Costs Rising Nonlinearly in High Leveraging Regime, though Macro Feedback Loops Might Be Weak. Initial Conditions $k(0) = 10$, $b(0) = 6$. Debt Dynamics Eventually Unstable, though GDP Growth Is by and Large Unaffected.

borrowing cost below some threshold. For these initial conditions we can observe the capital stock to converge to the steady state.

Note that in this scenario variant we have set here the macro feedback loops to aggregate demand to be weak. We still obtain the sovereign debt to be unstable eventually (see the upper trajectory in Figure 1), but output and capital accumulation stabilize. The black trajectory in Figure 1 represents the path of the capital stock (denoted by k) with low initial debt and weaker macro feedback loops, with a parallel evolution of output (not depicted here). But even at lower initial condition, the debt dynamics become unstable. What is modeled here is what has been called the feedback of financial market stress to aggregate demand and output.[17] Note that leveraging and credit cost above a certain threshold[18] may become unsustainable, due to our transition of Equation (7) to a higher stress regime.

[17] This is what a recent IMF study defines as follows: “The risk channel amplifies the transmission of shocks to aggregate demand, unless monetary policy manages to offset the spillover from sovereign default risk to private funding costs” (Corsetti et al., 2012).

[18] Those thresholds can be empirically estimated (see Schleer & Semmler, 2013).

2.3. Model Variant 2: Strong Macro Feedback Loops

We consider now a slightly modified variant of the above case. As mentioned above adverse macro feedback effects arising from sovereign leveraging can affect credit cost for consumption and investment as well as banking vulnerability. There are not only endogenous risk premia, rise of interest rates, and prices of assets declining but the macro feedback loops are likely to trigger a serious decline in aggregate demand and output[19] and thus banks' operating income and market valuation – with the consequence of a further reduction of credit supplies by banks. So the real side starts to have effects on the financial sector and the reverse. We thus focus here on economic mechanisms that entail endogenous feedback loops of the financial stress to macroeconomic activity, generating nonlinearities, possibly giving rise to greater instability. This is likely to occur if the central bank is not attempting – or not being able – to pursue a monetary policy to reduce financial market stress and to bring down credit cost through credit policies.

Though optimal payouts and investment might be targeted, actual operating income of banks, are likely to decline due to macroeconomic feedback loops. So overall we may experience that actual gross operating income y_t^a in Equation (8) may be only a fraction of y_t and negatively dependent on $r_t(|\gamma, c^*)$, namely

$$y_t^a = (1 - r(s_t|\gamma, c^*))y_t, \tag{8}$$

$$db_t = r(s_t|\gamma, c^*)b_t - (1 + r(s_t|\gamma, c^*))\big(y_t^a - c_t - i_t - \varphi(i_t)\big)dt. \tag{9}$$

Note that in Equation (8) we have defined actual operating income to be driven by aggregate activity in the regime of high financial stress $(1 - r(s_t|\gamma, c^*))$ $(i + c)$, where actual consumption and investment, responding to financial stress, $(1 - r(s_t|\gamma, c^*))$, are determining actual income. So the optimally chosen decision in each time period of the state variables are actually not realized, but the actual outcome depends on the degree of financial stress and the macro feedbacks triggered by this. The numerical results, obtained again through the application of the NMPC algorithm, are shown in Figure 2.

[19] See Blanchard and Leigh (2013) and Corsetti et al. (2012). They show how empirically, for example, sovereign debt and banking risk also increase private borrowing cost and thus make aggregate demand falling. They employ, as we do here, that the spillover effects of risk spread to aggregate demand, but one can also think of another channel through which macroeconomic contractions are triggered. A reduction of loan supplies by banks will set in when asset prices and net worth of banks fall, that is, they will reduce their loan supply to households and firms (see De Grauwe & Macchiarelli, 2013; Gerali, Neri, Sessa, & Signoretti, 2010).

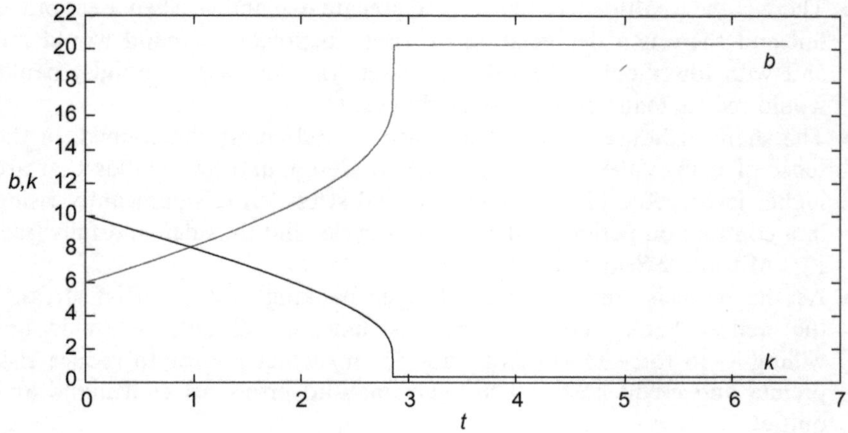

Figure 2: Dynamic Paths of Capital Stock k, and Debt b for Moderate Debt, but High Credit Spread and Default Risk. Initial Conditions $k(0)=10$, $b(0)=6$, Steady State Debt-to-Capital Ratio of $\mu^*=0.3$, with Debt Dynamics Quickly Unstable.

In Figure 2 we assume that the initial debt-to-capital stock ratio is roughly 0.6 which corresponds approximately to a sovereign debt to income ratio of 1.2. The function described by Equation (7), representing the steeply rising credit spread, makes credit cost rising with higher debt ratio and higher financial stress. Note also if in this case we were to look at the asset side of the economy, asset prices are likely to fall or do not grow anymore and capital gains could become negative and the income y would fall and surpluses would shrink, the debt service rise with higher interest rates and debt sustainability becomes threatened.

Since in our model we have also investment and capital accumulation we can trace better the macro feedback mechanisms that models based solely on consumption tend to overlook. The economic intuition of the upper and lower unstable trajectories is that stronger macroeconomic feedback loops with negative impact on demand, declining output and income and credit cost rise, may be due to the following:[20]

[20] A systematic study of macroeconomic feedback effect, known from the history of macroeconomics, partly stabilizing partly destabilizing, is extensively elaborated in Chiarella, Flaschel, and Semmler (2014). Note that we leave here aside the macro feedback effects of nominal type. Those can be built in as well in such a dynamic macro model, as it is, for example, done in Charpe et al. (2015).

- There is the wealth effect reducing aggregate demand – when asset prices fall and there is a depreciation of assets, aggregate demand would fall and with lower collateral value of assets (in our case of bonds) banks would reduce loans or increase credit cost.[21]
- The share of households that are income and credit constrained, in the sense of Galí, Vallés, and López-Salido (2007), and households that are higher leveraged and are under financial stress,[22] are significantly rising in a contraction period of the business cycle, and thus demand falls (see, e.g., Mittnik & Semmler, 2012, 2013).
- As the financial market forces trigger banking and financial stress,[23] the central bank may have no instruments available – or is not willing – to force the interest rate down further and/or to reduce risk premia and credit cost, which again may adversely affect demand and output.
- A fraction of private households starts strongly deleveraging that reduces income and liquidity of other households and firms (see, e.g., Eggertsson & Krugman, 2011). This might be accompanied by a Fisher debt deflation process, causing higher real debt and declining demand because of expected price fall (the Tobin effect).[24]
- Finally, there could occur even a worse feedback: a weak financial sector, holding risky sovereign bonds or other debt instruments, may come under severe stress, because debt may go into default and banks reduce lending to the real economy, or worse, may even default.[25]

We expect thus, starting with a leverage ratio roughly above normal, that the above feedback mechanisms are likely to lead to lower asset value, higher risk premia, higher credit costs, less credit supply – and thus higher financial market stress – and lower investment and consumption demand, lower output, leading to a contraction in the utilization of the capital stock,

[21] This has been called the "pass-through of sovereign risk" to the private sector.
[22] The share of those households matter, since there is empirical evidence that the drop in demand will be larger for households with larger debt that are forced to deleverage more (see Eggertsson & Krugman, 2011).
[23] This is documented by the ZEW financial condition index as presented in Schleer and Semmler (2013).
[24] Though we have not build into our model the described price dynamics, the reader might find the above mechanisms quite intuitive. A detailed discussion of such and further macroeconomic feedback effects can be found in Charpe et al. (2015).
[25] This is what Brunnermeier and Oehmke (2012) call "diabolic loop"; see also Bolton and Jeanne (2011) who present data on the sovereign debt holdings of banks.

and falling capital stock, with increasing credit spreads and so on. With the latter the excess sovereign debt rises due to high yields, low bond prices and insolvency risk is likely to rise.[26]

Given those above sketched adverse macro feedback loops, it is likely that a regime switch to a high-stress regime occurs where the vulnerability of financial intermediaries increases and a faster deterioration of demand and output, as well as capital stock, can be triggered which has then again feedback effects from the real to the financial side. This is likely to occur more often, the more central banks fail to successfully undertake an unconventional intervention into the money and asset markets. Conventional monetary policy will not help in this case but credit and financial market policies are needed instead.[27]

2.4. A Model Variant 3: Escape Routes from Sovereign Default Risk

Looking at the transition function given by Equation (7) escape routes from sovereign default risk might emerge, if credit costs are brought down and credit channels are unblocked by central banks credit and financial market policies. Such a low credit cost, low-stress regime, is characterized by low interest rates on borrowing, lower leveraging, and little credit spreads with an appropriate pass-through to households' and firms' borrowing conditions. This can be seen as equivalent to the case of the central bank successfully pursuing a low – or near zero – interest rate policy which keeps the economy in a low financial stress regime, where also the credit costs are low and rather constant, and in addition we have $y_t^a = y_t$.[28]

This more benign scenario is characterized by

$$\mathrm{d}b_t = (rb_t - (1+r)(y_t - c_t - i_t - \varphi(i_t)))\mathrm{d}t \tag{10}$$

with the agent's maximization problem still being given by Equation (4). As in the previous model variants, we have here again two decision variables and two state variables.

[26] This could equivalently create a downward spiral in net worth, if the model is written in terms of net worth, as in Stein (2012) and Brunnermeier and Sannikov (2014).
[27] See Correia, De Fiore, Teles, and Tristani (2013) who make a distinction between conventional monetary policies, reducing the interest rate and credit policies, and reducing the spread.
[28] A country in the euro area such as Germany seems to have enjoyed such conditions, after 2010.

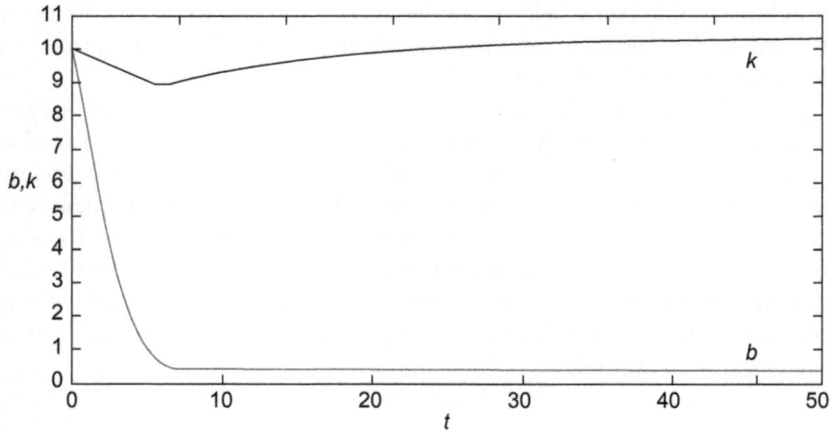

Figure 3: Stable Capital Stock k and Debt b. Dynamics under Low Interest Rates, and No Adverse Macro Feedback Loops, Both Starting from the Same Initial Conditions as in the Previous Cases.

We again have made a distinction between the discount rate and interest rate, the latter impacted by leveraging. Assuming here $r = 0.03$, the outcome of both the financial stress and the macro feedbacks is captured in the lower and upper trajectories of Figure 3.

As it can be clearly observed, when interest rate and bond yields are at a low level and do not react endogenously to adverse macroeconomic conditions, a positive primary surplus resulting from the excess of income over consumption and investment will reduce the sovereign leveraging over time. In this scenario – where adverse macroeconomic feedback loops are not present – sovereign debt can be stabilized by appropriate debt reduction policies and credit policies by the central bank, in a case when output is determined endogenously, as it is the case in the present framework. Those macro channels are however not available in model variants of Section 2.1. We will get back to the above three cases of Sections 2.2–2.4. In particular, we want to know if we could observe those cases in euro-area countries in recent times.

3. Empirical Analysis

Next we study such country differences with respect to their vulnerability to default traps. Can we detect our above mentioned three cases in the data? We explore a nonlinear linkage between sovereign debt, financial stress (as a proxy for sovereign default risk), and output growth, on the basis of quarterly data for 13 advanced countries. Though the financial stress index (FSI) we are using[29] contains also components other than bond yields, the index is constructed so that significant sovereign default risk should show up in the FSI. Our methodology is to investigate by means of nonlinear single-equation and panel estimation techniques if and for what countries or country groups, sovereign debt and financial stress affect economic activity in our sample of 13 industrialized countries.

3.1. Data Description

In our econometric analysis we use quarterly seasonally adjusted data on the net sovereign debt of the general government, GDP at constant prices, the financial stress index (FSI), and the real interest rate on long-term government bonds from 1981Q1 to 2013Q2 for the following 16 countries: Sweden (SWE), Austria (AUT), Belgium (BEL), Canada (CAN), Denmark (DNK), Germany (DEU), Spain (ESP), Finland (FIN), France (FRA), the United Kingdom (GBR), Greece (GRC), Italy (ITA), Japan (JPN), the Netherlands (NLD), Portugal (PRT), and the United States (USA). The data on real GDP and the interest rate on long-term government bonds stems from the OECD Economic Outlook database and Eurostat (for details on this data set, see Proaño, Schoder, & Semmler, 2014).

Figure 4 illustrates the evolution of the net sovereign debt-to-GDP ratio, the financial stress, and the output growth for 13 advanced economies over the period 1981Q1–2013Q2.

As it can be observed in Figure 4 while there is a significant heterogeneity between the net sovereign debt-to-GDP ratios across the considered countries (with Italy (ITA) and Japan (JPN) having the highest debt-to-GDP ratio at the end of the sample), a common feature among all EMU countries is the sizable deterioration of the fiscal balance (as measured by the sovereign debt-to-GDP ratio) resulting from the sharp drop in output growth associated to the 2007–2008 global economic recession and the subsequent euro-area crisis. This countercyclical response of the sovereign debt-to-GDP ratio is of course not surprising due to its construction (with the GDP level in the denominator of the ratio). However, the

[29] The financial stress index (FSI) – a composite indicator comprising information on the *banking-sector beta*, stock market returns, time-varying stock market return volatility, sovereign debt spreads, and an exchange market pressure index – stems from the IMF data set discussed in Danninger, Tytell, Balakrishnan, and Elekdag (2009) and Cardarelli, Elekdag, and Lall (2009).

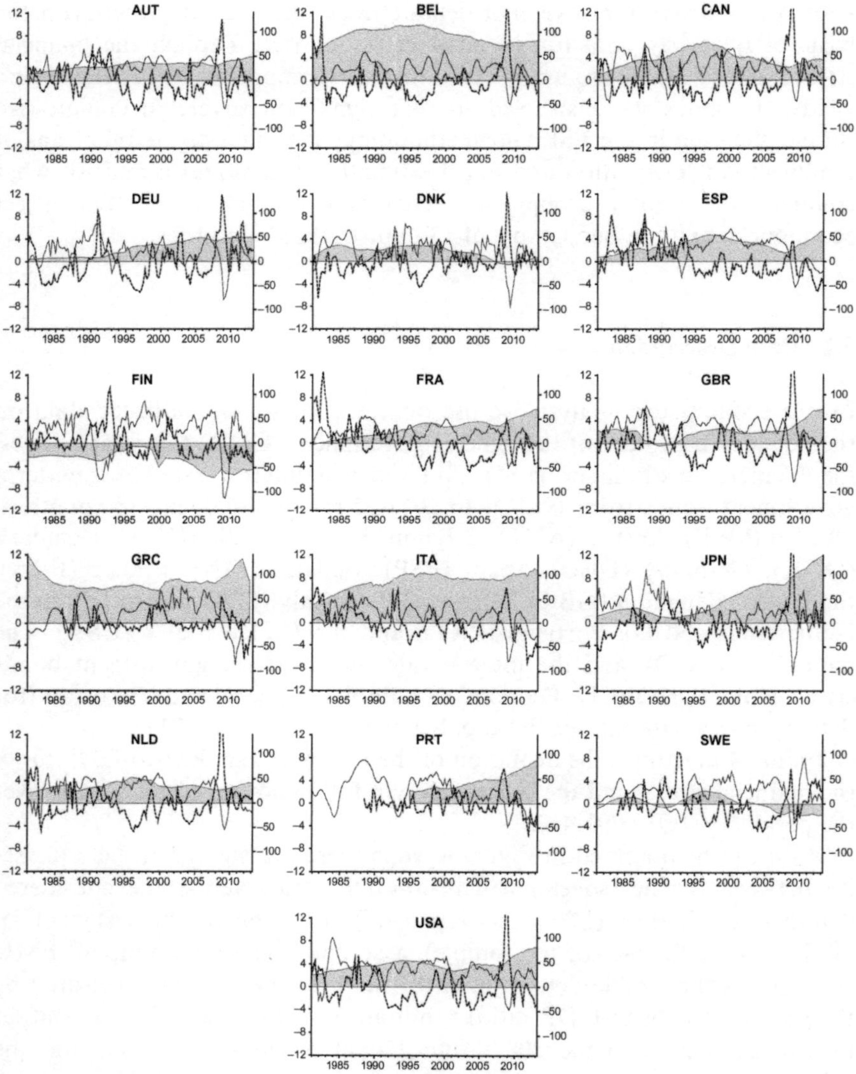

Figure 4: Net Sovereign Debt-to-GDP Ratio (Shaded Area, Left Axis), Year-to-Year GDP Growth Rate (Solid Line, Right Axis), and Financial Stress Index (Dashed Line, Right Axis) from 1981:1 to 2013:2. Seasonally Adjusted Quarterly Data. Source: OECD Economic Outlook Database, Eurostat, and IMF.

question of causality between these two variables can of course not be reduced to this simple construction, but has to be addressed by means of econometric methods, as it will be done below (see also Proaño et al., 2014).[30]

In general, concerning the dynamics and interaction of the FSI and the GDP growth, Figure 4 illustrates clearly that while the output contraction during the recent financial crisis was rather similar across all countries considered, the FSI reaction was, on the other hand, quite differentiated, with countries such as CAN, JPN, NLD, and USA soaring with their FSI about three times higher than the remaining countries. But, maybe with the exception of the United States, these were countries with little eminent default threat (see also the discussion in Proaño et al., 2014). These countries can be viewed as countries representing roughly the model variant 1 of Section 2.2.

At first sight, the sovereign leveraging does not seem to have generally triggered a transition to high-stress regimes with strong adverse macro feedback effects and eminent default threats. As to this nexus, the evolution of the sovereign debt-to-GDP ratios of Spain and the United Kingdom stand out, with an increase from a level of 20.4% in 2008Q3 to 63.5% in 2013Q2 of the former, and of 29.3% in 2008Q3 to 71.1% in 2012Q3 of the latter.[31] Yet, this dramatic increase in the debt-to-GDP ratio did not translate into a comparable reaction in the overall financial market stress – as the FSI in the United Kingdom increased to levels almost five times larger than in Spain at the height of the euro-area crisis in 2009 – nor to a similar reaction in GDP growth in the subsequent period. In this context an interesting case regards Italy, as one would expect its economic situation to be reflected by the model variant 1 or 2 discussed in the previous section. However, despite of the high level of the Italian debt-to-GDP ratio, the actual FSI in Italy did not increase significantly in the recent euro-area crisis, therefore not fully activating the adverse macroeconomic feedback mechanism previously discussed. Further, Sweden and Germany seem to belong more to the model variant 1 or 3 above, despite the significantly high levels of the FSI in the recent euro-area crisis. In contrast, in Portugal, a country that was close to sovereign default at some point, these adverse

[30] In contrast to the present study, Proaño et al. (2014) focus on the role of the sovereign debt-to-GDP as a transition variable determining the switching between two regimes, as well as the joint effect of this variable with the financial stress index in determining the switching between for regimes.

[31] Note that we consider here net sovereign debt, that is, sovereign debt held only by the public, because gross sovereign debt – which includes intra-governmental debt – may not have a direct impact on the economy.

macroeconomic feedback mechanisms seem to have been particularly active despite of the relatively low levels of the FSI.

So, there seem to be various types of nonlinearities at work in the different countries of our sample. In order to gain some first insights into the possibly nonlinear linkage between output growth, sovereign debt, and financial stress, in particular for subgroups of countries, we run first a battery of linear country-specific and dynamic panel regressions, which can be jointly represented through the following general specification:

$$y_{it} = \mu_i + \mathbf{x}_{it}\beta + \mathbf{w}_{it}\alpha + \varepsilon_{it}, \tag{11}$$

where $i = 1, \ldots, N$ is a country-index, $t = 1, \ldots, T$ is the time index, μ_i denotes a country-specific fixed effect, ε_{it} is an i.i.d. random disturbance with zero mean and a variance $\sigma^2_{\varepsilon i}$. y_{it} is the dependent variable (quarter-to-quarter real GDP growth), $\mathbf{x}_{it}$ is a vector of explanatory variables consisting of the main regressors y_{it-1}, b_{it-1}, f_{it-1}, that is, the lagged GDP growth rate, the government debt-to-GDP ratio, and the financial stress index, respectively, as well as the ex post real interest rate on long-term government bonds, as a control variable. Further, $\mathbf{w}_{it}$ is a vector of the main explanatory variables in their quadratic form, in its most general form given by

$$\mathbf{w}_{it} = \left(y^2_{it-1}, b^2_{it-1}, f^2_{it-1}\right).$$

Table 1 reports the estimation results of the most general specification where all quadratic terms are included in the set of regressors.[32] To start, it is interesting to note that the linear effect of debt-to-GDP ratio b_{t-1} on economic growth is statistically significant and negative only for a subset of countries, namely France, Greece, and Portugal, while for the remaining countries it is either statistically insignificant, or positive, as it is the case for Spain and Sweden. In contrast, the quadratic term b^2_{t-1} is negative and statistically significant only for Spain, which jointly with the first positive effect of b_{t-1}, seems to suggest that the – unexpectedly – positive effect of sovereign debt on GDP growth becomes smaller for larger values of b_{t-1}. By the same token, the positive and statistically significant coefficient of b^2_{t-1} in Greece suggests the negative effect of b_{t-1} on y_t decreases in absolute terms for larger values of b_{t-1}.

Further, concerning the effect of financial stress on GDP growth, our estimates deliver a much more uniform picture for the analyzed countries. Indeed, we find that the linear coefficient is negative for all countries and statistically significant for 9 out of the 13 countries analyzed, and that

[32] Additional regressions where the elements included in w_{it} were selectively included are available upon request.

Table 1: Country-Specific Least-Squares Regressions (Sample: 1981Q1–2013Q2)

	C	y_{t-1}	b_{t-1}	f_{t-1}	y^2_{t-1}	b^2_{t-1}	f^2_{t-1}	$\bar{R}^2$	DW-Stats
AUT	−0.345	0.113	0.069	−0.047*	0.123	−0.001	−0.016***	0.227	1.836
	(0.805)	(0.104)	(0.048)	(0.025)	(0.089)	(0.001)	(0.006)		
BEL	0.052	0.618***	0.001	−0.009	0.037	0.000	−0.001	0.479	1.594
	(1.508)	(0.096)	(0.033)	(0.018)	(0.085)	(0.000)	(0.003)		
CAN	−0.274	0.327***	0.023	−0.039	0.076	−0.000	−0.003	0.367	1.891
	(0.521)	(0.096)	(0.020)	(0.030)	(0.065)	(0.000)	(0.003)		
DEU	1.529***	−0.128	−0.042	−0.075**	0.113**	0.001	−0.021***	0.251	1.997
	(0.455)	(0.084)	(0.028)	(0.032)	(0.044)	(0.001)	(0.005)		
DNK	0.157	−0.285**	−0.003	−0.127***	0.006	0.001	−0.012*	0.218	2.053
	(0.210)	(0.115)	(0.024)	(0.046)	(0.054)	(0.001)	(0.007)		
ESP	−1.013*	0.310***	0.073***	0.057	−0.207***	−0.001***	−0.006	0.239	1.913
	(0.528)	(0.105)	(0.028)	(0.036)	(0.052)	(0.000)	(0.007)		
FIN	1.754***	0.083	0.049	−0.170***	−0.053**	0.000	0.018	0.239	1.985
	(0.560)	(0.091)	(0.026)	(0.065)	(0.024)	(0.000)	(0.011)		
FRA	1.392***	0.403***	−0.036***	−0.077***	−0.003	0.000	0.003	0.387	2.103
	(0.422)	(0.085)	(0.013)	(0.020)	(0.072)	(0.000)	(0.002)		
GBR	0.298	0.571***	0.006	−0.055**	−0.190**	−0.000	0.005	0.385	1.912
	(0.199)	(0.134)	(0.008)	(0.024)	(0.086)	(0.000)	(0.004)		
GRC	17.747	0.012	−0.337**	−0.152	−0.070	0.002**	−0.028	0.249	2.031
	(6.085)	(0.164)	(0.130)	(0.132)	(0.057)	(0.001)	(0.045)		
ITA	1.914	0.270***	−0.029	−0.007	−0.025	0.000	−0.024***	0.255	2.011
	(1.433)	(0.089)	(0.034)	(0.026)	(0.044)	(0.000)	(0.006)		
JPN	0.127	−0.037	−0.010	−0.052	0.082	0.000	−0.011*	0.073	2.043
	(0.533)	(0.124)	(0.013)	(0.047)	(0.063)	(0.000)	(0.007)		
NLD	0.735	−0.072	−0.020	−0.118***	0.053	0.000	−0.003	0.201	2.016
	(1.576)	(0.091)	(0.081)	(0.034)	(0.061)	(0.001)	(0.003)		
PRT	2.955**	0.032	−0.082*	−0.079	−0.062	0.001	−0.016	0.271	2.062
	(1.175)	(0.131)	(0.044)	(0.061)	(0.078)	(0.000)	(0.016)		
SWE	0.819	0.195**	0.012*	−0.079**	−0.044	−0.000	−0.006	0.296	1.945
	(0.238)	(0.093)	(0.007)	(0.033)	(0.042)	(0.000)	(0.006)		
USA	0.826	0.222*	−0.003	−0.078***	0.006	−0.000	0.000	0.270	2.017
	(0.905)	(0.126)	(0.031)	(0.025)	(0.080)	(0.000)	(0.003)		

Standard errors are in parenthesis.
***, **, and * denote the level of significance at 0.01%, 0.05%, and 0.1%, respectively.

the quadratic term f^2_{t-1} is also negative and statistically significant for Austria, Germany, Denmark, Italy, and Japan. This seems to corroborate – at least in a preliminary manner – the nonlinear effect of leveraging and financial stress on growth as discussed in the previous section of this chapter, for the model variants 1 and 3.[33]

Next we attempt some more general results from panel regressions. On the basis of the above preliminary least squares regressions, we estimate

[33] See also Brunnermeier and Sannikov (2014), for example.

dynamic panel regressions to exploit additionally the information along the cross-section dimension to obtain more robust results, as well as to identify potential differences between particular country subsamples. As subsamples we consider EMU and non-EMU countries, as well as Northern and Southern EMU countries. More specifically, we identify Austria, Belgium, Germany, Finland, France, and the Netherlands as "Northern" EMU countries, and Spain, Greece, Italy, and Portugal as "Southern" EMU countries.

Given the auto-regressive structure of the regression model given by Equation (11), we use the GMM estimator for dynamic panels proposed by Arellano and Bover (1995). Accordingly, in order to take care of the country-specific fixed effects in the dynamics panel structure, the variables are subject to a forward orthogonal deviation transformation, where each observation is subtracted by the mean of all future observations. This has the advantage of eliminating the fixed effects in a consistent manner while keeping the lags of the variables available as valid instruments. As dynamic instrumental variables, we use the first and second lags of the explanatory variables comprised in $\mathbf{x}_{it}$.

Table 2 reports our estimation results of these dynamic panel regressions. Our empirical findings can be summarized as follows: On the one hand, the coefficients of the lagged GDP growth rate are found to be statistically significant, of the expected sign and remarkably robust concerning their numerical value across all panels but the South EMU panel. Accordingly, GDP growth at date *t* depends positively on the GDP growth in the previous period. On the other hand, the coefficient of the debt-to-GDP ratio is found as negative and statistically significant not only in the panel of all countries considered, but also in the panel of all EMU countries. However, the validity of the instrument sets and regression estimates

Table 2: Dynamic Panel Regression Results (Sample: 1981Q1–2013Q2)

	y_{t-1}	b_{t-1}	f_{t-1}	r_{t-1}	b^2_{t-1}	f^2_{t-1}	*J*-Stat	*J*-Prob
All	0.239***	−0.004*	−0.075***	0.004	−0.000	−0.004***	522.291	0.000
	(0.021)	(0.002)	(0.006)	(0.006)	(0.000)	(0.001)		
EMU	0.327***	−0.004*	−0.052***	0.007	−0.000	−0.006***	477.800	0.000
	(0.019)	(0.002)	(0.007)	(0.006)	(0.000)	(0.001)		
Non-EMU	0.161***	0.002	−0.088***	0.005	−0.000	−0.002	386.598	0.369
	(0.020)	(0.002)	(0.005)	(0.005)	(0.000)	(0.001)		
North EMU	0.272***	−0.002	−0.068***	−0.001	−0.000	−0.002**	426.566	0.043
	(0.019)	(0.001)	(0.006)	(0.004)	(0.000)	(0.001)		
South EMU	0.226***	−0.002	−0.011**	−0.024***	−0.000***	−0.016***	321.283	0.501
	(0.009)	(0.002)	(0.005)	(0.003)	(0.000)	(0.001)		

Standard errors are in parenthesis.
***, **, and * denote the level of significance at 1%, 5%, and 10%, respectively.

is not corroborated by the *J*-statistics at standard significance levels, in contrast to the *J*-statistic associated with the dynamic panel regressions for the Non-EMU, North EMU, and South EMU subgroups.

This supports the differentiated analysis between these country subgroups and thus the validity of the estimates of the corresponding dynamic panel regressions, despite their reduced cross-sectional dimension. Focusing thus on these last three dynamic panel regressions, our estimates suggest that the linear effect of financial stress on GDP growth is negative and statistically significant for the three considered subgroups, being the linear effect largest in Non-EMU countries and smallest in the South EMU countries. This effect is however overturned by the significantly larger coefficient of the quadratic terms f_{t-1}^2 in the South EMU panel, which represents the countries more associated to the model variant 2 of the above section. This corroborates the notion that financial market stress may affect in a more nonlinear manner the Southern as well as the Northern EMU countries.

Next we use country-specific and panel threshold regressions of EMU and non-EMU countries, as well as of Northern and Southern EMU countries. Specifically, we consider the following dynamic threshold regression specification with the financial stress index not only as the threshold variable, but also as a regime-dependent regressor, that is,

$$\begin{aligned} y_{i,t} = {} & \alpha_y y_{i,t-1} + \alpha_r r_{i,t-1} + \alpha_b b_{i,t-1} + \beta_f^L f_{i,t-1} I\left(f_{i,t-1} \leq \gamma\right) \\ & + \beta_f^H f_{i,t-1} I\left(f_{i,t-1} > \gamma\right) + \delta I\left(f_{i,t-1} \leq \gamma\right) + \mu_i + \varepsilon_{i,t}, \end{aligned} \tag{12}$$

where $i = 1, \ldots, N$ denotes a country-index, $t = 1, \ldots, T$ the time index, μ_i a country-specific fixed effect, ε_{it} an i.i.d. country-specific random disturbance with zero mean and a variance $\sigma_{\varepsilon i}^2$, and $I(\cdot)$ is an indicator function which takes on the value of one if the condition in its argument holds and zero otherwise. Hence, the coefficients β^L and β^H represent the effect of $b_{i,t-1}$ on the dependent variable $y_{i,t}$ for $f_{i,t-1} \leq \gamma^f$ and $f_{i,t-1} > \gamma^f$, respectively. δ is the difference between the intercept in regime H, that is, μ_i, and the intercept in regime L, that is, $\mu_i + \delta$ (see Bick, 2010).

As previously mentioned, we estimate the regression model described by Equation (12) using both single-equation and panel estimation techniques. Concerning the single-equation regressions (where of course the index i is given and the information comes only from the variation in the time index t), we follow Caner and Hansen (2004) and employ their IV estimator to account for the possible endogeneity of the variables comprised in x_{it} and z_{it}. Further, also following Caner and Hansen (2004) the threshold value which determines the switch of the indicator function $I(\cdot)$ is identified as the value which minimizes the residual sum of squares.

Concerning the panel dimension of our analysis, despite the fact that, as recently pointed out by Baum, Checherita-Westphal, and Rother (2014), a full distribution theory for such type of models has not been developed so far,[34] we estimate the dynamic threshold panel regression described by Equation (12) following Kremer, Bick, and Nautz (2013), who extended the IV threshold estimation methodology developed in Caner and Hansen (2004) for the panel case using the data set of 13 countries spanning the same period (1981Q1–2013Q2) (see also Proaño et al., 2014).

Table 3 reports the estimation results for this specification, using the same country subgroups as in the previous regressions. As in the previous specification, despite the significant heterogeneity of the country-specific threshold values resulting from the single-equation regressions, the panel estimates of the different country subgroups are remarkably similar to each other with an average value of about 2.00. The parameter estimates for the lagged endogenous variable and for the interest rate are also broadly in line with the findings of the previous specifications.

The regime-independent estimate of the effect of the debt-to-GDP ratio on growth also reveals some interesting insights in the context of our previous finding that, at a given state of the financial markets, high indebtedness impairs growth only in the stand-alone countries of our sample and not in EMU countries. Yet, the results obtained in the present specification suggest that, overall, the debt-to-GDP ratio, here assumed to affect growth linearly and thus independently from its actual level, impairs growth more in the EMU countries, in particular the Northern EMU countries, than in the stand-alone countries.

Concerning the regime-dependent regressor in this equation, namely the FSI, our estimates suggest that the negative effect of the FSI on GDP growth is higher in absolute terms in the high financial stress regime than in the low financial stress regime in most countries considered. Comparing EMU and non-EMU countries reveals that, during times of low financial stress, the FSI has a more pronounced growth effect in the former group than in the latter. During times of high financial stress, the estimated coefficients are similar in both groups. Further, within the EMU we find similar growth effects of financial stress for both the Northern and Southern EMU countries for the low-stress regime. Yet, for the high-stress regime the growth effect of the FSI is rather pronounced in the Southern EMU countries. As expected, high financial stress seems to have had a strong effect on growth in these countries by triggering stronger adverse macro feedback effects.

In the context of the previous findings, these results imply that the FSI seems to be an important source of nonlinearities in its own relationship to

[34] The distribution theory developed in Hansen (1999) for threshold panels applies only for the case of non-dynamic panels.

Table 3: Country-Specific and Panel Dynamic Threshold GMM Estimation Results with the Financial Stress Index as the Threshold Variable and the Financial Stress Index as a Regime-Dependent Regressor

	γ	α_y	α_r	α_b	β_f^L	β_f^H	δ
Country-Specific Threshold Regressions							
Northern EMU countries							
AUT	1.35	0.200***	−0.006**	−0.063***	−0.051***	−0.310***	−0.921***
		(0.030)	(0.002)	(0.012)	(0.011)	(0.011)	(0.042)
BEL	3.60	0.594***	0.001	−0.006***	0.000	0.011	0.269
		(0.027)	(0.001)	(0.002)	(0.004)	(0.020)	(0.178)
DEU	−0.22	−0.092***	−0.012***	−0.164***	−0.120***	−0.254***	−0.543***
		(0.031)	(0.002)	(0.023)	(0.031)	(0.017)	(0.108)
FRA	1.97	0.366***	−0.015***	−0.016*	−0.077***	0.033**	0.639***
		(0.015)	(0.001)	(0.008)	(0.008)	(0.016)	(0.075)
NLD	1.12	−0.051	−0.001	−0.013	−0.108***	−0.216***	−0.667***
		(0.036)	(0.003)	(0.010)	(0.023)	(0.013)	(0.063)
Southern EMU countries							
ESP	0.22	0.129***	0.008***	−0.013	0.075***	0.046***	0.518***
		(0.043)	(0.002)	(0.012)	(0.025)	(0.016)	(0.075)
ITA	−0.65	0.452***	−0.002*	0.013**	−0.128***	−0.086***	−0.452***
		(0.028)	(0.001)	(0.007)	(0.013)	(0.012)	(0.043)
Non-EMU countries							
AUS	−0.43	−0.070*	0.019***	−0.056***	−0.052*	0.020	0.207***
		(0.036)	(0.003)	(0.006)	(0.026)	(0.013)	(0.053)
CAN	−0.13	0.438***	0.006***	−0.048***	−0.059***	−0.110***	−0.383***
		(0.032)	(0.002)	(0.007)	(0.021)	(0.016)	(0.072)
DNK	−0.30	−0.217***	0.016***	0.002	−0.155***	−0.272***	−0.561***
		(0.030)	(0.004)	(0.011)	(0.038)	(0.033)	(0.086)
GBR	0.27	0.354***	0.001	0.015**	0.049***	−0.069***	0.277***
		(0.019)	(0.001)	(0.008)	(0.015)	(0.010)	(0.045)
JPN	2.89	0.109***	−0.007***	0.021	0.006	−0.051	0.774***
		(0.028)	(0.001)	(0.018)	(0.012)	(0.056)	(0.221)
USA	1.58	0.271***	0.005**	0.032***	−0.009	−0.018	0.452***
		(0.024)	(0.002)	(0.005)	(0.009)	(0.015)	(0.061)
Panel threshold regressions							
All	1.86	0.253***	0.003	−0.001	−0.029***	−0.072**	0.138*
		(0.027)	(0.006)	(0.001)	(0.010)	(0.015)	(0.079)
EMU	1.84	0.310***	0.003	−0.004**	−0.085**	−0.070***	−0.226**
		(0.026)	(0.008)	(0.001)	(0.033)	(0.009)	(0.101)
Non-EMU	2.06	0.131***	0.007	0.000	−0.045***	−0.079***	0.288***
		(0.032)	(0.008)	(0.001)	(0.012)	(0.016)	(0.094)
North EMU	1.97	0.243***	0.006	−0.005***	−0.017*	−0.048**	0.270***
		(0.026)	(0.009)	(0.001)	(0.010)	(0.021)	(0.097)
South EMU	2.45	0.277***	−0.005*	−0.000	−0.026***	−0.203***	−0.794***
		(0.008)	(0.003)	(0.001)	(0.006)	(0.016)	(0.074)

Standard errors are in parenthesis.
***, **, and * denote the level of significance at 1%, 5%, and 10%, respectively.

economic activity. Since we control for the growth effect of sovereign debt, the nonlinear effects of the FSI on growth are independent of the sovereign debt-to-GDP ratio. This has important implications especially for the Southern EMU countries. Indeed, the estimation results of the last regression additionally suggest that much of the slowdown in economic growth over the recent years has been caused by high financial stress itself – and the possibly triggered macro feedback effects – and not directly by the increased level of sovereign debt.

So, as to our above three model variants of a transition to a high sovereign default risk countries it is not alone the increased level of sovereign leveraging, but rather the many feedback loops driving the financial stress, sovereign debt, and output, moving the country closer to default risk. Among them are important financial variables and macro feedback effects that make the destabilizing forces endogenous. But we should also note that similar mechanisms and feedback loops might work to move the economy out of the default risk trap. Yet, only with a more fully specified macro model which reveals the feedback variables and loops one can observe a variety of escape routes and one can make appropriate policy suggestions.

4. Conclusions

This chapter studied the macroeconomic consequences of a rise in the sovereign default risk and the overall financial market stress. To study these issues, we employed a theoretical model with two equilibria, one default risk equilibrium and one no-default equilibrium. We showed that such a framework is a useful modeling devise to understand default and non-default environments, and the switch between those two, as well as the role of macroeconomic amplification effects. As previously discussed, such model variants can also be solved when such amplifying macroeconomic feedback loops are operating in a finite decision horizon framework through the NMPC algorithm. We showed that this type of nonlinear macroeconomic models is useful to study recent financial turmoil episodes, such as the US financial and the EU sovereign debt crises. Indeed, it thus seems worthwhile to study earlier historical experiences on debt reduction policies – for example, the US post-WWII strategy to reduce its sovereign debt, Mexico's debt reduction after 1994, the Latin American debt of the 1990s, Argentinean debt reduction after 2001, and the debt reduction for African countries a decade ago – more extensively from the viewpoint of macroeconomic framework such as the one outlined in this chapter. Within such frameworks alternative economic policies can be studied which could allow the concerned economies to escape from the threat of sovereign default and move toward a more stable no-default macroeconomic environment.

As to the current regime, the euro area finds itself in a low-growth regime with financial stress potentially rising again, and thus monetary policy needs to be tailored toward this situation. In such regime, a general increase of the balance sheets of the Central Bank through Quantitative Easing may not be sufficient to get lending and economic activity again triggered. Specific credit policies are needed to aim at specific risk factors and specific bottlenecks. Liquidity mismatches resulting from such a regime will not disappear if interbank lending rates stay high in the near future. Moreover, the fragile situation of the balance sheets of households, firms, and the government may not get solved by extensive purchases of treasure bonds, such as the OMT program of the ECB suggests. If the financial system is still incapable to transmit the expansionary effects of such a general purchase of government bonds by the ECB to the private sector, more selective credit policies to affect specific credit spreads and funding cost and quantity measures to encourage credit flows to overcome credit bottlenecks might be needed. More research on specific risk factors and how to reduce their impact on economic activity appears to be advisable.

Acknowledgments

The research for this chapter was partly conducted while Willi Semmler was a visiting researcher at the European Central Bank (ECB), and Christian R. Proaño was a visiting researcher at the Deutsche Bundesbank. They would like to thank the ECB and the Deutsche Bundesbank for their hospitality and financial support, as well as Christian Schoder for helpful comments and suggestions. This chapter represents the authors' personal opinions and does not necessarily reflect the views of the ECB or the Deutsche Bundesbank.

References

Arellano, C. (2008). Default risk and income fluctuations in emerging economies. *American Economic Review*, *98*(3), 690–712.

Arellano, C., Maliar, L., Maliar, S., & Tsyrennikov, V. (2014). *Envelope condition method with an application to default risk models*. Unpublished manuscript, University of Minnesota.

Arellano, C., Mateos-Planas, X., & Rios-Rull, V. (2013). *Partial default*. Manuscript, University of Minnesota.

Arellano, M., & Bover, O. (1995). Another look at the instrumental variable estimation of error components models. *Journal of Econometrics*, *68*(1), 29–51.

Baum, A., Checherita-Westphal, C., & Rother, P. (2014). Debt and growth. New evidence for the euro area. *Journal of International Money and Finance*, *32*(February 2013), 809–821.

Baum, A., Poplawski-Ribeiro, M., & Weber, A. (2012, December). *Fiscal multipliers and the state of the economy*. Working Paper No. 12/286. International Monetary Fund.

Bick, A. (2010). Threshold effects of inflation on economic growth in developing countries. *Economics Letters*, *108*(2), 126–129.

Blanchard, O., Dell'Ariccia, G., & Mauro, P. (2013, April 15). *Rethinking macro policy II: Getting granular*. Staff Discussion Notes 13/3. International Monetary Fund.

Blanchard, O., & Leigh, D. (2013). *Growth forecast errors and fiscal multipliers*. IMF Study. Working Paper No. WP/13/1.

Bohn, H. (1998). The behavior of U.S. public debt and deficits. *The Quarterly Journal of Economics*, *113*(3), 949–963.

Bolton, P., & Jeanne, O. (2011). Sovereign default risk and bank fragility in financially integrated economies. *IMF Economic Review*, *59*, 162–194.

Brunnermeier, M. K., & Oehmke, M. (2012, September). *Bubbles, financial crises and systemic risk*. NBER Working Paper No. 18398.

Brunnermeier, M. K., & Sannikov, Y. (2014). A macroeconomic model with a financial sector. *American Economic Review*, *104*(2), 379–421.

Buiter, W. (2010). *Global economic view, sovereign debt problem in advanced industrial countries*. Citibank. Retrieved from http://www.finfacts.ie/biz10/Buiter-Sovereign-Debt-May052010.pdf. Accessed on April 26, 2010.

Caner, M., & Hansen, B. E. (2004). Instrumental variable estimation of a threshold model. *Econometric Theory*, *20*, 813–843.

Cardarelli, R., Elekdag, S., & Lall, S. (2009). *Financial stress, downturns, and recoveries*. Working Paper No. 09/100. International Monetary Fund, Washington, DC.

Charpe, M., Flaschel, P., Krolzig, H.-M. Proaño, C. R., Semmler, W., & Tavani, D. (2015, April). Credit-driven investment, labor market heterogeneity and macroeconomic dynamics. *Journal of Economic Interaction and Coordination*, *10*(1), 63–181.

Chiarella, C., Flaschel, P., & Semmler, W. (2014). *Reconstructing Keynesian economics, volume 3:* Macroeconomic activity, banking and financial market. London: Routledge.

Coimbra, N. (2014). *Sovereigns at risk: A dynamic model of sovereign debt and banking leverage*. Mimeo, London Business School.

Correia, S., De Fiore, F., Teles, P., & Tristani, O. (2013). *Credit spreads and the zero bound on interest rates*. Manuscript, ECB.

Corsetti, G., Meier, A., & Müller, G. (2012). *What determines government spending multipliers*? IMF Working Papers No. 12/150. International Monetary Fund.

Danninger, S., Tytell, I., Balakrishnan, R., & Elekdag, S. (2009). *The transmission of financial stress from advanced to emerging economies*. IMF Working Papers No. 09/133. International Monetary Fund, Washington, DC.

De Grauwe, P. (2012). The governance of a fragile Eurozone. *Australian Economic Review*, *45*(3), 255–268.

De Grauwe, P., & Ji, Y. (2012). Self-fulfilling crises in the Eurozone: An empirical test. *Journal of International Money and Finance*, *34*, 15–36.

De Grauwe, P., & Macchiarelli, C. (2013). *Animal spirits and credit cycles*. CESIFO Working Paper No. 4480. CESIFO.

Eggertsson, G. B., & Krugman, P. (2011). *Debt, deleveraging, and the liquidity trap: A Fisher-Minsky-Koo approach*. Retrieved from http://www.frbsf.org/economics/conferences/1102/PKGE_Feb14.pdf

Ernst, E., & Semmler, W. (2010). Global dynamics in a model with search and matching in labor and capital markets. *Journal of Economic Dynamics and Control*, *34*(9), 1651–1679.

Farmer, R. E. A., Waggoner, D. F., & Zha, T. (2009). Understanding Markov-switching rational expectations models. *Journal of Economic Theory*, *144*, 1849–1867.

Galí, J., Vallés, J., & López-Salido, J. D. (2007). Understanding the effects of government spending on consumption. *Journal of the European Economic Association*, *5*(1), 227–270.

Gavin, W., Keen, K., Richter, A., & Throckmorton, N. (2013). *Global dynamics at the zero lower bound*. Working Paper No. 2013-007A. Research Division, Federal Reserve Bank of St. Louis, St. Louis, MO.

Gerali, A., Neri, S., Sessa, L., & Signoretti, F. M. (2010). Credit and banking in a DSGE model of the euro area. *Journal of Money, Credit and Banking*, *42*(1), 107–141.

Gilchrist, S., & Zakrajsek, E. (2012). Credit spreads and business cycle fluctuations. *American Economic Review*, *102*, 1692–1720.

Grüne, L., & Pannek, J. (2011). *Nonlinear model predictive control*. New York, NY: Springer.

Grüne, L., & Semmler, W. (2004). *Solving asset pricing models with stochastic dynamic programming*. CEM Working Paper No. 54. Bielefeld University, Germany.

Grüne, L., Semmler, W., & Stieler, M. (2013). *Using nonlinear model predictive control for dynamic decision problems in economics*. SSRN. Retrieved from ssrn.com/sol3/Delivery.cfm?abstractid=2242339

Hansen, B. E. (1999). Threshold effects in non-dynamic panels: Estimation, testing, and inference. *Journal of Econometrics*, *93*, 345–368.

Kremer, S., Bick, A., & Nautz, D. (2013). Inflation and growth: New evidence from a dynamic panel threshold analysis. *Empirical Economics*, *44*(2), 861–878.

Lorenzoni, G., & Werning, I. (2013, July). *Slow moving debt crises*. National Bureau of Economic Research Working Paper No. 19228. National Bureau of Economic Research.

Mittnik, S., & Semmler, W. (2012). Regime dependence of the multiplier. *Journal of Economic Behavior and Organization*, *83*(3), 502–522.

Mittnik, S., & Semmler, W. (2013). The real consequences of financial stress. *Journal of Economic Dynamics and Control*, *37*(8), 1479–1499.

Proaño, C. R., Schoder, C., & Semmler, W. (2014). Financial stress, sovereign debt and economic activity in industrialized countries: Evidence from dynamic threshold regressions. *Journal of International Money and Finance*, *45*, 17–37.

Reinhart, C. M., & Trebesch, C. (2014). *A distant mirror of debt, default, and relief.* NBER Working Paper No. 20577.

Roch, F., & Uhlig, H. (2013). *The dynamics of sovereign debt crises and bailouts.* Unpublished Manuscript. University of Chicago, CentER, NBER, CERP.

Schleer, F., & Semmler, W. (2013). *Financial sector-output dynamics in the euro area: Non-linearities reconsidered.* ZEW Discussion Papers 13-068. Mannheim, Germany.

Semmler, W., & Gevorkyan, A. (2014). *Macroeconomic variables and the sovereign risk premia in EMU, EU and standalone countries.* Mimeo. The New School of Social Research, New York, NY.

Stein, J. L. (2012). *Stochastic optimal control and the US financial crisis.* New York, NY: Springer Publishing House.

Tobin, J. (1963). An essay on the principles of debt management. In Fiscal and debt management policies. Prepared for the Commission on Money and Credit. Englewood Cliffs, NJ: Prentice Hall. (Reprinted in Tobin, J. (1971). *Essays in economics* (Vol. 1). Amsterdam: North-Holland).

Tobin, J. (1987). Unemployment, interest, deficit and money. In P. M. Jackson (Ed.), *Policies for prosperity: Essays in a Keynesian mode.* Cambridge, MA: MIT Press.

Uhlig, H. (2014). *Sovereign default risk and banks in a monetary union.* Manuscript, University of Chicago, NBER and CEPR.

Appendix: Numerical Procedure

For the numerical solution of the optimal control problem we do not apply here the dynamic programming (DP) approach as in Ernst and Semmler (2010). Though DP method has the advantage that a global solution to the optimal control problem can be found, by first computing an approximation to the optimal value V and then the optimal control, and its time path, is computed from V. For a detailed description of the specifics of the DP algorithm we are using we refer to Grüne and Semmler (2004). The main disadvantage of DP, however, is that its numerical effort typically grows exponentially with the dimension of the state variable. Hence, even for moderate state dimensions it may be impossible to compute a solution with reasonable accuracy.[35]

A remedy to this problem can be obtained by using NMPC. Instead of computing the optimal value function for all possible initial states, NMPC only computes single (approximate) optimal trajectories. In order to describe the method, let us abstractly write the optimal decision problem as

$$\text{maximize} \quad \int_0^{\infty} e^{-\rho t} \ell(x(t), u(t)) \mathrm{d}t,$$

where $x(t)$ satisfies $\dot{x}(t) = f(x(t), u(t))$, $x(0) = x_0$ and the maximization takes place over a set of admissible control functions. By discretizing this problem in time, we obtain an approximate discrete time problem of the form

$$\text{maximize} \quad \sum_{i=0}^{\infty} \beta^i \ell(x_i, u_i), \tag{A.1}$$

where the maximization is now performed over a sequence u_i of control values and the sequence x_i satisfies $x_{i+1} = \Phi(h, x_i, u_i)$. Here $h > 0$ is the discretization time step, $\beta = e^{-\rho h}$ and Φ is a numerical scheme approximating the solution of $\dot{x}(t) = f(x(t), u(t))$ on the time interval $[ih, (i+1)h]$. For details and references in which the error of this discretization is analyzed we refer to Grüne and Semmler (2004).

[35] Another global algorithm that works with gridding and computation of the value function and computation of the decision variables at each grid point, is used in Gavin et al. (2013), where a New Keynesian model is solved globally. They point out quite different solutions far from the steady state as compared to close to the steady state. Thus, they also show that nonlinearities matter. Yet for their algorithm it also holds that there is a curse of dimension.

The idea of NMPC now lies in replacing the maximization of the infinite horizon functional (A.1) by the iterative maximization of finite horizon functionals

$$\text{maximize} \sum_{k=0}^{N} \beta^i \ell(x_{k,i}, u_{k,i}) \tag{A.2}$$

for a truncated finite horizon $N \in \mathbb{N}$ with $x_{k+1,i} = \Phi(h, x_{k,i}, u_{k,i})$ and the index i indicates the number of the iteration (cf. the algorithm below). Note that neither β nor ℓ nor Φ changes when passing from Equations (A.1) to (A.2), only the optimization horizon is truncated.

Problems of type (A.2) can be efficiently solved numerically by converting them into a static nonlinear program and solving them by efficient NLP solvers (see Grüne & Pannek, 2011). In our simulations, we have used a discounted variant of the MATLAB routine nmpc.m available from www.nmpc-book.com, which uses MATLAB's fmincon NLP solver in order to solve the resulting static optimization problem.

Given an initial value x_0, an approximate solution of (A.1) can now be obtained by iteratively solving (A.2) as follows:

(1) for $i = 1, 2, 3, \ldots$
(2) solve (2) with initial value $x_{0,i} := x_i$ and denote the resulting optimal control sequence by $u^*_{k,i}$
(3) set $u_i := u^*_{0,i}$ and $x_{i+1} := \Phi(h, x_i, u_i)$
(4) end of for-loop

This algorithm yields an infinite trajectory x_i, $i = 1, 2, 3, \ldots$ whose control sequence u_i consists of all the first elements $u^*_{0,i}$ of the optimal control sequences for the finite horizon subproblems (A.2).

Under appropriate assumptions on the problem, it can be shown that the solution (x_i, u_i) (which depends on the choice of N in (A.2)) converges to the optimal solution of (A.1) as $N \to \infty$. The main requirement in these assumptions is the existence of an optimal equilibrium for the infinite horizon problem (A.1). If this equilibrium is known, it can be used as an additional constraint in (A.2), in order to improve the convergence properties.

However, recent results have shown that without a priori knowledge of this equilibrium this convergence can also be ensured, and this is the approach we use in the computations in this chapter. It should be noted that the references just cited treat averaged instead of discounted infinite horizon problems. However, we conjecture that the main proofs carry over to the discounted case details which will be addressed in future research. In any case, the solution generated by NMPC will always provide a lower bound for the true optimal solution. The procedure also allows for irregular impacts on the dynamics of the state variables and regime switches.[36]

[36] Note that in DSGE models, regime switches are also perceived as something likely to occur, which some literature has started to explore (see Farmer et al., 2009).

Chapter 7

Actual versus Perceived Taylor Rules: How Predictable Is the European Central Bank?

Nikolay Markov

Pictet Asset Management, Route des Acacias 60, CH-1211 Geneva 73, Switzerland, e-mail: nmarkov@pictet.com

Abstract

This chapter investigates the predictability of the European monetary policy through the eyes of the professional forecasters from a large investment bank. The analysis is based on forward-looking Actual and Perceived Taylor Rules for the European Central Bank which are estimated in real-time using a newly constructed database for the period April 2000–November 2009. The former policy rule is based on the actual refi rate set by the Governing Council, while the latter is estimated for the bank's economists using their main point forecast for the upcoming refi rate decision as a dependent variable. The empirical evidence shows that the pattern of the refi rate is broadly well predicted by the professional forecasters even though the latter have foreseen more accurately the increases rather than the policy rate cuts. Second, the results point to an increasing responsiveness of the ECB to macroeconomic fundamentals along the forecast horizon. Third, the rolling window regressions suggest that the estimated coefficients have changed after the bankruptcy of Lehman Brothers in October 2008; the ECB has responded less strongly to macroeconomic fundamentals and the degree of policy inertia has decreased. A sensitivity analysis shows that the baseline results are robust to applying a recursive window methodology and some of the findings are qualitatively unaltered from using Consensus Economics forecasts in the regressions.

Keywords: European Central Bank, monetary policy predictability, policy reaction function, real-time forecasts, financial crisis

JEL Classifications: C26, E52, E58

International Symposia in Economic Theory and Econometrics, Vol. 24
William A. Barnett and Fredj Jawadi (Editors)

ISSN: 1571-0386/doi: 10.1108/S1571-038620150000024019

1. Introduction

It has often been argued in the recent monetary economics literature that modern Central Banks follow a Taylor Rule essentially as a guiding principle for the implementation of their monetary policy strategy rather than as a strict rule of thumb. In a forward-looking environment, monetary policy is mainly considered as the art of managing the expectations of private agents, as has well emphasized Michael Woodford (2003). In the same spirit, the President of the Governing Council of the European Central Bank (ECB), Jean-Claude Trichet, has defined the monetary policy strategy during a press conference on August 31, 2006: *"Our concept is very simple: we do what -in our opinion- is necessary to counter the inflationary risks that we see, to deliver price stability over the medium term and to be credible in the delivery of price stability [...] I do not want to qualify in any other manner what we will do in the future, because, once again, we will do what we have to do in order to deliver price stability, be credible in the delivery of price stability over the medium term and continue anchoring inflationary expectations."*

The previous statement points out that the ECB's strategy is based on the firm commitment to deliver price stability in the policy-relevant medium to long-term horizons within a flexible monetary policy framework.[1] In this perspective, the European monetary policy can be characterized as a constrained discretion framework which features the absence of precommitment to future policy decisions. Thus, while being fully transparent about the inflation objective, the Governing Council remains silent on the future orientation of monetary policy. Hence, with regard to the latter its communication with the relevant economic agents breaks down. This limited procedural transparency of the Central Bank might hamper the predictability of the future monetary policy stance which would adversely affect the credibility of the ECB.[2] De Haan, Amtenbrink, and Waller (2004) point out that the ECB does not seem to be perceived as transparent and credible based on a survey they have conducted among professional

[1] The Governing Council has defined price stability as a yearly rate of inflation below 2%. More precisely, members of the Council have declared that their inflation objective corresponds to an inflation rate that is below but close to 2%. The latter embodies inflationary expectations remaining in the range of 1.7–1.9% over the policy-relevant horizon. The ECB has also clarified that the medium term horizon corresponds to a period of approximately 2 years.

[2] For an extensive treatment of the relation between Central Bank transparency, communication and credibility one can refer to Blinder (2000), Blinder, Hildebrand, Lipton, and Wyplosz (2001), Blinder, Ehrmann, Fratzscher, de Haan, and Jansen (2008), Demertzis and Hallett (2007), Geraats (2007, 2008, 2009), and Woodford (2005).

economists in the first years of the common monetary policy. However, the policy statement of Mr. Trichet emphasizes the importance of being credible in order to shape the expectations of economic agents in line with the price stability goal of the ECB. An anchoring of the private sector expectations with those of the Central Bank reduces the overall macroeconomic uncertainty and enhances the predictability of monetary policy in the medium and longer terms. The alignment of expectations improves monetary policy effectiveness and fosters a low inflation credibility in the ECB. This strategy can be implemented by a transparent Central Bank that features excellent communication skills. In such a transparency enhanced framework the ECB could achieve a better anchoring of inflation expectations, thereby contributing to sustainable growth and employment creation in the medium to long terms. Monetary policy is hence more effective at stabilizing key macroeconomic aggregates.

Given that, on the one hand the ECB is fully committed to the delivery of price stability, while on the other it is never pre-committed to its future policy decisions, it is important to analyze the implications of the current monetary policy framework for the predictability of the European monetary policy stance. Most of the previous literature has studied this issue on the basis of the predictability of the money market interest rates derived from futures contracts, as for instance in Kuttner (2001) and in Ross (2002). The latter have found that future contracts provide broadly accurate predictions of the money market interest rates the Central Banks seek to influence. Swansson (2006) has found that an improvement of the Federal Reserve transparency has gradually lead to more accurate private sector forecasts of the fed funds since the 1990s. Rosa and Verga (2007) argue that the forecast accuracy of the forthcoming refi rate based on the ECB communication is similar to the market-based expectations for the main policy rate. Gerlach (2007) points out that the changes in the ECB's refi rate can be explained by subjective measures of the economic outlook based on the monthly bulletin of the Central Bank along with the growth rate of M3 and the nominal effective exchange rate. Conversely, the inflation rate and the output gap do not seem to play a role in the ECB's interest rate setting. More recently, using a new approach Hamilton, Pruitt, and Borger (2009) have specified a market-perceived monetary policy rule to measure how market participants understand the Federal Reserve policy rule using macroeconomic news at a monthly frequency. Their model relates the change in the forecast of the future fed funds to a change in the forecasts of macroeconomic variables through a perceived Taylor Rule. Within this framework, the authors find that the market participants indeed extract information from macroeconomic news in order to predict the future fed funds. Their findings also point out that the estimated policy rule has changed over time. Sauer and Sturm (2003) have estimated Taylor Rules for the ECB and have found that the Central Bank implements an inflation destabilizing policy for inflation when using a backward-looking specification; however, its policy is inflation stabilizing when including forward-looking variables in the policy rule. Along the same lines, Gorter, Jacobs, and de Haan (2008) show that the ECB responds to the expectations of inflation and real GDP growth using Consensus Economics Forecasts in real-time. The authors also point out that the estimates from a contemporaneous Taylor Rule do not imply an inflation-stabilizing policy of the Central Bank because of the lack of a forward-looking nature of the variables. Therefore, one should prefer a specification with expectations data in order to more properly model the preemptive behavior of Central Banks.

Consistently with this new line of research, this chapter contributes to the literature to the extent that it adopts an alternative approach to the analysis of monetary policy predictability. In contrast with the previous methodologies, I introduce a direct measure of the ECB's key policy rate point forecasts performed by the professional forecasters of a large investment bank. Thus, I examine whether the relevant market participants have accurately predicted the main policy rate of the Central Bank before each meeting of the Governing Council. An alignment between the private forecasts of the policy rate with the actual interest rate would point out that the Central Bank has used a similar information set on macroeconomic fundamentals when setting the refi rate as the professional forecasters. In that perspective, Berger, Ehrmann, and Fratzscher (2009) analyze the forecast accuracy of the ECB's main interest rate using the Reuters' poll of economic forecasters over the period September 2000–January 2005. Within a panel approach, the researchers show evidence in favor of an important degree of forecast heterogeneity which they explain by geographic factors, information clustering in important financial areas and country-specific macroeconomic variables. Finally, Boeckx (2011) uses monthly interpolated data from the quarterly ECB's Survey of Professional Forecasters (SPF) to estimate a policy reaction function for the ECB using inflation and real output growth forecasts within a discrete choice approach. He finds that the predictions from an ordered probit model are in general in line with the observed policy rate and that the Central Bank has responded less strongly to the economic forecasts since the height of the financial crisis in October 2008. However, a comparison of the results obtained from the probit model with the survey information from the Reuters' poll of forecasters points to some misalignments in the predictions. In contrast with the previous approaches, I assume that close to the monetary policy meetings, the market participants and the Central Bank should have broadly similar views on inflation and on the economic outlook, which are fostered by the economic transparency of the ECB and its desire to align the private sector expectations with its macroeconomic forecasts.

In order to investigate the predictability of the key policy rate, I estimate a forward-looking specification of the Taylor Rule for the ECB, as well as a perceived Taylor Rule for the investment bank professional forecasters. As a dependent variable for the Actual Taylor Rule, I use the ECB's refi rate set on the corresponding monetary policy meeting, while the Perceived Taylor Rule is based on the professional point forecasts of the refi rate for the upcoming meeting. Any difference in the estimated coefficients or in the implied predictions of the policy rules might point to a limited predictability of the monetary policy stance. Such a finding could hinder the anchoring of private agents' expectations with the Central Bank's objective and would impair the effectiveness of monetary policy. Modeling private agents' perceptions of the future policy stance is particularly valuable for the appropriate design of monetary policy, as pointed out by Van der Cruijsen and Eijffinger (2008) in a survey they have conducted on the perceived transparency of the ECB among the Dutch households. The researchers emphasize that the perceived transparency is more important than the actual one as the former permits to ensure a public support for the Central Bank. The authors show that the transparency perceptions can be further enhanced by improving the public knowledge about the Central Bank and increasing its degree of procedural and operational transparency. However, the ECB has an incentive to highlight its transparency strengths and not to disclose its weaknesses in order to foster pubic trust in the monetary institution.

The empirical results first suggest that the ECB's monetary policy is broadly well predicted by the professional forecasters within the estimated linear policy rules. However, the economists have foreseen more accurately the policy rate hikes than the interest rate cuts. There is also evidence for increasing Central Bank's reaction to inflation and output growth expectations along the forecast horizon. The evidence from the rolling and recursive window regressions indicates that there are some gaps between the actual and perceived point estimates over time, in particular since the height of the financial crisis in 2008. Finally, the results point out that the ECB has responded less strongly to key macroeconomic fundamentals and has adjusted faster the refi rate to the desired target level after the bankruptcy of Lehman Brothers. The time dummies show that the broadening of the financial crisis has exerted an important negative and significant effect on the estimated policy rules. Thereby, the evidence reveals that the ECB might have switched to a new monetary policy regime that occurs in periods of deep financial and economic slump.

The structure of the chapter is the following. Section 2 presents the theoretical framework, while the data and methodology used are outlined in Section 3. Section 4 contains the linear model estimations of the Actual and Perceived Taylor Rules, while the rolling window regressions are performed in Section 5. Section 6 presents the estimation results of the policy rules with some relevant time dummies and Section 7 conducts a sensitivity analysis of the baseline results. The final section provides some concluding remarks on the main empirical findings of the chapter.

2. Theoretical Framework

Following most of the recent literature, I specify a linear forward-looking policy reaction function.[3] This approach can be justified by the long and variable lags that are necessary for monetary policy to affect real economic activity. As in this perspective monetary policy becomes the art of managing the expectations of economic agents, the Central Bank is concerned about the predictability and credibility of its strategy. I assume that at the forthcoming monetary policy meeting, occurring in period $t+1$, the Central Bank sets the main interest rate based on the following Taylor Rule specification:

$$\bar{i}_{t+1} = r^* + \pi^* + \beta_\pi E_t\{\pi_{t+k} - \pi^* | \Omega_t\} + \beta_y E_t\{y_{t+k} - y^* | \Omega_t\} + \eta_{t+1}, \qquad (1)$$

where $\bar{i}_{t+1}$ denotes the Central Bank's target for the policy interest rate in period $t+1$, r^* and π^* are the equilibrium real interest rate and the inflation objective, respectively. $E_t\{\pi_{t+k} - \pi^* | \Omega_t\}$ and $E_t\{y_{t+k} - y^* | \Omega_t\}$ are the inflation and real output growth expectations, respectively, made in period t for a horizon $t+k$, in deviation from the inflation objective π^* and the trend real output growth rate y^*. Ω_t denotes the available information set in period t and η_{t+1} is a stochastic disturbance term.[4] Notice that this specification of the Taylor Rule is in line with the speed limit policy recommended by Walsh (2003). The latter has shown that a Central Bank that responds to the change in the output gap rather than to its level can deliver the optimal pre-commitment policy outcome. This policy is also welfare improving compared to inflation targeting if the inflation process is forward-looking. I also introduce interest rate smoothing in the specification to account for the fact that usually Central Banks adjust gradually their policy rate to

[3] The theoretical specification is based on Gorter et al. (2008), Clarida, Galí, and Gertler (1998, 1999, 2000) and Woodford (2001). This policy rule differs from the original Taylor Rule (1993) in that the former is forward-looking and the Central Bank responds to the growth rate of real GDP and not to the output gap.

[4] In the empirical part of the chapter, I use different forecast horizons in the estimation of the policy rules to determine to what extent the responsiveness of the Central Bank to macroeconomic fundamentals is sensitive to the measures of expectations and how it changes along the forecast horizon.

the desired level in order to avoid excess volatility in financial markets. The partial adjustment equation that accounts for this practice is the following:

$$i_{t+1} = \rho i_t + (1-\rho)\bar{i}_{t+1} + \xi_{t+1}, \tag{2}$$

where i_{t+1} is the observed interest rate in period $t+1$, ρ is the interest rate smoothing parameter, and ξ_{t+1} is a stochastic disturbance. This equation points out that the Central Bank implements a fraction $(1-\rho)$ of the desired policy rate target at each meeting of the policy committee. Combining Equations (1) and (2) yields the final specification to be estimated:

$$i_{t+1} = \rho i_t + (1-\rho)\left[\alpha + \beta_\pi E_t\{\pi_{t+k}|\Omega_t\} + \beta_y E_t\{y_{t+k}|\Omega_t\}\right] + \epsilon_{t+1}, \tag{3}$$

where $\alpha = r^* + \pi^*(1-\beta_\pi) - y^*\beta_y$.

Based on Equation (3) I estimate an Actual Taylor Rule for which the dependent variable is the observed refi rate as set at the policy meeting in period $t+1$:

$$i_{t+1} = \rho i_t + (1-\rho)\left[\alpha + \beta_\pi E_t\{\pi_{t+k}|\Omega_t\} + \beta_y E_t\{y_{t+k}|\Omega_t\}\right] + \epsilon_{1t+1}. \tag{4}$$

I also estimate a Perceived Taylor Rule which is based on the professional point forecast of the ECB's refi rate to be set at the forthcoming meeting of the policy committee performed by the economists of the investment bank one week ahead:

$$E_t\{i_{t+1}\} = \rho i_t + (1-\rho)\left[\alpha + \beta_\pi E_t\{\pi_{t+k}|\Omega_t\} + \beta_y E_t\{y_{t+k}|\Omega_t\}\right] + \epsilon_{2t}. \tag{5}$$

In the specification of the Taylor Rules, I have assumed that both the Central Bank and the market participants share the same information set about macroeconomic fundamentals one week ahead of the Governing Council meetings. This is a reasonable assumption given that the ECB Council often refers to the inflation and real GDP growth forecasts of market participants when explaining monetary policy decisions during the press conferences. On a regular basis, the Council compares the ECB's staff macroeconomic projections with the forecasts performed by the OECD, the IMF, the European Commission, and Consensus Economics. In addition, the Central Bank conducts its own survey of inflation and real output growth expectations among a wide range of professional forecasters in the euro zone at a quarterly frequency (the ECB SPF). Using all macroeconomic projections from different agencies and surveys, the ECB often highlights the fact that the forecasts are broadly well aligned. This evidence brings further support to the decisions taken on the main refinancing operations rate (the refi rate) of the ECB and should enhance their predictability. The current practice of the ECB points to a high level of economic transparency of the Central Bank even though the economic forecasts should be performed at the frequency of the Governing Council meetings. This practice would foster the predictability of the ECB's interest rate decisions by the relevant market participants. Another possibility would be to reduce the frequency of the monetary policy decisions and turn to quarterly policy meetings for instance.

3. Data and Methodology

The aim of this chapter is to assess the predictability of the ECB's main policy rate (the refi rate) by the professional forecasters of a large investment bank before each meeting of the Governing Council. This analysis is important as it will bring new light on determining whether the policy strategy of the Central Bank is well understood by the relevant economic agents and to what extent the monetary policy stance is accurately predicted in a real-time setting. While this issue is crucial for the communication strategy and transparency of the ECB with the markets, collecting data that are available to the market participants in real-time and at the frequency of the meetings of the monetary policy committee is a particularly difficult and challenging task. After a long and comprehensive exploration of numerous relevant data, I have collected the macroeconomic projections of a large investment bank that are available on a weekly frequency and in real-time. Based on these data, I have constructed a database that contains the real-time point forecasts of the refi rate for the upcoming policy meeting, inflation, and real GDP growth for the euro area as reported by the economists of the bank in their weekly economic research publications.[5] The macroeconomic forecasts are performed for the current quarter and the quarter ahead, as well as for the current year and the year ahead. This framework is particularly well suited for assessing the predictability of the European monetary policy stance based on the Actual and Perceived Taylor Rules derived in the previous section. Since there are no forecasts of the output gap performed at the frequency of the Governing Council meetings we use the projections of real GDP growth in the regressions. Orphanides and van Norden (2002) have highlighted the important revisions in the output gap

[5] I have built-up the database from their weekly economic reports made in general one week before the upcoming monetary policy meeting of the ECB. The forecasts are provided in real-time and thus are not subject to the Orphanides' critique (2001). The latter has shown that one should use real-time data for actual policy-making because revised data could yield misleading outcomes. Further evidence on the use of real-time rather than revised data is provided in Molodtsova, Nikolsko-Rzhevskyy, and Papell (2008).

estimates which render the use of real-time output gap forecasts unreliable. According to the authors the main problem lies in the end-of-period estimates of potential output which are not completely trustworthy with the methods applied to extract potential output, and hence could lead to mistaken policy recommendations. This is unlikely to be the case for the real GDP growth forecasts used in this chapter which are not revised.

The methodology is also in line with the approach adopted in Berger, Ehrmann and Fratzscher (2009) and Boeckx (2011) who have analyzed the forecast accuracy of the ECB's refi rate. In addition, Coibion and Gorodnichenko (2011) have recently shown that the Federal Reserve has responded to the inflation and output growth forecasts from the Greenbook data set they have used in estimating the monetary policy rules at the frequency of the FOMC meetings.

As pointed out previously, the investment bank's economists report the most likely point forecast for the refi rate set by the ECB Governing Council at the upcoming monetary policy meeting. The forecasts are usually made in the week before the corresponding policy decision and are based on the economists' projections of key macroeconomic variables for the euro area. The database spans the period from April 2000 until November 2009. The frequency of the observations corresponds to the meetings of the Governing Council of the ECB which are in general monthly.[6] A detailed description of the variables used is provided in Table A.1. Table A.2 reports some summary statistics of the series used in the estimations. At a first look at the table one can see that the average of the inflation expectations of the economists for the year ahead is 1.807% which is fully in line with the inflation objective of the ECB. This result is corroborated by the consensus average inflation forecast which is 1.814% for the year ahead. This evidence suggests that the Central Bank has been successful at anchoring the inflation expectations of the market participants. Data on the key policy interest rate are taken from the official website of the ECB. Figure 1 displays the timing of the model.

Figure 2 compares the actual refi rate set by the ECB with the refi rate point forecast from the economists of the investment bank before the

[6] The Governing Council has taken monetary policy decisions twice a month until October 2001. The estimation results of the policy rules with a dummy variable for the period when the Council has met more than once within a month are presented in the appendix. It is also important to emphasize that the frequency of the monetary policy meetings reflects the time period that is required to assess the monetary policy stance and is not necessarily associated with a change in the underlying monetary policy rule. Moreover, Berger et al. (2009) do not find evidence that the number of meetings of the Governing Council has altered the forecast accuracy of the refi rate.

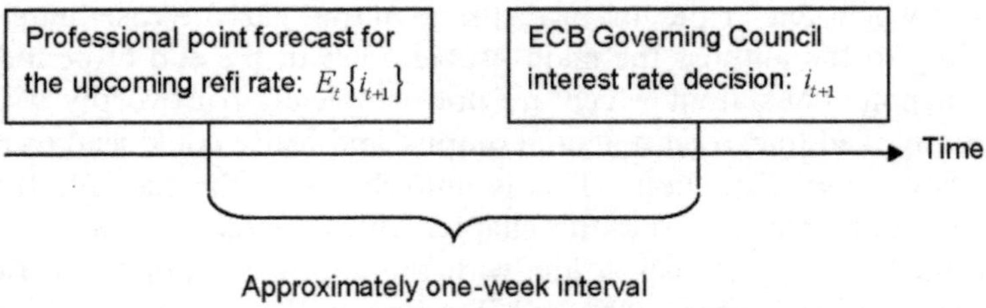

Figure 1: The Timing of the Model.

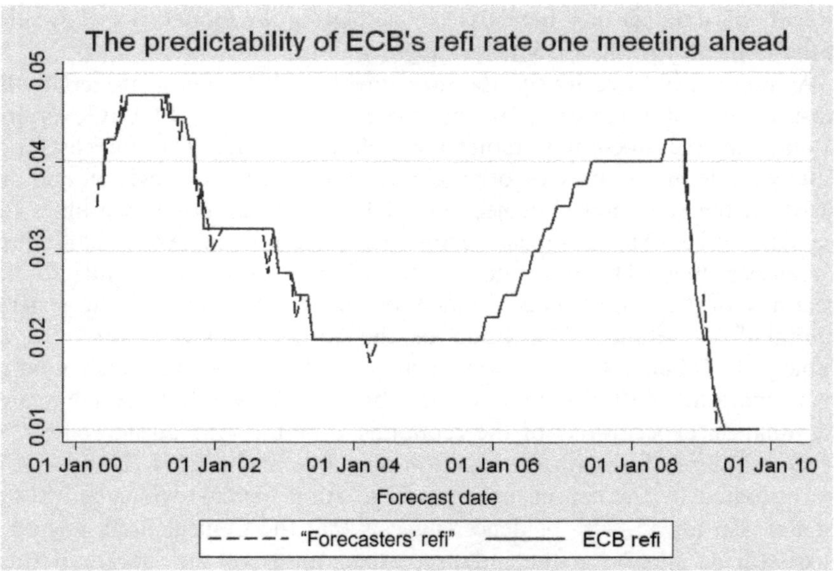

Figure 2: The Predictability of ECB's Main Policy Rate by the Professional Forecasters.

corresponding monetary policy meeting. This analysis provides a first evidence for understanding the forecasting of the main policy rate of the ECB. The figure points to a possibly limited predictability of the refi rate in the period from 2000 to the end of 2003 as indicated by the recurrent prediction errors. During the cycle of policy easing the forecasters have often expected higher refi rate cuts than the ones implemented by the Central Bank. Even though the economists have not predicted well the magnitude of the policy rate adjustments, they have managed to perceive broadly well the pattern of the policy rate in that period. Since June 2003 and until December 2005 the economists' point forecasts of the refi rate have

Table 1: The Refi Rate Adjustments

The magnitude of the changes in the refi rate							
	−75 b.p.	−50 b.p.	−25 b.p.	0 b.p.	+25 b.p.	+50 b.p.	+75 b.p.
Number of changes implemented	1	8	5	108	12	1	0
Number of changes predicted	1	7	9	106	11	1	0
Correct predictions	100%	50%	40%	94.4%	83.3%	0%	n.a.

Note: The table displays the changes of the refi rate expressed in basis points that the ECB has implemented along with the predictions performed by the investment bank's economists. The latter are used to determine the point forecasts of the policy rate.
n.a. refers to a rate change that is not observed during the period studied.

remained at 2% in line with the actual policy rate. There has been only one exception in March 2004, when the economists have perceived a further decline of the refi rate to a level of 1.75% which the ECB has not implemented. The gradual monetary policy tightening that the Central Bank has started in December 2005 has been remarkably well predicted by the market participants one meeting ahead. Finally, the professional forecasters have fallen short into perceiving the timing and magnitude of the refi rate cuts during the recent financial crisis, even though they have broadly well predicted the monetary policy easing that has been implemented since October 2008.

Table 1 reports the number of the refi rate adjustments the ECB has implemented along with the changes in the policy rate predicted by the professional forecasters from April 2000 to November 2009.[7] The results indicate that during most of the meetings the Governing Council has not changed the refi rate, while there have been almost as many rate cuts as interest rate hikes. The reported correct predictions take due account of the timing of the interest rate decisions. They point out that while the investment bank's economists have broadly well predicted the increases in the refi rate and the unchanged policy rate, the professional forecasters have experienced a hard time in forecasting the refi rate cuts of the Central Bank. This evidence mirrors the communication policy of the ECB. Indeed,

[7] Notice that as an alternative approach one could model the probability of having a particular change in the refi rate. However, this analysis has been performed to some extent in the recent literature. Instead, in this chapter I model the market participants' perception of the Central Bank's reaction function within a Taylor Rules framework.

given that the Governing Council has been perfectly clear on its firm commitment to foster price stability as its overriding goal, the market participants have remarkably well foreseen the timing and the size of the refi rate hikes the ECB has implemented to alleviate some inflationary pressures. However, as the Council has not explicitly clarified the weight it assigns to the economic outlook when deciding on the level of the refi rate, the investment bank's economists have not well predicted neither the timing nor the magnitude of the refi rate cuts the Central Bank has implemented in response to a fall in economic activity or to a financial slump. The results thus unveil the asymmetry inherent to the ECB's communication policy: the Central Bank signals in advance the forthcoming rate hikes while it often remains silent on the future rate cuts. Besides, Ehrmann and Fratzscher (2009) point out that the communication of the Central Bank during the press conferences exerts a clarification role of the monetary policy decisions especially in periods of heightened macroeconomic uncertainty.

On the one hand, the good predictability of the refi rate increases since December 2005 might be partly related to the use of some code words like "vigilance" and "strong vigilance" in the ECB's communication with the markets, as is emphasized in De Haan and Jansen (2009). On the other hand, Geraats, Giavazzi, and Wyplosz (2008) highlight that the system of code words has not been very successful because the market participants have not accurately foreseen the overall stance of policy tightening further in advance and the system has been used only to signal the policy rate hikes. This practice possibly explains the smaller forecast accuracy of the refi rate cuts one week ahead of the Governing Council meetings. As in general the "traffic light system" of the ECB seems to be quite confusing to the market participants for perceiving the overall policy rate strategy, one should rely on a Taylor Rule framework to better understand and predict the refi rate setting policy of the Central Bank.

Along with the point forecast for the policy rate, the economists report their prediction of inflation and real GDP growth for the current quarter and current year, and for the quarter and year ahead. Based on the methodology of Gorter et al. (2008), I use two approaches in constructing the expectations of inflation and real output growth that are used in the empirical analysis.

In a first step to modeling the expectations of inflation and real output growth, I use for each period t the inflation and real output growth forecasts for the quarter ahead or for the year ahead, respectively. The advantage of this methodology is that it is entirely forward-looking since I consider the economists' expectations for the upcoming quarter or for the upcoming year. This approach is also in line with the method applied by Poplawski-Ribeiro and Rülke (2010) in their investigation of the impact of the Stability and Growth Pact on the forecast accuracy of the public budget deficit in the euro area by the market participants. This methodology could also be consistent with the observed long and variable lags in the monetary policy transmission process.

The second methodology considers a fixed horizon of one-quarter which is computed for the inflation and real output growth forecasts using the following formula for the weighted average ($\bar{x}_{q,h}$):

$$\bar{x}_{q,h} = \frac{91-h}{90} x_{q,h} + \frac{h-1}{90} x_{q+1,h},$$

where $x_{q,h}$ is any of the current quarter (q) forecasts of the aforementioned variables reported on day h and $x_{q+1,h}$ stands for the quarter ahead ($q+1$) projections made in the same day. The indices q and h take, respectively, the values $q = 2000Q2, \ldots, 2009Q4$ and $h = 1, \ldots, 90$. I have considered 90 days within a quarter which is a standard assumption for financial markets' participants.

To obtain a one-year fixed horizon forecasts of the variables, I compute a weighted average ($\bar{x}_{y,h}$) of the current year and the year ahead forecasts using the following formula:

$$\bar{x}_{y,h} = \frac{361-h}{360} x_{y,h} + \frac{h-1}{360} x_{y+1,h},$$

where $x_{y,h}$ is any of the current year (y) forecasts of the macroeconomic variables reported on day h and $x_{y+1,h}$ stands for the year ahead ($y+1$) projections published on the same day. The indices y and h take, respectively, the values $y = 2000, \ldots, 2009$ and $h = 1, \ldots, 360$ assuming 360 days within a year.

The advantage of this approach is that one obtains a fixed horizon of one-quarter and of one-year, respectively, for the inflation and real GDP growth forecasts. However, there are also some drawbacks related to this methodology. First, the variables computed are not entirely forward-looking since they contain expectations of the series for the current quarter and the current year. Second, by applying this formula we cannot assign a specific forecasting period to the expectations variables because they span any time interval that is between the current quarter and the quarter ahead or between the current year and the year ahead. Moreover, given that these variables are constructed from the reported forecasts they may not correspond well to the way the economists form their expectations of macroeconomic fundamentals. Conversely, the quarter and the year ahead projections published by the economists are purely forward-looking and hence are more likely to correspond with the expectations formation mechanism of the market participants compared to the forecasts of macroeconomic fundamentals obtained with the second approach.

Tables A.3 and A.4 display the unit root tests of the variables that are used in the estimation of the Taylor Rules.[8] The results point out that most of the series seem to be stationary in light of the evidence from the Augmented Dickey–Fuller (ADF) and Kwiatkowski–Phillips–Schmidt–Shin (KPSS) tests. However, some of the Phillips–Perron (PP) tests do not show evidence against the null hypothesis of unit root, in particular for the actual and forecasted refi rates and for the real GDP growth forecasts. The latter results are at odds with the theoretical assumption of stationarity of the output growth rate and with the estimation results in the literature. In the empirical section I also report the unit root tests of the residuals along with the estimated coefficients. I have performed the Augmented Dickey–Fuller and the Phillips–Perron tests that point out that the residuals are all stationary. This brings evidence against any spurious regression problem that may arise along the lines of Granger and Newbold (1974). It should be emphasized that in the literature the researchers make the assumption of stationarity of the series when estimating Taylor Rules, even though it is often hard to reject the presence of a unit root in the macroeconomic time series used in the estimations. The latter assumption is justified by the generally low power of the unit root tests in small samples as outlined in Gorter et al. (2008), Clarida, Galí, and Gertler (2000) for instance. Thus, the absence of evidence against the unit root hypothesis found with the Phillips–Perron statistics for some of the series in this chapter is possibly due to the low power of the tests and the relatively short time period considered in the analysis. Therefore, given the strong theoretical arguments in favor of stationarity of the variables in the Taylor Rules, the series can be considered as stationary.

In line with the literature, I adopt a GMM approach to estimate the policy rules. As instruments for the lagged policy rate I use the first and second lags of the inflation and real output growth forecasts in the regressions.[9] To correct the standard errors of the estimates for heteroskedasticity and autocorrelation of unknown form, I follow the approach of Newey and West (1987) and apply a Bartlett kernel for the estimation of the variance-covariance matrix. This procedure yields consistent and unbiased coefficient estimates of the explanatory variables in the Taylor Rule. The inflation and output growth forecasts are exogenous

[8] A comprehensive overview of the testing procedures is available in Maddala and Kim (2004).

[9] This approach is in line with Fourçans and Vranceanu (2004) for instance who use the first and second lags of the series as instruments in estimating a policy rule for the ECB.

regressors for several reasons. First, these forecasts are used in real-time by the investment bank's economists to perform their refi rate point forecast approximately one week ahead of the Governing Council meetings and hence are observed before the realization of the refi rate. Second, I have performed some endogeneity tests of the inflation and output growth forecasts, and the difference-in-Sargan statistics all point out that there is no evidence against the null hypothesis of exogeneity in all regressions. Third, the evidence documented in the literature, as in Gorter et al. (2008) and Sturm and Wollmershäuser (2008) for instance, supports the view that in the Taylor Rule framework the projections of macroeconomic variables provided in real-time are exogenous. The Hansen's J-statistic is reported along with the coefficient estimates and shows that there is no evidence against the validity of the instruments used in the regressions.

I first perform the GMM estimations for the period April 2000–November 2009. Second, I run rolling window regressions to determine whether the coefficient estimates have remained stable over time as well as to infer some underlying learning process for the market participants about the ECB's policy rule. In the robustness section, I also implement some recursive window regressions to check the sensitivity of the results to the applied methodology. The rolling window approach explores the stability of the coefficient estimates of the Taylor Rules using a constant number of observations but over different periods, whereas the recursive windows account for the impact of an additional information set that is gradually extended over time on the estimation of the policy rules.

4. Linear Model Estimations

In this section, I present the estimation results for the Actual and Perceived policy reaction functions over the entire period: April 2000–November 2009. As previously mentioned the regressions are performed with the expectations variables for the quarter and year ahead, as well as for the one-quarter and one-year horizons, respectively. The goal of using different horizons is to understand how the ECB reacts to the forecasts of macroeconomic fundamentals for different time periods.

4.1. Estimations for the Quarter and Year Ahead Horizons

This subsection presents the estimation results for the policy rules with the quarter and year ahead horizons. The coefficient estimates are reported in Tables 2 and 3 for the Actual and Perceived Taylor Rules, respectively.

Table 2: Actual Taylor Rule, 2000–2009

	Quarter ahead	Year ahead
ρ	0.9225***	0.9561***
	(0.0199)	(0.0125)
β_π	0.3419**	2.2607***
	(0.1428)	(0.4307)
β_y	0.8068***	2.3241***
	(0.1726)	(0.4493)
α	0.0098***	−0.0611***
	(0.0025)	(0.0131)
R^2	0.9826	0.9842
Observations	133	133
Hansen J-statistic	1.6143	1.2654
ADF Z(t)	−5.294***	−4.832***
PP Z(t)	−10.156***	−11.274***

Note: GMM estimates, HAC standard errors are computed with the Delta method and are denoted in parentheses. The table reports the long-run response coefficients. The regressions are performed for the specifications with the forecasts for the quarter ahead and the year ahead, respectively. The Hansen J-statistic tests whether the over-identifying restrictions are satisfied. A statistically significant test shows evidence against the validity of the instruments. The ADF Z(t) and PP Z(t) refer to the Augmented Dickey–Fuller and Phillips–Perron statistics, respectively. Both are used to determine whether the residuals contain a unit root. A statistically significant test shows evidence against the null hypothesis of unit root. For the ADF test, three lags of the difference in the residuals have been used, while the number of lags used in the Phillips–Perron test is determined automatically based on Newey–West bandwidth selection.
***$p < 0.01$, **$p < 0.05$, *$p < 0.1$.

Before turning to the estimations, it is important to bear in mind that if the ECB is on the hawkish side it will mainly focus on stabilizing inflation expectations assigning a smaller weight to the economic outlook, whereas if it is more dovish its policy will gear toward stabilizing real output growth rather than inflation expectations.[10]

In a first step, based on the forecasts for the quarter ahead, the Central Bank responds positively and significantly to increases in the inflation forecasts but the Taylor Principle is not satisfied as the estimated inflation coefficient is below one in both policy rules.[11] In the event of a 1% increase in

[10] It is relevant to emphasize that the coefficients in the Taylor Rule embody both Central Bank preferences and structural characteristics of the economy. Thus, changes in the Taylor Rule coefficients reflect relative changes in the Central Bank preferences assuming that the structure of the economy is not altered.

[11] In order to exert a stabilizing policy on inflation, the nominal interest rate should rise more than proportionally to increases in inflation expectations in order for the real interest rate to augment. This proposition is known as the Taylor Principle.

Table 3: Perceived Taylor Rule, 2000–2009

	Quarter ahead	Year ahead
ρ	0.9122***	0.9060***
	(0.0110)	(0.0259)
β_π	0.5368***	2.1334***
	(0.1220)	(0.1793)
β_y	0.6761***	1.2351***
	(0.1055)	(0.2445)
α	0.0074***	−0.0343***
	(0.0020)	(0.0047)
R^2	0.9815	0.9828
Observations	133	133
Hansen J-statistic	1.7867	1.5091
ADF Z(t)	−4.361***	−3.894***
PP Z(t)	−10.633***	−10.306***

Note: GMM estimates, HAC standard errors are computed with the Delta method and are denoted in parentheses. The table reports the long-run response coefficients. The regressions are performed for the specifications with the forecasts for the quarter ahead and the year ahead, respectively. The Hansen J-statistic tests whether the over-identifying restrictions are satisfied. A statistically significant test shows evidence against the validity of the instruments. The ADF Z(t) and PP Z(t) refer to the Augmented Dickey–Fuller and Phillips–Perron statistics, respectively. Both are used to determine whether the residuals contain a unit root. A statistically significant test shows evidence against the null hypothesis of unit root. For the ADF test, three lags of the difference in the residuals have been used, while the number of lags used in the Phillips–Perron test is determined automatically based on Newey–West bandwidth selection.
***$p<0.01$, **$p<0.05$, *$p<0.1$.

inflation expectations, the refi rate will be raised by 0.34% and 0.54% according to the actual and perceived policy rules, respectively. One possible interpretation of this surprising result might be related to the fact that the ECB aims at stabilizing inflation in the medium and long terms and may not be worried by inflation deviations from its objective within the quarter ahead horizon. This explanation is further justified by the long and variable lags in the monetary policy transmission process which prevent the ECB from affecting inflation in the very short term.

Second, within the quarter ahead horizon, it seems that the Central Bank has more likely responded to the real output growth forecasts and has implemented a stabilizing policy for the economic outlook as indicated by the positive and significant coefficient estimates from both policy rules. A 1% increase in the output growth expectations will trigger an increase of 0.81% and 0.68% of the policy rate in the Actual and Perceived Taylor Rules, respectively. Indeed, the importance of the economic outlook has been regularly underlined by the ECB Governing Council in the introductory statements to the regular press conferences. However, the ECB has not clarified the relative weight it assigns to the economic outlook in the policy strategy. Finally, the policy inertia coefficient estimates point out that the refi rate is adjusted only gradually to the desired target rate given the high level of sluggishness in the interest rates. In addition, the market participants have foreseen a similar degree of policy inertia as the actual one since the point estimates are very close. Notice also that the professional forecasters have perceived the ECB to react more strongly to the inflation rather than to the real output growth expectations compared to the coefficient estimates from the Actual Taylor Rule.

As regards the estimations with the year ahead forecasts, one can observe an important difference in the magnitude of the estimated coefficients. Indeed, both the inflation and real output growth point estimates increase in both Taylor Rules when considering a longer forecast horizon. Importantly, Tables 2 and 3 point out that the coefficient estimates are broadly in line with the empirical findings for the ECB in the literature.[12] This result is consistent with the interpretation that within the quarter ahead horizon the ECB has mainly focused on stabilizing real output growth rather than inflation expectations, the latter being its major concern in the policy-relevant medium-term horizon. The evidence for increasing Central Bank's responsiveness coefficients along with the forecasting horizon is further corroborated in Hamilton et al. (2009). These authors have found increasing policy reaction coefficients with the forecasting horizon for the U.S. Federal Reserve. They have interpreted this finding as evidence for a gradual policy adjustment of the Central Bank to economic fundamentals.

Looking further ahead, the Actual and Perceived Taylor Rules show that the Taylor Principle is verified implying a stabilizing policy of the ECB on inflation expectations. This finding is in line with the ECB's objective of anchoring the inflation forecasts to its price stability objective in the medium to long terms. In addition, the positive and significant point estimates of the output growth forecasts indicate that the Central Bank has implemented a stabilizing policy for the economic outlook as well. In the event of a 1% increase in the output growth expectations, the policy rate will be raised by 2.32% and 1.24% based on the actual and perceived

[12] The reader could refer to Gorter et al. (2008), Fourçans and Vranceanu (2004), Gerdesmeier and Roffia (2004), and Sauer and Sturm (2003) for instance. These authors estimate a reaction function for the ECB using a partial adjustment mechanism. Their estimates show that the Central Bank has exerted a stabilizing effect on inflation and on the output gap when using only a forward-looking specification of the policy rule.

estimates, respectively. However, the estimated actual and perceived inflation coefficients are quite similar in both reaction functions. Thus, in the case inflation expectations increase by 1%, the Central Bank will augment the policy rate by 2.26% and 2.13% according to the actual and perceived policy rules correspondingly. These results show that the professional forecasters have perceived the ECB to respond relatively more strongly to the inflation than to the output growth forecasts in contrast with the findings for the actual reaction function. Indeed, the evidence points out that the Central Bank's responsiveness to the output growth forecasts is slightly higher than its reaction to the inflation forecasts according to the actual reaction function. As regards the policy inertia coefficient estimate, the latter has slightly decreased in the Perceived Taylor Rule while the Actual Taylor Rule points to a more sluggish adjustment of the policy rate compared to the results with the quarter ahead horizon. The following subsection presents the empirical findings with the one-quarter and one-year horizons.

4.2. Estimations for the One-Quarter and One-Year Horizons

Tables 4 and 5 display the coefficient estimates of the policy rules when considering a horizon of one-quarter and of one year, respectively, in the regressions. At a first glance, the evidence suggests that the empirical results previously obtained with the forecasts for the quarter and the year ahead remain qualitatively unaltered. Considering a horizon of one-quarter in the regressions, the ECB responds positively to the inflation and output growth forecasts in line with the above findings. Moreover, the Taylor Principle is not satisfied in both Taylor Rules as previously found. A 1% increase in inflation expectations will engineer a rise in the refi rate of about 0.26% and 0.40% in the Actual and Perceived Taylor Rules, respectively. Regarding the output growth forecasts, in the event of a 1% increase in the latter, the policy rate will be raised by 0.62% and 0.60% according to the actual and perceived reaction functions correspondingly. Thus, in the short term the Central Bank puts a higher emphasis on stabilizing the economic outlook rather than inflation expectations which is in line with the earlier evidence. Besides, the professional forecasters have perceived the ECB to respond relatively more strongly to inflation rather than to output growth expectations compared to the estimates from the actual policy rule.

The Central Bank's responsiveness to both the inflation and output growth forecasts increases when considering the one-year horizon in the estimations, in line with the findings for the year ahead horizon. The size of the estimated coefficients is quite smaller compared to the evidence for the year ahead forecasts. In the event of a 1% increase in inflation

Table 4: Actual Taylor Rule, 2000–2009 Alternative Model

	One-quarter horizon	One-year horizon
ρ	0.8775***	0.9000***
	(0.0290)	(0.0382)
β_π	0.2621**	0.7094***
	(0.1101)	(0.2075)
β_y	0.6174***	0.9718***
	(0.1024)	(0.3077)
α	0.0157***	−0.0004
	(0.0024)	(0.0051)
R^2	0.9801	0.9832
Observations	133	133
Hansen J-statistic	1.7440	1.5428
ADF Z(t)	−4.218***	−4.805***
PP Z(t)	−9.057***	−10.440***

Note: GMM estimates, HAC standard errors are computed with the Delta method and are denoted in parentheses. The table reports the long-run response coefficients. The regressions are performed for the specifications with the forecasts for a one-quarter and one-year horizon, respectively. The Hansen J-statistic tests whether the over-identifying restrictions are satisfied. A statistically significant test shows evidence against the validity of the instruments. The ADF Z(t) and PP Z(t) refer to the Augmented Dickey–Fuller and Phillips–Perron statistics, respectively. Both are used to determine whether the residuals contain a unit root. A statistically significant test shows evidence against the null hypothesis of unit root. For the ADF test, three lags of the difference in the residuals have been used, while the number of lags used in the Phillips–Perron test is determined automatically based on Newey–West bandwidth selection. ***$p < 0.01$, **$p < 0.05$, *$p < 0.1$.

expectations, the refi rate will be raised by 0.71% and 1.11%, respectively, according to the actual and perceived policy rules. As regards the output growth forecasts, a 1% increase in the latter will trigger a 0.97% and 0.83% rise in the policy rate for the actual and perceived reaction functions correspondingly. Therefore, the market participants perceive the ECB to respond more aggressively to inflation than to output growth expectations compared to the results from the actual reaction function. In contrast with the results for the year ahead horizon, the Taylor Principle is still not verified for the Actual Taylor Rule when including the one-year forecasts in the regressions. Regarding the Perceived Taylor Rule, the ECB implements a stabilizing policy for inflation expectations but the coefficient estimate is much smaller compared to the point estimate obtained with the forecasts for the year ahead. Moreover, the Central Bank reacts more strongly to the output growth rather than to the inflation forecasts as the Actual Taylor Rule estimates point it out. The degree of policy inertia is broadly close to the previous results with some exceptions concerning the size of the

Table 5: Perceived Taylor Rule, 2000–2009 Alternative Model

	One-quarter horizon	One-year horizon
ρ	0.8836***	0.8960***
	(0.0130)	(0.0212)
β_π	0.3989***	1.1110***
	(0.1064)	(0.1563)
β_y	0.5984***	0.8324***
	(0.0642)	(0.2384)
α	0.0126***	−0.0061
	(0.0025)	(0.0052)
R^2	0.9798	0.9823
Observations	133	133
Hansen J-statistic	1.7504	1.5486
ADF Z(t)	−3.596***	−3.899***
PP Z(t)	−9.819***	−10.826***

Note: GMM estimates, HAC standard errors are computed with the Delta method and are denoted in parentheses. The table reports the long-run response coefficients. The regressions are performed for the specifications with the forecasts for a one-quarter and one-year horizon, respectively. The Hansen J-statistic tests whether the over-identifying restrictions are satisfied. A statistically significant test shows evidence against the validity of the instruments. The ADF Z(t) and PP Z(t) refer to the Augmented Dickey–Fuller and Phillips–Perron statistics, respectively. Both are used to determine whether the residuals contain a unit root. A statistically significant test shows evidence against the null hypothesis of unit root. For the ADF test, three lags of the difference in the residuals have been used, while the number of lags used in the Phillips–Perron test is determined automatically based on Newey–West bandwidth selection.
***$p < 0.01$, **$p < 0.05$, *$p < 0.1$.

estimated coefficients. In both policy rules the adjustment coefficient is slightly smaller than found earlier and the perceived point estimate increases a little when moving from the one-quarter to the one-year horizon.

The estimation results are broadly in line with the evidence reported in Sturm and Wollmershäuser (2008) for the forward-looking ECB Taylor Rule they estimate over the period 1999–2006 at the frequency of the Governing Council meetings. The estimated degree of policy inertia is of about 0.90 and is statistically significant at the 5% level. The coefficient estimates of the inflation and output growth forecasts are 1.63 and 1.52, respectively, and are statistically significant at the 5% level. This suggests that the ECB responds strongly to the macroeconomic projections and that the Taylor Principle is satisfied. Even though these results are in general consistent with the evidence found in this chapter, the magnitude of the inflation and output growth point estimates is smaller than the findings for the Actual Taylor Rule and to some extent for the Perceived Taylor Rule within the year ahead horizon. However, the reaction of the ECB to macroeconomic fundamentals estimated in Sturm and Wollmershäuser (2008) is well above the point estimates reported with the one-year forecast horizon.

To sum up, the empirical findings suggest that the Central Bank responds more strongly to the inflation and output growth expectations and implements an inflation-stabilizing policy when considering the year ahead rather than the one-year forecasts in the regressions. The smaller responsiveness of the ECB with the one-quarter and the one-year forecasts could be related to the fact that the latter are not sufficiently forward-looking to engineer a stronger response of the ECB to the macroeconomic variables. The quarter and the year ahead forecasts are entirely forward-looking and are well suited to account for the lags in the monetary policy transmission process. They also seem to better correspond to the expectations formation process of the professional forecasters.

4.3. Actual and Perceived Fitted Policy Rules

In this subsection I compare the fitted policy rate targets with the actual refi rates in both Taylor Rules.[13] This analysis will help to understand whether the ECB has accurately set the refi rate based on the recommendations stemming from the policy rules and will determine to what extent the market participants have correctly predicted the pattern of the policy rate within the sample.

Figure 3 displays the predicted policy rate target from the Actual and Perceived Taylor Rules when considering the forecasts for the quarter ahead in the estimations. At first sight, the figures point out that the predicted refi rates from both reaction functions are very similar. Indeed for both Taylor Rules, the pattern of the refi rate is broadly close to the predicted target rate but there are some important discrepancies as regards their magnitude for some periods. A first gap occurs after the financial market turmoil of 2000, when the predictions from the policy rules suggest that the ECB should have implemented sharper interest rate cuts and a few months earlier than in May 2001. Nevertheless, the Central Bank has reached the recommended target rate of 2% for the refi rate but only in June 2003. Importantly, since that date the Central Bank has maintained the policy rate at the level of 2% for a rather protracted period of time.

[13] The fitted target rate can be computed as indicated by Equation (1) in the theoretical framework. It corresponds to the desired level of the refi rate that the Central Bank seeks to achieve. Notice that the refi rate fit would be closer to the policy rate when including the lagged refi rate in the prediction and therefore it is not reported.

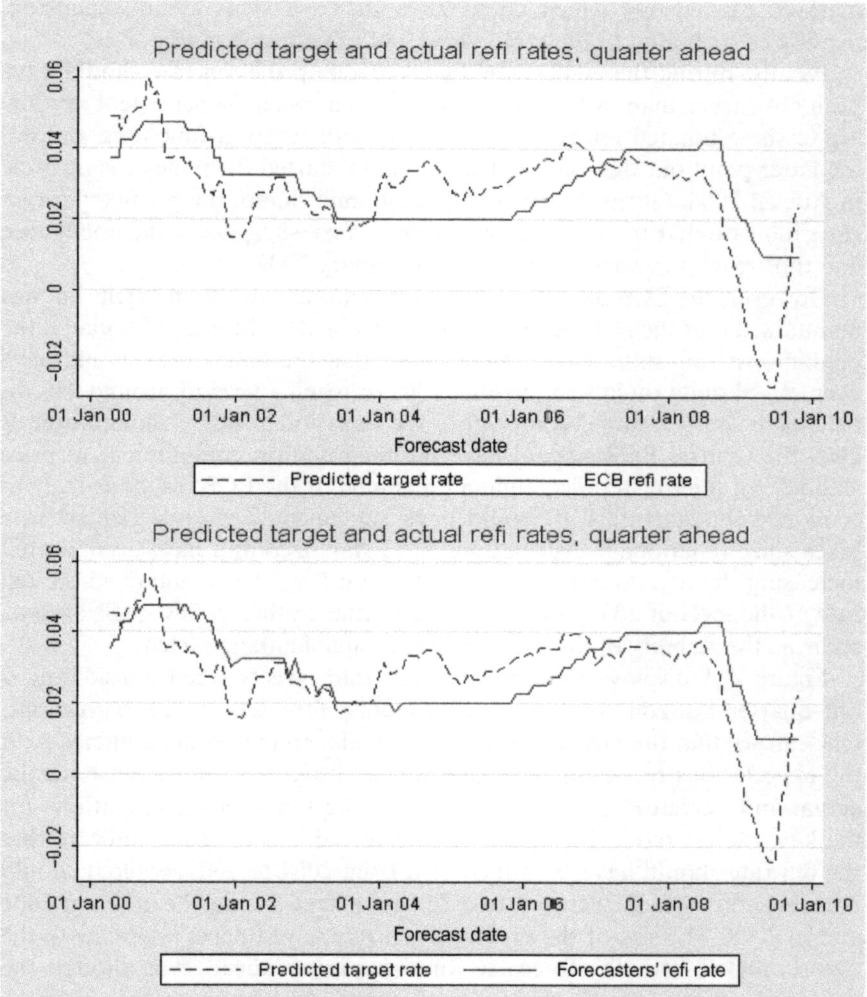

Figure 3: Actual and Perceived Taylor Rules, Quarter Ahead Forecasts.

The predicted target rates from both policy rules indicate that the ECB should have begun implementing a tightening cycle around January 2004. This result stands in contrast with December 2005 when the Central Bank started raising the refi rate for the first time. Hence, it seems that during a period of approximately two years the ECB has kept its policy rate at a too low level compared to the refi rate it should have set, has it followed the recommendations from the estimated Taylor Rules. This low level for the refi rate could have favored a risk-taking behavior on the part of financial markets participants which could have fueled a swift credit expansion, thereby contributing to the rapid growth of the housing market.

Finally, during the 2007–2009 financial slump the refi rate should have been cut earlier than in October 2008 and to a much deeper extent according to the estimated refi rate targets from both reaction functions. Indeed, the latter point out that the ECB should have started the policy easing cycle in August 2008. Given the size of the economic slump, the predicted target rates indicate that the Central Bank should have sharply cut the policy rate and thus reach the zero lower bound in January 2009.

However, the ECB has not lowered the refi rate to such an extent but has maintained it at the historically low level of 1% since May 2009. Finally, the predictions from both Taylor Rules show that the policy rate should have been raised quite rapidly in October 2009 to reach a level of around 2%. In fact, as the euro area has come out of the recession in the second quarter of 2009 the Central Bank should have resumed its firm commitment to price stability by entering a policy tightenting mode. If the ECB responds truly to economic fundamentals, it should have implemented gradual interest rate hikes since inflationary expectations have stabilized and have even started increasing slightly. Apparently, as the Central Bank has maintained the refi rate at the level of 1% it might have prioritized other policy goals such as securing the stability of the still fragile euro area banking system.

Figure A.1 displays the predicted refi rate targets when considering a one-quarter horizon for the macroeconomic forecasts in the regressions. One can see that the predictions are very similar to the results obtained with the expectations for the quarter ahead. The fitted refi rates from both the actual and perceived policy rules point to the same recommendations for the key interest rate. The Actual and Perceived Taylor Rules indicate that the refi rate should have been increased from 2004 to 2007, while it should have been lowered earlier and to a further extent during the crises in 2001 and in 2008. The size of the predicted refi rate adjustments is similar to the one estimated with the forecasts for the quarter ahead even though the predicted refi rate cuts are slightly smaller within the one-quarter horizon.

In a next step, I also compare the fitted target rates from the Actual and Perceived Taylor Rules when considering the forecasts for the year ahead in the regressions in Figure 4. The graphs show that the previous results remain qualitatively unaltered when considering a longer forecast horizon in the estimation of both policy rules. The predicted target rates point out that the Central Bank has not sufficiently cut the refi rate in periods of recessions and financial turmoil and should have implemented a tighter policy stance from 2004 to 2007. Besides, the refi rate predictions of the Actual and Perceived Taylor Rules seem to be overall well aligned. However, there is an important difference in the magnitude of the predicted policy rate targets compared to the previous evidence for the quarter ahead horizon. Figure 4 points out that

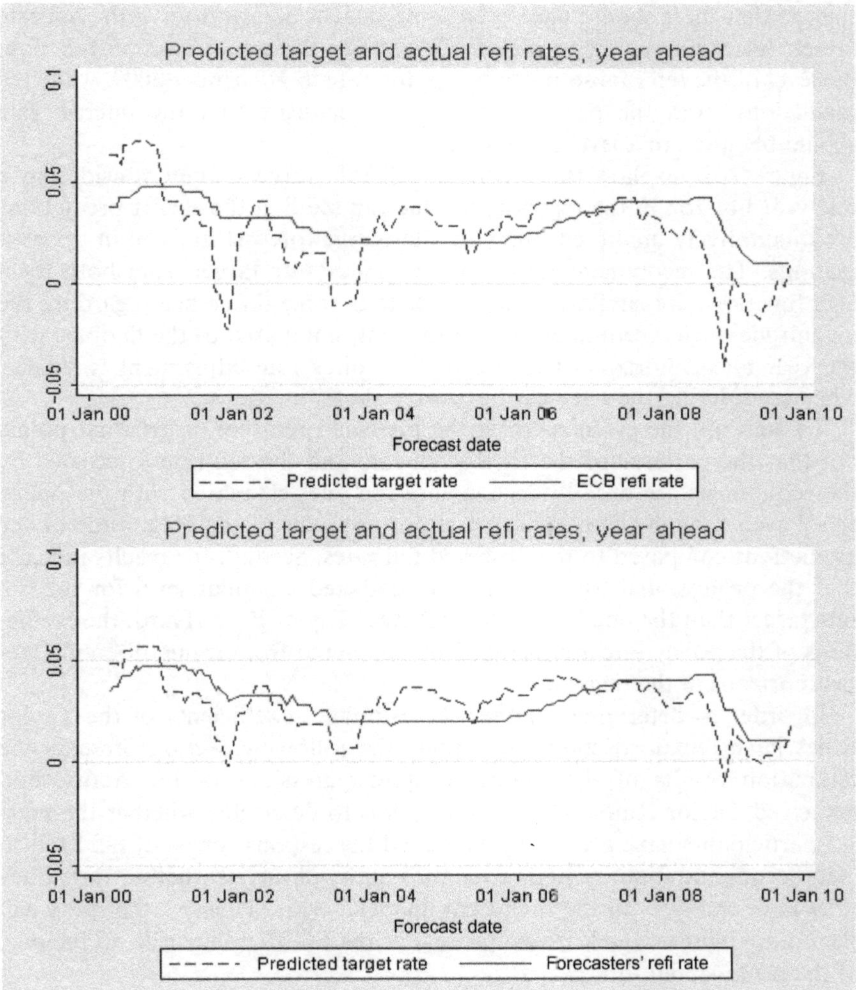

Figure 4: Actual and Perceived Taylor Rules, Year Ahead Forecasts.

in periods of economic slump the refi rate should have been cut more sharply compared to the one implemented and the actual policy rule estimates point to even more negative interest rates especially during the recent crisis.[14] The predictions from the Perceived Taylor Rule are qualitatively similar but

---

[14] Gorter, Jacobs, and de Haan (2009) do not find evidence for negative interest rates for the euro area during the crisis period. However, the three months' euribor rate they use in the estimations is substantially higher than the ECB's policy rate during the turmoil.

suggest that there should have been some smaller adjustments of the refi rate target. According to the in-sample forecasts of the actual reaction function, the level of the refi rate seems to be appropriate in November 2009, while the predictions from the perceived policy rule indicate that the interest rate should be raised to a level close to 1.75%.

Figure A.2 displays the predicted refi rate targets when considering a one-year horizon in the regressions. One can see that the earlier predictions are qualitatively unaltered using an alternative forecast horizon in the estimations. The recommendations for the policy rate target from both reaction functions are similar. However, there is some difference regarding the magnitude of the recommended refi rate cuts compared to the findings with the year ahead horizon. The size of the policy rate adjustment is smaller when considering the one-year horizon in the estimations.

To sum up, the evidence from the predicted refi rate targets first points out that the patterns of the ECB's refi rate and the refi rate forecasted by the economists are broadly in line with the ones estimated with the policy rules, even though there are some important gaps in the magnitude of the predictions compared to the observed refi rates. Second, the results indicate that the professional forecasters have predicted a similar level for the refi rate target than the one based on the Actual Taylor Rule. Third, the predictions of the policy rate are qualitatively unaltered from using different forecast horizons in the regressions.

In order to determine whether the estimated coefficients of the Taylor Rules have remained stable over time, the following section presents the estimation results of the rolling window regressions of the Actual and Perceived Taylor Rules. This analysis helps to determine whether the market participants have accurately estimated the responsiveness of the ECB to macroeconomic fundamentals over time and will unveil whether the policy rules have changed during the recent financial crisis. Thereby, the study will shed more light on the learning process of the ECB's policy rule on the part of the professional forecasters.

5. Rolling Window Estimations

In this part of the chapter, I estimate the policy inertia, expected inflation, and real output growth coefficients with rolling window regressions in order to determine whether the Central Bank's responsiveness to economic fundamentals has changed over time. This analysis will help to determine if a linear specification of the Taylor Rule is appropriate or whether one should consider a nonlinear model to account for a possible change in the coefficients of the policy reaction function for instance. The regressions are performed with the forecasts for the year ahead and the one-year horizons as they are more consistent with the standard view on the transmission of monetary policy impulses to the economy. They are also more in line with the horizon at which the ECB aims at stabilizing inflation expectations. The regressions are performed with the GMM method used for the estimation of the linear Taylor Rules presented in the previous section. The coefficients are estimated with a rolling window of 95 observations and a step that corresponds to each Governing Council meeting starting in April 2000.[15] The point estimates along with the corresponding 95% confidence intervals are displayed in the following graphs. Given that all estimations are performed in a real-time framework, this procedure is particularly valuable for understanding the monetary policy rule in light of the newly available information about macroeconomic fundamentals. Thereof, the results are especially useful for performing policy recommendations on the appropriate level of the policy rate in a real-time setting.

5.1. Coefficient Estimates of Policy Inertia

Figure 5 points out that both the actual and perceived point estimates have remained overall stable during most of the estimation period. This evidence suggests that the ECB has not significantly changed the speed of adjustment of the policy rate until the second half of 2008. Second, the results indicate that there is a substantial sluggishness in the adjustment of the refi rate as the magnitude of the estimated coefficients is quite high, which is in line with the results of the previous section. The actual and perceived point estimates are close indicating that the market participants have perceived a broadly similar degree of policy inertia compared to the one estimated with the Actual Taylor Rule. Third, it is compelling to notice the change in the policy inertia coefficient estimates that has occurred since the peak of the financial crisis in October 2008. Indeed, one can see that both the actual and perceived point estimates have substantially changed since the tipping point of the turmoil. The policy inertia has decreased and the uncertainty associated with the estimated coefficients has broadened during the period of financial turbulence.

The empirical evidence thus accounts for the peak of the financial slump that has occurred in October 2008 after the bankruptcy of Lehman Brothers and the bailouts of several other worldwide large investment banks. The

[15] The window of 95 observations is chosen in order to have sufficient observations for an accurate estimation of the response coefficients. The regressions have also been performed with a smaller window size but the results are not satisfactory.

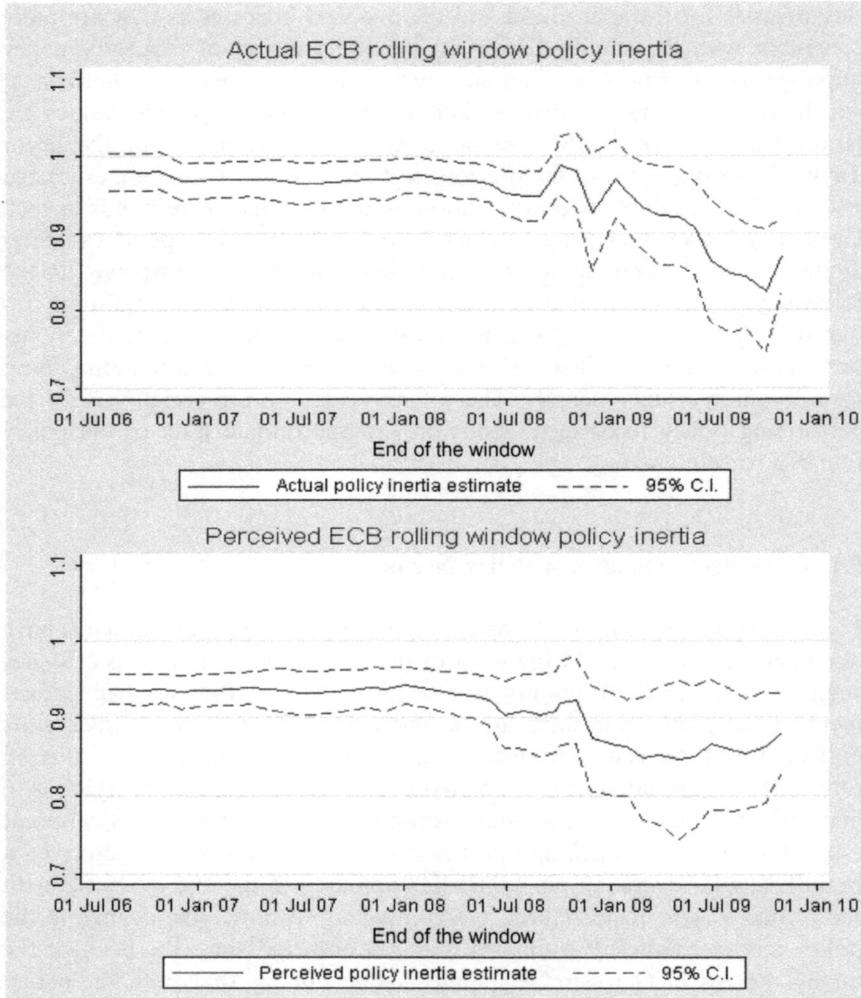

Figure 5: Policy Inertia Estimates, Year Ahead Forecasts (Rolling).

emergence of an exceptionally high systemic risk in the euro area banking sector has been followed by an unexpected reversal of the monetary policy-tightening stance that the ECB has implemented in the following month. The Central Bank has thus reduced the refi rate by 50 basis points on October 8, 2008 in order to enhance the liquidity provision operations in the euro interbank market which has been adversely affected by massive liquidity shortages. This policy shift has been initially largely unexpected by the economists.

Since the tipping point of the financial crisis, the actual policy inertia coefficient has substantially decreased. This result is not surprising given the fact that the ECB has quickly brought down the refi rate to a historically very low level in order to prevent a broadening of the crisis and a further decline in economic activity. Besides, the jump as well as the higher uncertainty in the actual and perceived point estimates are very similar. Since October 2008, the actual coefficient estimate has gradually decreased reflecting the higher speed of implementation of the desired level of the refi rate that the ECB has undertaken.[16] The perceived policy inertia estimate has started decreasing since the peak of the crisis, indicating that the professional forecasters have perceived a higher speed of adjustment of the ECB's refi rate as well. Furthermore, the confidence interval has widened substantially relative to the period before the unwinding of the crisis, possibly reflecting the broadening of macroeconomic uncertainty. The latter has been regularly emphasized by the Governing Council of the ECB on the monetary policy press conferences since October 2008.

Finally, Figure A.5 presents the policy inertia rolling window estimates using a one-year forecast horizon in the regressions. The figure points out that the previous results are qualitatively unaltered when considering an alternative horizon in the estimations. However, since the first half of 2009 the estimates from both Taylor Rules indicate that the policy inertia has decreased more substantially than estimated with the forecasts for the year ahead. The next subsection presents a similar analysis for the inflation forecast coefficient estimates.

5.2. Coefficient Estimates of Expected Inflation

At a first sight, Figure 6 indicates that the magnitude of the actual inflation coefficient estimate is relatively high but has not changed in an important way in the period before the financial crisis. The point estimate in the Actual Taylor Rule is also surrounded by a higher uncertainty compared to the narrower confidence interval of the perceived inflation coefficient estimate. One cannot state that the actual and perceived point estimates are different before October 2008 because of the wide confidence interval of the estimated actual inflation coefficient, even though the perceived point estimate is smaller than the actual one. This evidence is consistent with the baseline results. As regards the perceived inflation coefficient, it has remained broadly unaltered during most of the period featuring only a slightly upward trend. The actual point estimate has risen substantially since the second half of 2007, thereby reflecting a higher concern of the Central Bank about rising inflationary pressures. The perceived inflation

[16] From October 2008 to May 2009, the total reduction in the main policy rate has reached 325 basis points.

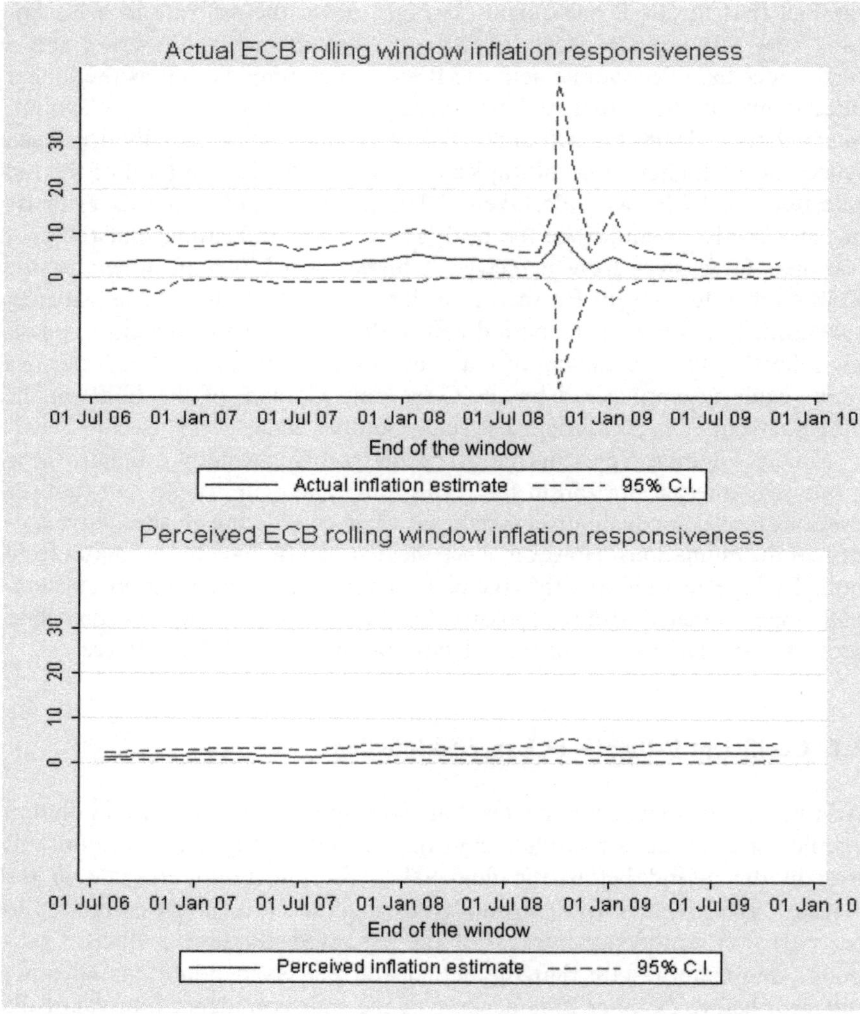

Figure 6: Inflation Coefficient Estimates, Year Ahead Forecasts (Rolling).

coefficient has also increased in that period but to a lesser extent.[17] Overall, the observed gap in the actual and perceived coefficient estimates accounts for a hampered predictability of the size of the actual ECB's inflation responsiveness during most of the estimation period.

[17] The change in the estimated coefficients doesn't seem to be important at a first look because of the wide confidence interval for the actual point estimate observed at the peak of the crisis.

Furthermore, Figure 6 reports an important change in the actual coefficient estimate which has occurred in the second half of 2008 and has peaked in October of that year precisely during the broadening of the financial crisis. The inflation point estimate has sharply jumped at the peak of the crisis and has reached a particularly high level. The actual inflation coefficient has swiftly increased in the second half of 2008 and then has rapidly declined after the tipping point of the turmoil. The observed sharp jump of the confidence interval reflects the exceptionally high level of uncertainty surrounding the coefficient estimate at the height of the financial turbulence. Thus, the observed behavior of the ECB's inflation responsiveness appears to be quite puzzling and should be attributed to the sudden reversal of the monetary policy stance that the ECB has implemented after the bankruptcy of Lehman Brothers.

Indeed, before the peak of the crisis the ECB was following a policy-tightening strategy facing increasing inflationary pressures stemming essentially from commodity and food price increases. In addition, the ECB was also concerned about some possible second round effects on prices and wages which could have triggered off an inflation spiral. The Central Bank has even further tightened the euro area refinancing conditions by bringing up the refi rate to the level of 4.25% in July 2008, just two months before the tipping point of the financial turmoil. Then, on October 8, 2008, the ECB has sharply and unexpectedly reduced the refi rate within a coordinated policy action implemented jointly with other major Central Banks. Hence, the observed pattern of the ECB's policy rate largely reflects the fact that the broadening of the financial crisis in September 2008 has not been anticipated by the Governing Council of the ECB. Therefore, the puzzling spike of the actual inflation coefficient estimate might indicate the switching to a new monetary policy stance that the ECB has implemented at the height of the financial turbulence.

Importantly, the perceived inflation coefficient estimate points out that the professional forecasters have not anticipated the swift change of the ECB's monetary policy strategy in 2008. The point estimate has remained quite stable over most of the estimation period. It has increased just slightly after the July 2008 policy hike and then has declined only modestly in October 2008. Overall, the coefficient estimate has not been particularly affected by the crisis and is estimated very accurately compared to the larger confidence interval obtained for the actual inflation point estimate.

Finally, since January 2009, the actual inflation coefficient has gradually declined whereas the perceived one has remained stable. Nevertheless, it seems that the market participants have foreseen a similar inflation responsiveness of the Central Bank in the aftermath of the financial turmoil to the one found with the actual policy rule. This result points out that the ECB might have well-anchored inflation expectations despite pursuing other policy goals in such a period of macroeconomic uncertainty. Figure A.6 displays the rolling window inflation coefficient estimates with the one-year forecast horizon. The estimated coefficients are broadly in line with the previous evidence even though they report a much smaller peak of the actual inflation point estimate during the crisis. Consistently with the findings for the year ahead horizon, the professional forecasters do not seem to have perceived a different inflation responsiveness of the Central Bank compared to the actual policy rule estimates before the financial turmoil, even though the former point estimates are smaller than the latter. The perceived inflation reaction of the ECB has remained relatively stable during most of the period as previously found. In the final subsection, I present the real output growth coefficient estimates from the rolling window regressions.

5.3. Coefficient Estimates of Expected GDP Growth

Figure 7 points out that the actual and perceived point estimates are broadly similar until the second half of 2008, except at the beginning of the estimation period. Besides, the output growth coefficient is estimated more accurately by the professional forecasters compared to the wider confidence interval obtained for the Actual Taylor Rule. This result is in line with the findings for the inflation coefficient estimates. Overall, it seems that the market participants have well perceived the actual ECB's responsiveness to the economic outlook in the first part of the estimation period. The figure points out that the perceived growth coefficient has remained broadly stable until January 2008 and then has gradually declined along with the actual point estimate during the first half of 2008. This evidence probably reflects a higher concern of the ECB and the economists for the inflation outlook. During that period the Governing Council has focused on preventing a surge in inflation expectations by tightening the policy stance.

Moreover, there is an important change in the dynamics of the actual output growth coefficient during the broadening of the financial crisis and particularly in October 2008 as found for the policy inertia and inflation coefficients previously estimated. In that period the actual point estimate has considerably increased pointing to a relatively high concern of the ECB about the magnitude of the economic slump. However, the perceived output growth coefficient has changed only a little and is estimated quite accurately as indicated by the narrow confidence interval. As with the inflation reaction of the ECB, the market participants have not anticipated the swift change in the responsiveness of the Central Bank to the economic outlook. Until the beginning of 2009 the actual point estimate has followed a shifting pattern possibly reflecting the exceptional degree of uncertainty

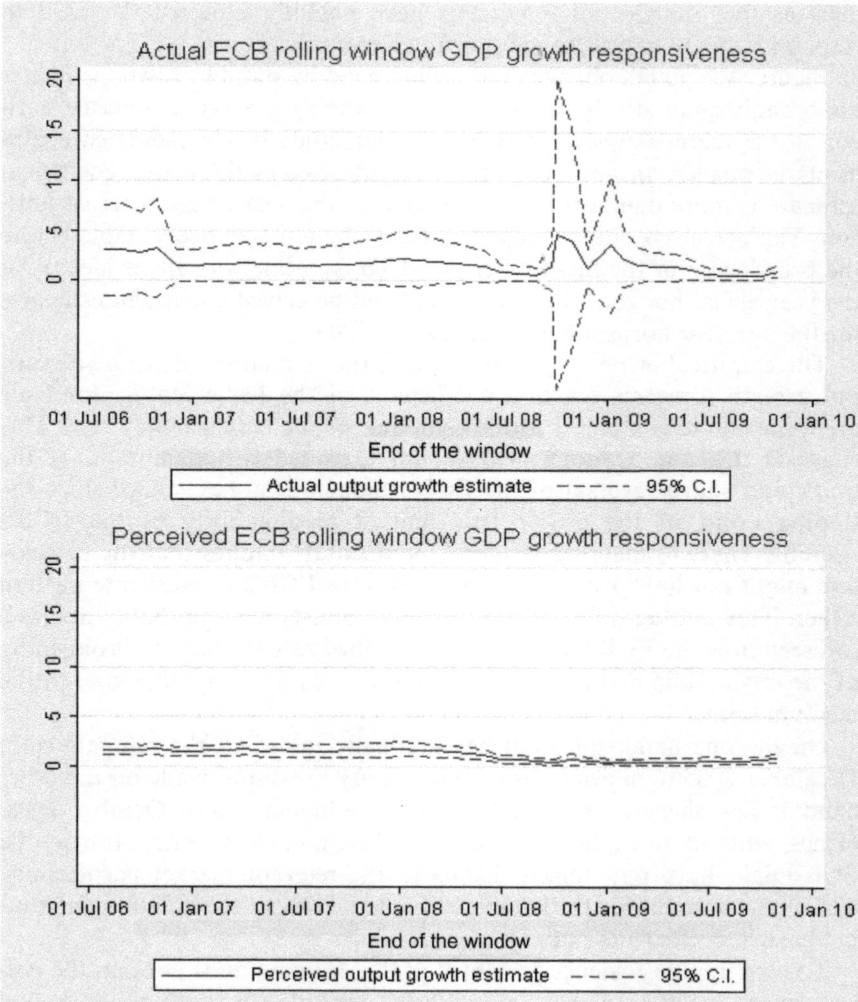

Figure 7: Output Growth Coefficient Estimates, Year Ahead Forecasts (Rolling).

surrounding the monetary policy framework, whereas the perceived coefficient has remained rather stable.

Finally, the actual output growth coefficient has steadily declined since January 2009 as found for the actual inflation estimate, probably indicating a higher concern of the ECB about the fragility of the euro area banking system and its impact on the economic outlook. However, the perceived inflation and output growth coefficients have remained broadly stable in

2009 as the professional forecasters have possibly expected the ECB to respond strongly to macroeconomic fundamentals.

Figure A.7 points out that the rolling window output growth estimates are broadly qualitatively similar when considering a one-year forecast horizon in the regressions even though the magnitude of the estimated coefficients is smaller. In addition, the observed peak in the actual coefficient estimate is more dampened than found with the year ahead forecast horizon. The perceived output growth point estimate is relatively stable before the broadening of the financial crisis which is in line with the evidence for the year ahead horizon. Both the actual and perceived coefficient estimates for the one-year horizon have decreased in 2009.

The empirical evidence points out that the estimated inflation and output growth forecasts reaction coefficients of the Perceived Taylor Rule are quite stable compared to the estimates of the actual policy rule. This suggests that the economists have not expected the magnitude of the quick and sharp reversal of the ECB's monetary policy stance since the tipping point of the crisis. This limited predictability of the ECB's responsiveness to macroeconomic fundamentals implies that the forecasters might not have well perceived the future ECB's interest rate pattern either. This finding indicates that the economists have probably not well foreseen how the ECB has adjusted the policy rate to face the broadening of the crisis while maintaining price stability as its overriding goal in the medium term.

On the one hand, the ECB has gradually increased the refi rate since December 2005 to alleviate rising inflationary pressures, while on the other hand it has sharply reversed the policy tightening since October 2008. Hence, without an explicit clarification of the monetary policy strategy the ECB might have sent mixed signals to the relevant market participants, which may account for the hampered predictability of the inflation and output growth coefficients since October 2008.[18]

To sum up, the evidence presented in this section points out that the policy response coefficients have more likely changed over time and the Actual Taylor Rule has been particularly affected by the financial turmoil in 2008. The observed spikes in the inflation and output growth point estimates

[18] The limited transparency of the ECB is extensively analyzed in Geraats (2008) and Geraats et al. (2008). The authors emphasize that the markets have well managed to predict the next policy move of the ECB but have fallen short into predicting the medium to long-term policy orientation. They conclude that the ECB should be more transparent in order to improve the predictability of its future policy actions by the relevant market participants. In particular, the authors point out that the ECB would have benefited from providing future guidance to the markets by publishing its expected future interest rate path.

indicate that the ECB has swiftly and sharply reversed its policy stance facing an environment of exceptional macroeconomic uncertainty with a high level of systemic risk in the banking sector. The results point out that there is more uncertainty surrounding the coefficient estimates of the Actual Taylor Rule within the year ahead than with the one-year horizons. Even though the professional forecasters have accurately estimated the Central Bank's responsiveness to macroeconomic fundamentals before the crisis, they have not well anticipated the policy reversal at the peak and in the aftermath of the financial turmoil. Thereby, the following section is focused on analyzing more in-depth the impact of the financial slump on the estimated policy reaction functions.

6. Estimation with Time Dummies

In view of the evidence from the rolling window results, in this section I investigate the size of the effect of the tipping point of the financial crisis and the subsequent broadening of the turmoil on the main policy rate of the ECB. For this purpose, I estimate the above Actual and Perceived Taylor Rules by including a time dummy that accounts for the peak of the crisis occurring on October 8, 2008, as well as a second time dummy for the period of economic slump, from October 8, 2008 until May 7, 2009. The final date corresponds to the end of the sharp policy rate cuts the ECB has implemented and coincides with the end of the economic recession according to the Euro Area Business Cycle Dating Committee. The coefficient estimates for the actual policy rule are presented in Table 6.

The table points out that the peak of the crisis has exerted an important negative effect on the policy rate as one could have expected in light of the previous results. However, even though the effect of the dummy variable on the refi rate is negative for both forecast horizons, the coefficient estimates are not statistically significant. Besides, when controlling for the tipping point of the financial turmoil the responsiveness of the Central Bank to macroeconomic fundamentals changes slightly compared to the baseline results. As regards the estimates for the year ahead horizon, the ECB features a higher inflation responsiveness relative to its reaction to the output growth forecasts while the policy inertia coefficient is in line with the previous evidence. Concerning the one-year forecast horizon, the inflation responsiveness coefficient has increased as well but the Central Bank still reacts more strongly to the economic outlook rather than to inflation expectations consistently with the baseline results. The policy inertia coefficient is not altered from including the dummy variable in the regressions for the year ahead and the one-year horizons.

Table 6: Actual Taylor Rule, 2000–2009 Crisis Dummies

	Year ahead 1	Year ahead 2	One-year horizon 1	One-year horizon 2
ρ	0.9606***	0.9584***	0.9045***	0.9638***
	(0.0135)	(0.0125)	(0.0444)	(0.0066)
β_π	3.4155***	2.2627***	0.8849***	0.4924
	(0.8312)	(0.2942)	(0.1894)	(0.3782)
β_y	2.0166***	1.5507***	0.9379**	1.2639***
	(0.5326)	(0.4012)	(0.3716)	(0.4493)
Crisis' peak	−0.1887		−0.0369	
	(0.1414)		(0.0240)	
Crisis		−0.0752***		−0.0779***
		(0.0229)		(0.0277)
α	−0.0748***	−0.0411***	−0.0031	−0.0006
	(0.0204)	(0.0101)	(0.0067)	(0.0110)
R^2	0.9839	0.9878	0.9840	0.9863
Observations	133	133	133	133
Hansen J-statistic	0.5300	1.2183	1.5292	1.6690
ADF Z(t)	−4.897***	−5.104***	−4.578***	−4.910***
PP Z(t)	−11.540***	−13.473***	−10.635***	−12.206***

Note: GMM estimates, HAC standard errors are computed with the Delta method and are denoted in parentheses. The table reports the long-run response coefficients. The regressions are performed for the specifications with the forecasts for the year ahead and the one-year horizons, respectively. The variable "Crisis' peak" is a dummy that takes the value 1 for October 8, 2008, while the variable "Crisis" is a dummy for the period of the financial turmoil from October 8, 2008 until May 7, 2009. The Hansen J-statistic tests whether the over-identifying restrictions are satisfied. A statistically significant test shows evidence against the validity of the instruments. The ADF Z(t) and PP Z(t) refer to the Augmented Dickey–Fuller and Phillips–Perron statistics, respectively. Both are used to determine whether the residuals contain a unit root. A statistically significant test shows evidence against the null hypothesis of unit root. For the ADF test, three lags of the difference in the residuals have been used, while the number of lags used in the Phillips–Perron test is determined automatically based on Newey–West bandwidth selection.
***$p < 0.01$, **$p < 0.05$, *$p < 0.1$.

Furthermore, the size of the impact of the period of financial crisis on the refi rate is particularly important and the coefficient estimates are negative and statistically significant. The point estimates indicate that the magnitude of the crisis is quite similar for the two forecast horizons and shows that the financial slump has lead to a policy rate cut of approximately 7.5% and 7.8% on average over that period for the year ahead and the one-year horizons, respectively. In addition, the estimated inflation coefficient is the same as found with the baseline model and the Central Bank responds less strongly to the output growth expectations within the year ahead forecast horizon. The estimated policy inertia is consistent with the earlier evidence. Regarding the one-year horizon, the inflation point estimate is not significant

Table 7: Perceived Taylor Rule, 2000–2009 Crisis Dummies

	Year ahead 1	Year ahead 2	One-year horizon 1	One-year horizon 2
ρ	0.8942***	0.9065***	0.8929***	0.9118***
	(0.0247)	(0.0198)	(0.0218)	(0.0106)
β_π	2.0037***	2.0705***	1.0213***	1.1697***
	(0.2148)	(0.1614)	(0.1776)	(0.1581)
β_y	1.2385***	1.0180***	0.8395***	0.8105***
	(0.2095)	(0.1957)	(0.2501)	(0.1496)
Crisis' peak	0.0319		0.0189	
	(0.0203)		(0.0132)	
Crisis		−0.0186***		−0.0086
		(0.0049)		(0.0061)
α	−0.0317***	−0.0276***	−0.0047	−0.0068*
	(0.0033)	(0.0043)	(0.0047)	(0.0041)
R^2	0.9821	0.9839	0.9822	0.9832
Observations	133	133	133	133
Hansen J-statistic	1.0109	1.5122	1.5197	1.5753
ADF Z(t)	−3.882***	−3.435***	−4.034***	−3.919***
PP Z(t)	−9.873***	−10.986***	−10.639***	−11.370***

Note: GMM estimates, HAC standard errors are computed with the Delta method and are denoted in parentheses. The table reports the long-run response coefficients. The regressions are performed for the specifications with the forecasts for the year ahead and the one-year horizons, respectively. The variable "Crisis' peak" is a dummy that takes the value 1 for October 8, 2008, while the variable "Crisis" is a dummy for the period of the financial turmoil from October 8, 2008 until May 7, 2009. The Hansen J-statistic tests whether the over-identifying restrictions are satisfied. A statistically significant test shows evidence against the validity of the instruments. The ADF Z(t) and PP Z(t) refer to the Augmented Dickey–Fuller and Phillips–Perron statistics, respectively. Both are used to determine whether the residuals contain a unit root. A statistically significant test shows evidence against the null hypothesis of unit root. For the ADF test, three lags of the difference in the residuals have been used, while the number of lags used in the Phillips–Perron test is determined automatically based on Newey–West bandwidth selection.
***$p < 0.01$, **$p < 0.05$, *$p < 0.1$.

and the ECB reacts more strongly to the economic outlook which is in line with the results from the baseline regression. The Taylor Principle is not verified with the one-year forecasts as previously found. Besides, the policy inertia coefficient estimate suggests that there is a higher sluggishness in the adjustment of the refi rate compared to the earlier findings for the one-year horizon. Table 7 displays the estimated results for the perceived policy rule.

The evidence from Table 7 suggests that the impact of the financial crisis on the policy rate is more dampened compared to the results obtained for the Actual Taylor Rule. As regards the peak of the crisis, the effect on the refi rate is positive and not significant for both forecast horizons, which stands in contrast with the negative estimates found for the actual policy rule. In addition, the responsiveness of the Central Bank to macroeconomic fundamentals and the degree of policy inertia are qualitatively unaltered from the baseline results when including the dummy variable for the crisis' peak in the regressions. However, the size of the ECB's reaction to inflation expectations is smaller relative to the output growth forecast point estimates in both horizons.

Concerning the period of financial turmoil, the effect on the refi rate is negative but the size of the estimated coefficients is smaller compared to the results found for the actual reaction function and is significant only for the year ahead horizon. This evidence points out that the economists have not foreseen the effect of the sharp reversal of the policy stance the ECB has implemented on October 8, 2008 and in the subsequent period on the refi rate. For the year ahead horizon the crisis dummy indicates that in that period the interest rate has been lowered by approximately 1.9%, while for the one-year horizon the financial slump has lead to a reduction of the policy rate by only 0.9% with an estimated coefficient that is not statistically significant. The inflation and output growth point estimates, as well as the degree of policy inertia are qualitatively similar to the baseline results, even though it seems that the ECB has slightly increased its responsiveness to inflation relative to output growth expectations. The Taylor Principle is verified with the one-year forecasts which is in line with the findings of Section 4.

The estimations with the crisis dummies as well as the evidence from the rolling window regressions reveal that the Actual and to a lesser extent the Perceived Taylor Rules have been particularly affected by the broadening of the financial turmoil since October 2008. Given that the ECB has quickly and sharply adjusted the policy rate to prevent a further decline in economic activity, it might have responded differently to macroeconomic fundamentals during this period by entering a crisis regime. During the financial turbulence, the Central Bank has focused on improving the liquidity provision of the interbank market and on restoring the orderly functioning of financial markets. Besides, the policy implemented seems to have affected the interest rate setting framework of the ECB. This evidence is in line with the view of Smets (2009) who has stated that the separation principle has been breached because the broadening of the financial turmoil has affected the interest rate setting strategy of the ECB. The rolling window estimates have shown that the inflation and output growth coefficient estimates of the Actual Taylor Rule have decreased in that period as the Governing Council's policy has geared towards securing the stability of the euro area financial system. The unconventional policy measures implemented by the ECB during the crisis are extensively documented in Wyplosz (2010). The author highlights that the delayed refi rate cuts undertaken only at the height of the turmoil could be related to the rising commodity and food prices in the fall of 2007 and the specific prioritization of the price stability objective in the ECB's mandate.

7. Robustness Analysis

The goal of this section is to conduct a sensitivity analysis of the results presented in Sections 4 and 5. For this purpose, I adopt an alternative methodology to estimate the response coefficients of the policy rules over time and I also include different forecasts of economic fundamentals in the regressions. In a first step, I adopt a recursive window approach in estimating the Actual and Perceived Taylor Rules using the forecasts for the year ahead and the one-year horizons. Then, I estimate the policy rules using Consensus Economics Forecasts (CEF) of inflation and output growth in order to determine whether the results are sensitive to the expectations variables used.[19]

With the recursive window procedure, the starting date of the regressions is fixed and the estimation range is progressively extended as the available information set increases over time. With this approach I investigate to what extent the policy rules coefficients are affected by an additional information on macroeconomic fundamentals. As for the rolling window methodology, I apply a step of one policy meeting in the estimations to track as closely as possible the monetary policy decision process. The coefficient estimates are displayed in Figures A.8–A.10 for the year ahead forecast horizon. The recursive point estimates are in general in line with the results found with the rolling window approach. In particular, the actual and perceived policy inertia estimates are of a similar size and are quite stable before the financial crisis. Since the tipping point of the turmoil the estimated coefficients tend to decrease but to a much smaller extent than found with the rolling window regressions. As regards the inflation response coefficient, the professional forecasters have not perceived a different responsiveness of the Central Bank from the actual one, even though the perceived point estimate is smaller than the actual coefficient as found with the rolling window methodology. The magnitude of the actual and perceived recursive point estimates is similar to the one estimated with the rolling window approach but the actual inflation reaction of the ECB is more dampened at the peak of the crisis than found earlier. As regards the output growth coefficient, the actual point estimate is not different from the perceived coefficient in the recursive regressions, and its

[19] The Consensus Economics Forecasts are reported for the current year and the year ahead. They are also provided in real-time and are not revised. The forecasts correspond to the average projections of inflation and real GDP growth which are performed by a panel of professional forecasters for the euro area. The author is particularly grateful to the Swiss National Bank which kindly provided access to the Consensus reports.

magnitude is relatively small at the broadening of the crisis compared to the results with the rolling windows. In line with the baseline results, the actual inflation and output growth coefficients have followed a downward pattern since 2009 as the Central Bank might have prioritized other goals such as maintaining the stability of the financial system. Importantly, the perceived coefficient estimates are more stable than the actual ones because the market participants have not expected the swift reversal of the ECB's policy during the financial turmoil. Consistently with the baseline results, the main message brought by the Actual Taylor Rule is that since the financial slump the ECB has adjusted more frequently the refi rate to the desired target level and has weakened its inflation and output growth responsiveness. Regarding the Perceived Taylor Rule, the estimated policy inertia has decreased since the peak of the crisis but there is no evidence that the Central Bank has responded less strongly to macroeconomic fundamentals. This is in line with the findings from the rolling window regressions.

The recursive window estimates for the one-year forecast horizon are also broadly consistent with the results from the one-year rolling window regressions as shown in Figures A.11–A.13. In particular, the actual and perceived policy rules point out that the policy inertia of the ECB has decreased and its responsiveness to the inflation and output growth expectations has weakened since the peak of the financial turmoil. In general, the magnitude of the recursive window coefficients is quite similar to the one estimated with the rolling window regressions for the one-year horizon. There is no evidence that the actual and perceived coefficients are different, even though the point estimates from the Perceived Taylor Rule are smaller than the actual ones before the crisis and for both horizons.

The observed gaps between the actual and perceived coefficient estimates can be attributed to the communication policy of the ECB which is rather opaque as regards the relative weighting scheme of the inflation and output growth stabilization objectives in its policy strategy. In line with this view, during the January 2004 introductory statement, Mr. Trichet has emphasized the following: "*...we are not the prisoner of an equation, we are not the prisoner of a system of equations, we are not the prisoner of an algorithm which would dictate our conduct and behavior. We take, I would say, all pertinent information-all pertinent analyses-and we make a judgment [...] Because by anchoring a low level of inflation in the years to come, and not in the medium term but also in the long term, we pave the way for this favorable financial environment which is conducive to growth.*" This constrained discretion approach points out that the Governing Council avoids any precommitment to a future course of policy actions but intends to be perfectly transparent about its long-run goal of price stability. Thereby, the ECB has not clarified the way it takes due account of the economic outlook while pursuing its overriding objective.

The estimations with the Consensus Economics Forecasts are presented in Tables A.7 and A.8. At a first glance, some of the results are broadly consistent with the previous evidence for the Perceived Taylor Rule even though there are some differences in the size of the estimated coefficients. Concerning the Actual Taylor Rule, the estimates suggest that the ECB has responded more strongly to the inflation rather than to the output growth expectations when considering the forecasts for the year ahead compared to the baseline results. However, the inflation point estimate is similar to the one obtained with the investment bank's forecasts. Regarding the forecasts for the one-year horizon, the results are in general close to the baseline evidence for the Actual Taylor Rule except for the inflation responsiveness coefficient which is negative but not significant. Besides, the CEF estimates of the policy inertia and output growth coefficients are in line with the evidence for the Perceived Taylor Rule except that the Taylor Principle is not satisfied for the one-year horizon. Figures A.3 and A.4 display the fitted policy rate targets using the consensus data for different forecast horizons. The predicted target refi rates fully corroborate the results obtained with the investment bank's forecasts for both the Actual and Perceived Taylor Rules. In particular, the graphs point out that the refi rate should have been raised earlier than in December 2005 and during the recent crisis the policy rate should have been cut more in advance and to a lower level than the one implemented. The estimations with the crisis dummies, which are not reported in the chapter reveal that the peak of the crisis has exerted a negative but not significant effect on the refi rate except for the Perceived Taylor Rule within the year ahead horizon. In the period of financial slump, from October 2008 to May 2009, the policy rate has been particularly affected by the crisis as the estimated coefficients of the dummy variables are negative and significant except for the Actual Taylor Rule within the one-year horizon. This evidence corroborates the previous results for the regressions with the investment bank's forecasts.

The rolling and recursive window regressions with the consensus forecasts are consistent with the previous evidence for the policy inertia point estimates. However, the reaction of the ECB to the inflation and output growth forecasts is quite dampened during the recent crisis in both policy rules.[20] Besides, the Consensus forecasters have estimated a similar responsiveness of the Central Bank to macroeconomic fundamentals to the one obtained with the actual policy rule and the uncertainty surrounding the point estimates is of the same size. Since 2009 the inflation and output

[20] The rolling and recursive window regressions with the CEF data are not reported in the chapter to save some space.

growth point estimates have declined which is consistent with the baseline results for the Actual Taylor Rule.

I have also estimated the policy rules with the Economic Sentiment Indicator (ESI), expressed in percentage point deviation from its long-run average of 100, as an alternative measure of the private sector expectations of the euro area economic outlook.[21] The ESI is a leading business cycle indicator and the ECB often refers to this variable when assessing the private agents' expectations on the future economic conditions in the monetary union. Tables A.9 and A.10 report the coefficient estimates for the Actual and Perceived Taylor Rules for different forecast horizons. The evidence indicates that the ECB does not react as strongly to the ESI as to the output growth expectations; however, the latter provides a relevant indication on the expected developments in the euro area economy. Tables A.11 and A.12 report the estimation results with the consensus inflation expectations and the deviation of the ESI from its long-run average included as regressors in the Taylor Rules. Overall, the evidence suggests that the Central Bank should have cut more quickly and sharply the refi rate during crises and should have raised more in advance and to a further extent the policy rate in periods of economic upturn.

The sensitivity analysis presented in this section shows that the actual and perceived response coefficients are likely to have changed over time regardless of the methodology and the data used in the estimations. However, the size of the change in the ECB's behavior during the financial crisis is sensitive to the forecast variables and to the horizons considered. A robust result to the data and to the estimation methodology is the finding that since the peak of the turmoil the degree of policy inertia has decreased in both policy rules. Some of the results have also shown evidence that the Central Bank has responded differently to macroeconomic fundamentals since the broadening of the financial crisis. Therefore, it is worth investigating more thoroughly the specification of the policy rules within an appropriate nonlinear model.

8. Conclusion

This chapter has brought new insights on understanding the predictability of the monetary policy stance of the European Central Bank through the

[21] The ESI is a weighted average of the confidence indicators in the industry, services, construction, retail trade, and consumers' sectors published by the European Commission on a monthly basis.

eyes of the professional forecasters from a large investment bank. The empirical evidence points to the following main results.

First, within the Actual and Perceived Taylor Rules framework the professional forecasters have accurately predicted the pattern of the refi rate even though they have perceived more properly the policy rate increases than the refi rate cuts. The predictions of the refi rate target from both policy rules are well aligned and point out that the ECB has maintained the policy rate at a too low level for a protracted period from 2004 until 2007. Thereby, the Central Bank might have favored a risk-taking behavior which could have fueled the rapid expansion of the housing market in the euro area. Besides, the estimates indicate that in periods of financial turmoil the ECB should have cut the refi rate earlier and to a deeper extent than the adjustments it has implemented. There is also evidence that the responsiveness of the Central Bank to inflation and output growth expectations increases along the forecast horizon in both Taylor Rules. This result is robust to the expectations variables considered in the estimations. The responsiveness of the ECB to macroeconomic fundamentals is stronger with the year ahead than with the one-year horizon, which suggests that the former are possibly more in line with the expectations formation process of the professional forecasters.

Second, the rolling window regressions show that the estimated coefficients have remained broadly stable until the second half of 2008. There is evidence that the reaction of the Central Bank to macroeconomic fundamentals has changed after the bankruptcy of Lehman Brothers as the ECB has focused on preventing a further decline in economic activity. The perceived coefficients are broadly similar to the actual ones given the wide confidence intervals of the Actual Taylor Rule, even though the economists have estimated a smaller policy inertia and ECB's reaction to the inflation and output growth expectations. The results from the estimations with the one-year horizon are qualitatively similar to the evidence for the year ahead forecasts; however, the magnitude of the estimated coefficients is smaller with the former. The estimations with the time dummies point out that during the broadening of the crisis the refi rate has been cut in an important way especially in the regressions with the year ahead horizon.

Third, the recursive window estimates corroborate the previous findings. Some of the results are also qualitatively unaltered from using Consensus Economics Forecasts and the ESI growth rate, even though there are some differences in the size of the point estimates. It is interesting to note that both the rolling and recursive window techniques point to a decreasing pattern of the inflation and real output growth coefficients since January 2009 for the actual policy rule. As previously highlighted, this finding might suggest a higher concern of the Central Bank about the stability of the banking system, which has been affected by an unforeseen level of systemic risk. An interesting topic would be to further investigate to what extent the financial stability issue could affect the monetary policy strategy of the ECB, and particularly the overriding price stability mandate in the medium and longer terms.

The analysis performed in the chapter points to some gaps between the actual and perceived coefficient estimates of inflation and real output growth expectations. The latter indicate that the learning process about the ECB's policy reaction function can be further improved by enhancing the transparency and communication strategy of the Central Bank. Regularly, the ECB has justified that this limited openness is implied by the very precise and simple policy framework: the delivery of price stability over the medium term. However, I would suggest the following policy recommendations to improve the effectiveness of the European monetary policy. First, the ECB should clarify the weight it assigns to the economic outlook and to the stability of the banking system when deciding on the appropriate level of the refi rate. Second, the Central Bank should publish its main macroeconomic projections at the frequency of the Governing Council meetings in order to enhance the predictability of its policy decisions by the relevant economic agents. Finally, the ECB would benefit from publishing the conditional future refi rate path along with the associated uncertainty of the point forecasts. This practice will not tie the hands of the Central Bank to a predetermined course of actions because the predicted future levels of the policy rate are conditional on the expected inflation and economic developments in the euro area. Instead, by anchoring the expectations of the private sector to the Central Bank's forecasts this enhanced transparency would help to credibilize the low inflation commitment of the ECB in the medium and longer terms. Lastly, the estimation results suggest that the monetary policy stance has been severely challenged by the recent financial crisis. Particularly, the broadening of the turmoil has not been anticipated by the Central Bank neither by the professional forecasters. Hence, in a future work it would be relevant to further analyze the responsiveness of the Central Bank to macroeconomic fundamentals within an appropriately designed regime switching model.

Acknowledgment

The author is particularly grateful to Henri Loubergé, Charles Wyplosz, Ulrich Kohli, Mathias Thoenig, Jürgen von Hagen, Arnaud Chéron, Jean-Paul L'Huillier, and to the colleagues from the Department of Economics for their valuable comments and insights. I also would like to thank the participants of the Annual conference T2M 2010 in Le Mans, in particular Paul Beaudry, Michel Normandin, Syed Rizvi and the participants of the 30th CIRET 2010 conference in New York, in particular Christian Conrad.

References

Berger, H., Ehrmann, M., & Fratzscher, M. (2009). Forecasting ECB monetary policy: Accuracy is a matter of geography. *European Economic Review*, *53*(8), 1028–1041.

Blinder, A. S. (2000). Central bank credibility: Why do we care? How do we build it? *American Economic Review*, *90*(5), 1421–1431.

Blinder, A. S., Ehrmann, M., Fratzscher, M., de Haan, J., & Jansen, D.-J. (2008). Central bank communication and monetary policy: A survey of theory and evidence. *Journal of Economic Literature*, *46*(4), 910–945.

Blinder, A. S., Hildebrand, P., Lipton, D., & Wyplosz, C. (2001). *How do central banks talk?* Geneva reports on the world economy 3. CEPR and ICMB.

Boeckx, J. (2011). *Estimating monetary policy reaction functions: A discrete choice approach*. National Bank of Belgium Working Paper No. 210.

Clarida, R., Galí, J., & Gertler, M. (1998). Monetary policy rules in practice: Some international evidence. *European Economic Review*, *42*(6), 1033–1067.

Clarida, R., Galí, J., & Gertler, M. (1999). The science of monetary policy: A new Keynesian perspective. *Journal of Economic Literature*, *37*(4), 1661–1707.

Clarida, R., Galí, J., & Gertler, M. (2000). Monetary policy rules and macroeconomic stability: Evidence and some theory. *Quarterly Journal of Economics*, *115*(1), 147–180.

Coibion, O., & Gorodnichenko, Y. (2011). *Why are target interest rate changes so persistent?* NBER Working Paper No. 16707.

De Haan, J., Amtenbrink, F., & Waller, S. (2004). The transparency and credibility of the European Central Bank. *Journal of Common Market Studies*, *42*(4), 775–794.

De Haan, J., & Jansen, D.-J. (2009). *The communication policy of the European Central Bank: An overview of the first decade*. De Nederlandsche Bank Working Paper No. 212.

Demertzis, M., & Hallett, A. H. (2007). Central bank transparency in theory and practice. *Journal of Macroeconomics*, *29*(4), 760–789.

Ehrmann, M., & Fratzscher, M. (2009). Explaining monetary policy in press conferences. *International Journal of Central Banking*, *5*(2), 41–84.

Fourçans, A., & Vranceanu, R. (2004). The ECB interest rate rule under the Duisenberg presidency. *European Journal of Political Economy*, *20*(3), 579–595.

Geraats, P. (2007). The mystique of central bank speak. *International Journal of Central Banking*, *3*(1), 37–80.

Geraats, P. M. (2008). ECB credibility and transparency, European economy. Economic Papers 330. Directorate General Economic and Financial Affairs (DG ECFIN), European Commission.

Geraats, P. M. (2009). Trends in monetary policy transparency. *International Finance*, *12*(2), 235–268.

Geraats, P., Giavazzi, F., & Wyplosz, C. (2008). *Transparency and governance: Monitoring the European Central Bank 6*. Centre for Economic Policy Research.

Gerdesmeier, D., & Roffia, B. (2004). *Taylor rules for the Euro area: The issue of real-time data*. Deutsche Bundesbank Discussion Paper No. 37.

Gerlach, S. (2007). Interest rate setting by the ECB, 1999–2006: Words and deeds. *International Journal of Central Banking*, *3*(3), 1–46.

Gorter, J., Jacobs, J., & de Haan, J. (2008). Taylor rules for the ECB using expectations data. *Scandinavian Journal of Economics*, *110*(3), 473–488.

Gorter, J., Jacobs, J., & de Haan, J. (2009). Negative rates for the Euro area. *Central Banking*, *2*(2), 61–66.

Granger, C. W. J., & Newbold, P. (1974). Spurious regressions in econometrics. *Journal of Econometrics*, *2*(2), 111–120.

Hamilton, J. D., Pruitt, S., & Borger, S. C. (2009). *The market-perceived monetary policy rule*. Federal Reserve International Finance Discussion Paper No. 982.

Kuttner, K. N. (2001). Monetary policy surprises and interest rates: Evidence from the fed funds futures market. *Journal of Monetary Economics*, *47*(3), 523–544.

Maddala, G. S., & Kim, I.-M. (2004). *Unit roots, cointegration, and structural change*. Cambridge: *Cambridge University Press*.

Molodtsova, T., Nikolsko-Rzhevskyy, A., & Papell, H. D. (2008). Taylor rules with real-time data: A tale of two countries and one exchange rate. *Journal of Monetary Economics*, *55* (Suppl.), S63–S79.

Newey, W. K., & West, K. D. (1987). A simple, positive semi-definite, heteroskedasticity and autocorrelation consistent covariance matrix. *Econometrica*, *55*(3), 703–708.

Orphanides, A. (2001). Monetary policy rules based on real-time data. *American Economic Review*, *91*(4), 964–985.

Orphanides, A., & van Norden, S. (2002). The unreliability of output-gap estimates in real time. *The Review of Economics and Statistics*, *84*(4), 569–583.

Poplawski-Ribeiro, M., & Rülke, J.-C. (2010). Market's expectations on the stability and growth pact: Evidence from survey data. Working paper presented at the 2010 CIRET conference in New York.

Rosa, C., & Verga, G. (2007). On the consistency and effectiveness of central bank communication: Evidence from the ECB. *European Journal of Political Economy*, *23*(1), 146–175.

Ross, K. (2002). *Market predictability of ECB monetary policy decisions: A comparative examination*. International Monetary Fund Working Paper No. 233.

Sauer, S., & Sturm, J.-E. (2003). *Using Taylor rules to understand ECB monetary policy*. CESifo Working Paper No. 1110.

Smets, F. (2009). The ECB's response to the current crisis: Experience and lessons. Financial forum presentation held at the National Bank of Belgium, June 29, 2009.

Sturm, J.-E., & Wollmershäuser, T. (2008). *The stress of having a single monetary policy in Europe*. CESifo Working Paper No. 2251.

Swansson, E. (2006). Have increases in federal reserve transparency improved private sector interest rate forecasts? *Journal of Money, Credit and Banking*, *38*(3), 791–819.

Taylor, J. (1993). Discretion versus policy rules in practice. *Carnegie-Rochester Conference Series on Public Policy*, p. 39.

Van der Cruijsen, C., & Eijffinger, S. (2008). *Actual versus perceived transparency: The case of the European Central Bank*. De Nederlandsche Bank Working Paper No. 163.

Walsh, C. (2003). Speed limit policies: The output gap and optimal monetary policy. *American Economic Review*, *93*(1), 265–278.

Woodford, M. (2001). The Taylor rule and optimal monetary policy. *American Economic Review*, *91*(2), 232–237.

Woodford, M. (2003). *Interest and prices: Foundations of a theory of monetary policy*. Princeton, NJ: *Princeton University Press*.

Woodford, M. (2005). *Central bank communication and policy effectiveness*. National Bureau of Economic Research Working Paper No. 11898.

Wyplosz, C. (2010). *The Eurozone in the current crisis*. ADBI Working Paper No. 207.

Appendix

Variables Used in the Estimations

Table A.1: List of Variables

Variable	Description
i_{t+1}	Refi rate set by the ECB at its policy meeting in period $t+1$.
$E_t i_{t+1}$	Refi rate point forecast reported by the investment bank's economists in period t for the refi rate decision in period $t+1$.
$E_t \pi_q$	Inflation point forecasts of the investment bank's economists for the current quarter horizon.
$E_t \pi_{q+1}$	Inflation point forecasts of the investment bank's economists for the quarter ahead horizon.
$E_t \overline{\pi}_q$	One-quarter inflation point forecasts horizon of the investment bank's economists.
$E_t \pi_y$	Inflation point forecasts of the investment bank's economists and Consensus Economics for the current year horizon.
$E_t \pi_{y+1}$	Inflation point forecasts of the investment bank's economists and Consensus Economics for the year ahead horizon.
$E_t \overline{\pi}_y$	One-year inflation point forecasts horizon of the investment bank's economists and Consensus Economics.
$E_t y_q$	Real GDP growth point forecasts of the investment bank's economists for the current quarter horizon.
$E_t y_{q+1}$	Real GDP growth point forecasts of the investment bank's economists for the quarter ahead horizon.
$E_t \overline{y}_q$	One-quarter real GDP growth point forecasts horizon of the investment bank's economists.
$E_t y_y$	Real GDP growth point forecasts of the investment bank's economists and Consensus Economics for the current year horizon.
$E_t y_{y+1}$	Real GDP growth point forecasts of the investment bank's economists and Consensus Economics for the year ahead horizon.
$E_t \overline{y}_y$	One-year real GDP growth point forecasts horizon of the investment bank's economists and Consensus Economics.
ESI	The difference between the euro area Economic Sentiment Indicator (ESI) and its long-run average of 100 expressed in percentage points of the long-run average. The ESI is published by the European Commission on a monthly basis.

Table A.2: Summary Statistics

Dependent and explanatory variables	Obs.	Mean	Std. deviation	Min	Max
ECB's main refinancing operations rate (refi rate) (%)	133	3.164	1.129	1.00	4.75
ECB's refi rate point forecast, investment bank (%)	133	3.160	1.135	1.00	4.75
Current quarter inflation, investment bank (%)	133	2.204	0.716	−0.50	4.00
Quarter ahead inflation, investment bank (%)	133	2.085	0.690	−0.40	4.00
One-quarter inflation, investment bank (%)	133	2.140	0.704	−0.27	3.98
Current year inflation, investment bank (%)	133	2.101	0.661	0.20	3.70
Year ahead inflation, investment bank (%)	133	1.807	0.358	1.00	2.60
One-year inflation, investment bank (%)	133	1.936	0.464	0.53	3.11
Current quarter real GDP growth, investment bank (%)	133	1.422	1.799	−5.20	4.20
Quarter ahead real GDP growth, investment bank (%)	133	1.538	1.725	−4.50	5.00
One-quarter real GDP growth, investment bank (%)	133	1.465	1.756	−4.61	4.33
Current year real GDP growth, investment bank (%)	133	1.497	1.719	−4.30	4.00
Year ahead real GDP growth, investment bank (%)	133	2.032	0.787	−0.50	3.60
One-year real GDP growth, investment bank (%)	133	1.700	1.219	−2.24	3.84
Current year inflation, consensus forecasts (%)	133	2.063	0.618	0.30	3.60
Year ahead inflation, consensus forecasts (%)	133	1.814	0.250	1.20	2.50
One-year inflation, consensus forecasts (%)	133	1.914	0.408	0.70	3.26
Current year real GDP growth, consensus forecasts (%)	133	1.548	1.627	−4.40	3.40
Year ahead real GDP growth, consensus forecasts (%)	133	2.030	0.765	−0.90	3.20
One-year real GDP growth, consensus forecasts (%)	133	1.777	1.116	−2.17	3.29
Economic Sentiment Indicator, deviation from long-run average (%)	133	0.968	10.413	−29.30	17.60

Note: The actual refi rate comes from the website of the ECB and the Economic Sentiment Indicator is taken from the European Commission's website. The long-run average of the ESI is equal to 100 as computed by the European Commission.

Unit Root and Stationarity Tests

Table A.3: Unit Root Tests, Investment Bank Forecasts

Variables	ADF Z(t)	PP Z(t)	KPSS	Integration order
Refi rate	−2.031**	−0.630	0.607**	I(0)
	(0.022)	(0.864)		
Forecasted refi rate	−1.594*	−0.711	0.588**	I(0)
	(0.057)	(0.844)		
Expected inflation, current quarter	−2.989***	−1.962	0.184	I(0)
	(0.002)	(0.303)		
Expected inflation, quarter ahead	−3.758***	−2.740*	0.138	I(0)
	(0.000)	(0.067)		
Expected inflation, current year	−2.410***	−2.099	0.132	I(0)
	(0.009)	(0.245)		
Expected inflation, year ahead	−3.112***	−2.962**	0.138	I(0)
	(0.001)	(0.039)		
Expected inflation, one-quarter horizon	−4.486***	−2.089	0.154	I(0)
	(0.000)	(0.249)		
Expected inflation, one-year horizon	−4.278***	−2.481	0.121	I(0)
	(0.000)	(0.120)		
Expected GDP growth, current quarter	−1.950**	−1.507	0.515**	I(0)
	(0.027)	(0.530)		
Expected GDP growth, quarter ahead	−2.647***	−2.358	0.570**	I(0)
	(0.005)	(0.154)		
Expected GDP growth, current year	−0.254	0.040	0.577**	I(1)
	(0.400)	(0.962)		
Expected GDP growth, year ahead	−2.866***	−2.929**	0.777***	I(0)
	(0.002)	(0.042)		
Expected GDP growth, one-quarter horizon	−2.395***	−1.782	0.543**	I(0)
	(0.009)	(0.389)		
Expected GDP growth, one-year horizon	−2.664***	−2.097	0.640**	I(0)
	(0.004)	(0.246)		
ESI percentage deviation from the long-run average	−2.306**	−1.497	0.524**	I(0)
	(0.011)	(0.535)		
Observations	131	133	135	

Note: The ADF Z(t) and PP Z(t) refer to the Augmented Dickey−Fuller and Phillips−Perron tests for unit root in the variables. A statistically significant test shows evidence against the null hypothesis of unit root. For the ADF test, three lags of the difference in the variables have been used, while the number of lags used in the Phillips−Perron test is determined automatically based on Newey−West bandwidth selection. The Kwiatkowski−Phillips−Schmidt−Shin (KPSS) test reports the statistic for testing the null hypothesis of level stationarity based on Newey−West automatic bandwidth selection. A statistically significant test shows evidence against the hypothesis of stationarity. The integration order is determined on the basis of the ADF, PP and KPSS test statistics. MacKinnon approximate p-values are reported in parentheses.

***$p < 0.01$, **$p < 0.05$, *$p < 0.1$.

Table A.4: Unit Root Tests, Consensus Economics Forecasts

Variables	ADF Z(t)	PP Z(t)	KPSS	Integration order
Expected inflation, current year	−2.910***	−2.168	0.0835	I(0)
	(0.002)	(0.218)		
Expected inflation, year ahead	−2.159**	−2.226	0.139	I(0)
	(0.016)	(0.197)		
Expected inflation, one-year horizon	−2.532***	−3.230**	0.073	I(0)
	(0.006)	(0.018)		
Expected GDP growth, current year	−0.719	0.541	0.614**	I(1)
	(0.237)	(0.986)		
Expected GDP growth, year ahead	−1.519*	−1.791	1.250***	I(1)
	(0.066)	(0.385)		
Expected GDP growth, one-year horizon	−2.755***	−1.686	0.834***	I(1)
	(0.003)	(0.438)		
Observations	131	133	135	

Note: The ADF Z(t) and PP Z(t) refer to the Augmented Dickey–Fuller and Phillips–Perron tests for unit root in the variables. A statistically significant test shows evidence against the null hypothesis of unit root. For the ADF test, three lags of the difference in the variables have been used, while the number of lags used in the Phillips–Perron test is determined automatically based on Newey–West bandwidth selection. The Kwiatkowski–Phillips–Schmidt–Shin (KPSS) test reports the statistic for testing the null hypothesis of level stationarity based on Newey–West automatic bandwidth selection. A statistically significant test shows evidence against the hypothesis of stationarity. The integration order is determined on the basis of the ADF, PP and KPSS test statistics. MacKinnon approximate p-values are reported in parentheses.

***$p < 0.01$, **$p < 0.05$, *$p < 0.1$.

Actual and Perceived Taylor Rules with a Dummy Variable for the ECB Meetings

Table A.5: Actual Taylor Rule, 2000–2009 Meeting Dummy

	Quarter ahead	Year ahead	One-quarter horizon	One-year horizon
ρ	0.8734***	0.9152***	0.7609***	0.8217***
	(0.0326)	(0.0203)	(0.0535)	(0.0517)
β_π	0.5503***	1.7607***	0.5569***	1.0949***
	(0.1183)	(0.2528)	(0.0792)	(0.1448)
β_y	0.4315***	1.2135***	0.2743***	0.3942***
	(0.1247)	(0.3101)	(0.0582)	(0.1478)
Meeting	0.0103***	0.0069**	0.0120***	0.0113***
	(0.0017)	(0.0028)	(0.0011)	(0.0014)
α	0.0094***	−0.0290***	0.0118***	−0.0002
	(0.0014)	(0.0078)	(0.0016)	(0.0019)
R^2	0.9816	0.9835	0.9738	0.9804
Observations	133	133	133	133
Hansen J-statistic	1.5172	1.4370	1.3877	1.3611
ADF Z(t)	−4.621***	−4.342***	−3.291**	−3.882***
PP Z(t)	−9.109***	−10.524***	−6.680***	−8.585***

Note: GMM estimates, HAC standard errors are computed with the Delta method and are denoted in parentheses. The table reports the long-run response coefficients. The regressions are performed for all forecast horizons. The variable "Meeting" is a dummy that takes the value of 1 when the Governing Council of the ECB has met more than once within a month until November 2001. The Hansen J-statistic tests whether the over-identifying restrictions are satisfied. A statistically significant test shows evidence against the validity of the instruments. The ADF Z(t) and PP Z(t) refer to the Augmented Dickey–Fuller and Phillips–Perron statistics, respectively. Both are used to determine whether the residuals contain a unit root. A statistically significant test shows evidence against the null hypothesis of unit root. For the ADF test, three lags of the difference in the residuals have been used, while the number of lags used in the Phillips–Perron test is determined automatically based on Newey–West bandwidth selection.
***$p < 0.01$, **$p < 0.05$, *$p < 0.1$.

Table A.6: Perceived Taylor Rule, 2000–2009 Meeting Dummy

	Quarter ahead	Year ahead	One-quarter horizon	One-year horizon
ρ	0.8818***	0.9046***	0.7627***	0.8398***
	(0.0119)	(0.0249)	(0.0263)	(0.0218)
β_π	0.6525***	2.2412***	0.6300***	1.3334***
	(0.0973)	(0.2803)	(0.0690)	(0.0988)
β_y	0.4283***	0.9098***	0.2618***	0.3734***
	(0.0783)	(0.2434)	(0.0440)	(0.1092)
Meeting	0.0095***	0.0087***	0.0114***	0.0109***
	(0.0017)	(0.0023)	(0.0011)	(0.0014)
α	0.0072***	−0.0320***	0.0107***	−0.0046**
	(0.0015)	(0.0087)	(0.0014)	(0.0021)
R^2	0.9808	0.9833	0.9725	0.9806
Observations	133	133	133	133
Hansen J-statistic	1.7722	1.5055	1.4961	1.4681
ADF Z(t)	−4.087***	−4.127***	−2.787*	−3.516***
PP Z(t)	−9.978***	−10.457***	−7.180***	−9.527***

Note: GMM estimates, HAC standard errors are computed with the Delta method and are denoted in parentheses. The table reports the long-run response coefficients. The regressions are performed for all forecast horizons. The variable "Meeting" is a dummy that takes the value of 1 when the Governing Council of the ECB has met more than once within a month until November 2001. The Hansen J-statistic tests whether the over-identifying restrictions are satisfied. A statistically significant test shows evidence against the validity of the instruments. The ADF Z(t) and PP Z(t) refer to the Augmented Dickey–Fuller and Phillips–Perron statistics, respectively. Both are used to determine whether the residuals contain a unit root. A statistically significant test shows evidence against the null hypothesis of unit root. For the ADF test, three lags of the difference in the residuals have been used, while the number of lags used in the Phillips–Perron test is determined automatically based on Newey–West bandwidth selection.
***$p < 0.01$, **$p < 0.05$, *$p < 0.1$.

Actual and Perceived Taylor Rules with Consensus Economics Forecasts

Table A.7: Actual Taylor Rule, 2000–2009 Consensus Forecasts

	Year ahead	One-year horizon
ρ	0.8928***	0.8923***
	(0.0194)	(0.0173)
β_π	2.1397***	−0.1349
	(0.3255)	(0.2434)
β_y	1.5716***	1.1680***
	(0.1740)	(0.1300)
α	−0.0410***	0.0119**
	(0.0083)	(0.0052)
R^2	0.9833	0.9806
Observations	133	133
Hansen J-statistic	1.1341	1.6593
ADF Z(t)	−4.162***	−4.310***
PP Z(t)	−10.445***	−9.618***

Note: GMM estimates, HAC standard errors are computed with the Delta method and are denoted in parentheses. The table reports the long-run response coefficients. The regressions are performed for the specifications with the forecasts for the year ahead and the one-year horizon, respectively. The Hansen J-statistic tests whether the over-identifying restrictions are satisfied. A statistically significant test shows evidence against the validity of the instruments. The ADF Z(t) and PP Z(t) refer to the Augmented Dickey–Fuller and Phillips–Perron statistics, respectively. Both are used to determine whether the residuals contain a unit root. A statistically significant test shows evidence against the null hypothesis of unit root. For the ADF test, three lags of the difference in the residuals have been used, while the number of lags used in the Phillips–Perron test is determined automatically based on Newey–West bandwidth selection.

***$p < 0.01$, **$p < 0.05$, *$p < 0.1$.

Table A.8: Perceived Taylor Rule, 2000–2009 Consensus Forecasts

	Year ahead	One-year horizon
ρ	0.9322***	0.8557***
	(0.0129)	(0.0242)
β_π	2.7004***	0.7590***
	(0.4857)	(0.1372)
β_y	1.7088***	0.8845***
	(0.3124)	(0.1286)
α	−0.0556***	−0.0001
	(0.0105)	(0.0043)
R^2	0.9809	0.9779
Observations	133	133
Hansen J-statistic	1.0823	1.6747
ADF Z(t)	−4.009***	−3.128**
PP Z(t)	−10.899***	−9.150***

Note: GMM estimates, HAC standard errors are computed with the Delta method and are denoted in parentheses. The table reports the long-run response coefficients. The regressions are performed for the specifications with the forecasts for the year ahead and the one-year horizon, respectively. The Hansen J-statistic tests whether the over-identifying restrictions are satisfied. A statistically significant test shows evidence against the validity of the instruments. The ADF Z(t) and PP Z(t) refer to the Augmented Dickey–Fuller and Phillips–Perron statistics, respectively. Both are used to determine whether the residuals contain a unit root. A statistically significant test shows evidence against the null hypothesis of unit root. For the ADF test, three lags of the difference in the residuals have been used, while the number of lags used in the Phillips–Perron test is determined automatically based on Newey–West bandwidth selection.
***$p<0.01$, **$p<0.05$, *$p<0.1$.

Actual and Perceived Taylor Rules with the Economic Sentiment Indicator

Table A.9: Actual Taylor Rule, 2000–2009 ESI

	Quarter ahead	Year ahead	One-quarter horizon	One-year horizon
ρ	0.8735***	0.8943***	0.8624***	0.8857***
	(0.0126)	(0.0110)	(0.0142)	(0.0177)
β_π	0.3254***	0.1467	0.3092***	0.4559**
	(0.0918)	(0.1978)	(0.0902)	(0.1797)
β_{esi}	0.1157***	0.1359***	0.1120***	0.1223***
	(0.0099)	(0.0108)	(0.0093)	(0.0169)
α	0.0225***	0.0262***	0.0230***	0.0203***
	(0.0021)	(0.0037)	(0.0020)	(0.0034)
R^2	0.9842	0.9847	0.9835	0.9846
Observations	133	133	133	133
Hansen J-statistic	1.5691	1.2861	1.4809	1.2772
ADF Z(t)	−4.624***	−5.044***	−4.306***	−4.953***
PP Z(t)	−10.371***	−10.833***	−10.060***	−10.753***

Note: GMM estimates, HAC standard errors are computed with the Delta method and are denoted in parentheses. The table reports the long-run response coefficients. The regressions are performed for the specifications with the forecasts for the quarter ahead and the year ahead, respectively. The Hansen J-statistic tests whether the over-identifying restrictions are satisfied. A statistically significant test shows evidence against the validity of the instruments. The ADF Z(t) and PP Z(t) refer to the Augmented Dickey–Fuller and Phillips–Perron statistics, respectively. Both are used to determine whether the residuals contain a unit root. A statistically significant test shows evidence against the null hypothesis of unit root. For the ADF test, three lags of the difference in the residuals have been used, while the number of lags used in the Phillips–Perron test is determined automatically based on Newey–West bandwidth selection.
***$p < 0.01$, **$p < 0.05$, *$p < 0.1$.

Table A.10: Perceived Taylor Rule, 2000–2009 ESI

	Quarter ahead	Year ahead	One-quarter horizon	One-year horizon
ρ	0.9267***	0.9287***	0.9182***	0.9222***
	(0.0094)	(0.0084)	(0.0115)	(0.0094)
β_{π}	0.3814***	1.3603***	0.3373**	0.9780***
	(0.1386)	(0.3204)	(0.1384)	(0.2036)
β_{esi}	0.1470***	0.1356***	0.1392***	0.1288***
	(0.0147)	(0.0136)	(0.0151)	(0.0134)
α	0.0192***	0.0024	0.0205***	0.0085*
	(0.0031)	(0.0062)	(0.0029)	(0.0044)
R^2	0.9839	0.9844	0.9837	0.9842
Observations	133	133	133	133
Hansen J-statistic	1.7572	1.5648	1.7001	1.5928
ADF Z(t)	−5.112***	−5.276***	−4.905***	−5.138***
PP Z(t)	−12.330***	−12.540***	−12.118***	−12.423***

Note: GMM estimates, HAC standard errors are computed with the Delta method and are denoted in parentheses. The table reports the long-run response coefficients. The regressions are performed for the specifications with the forecasts for the quarter ahead and the year ahead, respectively. The Hansen J-statistic tests whether the over-identifying restrictions are satisfied. A statistically significant test shows evidence against the validity of the instruments. The ADF Z(t) and PP Z(t) refer to the Augmented Dickey–Fuller and Phillips–Perron statistics, respectively. Both are used to determine whether the residuals contain a unit root. A statistically significant test shows evidence against the null hypothesis of unit root. For the ADF test, three lags of the difference in the residuals have been used, while the number of lags used in the Phillips–Perron test is determined automatically based on Newey–West bandwidth selection.

***$p<0.01$, **$p<0.05$, *$p<0.1$.

Actual and Perceived Taylor Rules with Consensus Inflation Forecasts and the Economic Sentiment Indicator

Table A.11: Actual Taylor Rule, 2000–2009 Consensus Forecasts and ESI

	Year ahead	One-year horizon
ρ	0.8796***	0.8805***
	(0.0117)	(0.0231)
β_π	0.6212***	0.2869**
	(0.2171)	(0.1348)
β_{esi}	0.1243***	0.1295***
	(0.0093)	(0.0181)
α	0.0178***	0.0233***
	(0.0042)	(0.0022)
R^2	0.9843	0.9841
Observations	133	133
Hansen J-statistic	1.4254	1.3470
ADF Z(t)	−4.779***	−4.862***
PP Z(t)	−10.552***	−10.513***

Note: GMM estimates, HAC standard errors are computed with the Delta method and are denoted in parentheses. The table reports the long-run response coefficients. The regressions are performed for the specifications with the forecasts for the year ahead and the one-year horizon, respectively. The Hansen J-statistic tests whether the over-identifying restrictions are satisfied. A statistically significant test shows evidence against the validity of the instruments. The ADF Z(t) and PP Z(t) refer to the Augmented Dickey–Fuller and Phillips–Perron statistics, respectively. Both are used to determine whether the residuals contain a unit root. A statistically significant test shows evidence against the null hypothesis of unit root. For the ADF test, three lags of the difference in the residuals have been used, while the number of lags used in the Phillips–Perron test is determined automatically based on Newey–West bandwidth selection.
***$p < 0.01$, **$p < 0.05$, *$p < 0.1$.

Table A.12: Perceived Taylor Rule, 2000–2009 Consensus Forecasts and ESI

	Year ahead	One-year horizon
ρ	0.9263***	0.8745***
	(0.0087)	(0.0197)
β_π	0.7741*	0.9538***
	(0.4045)	(0.1078)
β_{esi}	0.1559***	0.1108***
	(0.0145)	(0.0156)
α	0.0131*	0.0106***
	(0.0075)	(0.0026)
R^2	0.9838	0.9829
Observations	133	133
Hansen J-statistic	1.3553	1.6493
ADF Z(t)	−5.234***	−3.998**
PP Z(t)	−12.399***	−11.046***

Note: GMM estimates, HAC standard errors are computed with the Delta method and are denoted in parentheses. The table reports the long-run response coefficients. The regressions are performed for the specifications with the forecasts for the year ahead and the one-year horizon, respectively. The Hansen J-statistic tests whether the over-identifying restrictions are satisfied. A statistically significant test shows evidence against the validity of the instruments. The ADF Z(t) and PP Z(t) refer to the Augmented Dickey–Fuller and Phillips–Perron statistics, respectively. Both are used to determine whether the residuals contain a unit root. A statistically significant test shows evidence against the null hypothesis of unit root. For the ADF test, three lags of the difference in the residuals have been used, while the number of lags used in the Phillips–Perron test is determined automatically based on Newey–West bandwidth selection.
***$p < 0.01$, **$p < 0.05$, *$p < 0.1$.

Predicted Refi Rate Target, Investment Bank Forecasts

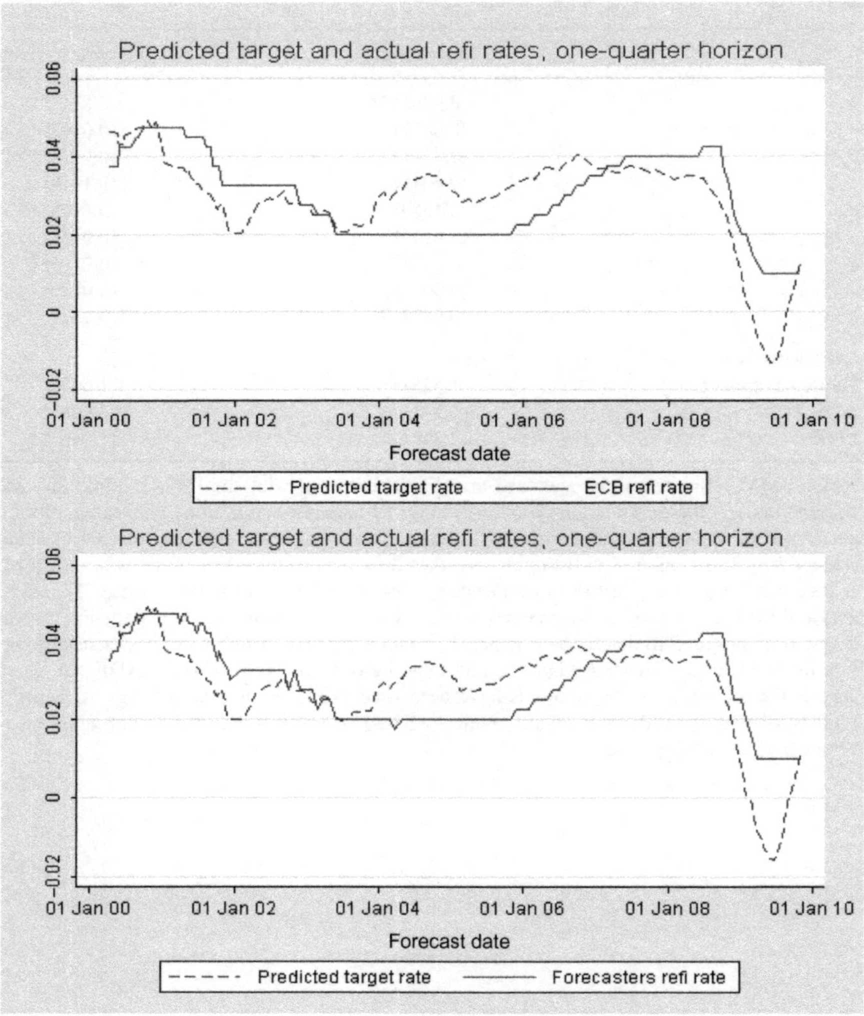

Figure A.1: Actual and Perceived Taylor Rules, One-Quarter Forecasts.

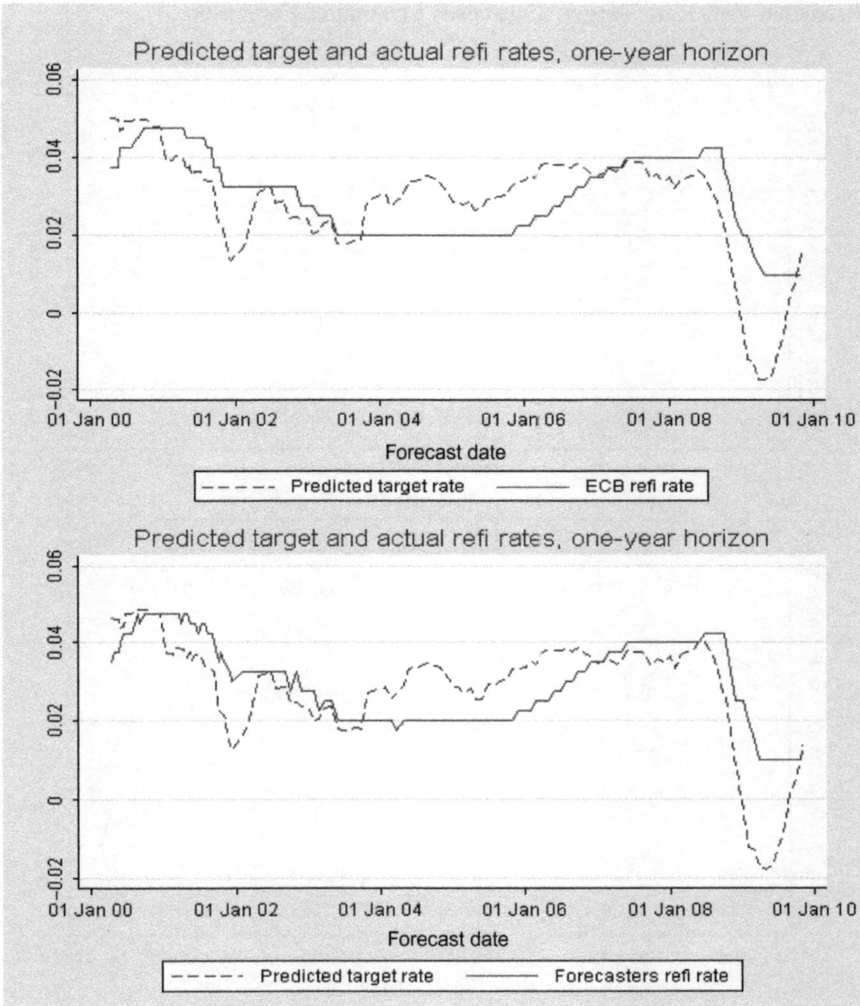

Figure A.2: Actual and Perceived Taylor Rules, One-Year Forecasts.

Predicted Refi Rate Target, Consensus Economics Forecasts

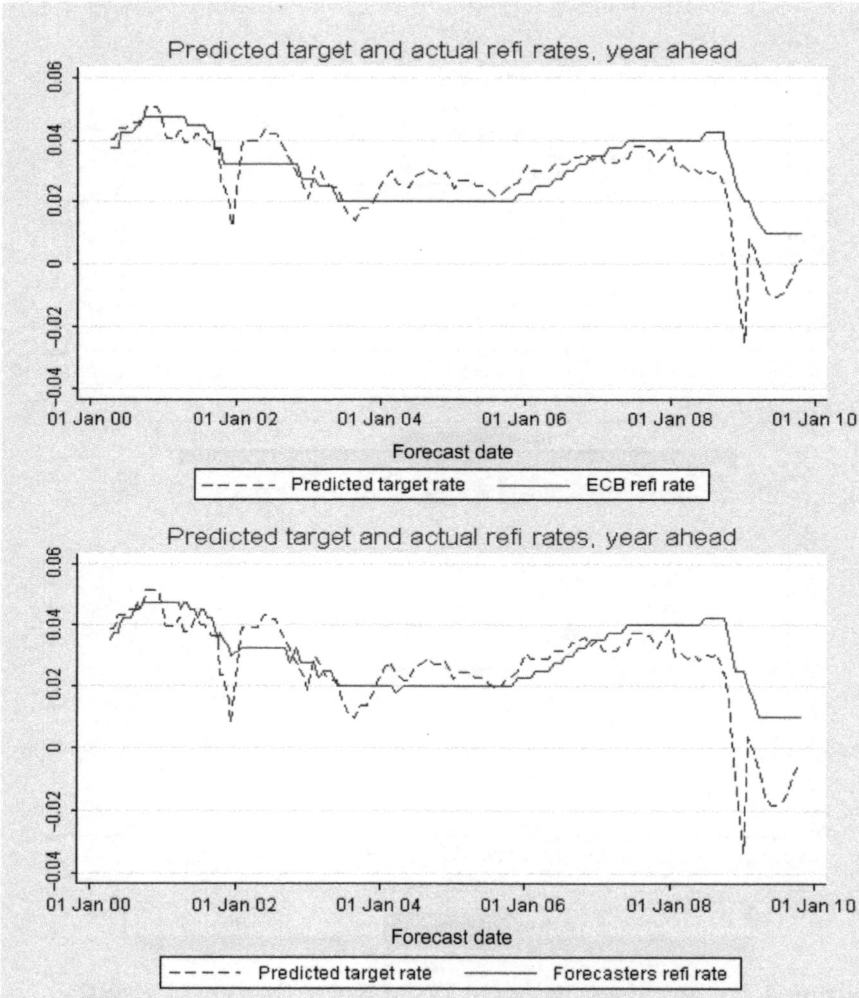

Figure A.3: Actual and Perceived Taylor Rules, Year Ahead Consensus Forecasts.

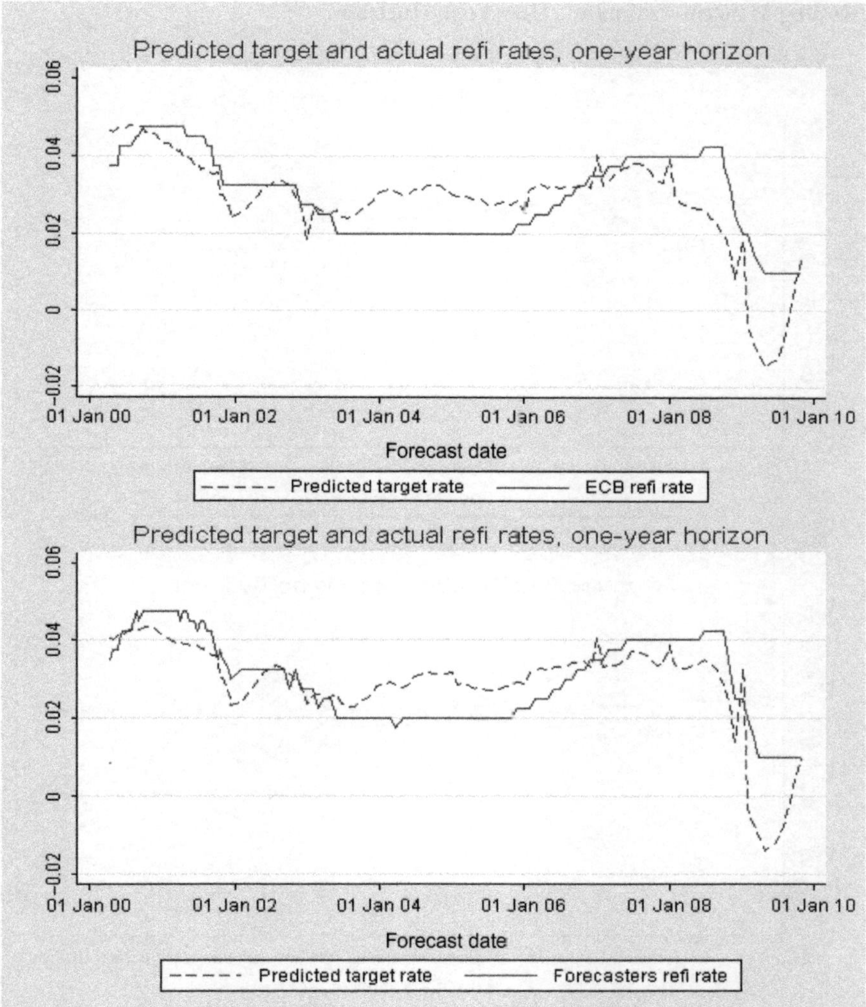

Figure A.4: Actual and Perceived Taylor Rules, One-Year Consensus Forecasts.

Rolling Window Estimates, One-Year Horizon

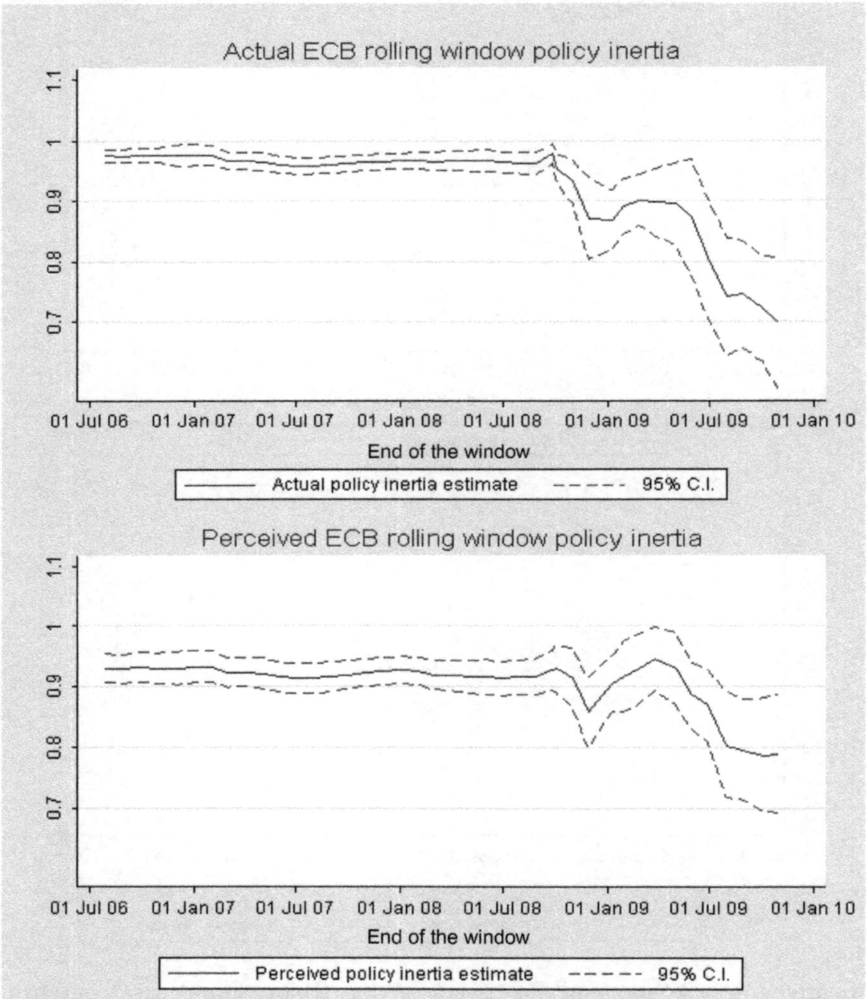

Figure A.5: Policy Inertia Estimates, One-Year Forecasts (Rolling).

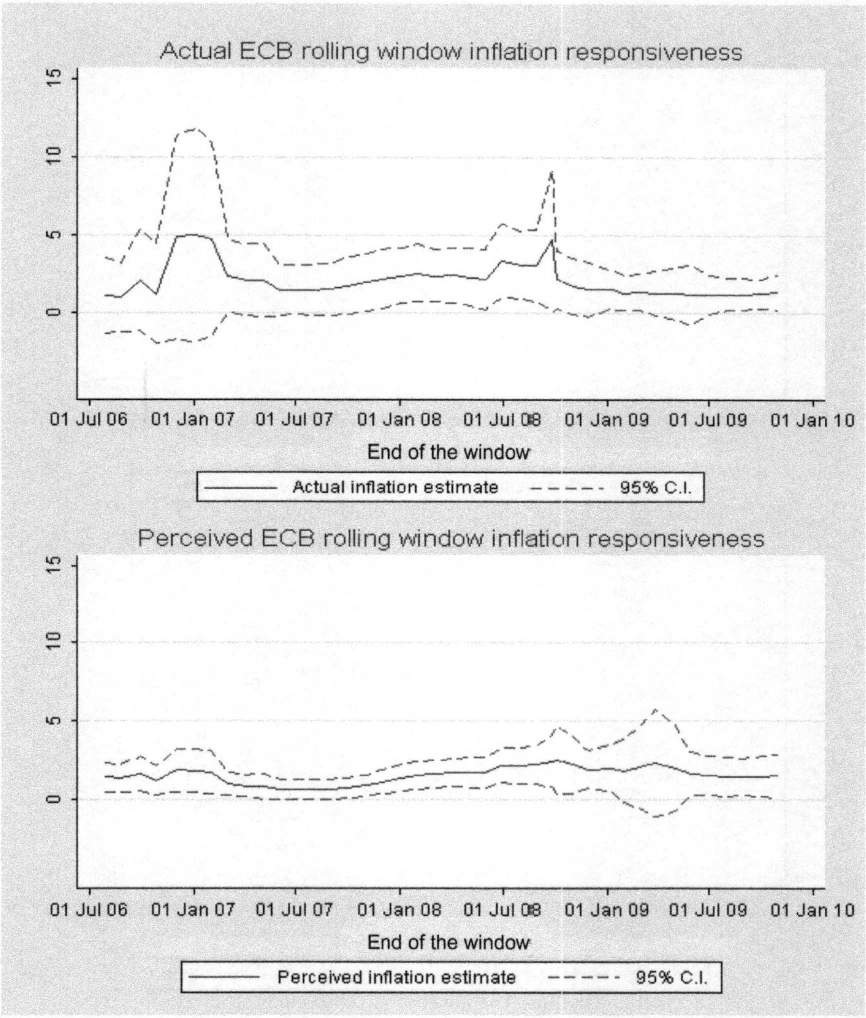

Figure A.6: Inflation Coefficient Estimates, One-Year Forecasts (Rolling).

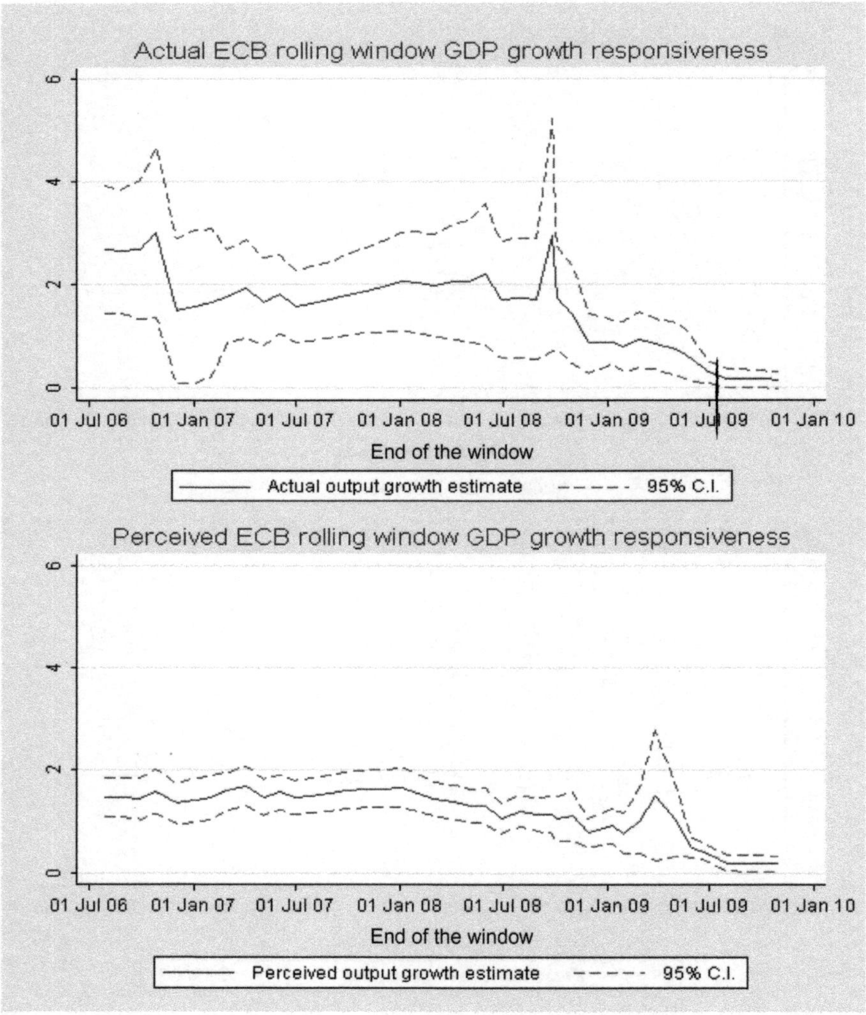

Figure A.7: Output Growth Coefficient Estimates, One-Year Forecasts (Rolling).

Recursive Window Estimates, Year Ahead Horizon

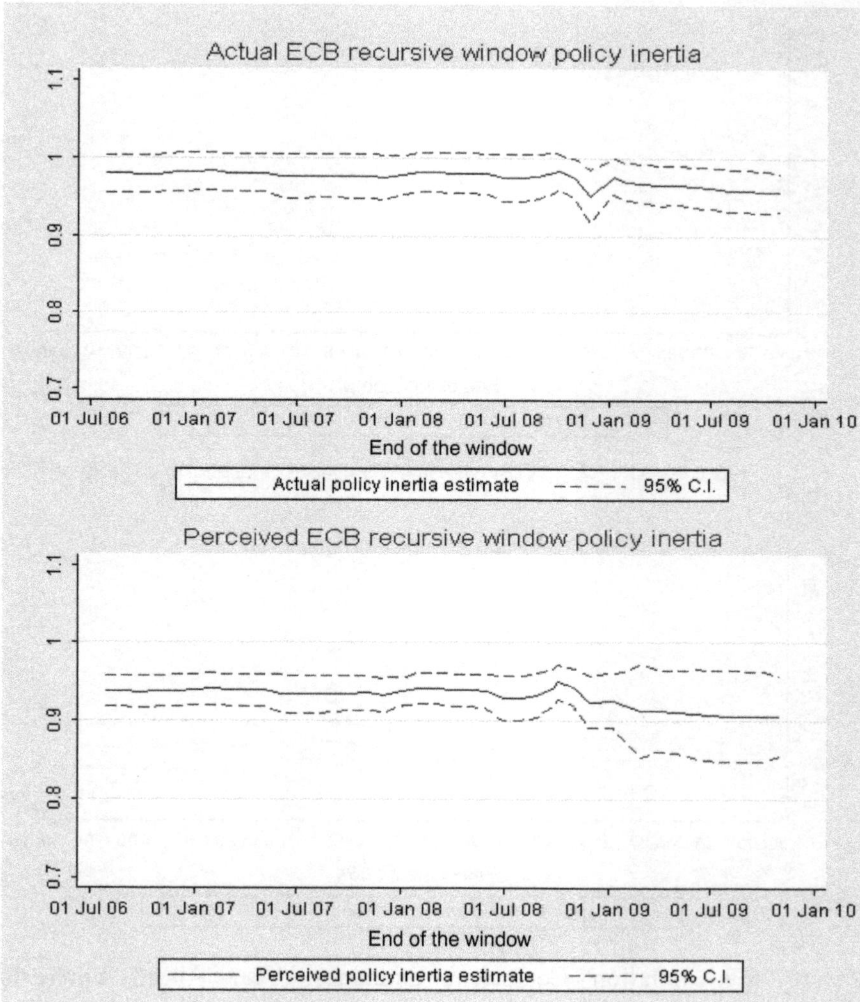

Figure A.8: Policy Inertia Estimates, Year Ahead Forecasts (Recursive).

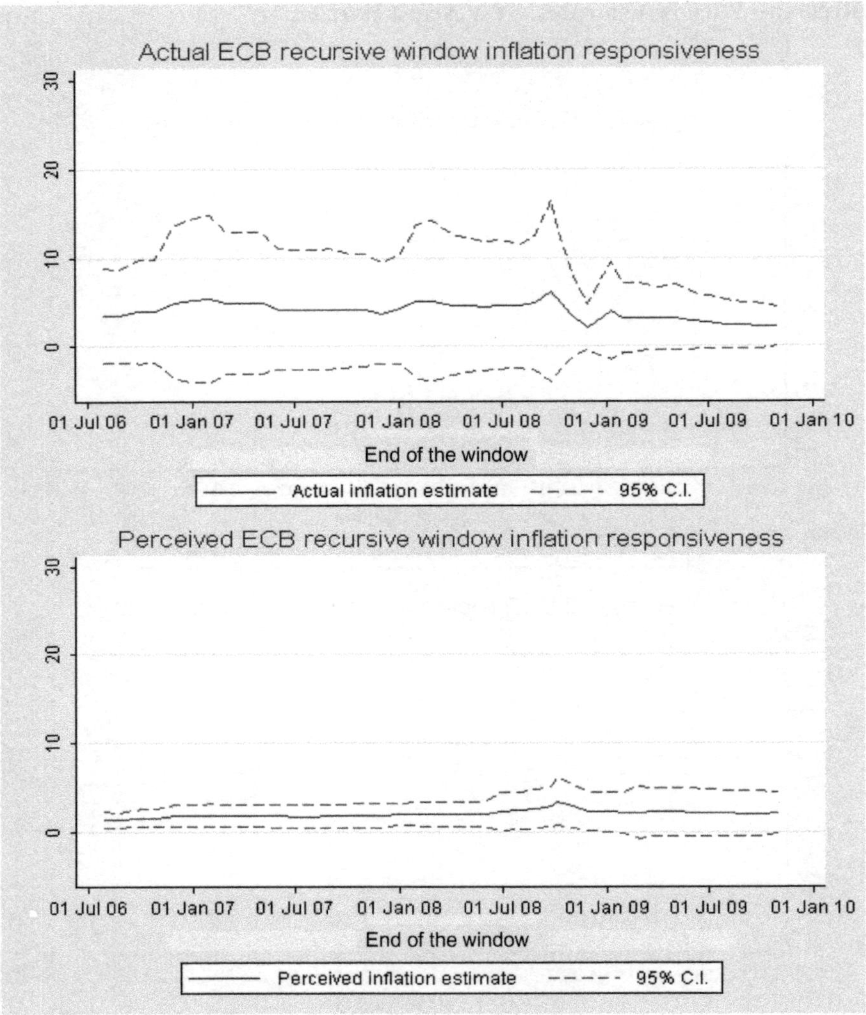

Figure A.9: Inflation Coefficient Estimates, Year Ahead Forecasts (Recursive).

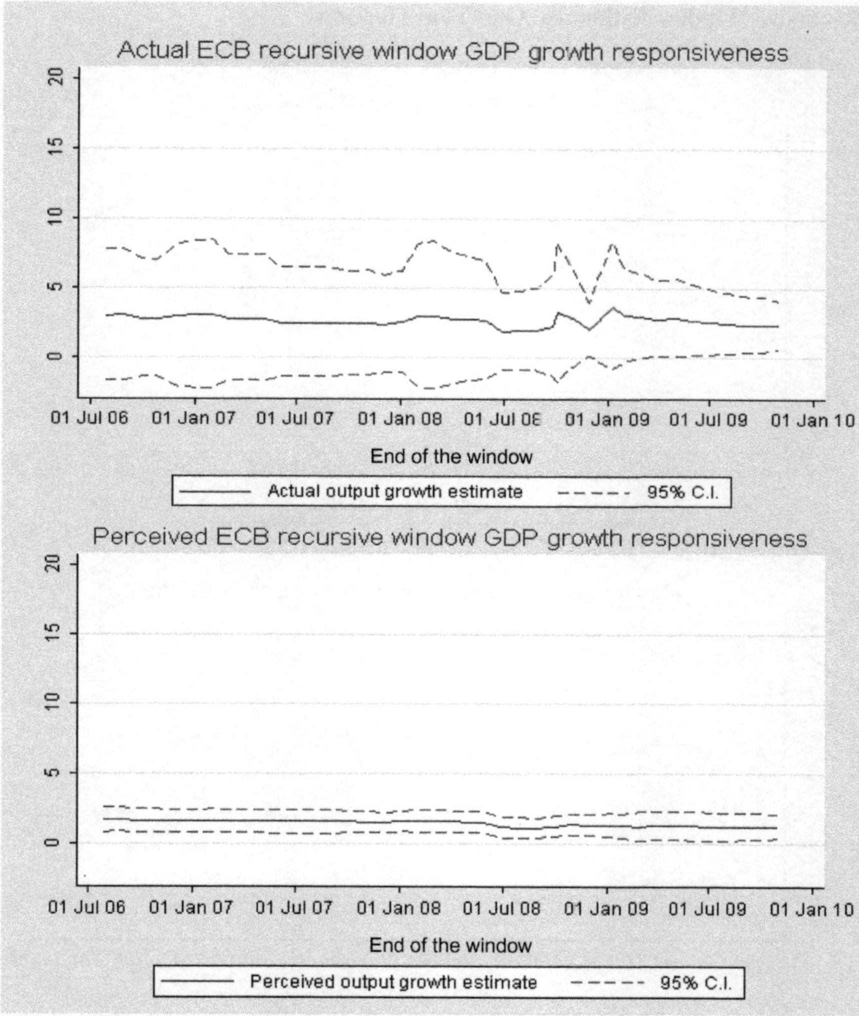

Figure A.10: Output Growth Coefficient Estimates, Year Ahead Forecasts (Recursive).

Recursive Window Estimates, One-Year Horizon

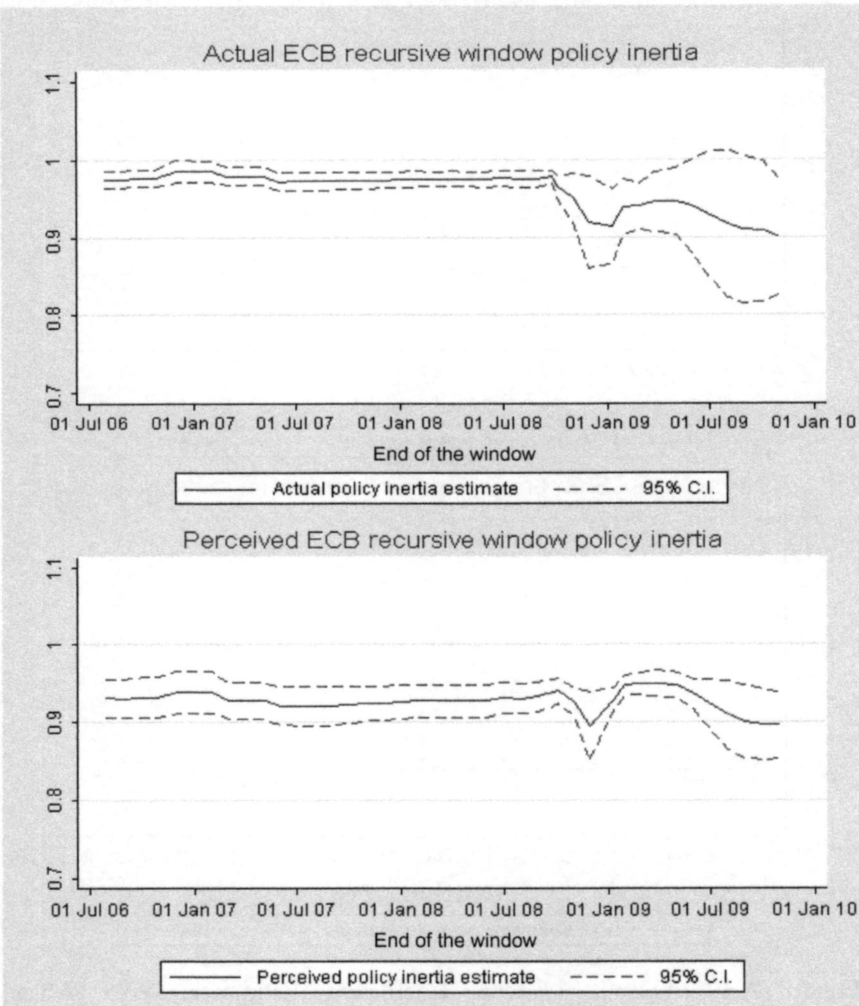

Figure A.11: Policy Inertia Estimates, One-Year Forecasts (Recursive).

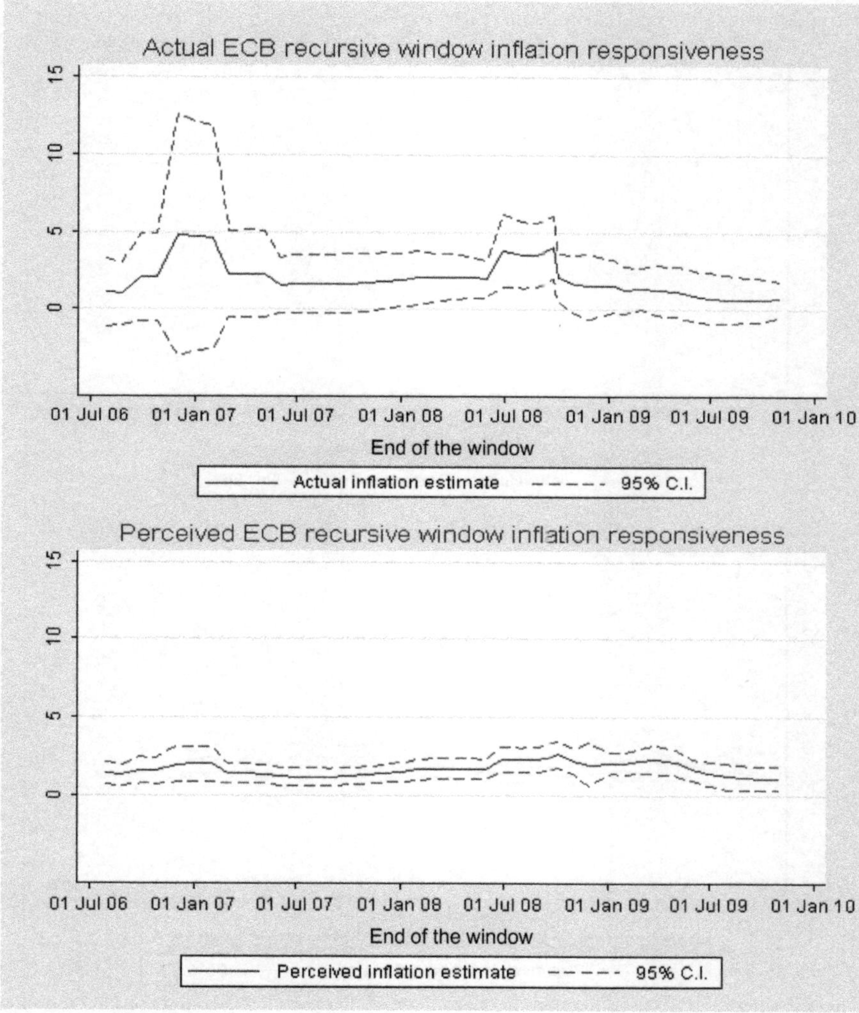

Figure A.12: Inflation Coefficient Estimates, One-Year Forecasts (Recursive).

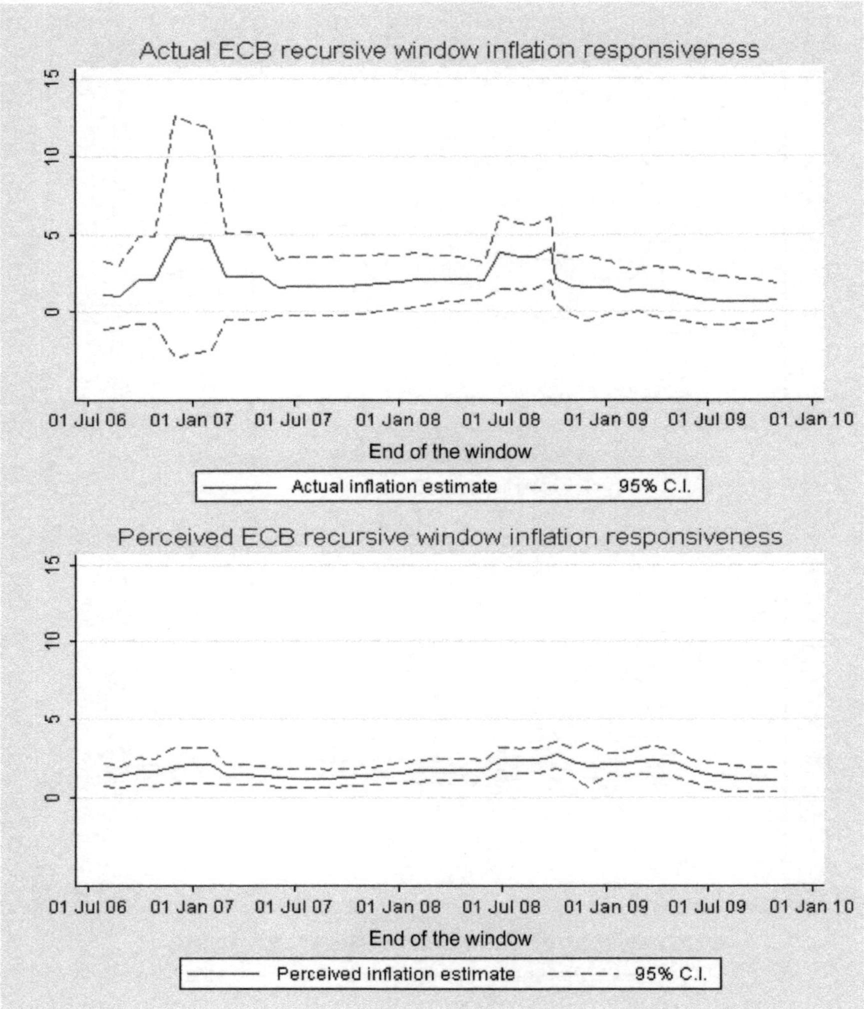

Figure A.13: Output Growth Coefficient Estimates, One-Year Forecasts (Recursive).

Chapter 8

A Regime Switching Model for the European Central Bank

Nikolay Markov

Pictet Asset Management, Route des Acacias 60, CH-1211 Geneva 73, Switzerland, e-mail: nmarkov@pictet.com

Abstract

This chapter estimates a regime switching Taylor Rule for the European Central Bank (ECB) in order to investigate some potential nonlinearities in the forward-looking policy reaction function within a real-time framework. In order to compare observed and predicted policy behavior, the chapter estimates Actual and Perceived regime switching Taylor Rules for the ECB. The former is based on the refi rate set by the Governing Council while the latter relies on the professional point forecasts of the refi rate performed by a large investment bank before the upcoming policy rate decision. The empirical evidence shows that the Central Bank's main policy rate has switched between two regimes: in the first one the Taylor Principle is satisfied and the ECB stabilizes the economic outlook, while in the second regime the Central Bank cuts rates more aggressively and puts a higher emphasis on stabilizing real output growth expectations. Second, the results point out that the professional forecasters have broadly well predicted the actual policy regimes. The estimation results are also robust to using consensus forecasts of inflation and real output growth. The empirical evidence from the augmented Taylor Rules shows that the Central Bank has most likely not responded to the growth rates of M3 and the nominal effective exchange rate and the estimated regimes are robust to including these additional variables in the regressions. Finally, after the bankruptcy of Lehman Brothers the policy rate has switched to a crisis regime as the ECB has focused on preventing a further decline in economic activity and on securing the stability of the financial system.

International Symposia in Economic Theory and Econometrics, Vol. 24
William A. Barnett and Fredj Jawadi (Editors)

ISSN: 1571-0386/doi: 10.1108/S1571-038620150000024020

Keywords: European Central Bank, monetary policy predictability, nonlinear policy reaction function, real-time forecasts, Markov regime switching

JEL Classifications: C24, E52, E58

1. Introduction

In the previous chapter I have investigated the predictability of ECB's monetary policy by the professional forecasters of a large investment bank within a forward-looking Taylor Rule framework.[1] In that chapter the dynamic stability of the response coefficients of the Taylor Rules has been analyzed within rolling and recursive window regressions. The results have shown a swift change in the coefficient estimates of the policy rules occurring since the broadening of the financial crisis in October 2008. At that moment, the ECB has sharply reversed its policy stance to foster liquidity provision on the interbank lending market, as well as to offset a further decline in the economic outlook. This finding points to some possible nonlinearities in the policy reaction functions. Indeed, the Central Bank might have responded in a different way to economic fundamentals depending on the state of the economy, being a financial crisis, an economic downturn or an expansion. Besides, the ECB might also have responded to other economic fundamentals when setting the policy rate. In order to investigate these issues more in-depth, the goal of this chapter is to examine some potential nonlinearities in the Central Bank's responsiveness to economic fundamentals within a Markov Regime Switching model for the Actual and Perceived Taylor Rules (MRS ATR and PTR).

The use of regime switching models has been introduced in macroeconomics by Quandt (1972), Goldfeld and Quandt (1973), and has been further investigated by Mankiw, Miron, and Weil (1987). The latter study the effect of the founding of the Federal Reserve on the stochastic process for the short-term interest rate. They have found a sharp switch of the interest rate to a new regime occurring at the inception of the Federal Reserve in 1914. The authors show that the transition has been sharp rather than gradual and has altered the stochastic process for the long-term interest rate as well, consistently with the expectations theory of the term structure of interest rates. Furthermore, in a seminal paper Hamilton (1989) has

[1] Markov (2009).

proposed a regime switching model for the U.S. business cycle. He has shown that the MRS framework provides an alternative objective method for measuring U.S. post-war business cycles that fits accurately the NBER's official measures. Garcia and Perron (1996) consider a three regimes model for the ex post real interest rate in the United States and find that it has different means and variances over specific time periods. As regards monetary policy, the empirical literature considers two approaches for modeling regime switching policy reaction functions.

The first approach suggests a gradual regime switching model which assumes that the transition between regimes takes place progressively and is driven by a specific variable with respect to some threshold value. In this framework the researchers estimate a logistic smooth transition regression (LSTR) as in Alcidi, Flamini, and Fracasso (2005). The latter have found that a linear Taylor Rule for the U.S. Federal Reserve might have hidden finer policy regimes in the period from 1988 to 2004. They have detected three policy regimes distinguishing between a general, a crash, and a Zero Lower Bound (ZLB) regimes. The authors have also emphasized that the linear Taylor Rule actually provides a weighted average of the policy regimes in place during the estimation period. Finally, at the research frontier on this topic, Gerlach (2011) and Gerlach and Lewis (2010) have estimated a gradual regime switching model for the European Central Bank within a logistic smoothed transition approach. They have found that the ECB's behavior has changed after the bankruptcy of Lehman Brothers in September 2008 since the Central Bank has adjusted its policy rate much more aggressively than before. Their findings are also consistent with one strand of the literature that postulates that the Central Bank cuts rates more strongly in the vicinity of the ZLB.[2]

The second approach is based on a Markov Regime Switching policy framework. This methodology is more general as it allows for discrete changes of regimes which do not depend on any specific transition variable. The MRS models assume an abrupt discrete switch that takes place between some unobservable states rather than considering a gradual transition between regimes. There are several authors who have followed the latter approach as Assenmacher-Wesche (2006). The latter has estimated Central Banks' preferences from time-varying reaction functions for the United States, the United Kingdom, and Germany within a two regimes MRS model. She has found that monetary policy in these countries features a low and a high inflationary regimes and that switching in the residuals' variance turns out to be important for the model's fit. Furthermore, the results

[2] See for instance Reifschneider and Williams (2000) among others.

indicate that the Deutsche Bundesbank has assigned a higher weight to inflation compared to the Federal Reserve and the main difference in monetary policies is driven by different preferences for interest rate smoothing. In addition, Owyang and Ramey (2004) estimate a MRS model for the United States over the period 1965–1999. Their estimates point to the presence of a "dove" and a "hawk" regimes in monetary policy. The researchers report evidence that the regime switches have also Granger caused both NBER's dating of recessions and Romer dates. Sims and Zha (2006) have investigated regime switches in the U.S. monetary policy over the period 1959–2003. Their best model features only a switching in the residuals' variance while among the coefficient switching models the best fit is given by a four regimes MRS model. More recently, Perruchoud (2009) has estimated a MRS forward-looking Taylor Rule for Switzerland over the period 1975–2007. He has found that Swiss monetary policy is described by a smooth and an active regimes. The latter involves a strong reaction of the Swiss National Bank to counteract large deviations of the exchange rate from its trend.

One should note that an alternative approach to the regime switching modeling would be to split the sample in different subsamples and estimate a model with breaks in the case of known break dates, or to estimate them endogenously.[3] In contrast with this method, the MRS model features much greater flexibility in dealing with nonlinearities since it estimates the regime switches using all available data. Moreover, it also differs from the LSTR specification in the sense that it is a more general framework to detect regime shifts without defining a priori any transition variable that drives the switch between regimes. Besides, the MRS model assumes that the regime shift occurs instantaneously as one would expect in a period of economic turmoil for instance. Therefore, in order to keep the model as flexible and general as possible in detecting all potential regime switches in the ECB policy rate, I have opted for the MRS approach in modeling the nonlinearity of the reaction function.

In that spirit, the chapter contributes to the aforementioned literature on MRS models in three aspects. First, it analyzes potential nonlinearities in the European monetary policy at the frequency of the ECB Governing Council meetings from April 2000 until June 2010. Second, in the theoretical specification and in the empirical investigation I specify Actual and Perceived MRS Taylor Rules for the ECB. The latter is based on the professional point forecasts from a large investment bank of the key policy rate (the refi rate) for the upcoming Governing Council interest rate decision, while the former is based on the actual refi rate set by the Council at

[3] In the latter case the researcher could follow the approach of Zivot and Andrews (1992) for instance.

the corresponding policy meeting. Such a comparison will unveil whether the economists have foreseen the nonlinearity of the ECB Taylor Rule and have accurately predicted the regime switches of the actual refi rate. Third, the empirical evidence sheds more light on understanding the behavior of the ECB during the recent financial crisis.

The estimation results point to several major findings. First, the MRS model has identified two regimes for the European monetary policy: in the first one the Taylor Principle is satisfied and the policy rate exhibits a high level of inertia, while in the second regime the Central Bank puts a higher emphasis on the economic outlook downplaying the stabilization of inflation expectations. Second, the professional forecasters have broadly well predicted the policy regimes, as well as the timing of the switches. The augmented Taylor Rules point out that the Central Bank has most likely not responded to the growth rates of M3 and to the nominal effective exchange rate when setting the policy rate. In addition, the estimated coefficients are sensitive to the measure of inflation and real output growth expectations used in the regressions while the estimated regimes remain qualitatively unaltered. The empirical evidence also suggests that there might be a third regime in the Central Bank's responsiveness to economic fundamentals. The latter tends to occur in periods of monetary policy tightening but is sometimes difficult to disentangle from the presence of the second regime.

The structure of the chapter is the following. Section 2 outlines the theoretical model, while the data and the methodological approach are described in Section 3. The main empirical results are reported in Section 4, while Section 5 provides a sensitivity analysis of the baseline results using consensus data, an alternative forecast horizon, and some additional variables. The extension to a three regimes switching model is presented in Section 6 and the final part of the chapter concludes on the empirical findings.

2. The Model

In line with most of the recent literature on Central Bank policy reaction functions, I estimate a forward-looking Taylor Rule which takes the following form:[4]

[4] The modeling approach is in line with the monetary policy rules estimated in Clarida, Galí, and Gertler (1998, 2000) for instance. The difference is that in this setting the Central Bank responds to the growth rate of real GDP in deviation from the growth rate of potential GDP instead to the output gap. Given the relatively short period since the inception of the ECB it is reasonable to assume that the potential GDP has remained constant.

$$\bar{i}_{t+1} = r^* + \pi^* + \beta_\pi E_t\{\pi_{t+k} - \pi^* | \Omega_t\} + \beta_y E_t\{y_{t+k} - y^* | \Omega_t\} + \eta_{t+1}, \tag{1}$$

where $\bar{i}_{t+1}$ denotes the Central Bank's target for the policy interest rate in period $t+1$, r^*, and π^* are the equilibrium real interest rate and the inflation objective, respectively. $E_t\{\pi_{t+k} - \pi^* | \Omega_t\}$ and $E_t\{y_{t+k} - y^* | \Omega_t\}$ are the inflation and real output growth expectations, respectively, formed in period t for a horizon $t+k$, in deviation from the inflation objective π^* and the trend real output growth rate y^*. Ω_t denotes the available information set in period t and η_{t+1} is a stochastic disturbance term. In order to account for the fact that Central Banks tend to adjust the policy rate gradually to the target level, I introduce the following partial adjustment mechanism for the policy rate:

$$i_{t+1} = \rho i_t + (1-\rho)\bar{i}_{t+1} + \xi_{t+1}, \tag{2}$$

where i_{t+1} is the observed interest rate in period $t+1$, ρ is the interest rate smoothing parameter, and ξ_{t+1} is a stochastic disturbance. This equation points out that the Central Bank implements a fraction $(1-\rho)$ of the desired policy rate target at each meeting of the policy committee. Combining Equations (1) and (2) yields the final specification to be estimated:

$$i_{t+1} = \rho i_t + (1-\rho)\left[\alpha + \beta_\pi E_t\{\pi_{t+k} | \Omega_t\} + \beta_y E_t\{y_{t+k} | \Omega_t\}\right] + \varepsilon_{t+1}, \tag{3}$$

where $\alpha = r^* + \pi^*(1-\beta_\pi) - y^*\beta_y$.

Furthermore, in order to consider some potential nonlinearities in the forward-looking Taylor Rule, I estimate a two regimes first order Markov Regime Switching model (MRS) for the policy rate in which the coefficients can switch from one regime to another with some probability estimated from the data. Hence, by relaxing the linearity assumption the MRS model should permit to unveil whether the European monetary policy could be described by a Taylor Rule whose coefficient estimates change along with the state of the economy. In addition, given the swift reversal of the single monetary policy stance that has occurred on October 8, 2008, this model will permit to reveal whether and possibly how the ECB's behavior has changed at the turning point of the financial crisis. Therefore, it will show in which manner the Taylor Rule has to be specified in order to more accurately describe the monetary policy stance in normal and in crisis periods.

Based on Equation (3), I estimate an Actual regime switching Taylor Rule which takes the following form:

$$\begin{aligned} i_{t+1} = {} & \rho_{S_{t+1}} i_t + \left(1-\rho_{S_{t+1}}\right) \\ & \left[\alpha_{S_{t+1}} + \beta_{\pi S_{t+1}} E_t\{\pi_{t+k} | \Omega_t\} + \beta_{y S_{t+1}} E_t\{y_{t+k} | \Omega_t\}\right] + \varepsilon_{1t+1}, \end{aligned} \tag{4}$$

where i_{t+1} denotes the refi rate set by the ECB Governing Council in period $t+1$.

I also estimate a Perceived regime switching Taylor Rule based on the professional point forecasts of the refi rate $E_t\{i_{t+1}\}$ one week ahead of the upcoming policy rate decision:

$$E_t\{i_{t+1}\} = \rho_{S_{t+1}} i_t + (1-\rho_{S_{t+1}}) \left[\alpha_{S_{t+1}} + \beta_{\pi S_{t+1}} E_t\{\pi_{t+k}|\Omega_t\} + \beta_{y S_{t+1}} E_t\{y_{t+k}|\Omega_t\}\right] + \varepsilon_{2t}, \quad (5)$$

where ε_{1t+1} is i.i.d. $N(0,\sigma^2_{\varepsilon_1})$, ε_{2t+1} is i.i.d. $N(0,\sigma^2_{\varepsilon_2})$.

The regime-dependent Actual Taylor Rule becomes the following:

$$i_{t+1} = \rho_{S_{t+1}} i_t + \gamma'_{S_{t+1}} x_t + \varepsilon_{1t+1}. \quad (6)$$

The regime switching Perceived Taylor Rule can be written in a similar way:

$$E_t\{i_{t+1}\} = \rho_{S_{t+1}} i_t + \gamma'_{S_{t+1}} x_t + \varepsilon_{2t}, \quad (7)$$

where

$$x_t = \left[1 \;\; E_t\{\pi_{t+k}|\Omega_t\} \;\; E_t\{y_{t+k}|\Omega_t\}\right]' \quad (8)$$

$$\gamma_{S_{t+1}} = \left[(1-\rho_{S_{t+1}})\alpha_{S_{t+1}} (1-\rho_{S_{t+1}})\beta_{\pi S_{t+1}} (1-\rho_{S_{t+1}})\beta_{y S_{t+1}}\right]'. \quad (9)$$

The parameters $\gamma_{S_{t+1}}$ are assumed to be driven by two regimes depending on the unobservable latent variable S_{t+1}. The latter takes the value 0 or 1 for the first and the second regimes correspondingly:

$$\rho_{S_{t+1}} = \rho_1(1-S_{t+1}) + \rho_2 S_{t+1} \quad (10)$$

$$\beta_{\pi S_{t+1}} = \beta_{\pi_1}(1-S_{t+1}) + \beta_{\pi_2} S_{t+1} \quad (11)$$

$$\beta_{y S_{t+1}} = \beta_{y_1}(1-S_{t+1}) + \beta_{y_2} S_{t+1} \quad (12)$$

$$\alpha_{S_{t+1}} = \alpha_1(1-S_{t+1}) + \alpha_2 S_{t+1}. \quad (13)$$

The dummy variable S_{t+1} is assumed to be driven by the Markov transition probabilities which can be written as follows:

$$p_{ij} = p(S_{t+1} = j | S_t = i), \quad i,j = 1,2 \quad (14)$$

$$\Pi = \begin{bmatrix} \pi_{11} & \pi_{21} \\ \pi_{12} & \pi_{22} \end{bmatrix},$$

where Π denotes the Markov transition probabilities matrix and the rows refer to regimes 1 and 2, respectively.[5]

3. Data and Methodology

The data set contains real-time point forecasts of inflation and real GDP growth for the euro area reported by the economists of Barclays in their weekly economic research publications.[6] Since the market participants do not report forecasts of the output gap I use the projections of real GDP growth in the regressions.[7] In addition, the professional forecasters of the bank also report the main point forecast of the refi rate for the upcoming interest rate decision of the ECB Governing Council. The forecasts are made in general one week before the corresponding monetary policy meeting and span the period from April 2000 until June 2010. The frequency of the observations thus corresponds to the meetings of the Governing Council of the ECB which are in general monthly.[8] Data on the key policy interest rate are taken from the official website of the ECB. Given that the weekly reports contain the economists' expectations about the future policy rate, this framework permits to assess the predictability of the European

[5] Each row indicates the probability to remain in the corresponding regime as well as the probability to switch to another regime. As the probabilities reported in each row represent all possible outcomes within each regime they have to sum to one.

[6] I have built-up the database from the euro weekly reports of Barclays made in general one week before the upcoming monetary policy meeting of the ECB. The forecasts are provided in real-time and thus are not subject to the Orphanides' critique (2001).

[7] This approach is consistent with the speed limit policy described by Walsh (2003). The latter has emphasized that a policy rule in which the Central Bank responds to the change in the output gap delivers the optimal pre-commitment policy outcome. This policy is welfare improving especially in the case of imperfect observation of the output gap. In the present setting I have assumed a constant level of potential output given the relatively short time period.

[8] The Governing Council has taken monetary policy decisions twice a month until October 2001. However, as shown in Markov (2009) accounting for the higher frequency of the meetings before October 2001 does not seem to be important for the interest rate setting policy. Besides, the regime switching estimates do not show evidence for a change in the Taylor Rules related to the frequency of the monetary policy meetings.

monetary policy within the regime switching Actual and Perceived Taylor Rules.

Regarding the forecasts of economic fundamentals, the economists report their main point projection of inflation and real GDP growth for the current year and the year ahead. As the latter are directly observed by the forecasters and the ECB and are used to predict the refi rate these variables are considered as exogenous. This assumption is corroborated by the formal difference-in-Sargan statistics which do not find evidence against the null hypothesis of exogeneity. A detailed description of the data and some summary statistics are provided in Tables A.1 and A.2. The average inflation expectations for the year ahead are 1.788% and 1.790% for the investment bank economists and the consensus forecasters respectively and they are fully consistent with the ECB's inflation objective. Tables A.3 and A.4 report the unit root and stationarity tests of the series used in the estimations. The Augmented Dickey–Fuller (ADF) and the Kwiatkowski–Phillips–Schmidt–Shin (KPSS) test statistics point out that in general the variables are stationary. However, as found in the first chapter some of the Phillips–Perron (PP) tests do not show evidence against the null hypothesis of unit root for some of the series, in particular for the actual and forecasted refi rates and for the GDP growth forecasts. This result is probably due to the low power of the test statistics in small samples and to the magnitude of the economic contraction during the recent financial crisis. The latter is explicitly accounted for in the regime switching specification. Based on the methodology of Gorter, Jacobs, and de Haan (2008) I use two approaches in constructing the expectations of inflation and real output growth that are used in the empirical analysis.

In a first approach to modeling the expectations of inflation and real output growth I use for each period t the inflation and real GDP growth forecasts for the year ahead. The attractiveness of this methodology is that it is entirely forward-looking since I consider the forecasters' expectations for the year ahead. It is also in line with the method used in Poplawski-Ribeiro and Rülke (2010) in their investigation of the impact of the Stability and Growth Pact on the forecast accuracy of the public budget deficit in the euro area by the market participants. This approach could also better reflect the observed long and variable lags in the monetary policy transmission process.

The second methodology considers a fixed forecast horizon of one year which is computed using the following formula:

$$\bar{x}_{y,h} = \frac{361 - h}{360} x_{y,h} + \frac{h-1}{360} x_{y+1,h},$$

where $x_{y,h}$ is any of the current year (y) forecasts of the macroeconomic variables reported on day h and $x_{y+1,h}$ stands for the year ahead ($y+1$) projections reported on the same day. The indices y and h take respectively the values $y=2000,\ldots,2010$ and $h=1,\ldots,360$ assuming 360 days within a year which is a standard assumption for financial markets participants.

The advantage of this approach is that one obtains a fixed horizon of one year for the inflation and real GDP growth forecasts. However, there are also some drawbacks related to this methodology. First, the variables computed are not entirely forward-looking because I consider the expectations of the series for the current year in their computation. Second, by applying this formula we cannot assign a specific forecasting horizon to the variables computed because they encompass any period that is between the current year and the year ahead. Moreover, given that these variables are constructed from the economists' reports they may not correspond well to the way the economists form their expectations of macroeconomic variables. Conversely, the year ahead forecasts are directly reported by the economists and are observed by the Central Bank in real-time, and hence are more likely to correspond to the expectations formation process of the private sector about macroeconomic fundamentals compared to the expectations variables obtained with the second approach.

Finally, in the empirical part of the chapter the first methodology yields better results which points out that the year ahead forecasts of the variables provide a good measure for the forward-looking expectations of inflation and output growth of the investment bank's economists and the consensus forecasters. The one-year fixed horizon forecasts obtained with the second approach are less likely to reflect the expectations formation process of the professional forecasters as they yield less satisfactory results and do not imply a preemptive behavior of the Central Bank.

The estimation approach closely follows the methodology developed in the seminal paper of Hamilton (1989), which is also explained in Hamilton (2005) and is derived in Kim and Nelson (1999). In the first paper, Hamilton develops a classical method for estimating regime switching models which is based on an iterative maximum likelihood estimation (I-MLE). This methodology provides the best unbiased estimator for linear and non-linear regressions with identically and independently distributed error terms. It is important to emphasize that in Markov switching models the GMM approach is not feasible because of the presence of the unobservable latent variable S_{t+1}. Therefore, all regressions are performed with the I-MLE algorithm of Hamilton. To control for a potential endogeneity that could arise when including the lagged dependent variable as a regressor, I have performed Portmanteau and BDS white noise tests as well as LM tests for serial correlation of the residuals. The test statistics point out that there is no evidence against the absence of autocorrelation in the residuals and the latter can be considered as white noise processes.

The estimation algorithm derived below is based on the methodology exposed in Kim and Nelson (1999). The Actual Taylor Rule of Equation (6) can be written in the following more compact form:[9]

$$i_{t+1} = \Theta'_{S_{t+1}} z_t + \varepsilon_{1t+1}, \quad t = 1, 2, \ldots, T, \tag{15}$$

where

$$\Theta_{S_{t+1}} = \begin{bmatrix} \rho_{S_{t+1}} \\ \gamma'_{S_{t+1}} \end{bmatrix}, \quad z_t = \begin{bmatrix} i_t \\ x_t \end{bmatrix} \tag{16}$$

and

ε_{1t+1} is i.i.d. $N\left(0, \sigma^2_{\varepsilon_1}\right)$.

First, in order to start the optimization algorithm one has to consider the joint density function of i_{t+1} and the unobserved state S_{t+1}:

$$f(i_{t+1}, S_{t+1}|\Psi_t) = f(i_{t+1}|S_{t+1}, \Psi_t) f(S_{t+1}|\Psi_t), \tag{17}$$

where Ψ_t refers to the available information set at time t. The marginal density function of i_{t+1} is then obtained in the following way:

$$\begin{aligned} f(i_{t+1}|\Psi_t) &= \sum_{S_{t+1}=0}^{1} f(i_{t+1}, S_{t+1}|\Psi_t) \\ &= \sum_{S_{t+1}=0}^{1} f(i_{t+1}|S_{t+1}, \Psi_t) f(S_{t+1}|\Psi_t) \\ &= f(i_{t+1}|S_{t+1}=0, \Psi_t)\Pr[S_{t+1}=0|\Psi_t] \\ &\quad + f(i_{t+1}|S_{t+1}=1, \Psi_t)\Pr[S_{t+1}=1|\Psi_t]. \end{aligned} \tag{18}$$

The associated log-likelihood function is a weighted average of the density functions in the two regimes and takes the following form:

$$\text{Log Lik} = \sum_{t=1}^{T} \text{Log}\left[\sum_{j=0}^{1} f(i_{t+1}|S_{t+1}, \Psi_t)\Pr[S_{t+1}=j|\Psi_t]\right]. \tag{19}$$

The weights are given by the transition probabilities and can be written as follows:

$$\Pr[S_{t+1}=j|\Psi_t] = \sum_{i=0}^{1} \Pr[S_{t+1}=j, S_t=i|\Psi_t] = \sum_{i=0}^{1} \Pr[S_{t+1}=j|S_t=i]\Pr[S_t=i|\Psi_t], \tag{20}$$

[9] The same algorithm can be applied to the Perceived Taylor Rule in a straightforward way.

where $\Pr[S_{t+1}=j|S_t=i]$ denotes the states' transition probabilities. At the end of each period $t+1$, i_{t+1} is observed and one has to apply an iterative filter to update the filtered probabilities:

$$\Pr[S_{t+1}=j|\Psi_{t+1}]=\Pr[S_{t+1}=j|\Psi_t,i_{t+1}]=\frac{f(S_{t+1}=j,i_{t+1}|\Psi_t)}{f(i_{t+1}|\Psi_t)}$$
$$=\frac{f(i_{t+1}|S_{t+1}=j,\Psi_t)\Pr[S_{t+1}=j|\Psi_t]}{\sum_{j=0}^{1}f(i_{t+1}|S_{t+1}=j,\Psi_t)\Pr[S_{t+1}=j|\Psi_t]}. \tag{21}$$

This approach can also be used to compute the smoothed regime probabilities (using all available information up to the final observation T):

$$\Pr[S_{t+1}=j|\Psi_t],\quad t=1,2,\ldots,T. \tag{22}$$

To start the filter in the first period one can use the unconditional states' probabilities for the first and the second regimes respectively:

$$\pi_1=\Pr[S_1=0|\Psi_0]=\frac{1-p}{2-p-q},\quad \pi_2=\Pr[S_1=1|\Psi_0]=\frac{1-q}{2-p-q}, \tag{23}$$

where p and q are the unconstrained parameters.

Using the described methodology the following section presents the estimation results for the Actual and Perceived MRS TR.[10]

4. Empirical Evidence

The goal of the MRS TR specification is to uncover whether the standard forward-looking policy reaction function hides any finer monetary policy regimes that could not have been detected by a linear policy rule. Moreover, a comparison between the Actual and Perceived Taylor Rules will reveal whether the investment bank's economists have accurately predicted the magnitude and the timing of the actual regime switches of the ECB's main policy rate. In the following subsection, I first present the estimation results for the Actual Taylor Rule using the inflation and real output growth forecasts for the year ahead.[11]

[10] All estimations are derived from numerical optimization that has been implemented in Matlab R (2010a) and are based on the estimation algorithm developed by Perlin (2009).

[11] The favorite specifications contain the real-time professional forecasts of inflation and real output growth for the year ahead instead of the one-year horizon forecasts computed with the second approach. Indeed, the former yield more satisfactory results compared to the latter. However, in Section 5, I also present the estimation results using the alternative one-year horizon forecasts.

4.1. Actual Regime Switching Taylor Rule

In a first approach, I estimate a baseline model which allows for a switching in the model's coefficients across two possible regimes. The model features regime shifts in the policy inertia, inflation and real GDP growth coefficients.[12] Indeed, in a general framework one can rationally assume that the Central Bank's responsiveness to key macroeconomic fundamentals, such as inflation and real output growth, might depend on the state of the euro area economy. The ECB might be more inclined to implement a more hawkish monetary policy in a highly inflationary environment consistently with its policy mandate, and to behave more dovishly in a state of economic downturn or in an economic crisis. The MRS model in this chapter assumes that the transition probabilities of the regimes are governed by a first order Markov chain process and are also reported along with the coefficient estimates. Table 1 reports the estimation results for the Actual Taylor Rule.

From the results of Table 1 one can observe the emergence of two different policy regimes with statistically significant parameter estimates. In the first one monetary policy is quite inertial and the ECB raises the refi rate in the event of an increase in the inflation and real output growth forecasts. Conversely, in the second one the policy stance becomes more aggressive as the Central Bank implements a larger fraction of the desired policy rate in each period. Besides, while the ECB responds positively to the economic outlook, the coefficient estimate on inflation expectations is negative in the second regime. The increasing aggressiveness of the Central Bank in the crisis regime is in line with the findings reported in the literature as in Belke and Klose (2010), Gerlach and Lewis (2010), and Mishkin (2009) for instance. As regards the estimated transition probabilities, one can see that the first regime is particularly persistent compared to the smaller probability of occurrence of the second regime. The average duration of the former is about 19.38 policy meetings while the latter lasts on average 1.71 meetings. Furthermore, there is a much higher probability of transiting into regime 1 conditional on being in the second regime compared to the lower probability of entering the second regime conditional on being in the first one. Indeed, once the policy rate has entered the second regime it has a greater chance to transit back again to the first one. The long-run response coefficients of the model, $\beta_{\pi_{S_{t+1}}}$ and $\beta_{y_{S_{t+1}}}$, as well as some relevant statistics are reported in Table 2.

[12] The models do not feature a switching in the constant term because it does not produce satisfactory results and there is evidence that the constant has not switched across regimes in the more general specification.

Table 1: Actual MRS Taylor Rule, Baseline Model (BM)

	Regime 1		Regime 2
$\rho_{S_{t+1}}$	0.9859***		0.9300***
	(0.0050)		(0.0190)
$\gamma_{\pi_{S_{t+1}}}$	0.0315***		−0.1864***
	(0.0040)		(0.0377)
$\gamma_{y_{S_{t+1}}}$	0.0052***		0.0441***
	(0.0001)		(0.0010)
γ_c		−0.0000	
		(0.0000)	
σ_ε		0.0009***	
		(2.350e−05)	
$P[S_{t+1}=i\|S_t=1]$	0.9484***		0.0516***
	(0.1393)		(0.0015)
$P[S_{t+1}=i\|S_t=2]$	0.5831***		0.4169***
	(0.1123)		(0.0521)
Observations		141	
Log-likelihood		749.329	

Note: The table displays the short-run coefficients. $\rho_{S_{t+1}}, \gamma_{\pi_{S_{t+1}}}, \gamma_{y_{S_{t+1}}}, \gamma_c$ denote the policy inertia, inflation and output growth expectations coefficients, respectively, and the constant term. Estimates in the middle of the columns refer to parameters that do not switch across regimes. Iterative MLE, HAC standard errors are reported in parentheses.
***$p<0.01$, **$p<0.05$, *$p<0.1$.

As Table 2 shows the estimated long-run coefficients are statistically significant in both regimes. In the first one, the refi rate is particularly inertial and the Central Bank implements a stabilizing policy for both the inflation and real output growth expectations.[13] As pointed out before, in the second regime monetary policy becomes more aggressive and it seems that the Central Bank does not prioritize the stabilization of inflation expectations since the estimated coefficient is negative. On the contrary, its policy is geared towards stabilizing the economic outlook as reflected in the increasing output growth forecasts responsiveness coefficient.

In order to corroborate the economic intuition about the estimated regimes it is important to test explicitly for the number of regimes against the null hypothesis of one regime estimated with a linear model. However, the testing procedure is complicated by the fact that there is a problem of

[13] For an inflation stabilizing regime $\beta_{\pi_{S_{t+1}}}$ should be higher than one according to the Taylor Principle, while $\beta_{y_{S_{t+1}}}$ should be positive to observe a stabilizing policy for the economic outlook.

Table 2: Actual MRS Taylor Rule, BM Long-Run Parameters

	Regime 1		Regime 2
$\rho_{s_{t+1}}$	0.9859***		0.9300***
	(0.0050)		(0.0190)
$\beta_{\pi_{s_{t+1}}}$	2.2400**		−2.6631***
	(1.0744)		(0.1951)
$\beta_{y_{s_{t+1}}}$	0.3688***		0.6304***
	(0.1378)		(0.1577)
Observations		141	
LL MRS model		749.329	
LL linear model		729.030	
LR test		40.598***	
AIC MRS model		−1474.659	
BIC MRS model		−1439.274	
AIC linear model		−1448.060	
BIC linear model		−1433.316	
RMSE MRS model		0.000899	
RMSE linear model		0.001375	

Note: The table displays the implied long-run coefficients. $\rho_{s_{t+1}}$, $\beta_{\pi_{s_{t+1}}}$, $\beta_{y_{s_{t+1}}}$ denote the policy inertia, inflation and output growth expectations coefficients, respectively. Estimates in the middle of the columns refer to parameters that do not switch across regimes. Standard errors are computed with the Delta method and are reported in parentheses.
$^{***}p<0.01$, $^{**}p<0.05$, $^{*}p<0.1$.

nuisance parameters as the transition probabilities are not identified under the null hypothesis of linearity.[14] To overcome this problem I follow the approach of Assenmacher-Wesche (2006), Tillmann (2003), and Jeanne and Masson (2000). Hence, in performing the likelihood-ratio (LR) test for the number of regimes the test statistic is compared to a $\chi^2(d+n)$ distribution where d corresponds to the number of restrictions tested and n indicates the number of unidentified nuisance parameters under the null hypothesis.[15] In the empirical literature it is commonly acknowledged that this is a rather conservative approach in testing the number of regimes as the test statistic fails to reject the null hypothesis of linearity too often when the latter is actually false (a type two error).

[14] This problem is extensively documented in Garcia (1998), Hamilton (1994), and Hansen (1992, 1996) for instance.

[15] The LR test statistic is computed in the following way:

$$\text{LR} = 2[\text{LL}(\gamma|Y) - \text{LL}(\gamma^*|Y)]$$

where $\text{LL}(\gamma^*|Y)$ denotes the value of the log-likelihood function obtained in the constrained linear model.

Table 2 indicates that the LR statistic is highly statistically significant and corroborates the presence of two regimes in the estimated monetary policy rule. Furthermore, a comparison of the AIC and BIC information criteria between the MRS and the linear models points out that the regime switching specification is also preferred from a model selection perspective. Finally, in line with the previous evidence it is also important to emphasize that the model performance is much better when using a regime switching specification rather than a linear model. Indeed, an inspection of the root mean squared error (RMSE) of the models indicates that the nonlinear specification should be preferred to the linear one as the former more accurately predicts the actual policy rate of the ECB within the sample.

In addition, one could also test for a higher number of regimes. Section 6 reports the estimation results from a three regimes model along with the LR test statistic. However, it should be noted that it seems rather implausible that a higher order of policy regimes has prevailed given the relatively short time span that has elapsed since the inception of the ECB. Even though there is some statistical evidence for a three regimes model the baseline specification features two regimes which are also more in line with the economic intuition.

In order to provide an economic interpretation of the policy behavior of the Central Bank in the estimated regimes one should examine the estimated filtered regime probabilities along with the refi rate set by the ECB and the one forecasted by the economists of the investment bank. These variables are displayed in Figure 1.[16]

Figure 1 shows that there have been several switches of the actual refi rate set by the ECB between the estimated regimes. With a view to providing an economic interpretation to the regime switches one should compare the actual filtered probabilities with the refi rate that has been effectively set by the ECB Governing Council. In that perspective one can see that regime 1 tends to occur both in periods of monetary policy easing and tightening, whereas regime 2 takes place only in periods that feature swift interest rate cuts. Therefore, periods of sharp reduction in the main policy rate are characterized by a change in the policy inertia, inflation and real output growth responsiveness of the Central Bank. Moreover, a switch to the second regime seems to occur during economic downturns that often require sharp interest rate cuts, as in the period from 2001 to 2003, and in

[16] I report the filtered probabilities instead of the smoothed ones because the former are estimated using only currently available information instead of considering all observations. This approach is more consistent with the real-time spirit of the chapter. The results are qualitatively very similar when using the estimated smoothed probabilities.

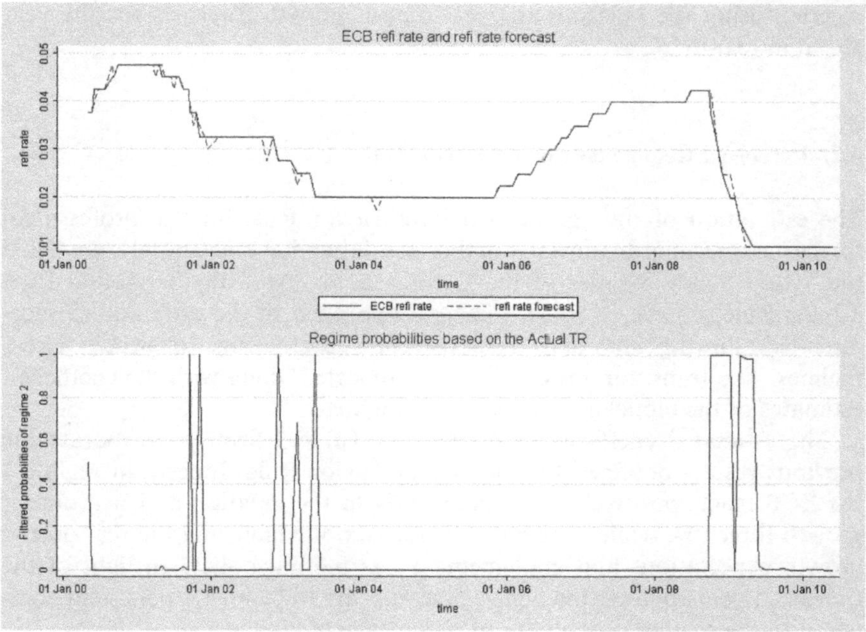

Figure 1: Actual Filtered Probabilities, Baseline Model.

particular during the recent financial crisis from October 2008 until the first half of 2009.[17]

The empirical evidence thus suggests that regime 1 could be attributed to a policy stance that takes place in normal (noncrisis) periods, while regime 2 points to a crisis behavior on the part of the Central Bank which occurs in times of economic turmoils. In fact, in the latter the ECB's responsiveness to economic fundamentals changes sharply: the Central Bank adjusts faster the refi rate and focuses on stabilizing the economic outlook rather than inflation expectations.

In the following subsection I present the estimation results for the Perceived regime switching Taylor Rule. The latter is based on the economists' point forecasts of the refi rate for the upcoming monetary policy

[17] It is important to emphasize, that in the 2001–2003 monetary policy easing the refi rate has been cut by 275 basis points, while in the 2008–2009 series of interest rate cuts it has been reduced by 325 basis points. While in terms of magnitude the reduction of the refi rate is of a similar order, the latter interest rate cuts have lasted only 8 months.

meeting using the inflation and real output growth forecasts for the year ahead in real-time.

4.2. Perceived Regime Switching Taylor Rule

The estimation of the regime switching Taylor Rule for the professional forecasters permits to unveil whether the latter have accurately predicted the actual policy regimes of the Central Bank. As with the Actual ECB Taylor Rule, I have adopted a general approach in the estimation procedure by allowing all policy responsiveness coefficients to switch across regimes. The transition probabilities are reported along with the coefficient estimates of the model as previously highlighted.

The estimated coefficients presented in Table 3 firmly corroborate the previous results obtained for the Actual Taylor Rule. Indeed, in regime 1 the ECB reacts positively and significantly to the inflation and real output growth forecasts, while in regime 2 it focuses on stabilizing the real output growth expectations and implements a less inertial policy. In light of the transition probabilities, the first regime appears to be highly persistent compared to the smaller probability of occurrence of regime 2.

Table 3: Perceived MRS TR, Baseline Model (BM)

	Regime 1		Regime 2
$\rho_{s_{t+1}}$	0.9737***		0.8900***
	(0.0053)		(0.0166)
$\gamma_{\pi_{s_{t+1}}}$	0.0360***		−0.1430***
	(0.0023)		(0.0033)
$\gamma_{y_{s_{t+1}}}$	0.0158***		0.0249***
	(0.0014)		(0.0011)
γ_c		0.0000	
		(0.0000)	
σ_ε		0.0010***	
		(3.297e−05)	
$P[S_{t+1}=i\|S_t=1]$	0.9501***		0.0499***
	(0.0177)		(0.0022)
$P[S_{t+1}=i\|S_t=2]$	0.7039***		0.2961***
	(0.0128)		(0.0149)
Observations		141	
Log-likelihood		736.512	

Note: The table displays the short-run coefficients. $\rho_{s_{t+1}}$, $\gamma_{\pi_{s_{t+1}}}$, $\gamma_{y_{s_{t+1}}}$, γ_c denote the policy inertia, inflation and output growth expectations coefficients respectively and the constant term. Estimates in the middle of the columns refer to parameters that do not switch across regimes. Iterative MLE, HAC standard errors are reported in parentheses.
$^{***}p<0.01$, $^{**}p<0.05$, $^{*}p<0.1$.

Indeed, the average duration of the former is 20.04 policy meetings, while the latter is much short-lived as it lasts on average 1.42 meetings of the Governing Council. In addition, similarly to the results obtained for the Actual Taylor Rule, there is a much higher probability of transiting back into the first regime conditional on being in the second one than to enter the second regime conditional on being in the first one. The long-run response coefficients of the model, $\beta_{\pi S_{t+1}}$ and $\beta_{y S_{t+1}}$, as well as some relevant statistics are reported in Table 4.

The empirical evidence points to the presence of two regimes for the perceived policy reaction function as well. In both regimes the estimated coefficients are significant and corroborate the results previously found for the actual policy rule. However, the LR test statistic does not show evidence against the restricted linear model. This result is possibly attributed to the particularly conservative approach adopted when computing the LR test statistic. The latter often fails to reject the null hypothesis of linearity even when it is actually false. In terms of the AIC information criterion the difference between the MRS and the linear models is very small, while the BIC criterion suggests that the linear model is more likely to be preferred from the perspective of model selection. Nevertheless, it is better to estimate a regime switching model in order to more accurately predict

Table 4: Perceived MRS Taylor Rule, BM Long-Run Parameters

	Regime 1		Regime 2
$\rho_{S_{t+1}}$	0.9737***		0.8900***
	(0.0053)		(0.0166)
$\beta_{\pi_{S_{t+1}}}$	1.3683***		−1.3002***
	(0.3408)		(0.1694)
$\beta_{y_{S_{t+1}}}$	0.6002***		0.2261***
	(0.1661)		(0.0439)
Observations		141	
LL MRS model		736.512	
LL linear model		730.705	
LR test		11.614	
AIC MRS model		−1449.023	
BIC MRS model		−1413.638	
AIC linear model		−1451.411	
BIC linear model		−1436.667	
RMSE MRS model		0.001011	
RMSE linear model		0.001359	

Note: The table displays the implied long-run coefficients. $\rho_{S_{t+1}}$, $\beta_{\pi_{S_{t+1}}}$, $\beta_{y_{S_{t+1}}}$ denote the policy inertia, inflation and output growth expectations coefficients, respectively. Estimates in the middle of the columns refer to parameters that do not switch across regimes. Standard errors are computed with the Delta method and are reported in parentheses.
$^{***}p<0.01$, $^{**}p<0.05$, $^{*}p<0.1$.

the policy rate as indicated by the lower RMSE of the MRS model compared to the higher RMSE of the linear specification.

The estimation results point out that the professional forecasters have quite accurately foreseen the Actual regime switching Taylor Rule. Indeed, based on the Perceived Taylor Rule regime 1 features a particularly inertial policy rate and monetary policy exerts a stabilizing effect both on inflation expectations and on the output growth forecasts. Notice that the estimated coefficients in the first regime are well in line with the empirical findings in the literature. Besides, the economists have perceived the ECB to put a higher emphasis on the economic outlook relative to inflation stabilization when switching to the second regime, consistently with the evidence for the actual policy rule. It is also important to highlight that, even though the inflation coefficient estimate is negative in the second regime for both the Actual and Perceived Taylor Rules, monetary policy is not necessarily destabilizing for inflation because of the short average duration of this regime and the fact that the algorithm maximizes the joint probability distribution of the policy rates and the regimes. Figure 2 displays the filtered probabilities of the second regime for the Perceived Taylor Rule.

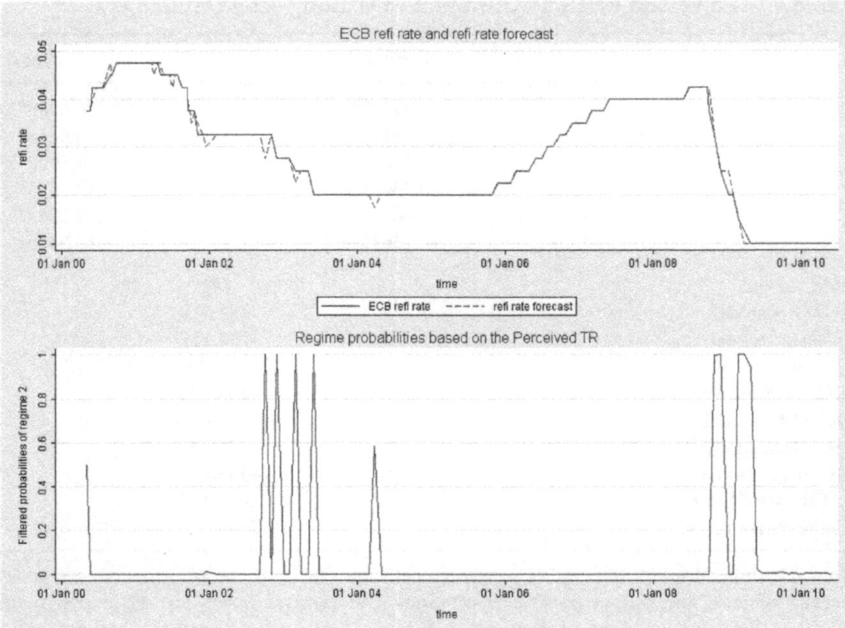

Figure 2: Perceived Filtered Probabilities, Baseline Model.

The perceived filtered probabilities provide evidence for the accurate perceptions of the professional forecasters about the actual regime switches of the main policy rate estimated with the actual policy rule. Indeed, the timing of the perceived regime switches is broadly well aligned with the actual dates of the regime shifts. As pointed out earlier, the first regime occurs both in periods of monetary policy easing and tightening, while the second one appears in times of economic downturns that require swift interest rate cuts. The economists have accurately perceived the switch to the second regime in the 2001–2003 policy easing, as well as more recently during the broadening of the financial crisis since October 2008 until the first half of 2009. However, there is a slight difference compared to the actual regime shifts because the economists have not foreseen the initial stage of the series of policy rate cuts that has started in the second half of 2001. Besides, the professional forecasters have also expected a higher probability of a switch to the second regime in March 2004 that has not been estimated with the actual policy reaction function. Indeed, this perception is related to the forecast of a policy rate cut for the April 1, 2004 meeting of the Governing Council which actually has not materialized. The next subsection presents a more detailed analysis of the timing of the regime switches based on a comparison between the actual and perceived filtered probabilities.

4.3. Actual and Perceived Filtered Probabilities

This subsection offers a detailed analysis of the actual and perceived filtered probabilities of the estimated regimes. The goal is to assess the accuracy of the professional economists' predictions of the actual filtered regime probabilities and to shed more light on understanding the driving factors of the regime switches during the first decade of single European monetary policy. Figure 3 displays the estimated filtered probabilities.

As previously reported, it is compelling to notice that the professional forecasters have quite accurately predicted the actual regime switches of the ECB over the last decade. However, as regards the 2001–2003 interest rate cuts a closer inspection of Figure 3 reveals that there have been some misalignments between the actual and perceived filtered probabilities. The first one occurs with the sharp 50 basis points reduction of the key policy rate that the ECB has implemented in September 2001. Indeed, the economists have not expected the exact magnitude of that rate cut as well as the subsequent switch of the refi rate to the second regime. The second mismatch appears in November 2001 when the professional forecasters have not expected the switch of the policy rate to the second regime that has occurred following the 50 basis points cut of the refi rate. Then, in October 2002, as well as in March 2004, the refi rate point forecast has switched to

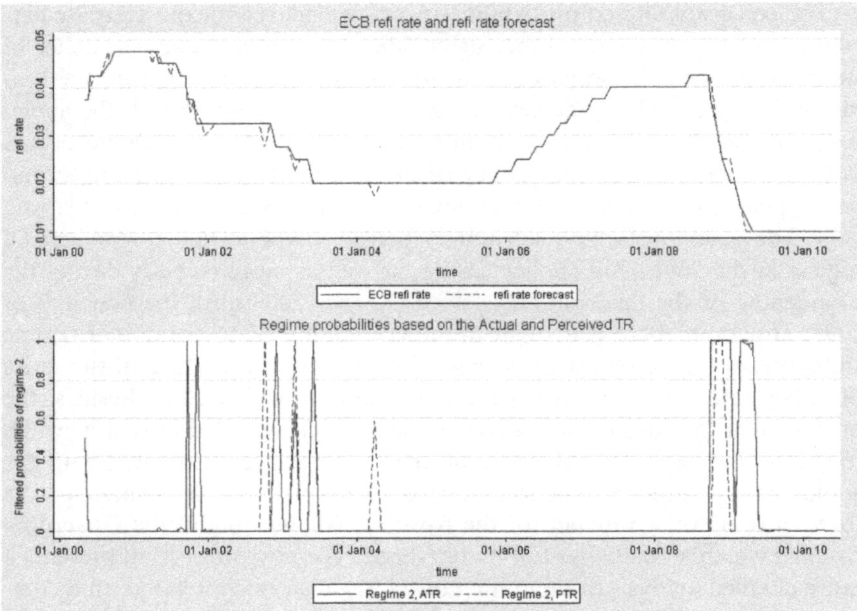

Figure 3: Actual and Perceived Filtered Probabilities, Baseline Model.

the second regime as the economists have expected further policy rate cuts that actually have not materialized.

Concerning the recent financial crisis, one can notice that until October 8, 2008 the actual and forecasted policy rates have remained in the first regime. Then, after the sharp reduction of the refi rate that has been implemented on the same day, the actual policy rate has switched to the second crisis regime. As regards the forecasted policy rate the observed pattern is broadly identical with some exceptions. The latter has switched to the second regime only at the following monetary policy meeting in November 2008, probably because the economists have not expected the sharp refi rate cut. Regarding the actual policy rate it has remained in the second regime until January 2009 and then has switched back to the first policy regime in February 2009. Turning to the perceived policy rule, the refi rate point forecast has remained in the second regime until December 2008 and then has switched back again to the first inflation stabilizing regime as the professional forecasters have not expected the 50 basis points rate cut occurring in January 2009. Then, as the ECB has resumed the interest rate cuts in the first half of 2009, the actual as well as the forecasted policy rates have switched back again to the second regime in March 2009 and have stayed there until May 2009. Since June 2009 both Taylor Rules have switched back to the first regime and have firmly remained there until June 2010 which is the final observation in the data set.[18]

Therefore, a closer analysis of the recent financial crisis reveals that while there have been broadly similar perceptions of the economists about the actual regime switches, it seems that the professional forecasters have exhibited a delayed perception of the actual timing of the ECB regime switches. This finding may be attributed to some gradual learning process about the actual monetary policy stance that has taken place especially in such a period of financial turbulence. Finally, in the period studied the switching to the crisis regime usually takes place once a sharp reduction of the main policy rate of about 50–75 basis points is either observed or/and expected. Furthermore, the empirical results obtained with the regime switching specification partly corroborate the findings of Gerlach and Lewis (2010). The authors model the ECB interest rate policy in the vicinity of the Zero Lower Bound within a logistic smooth transition regression. They have found that the best model for the ECB's key policy rate in the crisis regime is an AR(1) process for the interest rate. Indeed, in a period of economic downturn the ECB might respond less to economic fundamentals and could be more inclined to sharply cut the policy rate to secure the stability of the euro area financial system. Consistently with their results, I find that in a crisis period the Central Bank enters a second policy regime and cuts rates faster compared to a normal period. However, in contrast with their evidence, in the second regime the Central Bank still responds, but in a differentiated way to key macroeconomic fundamentals. The difference in the ECB's responsiveness between the 2000–2001 crisis and the 2007–2009 economic downturn lies in the duration of the crisis regime. In fact, while during the 2001–2003 cycle of policy rate cuts the second regime has occurred sporadically during very short periods, in the 2008–2009 series of interest rate cuts the refi rate has remained longer in the crisis regime. This evidence reflects the pronounced severity of the recent turmoil compared to the earlier crisis.

4.4. Actual and Perceived Fitted Policy Rates

In this subsection I present the graphs of the fitted policy rates obtained with the estimated Actual and Perceived regime switching Taylor Rules.

[18] It is interesting to notice that the switch back to the normal policy regime has occurred in the same quarter as the end of the recession in the euro area as announced by the Euro Area Business Cycle Dating Committee. Possibly, as economic fundamentals have improved the ECB has prioritized its long-run price stability goal.

This analysis is important as it permits to better understand whether a non-linear specification of the Taylor Rule fits more closely the actual policy rate.[19] The goal of this subsection is to provide a graphical analysis of the estimation results and to highlight the advantage of using a regime switching approach compared to a linear model in performing the in-sample predictions of the policy rate. Furthermore, the analysis should unveil whether there is any difference in the implied policy rate targets when using a non-linear specification compared to the policy rate target predicted from a linear model.[20]

I first start the analysis by comparing the actual and perceived fitted policy rates based on the previous estimations. The graphs are displayed in Figures A.1 and A.2, respectively. As expected, for both Taylor Rules the model's fit is clearly better when considering a regime switching specification compared to the fit from a linear model. Indeed, the figures point out that for both Taylor Rules the in-sample predicted interest rates follow more closely the actual and forecasted policy rates when considering the MRS specification rather than a linear model.

Therefore, accounting for different monetary policy regimes seems to provide an important improvement of the model specification as it permits to more accurately predict the Central Bank's key policy rate within the sample. Moreover, I also display the implied refi rate targets for both policy rules in Figure 4 and compare them to the policy rate targets estimated from a linear model. In order to provide an economic intuition for the results I also present a graph of the inflation and real output growth forecasts used in the regressions in Figure 5.

First, based on the results from the Actual Taylor Rule one can see that accounting for regime switches in the ECB's monetary policy results in a different implied target rate compared to the one estimated with a linear model. Indeed, within a normal policy regime the policy rate target predicted from the regime switching specification exceeds in general the one inferred from the linear model. In particular, the graph suggests that the ECB's refi rate has remained at a too low level for an extended period of time from June 2003 until December 2005. During this period the refi rate

[19] Actually, this issue has been investigated more formally in the previous subsection when comparing the RMSE of the MRS and the linear models.

[20] The implied policy rate target corresponds to the fitted policy rate of Equation (1). It is obtained by dividing the estimated short-run model coefficients by one minus the lagged refi rate within the corresponding policy regime. More precisely, I compute the expected refi rate target since the coefficient estimates are weighted by the probability of being in the different regimes. The results are almost identical when considering that the policy rate is in a particular regime according to a specific threshold value for the filtered probabilities.

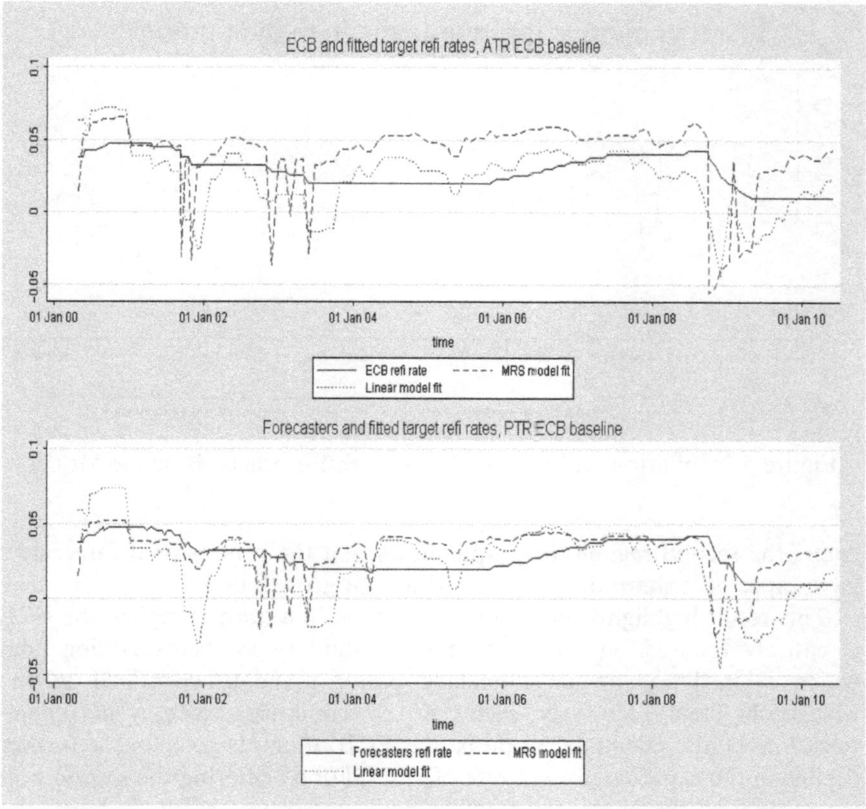

Figure 4: Actual and Perceived Fitted Target Rates, Baseline Model.

has been maintained at the level of 2%. Based on the MRS model the Central Bank should have started raising the main policy rate much earlier than in December 2005 and should have kept the refi rate at a higher level until the first half of 2008. The implied target rate from the linear model also points in the same direction even though it suggests that the refi rate should have been maintained at a lower level than the one predicted with the MRS specification.

Second, one can clearly see from Figure 4 that within a crisis regime the Central Bank cuts swiftly the policy rate and the implied target rate falls down sharply and reaches the Zero Lower Bound quite often. This evidence raises the question about what are the driving factors of the change in regime in the single European monetary policy.

An inspection of Figure 5 indicates that what drives mostly the switch from the normal to the crisis regime are the expectations of a sharp decline in the forecasts of the economic outlook: each time the main policy rate

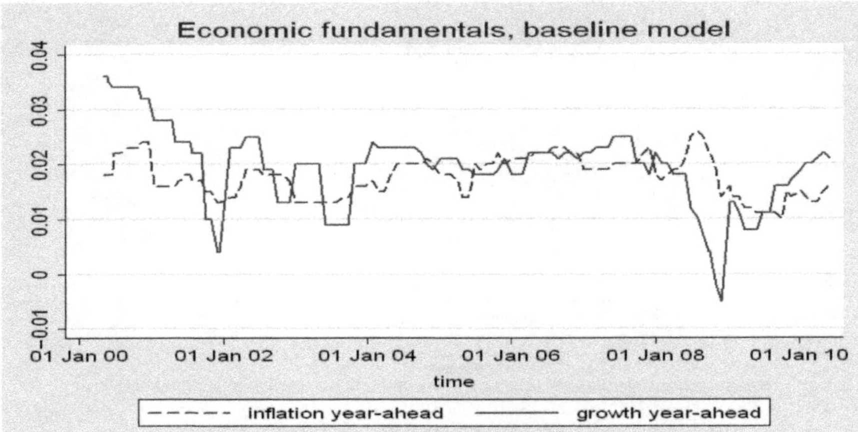

Figure 5: Inflation and Real GDP Growth Forecasts, Baseline Model.

enters the second regime the graph shows that the professional forecasters have expected a sharp drop in the real output growth rate.

This result highlights an important finding: in a normal regime the ECB is entirely focused on maintaining price stability as its overriding goal which is in line with its monetary policy mandate enshrined in the Maastricht Treaty. However, each time the economists expect a sharp deterioration of the economic outlook the ECB attempts to avoid a further decline in the expected growth rate of real GDP by entering the second policy regime. In the latter, the Central Bank cuts rates swiftly to boost the euro area economy and it temporarily puts aside its primary goal of price stability. It is also important to highlight that the second regime is not necessarily destabilizing for inflation expectations as it is on average rather short-lived. Finally, notice that according to the predicted policy rate target from the MRS model the ECB should have started increasing its policy rate since the second half of 2009 as the euro area economy has come out of the economic recession in line with the forecasts performed by the Euro Area Business Cycle Dating Committee.

As regards the evidence from the Perceived Taylor Rule the results are broadly in line with the previous findings. Nevertheless, there is an important difference in the magnitude of the predicted target rate especially in the first policy regime. Indeed, in normal periods the perceived policy rule predicts that in general the refi rate target should have been higher than the observed refi rate but to a lesser extent compared to the predictions from the actual reaction function. Consistently with the above results the switch to the crisis regime seems to have been driven primarily by the expectations of a sharp decline in the economic outlook. One can also notice that during the 2001–2003 series of policy rate cuts, as well as throughout the broadening of the financial crisis in 2008 the refi rate target seems to have reached the Zero Lower Bound as reflected in both the MRS and linear model predictions from both Taylor Rules. Finally, in the aftermath of the recent financial crisis the ECB should have started increasing the refi rate since the second half of 2009 as the recession has ended and the Central Bank has entered the first regime. This result is in line with the previous findings for the Actual Taylor Rule.

The empirical results presented in this section are consistent with the theoretical model of Agur and Demertzis (2011). The latter derive the optimal policy rate from a Central Bank loss function that contains a financial stability goal in addition to the objective of output gap stabilization. The authors show that following a negative demand shock a Central Bank that carries on a financial stability goal will implement larger cuts of the policy rate that will be rather short-lived compared to the policy response it would provide in the absence of such an objective. The authors argue that given that the rate cut has a short duration the Central Bank has to behave aggressively and implement large policy rate cuts in order to take into account the need to stabilize the output gap as well. In addition, Agur and Demertzis (2011) also show that if the rate cuts last for a prolonged period of time they may favor a risk taking behavior on the part of the banking sector. Therefore, the more a Central Bank is concerned about securing the stability of the financial system the shorter will be the rate cuts and the sharper their magnitude in order to take account of the other policy objectives.

The paper of Agur and Demertzis (2011) thus provides the theoretical underpinning of the regime switching Taylor Rules for the ECB. Consistently with their results, the second regime is rather short-lived and the Central Bank implements sharp policy rate cuts. The aggressive policy responsiveness of the ECB points out that when entering the crisis regime the Central Bank might be also concerned about the stability of the financial system in addition to stabilizing the economic outlook. Besides, this result suggests the presence of some asymmetry between the policy rate hikes and the rate cuts in the ECB's monetary policy. More precisely, the policy rate hikes of the ECB last longer than the rate cuts as the former occur in periods of economic expansion when the Central Bank is entirely focused on maintaining its price stability objective. Conversely, in periods of economic turmoil the policy rate enters a crisis regime and the ECB implements large interest rate cuts which are short-lived as indicated by the estimated filtered probabilities. Hence, this evidence might point out that in the second regime the ECB assigns some weight on securing the stability of the euro area financial system when setting the refi rate, while at the same time it accounts for the need to stabilize the economic activity. However, the observed behavior of the ECB contrasts with the optimal policy outlined in Agur and Demertzis (2011) in the sense that when switching back to the first regime the Central Bank maintains the policy rate at a low level for a rather prolonged period of time. Such a policy was implemented after the 2001–2003 series of rate cuts and more recently in the aftermath of the 2007–2009 financial crisis. In order to prevent the build-up of an excessive risk taking behavior in the banking sector, the Central Bank should not keep the policy rate at a too low level for a protracted period of time. Indeed, this proposition is fully in line with the implied refi rate targets estimated from the Actual and Perceived regime switching Taylor Rules which are displayed in Figure 4. The latter show that following an economic downturn the policy rate enters a normal regime and the ECB should raise the refi rate to foster its price stability commitment. This policy reversal is necessary for the firm anchoring of the long-run inflationary expectations to a level consistent with the policy objective. The latter is crucial for maintaining the low inflation credibility of the Central Bank in the medium and longer terms.

Furthermore, the empirical results for the regime switching policy rules are consistent with Mishkin (2009). The latter argues that monetary policy should be more aggressive in crisis periods as the Central Bank implements large interest rate cuts. According to the author this policy easing is necessary to alleviate the adverse effects of the financial turmoil on the economy and thus to prevent the emergence of an adverse feedback loop that could engineer a deeper economic contraction. Mishkin also argues that an important shortcoming of this policy is that it could lead to higher inflation expectations which would seriously challenge the price stability commitment of the Central Bank. Therefore, it is of the utmost importance that in the aftermath of financial crises Central Banks do not wait too long before implementing interest rate hikes in order to comply with their policy mandate. This proposition is also in line with the estimated refi rate targets from the regime switching Taylor Rules. Thereof, the more credible the Central Bank's commitment to a low level of inflation the more aggressive and shorter-lived the interest rate cuts in the event of a full-blown crisis and the more effective would be the policy outcome.

In the following section I conduct a sensitivity analysis of the baseline specifications previously estimated. In a first step, I consider the Consensus Economics Forecasts of inflation and real GDP growth in the regressions to infer whether the regimes previously obtained are robust to the forecast variables used. Then, I consider an alternative forecast horizon in the regressions to determine which forecast horizon is more in line with the expectations formation process of the economists. Finally, I estimate some augmented Taylor Rules to understand whether the ECB responds to other economic fundamentals as well. The extended model contains the growth rates of M3 and the nominal effective exchange rate as additional regressors.

5. Robustness Analysis

In order to perform a sensitivity analysis of the baseline results, the next subsection presents the estimation results for the actual and perceived policy rules using Consensus Economics Forecasts (CEF) of inflation and real output growth instead of the professional forecasts from the investment bank used in the benchmark regressions. The consensus forecasts data are particularly valuable since they are unrevised and are provided in a real-time setting. In the estimations I use the average of the inflation and real output growth forecasts provided by the panel of professional forecasters for the euro area.[21]

5.1. Actual and Perceived Taylor Rules with Consensus Forecasts

In this subsection I conduct a sensitivity analysis of the results obtained with the baseline model by considering the consensus forecasts of inflation and real GDP growth for the euro area and for the year ahead horizon in the regressions. In all estimations I have used the most recently available observations in order to preserve the real-time feature of the model. The estimation results for the Actual Taylor Rule are reported in Table 5.

At a first look one can see that the empirical results for the baseline specification are qualitatively unaltered when considering the consensus forecasts of economic fundamentals instead of the professional forecasts from the investment bank. More specifically, the empirical evidence suggests that there are two different regimes for the main policy rate as previously estimated with the baseline model. Hence, in the first regime the Central Bank implements a particularly inertial policy and responds positively and significantly to the inflation and real output growth expectations. Conversely, in the second regime the ECB enters in a crisis mode and implements the desired policy rate faster than in normal times. As previously found the Central Bank puts a higher emphasis on the economic outlook rather than on inflation expectations in the second regime.

Furthermore, Table 5 points out that the transition probabilities are very similar to those obtained with the baseline model. Indeed, regime 1 is particularly persistent featuring an average duration of 18.62 monetary policy meetings while the second regime is rather short-lived since it lasts on average 1.69 meetings. In line with the previous results, there is a much

[21] The Consensus Economics Forecasts are reported by a large panel of professional forecasters for the current year and the year ahead. The data are provided by the Swiss National Bank and Thomson Reuters Datastream.

Table 5: Actual MRS Taylor Rule, CEF

	Regime 1		Regime 2
$\rho_{s_{t+1}}$	0.9925***		0.9246***
	(0.0038)		(0.0045)
$\gamma_{\pi_{s_{t+1}}}$	0.0245***		−0.1654***
	(0.0026)		(0.0058)
$\gamma_{y_{s_{t+1}}}$	0.0010***		0.0603***
	(0.0001)		(0.0062)
γ_c		−0.0000	
		(0.0000)	
σ_ε		0.0009***	
		(6.140e−05)	
$P[S_{t+1}=i\|S_t=1]$	0.9463***		0.0537***
	(0.0590)		(0.0051)
$P[S_{t+1}=i\|S_t=2]$	0.5908***		0.4092**
	(0.0521)		(0.1750)
Observations		141	
Log-likelihood		748.636	

Note: The table displays the short-run coefficients. $\rho_{s_{t+1}}, \gamma_{\pi_{s_{t+1}}}, \gamma_{y_{s_{t+1}}}, \gamma_c$ denote the policy inertia, inflation and output growth expectations coefficients respectively and the constant term. Estimates in the middle of the columns refer to parameters that do not switch across regimes. Iterative MLE, HAC standard errors are reported in parentheses.
$^{***}p<0.01$, $^{**}p<0.05$, $^{*}p<0.1$.

higher probability of transiting to the first regime conditional on being in the second one rather than to enter the crisis regime conditional on being in the normal one. Table 6 displayed above reports the implied long-run model coefficients along with some relevant statistics.

The implied long-run coefficients of the model with the consensus forecasts are broadly in line with the results obtained for the benchmark model. In particular one can see that in the first regime the Taylor Principle is satisfied as the ECB implements a particularly stabilizing policy with respect to inflation expectations. This result is also consistent with the long-run objective of price stability that is embedded in the monetary policy mandate. Without prejudice to this overriding goal the Central Bank also takes into account the need to stabilize the economic outlook as indicated by the significant and positive coefficient estimate of the real output growth forecasts. Second, the ECB focuses primarily on stabilizing the latter rather than inflation expectations when entering the crisis regime thus putting temporarily aside its overriding goal. However, it is important to emphasize that given that the second regime has a short duration, the negative coefficient estimate on inflation expectations does not necessarily imply that the Central Bank implements a destabilizing policy with respect to inflation expectations.

Table 6: Actual MRS Taylor Rule, CEF Long-Run Parameters

	Regime 1		Regime 2
$\rho_{s_{t+1}}$	0.9925***		0.9246***
	(0.0038)		(0.0045)
$\beta_{\pi_{s_{t+1}}}$	3.2890*		−2.1930***
	(1.9589)		(0.1709)
$\beta_{y_{s_{t+1}}}$	0.1320*		0.8000***
	(0.0771)		(0.1028)
Observations		141	
LL MRS model		748.636	
LL linear model		726.111	
LR test		45.050***	
AIC MRS model		−1473.271	
BIC MRS model		−1437.886	
AIC linear model		−1442.222	
BIC linear model		−1427.479	
RMSE MRS model		0.000881	
RMSE linear model		0.001404	

Note: The table displays the implied long-run coefficients. $\rho_{s_{t+1}}$, $\beta_{\pi_{s_{t+1}}}$, $\beta_{y_{s_{t+1}}}$ denote the policy inertia, inflation and output growth expectations coefficients, respectively. Estimates in the middle of the columns refer to parameters that do not switch across regimes. Standard errors are computed with the Delta method and are reported in parentheses.
***$p<0.01$, **$p<0.05$, *$p<0.1$.

In addition, the LR test statistic shows strong evidence in favor of the regime switching specification compared to the linear model. The AIC and BIC information criteria suggest that the nonlinear model should be preferred to the linear one from a model selection perspective. Finally, the MRS specification permits to more accurately predict the refi rate within the sample as indicated by the smaller RMSE compared to the one of the linear model. This result corroborates the previous findings that the fitted policy rate follows more closely the actual refi rate within the regime switching specification. In order to check whether the baseline results for the professional forecasters are robust to using consensus data, Table 7 reports the empirical evidence for the Perceived Taylor Rule.

As regards the Perceived Taylor Rule the regime switching model does not converge well when considering a switching in all policy responsiveness coefficients. The best model is obtained by considering a switching in the policy inertia coefficient only. Nevertheless, the results obtained with this specification are in line with the previous economic intuition about the policy regimes. In light of the results from Table 7 one can see that when switching from the first to the crisis regime the perceived policy stance is less inertial. However, the ECB responds positively and significantly to the inflation and real output growth forecasts in both regimes. The estimated

Table 7: Perceived MRS Taylor Rule, CEF

	Regime 1		Regime 2
$\rho_{s_{t+1}}$	0.9836***		0.8029***
	(0.0050)		(0.0029)
$\gamma_{\pi_{s_{t+1}}}$		0.0178***	
		(0.0005)	
$\gamma_{y_{s_{t+1}}}$		0.0152***	
		(0.0008)	
γ_c		−0.0000	
		(0.0000)	
σ_ε		0.0011***	
		(3.125e−05)	
$P[S_{t+1}=i\|S_t=1]$	0.9485***		0.0515***
	(0.0280)		(0.0007)
$P[S_{t+1}=i\|S_t=2]$	0.7047***		0.2953***
	(0.0217)		(0.0030)
Observations		141	
Log-likelihood		731.921	

Note: The table displays the short-run coefficients. $\rho_{s_{t+1}}, \gamma_{\pi_{s_{t+1}}}, \gamma_{y_{s_{t+1}}}, \gamma_c$ denote the policy inertia, inflation and output growth expectations coefficients, respectively, and the constant term. Estimates in the middle of the columns refer to parameters that do not switch across regimes. Iterative MLE, HAC standard errors are reported in parentheses.
$^{***}p<0.01$, $^{**}p<0.05$, $^{*}p<0.1$.

transition probabilities are also fully in line with those obtained for the Perceived Taylor Rule in the baseline specification. Thereby, regime 1 is particularly persistent compared to the smaller probability of occurrence of the crisis regime. The average duration of the former is 19.42 policy meetings while the latter lasts 1.42 meetings on average. Table 8 reports the implied long-run coefficient estimates and some relevant statistics.

The estimated long-run coefficients suggest that the Taylor Principle seems to be satisfied in the normal regime. Indeed, in the latter the ECB implements a stabilizing policy with respect to inflation expectations. The Central Bank also takes due account of the need to stabilize the economic activity in the euro area as reflected by the significant and positive real output growth forecasts coefficient. In contrast with these results, in the crisis regime the ECB implements a larger fraction of the desired policy rate as indicated by the smaller policy inertia coefficient. Besides, the Central Bank's long-run responsiveness to both the inflation and real output growth expectations seems to have been dampened and the Taylor Principle is not fulfilled. This evidence is related to the fact that the variables do not switch across regimes and the change in the long-run coefficients is entirely due to a change in the policy inertia point estimate.

Table 8: Perceived MRS Taylor Rule, CEF Long-Run Parameters

	Regime 1		Regime 2
$\rho_{s_{t+1}}$	0.9836***		0.8029***
	(0.0050)		(0.0029)
$\beta_{\pi_{s_{t+1}}}$	1.0876***		0.0904***
	(0.3521)		(0.0021)
$\beta_{y_{s_{t+1}}}$	0.9256***		0.0769***
	(0.3144)		(0.0040)
Observations		141	
LL MRS model		731.921	
LL linear model		715.022	
LR test		33.798***	
AIC MRS model		−1443.841	
BIC MRS model		−1414.354	
AIC linear model		−1420.045	
BIC linear model		−1405.301	
RMSE MRS model		0.001061	
RMSE linear model		0.001519	

Note: The table displays the implied long-run coefficients. $\rho_{s_{t+1}}$, $\beta_{\pi_{s_{t+1}}}$, $\beta_{y_{s_{t+1}}}$ denote the policy inertia, inflation and output growth expectations coefficients, respectively. Estimates in the middle of the columns refer to parameters that do not switch across regimes. Standard errors are computed with the Delta method and are reported in parentheses.
***$p<0.01$, **$p<0.05$, *$p<0.1$.

Moreover, the LR test statistic indicates that there is evidence in favor of a regime switching specification compared to a linear model. Both the AIC and BIC information criteria also point out that the nonlinear specification should be preferred to a linear model. Finally, a comparison of the RMSE between the models points out that the fitted policy rate forecast in the MRS model follows more closely the actual policy rate forecast and should be preferred to a linear specification. The estimated filtered probabilities are displayed in Figure 6.

It is compelling to notice from the following figure that the actual and perceived filtered probabilities are consistent with the results obtained for the baseline model. Indeed, the estimated regimes and the timing of the switches are identical using either the investment bank forecasts or the consensus data. In line with the previous findings the economists have broadly well predicted the actual regime switches of the Central Bank with some minor exceptions. The regimes are the same as in the previous subsection and the second relates to the 2001–2003 cycle of policy easing, and more recently to the sharp refi rate cuts implemented during the broadening of the financial crisis in 2008. The timing of the regimes points out that when switching to the second regime the ECB temporarily deviates from its primary goal of price stability and attempts to offset a further decline in

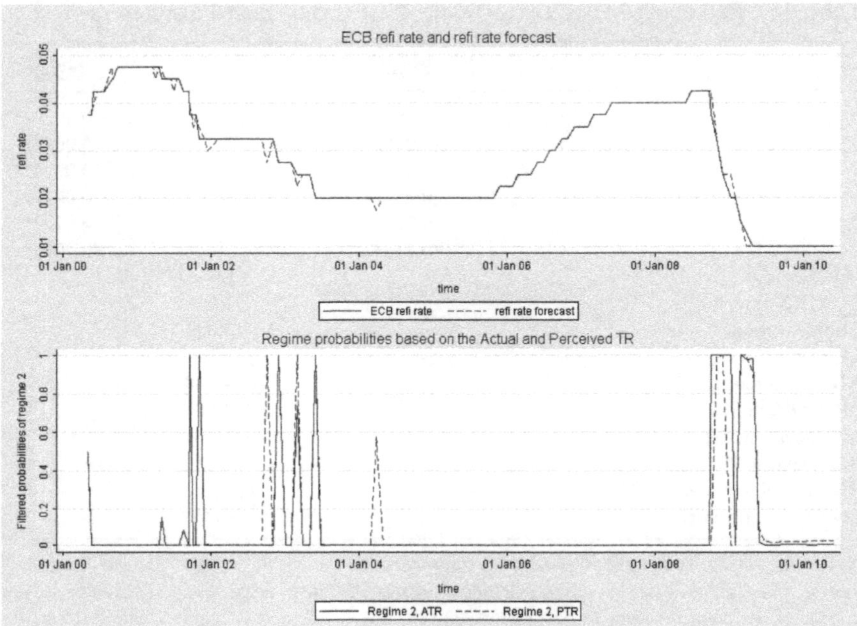

Figure 6: Actual and Perceived Filtered Probabilities, Consensus Forecasts.

economic activity. Given that the second regime occurs in periods of crisis or financial turbulence the Central Bank has to react very quickly to the economic downturn by adjusting its policy rate accordingly and by taking all necessary measures to secure the stability of the euro area financial system.

As a concluding remark of this subsection one can clearly state that the baseline results remain qualitatively unaltered from including the consensus forecasts of inflation and real output growth in the regressions. This evidence emphasizes the importance of modeling a regime switching policy reaction function in order to more accurately predict the ECB's main policy rate. Even though the estimation of the Perceived Taylor Rule with the consensus forecasts does not feature a switching in all policy reaction coefficients, the results obtained corroborate the policy regimes and the economic intuition of the benchmark model.

In order to check whether the empirical evidence is sensitive to the measure of expectations used in the estimations, the following subsection presents the results obtained with a one-year fixed forecast horizon using the expectations of inflation and real output growth from the investment bank's economists in the regressions.

5.2. Actual and Perceived Taylor Rules with an Alternative Forecast Horizon

In this subsection I present the estimation results for the regime switching policy rules using the inflation and real output growth forecasts with a fixed horizon of one year. It is important to emphasize that while this methodology permits to keep a fixed forecast horizon at each policy meeting the latter is obtained using the forecasts for the current year and the year ahead in computing the expectations. The goal of this approach is to determine whether the fixed forecast horizon corresponds more accurately with the expectations formation process of the economists compared to the previous methodology used in the baseline regressions. The regression results obtained with this approach are less satisfactory compared to the results obtained for the baseline model using the forecasts for the year ahead in the regressions. The estimation procedure does not converge well when allowing for a switching in all policy responsiveness coefficients and the model produces satisfactory results when a switching in the policy inertia and inflation responsiveness coefficients is permitted for the Actual and Perceived Taylor Rules respectively. I first present the empirical evidence for the actual reaction function in Table 9.

Table 9: Actual MRS Taylor Rule, Alternative Model (AM)

	Regime 1		Regime 2
$\rho_{S_{t+1}}$	0.9761***		0.8372***
	(0.0035)		(0.0090)
$\gamma_{\pi_{S_{t+1}}}$		0.0156***	
		(0.0012)	
$\gamma_{y_{S_{t+1}}}$		0.0349***	
		(0.0005)	
γ_c		0.0000	
		(0.0000)	
σ_ε		0.0009***	
		(1.521e–05)	
$P[S_{t+1}=i\|S_t=1]$	0.9483***		0.0517***
	(0.1491)		(0.0097)
$P[S_{t+1}=i\|S_t=2]$	0.6194***		0.3806***
	(0.1186)		(0.0134)
Observations		141	
Log-likelihood		752.061	

Note: The table displays the short-run coefficients. $\rho_{S_{t+1}}$, $\gamma_{\pi_{S_{t+1}}}$, $\gamma_{y_{S_{t+1}}}$, γ_c denote the policy inertia, inflation and output growth expectations coefficients respectively and the constant term. Estimates in the middle of the columns refer to parameters that do not switch across regimes. Iterative MLE, HAC standard errors are reported in parentheses.
***$p<0.01$, **$p<0.05$, *$p<0.1$.

The results from Table 9 highlight the presence of two regimes for the policy inertia coefficient. In the first one monetary policy is quite inertial while in the second regime the Central Bank implements a larger fraction of the desired policy rate at each monetary policy meeting. Moreover, the ECB seems to respond positively to the inflation and real output growth forecasts and puts a higher emphasis on the latter. Finally, notice that in line with the empirical findings for the baseline specification regime 1 appears to be particularly persistent, contrarily to the smaller probability of occurrence of the second regime. In fact, the crisis regime is a rather infrequent event that occurs with a small conditional probability of the policy rate being in the normal regime. However, once the refi rate gets into the second regime it has a much greater chance to transit back to the first one rather than to remain in the second regime. Hence, the average duration of the former and the latter are respectively 19.34 and 1.61 policy meetings. The long-run response coefficients and the relevant statistics are reported in Table 10.

Table 10 points out that the Taylor Principle does not seem to be satisfied in either regime when using a fixed horizon of one year in the estimations. Hence, it might be the case that these forecast variables do not accurately reflect the forward-looking nature of the expectations formation

Table 10: Actual MRS Taylor Rule, AM Long-Run Parameters

	Regime 1		Regime 2
$\rho_{s_{t+1}}$	0.9761***		0.8372***
	(0.0035)		(0.0090)
$\beta_{\pi_{s_{t+1}}}$	0.6530***		0.0957***
	(0.1390)		(0.0126)
$\beta_{y_{s_{t+1}}}$	1.4629***		0.2143***
	(0.1963)		(0.0093)
Observations		141	
LL MRS model		752.061	
LL linear model		727.479	
LR test		49.164***	
AIC MRS model		−1484.121	
BIC MRS model		−1454.634	
AIC linear model		−1444.959	
BIC linear model		−1430.215	
RMSE MRS model		0.000890419	
RMSE linear model		0.001390119	

Note: The table displays the implied long-run coefficients. $\rho_{s_{t+1}}$, $\beta_{\pi_{s_{t+1}}}$, $\beta_{y_{s_{t+1}}}$ denote the policy inertia, inflation and output growth expectations coefficients respectively. Estimates in the middle of the columns refer to parameters that do not switch across regimes. Standard errors are computed with the Delta method and are reported in parentheses.
***$p<0.01$, **$p<0.05$, *$p<0.1$.

process of the professional forecasters. This evidence could stem from the fact that the one-year forecasts are not entirely forward-looking and do not refer to a specific period between the current year and the year ahead. From this perspective, the forecasts for the year ahead clearly permit greater flexibility in the regime switching modeling of the forward-looking Taylor Rules and are likely to more accurately correspond with the expectations formation process of the professional forecasters. The latter is crucial for understanding the predictability of the European monetary policy within the Taylor Rule framework.

Furthermore, the results from Table 10 suggest first that the ECB has assigned a higher weight to stabilizing the real output growth rather than the inflation expectations in both regimes. Besides, when switching from the first to the second regime the Central Bank's policy inertia decreases and the reaction to both the inflation and real output growth forecasts is dampened. This result is close to the findings of Gerlach and Lewis (2010) who report that in a crisis regime the ECB responds very little to economic fundamentals. As regards the test for the two regimes model, the LM statistic points out that there is evidence in favor of the MRS specification compared to the linear model. This result is further corroborated by the AIC and BIC information criteria which indicate that the regime switching policy rule should be preferred from a model selection perspective as well. Finally, a comparison of the RMSE between the models reveals that one should use the nonlinear specification in order to reduce the in-sample prediction error for the main policy rate given the higher RMSE of the linear model. The specification that converges properly for the Perceived Taylor Rule embeds a switching only in the inflation responsiveness coefficient and is reported in Table 11.

The Table 11 indicates that there are two policy regimes for the inflation expectations coefficient in the Perceived Taylor Rule using the one-year fixed horizon forecasts in the estimations. In the first regime, the Central Bank responds positively to the inflation and real output growth forecasts putting a higher emphasis on the stabilization of the real output growth expectations as found for the Actual Taylor Rule. In the second regime, the ECB's reaction to inflation expectations sharply changes since the coefficient estimate becomes significantly negative. Besides, it seems that in both regimes the ECB has put a greater emphasis on stabilizing the real output growth rather than the inflation expectations. Consistently with all previous results the transition probabilities point out that the first regime is particularly persistent compared to the smaller probability of occurrence of the second one. Table 12 displays the long-run response coefficients along with some relevant statistics.

In line with the results for the Actual Taylor Rule, the estimated long-run coefficients point out that the Taylor Principle is not satisfied

Table 11: Perceived MRS Taylor Rule, Alternative Model (AM)

	Regime 1		Regime 2
$\rho_{s_{t+1}}$		0.9625***	
		(0.0059)	
$\gamma_{\pi_{s_{t+1}}}$	0.0270***		−0.2499***
	(0.0035)		(0.0046)
$\gamma_{y_{s_{t+1}}}$		0.0419***	
		(0.0004)	
γ_c		0.0000	
		(0.0000)	
σ_ε		0.0010***	
		(0.0001)	
$P[S_{t+1}=i \mid S_t=1]$	0.9503***		0.0497***
	(0.1753)		(0.0036)
$P[S_{t+1}=i \mid S_t=2]$	0.7492***		0.2508***
	(0.1081)		(0.0039)
Observations		141	
Log-likelihood		736.484	

Note: The table displays the short-run coefficients. $\rho_{s_{t+1}}$, $\gamma_{\pi_{s_{t+1}}}$, $\gamma_{y_{s_{t+1}}}$, γ_c denote the policy inertia, inflation and output growth expectations coefficients respectively and the constant term. Estimates in the middle of the columns refer to parameters that do not switch across regimes. Iterative MLE, HAC standard errors are reported in parentheses.
$^{***}p<0.01$, $^{**}p<0.05$, $^{*}p<0.1$.

for the Perceived Taylor Rule as well. Furthermore, in the first regime the Central Bank responds more strongly to the real output growth rather than to the inflation expectations. In a similar way, when switching to the second regime the inflation responsiveness coefficient becomes even negative possibly indicating that the latter occurs in periods of economic downturn when some exceptional circumstances lead the Central Bank to deviate temporarily from its overriding price stability objective. As previously emphasized, this result does not necessarily imply that the ECB implements a destabilizing policy with respect to inflation but more likely reflects the fact that in a period of economic turmoil the Central Bank's priority gears towards preventing a further decline in the economic outlook. The monetary institution also focuses on securing the stability of the financial system rather than anchoring inflation expectations with its price stability objective. The likelihood-ratio test of nonlinearity indicates that there is evidence in favor of the regime switching model compared to the linear one. Moreover, the AIC statistic shows that the MRS model should be preferred to the linear one in contrast to the evidence stemming from the BIC information criterion. Finally, from the perspective of minimizing the in-sample prediction error the RMSE

Table 12: Perceived MRS Taylor Rule, AM Long-Run Parameters

	Regime 1		Regime 2
$\rho_{s_{t+1}}$		0.9625***	
		(0.0059)	
$\beta_{\pi_{s_{t+1}}}$	0.7200***		−6.6714***
	(0.1998)		(0.9444)
$\beta_{y_{s_{t+1}}}$		1.1197***	
		(0.1863)	
Observations		141	
LL MRS model		736.484	
LL linear model		725.544	
LR test		21.880***	
AIC MRS model		−1452.967	
BIC MRS model		−1423.480	
AIC linear model		−1441.087	
BIC linear model		−1426.343	
RMSE MRS model		0.001001	
RMSE linear model		0.001409	

Note: The table displays the implied long-run coefficients. $\rho_{s_{t+1}}$, $\beta_{\pi_{s_{t+1}}}$, $\beta_{y_{s_{t+1}}}$ denote the policy inertia, inflation and output growth expectations coefficients respectively. Estimates in the middle of the columns refer to parameters that do not switch across regimes. Standard errors are computed with the Delta method and are reported in parentheses.
*** $p < 0.01$, ** $p < 0.05$, * $p < 0.1$.

points out that one should select the regime switching Taylor Rule instead of the linear specification. Figure 7 displays the actual and perceived filtered regime probabilities.

As a first remark, it is compelling to notice that the actual and perceived filtered regime probabilities are well aligned over most of the estimation period. This result shows that the professional forecasters have broadly well predicted the timing of the regime switches in the ECB's main policy rate. In addition, this evidence corroborates the results obtained for the baseline specification of the Taylor Rules. In particular, the estimations are in line with the previous economic intuition about the estimated regimes. Indeed, regime 1 occurs in normal periods when the Central Bank is focused on maintaining its primary objective of price stability, while the second regime takes places in times of economic downturn when the ECB has to react quickly to the turmoil by cutting swiftly its main policy rate. Consistently with the benchmark results there are, however, some small misalignments between the actual and perceived filtered probabilities. The first one occurs in the 2001–2003 cycle of interest rate cuts when the economists have not expected the temporary switch to the second regime occurring at the end of 2001. In fact, with the start of this interest rate easing cycle the actual policy rate has switched to the second regime in September

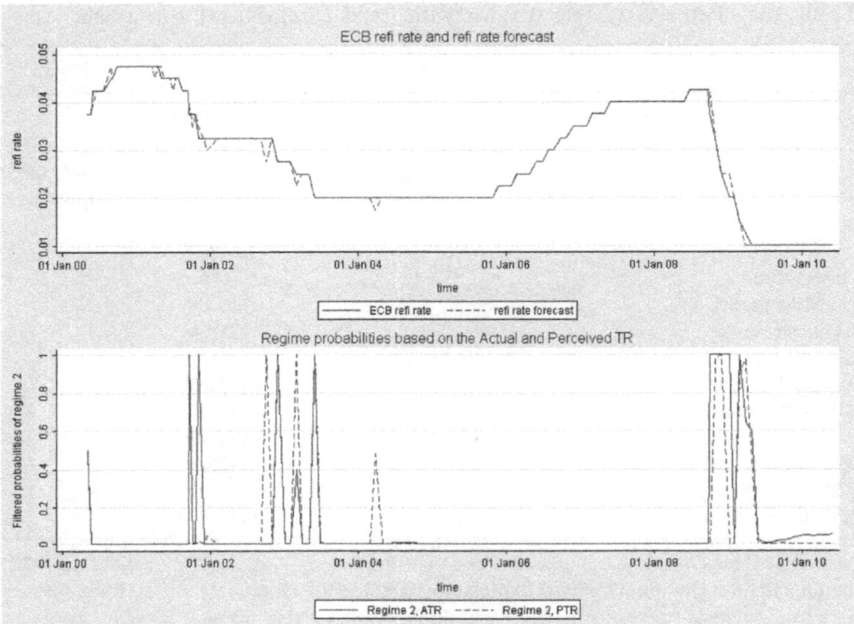

Figure 7: Actual and Perceived Filtered Probabilities, Alternative Model.

and in November 2001, while the refi rate point forecast has switched to the latter only consecutively to the 2002 policy rate cuts. Besides, the economists have perceived a temporary switch to the crisis regime in October 2002 and in March 2003 since they have expected sharp interest rate cuts which have not materialized. Then, in March 2004 as the professional forecasters have expected a 25 basis points rate cut the perceived filtered probability of the second regime has increased substantially even though the actual policy rate has not changed. Finally, at the broadening of the financial crisis in 2008, the economists have well predicted the occurrence of the crisis regime, even though the switch of the forecasted refi rate to the second regime has been delayed by one meeting of the Governing Council. The latter has switched back to the normal regime earlier than the actual refi rate in January 2009 as the economists have not expected the sharp rate cut occurring in that month. The Actual and Perceived Taylor Rules have switched again to the crisis regime in March 2009 as the Central Bank has resumed the series of refi rate cuts after the February 2009 break. Then, the actual and perceived policy rates have transited back to the normal regime since June and May 2009 respectively.

The empirical results of this subsection are also robust to using the inflation and real GDP growth consensus forecasts with the one-year fixed horizon. In particular the transition probabilities point to the same regimes previously estimated. The results are not presented since they are qualitatively very similar. In the next subsection I conduct some robustness analysis of the Taylor Rule specification considered in the previous regressions. In particular, I estimate an augmented Taylor Rule which contains a policy response of the Central Bank to the growth rate of M3 and to the nominal effective exchange rate. Indeed, given the two-pillar approach of the European monetary policy strategy it might be relevant to include the growth rate of M3 to account for the importance of the monetary pillar in the ECB's interest rate setting. In addition, this monetary aggregate could provide some additional indication on the long-run inflationary pressures in the euro area that might represent a valuable information for the decisions on the appropriate monetary policy stance. The nominal effective exchange rate is included in the regressions to control for the Central Bank's responsiveness to this variable when setting the refi rate as well. Actually, as the ECB might be concerned about the impact of the nominal effective exchange rate fluctuations on the euro area current account it could potentially respond to this variable when deciding on the level of the refi rate.

5.3. Augmented Taylor Rules

The goal of this subsection is to challenge the standard specification of the Taylor Rule by considering an augmented model with some additional explanatory variables. As previously indicated, I include the growth rate of the monetary aggregate M3 and the growth rate of the nominal effective exchange rate in the regressions.[22] Hence, for a well specified model the regressors included in the baseline specification should contain all relevant information in determining the policy interest rate and including additional variables in the estimations should not improve upon significantly the model. In that sense, the M3 and the nominal effective exchange growth rates should not provide relevant information for the decisions on the appropriate monetary policy stance. Table 13 reports the estimation results for the linear Actual and Perceived Taylor Rules. In line with the MRS methodology, the linear policy rules are estimated with the maximum likelihood method since the Portmanteau test statistics and the LM tests for

[22] The nominal effective exchange rate refers to a broad basket of currencies of the euro area trading partners. An increase of the former leads to an appreciation of the euro vis-à-vis this basket of currencies. The growth rates of both the M3 and the nominal effective exchange rate are obtained from the real-time database of the European Central Bank.

Table 13: Augmented Taylor Rules, Linear Model

	Actual Taylor Rule	Perceived Taylor Rule
ρ	0.9514***	0.9549***
	(0.0121)	(0.0110)
γ_π	0.1091**	0.1558***
	(0.0471)	(0.0451)
γ_y	0.1274***	0.1085***
	(0.0309)	(0.0301)
γ_m	0.0074*	0.0056
	(0.0044)	(0.0041)
γ_e	0.0032	0.0025
	(0.0030)	(0.0032)
γ_c	−0.0038***	−0.0043***
	(0.0009)	(0.0009)
σ_ε	0.00135***	0.0013***
	(0.0001)	(0.0001)
Observations	141	141
Log-likelihood	732.012	732.501

Note: The table displays the short-run coefficients. ρ, γ_π, γ_y, γ_m, γ_e, γ_c denote the policy inertia, inflation and output growth expectations, the M3 and the nominal effective exchange rate coefficients respectively and the constant term. MLE, robust standard errors are reported in parentheses.
***$p<0.01$, **$p<0.05$, *$p<0.1$.

serial correlation indicate that there is not any structure in the residuals and that the latter can be considered as white noise.

The results from Table 13 point out that the baseline specification of the Taylor Rule is quite robust to including the growth rate of M3 and the nominal effective exchange rate in the regressions. Indeed, the coefficient estimates for these variables are statistically insignificant except for the M3 growth rate coefficient in the Actual Taylor Rule which is significant only at the 10% level. Besides, the magnitude of the estimated additional parameters is very small suggesting that most likely the ECB does not respond to these variables when setting its main policy rate. Therefore, the evidence from both the actual and perceived augmented linear policy rules suggests that the inflation and real output growth forecasts contain all relevant information for determining the policy interest rate and one does not have to include the additional variables in the estimations. Table 14 reports the results from the augmented regime switching Taylor Rules.

One can see from the evidence of Table 14 that including the growth rate of M3 and the nominal effective exchange rate in the regressions does not provide important additional information to the model. Indeed, even though the estimated coefficients of the supplementary variables are significant in both regimes, the magnitude of the point estimates is very small to

Table 14: Actual and Perceived MRS Taylor Rules, Augmented Model

	Actual Taylor Rule		Perceived Taylor Rule	
	Regime 1	Regime 2	Regime 1	Regime 2
$\rho_{s_{t+1}}$	0.9840***	0.9392***	0.9765***	0.5848***
	(0.0036)	(0.0038)	(0.0037)	(0.0593)
$\gamma_{\pi_{s_{t+1}}}$	0.0238***	−0.2231***	0.0178***	0.4735***
	(0.0015)	(0.0114)	(0.0045)	(0.1652)
$\gamma_{y_{s_{t+1}}}$	−0.0001***	0.0508***	0.0056***	0.2189***
	(0.0000)	(0.0003)	(0.0011)	(0.0562)
$\gamma_{m_{s_{t+1}}}$	0.0053***		0.0059***	
	(0.0000)		(0.0015)	
$\gamma_{e_{s_{t+1}}}$	−0.0037***		−0.0065***	
	(0.0003)		(0.0001)	
γ_c	0.0000		0.0000	
	(0.0000)		(0.0000)	
σ_ε	0.0009***		0.0013***	
	(1.010e−05)		(3.970e−05)	
$P[S_{t+1}=i\|S_t=1]$	0.9511***	0.0489***	0.9774***	0.0226***
	(0.0841)	(0.0051)	(0.2613)	(0.0009)
$P[S_{t+1}=i\|S_t=2]$	0.5705***	0.4295***	0.1442***	0.8558***
	(0.0832)	(0.0280)	(0.0253)	(0.0353)
Observations	141		141	
Log-likelihood	751.990		722.963	

Note: The table displays the short-run coefficients. $\rho_{s_{t+1}}$, $\gamma_{\pi_{s_{t+1}}}$, $\gamma_{y_{s_{t+1}}}$, $\gamma_{m_{s_{t+1}}}$, $\gamma_{e_{s_{t+1}}}$, γ_c denote the policy inertia, inflation and output growth expectations, the M3 and the nominal effective exchange rate coefficients respectively and the constant term. Estimates in the middle of the columns refer to parameters that do not switch across regimes. Iterative MLE, HAC standard errors are reported in parentheses.
***$p<0.01$, **$p<0.05$, *$p<0.1$.

infer that the ECB has indeed taken them into account when setting the policy rate. The results are consistent with Berger, de Haan, and Sturm (2006) who find that the ECB has most likely not responded to the growth rate of M3 based on newly constructed communication indicators from the introductory statements of the Governing Council's press conferences. The estimates from Table 14 are also in line with Gerlach and Lewis (2010) who find little evidence for the importance of M3 and the nominal effective exchange rates in the ECB's policy rule. Besides, it is also consistent with Taylor and Williams (2010) who states that simple rules are robust to various specifications of the reaction function and additional regressors. Considering some augmented Taylor Rules, Siklos, Werner, and Bohl (2004) do not find evidence that the ECB has responded directly to asset prices in the estimated policy rules even though they can be considered as useful indicators for monetary policy. Their results corroborate the simulation exercise of Bernanke and Gertler (2001) who show that an optimal policy rule does not involve a response of the Central Bank to asset prices, even if it is known to policymakers that the market is driven by a bubble because the response can be harmful to the economy.

Table 14 points out the estimated coefficients of the growth rate of M3 and the nominal effective exchange rate feature the expected sign. Hence, if there is an increase in the monetary aggregate M3, the Central Bank will raise the refi rate to prevent the build-up of medium to long-term inflationary pressures in the euro area. Conversely, an appreciation of the euro vis-à-vis the trading partners' currencies will call for a rate cut in order to alleviate the negative impact on the euro area exports. Finally, it is important to highlight that the additional explanatory variables do not alter the results from the baseline specification. Indeed, when switching from the first to the second regime the policy inertia decreases and the ECB attempts to stabilize the economic outlook rather than inflation expectations, consistently with the previous results for the Actual Taylor Rule. However, for the Perceived Taylor Rule it seems that when switching to regime 2 the Central Bank tries to stabilize both the inflation and real output growth expectations with a higher emphasis on the former. The actual transition probabilities are well aligned with the results for the benchmark model. For the Perceived Taylor Rule, the transition probability of the first regime is also consistent with the previous estimations, while it seems that the second regime is more persistent than previously found.

Figure 8 displays the estimated filtered probabilities from both reaction functions. A comparison of Figures 3 and 8 reveals that the estimated filtered probabilities of the augmented model are broadly in line with the results from the benchmark specification. The evidence from the Actual Taylor Rule points out that the timing of the regime switches in the augmented model corresponds well to the one estimated with the benchmark specification. There is only one exception occurring in March 2003 when the actual refi rate has not switched to the second regime in the augmented model. The Perceived Taylor Rule estimates indicate that the timing of the regime switches is in line with the previous findings especially during the financial crisis in 2008 and 2009. However, there are some small differences at the beginning of the decade as the professional forecasters have perceived some switching to the second regime occurring in the second half of 2000. Then, they have perceived a longer duration of the second regime as the forecasted policy rate has remained in the crisis regime from December 2002 until October 2003 compared to the shorter duration of this regime as estimated in the baseline model for the same period. Finally, in the augmented model the economists have not forecasted a temporary switch to the second regime occurring in March 2004 as they have expected in the benchmark model. However,

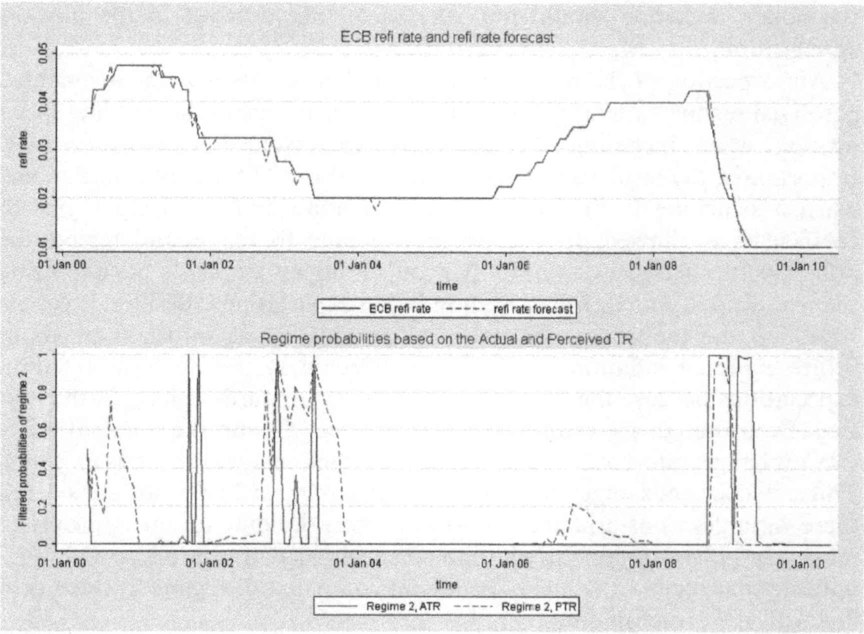

Figure 8: Actual and Perceived Filtered Probabilities, Augmented Model.

the professional forecasters have predicted the transition to the crisis regime at the broadening of the financial crisis in November 2008 in line with the previous estimates. They have also perceived a shorter duration of the turmoil as the policy rate point forecast has switched to the first regime in March 2009. The empirical evidence from the baseline model is therefore broadly corroborated from the estimation results with the augmented Taylor Rules.

Table A.5 presents the estimation results of the augmented model using the inflation and real output growth forecasts with a one-year horizon in the regressions. The table points out that the previous findings are further confirmed since the estimated coefficients of the additional explanatory variables are statistically insignificant. Hence, including the growth rate of the monetary aggregate M3 and the nominal effective exchange rate does not seem to provide additional insights on both the Actual and Perceived Taylor Rules within the one-year fixed horizon framework. Notice, however, that in the actual reaction function the inflation point estimate becomes insignificant as there might be some interaction between inflation expectations and the growth rate of M3. Therefore, as it seems that the ECB does not respond to these additional variables when setting the policy rate, one should not take them into account in the model's specification.

An inspection of the results from Table A.6 reveals that the augmented perceived regime switching model yields similar results to the baseline specification when including the additional regressors in the estimations. Importantly, the results are comparable with those of the benchmark model when a switching in the policy inertia, inflation and real output growth coefficients is allowed. Indeed, when switching to the second regime the policy inertia decreases and the ECB puts a higher emphasis on stabilizing the real output growth rather than inflation expectations. Besides, it is possible that the monetary aggregate M3 provides some information about future expected inflation which is not reflected in the one-year inflation expectations because the latter are not entirely forward-looking in this setting. Even though the estimated coefficients of M3 and the nominal effective exchange rate have the expected sign their magnitude is very small. This evidence thus suggests that the ECB has most likely not considered these variables as of primary importance when deciding on the appropriate monetary policy stance. In addition, the estimated transition probabilities indicate that regime 1 is highly persistent compared to regime 2 which is in line with the earlier findings.

Finally, the estimated filtered probabilities which are displayed in Figure A.3, point out that the timing of the regime switches is consistent with the baseline results. However, there are some exceptions occurring in the period from 2000 to 2003 when the actual and forecasted refi rates have switched more frequently to the second regime. In addition, after the bankruptcy of Lehman Brothers the policy rates have entered the second regime consistently with the previous results. Nevertheless, the actual and forecasted refi rates have switched back to the first regime in April and in May 2009 for the Actual and Perceived Taylor Rules respectively which is earlier than previously found. Therefore, the empirical evidence suggests that the estimated regimes and the filtered probabilities of the baseline and the alternative models are in general robust to including the monetary aggregate M3 and the nominal effective exchange rate as additional regressors in the model.

The regime switching policy rules have also been estimated with the Economic Sentiment Indicator (ESI) growth rate with respect to its long-run average as an additional sensitivity analysis. Overall, the results show that the estimated regimes and the timing of the transitions are robust to including the ESI growth rate in the regressions both for the year ahead and the one-year horizons. Consistently with the previous findings, the results point out that the policy inertia has decreased substantially and the ECB responds relatively more strongly to the deviations of the business cycle indicator from its long-run average in the crisis regime. This evidence is also corroborated from the estimations with the consensus inflation forecasts and the ESI growth rate for the year ahead and the one-year horizons.[23]

The empirical results previously presented indicate that it is appropriate to consider a two regimes switching specification of the Actual and Perceived Taylor Rules. Moreover, one could also envisage the possibility that the ECB might respond differently to macroeconomic fundamentals within a higher order of policy regimes. Therefore, the aim of the next section is to further investigate the relevance of a third regime for the key ECB's policy rate. However, one should be aware of the fact that estimating a three regimes MRS model involves a higher computational burden and one should not heavily rely on the estimation results. The latter should be considered more likely as indicative rather than as a formal evidence for the possibility of detecting a third regime in the ECB's interest rate setting policy.

6. A Three Regimes Switching Model

This section is devoted to further investigating the presence of a third regime in the ECB's refi rate. The previous empirical evidence has highlighted the occurrence of two policy regimes: the first one occurs in normal times and the second regime takes place in periods of economic turmoil. In addition, one could also determine whether the key interest rate enters a third regime that might appear in particularly turbulent periods as for instance during the broadening of the financial crisis in 2008. This investigation will thus shed new light on understanding more in-depth the ECB's policy responsiveness to economic fundamentals within a three regimes switching specification. Table 15 reports the results for the baseline model when considering a switching in the policy inertia, inflation and real output growth expectations.

At a first glance, Table 15 points to the presence of three regimes for the ECB's refi rate. First, one can easily identify the two regimes previously estimated. In line with the core results, when switching from the first to the second regime monetary policy becomes less inertial and the ECB focuses on stabilizing real output growth rather than inflation expectations. There is a small difference as regards the real output growth forecasts point estimate in the first regime which is slightly negative when estimated within the three regimes model. Importantly, the third regime features the least

[23] The results are qualitatively similar to the previous empirical evidence and therefore are not reported in the chapter.

Table 15: Actual MRS Taylor Rule, Three Regimes Model (TRM)

	Regime 1	Regime 2	Regime 3
$\rho_{s_{t+1}}$	0.9896***	0.8262***	0.4095***
	(0.0009)	(0.0317)	(0.0318)
$\gamma_{\pi_{s_{t+1}}}$	0.0368***	−0.4319***	0.9163***
	(0.0008)	(0.0069)	(0.0490)
$\gamma_{y_{s_{t+1}}}$	−0.0102***	0.5521***	0.2288***
	(0.0004)	(0.0381)	(0.0068)
γ_c		−0.0000	
		(0.0000)	
σ_ε		0.0006***	
		(3.595e−05)	
$P[S_{t+1}=i\|S_t=1]$	0.8631***	0.0753***	0.0616***
	(0.1091)	(0.0095)	(0.0022)
$P[S_{t+1}=i\|S_t=2]$	0.7826***	0.2174***	0.0000
	(0.0748)	(0.0113)	(0.0000)
$P[S_{t+1}=i\|S_t=3]$	0.5158***	0.1038***	0.3804***
	(0.0096)	(0.0102)	(0.0514)
Observations		141	
Log-likelihood		780.598	

Note: The table displays the short-run coefficients. $\rho_{s_{t+1}}$, $\gamma_{\pi_{s_{t+1}}}$, $\gamma_{y_{s_{t+1}}}$, γ_c denote the policy inertia, inflation and output growth expectations coefficients respectively and the constant term. Estimates in the middle of the columns refer to parameters that do not switch across regimes. Iterative MLE, HAC standard errors are reported in parentheses.
***$p<0.01$, **$p<0.05$, *$p<0.1$.

inertial monetary policy and the Central Bank responds quite strongly to both the inflation and real output growth expectations compared to the previous regimes. Consistently with the earlier intuition, regime 1 is the most persistent and regime 2 has the smallest probability of occurrence. Indeed, the former lasts on average 7.30 policy meetings and the latter features an average duration of 1.28 meetings. As regards the third regime it lasts on average 1.61 meetings. Finally, notice that conditional on being in either the third or in the second regime there is a high probability to transit to the first one, while it is much less likely to switch to the third one conditional on being in either the first or in the second regimes. Table 16 presents the estimated long-run coefficients along with some relevant statistics.

The previous evidence suggests that in regime 1 the policy rate is the most inertial and the Central Bank responds strongly to inflation expectations. In fact, given that the Taylor Principle is clearly satisfied the ECB exerts a stabilizing effect on inflation while its response to the real output growth forecasts is at odds with the baseline results. In the second regime, the ECB implements a higher fraction of the desired policy rate target and focuses on stabilizing the real output growth rather than the inflation

Table 16: Actual MRS Taylor Rule, TRM Long-Run Parameters

	Regime 1	Regime 2	Regime 3
$\rho_{s_{t+1}}$	0.9896***	0.8262***	0.4095***
	(0.0009)	(0.0317)	(0.0318)
$\beta_{\pi_{s_{t+1}}}$	3.5460***	−2.4848***	1.5516***
	(0.2487)	(0.4512)	(0.1665)
$\beta_{y_{s_{t+1}}}$	−0.9873***	3.1760***	0.3875***
	(0.1155)	(0.7945)	(0.0322)
Observations		141	
LL MRS three regimes		780.598	
LL MRS two regimes		749.329	
LR test		62.538***	
AIC MRS three regimes		−1521.195	
BIC MRS three regimes		−1462.220	
AIC MRS two regimes		−1474.659	
BIC MRS two regimes		−1439.274	
RMSE MRS three regimes		0.000628	
RMSE MRS two regimes		0.000899	

Note: The table displays the implied long-run coefficients. $\rho_{s_{t+1}}$, $\beta_{\pi_{s_{t+1}}}$, $\beta_{y_{s_{t+1}}}$ denote the policy inertia, inflation and output growth expectations coefficients respectively. Estimates in the middle of the columns refer to parameters that do not switch across regimes. Standard errors are computed with the Delta method and are reported in parentheses.
***$p < 0.01$, **$p < 0.05$, *$p < 0.1$.

expectations consistently with the benchmark results. Finally, in the third regime it is compelling to notice that the coefficient estimates are the closest to the original findings of Taylor (1993). In the latter, the point estimates indicate that the Central Bank attempts to stabilize both the inflation and real output growth expectations. Furthermore, the LR test points out that there is evidence in favor of a three regimes specification compared to a two regimes switching model. The AIC and BIC information criteria further suggest that the former should be preferred to the latter. As regards the RMSE there is a slight advantage of using the three regimes model compared to the specification with two regimes, as the former permits to reduce a little the in-sample prediction error of the policy rate. Table 17 reports the estimation results for the Perceived Taylor Rule.

Table 17 points out that the results are in line with the empirical evidence for the Actual Taylor Rule. More precisely, a robust finding is that when switching from the first to second regimes monetary policy is less inertial and the ECB is focused on stabilizing the real output growth rather than the inflation expectations. Besides, in the third regime the Central Bank's policy is the least inertial and exerts a stabilizing effect on both the inflation and real output growth expectations. The estimated transition

Table 17: Perceived MRS Taylor Rule, Three Regimes Model (TRM)

	Regime 1	Regime 2	Regime 3
$\rho_{s_{t+1}}$	0.9901***	0.8852***	0.6468***
	(0.0013)	(0.0142)	(0.0470)
$\gamma_{\pi_{s_{t+1}}}$	0.0315***	−0.1373***	0.6057***
	(0.0024)	(0.0237)	(0.0736)
$\gamma_{y_{s_{t+1}}}$	−0.0060***	0.0346***	0.1422***
	(0.0003)	(0.0006)	(0.0039)
γ_c		0.0000	
		(0.0000)	
σ_ε		0.0006***	
		(1.951e−06)	
$P[S_{t+1}=i\|S_t=1]$	0.8291***	0.0605***	0.1104***
	(0.1310)	(0.0006)	(0.0146)
$P[S_{t+1}=i\|S_t=2]$	0.7072***	0.2928***	0.0000
	(0.1918)	(0.1035)	(0.0000)
$P[S_{t+1}=i\|S_t=3]$	0.9168***	0.0000	0.0832***
	(0.0537)	(0.0000)	(0.0017)
Observations		141	
Log-likelihood		764.723	

Note: The table displays the short-run coefficients. $\rho_{s_{t+1}}$, $\gamma_{\pi_{s_{t+1}}}$, $\gamma_{y_{s_{t+1}}}$, γ_c denote the policy inertia, inflation and output growth expectations coefficients respectively and the constant term. Estimates in the middle of the columns refer to parameters that do not switch across regimes. Iterative MLE, HAC standard errors are reported in parentheses.
***$p<0.01$, **$p<0.05$, *$p<0.1$.

probabilities indicate that regime 1 is the most persistent while regime 3 features the smallest probability of occurrence. In line with the evidence for the actual reaction function, there is a higher probability to switch to the first regime conditional on being in the second or in the third regimes rather than to transit to the third one conditional on being in either the first or in the second regimes. The implied long-run coefficients are reported in Table 18.

The results of Table 18 are qualitatively similar to the evidence from Table 16. Indeed, in the first regime the ECB stabilizes inflation expectations and implements a particularly inertial policy, while in the second regime it aims at stabilizing the economic outlook. Finally, the policy stance is the least inertial in regime 3 and the Central Bank's policy switches towards stabilizing both the inflation and real output growth expectations in line with the recommendation stemming from a standard Taylor Rule. The LR test shows evidence in favor of a three regimes specification and the AIC and BIC information criteria also point in the same direction. Based on the RMSE evidence one should also prefer the three regimes model to reduce the in-sample prediction error of the policy rate.

Table 18: Perceived MRS Taylor Rule, TRM Long-Run Parameters

	Regime 1	Regime 2	Regime 3
$\rho_{s_{t+1}}$	0.9901***	0.8852***	0.6468***
	(0.0013)	(0.0142)	(0.0470)
$\beta_{\pi_{s_{t+1}}}$	3.1676***	−1.1961***	1.7148***
	(0.5255)	(0.0835)	(0.4366)
$\beta_{y_{s_{t+1}}}$	−0.5994***	0.3018***	0.4027***
	(0.0737)	(0.0328)	(0.0458)
Observations		141	
LL MRS three regimes		764.723	
LL MRS two regimes		736.512	
LR test		56.422***	
AIC MRS three regimes		−1489.446	
BIC MRS three regimes		−1430.470	
AIC MRS two regimes		−1449.023	
BIC MRS two regimes		−1413.638	
RMSE MRS three regimes		0.000603	
RMSE MRS two regimes		0.001011	

Note: The table displays the implied long-run coefficients. $\rho_{s_{t+1}}$, $\beta_{\pi_{s_{t+1}}}$, $\beta_{y_{s_{t+1}}}$ denote the policy inertia, inflation and output growth expectations coefficients respectively. Estimates in the middle of the columns refer to parameters that do not switch across regimes. Standard errors are computed with the Delta method and are reported in parentheses.
***$p<0.01$, **$p<0.05$, *$p<0.1$.

The estimated actual and perceived filtered probabilities are displayed in Figure 9.

Figure 9 shows that regime 2 corresponds to the one estimated within the two regimes switching specifications. Indeed, the latter occurs in crisis periods when the Central Bank cuts swiftly the policy rate to prevent a further decline in the economic outlook. This finding is thus robust to the number of regimes considered for the main policy rate. However, it is more difficult to understand the economic intuition about the third regime. In the latter, the policy inertia is the lowest among all regimes and the ECB stabilizes both the inflation and real output growth forecasts. Figure 9 points out that this regime tends to occur in periods of monetary policy tightening as observed in 2000 or from 2007 to 2008 which corresponds with the last tightening cycle. As the ECB implements more frequent adjustments of the refi rate the policy stance is less inertial and the Central Bank attempts to stabilize both the inflation and real output growth expectations as recommended by a standard Taylor Rule specification. Hence, not surprisingly the estimated coefficients in the third regime are the closest to the original findings of Taylor (1993). Even though the latter regime takes place in periods of policy tightening and features the lowest policy inertia across all regimes, it is sometimes difficult to disentangle from the presence of the second regime.

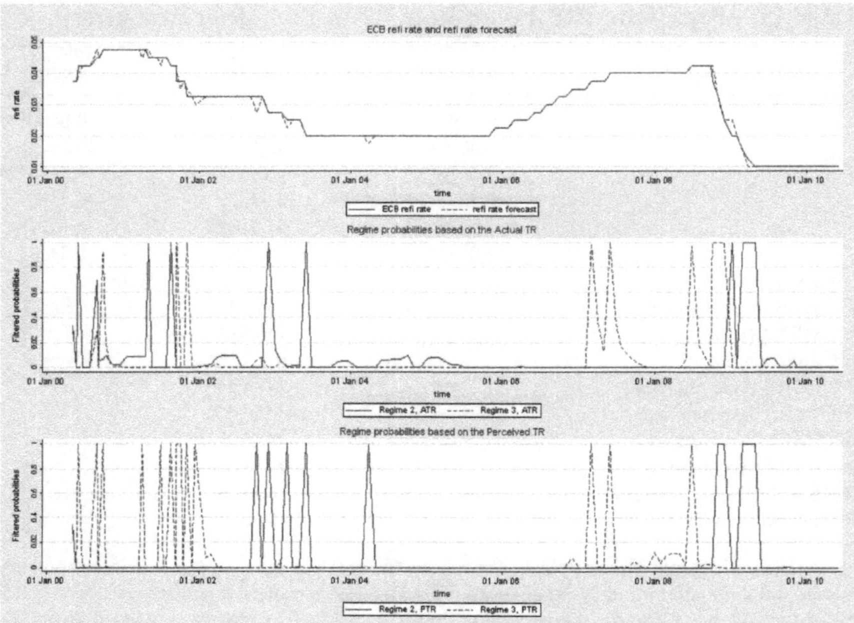

Figure 9: Actual and Perceived Filtered Probabilities, Three Regimes Model.

The first evidence occurs in April 2001 when the economists have perceived a policy rate cut. Then the refi rate enters sporadically the third regime rather than the second one during the 2001–2003 cycle of policy rate cuts the ECB has implemented. At the July 2008 rate hike both the actual and perceived policy rates have switched to the third regime as one should have expected. During the large rate cuts the ECB has implemented since October 2008 the refi rate has mainly switched to the second regime but it has also transited to the third one in October, November and December 2008 as regards the Actual Taylor Rule. Concerning the Perceived Taylor Rule the policy rate has not entered the third regime during the implemented policy rate cuts which is consistent with the estimation results from the two regimes framework. Therefore, the empirical evidence on the third regime is rather mixed. While on the one hand, it seems that the latter occurs in periods of policy tightening when the Central Bank raises the policy rate, on the other hand this regime takes place also during some interest rate cuts and is sometimes difficult to disentangle from the occurrence of the second regime. One may conclude that estimating a two regimes model provides more clearly-cut results that are in line with the economic intuition and one does not have to rely too much on the three regimes specification. The latter is computationally less reliable given the higher number of parameters that are estimated.

Tables A.7 and A.8 report the estimation results for the three regimes Actual Taylor Rule when considering a one-year fixed forecast horizon in the regressions. The evidence suggests that there are three regimes for the policy inertia coefficient which are consistent with the findings for the year ahead forecast horizon. Indeed, the policy rate is the most persistent in the first regime and the least inertial in regime 3. In addition, the ECB responds positively to both the inflation and real output growth forecasts whose coefficient estimates do not switch across regimes. The transition probabilities are in line with the findings obtained with the two regimes model. In particular, regime 1 is the most persistent and there is a high probability to switch to the latter conditional on being in regime 2. The former lasts 18.76 and the latter 1.20 policy meetings respectively. Conversely, regime 3 should not occur on average as the estimated probability is zero but is not significant.

Table A.8 points out that the Taylor Principle is not satisfied in neither regime as the Central Bank has focused more on stabilizing the economic outlook. This result is in line with the empirical findings for the two regimes model. The LR test statistic shows that there is no evidence against the model with two regimes. This result is corroborated by the AIC and BIC criteria which point out that one should prefer the two regimes model. The RMSE also indicate that there is almost no difference in the prediction error between the two specifications within the sample.

Finally, Tables A.9 and A.10 report the results for the Perceived Taylor Rule when considering the one-year fixed forecast horizon in the estimations. The results point out that the inflation responsiveness parameter has switched across three regimes. In the first one the ECB does not seem to respond very much to inflation expectations while in the second it responds negatively to the inflation forecasts. This evidence is broadly consistent with the results obtained for the model with two regimes. In addition, in the third regime the Central Bank responds positively to inflation expectations and implements a stabilizing policy for the latter.[24] Notice also that, even though the first regime is the most persistent featuring an average duration of 19.84 policy meetings, the third regime seems to be persistent as well to some extent as it lasts 6.55 meetings on average. Finally, the LR test statistic suggests that there is no evidence in favor of the three regimes specification and the AIC and BIC criteria broadly indicate that the two regimes model should be preferred. Nevertheless, in terms of the RMSE

[24] The long-run inflation coefficient indicates that the Taylor Principle is satisfied in regime 3.

there is some gain in choosing the three regimes model as it yields a slightly smaller prediction error of the main policy rate.

Figure A.4 shows the actual and perceived filtered probabilities using the one-year horizon forecasts in the regressions. The estimated probabilities indicate that the occurrence of the second regime is fully in line with the above findings and the results from the model featuring two regimes with only two exceptions in December 2008 and in May 2009. Indeed, regime 2 takes place in crisis periods when the Central Bank has to cut swiftly the policy rate. However, the interpretation of the third regime is less clear-cut. As found with the year ahead forecasts, the latter tends to occur in periods of monetary policy tightening as the Central Bank focuses on stabilizing inflation expectations. Hence, the policy rate point forecast switches to the third regime in 2000 and during the 2006–2008 cycle of policy rate hikes. Besides, as previously highlighted the occurrence of the third regime is sometimes difficult to disentangle from the transition to the second one. In fact, the forecasted policy rate has switched to the third regime during the refi rate cuts in November 2002 and in 2003, as well as in the first half of 2009. In contrast, the actual policy rate has switched to the third regime only at the December 2008 meeting of the Governing Council. A possible explanation is that in view of reaching the ZLB the refi rate has switched to a regime in which the ECB implements a more aggressive policy than in normal periods to stabilize both the inflation and real output growth expectations. The Perceived Taylor Rule has also switched to the third regime of policy tightening in May 2009 as the economists may have perceived a higher responsiveness of the Central Bank to economic fundamentals. As the ECB has maintained the policy rate at the historically low level of 1% the refi rate point forecast has transited to the first regime in January 2010.

7. Conclusion

This chapter has shed more light on understanding the European monetary policy within Actual and Perceived regime switching Taylor Rules. The former is based on the actual refi rate set by the ECB Governing Council while the latter relies on the professional point forecasts for the refi rate made before the upcoming monetary policy meeting. There are several main results that can be drawn from the empirical evidence of this chapter.

First, the standard linear Taylor Rule has hidden finer policy regimes that have been identified within the MRS framework. Indeed, the results have shown that the Central Bank has switched between a regime that occurs in normal (noncrisis) periods to a regime of economic downturn that features sharp interest rate cuts. In the former, the ECB attempts to stabilize both the inflation and real output growth expectations and the policy rate features substantial inertia. In the latter the Central Bank implements a larger fraction of the desired policy rate and switches towards stabilizing the economic outlook rather than inflation expectations. This evidence points out that in crisis periods, as the Central Bank has to react quickly, it puts temporarily aside its overriding price stability goal and focuses mainly on preventing a further decline in economic activity and on securing the stability of the financial system. The empirical results are consistent with a Central Bank loss function that contains a financial stability objective as outlined in Agur and Demertzis (2011). The evidence shows that the coefficient estimates in the corresponding regimes are sensitive to the measure of expectations used in the regressions. However, the estimated regimes are robust to using either the year ahead or the one-year fixed forecasting horizons. The estimations with the year ahead forecasts provide better results as they reflect more accurately the forward-looking nature of the expectations formation process, which is a salient feature of the Taylor Rules framework.

Second, the results point out that the professional forecasters have broadly well predicted the Central Bank's responsiveness to economic fundamentals in the corresponding policy regimes as well as the timing of the regime switches. Moreover, the results are robust to including consensus forecasts of inflation and real output growth instead of the investment bank forecasts in the regressions. The augmented Taylor Rule specification further suggests that including the growth rates of M3 and the nominal effective exchange rate in the estimations does not provide further insights on understanding the policy reaction function of the ECB. Besides, the estimated regimes remain robust to including these additional variables in the regressions.

Finally, the empirical evidence for the two regimes is broadly unaltered when estimating a model with three regimes. Even though some of the LM test statistics show evidence in favor of the three regimes specification, the economic evidence is rather mixed about the relevance of a third regime. Indeed, regime 3 seems to correspond to periods of monetary policy tightening when the Central Bank's policy switches towards stabilizing both the inflation and real output growth forecasts. However, for some periods the latter is quite difficult to disentangle from the occurrence of the second regime. In terms of policy recommendation, this chapter has shown that it is particularly important to consider a regime switching specification of the Taylor Rules in order to better understand the behavior of the ECB and to more accurately predict its main interest rate. Following a regime switching policy rule will help the Governing Council to set the appropriate level of the refi rate according to the specific state of the economy. As avenues for future research, it would be valuable to understand more thoroughly the nature and sources of nonlinearities in monetary policy rules.

Acknowledgments

The author is particularly grateful to Henri Loubergé, Charles Wyplosz, Ulrich Kohli, Jean-Marc Natal, Alessandro Missale, the colleagues from the Department of Economics, as well as the participants of the Young Researchers Seminar of the University of Geneva for their valuable comments and insights.

References

Agur, I., & Demertzis, M. (2011). *Leaning against the wind and the timing of monetary policy*. DNB Working Paper No. 303.

Alcidi, C., Flamini, A., & Fracasso, A. (2005). *Taylored rules. Does one fit (or hide) all?* HEI Working Paper No. 04/2005.

Assenmacher-Wesche, K. (2006). Estimating central banks' preferences from a time-varying empirical reaction function. *European Economic Review*, *50*(8), 1951–1974.

Belke, A., & Klose, J. (2010). *(How) do the ECB and the fed react to financial market uncertainty? The Taylor rule in times of crisis*. DIW Working Paper. No. 972.

Berger, H., de Haan, J., & Sturm, J. E. (2006). *Does money matter in the ECB strategy? New evidence based on ECB communication*. CESifo Working Paper No. 1652.

Bernanke, B., & Gertler, M. (2001). Should Central Banks Respond to Movements in Asset Prices? *American Economic Review*, *91*(2), 253–257.

Clarida, R., Galí, J., & Gertler, M. (1998). Monetary policy rules in practice: Some international evidence. *European Economic Review*, *42*(6), 1033–1067.

Clarida, R., Galí, J., & Gertler, M. (2000). Monetary policy rules and macroeconomic stability: Evidence and some theory. *Quarterly Journal of Economics*, *115*(1), 147–180.

Garcia, R. (1998). Asymptotic null distribution of the likelihood ratio test in Markov Switching models. *International Economic Review*, *39*(3), 763–788.

Garcia, R., & Perron, P. (1996). An analysis of the real interest rate under regime shifts. *Review of Economics and Statistics, MIT Press*, *78*(1), 111–125.

Gerlach, S. (2011). ECB repo rate setting during the financial crisis. *Economics Letters*, *112*(2), 186–188.

Gerlach, S., & Lewis, J. (2010). *The zero lower bound, ECB interest rate policy and the financial crisis*. De Nederlandsche Bank Working Paper No. 254.

Goldfeld, S., & Quandt, R. (1973). A Markov model for switching regressions. *Journal of Econometrics*, *1*(1), 3–15.

Gorter, J., Jacobs, J., & de Haan, J. (2008). Taylor rules for the ECB using expectations data. *Scandinavian Journal of Economics*, *110*(3), 473–488.

Hamilton, J. D. (1989). A new approach to the economic analysis of nonstationary time series and the business cycle. *Econometrica*, *57*(2), 357–384.

Hamilton, J. D. (1994). *Time series analysis*. Princeton, NJ: Princeton University Press.

Hamilton, J. D. (2005). Regime-switching models. *Palgrave dictionary of economics*. New York: Palgrave McMillan Ltd.

Hansen, B. E. (1992). The likelihood ratio test under nonstandard conditions: Testing the Markov switching model of GNP. *Journal of Applied Econometrics, Special Issue on Nonlinear Dynamics and Econometrics*, *7*(S1), S61–S82.

Hansen, B. E. (1996). Erratum: The likelihood ratio test under nonstandard conditions: Testing the Markov switching model of GNP. *Journal of Applied Econometrics*, *11*(2), 195–198.

Jeanne, O., & Masson, P. (2000). Currency crises, sunspots and Markov-switching regimes. *Journal of International Economics*, *50*(2), 327–350.

Kim, C.-J., & Nelson, C. (1999). *State-space models with regime switching*. Cambridge, MA: MIT Press.

Mankiw, G., Miron, J., & Weil, D. (1987). The adjustment of expectations to a change in regime: A study of the founding of the federal reserve. *American Economic Review*, *77*(3), 358–374.

Markov, N. (2009). *Actual versus perceived Taylor rules. How predictable is the European central bank?* University of Geneva Working Paper No. 11209.

Mishkin, F. (2009). Is monetary policy effective during financial crises. *American Economic Review: Papers and Proceedings*, *99*(2), 573–577.

Orphanides, A. (2001). Monetary policy rules based on real-time data. *American Economic Review*, *91*(4), 964–985.

Owyang, M., & Ramey, G. (2004). Regime switching and monetary policy measurement. *Journal of Monetary Economics*, *51*(8), 1577–1597.

Poplawski-Ribeiro M., & Rülke, J.-C. (2010). *Fiscal expectations on the stability and growth pact: Evidence from survey data*. Working Papers 2010-05. CEPII Research Center.

Perlin, M. (2009). *MS regress – A package for Markov regime switching models in matlab*. Matlab Central.

Perruchoud, A. (2009). Estimating a Taylor rule with Markov switching regimes for Switzerland. *Swiss Journal of Economics and Statistics*, *145*(2), 187–220.

Quandt, R. (1972). A new approach to estimating switching regressions. *Journal of the American Statistical Association*, *67*(338), 306–310.

Reifschneider, D., & Williams, J. (2000). Three lessons for monetary policy in a low-inflation era. *Journal of Money, Credit and Banking*, *32*(4), 936–966.

Siklos, P. L., Werner, T., & Bohl, M. T. (2004). *Asset prices in Taylor rules: Specification, estimation, and policy implications for the ECB*. Deutsche Bundesbank Discussion Paper, 22.

Sims, C., & Zha, T. (2006). Were there regime switches in U.S. monetary policy? *American Economic Review*, *96*(1), 54–81.

Taylor, J. (1993). Discretion versus Policy Rules in Practice. *Carnegie-Rochester Conference Series on Public Policy*, 39.

Taylor J., & Williams J. (2010). *Simple and robust rules for monetary policy*. Federal Reserve Bank of San Francisco Working Paper 2010-10.

Tillmann, P. (2003). The regime-dependent determination of credibility: A new look at European interest rate differentials. *German Economic Review*, *4*(4), 409–431.

Walsh, C. (2003). Speed limit policies: The output gap and optimal monetary policy. *American Economic Review*, *93*(1), 265–278.

Zivot, E., & Andrews, D. (1992). Further evidence on the great crash, the oil-price shock, and the unit-root hypothesis. *Journal of Business and Economic Statistics*, *10*(3), 251–270.

Appendix

Variables Used in the Estimations

Table A.1: List of Variables

Variables	Descriptions
i_{t+1}	Refi rate set by the ECB at its policy meeting in period $t+1$.
$E_t i_{t+1}$	Refi rate point forecast reported by the investment bank's economists in period t for the refi rate decision in period $t+1$.
$E_t \pi_y$	Inflation point forecasts of the investment bank's economists and Consensus Economics for the current year horizon.
$E_t \pi_{y+1}$	Inflation point forecasts of the investment bank's economists and Consensus Economics for the year ahead horizon.
$E_t \overline{\pi}_y$	One-year inflation point forecasts horizon of the investment bank's economists and Consensus Economics.
$E_t y_y$	Real GDP growth point forecasts of the investment bank's economists and Consensus Economics for the current year horizon.
$E_t y_{y+1}$	Real GDP growth point forecasts of the investment bank's economists and Consensus Economics for the year ahead horizon.
$E_t \overline{y}_y$	One-year real GDP growth point forecasts horizon of the investment bank's economists and Consensus Economics.
M3	The yearly growth rate of the monetary aggregate M3 which is taken from the ECB's real-time database.
Nominal exchange rate	The yearly growth rate of the nominal effective exchange rate of the euro against a broad basket of currencies. A positive growth rate implies an appreciation of the euro vis-à-vis this basket of currencies. The series is from the ECB's real-time database.
ESI	The difference between the euro area Economic Sentiment Indicator (ESI) and its long-run average of 100 expressed in percentage points of the long-run average. The ESI is published by the European Commission on a monthly basis.

Table A.2: Summary Statistics

Dependent and explanatory variables	Obs.	Mean	Std. deviation	Min	Max
ECB's main refinancing operations rate (refi rate) (%)	141	3.060	1.194	1.00	4.75
ECB's refi rate point forecast, investment bank (%)	141	3.057	1.200	1.00	4.75
Current year inflation, investment bank (%)	141	2.060	0.671	0.20	3.70
Year ahead inflation, investment bank (%)	141	1.788	0.358	1.00	2.60
One-year inflation, investment bank (%)	141	1.911	0.464	0.53	3.11
Current year real GDP growth, investment bank (%)	141	1.465	1.744	−4.30	4.00
Year ahead real GDP growth, investment bank (%)	141	2.042	0.776	−0.50	3.60
One-year real GDP growth, investment bank (%)	141	1.699	0.012	−2.24	3.87
Current year inflation, consensus forecasts (%)	141	2.005	0.655	0.30	3.60
Year ahead inflation, consensus forecasts (%)	141	1.790	0.265	1.10	2.50
One-year inflation, consensus forecasts (%)	141	1.871	0.442	0.32	3.26
Current year real GDP growth, consensus forecasts (%)	141	1.471	1.712	−4.40	3.40
Year ahead real GDP growth, consensus forecasts (%)	141	2.008	0.759	−0.90	3.20
One-year real GDP growth, consensus forecasts (%)	141	1.722	1.193	−3.80	3.29
M3 yearly growth rate (%)	141	6.660	2.751	−0.30	12.50
Nominal effective exchange rate, yearly rate of change (%)	141	1.723	6.276	−12.91	17.29
Economic Sentiment Indicator, deviation from long-run average (%)	141	0.804	10.287	−29.30	17.60

Note: The actual refi rate, the M3 growth rate and the nominal effective exchange rate are taken from the website of the ECB. The Economic Sentiment Indicator comes from the European Commission's website. The long-run average of the ESI is equal to 100 as computed by the Commission.

Unit Root and Stationarity Tests

Table A.3: Unit Root Tests, Investment Bank Forecasts

Variables	ADF Z(t)	PP Z(t)	KPSS	Integration order
Refi rate	−1.940** (0.027)	−0.682 (0.851)	0.585**	I(0)
Forecasted refi rate	−1.600* (0.056)	−0.753 (0.833)	0.567**	I(0)
Expected inflation, current year	−3.102*** (0.001)	−2.845* (0.052)	0.186	I(0)
Expected inflation, year ahead	−2.993*** (0.002)	−2.980** (0.037)	0.134	I(0)
Expected inflation, one-year horizon	−3.795*** (0.000)	−2.626* (0.088)	0.162	I(0)
Expected GDP growth, current year	−2.348*** (0.010)	−2.375 (0.149)	0.521**	I(0)
Expected GDP growth, year ahead	−2.987*** (0.002)	−3.055** (0.030)	0.657**	I(0)
Expected GDP growth, one-year horizon	−2.809*** (0.003)	−2.317 (0.166)	0.566**	I(0)
M3 yearly growth rate	−1.117 (0.133)	−0.288 (0.927)	0.257	I(1)
Nominal exchange rate, yearly rate of change	−2.696*** (0.004)	−2.453 (0.127)	0.281	I(0)
ESI percentage deviation from the long-run average	−2.712*** (0.004)	−1.923 (0.321)	0.480**	I(0)
Observations	137	140	141	

Note: The ADF Z(t) and PP Z(t) refer to the Augmented Dickey–Fuller and Phillips–Perron tests for unit root in the variables. A statistically significant test shows evidence against the null hypothesis of unit root. For the ADF test 3 lags of the difference in the variables have been used, while the number of lags used in the Phillips–Perron test are determined automatically based on Newey–West bandwidth selection. The Kwiatkowski–Phillips–Schmidt–Shin (KPSS) test reports the statistic for testing the null hypothesis of level stationarity based on Newey–West automatic bandwidth selection. A statistically significant test shows evidence against the hypothesis of stationarity. The integration order is determined on the basis of the ADF, PP and KPSS test statistics. MacKinnon approximate *p*-values are reported in parentheses.
***$p<0.01$, **$p<0.05$, *$p<0.1$.

Table A.4: Unit Root Tests, Consensus Economics Forecasts

Variables	ADF Z(t)	PP Z(t)	KPSS	Integration order
Expected inflation, current year	−3.165*** (0.001)	−2.681* (0.077)	0.167	$I(0)$
Expected inflation, year ahead	−2.316** (0.011)	−2.447 (0.129)	0.111	$I(0)$
Expected inflation, one-year horizon	−2.393*** (0.009)	−3.296** (0.015)	0.142	$I(0)$
Expected GDP growth, current year	−2.467*** (0.007)	−2.251 (0.188)	0.564**	$I(0)$
Expected GDP growth, year ahead	−1.879** (0.031)	−2.011 (0.282)	1.090***	$I(1)$
Expected GDP growth, one-year horizon	−1.897** (0.030)	−2.947** (0.040)	0.772***	$I(0)$
Observations	137	140	141	

Note: The ADF Z(t) and PP Z(t) refer to the Augmented Dickey–Fuller and Phillips–Perron tests for unit root in the variables. A statistically significant test shows evidence against the null hypothesis of unit root. For the ADF test 3 lags of the difference in the variables have been used, while the number of lags used in the Phillips–Perron test are determined automatically based on Newey–West bandwidth selection. The Kwiatkowski–Phillips–Schmidt–Shin (KPSS) test reports the statistic for testing the null hypothesis of level stationarity based on Newey–West automatic bandwidth selection. A statistically significant test shows evidence against the hypothesis of stationarity. The integration order is determined on the basis of the ADF, PP, and KPSS test statistics. MacKinnon approximate p-values are reported in parentheses.

***$p < 0.01$, **$p < 0.05$, *$p < 0.1$.

Fitted Policy Rates of the Baseline Model

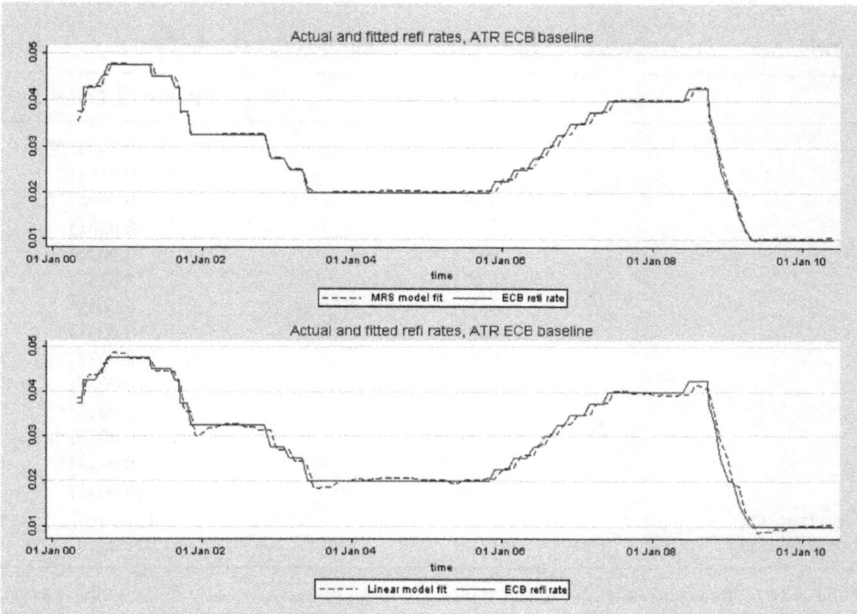

Figure A.1: MRS and Linear Model Fitted Rates, ATR Baseline Model.

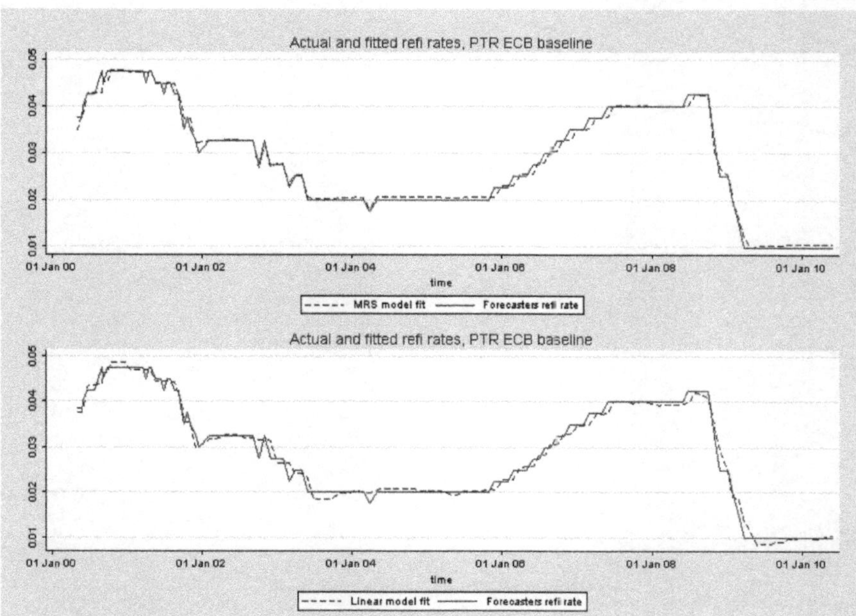

Figure A.2: MRS and Linear Model Fitted Rates, PTR Baseline Model.

Augmented Taylor Rules with a One-Year Forecast Horizon

Table A.5: Augmented Taylor Rules, Linear Model (One-Year)

	Actual Taylor Rule	Perceived Taylor Rule
ρ	0.9416***	0.9446***
	(0.0124)	(0.0113)
γ_π	0.0300	0.0690***
	(0.0472)	(0.0381)
γ_y	0.0792***	0.0620***
	(0.0216)	(0.0201)
γ_m	0.0068	0.0065
	(0.0042)	(0.0041)
γ_e	−0.0020	−0.0037
	(0.0026)	(0.0027)
γ_c	−0.0007	−0.0013***
	(0.0006)	(0.0005)
σ_ε	0.0014***	0.0014***
	(0.0001)	(0.0001)
Observations	141	141
Log-likelihood	728.351	727.022

Note: The table displays the short-run coefficients. ρ, γ_π, γ_y, γ_m, γ_e, γ_c denote the policy inertia, inflation and output growth expectations, the M3 and the nominal effective exchange rate coefficients respectively and the constant term. MLE, robust standard errors are reported in parentheses.

***$p < 0.01$, **$p < 0.05$, *$p < 0.1$.

Table A.6: Actual and Perceived MRS Taylor Rules, Augmented Model (One-Year)

	Actual Taylor Rule		Perceived Taylor Rule	
	Regime 1	Regime 2	Regime 1	Regime 2
$\rho_{s_{t+1}}$	0.9753***	0.8844***	0.9685***	0.9244***
	(0.0027)	(0.0145)	(0.0030)	(0.0088)
$\gamma_{\pi_{s_{t+1}}}$	0.0022***	−0.1149***	0.0196***	−0.1768***
	(0.0003)	(0.0079)	(0.0002)	(0.0049)
$\gamma_{y_{s_{t+1}}}$	0.0257***	0.2303***	0.0137***	0.2317***
	(0.0004)	(0.0324)	(0.0004)	(0.0048)
$\gamma_{m_{s_{t+1}}}$	0.0078***		0.0086***	
	(0.0020)		(0.0001)	
$\gamma_{e_{s_{t+1}}}$	−0.0033***		−0.0048***	
	(0.0008)		(0.0001)	
γ_c	−0.0000		−0.0000	
	(0.0000)		(0.0000)	
σ_ε	0.0009***		0.0010***	
	(1.514e−05)		(9.354e−06)	
$P[S_{t+1}=i\|S_t=1]$	0.8338***	0.1662***	0.7783***	0.2217***
	(0.0814)	(0.0080)	(0.0166)	(0.0048)
$P[S_{t+1}=i\|S_t=2]$	0.7725***	0.2275***	0.8333***	0.1667***
	(0.0838)	(0.0187)	(0.0294)	(0.0029)
Observations	141		141	
Log-likelihood	755.072		744.779	

Note: The table displays the short-run coefficients. $\rho_{s_{t+1}}$, $\gamma_{\pi_{s_{t+1}}}$, $\gamma_{y_{s_{t+1}}}$, $\gamma_{m_{s_{t+1}}}$, $\gamma_{e_{s_{t+1}}}$, γ_c denote the policy inertia, inflation and output growth expectations, the M3 and the nominal effective exchange rate coefficients respectively and the constant term. Estimates in the middle of the columns refer to parameters that do not switch across regimes. Iterative MLE, HAC standard errors are reported in parentheses.
***$p<0.01$, **$p<0.05$, *$p<0.1$.

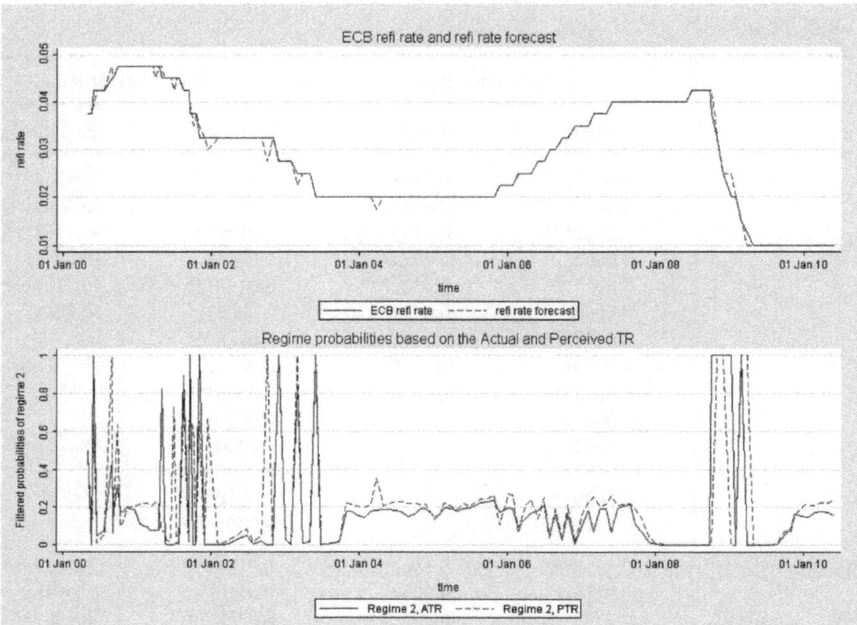

Figure A.3: Actual and Perceived Filtered Probabilities, Augmented Model (One-Year).

A Three Regimes Switching Model with a One-Year Forecast Horizon

Table A.7: Actual MRS TR, Three Regimes Model (TRM, One-Year)

	Regime 1	Regime 2	Regime 3
$\rho_{s_{t+1}}$	0.9784***	0.8479***	0.7683***
	(0.0030)	(0.0069)	(0.0665)
$\gamma_{\pi_{s_{t+1}}}$		0.0165***	
		(0.0009)	
$\gamma_{y_{s_{t+1}}}$		0.0304***	
		(0.0010)	
γ_c		−0.0000	
		(0.0000)	
σ_ε		0.0009***	
		(1.913e−05)	
$P[S_{t+1}=i\|S_t=1]$	0.9467***	0.0482***	0.0051***
	(0.0656)	(0.0024)	(0.0005)
$P[S_{t+1}=i\|S_t=2]$	0.7200***	0.1665***	0.1135***
	(0.0288)	(0.0122)	(0.0030)
$P[S_{t+1}=i\|S_t=3]$	0.0785***	0.9215***	0.0000
	(0.0041)	(0.0536)	(0.0000)
Observations		141	
Log-likelihood		754.851	

Note: The table displays the short-run coefficients. $\rho_{s_{t+1}}, \gamma_{\pi_{s_{t+1}}}, \gamma_{y_{s_{t+1}}}, \gamma_c$ denote the policy inertia, inflation and output growth expectations coefficients respectively and the constant term. Estimates in the middle of the columns refer to parameters that do not switch across regimes. Iterative MLE, HAC standard errors are reported in parentheses.
$***p<0.01$, $**p<0.05$, $*p<0.1$.

Table A.8: Actual MRS TR, TRM Long-Run Parameters (One-Year)

	Regime 1	Regime 2	Regime 3
$\rho_{s_{t+1}}$	0.9784***	0.8479***	0.7683***
	(0.0030)	(0.0069)	(0.0665)
$\beta_{\pi_{s_{t+1}}}$	0.7625***	0.1083***	0.0711***
	(0.0804)	(0.0020)	(0.0243)
$\beta_{y_{s_{t+1}}}$	1.4050***	0.1996***	0.1310***
	(0.2310)	(0.0149)	(0.0336)
Observations		141	
LL MRS three regimes		754.851	
LL MRS two regimes		752.061	
LR test		5.580	
AIC MRS three regimes		−1477.701	
BIC MRS three regimes		−1430.521	
AIC MRS two regimes		−1484.121	
BIC MRS two regimes		−1454.634	
RMSE MRS three regimes		0.000889	
RMSE MRS two regimes		0.000890	

Note: The table displays the implied long-run coefficients. $\rho_{s_{t+1}}$, $\beta_{\pi_{s_{t+1}}}$, $\beta_{y_{s_{t+1}}}$, denote the policy inertia, inflation and output growth expectations coefficients respectively. Estimates in the middle of the columns refer to parameters that do not switch across regimes. Standard errors are computed with the Delta method and are reported in parentheses.
***$p<0.01$, **$p<0.05$, *$p<0.1$.

Table A.9: Perceived MRS TR, Three Regimes Model (TRM, One-Year)

	Regime 1	Regime 2	Regime 3
$\rho_{s_{t+1}}$		0.9624***	
		(0.0041)	
$\gamma_{\pi_{s_{t+1}}}$	0.0006***	−0.2569***	0.0413***
	(0.0000)	(0.0118)	(0.0019)
$\gamma_{y_{s_{t+1}}}$		0.0466***	
		(0.0002)	
γ_c		−0.0000	
		(0.0000)	
σ_ε		0.0009***	
		(1.196e−05)	
$P[S_{t+1}=i\|S_t=1]$	0.9496***	0.0000	0.0504***
	(0.0232)	(0.0000)	(0.0003)
$P[S_{t+1}=i\|S_t=2]$	0.0000	0.2729***	0.7271***
	(0.0000)	(0.0056)	(0.0256)
$P[S_{t+1}=i\|S_t=3]$	0.0602***	0.0924***	0.8474***
	(0.0007)	(0.0047)	(0.0195)
Observations		141	
Log-likelihood		742.773	

Note: The table displays the short-run coefficients. $\rho_{s_{t+1}}, \gamma_{\pi_{s_{t+1}}}, \gamma_{y_{s_{t+1}}}, \gamma_c$ denote the policy inertia, inflation and output growth expectations coefficients respectively and the constant term. Estimates in the middle of the columns refer to parameters that do not switch across regimes. Iterative MLE, HAC standard errors are reported in parentheses.
$^{***}p<0.01$, $^{**}p<0.05$, $^{*}p<0.1$.

Table A.10: Perceived MRS TR, TRM Long-Run Parameters (One-Year)

	Regime 1	Regime 2	Regime 3
$\rho_{s_{t+1}}$		0.9624***	
		(0.0041)	
$\beta_{\pi_{s_{t+1}}}$	0.0158***	−6.8279***	1.0967***
	(0.0009)	(1.0520)	(0.1688)
$\beta_{y_{s_{t+1}}}$		1.2394***	
		(0.1394)	
Observations		141	
LL MRS three regimes		742.773	
LL MRS two regimes		736.484	
LR test		12.578	
AIC MRS three regimes		−1453.545	
BIC MRS three regimes		−1406.365	
AIC MRS two regimes		−1452.967	
BIC MRS two regimes		−1423.480	
RMSE MRS three regimes		0.000891	
RMSE MRS two regimes		0.001001	

Note: The table displays the implied long-run coefficients. $\rho_{s_{t+1}}$, $\beta_{\pi_{s_{t+1}}}$, $\beta_{y_{s_{t+1}}}$, denote the policy inertia, inflation and output growth expectations coefficients respectively. Estimates in the middle of the columns refer to parameters that do not switch across regimes. Standard errors are computed with the Delta method and are reported in parentheses.
***$p < 0.01$, **$p < 0.05$, *$p < 0.1$.

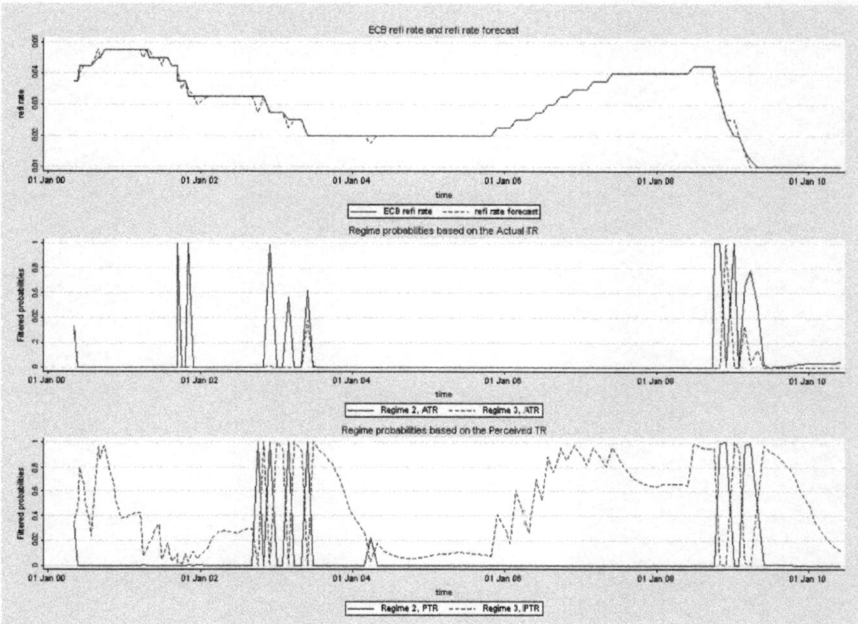

Figure A.4: Actual and Perceived Filtered Probabilities, Three Regimes Model (One-Year).

Chapter 9

International Trade Imbalance: The Amplification of Monetary Policy Effects through Financial Markets

Qiheng Han[a], Junqing Li[b] and Jianbo Zhang[c]

[a]*Department of Securities and Futures, Shanghai University of Finance and Economics, Shanghai, PR China, e-mail: hqheng@mail.shufe.edu.cn*
[b]*Department of Economics, Nankai University, Tianjin, PR China, e-mail: leejqdoc@163.com*
[c]*Department of Economics, University of Kansas, Lawrence, KS, USA, e-mail: jbzhang@ku.edu*

Abstract

Based on an uncertainty model with an infinite horizon, this chapter analyzes how financial development and monetary policy in two countries can impact international trade and capital flows and influence individual behavior and welfare. Our study shows that differences in capital market development are the major contributing factors for trade imbalance and investment among countries. We also find that monetary policies are important factors affecting the trade balance, consumption, and investment. Countries with one-sided, pegging exchange rate policies tend to buy more bonds and enjoy larger trade surpluses. This effect is closely related to the level of capital market development: in these two countries, at higher stages of development, the effects of idiosyncratic monetary policy on imbalance are amplified.

Keywords: incomplete financial market, monetary policy combination, global imbalances

JEL Classifications: D52, F17, F34

International Symposia in Economic Theory and Econometrics, Vol. 24
William A. Barnett and Fredj Jawadi (Editors)

ISSN: 1571-0386/doi: 10.1108/S1571-038620150000024021

1. Introduction

Global current account imbalances have received considerable attention in recent years. These unprecedented global imbalances are the subject of heated debates in academic and policy circles. Most prominently, the U.S. current account deficit has widened to over 3.16% of U.S. GDP in 2011; this deficit is mirrored by surpluses for some of the United States' trading partners. The current account balance in China has moved from a small aggregate deficit in 1995 to a surplus of 2.76% of GDP in 2011.

In this chapter we argue that large global imbalances could be attributed to financial integration among countries with heterogeneous domestic financial market development, as well as to differences in monetary policy across countries. Today, financial systems differ substantially across countries despite the globalization of capital markets since the 1980s. Financial integration is a global phenomenon, but financial development was not. Countries with less-sophisticated financial markets and monetary policies of *one-sided pegging* are more likely to run trade surpluses compared to countries with more sophisticated financial markets, all else being equal. Furthermore, heterogeneous financial markets amplify the effect of monetary policy on international trade. When two otherwise identical countries trade, the nation with higher demand for precautionary savings will save more and run a trade surplus. At the same time, different monetary policies cause the real return of nominal bonds to vary greatly, influencing an agent's choice of assets in his or her portfolio and, in turn, affecting international trade. The chapter finds that a one-sided peg monetary policy sustains a more advantageous financial environment and promotes persistent trade surpluses.

The motivation for studying global imbalances from this perspective derives from three key observations since the 1990s.

1.1. Global Trade Imbalance

Since 2000, a notable characteristic of the global economy has been global economic imbalance. In particular, this imbalance refers to large current account deficits in mature market economies, represented primarily by the United States, and massive current account surpluses in emerging market economies – chiefly, Asia and oil exporters. Since the 1990s, trade deficits in developed countries have increased steadily. The World Bank indicates that in 2008, current account deficits in developed countries reached 465 billion U.S. dollars (1.1% of world GDP), the highest level in recent years. In 2006, the U.S. total current account deficit rose to the highest level recorded in history, $788.1 billion (6% of U.S. GDP). Although

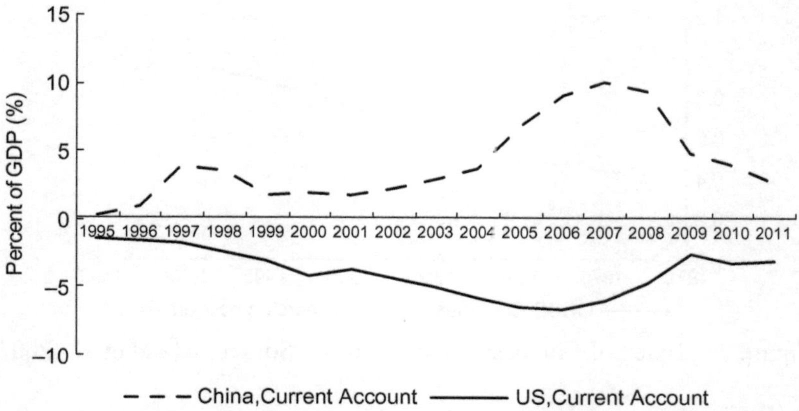

Figure 1: Current Accounts in China and the United States. Source: McKinnon and Schnabl (2009).

the U.S. current account deficit decreased in 2008 as a result of the global financial crisis, it remained at $673.3 billion (4.7% of GDP) (see Figure 1).

The current account surplus in emerging market countries exhibited vigorous growth in the 1990s. In 2008, this surplus was equal to 3.8% of world GDP ($714.4 bln). The trade surpluses of Asia and OPEC constituted the largest portion of this surplus. In 2008, the current account surpluses of developing countries in Asia exceeded $282.4 bln (5.8% of regional GDP); trade surpluses of Middle Eastern countries totaled $341.6 bln (18.8% of regional GDP). China's current account trade surplus was $426.1 bln in 2008 (10% of China's GDP). After the global financial crisis, China's trade surplus decreased to some extent but remained at a level of 1216.3 bln RMB in 2011 (see Figure 1).

1.2. Differences in the Development of Financial Markets across Countries

While financial markets in both emerging and developed countries have grown greatly, the gap in financial market development between developed and emerging nations has not exhibited any degree of change. As shown in Figure 2, this is evident from an index of financial development constructed by Abiad, Detragiache, and Tressel (2007) for industrial and emerging economies for 1973–2005. The high degree of heterogeneity in domestic financial market development across countries causes these differences to persist despite financial globalization and financial development (Mendoza, Quadrini, & Rios-Rull, 2009).

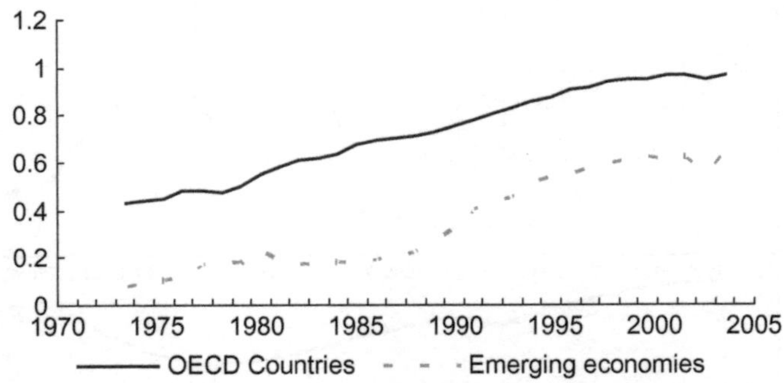

Figure 2: Index of Financial Liberalization. Source: Abiad et al. (2007).

1.3. Differences in Exchange Rate and Monetary Policy across Countries

Almost all emerging countries, including China, for example, have taken exchange rate policies into account when constructing monetary policy by pegging domestic currency to the dollar in various degrees. On the other hand, developed countries – in particular the United States – have continued to place stable GDP growth at the center of their monetary policy decisions, declining to prioritize exchange rate stability.

For a long period of time, monetary policy in China worked in conjunction with exchange rate policies pegging domestic currency to the US dollar. From 1994 to 2005, China operated a fixed exchange rate regime, which gained additional importance in 1998 following the financial crisis in Asia. Up until 2005, there was almost no fluctuation in the exchange rate between RMB (Yuan) and the U.S. dollar; only in July 2005 did the RMB begin to climb gradually against the dollar. From 2005 onward, the Chinese government began to adopt a managed floating exchange rate system based on market supply and demand that is adjusted by a basket of currencies and regulated by the central bank.

In response to domestic economic growth and sustained development of financial markets, U.S. monetary policy has repeatedly involved adjustment. After the 1970s, the intermediate target of monetary policy was changed from nominal interest rates (following Keynesian policy) to money supply (particularly M1, following the advice of Friedman). After the 1990s, financial innovation and economic globalization caused the United States to gradually move toward neutral monetary policy pegging real interest rate, but the Federal Reserve still had not completely abandoned money supply as a target of regulation. Although the intermediate targets of U.S. monetary policy have been increasingly integrated, including multi-term financial variables, the United States has not made its exchange rate a focus of monetary policy, consistently pursuing floating exchange rate policies. We should note that money supply targeting for Fed policy is not ideal, but is done for modeling simplicity in this chapter.

In order to explain the characteristics of the global economy that were mentioned above, this chapter uses a heterogeneous agent model with an infinite horizon to analyze the far-reaching influence of one country's financial development on its individual behavior and international trade. We emphasize the impact of heterogeneous monetary policy on individual consumption and investment decisions and its effects on trade imbalance, and we investigate the amplification of this impact by examining capital markets in each nation.

The rest of the chapter is organized as follows: Section 2 summarizes the relevant literature, Section 3 establishes the main analytical model, Section 4 conducts quantitative analysis, and Section 5 presents the chapter's conclusions.

2. Survey of Literature

Since global economic imbalance has recently intensified, there have been various efforts to explain this phenomenon, including the twin deficits hypothesis (Cline, 2005; Mann, 2002), the exchange rate devaluation hypothesis (Blanchard & Giavazzi, 2002; Lane & Milesi-Ferretti, 2005), the savings glut hypothesis (Bernanke, 2005; Gruber & Kamin, 2007), and the Bretton Woods II hypothesis (Dooley, Folkerts-Landau, & Garber, 2003, 2004). However, the most influential has been the hypothesis of comparative advantages in financial market development. Many studies believe that the main reason for global imbalance is that differential financial market development in developing and developed countries leads to advantages in receiving international capital flows. This hypothesis is the basic viewpoint of our chapter.

Many papers support this argument. Svensson (1988, 1989) believes that, under incomplete financial markets, the impact of various monetary policies on international trade and the international assets portfolio is ultimately what determines international capital flows. However, the focus on monetary policy's influence on the trade deficit in a two-period framework has not resolved details surrounding how incomplete markets influence capital flows. Our chapter adopts Svensson's method of classifying monetary policy.

Willen (2004) studied the qualitative predictions of a two-period endowment economy model with exponential utility and normal, i.i.d. shocks. He showed that under incomplete markets, trade imbalances emerge due to reduced savings by agents residing in countries with "more complete" asset markets. However, Willen's paper is also a two-period model and focuses on purely theoretical analysis. Our chapter adopts an infinite horizon model with heterogeneous agents and uses the method of quantity analysis to explore different factors that influence trade deficits and capital flows.

Caballero, Farhi, and Gourinchas (2008) also emphasize the role of heterogeneous domestic financial systems in explaining global imbalances, but they use a model in which financial imperfections are captured by a country's ability to supply assets in a world without uncertainty. While their analysis is done in a deterministic environment, our research is completed under the framework of uncertainty. In addition, Caballero's analysis stems from asset supply; ours is based mainly on asset demand.

Gourinchas and Rey (2005) explained why capital has not flowed from rich countries to poor countries, but instead from developing countries to developed countries. The author regards the main factors affecting capital flow as individual savings behavior, maturity of financial markets, and productivity of export sectors. Rather than using theoretical methods, their paper focuses on historical and empirical analysis.

Mendoza et al. (2009) explained the characteristics of international capital flows for financial markets with varying degrees of completeness. Countries with developed financial markets allocate risky assets globally, whereas nations with underdeveloped financial markets export capital mainly by purchasing bonds from developed countries. The analysis of Mendoza, Quadrini, and Rios-Rull (2007) regarding the influence of financial globalization on the welfare of individuals from financially underdeveloped regions considers only idiosyncratic risk; that this work does not consider aggregate risk makes it impossible to lend study to the influence of monetary policy on international trade. Our study, on the other hand, adds aggregate fluctuations, allowing us to investigate monetary policy combinations across countries. Our chapter also uses their quantitative description of the incompleteness of financial markets.

A common shortcoming of the above research is the failure to link aggregate risk from previous research to the international trade imbalance. For example, Mendoza et al. (2007, 2009) studies only idiosyncratic risk in a country; that is, only individual income risk with average national income remaining constant. Without aggregate risk, it is impossible to study the influence of monetary policy on international trade imbalance since monetary policy can take effect only through aggregate fluctuation. This chapter uses the classification method of monetary policies from Svensson (1988, 1989) to discuss the role of various monetary policies, analyze their influence on the real returns of nominal bonds in various countries, and investigate their effects on individual asset choice and the international trade imbalance. We find that the heterogeneity across the two countries' monetary policies has a deep impact on consumption and investment behavior as well as the trade imbalance. This impact is nonlinear in nature and is amplified through heterogeneity in capital markets. Moreover, integration of world capital markets exacerbates the trade imbalance across countries that is caused by distinct monetary policies.

3. The Basic Model

This section describes the model and defines its equilibrium.

3.1. The Basic Environment

Consider an economy composed of two countries, country one and country two ($i = 1, 2$). Each country is populated by a continuum of agents of total mass 1. Each agent maximizes expected lifetime utility

$$E_0\left(\sum_{t=0}^{\infty} \beta^t U(c_t)\right).$$

Here, E_0 denotes the expectation at the initial period, c_t is consumption of the nondurable good in period t, and $\beta (0 < \beta < 1)$ is the intertemporal discount factor. The utility function $U(\bullet)$ is twice continuously differentiable, strictly increasing and concave in c_t, and has the following CRRA (constant relative risk aversion) form:

$$U(c_t) = \frac{c_t^{1-\sigma}}{1-\sigma},$$

where $\sigma > 0$ is the relative risk aversion coefficient.

State variable $s_t = s_{d,t} \times s_{w1,t} \times s_{w2,t}$, where $s_{d,t}$ represents the idiosyncratic risk within a country and $s_{w_i,t}$ represents the aggregate risk in country i. $s_{d,t}$ and $\left\{s_{w_i,t}\right\}_{i=1}^{2}$ follow Markov chains. They induce a Markov chain on s_t with transition probabilities $\left\{\pi(s_{t+1}|s_t)\right\}$. We also denote $s_{w,t} = s_{w1,t} \times s_{w2,t}$.

There are two states of $s_{d,t}$, employed and unemployed; that is, $s_{d,t} = \{e, u\}$. There are also two states of $s_{w_i,t}$: good and bad. Thus, $s_{w_i,t} = \left\{g_i, b_i\right\}$.

We include an aggregate consumption good. Domestic risk sharing is accomplished with contingent claims for states $s_{d,t}$. International risk sharing is done through trade of a nominal, risk-free bond.

Subscript i indicates the country index; for example, $P_{1,t}$ is the price level in country 1.

Superscript j represents an agent in country j. For example, $c^1_{2,t}$ indicates consumption by an agent in country 1 of goods "produced" in country 2.

Each agent in country i is endowed with a perishable consumption good, each period, as follows:

$$y^i(s_t) = \bar{y}^i(s_{w,t}) + \tilde{y}^i(s_{d,t}) = \begin{cases} \bar{y}^i(s_{w,t})(1+\Delta^i) & \text{when } s_{d,t} = e \\ \bar{y}^i(s_{w,t})(1-\Delta^i) & \text{when } s_{d,t} = u \end{cases}. \quad (1)$$

3.1.1. Currency Demand

For currency demand, we have adopted the Clower (1967) Cash-in-Advance model in which an agent must purchase one country's products with that country's currency.

3.1.2. Monetary Policy

We separate a country's monetary policy into two categories: independent monetary policy and coordinated monetary policy. By independent we mean that policy in one country is independent of variables in the other country. Coordinated refers to policy in one country that depends on variables from both countries. Among possible independent policies, we only consider output-dependent monetary policy with a constant elasticity k of one country's money supply with respect to its output; that is, $M = y^k$. We refer to the case where $k > 0$ as pro-cyclical monetary policy, and where $k < 0$ as counter-cyclical monetary policy. The case where $k = 0$ can be called passive monetary policy, with money supply constant and state-independent. Here $M = 1$, and since M represents a country's nominal GDP ($M = py$), we can say that this policy stabilizes nominal GDP. When $k = 1$, $M = y$, implying the price level is constant ($p = 1$), we refer to this as price-stabilizing monetary policy. Among coordinated monetary policies designed to affect the exchange rate, we focus on one-sided peg monetary policy, the fixed exchange rate regime in which country two pursues output-dependent monetary policy and country one sets the money supply according to $M = eM^*y/y^*$ so as to hold the exchange rate constant. Here, M and M^* are country one and country two's monetary supplies, respectively, y and y^* are country one and country two's production quantities, respectively. Therefore, if country one adopts a GDP-stabilizing monetary policy and country two adopts a one-sided peg monetary policy, the equation $M = ey/y^*$ must hold.

3.1.3. The Incompleteness of Financial Markets

In this chapter, we refer to Mendoza et al. (2009) for a description of incomplete financial markets. If financial markets were complete – that is, there were no restrictions on the set of feasible claims (commercial insurance products, noncommercial, government-provided pensions, and medical and unemployment insurance) – agents would be able to perfectly insure against idiosyncratic endowment risk. Because of market frictions, however, the set of feasible claims is constrained in each country. In particular, we assume that contracts are not perfectly enforceable due to the limited (legal) verifiability of shocks. Because of this limited verifiability, an agent may divert part of his income from idiosyncratic endowment risk, but will lose a fraction Φ^i of the diverted income. The nonnegative parameters $\Phi = \{\Phi^1, \Phi^2\}$ are the financial incompleteness coefficients of country one and country two characterizing the degree of enforcement of financial contracts in both countries.

The financial incompleteness coefficients Φ ranges from 0 to 1. Higher values of Φ indicate more complete financial markets.

3.2. Consumer Optimization

For an agent in country 1,

$$E_0\left(\sum_{t=0}^{\infty}\beta^t U\left(c_{1t}^1 + c_{2t}^1\right)\right) \tag{2}$$

subject to

$$P_{1,t}a_t^1 = M_{1,t}^1 + e_t M_{2,t}^1 + B_{1,t}^1 + e_t B_{2,t}^1 + \sum_{s_{d,t+1}} A_t^1(s_{d,t+1})Q(s_{d,t+1}|s_t), \tag{3}$$

$$M_{1,t}^1 \geq P_{1,t}c_{1,t}^1 \tag{4}$$

$$M_{2,t}^1 \geq P_{2,t}c_{2,t}^1 \tag{5}$$

$$\begin{aligned} P_{1,t+1}a_{t+1}^1(s_{t+1}) = {} & P_{1,t+1}y_{t+1}^1 + B_{1,t}^1(1+i_{1,t}) + e_{t+1}B_{2,t}^1(1+i_{2,t}) \\ & + A_t^1(s_{d,t+1}) + X_t^1 \end{aligned} \tag{6}$$

$$a_{t+1}^1(e) - a_{t+1}^1(u) \geq (1-\Phi^1)\left(y_{t+1}^1(e) - y_{t+1}^1(u)\right) \tag{7}$$

$$M_{1t}^1, M_{2t}^1, e_t, p_t^1, p_t^2, y_t^1, c_{1t}^1, c_{2t}^1, i_t^1 \geq 0. \tag{8}$$

In Equation (3), a_t^1 is the agent's total wealth at time t (in state s_t) that can be used to purchase domestic and foreign currency $\left\{M_{i,t}^1 : i=1,2\right\}$, domestic and foreign bonds $\left\{B_{i,t}^1 : i=1,2\right\}$, and the state contingent claims $A_t^1\left(s_{d,t+1}\right)$ that pay $A_t^1\left(s_{d,t+1}\right)$ of domestic currency at time $t+1$ if in state $s_{d,t+1}$. The no-arbitrage condition for bond and Arrow securities in the first country implies $Q\left(s_{d,t+1}|s_t\right)=\pi\left(s_{d,t+1}|s_t\right)/\left(1+i_{1,t}\right)$. e_t is the exchange rate between domestic and foreign currency (in units of domestic currency per unit of foreign currency), and $\left\{P_{i,t} : i=1,2\right\}$ and $\left\{i_{i,t} : i=1,2\right\}$ are the domestic and foreign price levels and interest rates, respectively.

Equations (4) and (5) are CIA (cash in advance) constraints.

Equation (6) says that when state $s_{d,t+1}$ occurs at $t+1$, the wealth in country 1 is $P_{1,t+1}a_{t+1}^1(s_{t+1})$. $y_{t+1}^1=y^1(s_{t+1})$ is the agent's endowment at time $t+1$. The payoffs to bonds issued by the two countries in period t are $B_{1,t}^1\left(1+i_{1,t}\right)$and $e_{t+1}B_{2,t}^1\left(1+i_{2,t}\right)$, respectively, and the payoff from an Arrow security is $A_t^1\left(s_{d,t+1}\right)$. X_t^1 represents money transfer and any unused money in period t that the agent brings into period $t+1$.

Equation (7) indicates the effect of capital market incompleteness on wealth across different states.

Equation (8) imposes nonnegativity of relevant economic variables.

We also impose a necessary transversality condition to rule out Ponzi schemes.

3.3. Stationary Equilibrium

Let $D^i(s,a)$ denote the distribution of agents in country i, state s, and wealth a, where $s=s_d\times s_{w1}\times s_{w2}=s_d\times s_w$. At equilibrium, the following market clearing conditions must be satisfied:

Goods market:

$$\sum_i\sum_{s_{d,t}}\sum_{a_t}\left(c_{1,t}^i+c_{2,t}^i\right)D^i(s_t,a_t)=\sum_i\bar{y}^i\left(s_{w,t}\right),\quad \text{for each } s_{w,t}. \tag{9}$$

Bond market:

$$\sum_i\sum_{s_{d,t}}\sum_{a_t}B_{j,t}^iD^i(s_t,a_t)=0,\quad \text{for } j=1,2,\quad \text{for each } s_{w,t}. \tag{10}$$

Arrow-security market:

$$\sum_{a_t}A_t^iD^i(s_t,a_t)=0,\quad \text{for } i=1,2,\quad \text{for each } s_t. \tag{11}$$

Money market:

$$\sum_{i}\sum_{s_{d,t}}\sum_{a_t} M_{j,t}^{i} D^{i}(s_t, a_t) = M_{j,t}\left(s_{w,t}\right), \quad \text{for } j = 1, 2, \quad \text{for each } s_{w,t}. \tag{12}$$

A distribution $D^i(s,a)$ is stationary if

$$D^i(s', a') = \sum_{s} \sum_{a \in \Omega(s,a')} D^i(s,a)\pi(s'|s), \tag{13}$$

where $\Omega(s,a') = \{a : a' = a'(s,a)\}$ indicates our interest in the stationary equilibrium whose distribution of agents with respect to (s,a) remains constant over time.

We also assume that 50% of each country's agents lie in each idiosyncratic state:

$$\pi(e) = \sum_{a} D^i(s, a | s_d = e) = 0.5 \tag{14}$$

$$\pi(u) = \sum_{a} D^i(s, a | s_d = u) = 0.5. \tag{15}$$

Because this chapter considers only two micro-states, the computational strategy for the simulation can be simplified. The equivalent model is described in Appendix A and the computational procedures for the stationary equilibrium are detailed in Appendix B.

4. Quantitative Analysis

In this section, we study the quantitative implications of the model. Using comparative static analysis, we discuss agent behavior in an open economy with various economic parameters. We use a two-country model in which the parameters of country one submit a nation with mature markets and the parameters of country two describe a developing country. We analyze the influence of monetary policy combinations and the maturity effects of capital markets on capital flow, international trade, individual consumption, and welfare.

4.1. The Set of Parameters

We set the main parameters as follows:

The intertemporal discount factor β is set to 0.925, following Mendoza et al. (2009). Many theoretical studies regard the range of the relative risk aversion coefficient σ to be from 1 to 4, so we set σ to a value of 1.5 (Li & Han, 2009).

Stock and Watson (1998) and Zhang (2006) state that the standard deviation of the GDP growth rate in the United States between 1979 and 2005 is 1.82. As a result, we set the average income of each country $\overline{y}^i(s_{w,t})$ to be 1.02 under good macroeconomic conditions and 0.98 under bad macroeconomic condition. We also set $\Delta^i = 0.5$ and $\tilde{y}^i(s_{d,t}) = \pm 0.5\overline{y}^i(s_{w,t})$, meaning that the income for the "employed" is about three times that of the "unemployed."

According to Liu (2006), the economic cycle EC in the United States is about 10 years; thus, we set the economic cycles in both countries to 10 years. From this one can derive the probability of $s_{d,t}$ remaining constant: $1-2/\text{EC}=1-2/10$ (Li & Han, 2009). We can now calculate the transition matrix for $s_{w,t}$:

$$\begin{bmatrix} 0.64 & 0.16 & 0.16 & 0.04 \\ 0.16 & 0.64 & 0.04 & 0.16 \\ 0.16 & 0.04 & 0.64 & 0.16 \\ 0.04 & 0.16 & 0.16 & 0.64 \end{bmatrix}.$$

We also assume the transition probabilities from "employed" to "unemployed" and from "unemployed" to "employed" are equal. In both countries, the individual income transition matrix for $s_{d,t}$ is:

$$\begin{pmatrix} 0.9500 & 0.0500 \\ 0.0500 & 0.9500 \end{pmatrix}.$$

4.2. Benchmark Model: The Influence of Different Monetary Policy Combinations on Agent Behavior

Monetary policy can be divided into two categories: independent monetary policy and coordinated monetary policy. This chapter discusses three prevalent combinations of monetary policies in order to examine their influence on bond trading, international trade deficits, and individual welfare in each nation.

- Monetary policy combination one: both countries adopt price-stabilizing monetary policies. In this case, each nation's bonds are viewed as identical, risk-free bonds, each being perfect substitutes for the other. The exchange rate between the two countries is fixed at 1.
- Monetary policy combination two: country one employs a nominal GDP-stabilizing policy and country two adopts a one-side peg policy. In

this case, the bonds of country one and country two are perfect substitutes for each other and are equivalent to a claim on country one's output. The exchange rate is again fixed at 1.

- Monetary policy combination three: both countries adopt nominal GDP-stabilizing monetary policies. In this case, each nation's bonds are considered risky. Country one's bond is a perfect substitute for a claim on country one's output, while country two's bond is, likewise, a perfect substitute for a claim on country two's output. In this case, the exchange rate between the two countries floats.

Owing to different monetary policies, prices of goods in each country may be different depending on macroeconomic conditions. If nominal returns of each country's bonds are equal to 1, their real returns (real purchasing power) do not always equal 1. Table 1 shows the real returns of country one and country two bonds under different monetary policy combinations.

We assume the two countries are identical in all aspects other than choice of monetary policy. This allows us to isolate the effects of monetary policy on the behavior of both countries' agents. The key parameters of two countries are listed below in Table 2. Now, under different monetary policy combinations, we discuss each country's bond trading, explain capital flows between the two countries, and show the impact on one country's trade balance and agent welfare. The average simulation results of all macro-states are displayed in Table 3.

Table 1: Real Returns of Bonds under Different Monetary Policy Combinations

Macroeconomic condition	Monetary policy combination one		Monetary policy combination two		Monetary policy combination three	
	Real return of country one bond	Real return of country two bonds	Real return of country one bond	Real return of country two bond	Real return of country one bond	Real return of country two bond
Gg	1	1	1.02	1.02	1.02	1.02
Gb	1	1	1.02	1.02	1.02	0.98
Bg	1	1	0.98	0.98	0.98	1.02
Bb	1	1	0.98	0.98	0.98	0.98

Notes: In the above table, Gg represents both the macroeconomic condition in both countries are good. Gb indicating the first country has a good macroeconomics situation while the second country has a bad one.

Table 2: Economic Parameters of the Two Countries

Incompleteness of financial market (Φ)	Employed-unemployed gap (Δ)	Economic cycle (EC)	Endowment in macro-state	
			yh^1	yh^2
{0.5, 0.5}	{0.5, 0.5}	{10, 10}	{1.02, 0.98}	{1.02, 0.98}

Table 3: Agent Behavior under Different Monetary Policy Combinations (Benchmark Model, Φ = [0.50, 0.50])

Φ = [0.50, 0.50]	Monetary policy combination one		Monetary policy combination two		Monetary policy combination three	
	C_1	C_2	C_1	C_2	C_1	C_2
C	1.0000	1.0000	0.9917	1.0083	1.0000	1.0000
CAD	0.0000	0.0000	0.1502	−0.1502	0.0000	0.0000
U	−27.0935	−27.0935	−28.5987	−28.2794	−27.5124	−27.5124
B_1	0.0000	0.0000	−0.0751	0.0751	−0.6304	0.6304
B_2	0.0000	0.0000	−0.0751	0.0751	0.6304	−0.6304
i	0.0593	0.0593	0.0549	0.0549	0.0720	0.0720
r	0.0593	0.0593	0.0551	0.0551	0.0721	0.0721

Abbreviations: C denotes average consumption; CAD stands for average current account deficit (positive number for trade deficit and a negative number for trade surplus); U denotes average utility; B_1 denotes the average net position of country one's bonds; B_2 denotes the average net position of country two's bonds; i is the nominal interest rate; r is the real interest rate; and C_1 and C_2 refer to country one and country two, respectively.

(1) Agent behavior under monetary policy combination one
Since the countries are identical in all aspects, the position of net bond assets of each country's agents is zero and the corresponding trade deficits in each country is zero. Because the two types of bonds are perfect substitutes, they have the same effects in smoothing agents' consumption. So, welfare level in both countries will be the same under this monetary policy combination.

(2) Agent behavior under monetary policy combination two
In this case, the bonds from both countries can be used to hedge against output from country two. Therefore, country two will buy bonds from both countries (0.0751). Its financial accounts will show a capital outflow and its current accounts will show a trade surplus (−0.1502). Compared to other monetary policy combinations, country two has the strongest tendency to run a trade surplus; this surplus is the largest among all cases. Country one will sell bonds of both countries (−0.0751), generating a capital inflow and trade deficit (0.1502). In this scenario, it will be easier for country one to run a trade deficit than

under other monetary policy combinations; additionally, this trade deficit will also be larger than in all other cases.

With this combination of monetary policy, country two may use bonds from both countries to hedge its labor endowment. The real returns from both countries' bonds will be perfectly positively correlated with macroeconomic fluctuations in country one. Country one does not have the financial assets to hedge its risk (recall Table 1); therefore, the financial asset environment is favorable to country two. Country two responds by pegging its currency to country one's currency. Agent welfare in country two (−28.2794) is higher than in country one (−28.5987).

(3) Agent behavior under monetary policy combination three

In this scenario, only country two's bonds can be used to hedge against country one output. Regardless of which macro-state appears, country one will purchase country two's bonds (0.6304) also short sell its own bonds (−0.6304). Similarly, country two will purchase country one's bonds (0.6304) and also short sell its own bonds (−0.6304).

This can be seen in Figure 3, which plots the bond purchase decision function of each country's agents. Figure 3a shows how country two's agents

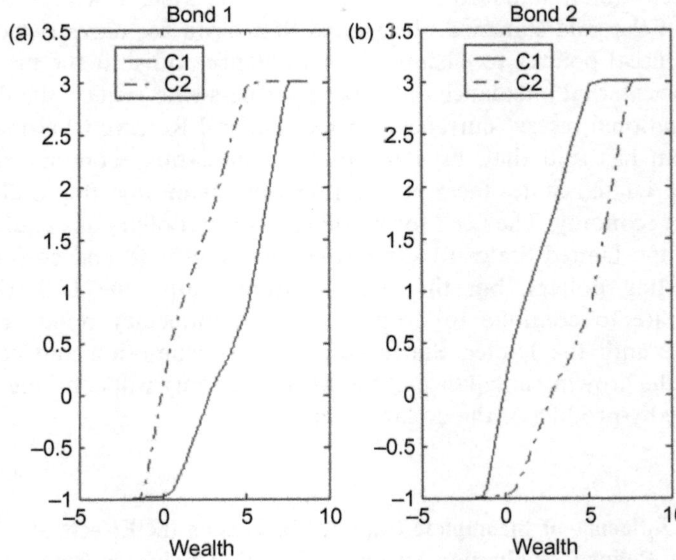

Figure 3: The Bond Purchase Decision Functions of Two Countries' Agents under Monetary Policy Combination Three: (a) The Purchase Decision Function of Country One's Bond; (b) The Purchase Decision Function of Country Two's Bond.

will buy more country one bonds than country one's agents at any level of wealth. Figure 3b shows how country one's agents will buy more country two bonds than country two's agents at any level of wealth.

Each country finances bond purchases by selling its own bonds. Since the amount of bonds bought and sold by each country is the same, it follows that both countries have neither trade deficits nor trade surpluses.

Under this monetary policy combination, country two can smooth its consumption only by purchasing country one's bonds. Country one can smooth its own consumption only by purchasing country two's bonds. Because the financial asset environment for both countries is the same, welfare in each country is equal.

In summary, in our two-country model, when the foreign country adopts a policy designed to stabilize nominal GDP and the home country adopts a one-sided peg monetary policy (i.e., monetary policy combination two), the latter tends to exhibit larger capital outflows and trade surpluses. The foreign nation choosing the nominal GDP-stabilizing policy tends to experience a trade deficit. When country two adopts a one-sided pegging policy, it demands more bonds from both markets (0.1502 = 0.0751 + 0.0751), driving down the world interest rate to 0.0549, lowest among the three cases.

McKinnon calls this phenomenon (monetary policy combination two) the de facto dollar standard. In today's monetary system, without the constraints of the gold standard, the United States can use unrestricted monetary and fiscal policies to ensure internal balance and shift the pressure to adjust for external imbalance onto trade partners who require the dollar as an international reserve currency. Former Federal Reserve Chairman Alan Greenspan has said that, as a means for stimulating economic development, the United States faces no legal restrictions on injecting dollars into the world economy. The need for world reserves in dollars has made it possible for the United States to support economic growth and consumption by exporting dollars, but this will inevitably cause the U.S. domestic savings rate to continue to drop. Given the monetary policy of other countries, until the United States adjusts its consumption and economic policies, the growing imbalance in the world economy will continue. It is an inevitable by-product of the dollar system.

4.3. The Influence of Incomplete Capital Markets on the Effects of Monetary Policy Combination Two under Equal Φ Values in Both Countries

Due to the fact that China pegged its currency to the U.S. dollar for a relatively long period of time while the United States paid more attention to nominal GDP stability, this section focuses on the impact of financial

Table 4: Economic Parameters of Two Countries

Monetary policy combination	Employed-unemployed gap (Δ)	Economic cycle (EC)	Endowment in macro-state	
			yh^1	yh^2
Monetary policy combination two	{0.5, 0.5}	{10, 10}	{1.02, 0.98}	{1.02, 0.98}

market development (the value of Φ) on both countries' trade deficits and agent welfare under monetary policy combination two. Here, the two countries are the same in all aspects other than monetary policy. The values of the parameters besides Φ are listed below in Table 4.

The results in the last section show that policy combination two is more likely to create a larger trade imbalance by inducing a larger trade surplus for country two. We shall now focus on the influence of incomplete capital markets on the effects of the monetary policy combination two.

According to theory, when capital market completeness increases in both countries, it is easier for individuals to smooth consumption by searching for better investment opportunities in both markets, increasing the demand for bonds in both nations' capital markets and leading to more stable consumption and higher welfare. On the other hand, in terms of country trade of goods and bonds, the imbalance will get worse, with country one bearing a larger trade deficit and country two experiencing higher trade surplus. Thus, increases in the completeness of capital markets amplify the effects of monetary policy. With more complete capital markets, domestic consumption behavior is amplified, inducing larger trade imbalances.

As we can see in Figure 4 and Table 5, the results of our simulation illustrate precisely this phenomenon that is predicted by the theory. Under policy combination two, as capital markets become more complete, country two residents hold more securities, increasing from 0.0049 to 0.2941 when capital market completeness, Φ, increases from [0, 0] to [1.0, 1.0]. Due to higher bond demand, the interest rate on bonds rises from 0.0081 to 0.0691, inducing capital flows from country two to country one. The trade surplus for country two increases from 0.0098 to 0.5882 and consumption becomes more stable (standard deviation moves from 0.4385 to 0.2076).

4.4. Differential Incompleteness of Capital Markets and Consumption/Investment in Two Countries

As shown in Figure 2, although the United States and Chinese capital markets have become more complete over time, the difference in the degree of

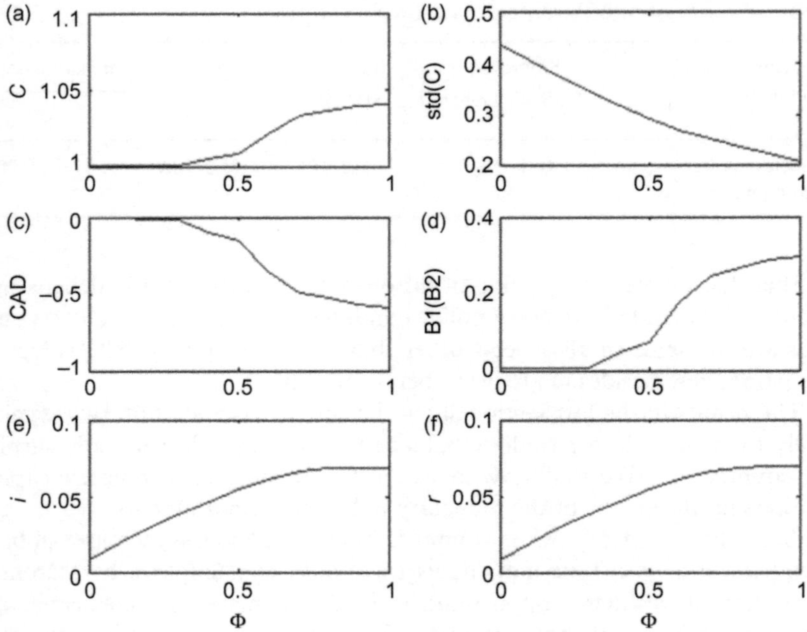

Figure 4: The Effects of Incomplete Capital Markets on Policy Combination Two. (a) Consumption; (b) Fluctuations in Consumption; (c) Trade Imbalance; (d) Bond Purchase; (e) Nominal Interest Rates; and (f) Real Interest Rates.

completeness in both countries has remained constant. The Chinese market continues to lag; as a result, Chinese residents may only partially hedge their risk from the consumption process and must absorb a large share themselves. This has been empirically proven by many studies.

Many papers have performed empirical analyses on the influence of the incompleteness of China's financial markets on the ability to smooth consumption, finding that, in China and other Asian countries, the underdevelopment of financial markets weakens an agent's ability to share risk and decreases welfare. These findings support our claims. Kim, Kim, and Wang (2006) studied consumption risk sharing in 10 East Asian countries and showed that the ability of residents to share risk in these regions is highly limited. In these regions, 80% of GDP volatility has not been smoothed, and overall, the smoothing effect on residents' consumption is extremely small. Xu (2008) showed that interprovince risk sharing in China is less than interstate/interprovince risk sharing in the United States and Canada. Chinese residents have a very strong incentive to insure against

Table 5: Agent Behavior Under Various Levels of Financial Market Development (Monetary Policy Combination Two)

		C	std(*C*)	CAD	*U*	B_1	B_2	*i*	*r*
Φ = [0.00, 0.00]	C_1	0.9998	0.4385	0.0098	−28.6847	−0.0049	−0.0049	0.0081	0.0083
	C_2	1.0002	0.4384	−0.0098	−28.6791	0.0049	0.0049	0.0081	0.0083
Φ = [0.10, 0.10]	C_1	0.9997	0.4079	0.0087	−28.8559	−0.0044	−0.0044	0.0181	0.0183
	C_2	1.0003	0.4077	−0.0087	−28.8545	0.0044	0.0044	0.0181	0.0183
Φ = [0.20, 0.20]	C_1	0.9995	0.3759	0.0138	−28.7447	−0.0069	−0.0069	0.0287	0.0289
	C_2	1.0005	0.3756	−0.0138	−28.7347	0.0069	0.0069	0.0287	0.0289
Φ = [0.30, 0.30]	C_1	0.9993	0.3472	0.0162	−28.7828	−0.0081	−0.0081	0.0377	0.0379
	C_2	1.0007	0.3475	−0.0162	−28.7676	0.0081	0.0081	0.0377	0.0379
Φ = [0.40, 0.40]	C_1	0.9952	0.3154	0.1013	−28.6950	−0.0506	−0.0506	0.0465	0.0467
	C_2	1.0048	0.3175	−0.1013	−28.4827	0.0506	0.0506	0.0465	0.0467
Φ = [0.50, 0.50]	C_1	0.9917	0.2862	0.1502	−28.5987	−0.0751	−0.0751	0.0549	0.0551
	C_2	1.0083	0.2908	−0.1502	−28.2794	0.0751	0.0751	0.0549	0.0551
Φ = [0.60, 0.60]	C_1	0.9785	0.2559	0.3521	−28.6237	−0.1760	−0.1760	0.0612	0.0615
	C_2	1.0215	0.2703	−0.3521	−27.8671	0.1760	0.1760	0.0612	0.0615
Φ = [0.70, 0.70]	C_1	0.9675	0.2265	0.4932	−28.6717	−0.2466	−0.2466	0.0660	0.0663
	C_2	1.0325	0.2545	−0.4932	−27.6404	0.2466	0.2466	0.0660	0.0663
Φ = [0.80, 0.80]	C_1	0.9637	0.1963	0.5315	−28.6157	−0.2658	−0.2658	0.0684	0.0686
	C_2	1.0363	0.2370	−0.5315	−27.5365	0.2658	0.2658	0.0684	0.0686
Φ = [0.90, 0.90]	C_1	0.9607	0.1690	0.5715	−28.5330	−0.2857	−0.2857	0.0689	0.0692
	C_2	1.0393	0.2237	−0.5715	−27.3944	0.2857	0.2857	0.0689	0.0692
Φ = [1.00, 1.00]	C_1	0.9595	0.1441	0.5882	−28.5363	−0.2941	−0.2941	0.0691	0.0693
	C_2	1.0405	0.2076	−0.5882	−27.3855	0.2941	0.2941	0.0691	0.0693

Abbreviations: *C* denotes average consumption; std(*C*) denotes the standard deviation of consumption; CAD stands for average current account deficit (positive number for trade deficit and a negative number for trade surplus); *U* denotes average utility; B_1 denotes the average net position of country one's bonds, B_2 denotes the average net position of country two's bonds; *i* is the nominal interest rate; *r* is the real interest rate; and C_1 and C_2 refer to country one and country two, respectively.

heterogeneous risk. Ho, Ho, and Li (2010) believe that the degree of consumption, risk sharing, and smoothing in China is much lower than in other developed economies and, occasionally, even lower than in OECD countries. Moreover, consumption risk sharing has not improved following the shift from a planned economy to the current transitional economy. Strikingly, consumption smoothing has become even weaker in the post-reform period. This also indicates that eliminating consumption fluctuation yields substantial welfare gain. Relative to Asia, U.S. financial markets provide residents more chances for consumption risk sharing. Asdrubali, Sorensen, and Yosha (1996) argue that from 1963 to 1990, 39% of the income volatility of the residents of every state was smoothed by financial markets; 13% by federal government tax revenue, transfer payments, and subsidies; and 23% by credit markets, leaving only 25% of risk

Table 6: Differential Capital Markets and Their Effects on Monetary Policies

	Monetary policy combination one		Monetary policy combination two		Monetary policy combination three	
	C_1	C_2	C_1	C_2	C_1	C_2
			A: $\Phi = [0.25, 0.00]$			
C	0.9823	1.0177	0.9815	1.0185	0.9597	1.0403
std(C)	0.3491	0.4420	0.3548	0.4473	0.3728	0.4825
CAD	0.6850	−0.6850	0.8344	−0.8344	0.7860	−0.7860
U	−27.5003	−26.9996	−28.4581	−27.9214	−28.5059	−28.2441
B_1	−0.3425	0.3425	−0.4172	0.4172	−1.0033	1.0033
B_2	−0.3425	0.3425	−0.4172	0.4172	0.2173	−0.2173
i	0.0260	0.0260	0.0223	0.0223	0.0512	0.0512
r	0.0259	0.0259	0.0225	0.0225	0.0513	0.0513
			B: $\Phi = [0.5, 0.25]$			
C	0.9566	1.0434	0.9463	1.0537	0.9397	1.0603
std(C)	0.2538	0.3597	0.2667	0.3794	0.2762	0.3980
CAD	0.8790	−0.8790	1.1430	−1.1430	0.9128	−0.9128
U	−27.8656	−26.6970	−28.9249	−27.3873	−28.3366	−27.3840
B_1	−0.4395	0.4395	−0.5715	0.5715	−1.0110	1.0110
B_2	−0.4395	0.4395	−0.5715	0.5715	0.0982	−0.0982
i	0.0494	0.0494	0.0472	0.0472	0.0660	0.0660
r	0.0494	0.0494	0.0474	0.0474	0.0661	0.0662
			C: $\Phi = [0.75, 0.5]$			
C	0.9175	1.0825	0.8864	1.1136	0.9141	1.0859
std(C)	0.1546	0.2763	0.1659	0.3158	0.1767	0.3105
CAD	1.2150	−1.2150	1.7141	−1.7142	1.1066	−1.1066
U	−28.1693	−26.0104	−29.5433	−26.3359	−28.2131	−26.4387
B_1	− 0.6075	0.6075	−0.8571	0.8571	−1.0155	1.0155
B_2	− 0.6075	0.6075	−0.8571	0.8571	−0.0910	0.0910
i	0.0680	0.0680	0.0664	0.0664	0.0776	0.0776
r	0.0680	0.0680	0.0666	0.0666	0.0778	0.0778

Abbreviations: C denotes average consumption; std(C) denotes the standard deviation of consumption; CAD stands for average current account deficit (positive number for trade deficit and a negative number for trade surplus); U denotes average utility; B_1 denotes the average net position of country one's bonds, B_2 denotes the average net position of country two's bonds; i is the nominal interest rate; r is the real interest rate; and C_1 and C_2 refer to country one and country two, respectively.

unsmoothed. Canova and Ravn (1996) have shown that in industrial countries, the aggregate domestic consumption risk posed by demographic, fiscal, and monetary shocks over short cycles is basically hedged and insured against. Their conclusion is consistent with those of Obstfeld

(1993), Atkeson and Bayoumi (1993), and Kollmann (1996), and also agrees with the conclusions of Backus, Kehoe, and Kydland (1992) and Devereux, Gregory, and Smith (1992).

To more accurately model reality, we maintain a 0.25 difference in capital market completeness between the two countries and simulate with increasing degrees of completeness. The effects are summarized in Table 6.

Under policy combination two, as we increase the degree of completeness in both nations from [0.25, 0] in A to [0.75, 0.5] in C of Table 6, country two buys more bonds than country one, moving net purchases from 0.8344 (= 0.4172 + 0.4172) in A to 1.7142 (= 0.8571 + 0.8571) in C of Table 6. This also increases the trade imbalance, which rises from 0.8344 in A to 1.7141 in C of Table 6. Simultaneously, the nominal interest rate on bonds increases, from 0.0223 in A to 0.0664 in C of Table 6, and consumption fluctuation decreases, from 0.4473 in A to 0.3158 in C of Table 6.

We can also conclude from the simulation data that under differentiated capital markets, policy combination two will cause country two to buy more bonds and enjoy larger trade surpluses. As seen in A of Table 6, the trade surplus and net bond purchases for country two is 0.8344 under policy combination two, while similar figures for policy combinations 1 and 3 are 0.6850 and 0.7860, respectively. The results are the same in B and C of Table 6.

To summarize, the degree of completeness in both nations' capital markets has great influence on consumption, investment, and the trade imbalance in the two countries. In addition, the effects of each country's monetary policy combination also have a great impact. This is especially significant when one country adopts the policy of one-sided pegging. Under this policy, a nation tends to buy more bonds from the other capital market and enjoy a larger trade surplus. As both markets evolve and become more complete, the effect of the one-sided monetary policy on bond purchases and the trade imbalance tends to be exacerbated.

5. Conclusion

The development of a country's financial markets has great influence on its individual behavior and, in an open economy, significant consequences for international capital flows and trade. Different monetary policies exert distinct influences on each country's individual behavior and international trade. China's one-sided pegging policy and its less-developed capital markets together play a large role in preserving its trade surplus status with the United States.

On one hand, the larger the gap is between two countries' financial markets, the larger the trade imbalance between the two nations. An undeveloped financial market will increase an agent's precautionary savings significantly. In contrast to a trade deficit, capital moves from the country with undeveloped financial markets to the country with developed markets by way of bond purchases. In this case, countries with undeveloped financial markets exhibit trade surpluses.

On the other hand, residents in one-sided pegging countries tend to buy more securities to hedge consumption risk, leading to more severe trade imbalances. This phenomenon will become more significant with continued development of capital markets. Integration and development of capital markets amplify the effects of idiosyncratic monetary policy (more so under the one-sided pegging policy).

Our study concludes that, over the past 20 years, rapid integration of international finance and heterogeneity of monetary policy has provided a basis for international imbalance. Under the international financial system based on the dollar standard, the United States has inherited the core role from the Bretton Woods system. The U.S.' role is reflected in two ways: first, by providing dollar assets as international dollar reserves, and second, by providing a mature market for efficient allocation and trade of financial assets. Behind these two advantages, the United States can continue to finance its large trade deficit via the sale of bonds.

In the long run, the main way to alleviate trade imbalance is to narrow the gap in financial market development between nations, especially in regions where financial markets are underdeveloped. Development of various commercial insurance products and government provision of noncommercial insurance such as pensions and medical and unemployment insurance enhance agents' ability to smooth consumption under shocks. Additionally, to reduce the trade imbalance between China and the world, China needs to adjust its exchange rate policy and adopt a more flexible exchange rate regime. Not only will this benefit the global trade balance in the long run, but it will also reduce volatility in consumption and increase agent welfare.

References

Abiad, A., Detragiache, E., & Tressel, T. (2007). *A new database of financial reforms*. IMF Working Paper No. 07/XX.

Asdrubali, P., Sorensen, B. E., & Yosha, O. (1996). Channels of interstate risk sharing: United States 1963–1990. *The Quarterly Journal of Economics*, *111*(4), 1081–1110.

Atkeson, A., & Bayoumi, T. (1993). Do private capital markets insure regional risk? Evidence from the United States and Europe. *Open Economies Review*, *4*(3), 303–324.

Backus, D. K., Kehoe, P. J., & Kydland, F. E. (1992). *Relative price movements in dynamic general equilibrium models of international trade*. NBER Working Paper No. 4243. National Bureau of Economic Research, Inc.

Bernanke, B. S. (2005). *The global saving glut and the U.S. current account deficit*. St. Louis, MO: Homer Jones Lecture.

Blanchard, O., & Giavazzi, F. (2002). Current account deficits in the Euro area: The end of the Feldstein-Horioka puzzle? *Brookings Papers on Economic Activity*, 147–186.

Caballero, R. J., Farhi, E., & Gourinchas, P.-O (2008). An equilibrium model of "global imbalances" and low interest rates. *American Economic Review*, *98*(1), 358–393.

Canova, F., & Ravn, M. O. (1996). International consumption risk sharing. *International Economic Review*, *37*(3), 573–601.

Cline, W. R. (2005). *The United States as a debtor nation: Risks and policy reform*. Washington, DC: Institute for International Economics.

Clower, R. W. (1967). A reconsideration of the micro-foundations of monetary theory. *Western Economic Journal*, *6*(1), 1–8.

Devereux, M. B., Gregory, A., & Smith, G. (1992). Realistic cross-country consumption correlations in a two-country real business cycle model. *Journal of International Money and Finance*, *11*, 3–16.

Dooley, M. P., Folkerts-Landau, D., & Garber, P. (2003). *An essay of revived Breton woods system*. NBER Working Paper No. 9971.

Dooley, M. P., Folkerts-Landau, D., & Garber, P. (2004). *The revived Bretton Woods system: The effects of periphery intervention and reserve management on interest rates and exchange rates in center countries*. NBER Working Paper No. 10332.

Gourinchas, P.-O., & Rey, H. (2005). *From world banker to world venture capitalist: US external adjustment and the exorbitant privilege*. NBER Working Paper No. 11563. National Bureau of Economic Research, Inc.

Gruber, J. W., & Kamin, S. B. (2007). Explaining the global pattern of current account imbalances. *Journal of International Money and Finance*, *26*(4), 500–522.

Ho, C., Ho, W. A., & Li, D. (2010). Consumption fluctuations and welfare: Evidence from China. *World Development*, *38*(9), 1315–1327.

Kim, S., Kim, S. H., & Wang, Y. (2006). Financial integration and consumption risk sharing in East Asia. *Japan and the World Economy*, *18*(2), 143–157.

Kollmann, R. (1996). Incomplete asset markets and the cross-country consumption correlation puzzle. *Journal of Economic Dynamics and Control*, *20*, 945–962.

Lane, P. R., & Milesi-Ferretti, G. M. (2005). *A global perspective on external positions*. CEPR Discussion Papers No. 5234.

Li, J., & Han, Q. (2009). Incomplete financial market, precautionary saving and welfare cost of inflation. *China Economic Quarterly*, *9*(1), 191–212.

Liu, S. (2006). *Report of research on Chinese economic cycle*. China, Beijing: Social Sciences Academic Press.

Mann, C. L. (2002). Perspectives on the US current account deficit and sustainability. *Journal of Economics Perspectives*, *16*, 131–152.

McKinnon, R., & Schnabl, G. (2009, March). *China's financial conundrum and global imbalances*. BIS Working Papers No. 277.

Mendoza, E. G., Quadrini, V., & Rios-Rull, J.-V. (2007). *On the welfare implications of financial globalization without financial development*. NBER Working Paper No. 13412. National Bureau of Economic Research.

Mendoza, E. G., Quadrini, V., & Rios-Rull, J.-V. (2009). Financial integration, financial development, and global imbalances. *Journal of Political Economy*, *117*(3), 371–416.

Obstfeld, M. (1993). *Are industrial-country consumption risks globally diversified?* Center for International and Development Economics Research (CIDER) Working Paper No. C93-014. University of California at Berkeley.

Stock, J. H., & Watson, M. W. (1998). *Business cycle fluctuations in U.S. macroeconomic time series*. NBER Working Paper No. 6528.

Svensson, L. E. O. (1988). Trade in risky assets. *American Economic Review*, *78*(3), 375–394.

Svensson, L. E. O. (1989). Trade in nominal assets: Monetary policy, and price level and exchange rate risk. *Journal of International Economics*, *26*(1–2), 1–28.

Willen, P. S. (2004). *Incomplete markets and trade*. Working Paper Series No. 04-8. Federal Reserve Bank of Boston.

Xu, X. (2008). Consumption risk-sharing in China. *Economica*, *75*(298), 326–341.

Zhang, B. (2006). Analysis on synchronization and transmission mechanisms of Sino-US business cycles. *World Economy Study*, (10), 31–38.

Appendix A: Equivalent Model

The following model is equivalent to the basic model described in Section 3. It is an optimization problem for an agent in country one. The optimization problem for an agent in country two can be derived similarly.

When nominal interest rates $i_{1,t}$ and $i_{2,t}$ are nonnegative for each state s_{wt}, there will be no need for an agent to hold currencies into the next period. Therefore, unused money in period t that the agent brings into period $t+1$ in Equation (6) is equal to zero, and inequalities (4) and (5) become equalities. In addition, there are only two micro-states, employed and unemployed. Constraints (3)–(8) can be simplified into the following constraints:

$$P_{1,t}a_t^1 = P_{1,t}c_{1,t}^1 + e_t P_{2,t}c_{2,t}^1 + B_{1,t}^1 + e_t B_{2,t}^1 + \frac{0.5A_t^1(e) + 0.5A_t^1(u)}{1+i_{1,t}} \tag{A.1}$$

$$P_{1,t+1}a_{t+1}^1(s_{t+1}) = P_{1,t+1}y_{t+1}^1 + B_{1,t}^1(1+i_{1,t}) + e_{t+1}B_{2,t}^1(1+i_{2,t}) + A_t^1(s_{d,t+1}) \tag{A.2}$$

$$a_{t+1}^1(e) - a_{t+1}^1(u) \geq (1-\Phi^1)\left(y_{t+1}^1(e) - y_{t+1}^1(u)\right) \tag{A.3}$$

$$c_{1t}^1, c_{2t}^1 \geq 0. \tag{A.4}$$

Using Equation (A.3) and the zero-profit condition $0.5A_t^1(e) + 0.5A_t^1(u) = 0$ (Mendoza, 2009), we obtain

$$\frac{A_t^1(u)}{p_{1,t+1}} = -\frac{A_t^1(r)}{p_{1,t+1}} = \bar{y}^1(s_{w,t})\Phi^1\Delta^1.$$

Thus, the "Arrow-Debreu Security" market clears, and Equation (10) is satisfied. Assume that purchasing power parity applies $(p_{1,t} = e_t p_{2,t})$, then, the optimization problem of an agent in country one is equivalent to[1]

[1] The optimization problem of Equation (A.5) is a dynamic programming problem. The basic approach is to start with the initial approximation $V0$ of the value function, compute the next approximation of the value function, and continue this process until the sequence of value functions converges to V.

$$V_t^1\left(s, a_t^1\right) = \max_{c_{1,t}^1, c_{2,t}^1, B_{1,t}^1, B_{2,t}^1, A_t^1} \left\{ U\left(c_{1,t}^1 + c_{2,t}^1\right) + \beta \sum_{s'} V_{t+1}^1\left(s', a_{t+1}^1(s')\right)\pi(s'|s) \right\} \tag{A.5}$$

Subject to:

$$a_t^1 = c_{1,t}^1 + c_{2,t}^1 + b_{1,t}^1 + b_{2,t}^1 \tag{A.6}$$

$$a_{t+1}^1(s_{t+1}) = \bar{y}^1\left(s_{w,t}\right) + \frac{b_{1,t}^1(1+i_{1,t})}{1+\pi_{1,t+1}} + \frac{b_{2,t}^1(1+i_{2,t})}{1+\pi_{2,t+1}} + \left(1-\Phi^1\right)\tilde{y}^i\left(s_{d,t}\right)\Delta^1 \tag{A.7}$$

$$c_{1,t}^1, c_{2,t}^1 \geq 0, \tag{A.8}$$

where $b_{1,t}^1 = B_{1,t}^1/p_{1,t}$ and $b_{2,t}^1 = B_{2,t}^1/p_{2,t}$. For country $i = 1, 2$, price $p_{i,t} = M_{i,t}/\left(\bar{y}^i\left(s_{w,t}\right)\right)$ and the inflation rate $\pi_{i,t+1} = (p_{i,t+1} - p_{i,t})/p_{i,t}$.

Appendix B: Computational Procedure

1. Given the intertemporal discount factor β and the relative risk aversion coefficient σ.
2. Given the economic cycles EC of two countries, calculate the 2×2 macro-state ($s_{w1,t}$ and $s_{w2,t}$) transition matrices. Since these two transition matrices are independent of each other, one can derive a 4×4 macro-state $\left(s_{w,t}=s_{w1,t}\times s_{w2,t}\right)$ transition matrix.
3. Given the 2×2 micro-state $\left(s_{d,t}\right)$ transition matrix for country one and country two. From the 4×4 macro-state transition matrix and the 2×2 micro-state transition matrix, one can obtain a 8×8 state $\left(s_t=s_{d,t}\times s_{w1,t}\times s_{w2,t}\right)$ transition matrix π.
4. Given the aggregate endowments of country one and country two, $\bar{y}^i\left(s_{w,t}\right)$.
5. Given employed-unemployed gap Δ^i of country one and country two, one can obtain the endowments for any s_t.
6. Given the monetary policies of country one and country two.
7. Given the financial incompleteness coefficients Φ^i of country one and country two.
8. For $i=1,2$ and any state s_t, discretize the net worth a_t^i into a grid of 301 points between 0 and 3.0.
9. Given the eight initial guesses of nominal interest rates $i_{1,t}$ and $i_{2,t}$ for the four macro-states.
10. An agent in country $i=1,2$ solves the optimization problem (A.5) under constraints (A.6) to (A.8) using dynamic programming, obtaining the decision rules $c_{1,t}^i, c_{2,t}^i, b_{1,t}^i, b_{2,t}^i$, and value function $V_t^i(s,a)$. Now Equation (11) is valid; that is, the "Arrow-Debreu Security" market clears.
11. Using Equation (13), for $i=1,2$, one can solve for the invariant two-dimensional distribution function $D^i(s,a)$. Now Equations (14) and (15) will be valid; that is, the agent constraint holds.
12. If Equation (10) is not true, update the guess for the sequences of the interest rates (step 9), and return to step 10 until the bonds market clearing conditions are satisfied. Now Equations (9) and (12) hold, that is, the "goods market" and the "money market" clear.

Chapter 10

Modern Monetary Rules: Any Role for Financial Targeting?☆

Marcin Wolski

European Investment Bank, Luxembourg, Luxembourg,
e-mail: m.wolski@eib.org

Abstract

We test the determinacy properties of the standard and financial-sector-augmented Taylor rules in a new Keynesian model with a presence of banking activities. We extend the basic fully rational environment to the setting with heterogeneous expectations. We observe that the benefits from extra financial targeting are limited. Financial targeting, if well designed, can compensate for the improper output-gap targeting through the financial-production channel. The analysis demonstrates however possible threats resulting from the misspecification of the augmented rule. A determinate mix of output-gap and inflation weights can turn indeterminate if compensated by too extreme financial targeting. The results are robust to the presence of heterogeneous expectations.

Keywords: monetary rules, financial frictions, heterogeneous agents

JEL Classifications: E52, D84, C62

1. Introduction

Monetary rules, that is, the rules which set the level of nominal interest rates as a function of the basic economic characteristics, have gained a

☆This research has been partly conducted while my PhD studies (European Doctorate in Economics - Erasmus Mundus) at the University of Amsterdam and Bielefeld University. Any views expressed are only those of author and do not necessarily represent the views of the EIB.

International Symposia in Economic Theory and Econometrics, Vol. 24
William A. Barnett and Fredj Jawadi (Editors)

ISSN: 1571-0386/doi: 10.1108/S1571-038620150000024022

lot of attention in the recent decades, starting with the seminal works of Taylor (1993) and Henderson and McKibbin (1993). Their simplicity and intuitive structure made them popular tools in macro policy and economic modeling. In particular, they proved to be of great importance in the Dynamic Stochastic General Equilibrium (DSGE) models, largely applied by the policy makers and central bankers around the world.

Nevertheless, the standard modeling techniques turned out to be insufficient to counteract (or even to predict) the recent global financial crisis. The failure of these models might be largely attributed to several simplifying assumptions which they are built upon. To the most widely criticized belong the Rational Expectations Hypothesis (REH) and representative agent structure (Frydman & Goldberg, 2007), linear dependencies (Hommes, 2013) and the absence of the well-characterized financial sector (Bernanke, Gertler, & Gilchrist, 1999; Tovar, 2008). Those shortcomings used to be neglected for many years as the global economy was growing steadily with little fluctuations, making the DSGE models powerful tools which provide a coherent framework for policy discussion and analysis. The beauty of their simplicity turned, however, into their biggest nightmare as the recent financial crisis erupted. Their forecasting accuracy, highlighted on pre-crisis samples (see e.g., Christoffel, Coenen, & Warne, 2010), in terms of Root Mean Square Error (RMSE), proved to be no better than naive forecasts (Edge & Gürkaynak, 2010). In short, as pointed out by Tovar (2008) "[d]espite the rapid progress made in recent years, at their current stage of development, these [DSGE] models are not fully ready to accomplish all what is being asked from them."

Despite the fact that a lot of attention has been paid to the improvement of the DSGE models, there has been only a few attempts to update the structure of monetary rules. In fact, many of the recent DSGE models still rely on the functional form provided by Taylor (1993), which sets the level of nominal interest rate as a function of the deviations in output gap and inflation.[1] The goal of this chapter is therefore to provide a formal investigation of a new monetary rule in a complex environment. In particular, we take into account a new Keynesian economy with financial frictions and heterogeneous expectations, as proposed by Goodfriend and McCallum (2007), Branch and McGough (2009) and Wolski (2013). We propose a new monetary rule which in addition to the standard output gap and inflation targeting, comprises a banking variable. In other words, according to our new rule, a policy maker is aware of the presence and importance of the financial sector and takes into account financial circumstances when making decisions.

[1] See for instance Goodfriend and McCallum (2007); Branch and McGough (2009, 2010).

Our new rule is mostly in line with those proposed by Gambacorta and Signoretti (2014), where they study asset prices and credit indicators. In fact, financial conditions are among some of the most widely advertized characteristics to be included in macro-prudential policies. Most recently, Adrian and Liang (2014) proposed four aspects of financial conditions which could be included in policy rules, that is, asset markets, banking sector, shadow banking, and financial interconnectedness. Our new rule comprises mostly the stance of the banking sector, however, it indirectly influences the remaining three aspects. In particular, we develop a formal DSGE framework where the banking sector has its own aggregate representation in the form of the marginal banking cost. The variable is in fact parallel to the output-gap measure, or the marginal production cost, known from the new Keynesian literature. The larger it gets, the more difficult banking becomes so that the credit supply decreases, the same as the bank risk-taking capacity. In a perfect-foresight economy, like the standard DSGE models, the effects of a new rule are negligible as individuals are fully aware of policy targets. In other words, the value added of the banking target is fully offset by the opposite effects in the production sectors. The analysis demonstrates possible threats resulting from the misspecification of the augmented rule. A determinate mix of output-gap and inflation weights can turn indeterminate if compensated by too extreme financial targeting. We argue that in an economy with no perfect-foresight equilibrium, the effects of an extra target are similar. However, in an environment with heterogeneous agents, we see a new indeterminacy region for too lenient inflation targeting – a phenomenon not observed in the framework with no financial frictions.

Having pointed that out, in order to get a comprehensive assessment of the new rule, we investigate its behavior in two types of economies. The first one is a standard fully rational DSGE environment where all agents are forward-looking fundamentalists and have perfect foresight. The second type is a heterogeneous setting where all the individuals are split into two groups. In addition to fundamentalists, we assume a constant fraction of boundedly rational agents who use simple heuristics to form their expectations. We focus on two types of heuristics which are most commonly referred to throughout the literature (Hommes, 2013), that is, adaptive and extrapolative expectations. Both assume that future realizations depend on the past performance of particular variables, however, the former assumes that the influence of past realizations decreases over time whereas the latter manifests the opposite. In both environments we compare the performance of our new monetary rule to the standard one.

The remainder of this chapter is organized as follows. The next section describes the evolution of the monetary policy models and the role of monetary rules in economic modeling. Section 3 describes the workhorse model with financial frictions and investigates the performance of the new rule compared to the standard one. Section 4 proposes an extension of the analysis to the heterogeneous environment and studies the new rule in a presence of boundedly rational agents. Finally, Section 5 concludes.

2. Motivation and Literature Review

The need for a framework which would incorporate financial frictions in DSGE models was stressed long before the 2007–2009 financial crisis (Bernanke & Gertler, 1989; Kiyotaki & Moore, 1997). The body of literature in this topic has grown substantially thereafter, bringing significant changes to monetary policy conduct (Rotemberg & Woodford, 1997; Woodford, 2003). It is surprising, as argued by Goodfriend and McCallum (2007) and Casares and Poutineau (2010), that the role of the banking sector was left unexplored in the monetary policy analysis until recently.

The framework used in this study clarifies this oversight. Firstly, by introducing profit-maximizing bankers at the micro level, one may explicitly study the impact of their individual behavior on the macro aggregates. Secondly, the differentiation of the capital market allows to investigate the relationship between various types of interest rates (Goodfriend, 2005). Thirdly, by having government bonds which serve for collateral purposes, one observes the direct influence of public policy on the monetary aggregates.

Most noticeably, however, a banking sector *per se* is an important, if not the most important part of each economy (Levine, 1997). Since it is a general source of liquidity, its problems may easily spread over the other sectors, bringing them down eventually. Especially, the recent history proves that banking sector disturbances might result in sovereign crises, as recently took place in the euro zone (Grammatikos & Vermeulen, 2012). Therefore, a detailed study of the banking sector's role in the monetary framework is required in order to (i) understand its transmission mechanism and (ii) endow the monetary authorities with the sufficient preventive tools.

Having pointed that out, the main question of this chapter is to investigate if a policy maker can benefit from including financial variables in the monetary rule. As advertized by Goodhart, Sunirand, and Tsomocos (2011), the interest rate rules are much better instruments for maintaining financial stability, compared to their monetary-base equivalents. This guarantees consistency with the question raised by this chapter and we proceed with interest rate rule as the main monetary instrument.[2] The idea behind a standard monetary rule is to represent the level of nominal interest rates in the economy as a function of aggregate variables in a given period. The basic build-up of a rule comprises the real interest rate and the deviations of production and inflation from their target levels as the input variables (Taylor, 1993). Formally, one can represent the nominal level of interest rates as

$$i_t = r_t + \lambda_x(x_t - x_t^*) + \lambda_\pi(\pi_t - pi_t^*), \tag{1}$$

where r_t is the real interest rate, $(x_t - x_t^*)$ and $(\pi_t - pi_t^*)$ are the deviations of output gap and inflation from their target values, respectively, and λs represent the weights a policy maker puts on production and inflation variables. Since the presence of the banking sector changes the dynamics of the macroeconomic performance (Goodfriend, 2005; Goodfriend & McCallum, 2007) as well as it can largely affect financial stability (Adrian & Liang, 2014), it is reasonable for a policy maker to include banking variables in the monetary rule as well. In other words, by the new (or augmented) monetary rule we formally understand that

$$i_t = r_t + \lambda_x(x_t - x_t^*) + \lambda_\pi(\pi_t - pi_t^*) + \lambda_f(f_t - f_t^*), \tag{2}$$

where f is a representation of financial conditions and the remaining notation is the same as in Equation (1). In this study, by f we consider the marginal banking cost, that is, the cost of running banking activities. There were several other attempts in the literature to add financial characteristics to the monetary rule. Benchimol and Fourans (2012) consider the money gap, revealing that its role is negligible unless there is a significant risk aversion in the private sector. Gilchrist and Zakrajek (2011, 2012) augment the standard Taylor rule with a credit spread as a measure of asset prices. They show that such a new rule is beneficial in mitigating aggregate credit frictions. Bekaert and Hoerova (2013) find that the standard Taylor rule residuals are strongly correlated with the uncertainty component of VIX and therefore propose to add financial market risk and uncertainty to the basic rule. Finally, Gambacorta and Signoretti (2014) argue that even if asset prices and credit indicators are not an explicit target of a policy maker, they enhance financial stability in a presence of supply shocks.

[2] One of the most widely known alternative rules is the so-called McCallum rule. McCallum (1987, 1988, 1993) propose to target the money growth instead of the interest rates directly. For instance, McCallum (2000) studies the performance of the McCallum rule in the United States, the United Kingdom and Japan, proving that its effectiveness largely depends on the period of interest. In this study we abstract from the money-growth rules and we focus entirely on the interest rate rules, as being more prominent in economic modeling and policy applications.

In this chapter we firstly propose a condensed form of the new Keynesian model with a banking sector of Goodfriend and McCallum (2007), where financial aggregates have their own representation. Secondly, we relax the assumption of agents' homogeneity and investigate how the presence of the backward-looking (or boundedly rational after Hommes (2013)) agents influences the determinacy of the equilibrium, given the standard and the banking-sector-augmented Taylor rules. We introduce agents' heterogeneity at the micro level, which means that each agent is solving the individual optimization problem simultaneously. It is an important distinction from a variety of models which neglect this aspect and allow for agents' heterogeneity at the macro level only. Clearly, such a concept violates the Subjective Expected Utility (SEU) theory and in our view is inappropriate. Instead, we follow the classical approach where the macro behavior is a direct consequence of agents' micro optimal plans.

The latter part of this study is motivated by a growing body of research which shows explicitly that agents differ in forming expectations. This phenomenon was confirmed by both survey data analysis (Branch, 2004; Carroll, 2003; Mankiw, Reis, & Wolfers, 2003) as well as laboratory experiments with human subjects (Assenza, Heemeijer, Hommes, & Massaro, 2011; Hommes, 2011; Hommes, Sonnemans, Tuinstra, & van de Velde, 2005; Pfajfar & Zakelj, 2011). The heterogeneity among agents was proved to have important implications on the determinacy properties in the new Keynesian models (Branch & McGough, 2009; Massaro, 2013). We follow this approach and assess its implication within the framework with a banking sector.

3. Monetary Rules under the Basic Scenario

In this section we develop the workhorse version of the model. Since the complete derivation, with the first order conditions and aggregation, is described in detail in the original paper of Goodfriend and McCallum (2007), we skip it in the main part of this text. However, for the reader's convenience, the complete derivation is given in Appendix A.

The model space consists of a continuum of farmers who provide labor supply to the production and banking sectors at the same time t (n_t and m_t, respectively). Additionally, each farmer manufactures a differentiated product and sells it in the monopolistically competitive environment. As in the standard new Keynesian framework, it is assumed that only a fraction $(1-\omega)$ of all farmers can adjust their prices fully flexibly. The remaining part takes the prices from the previous period (Calvo, 1983). Given these conditions, the goal of each farmer is to maximize her expected utility, which is a linear combination of consumption and leisure, over the infinite horizon.

In the utility maximization problem, each farmer has to take into account three constraints: (i) the budget constraint, (ii) the production constraint, and (iii) the banking constraint. The first of these is the standard intertemporal budget constraint which ensures that the net income and bond/money holdings in one period are being transmitted to the next period. The second constraint is a direct consequence of the production technology, which in this case is of the Cobb-Douglas type. Assuming market clearing, the production (Y_t) in each period is the consequence of the amount of capital (K_t) and labor (n_t^d) involved, corrected for their output elasticities: η and $(1-\eta)$, respectively. The banking constraint assumes that the level of consumption (C_t) has to be rigidly related to the level of deposits held at a bank. One may view this as if all the transactions were being facilitated through the banking sector and each agent may consume a part V of her wealth only. A bank is then allowed to use $(1-rr)$ fraction of the deposits to produce loans using the Cobb-Douglas production function with collateral (col_t) and labor (m_t^d) as production factors and α and $(1-\alpha)$ being the output elasticities. The collateral consists of two parts, that is, the discounted level of real bond holdings $B_{t+1}/(P_t^A(1+r_t^B))$, with P_t^A being the aggregate price level and r_t^B the interest rate on bonds, and real level of capital q_tK_{t+1}, corrected for the inferiority of capital to bonds for collateral purposes, υ. The last term results from the fact that bonds, contrary to capital goods, do not require substantial monitoring effort in order to verify their market value (Goodfriend & McCallum, 2007).

Such a banking sector setting captures several important aspects of financial intermediation. Firstly, it enters the consumer utility maximization problem at the micro level. Secondly, it builds a clear link between households and a production sector. Thirdly, because of its dependence on governmental securities, it comprises the monetary policy transmission mechanism (through the repo market).

There are two main simplifications of the original model. Firstly, we abstract from the capital shocks in the loan production function. We assume that the capital level is at its steady state level and the productivity shocks are transmitted through the labor channels only. This simplification does not affect the final results as in the determinacy analysis the stochastic terms do not play a role (Blanchard & Kahn, 1980). Secondly, we assume a zero tax rate. Eventually, the role of government is narrowed to issuing bonds in each period at some exogenously given level, and paying the interest.

Given the specification above, we may now turn to derivation of three model equations: the Investment-Savings (IS) curve, the Phillips curve, and the banking curve. The first two of these build the standard new Keynesian model. The last one is the direct consequence of the presence of the banking sector and describes its role in the aggregate dynamics explicitly.

3.1. The IS Curve

The model implies the presence of two Lagrange multipliers: λ_t for the budget constraint and ξ_t for the production constraint. They represent the shadow values, or the utility gains, of unit values of consumption and production, respectively (Casares & Poutineau, 2010). In particular, from the banking labor demand optimality condition we know that

$$\lambda_t^i = \frac{\xi_t^i}{\varphi_t^i} = \frac{\frac{\phi}{C_t^i}}{1 + \left(\frac{1-rr}{V}\right)\chi_t^i}, \tag{3}$$

where φ_t^i is the individual marginal production cost, ϕ is the utility weight on consumption and we explored the fact that the χ_t^i might be viewed as the individual marginal loan management cost, or simply the marginal banking cost (Casares & Poutineau, 2010; Goodfriend & McCallum, 2007).[3] To put it more formally, imagine the cost minimization problem of a representative bank in a situation without collateral cost. The total cost function may be rewritten as $\mathrm{TC}_t = m_t^d w_t$, where w_t is the real wage. The minimization problem includes the loan production constraint with a Lagrangian multiplier (here perceived as a marginal cost, Walsh, 2010), denoted by χ_t. The first order condition implies that $\chi_t = V w_t m_t^d / ((1-rr)(1-\alpha)C_t)$. In fact, χ_t^i is parallel to the individual marginal production cost that is being often referred to in the standard new Keynesian framework (Walsh, 2010). One may view that as a general variable describing the situation in the banking sector, that is, the higher it is the less effective the loan management is. As it is shown later, this variable is of crucial importance as it becomes a link between a standard new Keynesian model and the banking system.

Equation (3) gives the first overview of the model behavior. Firstly, the shadow value of production equals the shadow value of consumption corrected for the marginal production cost. In other words, additional consumption has to turn up in either increased production or decreased production costs. Secondly, λ_t is the marginal utility of consumption corrected for the marginal banking cost. Put differently, each additional unit of consumption requires more deposits, which may be raised at the

[3] We include superscript i to underline the individual level of the relationship which is explored in detail later. In the representative agent structure it may be omitted as every agent behaves the same.

cost χ_t. It is straightforward to notice that the lower the marginal banking cost, the relatively cheaper the additional consumption. On the other hand, a highly inefficient banking sector limits the incentives to increase consumption.

Substituting Equation (3) into the bond optimality condition, we finally arrive at the familiar Euler equation

$$\beta E_t^i\left(\frac{\frac{\phi}{C_{t+1}^i}}{1+\left(\frac{1-rr}{V}\right)\chi_{t+1}^i}\right)=\frac{\frac{\phi}{C_t^i}}{1+\left(\frac{1-rr}{V}\right)\chi_t^i}(1+E_t^i\pi_{t+1})\left(\frac{1-\frac{1-rr}{V}\chi_t^i\Omega_t^i}{1+r_t^B}\right), \tag{4}$$

where $(1+E_t^i\pi_{t+1})=P_{t+1}^A/P_t^A$ is the inflation rate and $\Omega_t^i=\alpha C_t^i/col_t^i$.

Following Goodfriend (2005), let us introduce a one-period default-free security with the nominal rate denoted by r_t^T. Since we additionally assume that it cannot serve for collateral purposes, r_t^T represents a pure intertemporal rate of interest and serves as a benchmark for other interest rates. From the agent optimization problem, we know that $1+r_t^{i,T}=E_t^i\lambda_t^i P_{t+1}^i/(\beta\lambda_{t+1}^i P_t^i)$ so that it includes the discounted difference between expected changes in shadow prices and actual prices. An important distinction is that the pricing of this fictitious security is done at the individual level which is not strange given its completely artificial and agent-dependent nature. Eventually, the last term of Equation (4) might be rewritten as the reciprocal of $(1+r_t^{i,T})$.

At the same time, let us assume that each bank can obtain funds from the interbank market at the common rate r_t^{IB}. It can then loan them to agents at the rate $r_t^{i,T}$. The profit maximization of a bank implies that the marginal costs of obtaining funds has to be equal their marginal profit so that

$$(1+r_t^{\mathrm{IB}})(1+\chi_t^i)=(1+r_t^{i,T}). \tag{5}$$

Inserting Equation (5) into Equation (4) and taking the log approximation around the steady state we have

$$\hat{Y}_t^i=E_t^i\hat{Y}_{t+1}^i+\left(\frac{1-rr}{V}\right)E_t^i\tilde{\chi}_{t+1}^i-\left(\frac{1-rr}{V}+1\right)\tilde{\chi}_t^i-(\hat{r}_t^{\mathrm{IB}}-E_t^i\pi_{t+1}), \tag{6}$$

where tildes and hats denote deviations and percentage deviations from the steady state, respectively, and we explored the market clearing condition.[4]

As in the standard new Keynesian framework, we define the potential output as the output under completely flexible prices and wages (Walsh, 2010). We additionally assume that in such a situation there is a fixed

[4] Following literature, we take the zero inflation steady state.

proportion between employment in the production and banking sector, $n_t^d \propto m_t^d$. Following Walsh (2010), price flexibility implies that all agents can adjust their prices immediately, which gives that the marginal cost of production φ_t is equal to $(\theta - 1)/\theta$ across all individuals, where θ is the elasticity of substitution between consumption goods. The labor optimality condition implies that the real wage has to be equal to the marginal rate of substitution between leisure and consumption, corrected for the presence of the banking sector. Combining the above-mentioned points with Equation (3) and the production constraint, we finally get that under flexible prices and wages, the supply of labor of each individual is fixed so that if the capital stock is in the steady state (as we assume throughout the model) the log deviations of the potential product depend only on exogenous disturbances, $\hat{Y}_t^f = (1-\eta)(A1_t - \bar{A}1)$. Subtracting them from both sides of Equation (5) and omitting the i superscript, we finally arrive at the aggregate IS curve corrected for the presence of a banking sector

$$x_t = E_t x_{t+1} + \left(\frac{1-rr}{V}\right) E_t \tilde{\chi}_{t+1} - \left(\frac{1-rr}{V} + 1\right) \tilde{\chi}_t - \left[\hat{r}_t^{\mathrm{IB}} - E_t \pi_{t+1}\right] + u_t, \quad (7)$$

where $x_t = \hat{Y}_t - \hat{Y}_t^f$ is the output-gap measure and u_t is the disturbance term that depends only on exogenous productivity shocks.

It is straightforward to notice that when skipping the banking sector variables from Equation (7) we obtain the standard new Keynesian IS curve. What is important, is that the aggregate dynamics is affected not only by the current, but also by the expected future values of the banking variables. In other words, the way the agents form their expectations about future banking sector conditions seems to play a role in determining current production. The impact of the banking sector is limited by (i) the reserve requirement, rr, and (ii) the proportion of consumption that has to be covered by deposits, V. Clearly, the lower the minimum reserve requirement, the larger the loan production so that the importance of the banking sector increases, *ceteris paribus*. At the same time, if the consumption-to-deposits coverage ratio is large, relative size of the banking sector is smaller so that its impact decreases.

3.2. The Phillips Curve

The model allows us also to derive the explicit formula for the Phillips (or Aggregate Supply) curve. We know that all the farmers share the same production technology and face the same constant demand elasticities. We know from the Calvo lottery that a fraction ω of agents cannot adjust their prices in a given period t. Profits of some future date $t+k$ are affected only if an agent did not receive a chance to adjust prices between t and $t+k$. Therefore, the probability of having lower expected profits in period k is ω^k. Having pointed that out, the price optimality condition has to be corrected for the nominal price rigidities in the long run and by iterating forward it might be viewed as

$$E_t^i \sum_{k=0}^{\infty} \beta^k \omega^k \left[(1-\theta)\left(\frac{P_t^i}{P_{t+k}^A}\right) + \theta\left(\frac{\xi_{t+k}^i}{\lambda_{t+k}^i}\right)\right]\left(\frac{1}{P_t^i}\right)\left(\frac{P_t^i}{P_{t+k}^A}\right) C_{t+k}^A = 0. \tag{8}$$

Solving for optimal price setting, we arrive at

$$\frac{P_t^i}{P_t^A} = \frac{E_t^i \sum_{k=0}^{\infty} \beta^k \omega^k C_{t+k}^A \varphi_{t+k}^i \left(\frac{P_{t+k}^A}{P_t^A}\right)^{\theta}}{E_t^i \sum_{k=0}^{\infty} \beta^k \omega^k C_{t+k}^A \left(\frac{P_{t+k}^A}{P_t^A}\right)^{\theta-1}}, \tag{9}$$

where $\varphi_t^i = \xi_t^i / \lambda_t^i$ is the individual marginal production cost (Goodfriend & McCallum, 2007). Skipping the i superscript and taking a log approximation, after some algebra we obtain[5]

$$\pi_t = \beta E_t \pi_{t+1} + k\hat{\varphi}_t, \tag{10}$$

where $k = (1-\omega)(1-\beta\omega)/\omega$. We further explore the fact that given the Cobb-Douglas production function, the steady state log deviations of the marginal production cost might be viewed as an output-gap measure (Goodfriend & McCallum, 2007). Finally, we arrive at the standard new Keynesian Phillips curve

$$\pi_t = \beta E_t \pi_{t+1} + kx_t. \tag{11}$$

What is important is that the situation in the banking sector does not affect the inflation level directly but only through the consumption channel. The absence of the banking variables in Equation (11) is a consequence of the banking sector specification. The level of consumption is rigidly related to the amount of deposits in the banking sector. Therefore, changes in the banking sector would result in a different deposit level, which would shake the consumption eventually. However, there is no direct link to the inflation in the meantime.

[5] For a detailed derivation see the appendix of Chapter 8 from Walsh (2010).

3.3. The Banking Sector Curve

Since the presence of the banking sector affects the aggregate evolution of the IS and (indirectly) Phillips curves, it is also necessary to describe its dynamics. Observing that $\varphi_t = q_t K_t/(\eta C_t)$, the capital optimality condition implies

$$1 - \frac{\upsilon(1-rr)}{V}\Omega_t^i \chi_t^i = \beta(2-\delta)E_t^i\left[\frac{\left(1+\left(\frac{1-rr}{V}\right)\chi_t^i\right)\varphi_{t+1}^i}{\left(1+\left(\frac{1-rr}{V}\right)\chi_{t+1}^i\right)\varphi_t^i}\right]. \tag{12}$$

Observe that the LHS of Equation (12) is almost identical with the numerator of the last term in Equation (4). The only difference comes from the inferiority of capital to bonds for collateral purposes, υ. Applying the same interest rate reasoning to the log approximation of the LHS of Equation (12), we see that $-\upsilon(1-rr)\Omega_t^i\chi_t^i/V = -\upsilon(r_t^{\mathrm{IB}} - r_t^B + \chi_t^i)$. Since the interbank rate r_t^{IB} and the government bond rate r_t^B are both short-term rates, they should be close to each other around the equilibrium (Goodfriend & McCallum, 2007). Additionally, given the fact that υ is relatively small, we neglect the influence of $\upsilon(r_t^{\mathrm{IB}} - r_t^B)$. Eventually, after taking the deviations from the steady state of Equation (12), iterating forward and skipping the i superscript, we get

$$\left(\upsilon + \frac{1-rr}{V}\right)\tilde{\chi}_t = \frac{1-rr}{V}E_t\tilde{\chi}_{t+1} - (E_t x_{t+1} - x_t). \tag{13}$$

Given Equation (13) it is clear that the marginal cost of banking depends on (i) expectations about the banking situation in the future and (ii) the current and expected future production. In particular, the expectations about higher next period marginal banking costs work as a self-fulfilling prophecy, increasing also today's cost. This positive feedback structure reflects, to at least some degree, financial market sentiment and herding behavior. When investors see that the banking sector is going to face difficulties the next day, they will adjust their today's positions accordingly. On the other hand, given the link between the banking sector and consumption, high expectations about next period output gap decrease today's marginal banking cost (negative feedback). Imagine that people expect that there will be a decrease in production in the next period. Since the banking sector is a source of funding, there will be gradually less effort involved in the loan production, bringing today's marginal cost down.

The effects on the current banking situation are proportional to the size of the banking sector, expressed by $(1-rr)/V$, being more prominent for smaller banking sectors. Smaller banking sectors are more vulnerable to changes in the production sector as the relatively higher part of the banking capital is involved. On the other side, a bigger banking sector might be viewed as being more stable in the sense that the production sector affects it to the lower extent. It should be kept in mind, however, that the model does not say that big banks are ultimately stable as a high drop in today's production can cause the marginal banking cost to skyrocket. Equation (13) predicts only that this effect will be more prominent in the environment with a smaller banking sector.

At the same time, the inferiority of capital to bonds for collateral purposes, υ, also plays a role in determining the current marginal banking cost. In particular, let us consider the extreme case when capital cannot serve as a collateral, that is, $\upsilon = 0$. Banks do not have access to capital then so that the only link between them and the production sector is through loans. If there is a production shock, it affects the bond holdings and labor in the banking sector, making it more severe. In this sense, using capital as collateral serves as a hedge against production sector disturbances. When banks can access capital, in the presence of a production shock, its magnitude is being partially absorbed by the capital part.

We can sum up our reasoning in the following proposition.

Proposition 1. *In a new Keynesian economy with a presence of a banking sector as described above, the aggregate dynamics around the steady state can be rewritten as*

$$x_t = E_t^{\mathrm{RE}} x_{t+1} + \left(\frac{1-rr}{V}\right) E_t^{\mathrm{RE}} \tilde{\chi}_{t+1} - \left(\frac{1-rr}{V} + 1\right) \tilde{\chi}_t - \left[\hat{r}_t^{\mathrm{IB}} - E_t^{\mathrm{RE}} \pi_{t+1}\right] + u_t, \tag{14}$$

$$\pi_t = \beta E_t^{\mathrm{RE}} \pi_{t+1} + \kappa x_t, \tag{15}$$

$$\left(\upsilon + \frac{1-rr}{V}\right) \tilde{\chi}_t = \frac{1-rr}{V} E_t^{\mathrm{RE}} \tilde{\chi}_{t+} 1 - \left(E_t^{\mathrm{RE}} x_{t+1} - x_t\right), \tag{16}$$

where E_t^{RE} is the rational expectations operator.

3.4. Performance of the Monetary Rules

As opposed to the standard framework, the central bank policy instrument is the interbank interest rate, $\hat{r}_t^{\mathrm{IB}}$ (not the bond rate). In fact, this is the monetary policy tool used in practice (Goodfriend & McCallum, 2007). In this section we compare the performance of two monetary rule, parallel to the ones proposed in Equations (1) and (2) We rely here on their forward-looking representation, that is, the variables of interest come at the expected values. This type of representation has been largely supported in the theoretical and empirical literature as it focuses on the expectational component of the central bank's decisions (Clarida, Gali, & Gentler, 2000). In such a framework the role of a central bank is to act in anticipation of the possible disturbances rather than to act to late. One can compare this situation as parallel to driving a car and looking ahead rather than into the rear-view mirror. The results are robust, however, to a mixed specification.[6] We consider the standard Taylor rule to have the following functional form

$$\hat{r}_t^{\mathrm{IB}} = \rho_x E_t^{\mathrm{RE}} x_{t+1} + \rho_\pi E_t^{\mathrm{RE}} \pi_{t+1}, \tag{17}$$

where ρ_x and ρ_π are constant weights on output and inflation, respectively. Alternatively, the banking-sector-augmented Taylor rule is of the form

$$\hat{r}_t^{\mathrm{IB}} = \rho_x E_t^{\mathrm{RE}} x_{t+1} + \rho_\pi E_t^{\mathrm{RE}} \pi_{t+1} + \rho_\chi E_t^{\mathrm{RE}} \chi_{t+1}, \tag{18}$$

where ρ_χ is a weight the policy maker puts on the banking sector variable. In the analysis we do not restrict the parameter to positive values, as ρ_x and ρ_π parameters are often assumed. The reason for that is twofold. Firstly, we would like to get a comprehensive overview of the inclusion of the new parameter in the Taylor rule. Secondly, in contrast to two other variables, a policy maker may have an incentive to lower interest rates when the banking activities are too costly. Inefficient financial intermediation can result in the lower long-term consumption path, creating possible welfare losses. Therefore it is likely that in the equilibrium it is optimal to loosen the monetary policy when the banking sector is too ineffective.

DSGE models often exhibit indeterminacy, that is, there is no unique path guiding the equilibrium or, to put it differently, there is a continuum of equilibria in any neighborhood of it. In such a situation, the quantities and prices might not be even locally determinate, making the monetary policy conduct more unstable (Woodford, 1994). Therefore, it is important to make sure that the monetary tools provide a determinate structure of the economy.

Let us write the complete model in the matrix form. The condensed homogeneous version of the model can be rewritten as

$$By_{t+1} = Fy_t + \varepsilon_t, \tag{19}$$

[6] By a mixed specification we consider a weighted average of groups' expectations. In a homogeneous setting a mixed specification is parallel to the forward-looking one.

where $y=(x,\pi,\tilde{\chi})'$, $\varepsilon=(u,0,0)$ is a vector of exogenous shocks and B and F are the coefficient matrices described as

$$B=\begin{pmatrix} 1-\rho_x & 1-\rho_\pi & \frac{(1-rr)}{V}\left[-\rho_\chi\right] \\ 0 & \beta & 0 \\ -1 & 0 & \frac{(1-rr)}{V} \end{pmatrix}, \tag{20}$$

$$F=\begin{pmatrix} 1 & 0 & \frac{(1-rr)}{V}+1 \\ -\kappa & 1 & 0 \\ -1 & 0 & \upsilon+\frac{(1-rr)}{V} \end{pmatrix}. \tag{21}$$

Here we deliberately put the ρ_χ parameter in square brackets as it enters the systems only when we study the augmented Taylor rule. In the simple specification we omit the ρ_χ parameter.

To study the determinacy properties, we apply the methodology developed by Blanchard and Kahn (1980). Since it does not depend on the exogenous disturbances, we omit ε in our further analysis. The determinacy is a result of the properties of the solution matrix M, where

$$M=B^{-1}F. \tag{22}$$

Observe that the system described by matrix M consists of predetermined and non-predetermined variables. The equilibrium of such a system is determinate only if the number of eigenvalues that are outside the unit circle is equal to the number of non-predetermined variables (or the forward-looking variables, Walsh, 2010), which is 3 in this case. Having more eigenvalues outside the unit circle implies explosiveness and fewer of them implies indeterminacy. The degree of indeterminacy is equal to the number of non-predetermined variables less the number of eigenvalues outside the unit circle (Evans & McGough, 2005).

We calibrate our model accordingly to Goodfriend and McCallum (2007) for the end of 2005. Parameter $V=0.31$ represents the ratio of U.S. GDP to M3 aggregate for the fourth quarter of 2005. The reserve requirement rate $rr=0.005$ is the ratio of U.S. total bank reserves to M3 aggregate in the last month of 2005. Parameter $\upsilon=0.2$ corresponds to the relatively low productivity of capital observed in information-intensive lending. Parameters κ and β are the standard new Keynesian calibration parameters (see for instance Woodford (2003) or Branch and McGough (2010)). The detailed calibration values are presented in Table 1, whereas the determinacy structures are presented in Figures 1 and 2 for the standard and the banking-sector-augmented Taylor rules, respectively. For the latter we show the full scope of the inflation and banking-sector weights as it provides the most transparent structure of the equilibrium. The range for policy parameters ρ_x is set from 0 to 5, for inflation ρ_π from 0 to 10 and for ρ_χ from −5 to 5, in order to show the complete behavior of the system.

Figure 1 represents the benchmark model. In an environment with fully rational agents, the standard Taylor rule provides a well-documented lesson, often referred to as the Taylor principle (Woodford, 2003). In order to determine the equilibrium price level, the sum of the ρ_π and scaled ρ_x should be

Table 1: Calibration Values for the Model Parameters

Parameter	V	rr	υ	κ	β
Value	0.31	0.005	0.2	0.05	0.99

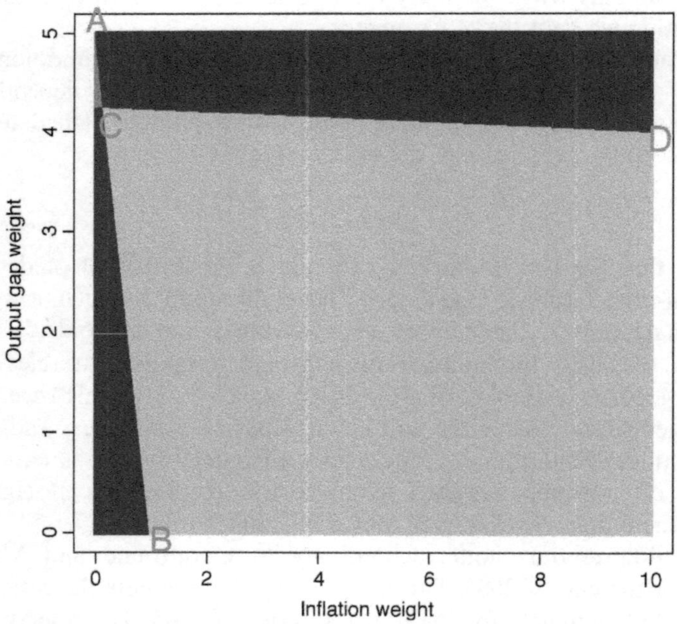

Figure 1: Determinacy Properties of the System's Equilibrium for the Standard Taylor Rule (Equation (17)) in an Environment with Fully Rational Agents. Light Gray Color Describes Determinacy, Dark Gray Order 1 Indeterminacy and Mid Gray Order 2 Indeterminacy.

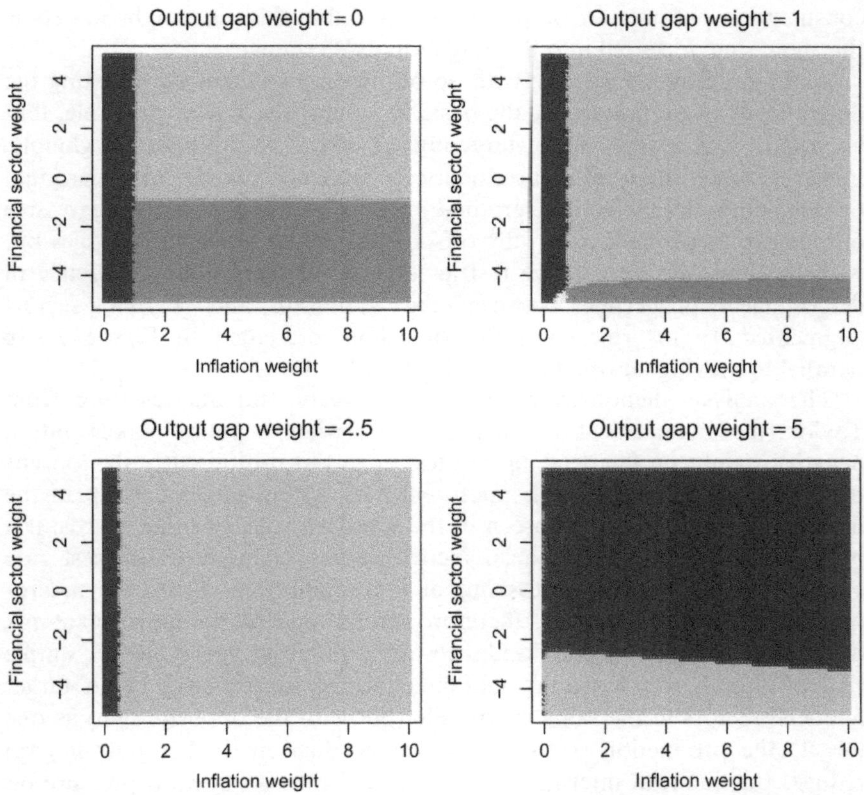

Figure 2: Determinacy Properties of the System's Equilibrium for the Augmented Taylor Rule (Equation (18)) in an Environment with Fully Rational Agents. Light Gray Color Describes Determinacy, Dark Gray Order 1 Indeterminacy, Mid Gray Order 2 Indeterminacy and White Order 3 Indeterminacy.

larger than 1. The formal condition implies that $\rho_\pi + (1-\beta)/\kappa\rho_x > 1$. In an environment of prolonged inflation the average long-term output gap increases by $(1-\beta)/\kappa$ for each additional percentage point of inflation. Therefore, in order to keep the prices determinate the nominal rates should increase more than the increase in inflation and output gap together. The line of the Taylor principle in our model is denoted by the line A-B in Figure 1. However, we observe that there is a cap on output-gap weight (denoted by the C-D line). In other words, if a policy maker puts too much weight on output-gap, relative to inflation, the system is driven out of control and the prices become indeterminate. A similar observation has been pointed out by Branch and McGough (2009). This can be the result of a feedback-type relation between inflation and output gap. Clearly, increased consumption put pressure on prices and given that this pressure breaks some threshold, the prices fell into the long-term indeterminacy.

As Figure 2 demonstrates, with no output-gap or financial targeting the determinacy is guaranteed by the basic version of the Taylor principle, that is, $\rho_\pi > 1$. The effects from targeting an extra variable are negligible, however. Since the level of production is inversely linked to the marginal banking cost, clearly the indeterminacy effects resulting from too aggressive output-gap targeting can be fully offset by targeting financial variables but with the opposite sign. If we restrict that $\rho_\chi > 0$ there is no difference in determinacy properties between the standard and banking-sector-augmented Taylor rules and the snapshots presented in Figure 2 are parallel to moving across the vertical axis in Figure 1.

The analysis demonstrates, however, possible threats resulting from Taylor rule misspecification. In a situation when a policy maker puts a negative weight on financial aggregates, or to put it differently she loosens the rate when the banking is inefficient, the system might end up in the indeterminacy of order 3, unseen in the standard rule. In other words, if a policy maker reacts to financial ineffectiveness by nominal interest rate cuts, she may drive the prices out of the equilibrium. From the macro-prudential point of view, it is therefore crucial to select an appropriate mix of targeting weights, if one decides to target financial aggregates. A simple rule of thumb which would guarantee determinacy would be to target financial factors in the same magnitude (but with the opposite sign) as one targets the production sector. Increased production (higher output gap) reduces the financial intermediation costs and puts an upward pressure on the nominal interest rate. If this pressure is exacerbated by a large weight, the system ends up out of determinacy. A quick solution is therefore to reduce this pressure with a negative weight on the financial aggregates.

4. Monetary Rules in Heterogeneous Environment

So far, we assumed that all the agents are the same and each of them faces the same optimization problem. Let us now consider what happens in the environment with heterogeneous agents. Contrary to the standard representative agent framework, we allow a part $(1-\gamma)$ of agents to be boundedly rational in forming their expectations.[7] In other words, we assume that a constant proportion of agents is uniformed or

[7] Throughout this chapter we use the term "rational" to refer to forward-looking whereas "boundedly rational" to express backward-looking expectations.

unable to form rational expectations. This implies that we may divide our continuum of farmers into two groups: those with rational expectations (E^{RE}) producing good $j \in [0, \gamma]$ and those with boundedly rational expectations (E^{BRE}) producing good $j \in [\gamma, 1]$. By rational agents we mean forward-looking fundamentalists who try to analyze the economy and form their expectations accordingly. Boundedly rational agents are unable to perfectly predict the future and use simple backward-looking heuristics instead.

To be able to aggregate the results over both groups, we follow the methodology proposed by Branch and McGough (2009) and we impose similar seven axioms on expectation operators:

1. expectations operators fix observables,
2. if z is a forecasted variable and has a steady state, then $E^{\mathrm{RE}}\bar{z} = E^{\mathrm{BRE}}\bar{z} = \bar{z}$,
3. expectations operators are linear,
4. if for all $k \geq 0$, z_{t+k} and $\sum_{k=0}^{\infty} \beta^{t+k} z_{t+k}$ are forecasted variables then $E_t^{\tau}\left(\sum_{k=0}^{\infty} \beta^{t+k} z_{t+k}\right) = \sum_{k=0}^{\infty} \beta^{t+k} E_t^{\tau} z_{t+k}$ for $\tau \in \{\mathrm{RE}, \mathrm{BRE}\}$,
5. expectation operators satisfy the law of iterative expectations,
6. if z is a forecasted variable at time t and time $t+k$ then $E_t^{\tau} E_{t+k}^{\tau'} z_{t+k} = E_t^{\tau} z_{t+k}$ for $\tau \neq \tau'$,
7. all agents have common expectations on expected differences in limiting wealth and marginal banking cost.

Our contribution to the original methodology comprises axiom 7, which describes the limiting behavior of the expectation operators. Since we add the banking sector to the model, we have to include it also in the expectation formation. Branch and McGough (2009) assume that both types of agents have common expectation on their limiting wealth. It allows to represent the aggregate expectations operator as a weighted average of group expectations. Otherwise, there is an extra term on the limiting behavior of expectations that complicates the dynamics (see Equation (B.7)). A similar pattern might be observed when aggregating the banking sector (Equation (B.15)). The aggregate dynamics of the system is therefore influenced by how agents predict the banking sector behaves over the infinite horizon.

Axiom 7 might be viewed as an agreement among all agents that in the far future their banking sectors will be equivalent or will at least generate the same marginal costs. From the macroeconomic perspective, one may think of it as if both groups of agents were trying to reach the banking sector technological frontier. Since there is a common technology, both types of agents should be heading toward the same frontier eventually, satisfying axiom 7.

Proposition 2. *In the presence of fraction* $(1-\gamma)$ *of boundedly rational agents, if agents' expectations satisfy axioms 1–7 then the model from Equations (7), (11), and (13) can be rewritten as*

$$x_t = \overline{E}_t x_{t+1} + \left(\frac{1-rr}{V}\right)\overline{E}_t\tilde{\chi}_{t+}1 - \left(\frac{1-rr}{V}+1\right)\tilde{\chi}_t - \left[\hat{r}_t^{\mathrm{IB}} - \overline{E}_t\pi_{t+1}\right] + u_t, \tag{23}$$

$$\pi_t = \beta\overline{E}_t\pi_{t+1} + \kappa x_t, \tag{24}$$

$$\left(\upsilon + \frac{1-rr}{V}\right)\tilde{\chi}_t = \frac{1-rr}{V}\overline{E}_t\tilde{\chi}_{t+1} - \left(\overline{E}_t x_{t+1} - x_t\right), \tag{25}$$

where $\overline{E}_t = \gamma E_t^{\mathrm{RE}} + (1-\gamma)E_t^{\mathrm{BRE}}$.

The proof of Proposition 2 can be found in Appendix B.

4.1. Performance of the Monetary Rules

Throughout the model, we assume that the economy consists of two types of agents that are homogeneous within each group. The first type of agents, $i=\mathrm{RE}$, are those who form rational expectations. We abstract here from the standard understanding of rationality, where agents have full knowledge and capacities to perfectly predict the future. Instead, we rather view them as being forward-looking fundamentalists, who collect information and form their expectations accordingly. They are not aware of the presence of the other type of agents so that they form their expectations as if everybody in the economy was rational in forming the expectations (Branch & McGough, 2009).

The second type of agents is not able to form rational expectations and use simple backward-looking heuristics instead to predict the future. Following Evans and Honkapohja (2001) we assume them to have adaptive expectations of the form

$$E_t^{\mathrm{BRE}} z_{t+1} = \mu^2 z_{t-1}, \tag{26}$$

where z is either x, π, or $\tilde{\chi}$. Parameter $\mu > 0$ describes the magnitude and the direction of the expectations. If $\mu > 1$, the influence of the past is being extrapolated to the future so that we would call those expectations extrapolative. On the other hand, when $\mu < 1$, this influence disappears over time and we would call those expectations adaptive.[8] When $\mu = 1$, the boundedly rational agents form naive expectations (Evans & Honkapohja, 2001). For simplicity of calculations and clarity of presentation we assume that parameter μ is the same across variables. Nevertheless, the reasoning and the main results hold as long as all the variables are forecasted by the same type of rule (extrapolative or adaptive), however, the magnitude of determinacy/indeterminacy regions will shift in the directions of the variables with the strongest effects.

Given the expectation operators for both groups of agents, we may rewrite the aggregate expectations as

$$\overline{E}_t z_{t+1} = \gamma E_t^{\mathrm{RE}} z_{t+1} + (1-\gamma)\mu^2 z_{t-1}, \tag{27}$$

with z being either x, π, or $\tilde{\chi}$.

In the analysis we rely on the same Taylor rules' specifications as in the homogeneous economy. This allows us to rewrite the complete model in the matrix form

$$\begin{pmatrix} B & 0 \\ 0 & I_3 \end{pmatrix} \begin{pmatrix} y_{t+1} \\ y_t \end{pmatrix} = \begin{pmatrix} F & -C \\ I_3 & 0 \end{pmatrix} \begin{pmatrix} y_t \\ y_{t-1} \end{pmatrix} + \begin{pmatrix} \varepsilon_t \\ 0 \end{pmatrix}, \tag{28}$$

where $y = (x, \pi, \tilde{\chi})'$, $\varepsilon = (u, 0, 0)$ is a vector of exogenous shocks and B, F, and C are the coefficient matrices described in detail in Appendix C.

The determinacy properties are studied for extrapolative and adaptive expectations separately. For the former, the μ parameter is set to 1.1 and for the latter to 0.9 (Branch & McGough, 2009). For clarity purposes we, for the standard Taylor rule we focus, show the full range of ρ_x and ρ_π parameters for $\gamma \in \{1, 0.99, 0.9, 0.8\}$. For the augmented Taylor rule we show the full ranges of ρ_χ and ρ_π parameters for different values of the ρ_x and γ fixed at 0.8. The ranges for policy parameters correspond to the setting with fully rational agents. The results are presented in Figures 3 and 4.

For the standard Taylor rule we firstly observe a "rotating" behavior of the system (Figure 3) when we vary the γ fraction of rational agents. With adaptive expectations the system rotates counterclockwise so that the determinacy area increases. With extrapolative expectations the system rotates clockwise decreasing the determinacy area, similarly to Branch and McGough (2009).

[8] In the literature, adaptive expectations are being recognized as the whole group of operators of the form similar to Equation (4). However, for clarity purposes, we distinguish here between extrapolative and adaptive expectations when $\mu > 1$ and $\mu < 1$, respectively.

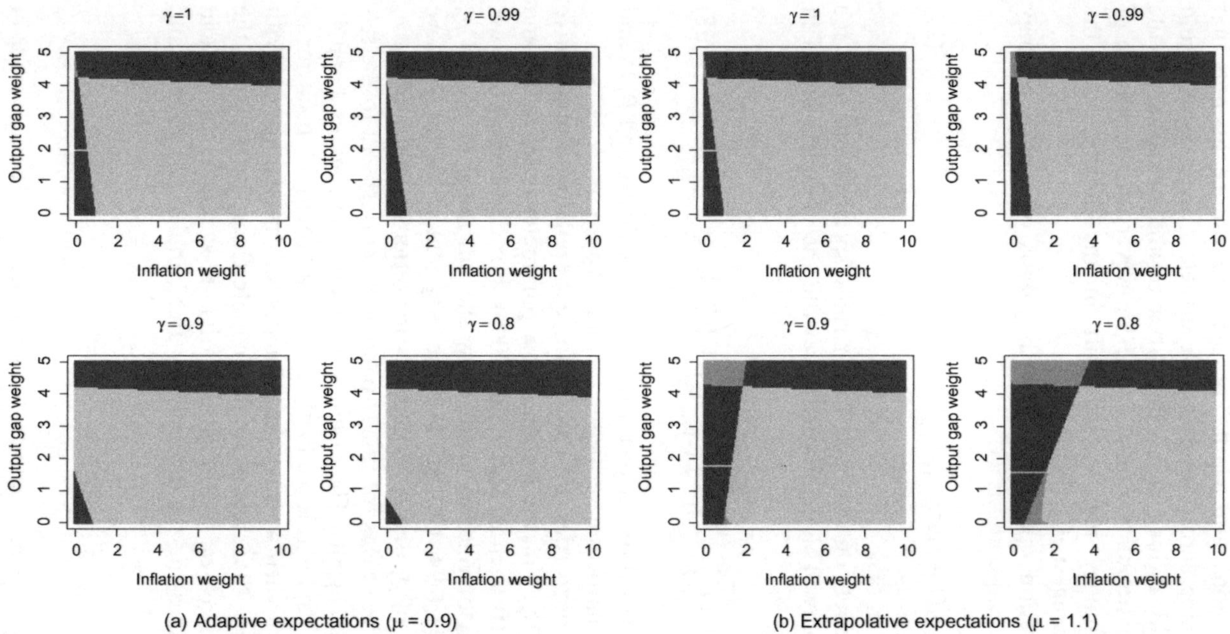

Figure 3: Determinacy Properties of the System's Equilibrium for the Standard Taylor Rule (Equation (17)) in a Presence of $1-\gamma$ Fraction of Boundedly Rational Agents. Part (a) Refers to Adaptive Expectations and (b) to Extrapolative Expectations. Light Gray Color Describes Determinacy, Dark Gray Order 1 Indeterminacy and Mid Gray Order 2 Indeterminacy.

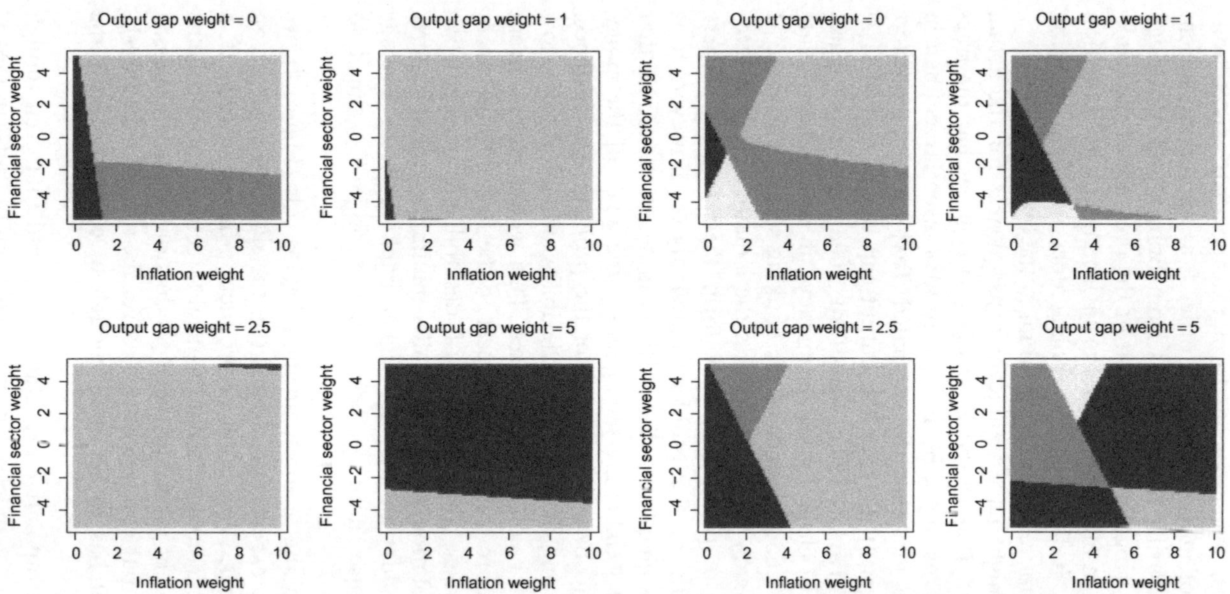

(a) Adaptive expectations (μ = 0.9) (b) Extrapolative expectations (μ = 1.1)

Figure 4: Determinacy Properties of the System's Equilibrium for the Augmented Taylor Rule (Equation (18)) in a Presence of 0.2 Fraction of Boundedly Rational Agents. Part (a) Refers to Adaptive Expectations and (b) to Extrapolative Expectations. Light Gray Color Describes Determinacy, Dark Gray Order 1 Indeterminacy, Mid Gray Order 2 Indeterminacy and White Order 3 Indeterminacy.

Secondly, the relative location of the determinacy and indeterminacy areas is preserved when we decrease the fraction of rational agents in a case of adaptive expectations. When agents form extrapolative expectations ($\mu = 1.1$), a new region of indeterminacy of order 2 arises for too lenient inflation targeting. Comparing to the results from Branch and McGough (2009), we find that this irregularity is a result of the presence of the banking sector in our model. In other words, in the environment with a fraction of extrapolative agents, if the monetary policy does not fight inflation sufficiently well, it may not reach the equilibrium in the long run.

In fact this pattern might have significant consequences for the actual monetary policy conduct. Pfajfar and Zakelj (2011) suggest that the fraction of extrapolative agents might be as high as 30%, even larger than in our analysis. Given the fact that the estimated Taylor rule parameters vary usually in the region of (0,1) for the output-gap weight and of (1,2) for the inflation weight (Taylor, 1999; Woodford, 2003), this may suggest that the system is very close to indeterminacy, if not indeterminate already, which arises as a consequence of the banking sector. Therefore, it seems vital for the monetary policy to address the issue of agents' heterogeneity and investigate in detail how they form their forecasts. There could be many solutions to the problem raised above, however, it is beyond the scope of this chapter to discuss them in detail. Assuming that the inflation and output weights are set to satisfy the goals of the monetary policy, there seem to be still ways out of the problem. For instance, one may think of increasing the clarity and flexibility of capital, somehow reducing its inferiority for collateral purposes. This would make current marginal banking cost more robust with respect to the future disturbances and thereof could decrease the influence of destabilizing extrapolative expectations. Another solution would be smaller minimum capital requirement, however, this could translate into higher banking sector leverage and eventually may cause more problems than it originally aimed to solve.

If we look at the banking-sector-augmented Taylor rule (Figure 4), we see that for the adaptive expectations (panel (a)) the situation is largely in line with previous findings. As a result of production-financial tradeoff, a policy maker can benefit from additional financial targeting. Those benefits are however fully dependent on the financial-production linkages discussed before, so that as the output-gap weight raises over the determinacy threshold, the financial weight has to be small enough to compensate for the production disturbances.

In the model with extrapolative expectations we find that even though financial targeting offsets the indeterminacy effects from output-gap targeting, it does not offset the inflation indeterminacy. Looking at panel (b) from Figure 4, for no output-gap targeting we see that the determinacy comes from a certain minimal threshold for inflation weight. If a policy maker increases the output-gap weight this effect is preserved, however by balancing inflation and financial weights it is now possible to reach determinacy even for aggressive output-gap targeting. Interestingly, financial targeting alone does not offer a clear-cut solution for the price indeterminacy arising from the presence of the banking sector.

There are therefore three main lessons to be drawn from this analysis. Firstly, in an environment with fully rational agents extra financial targeting in the Taylor rule does not bring clear-cut determinacy effects. This results mostly from the financial-production link entailed in the economy. Since financial aggregates affect inflation only through the production channel, a policy maker cannot simply benefit by targeting banking-sector aggregates. Instead, financial targeting serves as a compensation for the output-gap targeting, offering determinacy when the standard Taylor rule was lost. Secondly, we see that the presence of boundedly rational agents changes the determinacy structure of the economy. The determinacy region can either increase or decrease, depending on whether the heuristics used are adaptive or extrapolative. We find that the augmented Taylor rule does not serve as a clear-cut solution in such an environment either. Nevertheless, similarly to the standard Taylor rule, a proper mix of financial, output-gap and inflation weight can however lead to a determinate equilibrium. Thirdly, we see the threats of improper financial targeting. In a situation when a policy maker has pre-specified output-gap- and inflation targeting, an extra targeting variable can cause an extra indeterminacy problem.

5. Conclusions and Discussion

In this chapter we derived a workhorse model for monetary policy analysis which takes into account a presence of the banking sector. We then relaxed the assumption of the representative agent structure and investigated the determinacy effects of the monetary policy driven by the standard and banking-sector-augmented Taylor rules.

There are a couple of main observations. For the standard Taylor rule, the results suggest that the presence of a banking sector changes the determinacy structure of the equilibrium. Given that agents form adaptive expectations, the determinacy structure rotates counterclockwise, so that more lenient output-gap and inflation targeting still guarantees determinacy. The problem arises when backward-looking agents extrapolate the past performance over their future forecasts. The presence of the banking sector brings additional indeterminacy area for lower inflation-targeting parameter. In other words, in the environment with a fraction of extrapolative agents, if the monetary policy does not fight inflation sufficiently well, it may not reach the equilibrium in the long run.

We find that the benefits from extra financial targeting are limited. In an environment with fully rational agents, it compensates improper output-gap targeting. Since the level of production is inversely linked to the marginal banking cost, the indeterminacy effects resulting from too aggressive output-gap targeting can be fully offset by targeting financial variables but with the opposite sign. Financial targeting alone does not offer a clear-cut solution for the price indeterminacy arising from the presence of the banking sector in an environment with extrapolative expectations.

The analysis demonstrates possible threats resulting from Taylor rule misspecification. A determinate mix of output-gap and inflation weights can turn indeterminate if compensated by too extreme financial targeting. This result does not depend on the presence of boundedly rational agents and is rather a result of financial-production link.

In a discussion on the future of monetary rules one should bear in mind not only possible benefits of a new rule, but also its threats. McCallum (1987) points out that because of difficulties in economic measurement, a policy maker should focus on aggregates of the highest measurement quality and which might be directly controlled. Clearly, financial variables raise a number of possible measurement imperfections. This study advocates that there might be some gains from extra financial targeting, however, they come at a price of possible indeterminacy, if the weights are misspecified. Nevertheless, more study is needed in order to get an overall picture of the performance of the augmented Taylor rules. A comparison of two types of rules in a more dynamic setting, like in Branch and McGough (2010), is a natural continuation of this research.

References

Adrian, T., & Liang, N. (2014). Monetary policy, financial conditions and financial stability. *FED New York Staff Reports*, pp. 1–35.

Assenza, T., Heemeijer, P., Hommes, C., & Massaro, D. (2011). *Individual expectations and aggregate macro behavior*. CeNDEF Working Paper 11-01, University of Amsterdam.

Bekaert, G., & Hoerova, M. (2013). *The VIX, the variance premium and stock market volatility*. NBER Working Papers 18995, National Bureau of Economic Research, Inc.

Benchimol, J., & Fourans, A. (2012). Money and risk in a {DSGE} framework: A Bayesian application to the Eurozone. *Journal of Macroeconomics*, *34*, 95–111.

Bernanke, B. S., & Gertler, M. (1989). Agency costs, net worth, and business fluctuations. *The American Economic Review*, *79*, 14–31.

Bernanke, B. S., Gertler, M., & Gilchrist, S. (1999). The financial accelerator in a quantitative business cycle framework. In J. B. Taylor & M. Woodford (Eds.), *Handbook of macroeconomics* (pp. 1341–1393). New York, NY: Elsevier.

Blanchard, O. J., & Kahn, C. M. (1980). The solution of linear difference models under rational expectations. *Econometrica*, *48*, 1305–1311.

Branch, W. A. (2004). The theory of rationally heterogeneous expectations: Evidence from survey data on inflation expectations. *The Economic Journal*, *114*, 592–621.

Branch, W. A., & McGough, B. (2009). A new Keynesian model with heterogeneous expectations. *Journal of Economic Dynamics and Control*, *33*, 1036–1051.

Branch, W. A., & McGough, B. (2010). Dynamic predictor selection in a new Keynesian model with heterogeneous expectations. *Journal of Economic Dynamics and Control*, *34*, 1492–1508.

Calvo, G. A. (1983). Staggered prices in a utility-maximizing framework. *Journal of Monetary Economics*, *12*, 383–398.

Carroll, C. D. (2003). Macroeconomic expectations of households and professional forecasters. *Quarterly Journal of Economics*, *118*, 269–298.

Casares, M., & Poutineau, J.-C. (2010). Short-run and long-run effects of banking in a new Keynesian model. *The B.E. Journal of Macroeconomics*, *11*, 1–34.

Christoffel, K., Coenen, G., & Warne, A. (2010). *Forecasting with DSGE models*. Working Paper 1185, European Central Bank.

Clarida, R., Gali, J., & Gentler, M. (2000). Monetary policy rules and macroeconomic stability: Evidence and some theory. *Quarterly Journal of Economics*, *115*, 147–180.

Dixit, A. K., & Stiglitz, J. E. (1977). Monopolistic competition and optimum product diversity. *The American Economic Review*, *67*, 297–308.

Edge, R. M., & Gürkaynak, R. S. (2010). *How useful are estimated DSGE model forecasts for central bankers?* Discussion Paper 8158, Centre for Economic Policy Research.

Evans, G. W., & Honkapohja, S. (2001). *Learning and expectations in macroeconomics*. Princeton, NJ: Princeton University Press.

Evans, G. W., & McGough, B. (2005). Monetary policy, indeterminacy and learning. *Journal of Economic Dynamics and Control*, *29*, 1809–1840.

Frydman, R., & Goldberg, M. D. (2007). *Imperfect knowledge economics: Exchange rates and risk*. Princeton, NJ: Princeton University Press.

Gambacorta, L., & Signoretti, F. M. (2014). Should monetary policy lean against the wind? *Journal of Economic Dynamics and Control*, 43, 146–174.

Gilchrist, S., & Zakrajek, E. (2011). Monetary policy and credit supply shocks. *IMF Economic Review*, *59*, 195–232.

Gilchrist, S., & Zakrajek, E. (2012). Credit supply shocks and economic activity in a financial accelerator model. In A. Blinder, A. Lo, & R. Solow (Eds.), *Rethinking the financial crisis*. New York: Zakrajsek.

Goodfriend, M. (2005). Narrow money, broad money, and the transmission of monetary policy. In J. Faust, A. Orphanides, & A. Reifschneider (Eds.), *Models and monetary policy: Research in the tradition of Dale Henderson, Richard Porter, and Peter Tinsley*. Washington, DC: Board of Governors of the Federal Reserve System.

Goodfriend, M., & McCallum, B. T. (2007). Banking and interest rates in monetary policy analysis: A quantitative exploration. *Journal of Monetary Economics*, *54*, 1480–1507.

Goodhart, C., Sunirand, P., & Tsomocos, D. (2011). The optimal monetary instrument for prudential purposes. *Journal of Financial Stability*, *7*, 70–77.

Grammatikos, T., & Vermeulen, R. (2012). Transmission of the financial and sovereign debt crises to the EMU: Stock prices, CDS spreads and exchange rates. *Journal of International Money and Finance*, *31*, 517–533.

Henderson, D. W., & McKibbin, W. J. (1993). A comparison of some basic monetary policy regimes for open economies: Implications of different degrees of instrument adjustment and wage persistence. *Carnegie-Rochester Conference Series on Public Policy*, *39*, 221–317.

Hommes, C. (2011). The heterogeneous expectations hypothesis: Some evidence from the lab. *Journal of Economic Dynamics and Control*, *35*, 1–24.

Hommes, C. (2013). *Behavioral rationality and heterogeneous expectations in complex economic systems*. Cambridge: Cambridge University Press.

Hommes, C., Sonnemans, J., Tuinstra, J., & van de Velde, H. (2005). Coordination of expectations in asset pricing experiments. *Review of Financial Studies*, *18*, 955–980.

Kiyotaki, N., & Moore, J. (1997). Credit cycles. *The Journal of Political Economy*, *105*, 211–248.

Levine, R. (1997). Financial development and economic growth views and agenda. *Journal of Economic Literature*, *35*, 688–726.

Mankiw, N. G., & Reis, R. (2007). Sticky prices in general equilibrium. *Journal of European Economic Association*, *5*, 603–613.

Mankiw, N. G., Reis, R., & Wolfers, J. (2003). Disagreement about inflation expectations. In M. Gertler & K. Rogoff (Eds.), *NBER macroeconomics annual* (pp. 209–248). Cambridge: MIT Press, December 2002.

Massaro, D. (2013). Heterogeneous expectations in monetary DSGE models. *Journal of Economic Dynamics and Control*, *37*, 680–692.

McCallum, B. T. (1987). The case for rules in the conduct of monetary policy: A concrete example. *Economic Review*, September/October, 10–18.

McCallum, B. T. (1988). Robustness properties of a rule for monetary policy. *Carnegie-Rochester Conference Series on Public Policy*, *29*, 173–203.

McCallum, B. T. (1993). *Specification and analysis of a monetary policy rule for Japan*. NBER Working Papers 4449, National Bureau of Economic Research, Inc.

McCallum, B. T. (2000). *Alternative monetary policy rules: A comparison with historical settings for the United States, the United Kingdom, and Japan*. NBER Working Papers 7725, National Bureau of Economic Research, Inc.

Pfajfar, D., & Zakelj, B. (2011). *Inflation expectations and monetary policy design: Evidence from the laboratory*. CentER Working Paper 2011-091, Tilburg University.

Rotemberg, J. J., & Woodford, M. (1997). An optimization based econometric framework for the evaluation of monetary policy. *NBER Macroeconomics Annual*, *12*, 297–346.

Shi, S. (1999). Search, inflation and capital accumulation. *Journal of Monetary Economics*, *44*, 81–103.

Taylor, J. B. (1993). Discretion versus policy rules in practice. *Carnegie-Rochester Conference Series on Public Policy*, *39*, 195–214.

Taylor, J. B. (1999). A historical analysis of monetary policy rules. In *Monetary policy rules*. Cambridge: National Bureau of Economic Research, Inc.

Tovar, C. (2008). *DSGE models and central banks* Working Paper 258, Bank for International Settlements.

Walsh, C. E. (2010). *Monetary theory and policy* (3rd ed.). Cambridge/London: MIT Press.

Wolski, M. (2013). *Monetary policy, banking and heterogeneous expectations*. Working Paper 136, National Bank of Poland.

Woodford, M. (1994). Determinacy of equilibrium under alternative policy regimes. *Economic Theory*, *4*, 323–326.

Woodford, M. (2003). *Interest and prices*. Princeton, NJ: Princeton University Press.

Appendix A: Baseline Derivation

The utility of a farmer is defined as a weighted average of her consumption and leisure and takes the form

$$U^i(C_t^i, n_t^i, m_t^i) = \phi \log(C_t^i) + (1 - \phi) \log(1 - n_t^i - m_t^i), \quad \text{(A.1)}$$

where ϕ is the relative preference weight on consumption and t is the time subscript. C_t^i represents a composite consumption good and is of the standard Constant Elasticity of Substitution (CES) form, as in Dixit and Stiglitz (1977)

$$C_t^i = \left(\int_0^1 c_{jt}^{\frac{\theta-1}{\theta}} \mathrm{d}j \right)^{\frac{\theta}{\theta-1}}, \quad \text{(A.2)}$$

with θ being the elasticity of substitution.

The farmer's decision problem is to maximize her discounted expected utility subject to the budget and technology constraints. Assuming a cashless limit (Branch & McGough, 2009; Woodford, 2003), we may define the former in real terms as

$$w_t(n_t^i + m_t^i) + q_t(1 - \delta)K_t^i + \frac{Y_t^i P_t^i}{P_t^A} + \frac{B_t^i}{P_t^A} = w_t(n_t^{i,d} + m_t^{i,d}) + C_t^i + q_t K_{t+1}^i + \frac{B_{t+1}}{P_t^A\left(1 + r_t^B\right)}, \quad \text{(A.3)}$$

where K_t^i is capital level with q_t being its real price and δ the depreciation rate, w_t is the real wage and B_t^i are the nominal bond holdings with the nominal interest equal r_t^B. Y_t^i is the production level, P^i is the price of the individual good, and P_t^A is the aggregate price level, as in the Dixit-Stiglitz setup. Superscript d denotes the amount of labor demanded by a given farmer. Superscript i and subscript t relate to the agent and time dimensions, respectively.

Contrary to the standard new Keynesian framework, there is a capital market in the model. Its role is twofold. Firstly, capital serves as a production factor in the farmers' technology. Secondly, it is used as a collateral in the banking sector to produce loans. For simplicity, it is assumed that the aggregate capital stock is on a steady state growth path (Goodfriend & McCallum, 2007). What is important is that farmers are allowed to trade it so that its market price q_t may fluctuate.

The production constraint requires that

$$Y_t^i = K_t^{i\eta}\left(e^{A1_t} n_t^{i,d}\right)^{1-\eta}, \quad \text{(A.4)}$$

where $A1_t$ is an aggregate productivity disturbance and η is the capital elasticity measure.

A novelty in the model is the presence of the banking sector. Its main role is to facilitate transactions between production and consumption sides of the economy. Since the medium of exchange is the crucial role of the monetary policy analysis, the model does not distinguish between transaction balances and time deposits at the banks. In this simple form, it implies that the farmer's consumption in each period has to be rigidly related to the deposits held at a bank (Goodfriend & McCallum, 2007). In other words, in each period, the level of consumption (C_t^i) has to be covered by some constant fraction of the real deposits (VD_t^i/P_t^A). Since each bank has to hold a given level of reserves at the central bank (rr), the nominal amount of loans it may produce from deposits held by farmer i is constrained by $L_t^i = (1-rr)D_t^i$. At the same time, the real loan production depends on the collateral and loan monitoring, and is assumed to be of a Cobb-Douglas form

$$\frac{L_t^i}{P_t^A} = F\left(\frac{B_{t+1}^i}{P_t^A(1+r_t^B)} + \upsilon q_t K_{t+1}^i\right)^{\alpha} \left(e^{A2_t} m_t^{i,d}\right)^{1-\alpha}. \tag{A.5}$$

The loan monitoring is assumed to be proportional to the labor supplied to the banking sector by farmer i and $A2_t$ is the productivity disturbance similar to the one in the production sector. Since capital stock require a substantial monitoring effort to confirm its physical condition, its inferiority to bonds for collateral purposes is expressed by υ (Goodfriend & McCallum, 2007).

The complete intertemporal farmers's maximization problem (with a presence of the banking sector) may be written as

$$\max_{n_t^i, m_t^i, n_t^{i,d}, m_t^{i,d}, P_t^i, K_{t+1}^i, B_{t+1}^i} E_t^i \sum_{k=0}^{\infty} \beta^k \left[\phi \log(C_{t+k}^i) + (1-\phi)\log\left(1 - n_{t+k}^i - m_{t+k}^i\right)\right]. \tag{A.6}$$

subject to the budget constraint (Equation (A.3)) and production constraint (Equation (A.4)).

Before solving the optimization problem, from Equation (A.5) we know that

$$C_t^i = \frac{VF}{1-rr}\left(b_{t+1}^i + \upsilon q_t K_{t+1}^i\right)^{\alpha} \left(e^{A2_t} m_t^{i,d}\right)^{1-\alpha}, \tag{A.7}$$

where $b_{t+1}^i = B_{t+1}^i/(P_t^A(1+r_t^B))$. Additionally, by imposing market clearing we know that the good produced by farmer i is equal to its demand

$$Y_t^i = \left(\frac{P_t^i}{P_t^A}\right)^{-\theta} C_t^A, \tag{A.8}$$

where C_t^A is the aggregate consumption level that each individual takes as given.

Let the Lagrange multipliers be λ_t and ξ_t for the budget and production constraints, respectively. By including Equations (A.7) and (A.8) into the maximization problem and assuming market symmetry (Goodfriend & McCallum, 2007), the first order conditions provide

$$\frac{-(1-\phi)}{1-n_t^i-m_t^i} + \lambda_t^i w_t = 0, \tag{A.9}$$

$$-\lambda_t^i w_t + \xi_t^i e^{A1_t}(1-\eta)\left(\frac{K_t^i}{e^{A1_t} n_t^i}\right)^{\eta} = 0, \tag{A.10}$$

$$\left(\frac{\phi}{C_t^i} - \lambda_t^i\right)\frac{C_t^i(1-\alpha)}{m_t^i} - \lambda_t^i w_t = 0, \tag{A.11}$$

$$C_t^A\left(\frac{P_t^i}{P_t^A}\right)^{-\theta}\left(\frac{(1-\theta)\lambda_t^i}{P_t^A} + \frac{\theta\xi_t^i}{P_t^i}\right) = 0, \tag{A.12}$$

$$\begin{aligned}\left(\frac{\phi}{C_t^i\lambda_t} - 1\right)\Omega_t^i \upsilon q_t - q_t + \beta(1-\delta)E_t^i\left(\frac{\lambda_{t+1}^i}{\lambda_t^i} q_{t+1}\right)\\ + \beta\eta E_t^i\left(\frac{\xi_{t+1}^i}{\lambda_t^i}\left(\frac{e^{A1_{t+1}} n_{t+1}^i}{K_{t+1}^i}\right)^{1-\eta}\right) = 0,\end{aligned} \tag{A.13}$$

$$\left(\frac{\phi}{C_t^i\lambda_t^i} - 1\right)\Omega_t^i - 1 + \beta E_t^i\left(\frac{\lambda_{t+1}^i}{\lambda_t^i}\frac{P_t^A}{P_{t+1}^A}\left(1 + r_t^B\right)\right) = 0, \tag{A.14}$$

where Ω_t^i is the partial derivative of the deposit constraint $C_t^i = \frac{VL_t^i}{(1-rr)P_t^A}$ with respect to collateral

$$\Omega_t^i = \frac{\alpha C_t^i}{b_{t+1}^i + \upsilon q_t K_{t+1}^i}. \tag{A.15}$$

Appendix B: The Influence of Heterogeneous Agents

Throughout the following derivation, we assume that each agent belongs to one of the two groups, that is, $i=\tau\in\{\mathrm{RE},\mathrm{BRE}\}$. By superscript A we will refer to the aggregate values.

B.1 The Heterogeneous IS Curve

Let us first introduce a benevolent financial institution that helps farmers in hedging the risk associated with the Calvo lottery (Mankiw & Reis, 2007; Shi, 1999). In each period it collects all the income from the market and then redistribute it evenly across farmers. Given this property and assuming cashless limit, the agents' budget constraint becomes

$$w_t\left(n_t^i+m_t^i\right)+q_t(1-\delta)K_t^i+\frac{Y_t^iP_t^i}{P_t^A}+\frac{B_t^i}{P_t^A}+I_{r,t}^i=w_t\left(n_t^{i,d}+m_t^{i,d}\right)+C_t^i+q_tK_{t+1}^i$$
$$+\frac{B_{t+1}}{P_t^A\left(1+r_t^B\right)}+I_{p,t}^i, \qquad \text{(B.1)}$$

where $I_{r,t}^i$ and $I_{r,t}^i$ are the real receipts from and payments to the insurance agency. Each agent maximizes her expected utility over an infinite horizon, subject to Equation (B.1) instead of (Equation (A.3)).

We know that the average real income (denoted by Ψ_t^τ) and the average marginal banking cost χ_t^τ obtained by rational and boundedly rational agents are

$$\Psi_t^{\mathrm{RE}}=\frac{1}{\gamma P_t^A}\int_0^\gamma P_t^iY_t^i\mathrm{d}i \quad \text{and} \quad \Psi_t^{\mathrm{BRE}}=\frac{1}{(1-\gamma)P_t^A}\int_\gamma^1 P_t^iY_t^i\mathrm{d}i, \qquad \text{(B.2)}$$

$$\chi_t^{\mathrm{RE}}=\frac{1}{\gamma}\int_0^\gamma \chi_t^i\mathrm{d}i \quad \text{and} \quad \chi_t^{\mathrm{BRE}}=\frac{1}{1-\gamma}\int_\gamma^1 \chi_t^i\mathrm{d}i. \qquad \text{(B.3)}$$

From the above equations it is clear that we may view the aggregate production and aggregate real marginal banking cost as a weighted average of their components, that is, $Y_t^A=\gamma Y_t^{\mathrm{RE}}+(1-\gamma)Y_t^{\mathrm{BRE}}$ and $\chi_t^A=\gamma\chi_t^{\mathrm{RE}}+(1-\gamma)\chi_t^{\mathrm{BRE}}$.

Following Branch and McGough (2009), if an agent is of type τ, then her real receipts from and payments to the insurance agency are $I_{r,t}^i=\Psi_t^\tau$ and $I_{p,t}^i=Y_t^iP_t^i/P_t^A$. By market clearing and axiom A2 the steady states of consumption and production are equal at individual and group levels. By imposing market symmetry, the budget constraint (Equation (B.1)) yields

$$\hat{C}_t^\tau = \hat{\Psi}_t^\tau + \frac{B_t^\tau/P_t^A}{\overline{Y}_t^A} - \frac{B_{t+1}^\tau/(P_t^A(1+\overline{r}_t^B))}{\overline{Y}_t^A} + \frac{q_t(1-\delta)K^\tau}{\overline{Y}_t^A} - \frac{q_t K_{t+1}^\tau}{\overline{Y}_t^A}, \tag{B.4}$$

where the bars indicate the steady state levels. Bond and capital market clearing require that $\alpha B_t^{\text{RE}} = -(1-\alpha)B_t^{\text{BRE}}$ and $\alpha K_t^{\text{RE}} = -(1-\alpha)K_t^{\text{BRE}}$. After multiplying Equation (B.4) by γ for rational and by $(1-\gamma)$ for boundedly rational agents and summing up, we arrive at

$$\hat{Y}_t^A = \gamma\hat{\Psi}_t^{\text{RE}} + (1-\gamma)\hat{\Psi}_t^{\text{BRE}}. \tag{B.5}$$

From Equations (6), (B.3), and (B.4) we have

$$\hat{\Psi}_t^\tau = E_t^\tau \hat{\Psi}_{t+1}^\tau + \left(\frac{1-rr}{V}\right) E_t^\tau \tilde{\chi}_{t+1}^\tau - \left(\frac{1-rr}{V}+1\right)\tilde{\chi}_t^\tau - \left(\hat{r}_t^{\text{IB}} - E_t^\tau \pi_{t+1}\right). \tag{B.6}$$

Iterating this equation forward and substituting into Equation (B.5) we finally get

$$\begin{aligned}\hat{Y}_t^A = {} & \overline{E}_t \hat{Y}_{t+1}^A + \left(\frac{1-rr}{V}\right) \overline{E}_t \tilde{\chi}_{t+1}^A - \left(\frac{1-rr}{V}+1\right)\tilde{\chi}_t^A - \left(\hat{r}_t^{\text{IB}} - \overline{E}_t \pi_{t+1}\right) \\ & + \left(\gamma\hat{\Psi}_\infty^{\text{RE}} + (1-\gamma)\hat{\Psi}_\infty^{\text{BRE}}\right) - \overline{E}_t\left(\gamma\hat{\Psi}_\infty^{\text{RE}} + (1-\gamma)\hat{\Psi}_\infty^{\text{BRE}}\right),\end{aligned} \tag{B.7}$$

with $\overline{E}_t = \gamma E_t^{\text{RE}} + (1-\gamma)E_t^{\text{BRE}}$ and $\hat{\Psi}_\infty^\tau = \lim_{k\to\infty} E_t^\tau \hat{\Psi}_{t+k}^\tau$. In fact, Equation (B.7) is of exactly the same form as in Branch and McGough (2009) but with a banking sector present. Axiom 7 indicates that agents predict their limiting wealth identically, which makes

$$\left(\gamma\hat{\Psi}_\infty^{\text{RE}} + (1-\gamma)\hat{\Psi}_\infty^{\text{BRE}}\right) = \overline{E}_t\left(\gamma\hat{\Psi}_\infty^{\text{RE}} + (1-\gamma)\hat{\Psi}_\infty^{\text{BRE}}\right). \tag{B.8}$$

Subtracting the log deviations of the potential product from both sides, we finally arrive at the heterogeneous IS curve with a present banking sector

$$x_t = \overline{E}_t x_{t+1} + \left(\frac{1-rr}{V}\right) \overline{E}_t \tilde{\chi}_{t+1}^A - \left(\frac{1-rr}{V}+1\right)\tilde{\chi}_t^A - \left[\hat{r}_t^{\text{IB}} - \overline{E}_t \pi_{t+1}\right] + u_t, \tag{B.9}$$

where $x_t = \hat{Y}_t^A - \hat{Y}_t^{f,A}$ is the output-gap measure, the expectation operator is the weighted average of the group expectations $\overline{E}_t = \gamma E_t^{\text{RE}} + (1-\gamma)E_t^{\text{BRE}}$ and u_t is a disturbance term that depends only on exogenous productivity shocks.

B.2 The Heterogeneous Phillips Curve

It is important to note that when farmers may hedge against the Calvo risk their production level would be 0 in equilibrium as a result of the free-riding problem. Therefore, following Branch and McGough (2009), we assume that farmers make their pricing decisions as if there was no insuring agency.

Let us take the log approximation of Equation (9)

$$\log P_t^\tau - \log P_t^A = (1-\omega\beta)\hat{\varphi}_t^\tau + \omega\beta E_t^\tau \pi_{t+1} + \omega\beta E_t^\tau \log P_{t+1}^\tau / P_{t+1}^A. \quad \text{(B.10)}$$

Branch and McGough (2009) show that the Calvo lottery implies aggregate inflation to follow

$$\pi_t = \frac{1-\omega}{\omega}\left(\gamma \log P_t^{\mathrm{RE}}/P_t^A + (1-\gamma)\log P_t^{\mathrm{BRE}}/P_t^A\right). \quad \text{(B.11)}$$

As long as the pricing decisions are homogeneous within each group τ, by multiplying Equation (B.10) by γ for rational and by $(1-\gamma)$ for boundedly rational agents and adding up, after some algebra we arrive at the final aggregate heterogeneous Phillips curve

$$\pi_t = \beta \overline{E}_t \pi_{t+1} + \kappa \varphi_t^A, \quad \text{(B.12)}$$

where $\kappa = (1-\omega)(1-\beta\omega)/\omega$.

Finally, noting that the aggregate marginal production cost is the aggregate output-gap measure, the heterogeneous new Keynesian Phillips curve amended for the banking sector may be viewed as

$$\pi_t = \beta \overline{E}_t \pi_{t+1} + \kappa x_t, \quad \text{(B.13)}$$

where $\overline{E}_t = \gamma E_t^{\mathrm{RE}} + (1-\gamma)E_t^{\mathrm{BRE}}$.

B.3 The Heterogeneous Banking Sector Curve

Taking the steady state log deviations of Equation (12) and iterating forward we get for each group of agents

$$\tilde{\chi}_t^\tau = \left(\frac{1-rr}{V}\right)^{-1}\left[-\upsilon E_t^\tau \sum_{j=0}^{\infty} \tilde{\chi}_{t+j}^\tau + \left(\frac{1-rr}{V}\right)\tilde{\chi}_\infty^\tau - \left(x_\infty^\tau - x_t^\tau\right)\right], \quad \text{(B.14)}$$

where $\hat{\chi}_\infty^\tau = \lim_{k\to\infty} E_t^\tau \hat{\chi}_{t+k}^\tau$ and $x_\infty^\tau = \lim_{k\to\infty} E_t^\tau x_{t+k}^\tau$.

Given Equations (B.3) and (B.14), we get

$$\begin{aligned}
\tilde{\chi}_t^A &= \gamma\tilde{\chi}_t^{\mathrm{RE}} + (1-\gamma)\tilde{\chi}_t^{\mathrm{BRE}} \\
&= \left(\frac{1-rr}{V}\right)^{-1}\Bigg[-\upsilon\left(\gamma E_t^{\mathrm{RE}}\sum_{k=0}^{\infty}\tilde{\chi}_{t+k}^{\mathrm{RE}} + (1-\gamma)E_t^{\mathrm{BRE}}\sum_{k=0}^{\infty}\tilde{\chi}_{t+k}^{\mathrm{BRE}}\right) + x_t \\
&\quad + \left(\frac{1-rr}{V}\right)\left(\gamma\tilde{\chi}_\infty^{\mathrm{RE}} + (1-\gamma)\tilde{\chi}_\infty^{\mathrm{BRE}}\right) - \left(\gamma x_\infty^{\mathrm{RE}} + (1-\gamma)x_\infty^{\mathrm{BRE}}\right)\Bigg] \\
&= \overline{E}_t\tilde{\chi}_{t+1}^A - \frac{\upsilon V}{1-rr}\tilde{\chi}_t^A - \left(\frac{1-rr}{V}\right)^{-1}\left(\overline{E}_t x_{t+1} - x_t\right) \\
&\quad + \left[\left(\gamma\tilde{\chi}_\infty^{\mathrm{RE}} + (1-\gamma)\tilde{\chi}_\infty^{\mathrm{BRE}}\right) - \overline{E}_t\left(\gamma\tilde{\chi}_\infty^{\mathrm{RE}} + (1-\gamma)\tilde{\chi}_\infty^{\mathrm{BRE}}\right)\right] \\
&\quad - \left(\frac{1-rr}{V}\right)^{-1}\left[\left(\gamma x_\infty^{\mathrm{RE}} + (1-\gamma)x_\infty^{\mathrm{BRE}}\right) - \overline{E}_t\left(\gamma x_\infty^{\mathrm{RE}} + (1-\gamma)x_\infty^{\mathrm{BRE}}\right)\right].
\end{aligned} \tag{B.15}$$

The last two lines disappear due to Axiom 7, which gives

$$\left(\gamma\tilde{\chi}_\infty^{\mathrm{RE}} + (1-\gamma)\tilde{\chi}_\infty^{\mathrm{BRE}}\right) = \overline{E}_t\left(\gamma\tilde{\chi}_\infty^{\mathrm{RE}} + (1-\gamma)\tilde{\chi}_\infty^{\mathrm{BRE}}\right) \tag{B.16}$$

$$\left(\gamma x_\infty^{\mathrm{RE}} + (1-\gamma)x_\infty^{\mathrm{BRE}}\right) = \overline{E}_t\left(\gamma x_\infty^{\mathrm{RE}} + (1-\gamma)x_\infty^{\mathrm{BRE}}\right) \tag{B.17}$$

so that the final banking curve equation may be written as Equation (25).

Appendix C: Model Dynamics

The condensed model can be viewed as

$$\begin{pmatrix} B & 0 \\ 0 & I_3 \end{pmatrix} \begin{pmatrix} y_{t+1} \\ y_t \end{pmatrix} = \begin{pmatrix} F & -C \\ I_3 & 0 \end{pmatrix} \begin{pmatrix} y_t \\ y_{t-1} \end{pmatrix}, \tag{C.1}$$

where $y = (x, \pi, \tilde{\chi})'$ and

$$B = \begin{pmatrix} \gamma - \rho_x & \gamma - \rho_\pi & \dfrac{\gamma(1-rr)}{V}\left[-\rho_\chi\right] \\ 0 & \beta\gamma & 0 \\ -\gamma & 0 & \dfrac{\gamma(1-rr)}{V} \end{pmatrix}, \tag{C.2}$$

$$F = \begin{pmatrix} 1 & 0 & \dfrac{(1-rr)}{V} + 1 \\ -\kappa & 1 & 0 \\ -1 & 0 & \upsilon + \dfrac{(1-rr)}{V} \end{pmatrix}, \tag{C.3}$$

$$C = \begin{pmatrix} (1-\gamma)\mu^2 & (1-\gamma)\mu^2 & \dfrac{(1-\gamma)\mu^2(1-rr)}{V} \\ 0 & \beta(1-\gamma)\mu^2 & 0 \\ -(1-\gamma)\mu^2 & 0 & \dfrac{(1-\gamma)\mu^2(1-rr)}{V} \end{pmatrix}. \tag{C.4}$$

Here we also exploited the fact that the ρ_χ parameter appears only in the augmented Taylor rule. In the simple version it vanishes.

Chapter 11

The Taylor Rule, the Zero Lower Bound, and the Term Structure of Interest Rates

J. Huston McCulloch

Department of Economics (Emeritus), Ohio State University, Columbus, OH, USA; FAS Economics Department (Adjunct), New York University, New York, NY, USA, e-mail: mcculloch.2@osu.edu

Abstract

The Taylor Rule's Zero Lower Bound problem can be solved by pegging interest rates on longer-maturity loans than the 6 weeks implicit in the Fed's current operating procedures. However, the Fed's policy since 2008 of reducing the opportunity cost of excess reserves to zero (or even negative) has neutralized the stimulative effect of the Fed's low interest rate policy. Eliminating interest on excess reserves would restore the effectiveness of monetary policy, but would require promptly unwinding the Fed's "Quantatitve Easing" acquisitions.

It is argued that the Fed's reaction function should contain no pure inertial terms, and that the "output gap" as originally conceived by Taylor is a statistical illusion. Although the unemployment gap is statistically meaningful, it is not clear that it should be directly included in the Taylor Rule unless it serves as a proxy for the equilibrium real interest rate.

Keywords: Taylor Rule, Zero Lower Bound, term structure of interest rates

JEL Classifications: E52, E43, E58

1. The Zero Lower Bound Issue

The so-called Taylor Rule is an equation relating the Federal Reserve System's Federal Funds rate target i^* to anticipated inflation $E\pi$ and, in its

International Symposia in Economic Theory and Econometrics, Vol. 24
William A. Barnett and Fredj Jawadi (Editors)

ISSN: 1571-0386/doi: 10.1108/S1571-038620150000024023

original formulation, the estimated percentage deviation of real output from its trend, *ygap*. The "benchmark" version of the equation, with coefficients as estimated by Taylor (1993) on the basis of the Fed's behavior in the 1980s and early 1990s, is

$$i^* = 1.0 + 1.5E\pi + 0.5ygap.$$

There is widespread agreement among economists that weak (i.e., less than 100%) feedback from expected inflation to i^* was responsible for accelerating inflation prior to 1979, while strong (i.e., greater than 100%) feedback was responsible for bringing inflation down from double digits at the beginning of the 1980s to approximately 2% since 1990 (see, e.g., Clarida, Galí, & Gertler, 2000). The actual coefficients depend on the Fed's inflation target, on its estimate of the equilibrium real interest rate, and on how aggressively it wants to fight inflation and/or the output gap. Furthermore, the coefficients appear to have varied over time (Clarida et al., 2000; McCulloch, 2007). This note will use the above "benchmark" coefficients for the sake of illustration, with the understanding that the Fed may in fact choose to modify these coefficients. The output gap variable, discussed below, is problematic, but by definition averages out to zero, so that the long-run inflation implications of the Taylor Rule lie entirely in the first two terms.

If inflation has been running at the Fed's announced target of 2% and is expected to continue at this level, the above rule calls for a "normal" level of i^* of 4%. This will be neutral with respect to inflation if the equilibrium short-term real interest rate is 2%.[1] If inflation falls to say 0% and is expected from the time series evidence to stay there, the benchmark rule calls for an i^* of 1%, or 3% below its normal level of 4%. This implies a real rate of 1%, which is less than its assumed equilibrium level of 2%, and hence would put upward pressure on inflation, driving it back toward the Fed's announced target of +2%.

But if inflation falls to say −2% (i.e., 2% *de*flation) and is expected to stay there, the benchmark rule calls for an impossibly negative i^* of −2%. Because of the Zero Lower Bound (ZLB) on nominal interest rates, the lowest i^* can ordinarily go is 0%. This would imply a real rate of +2%, which would not be stimulative at all, and so would permit inflation to drift even lower. With any deeper expected deflation, the ZLB would actually lead to an even higher real rate and further *downward* pressure on inflation,

[1] The equilibrium real interest rate is that determined in the absence of a monetary disequilibrium by the supply and demand for saving, as in the "Loanable Funds Model" of Irving Fisher (1930/1974). This is equivalent to Knut Wicksell's "Natural Rate of Interest," as discussed by Friedman (1968).

which has led many economists to fear the possibility of an unstoppable deflationary spiral. This supposed ZLB threat has been used as a rationale for deliberately targeting a positive inflation rate in order to give the Fed some additional space to reduce nominal rates before hitting the ZLB, in spite of the Fed's legislative mandate to stabilize prices. In 2012, the Fed in fact announced its intention to target 2% inflation, in part for this very reason.

We will see that this fear is unwarranted. But first, let us consider how the Taylor Rule may be expected to operate when the ZLB is not binding.

2. The Taylor Rule When the ZLB Is Not Binding

Lowering the nominal interest rate i on loans of maturity m by Δi, while holding forward rates beyond m constant, reduces the cost of borrowing to any maturity beyond m by $m\Delta i$.[2] Holding the public's inflationary expectations constant, this creates a proportionate Excess Demand for Credit (command over current output), offset by an equal and opposite Excess Supply of Money, and generates proportionate inflationary pressure over and above expectations.[3] The opposite is true for an increase in interest rates.

The Federal Funds rate itself is overnight ($m = 1/365$), and so in itself has only negligible effect on the cost of credit or inflationary pressure. However, the Fed's Federal Open Market Committee (FOMC) only meets eight times a year, so that the effective m of the Fed's i^* is 1/8 year or about 6 weeks.[4] The Fed typically manipulates short-term rates through overnight loans to dealers via the repo market.[5] However, if dealers can count on a particular value of i^* continuing for 6 weeks, they can make a virtually

[2] If $i(m)$ is the continuously compounded nominal zero-coupon yield to maturity m, the discount factor $\delta(m) = \exp(-m\, i(m))$ is the current price of \$1 payable at maturity m, and $f(m) = -\mathrm{d}/\mathrm{d}m \log \delta(m) = i(m)+m\, i'(m)$ is the instantaneous forward interest rate at maturity m. Raising (or lowering) $i(m)$ by Δi while holding $f(m)$ unchanged for all $m > m_0$ will lower (or raise) $\log \delta(m)$ by $m_0\, \Delta i$ for all $m > m_0$.

[3] See McCulloch (2014).

[4] The FOMC has occasionally changed its Fed Funds target between regular meetings, via an emergency conference-call meeting, but such events are rare enough to ignore for present purposes.

[5] A repurchase agreement, or repo for short is in effect a short-term loan secured with Treasury securities. Legally, the effective lender or "seller" buys the security, and the same time agrees to buy it back in the near future at a slightly higher price, reflecting the effective interest rate. In practice, "triparty" repos are often used, in which a custodial bank is the legal owner of the collateral securities throughout.

riskless arbitrage profit by using 6-week Treasury bills as collateral for a series of overnight loans until the 6-week T-bill rate equals i^*. The Fed could achieve a very similar result without the intermediation of dealers by pegging the rate on T-bills maturing on or before the next FOMC meeting to i^*.[6] Since there is no reason for the credit premium on private loans to have changed, private loan rates will be similarly reduced, unless the Fed ends up holding a dominant fraction of all the maturing T-bills.

The direct effect of say a 100 basis point (1 percentage point) reduction in rates at even a 1/8 year maturity is still too subtle to create much inflationary pressure. However, if the market realizes this, it will recognize that conditions will most likely be similar to the present at the next FOMC meeting, and therefore that the FOMC will mostly likely choose a similar i^*. This will create speculative demand for longer-term Treasury securities, financed by further short-term borrowing from the Fed, until forward rates beyond m on Treasury debt, and therefore private debt, reflect the probable trajectory of i^*, as adjusted for the empirical term premium.[7] This speculative demand for short-term loans from the Fed will magnify the direct and arbitrage demand, and can greatly increase the inflationary pressure of the low interest rate policy.

So long as the market is confident that the Fed will continue to fight high inflation (or below target inflation) with continuing tight (or easy) interest rate policy until inflation is back on target, there is therefore no need for the Fed to use "forward guidance" by announcing in advance a specific future interest rate target trajectory. Doing so is in fact counterproductive, because it may lead the Fed to feel bound to retain its promised interest rate trajectory despite conditions that in all likelihood will have changed somewhat, one way or the other. It is sufficient for the market simply to expect the Fed to aggressively follow a policy that will stabilize inflation as well as may be expected under a Taylor-type rule, with hands untied by the past.

The Taylor Rule approach to monetary policy has the advantage over a money growth rule motivated by the Quantity Theory of Money that it does not rely on knowledge or stability of the demand for real money balances. At the same time, it has the disadvantage, even in the absence of the ZLB, that it relies instead on the knowledge and stability of

[6] Historically, maturing Treasury bills typically yield approximately 90% of the effective Federal Funds Rate. This is presumably due to their exemption from state and local income taxes. The Fed would therefore in practice target a T-bill rate about 10% below its Fed Funds target. In the text I have abstracted from this minor technicality.

[7] See, for example, McCulloch (1975).

the equilibrium real interest rate. In practice, neither is fully known or stable, so that the monetary policy maker's choice is between the less imperfect of two options.

3. The Taylor Rule When the ZLB is Binding

Now suppose that the ZLB on i^* is binding. To take our hypothetical example, suppose that experience and other variables would lead one to expect it to continue at –2%, so that the benchmark Taylor Rule calls for $i^* = -2\%$, or 6% below the "normal" nominal rate of 4%. However, the most it can lower i^* before hitting the ZLB is 4%, which would be only 2/3 of the desired stimulus. Nevertheless, it can still achieve the equivalent of a 6% reduction out to a 6-week maturity, simply by lowering rates to 0 (i.e., by 4% below normal) out to 9 weeks (3/2 of the 6-week meeting interval) instead.

Doing this with no direct disturbance to forward rates beyond 9 weeks would simply require the Open Market Desk to peg the interest rate on T-bills maturing within 9 weeks of the current FOMC meeting to 0, and to hold them there until the next FOMC meeting.[8] At that time, the FOMC would then be free to continue the stimulus by moving the peg out another 6 weeks, or to alter the strength of the stimulus in either direction.

If the Fed, in our example, ends up a holding dominant share of all the outstanding T-bills maturing within 9 weeks of the current meeting, it may have to supplement T-bill purchases with term repurchase agreements or term discount loans to insured Commercial Banks up to the same maturity date, in order to prevent private loans from paying a higher risk-adjusted rate.

Thus, although the ZLB may require some adjustment of procedures, it does not in itself prevent the functioning of the Taylor Rule. In particular it does not justify the adoption of a positive inflation target instead of price stability, or the Fed's extraordinary "Quantitative Easing" programs since 2008.

4. Why Hasn't Inflation Accelerated?

Despite an essentially zero Federal Funds Rate since 2008, and a more than quadrupling of the monetary base through the Fed's "Quantitative

[8] Alternatively, the Fed could achieve the same stimulus, relative to a norm of 4%, without the complication of 0 interest rates, by pegging rates at say 1% out to 12 weeks from the current meeting.

Easing" programs, inflation has shown no signs of accelerating, and in fact has been lingering somewhat below the Fed's official 2% target. This has been quite puzzling in terms of either the conventional theory of the Taylor Rule or the traditional Quantity Theory of Money.

Ordinarily, as in the pre-2008 environment, the Taylor Rule works by creating an excess supply or demand for zero-interest monetary base. This in turn has an inflationary wealth effect to the extent the new base has an opportunity cost in terms of foregone interest (Johnson, 1969, Serletis & Barnett, 2000). Even if short-term market rates are currently up against the ZLB, the banks' expected holding period of excess reserves will simply increase until a maturity is inevitably reached with a positive interest rate.[9]

Since 2008, however, the Fed has had the authority to pay interest on reserve deposits, including excess reserves, and has used this authority to reduce the opportunity cost of excess reserves to zero (or even slightly negative).[10] As a consequence, the newly created excess reserves have no opportunity cost and therefore no inflationary impact per se. While it is true that at present the difference between the 25 basis points the Fed has been paying banks and zero may be virtually negligible, banks that hold these excess reserves can rest assured that they will *never* have an opportunity cost, so long as the Fed continues its current policy, even after short-term rates return to normal levels, and therefore have no incentive to lend them out today as opportunities arise. These excess reserves, and the assets whose purchase they have paid for, therefore constitute non-inflationary financial intermediation on the part of the Fed rather than inflationary money creation. Interest on excess reserves has therefore neutralized the effectiveness of monetary policy.

In order for the Taylor Rule to resume being a useful tool for inflation control, it is therefore important that Congress repeal the Fed's authority to pay interest on excess reserves. Interest on *required* reserves, on the other

---

[9] The famous Baumol-Tobin (Baumol, 1952) inventory model of money demand predicts that the maximum holding period for zero-interest cash inventories will be inversely proportional to the square root of the nominal interest rate i. The standard form of this model takes no account of the maturity structure of interest rates. However, it can be shown that with a yield curve $i(m)$ and forward curve $f(m)$ as defined in footnote 3, the same money demand formula is approximately valid, with the common interest rate i replaced by $i(m_0)^2/f(m_0)$, where m_0 is the maximum holding period of money, as determined by the model. With a rising yield curve, $f(m) > i(m)$, so that this expression is positive so long as $i(m_0)$ is positive, but somewhat smaller than $i(m_0)$ itself. The Miller-Orr (1966) model has random cash inflows and outflows that more realistically model bank excess reserve inventories. However, it will have a qualitatively similar implication.

[10] This authority was included in the October 2008 TARP bill.

hand, is a very different matter, and should in fact be retained. This has long been recommended by Friedman (1960) in order to prevent banks from gaming the reserve requirement and to maximize payment of interest on transactions accounts.[11]

To be sure, eliminating interest on excess reserves without massive inflation would require the Fed at the same time to promptly unwind its massive "Quantitative Easing" purchases of Treasury debt and Mortgage-Backed Securities. However, once excess reserves no longer earn interest, banks will be eager to buy even low-yielding Treasuries back from the Fed. The Fed's unfortunate $1.7 trillion of risky Mortgage-Backed Securities will be much harder to sell outright, since the market for them is nowhere near as deep as that for Treasury debt. However, mortgages continually return principal and frequently are prepaid when the house is sold or refinanced. The Fed should therefore allow its MBS position to wind down naturally as promptly as possible, and not roll over return of principal as it has been doing. In the meanwhile, it may temporarily be required to sell additional Treasury securities in order to absorb the excess reserves corresponding to its gradually declining mortgage position.[12]

The opportunity cost of excess reserves, and therefore their expansionary impact, could in principle be increased by actually charging interest on them when the Fed Funds rate falls below a certain threshold. For example, their opportunity cost could be raised to at least 2% by charging the greater of 2% minus Funds rate (averaged over say the last 2 weeks) or 0. At the margin this might lead banks to charge comparable interest on demand deposits, and/or lend at moderately negative nominal interest rates. The ramifications of such a rule should be thoroughly explored before it is actually put into practice.[13] But clearly *paying* interest on excess reserves, as has been done since 2008, is a move in the wrong direction.

[11] In order to relieve the burden of zero-interest reserve requirements on small banks, Congress long ago reduced the reserve requirement on the first several million dollars of deposits at each individual bank to 3%, or even 0%. This has made the effective reserve requirement less than its current nominal level of 10%, and has made it sensitive to changes in the size-composition of banks. But if required reserves pay competitive interest, they are no longer a burden, and hence there is no longer a political rationale for this exemption. Likewise, retail "sweep" accounts (Anderson & Rasche, 2001) should be made subject to the uniform reserve requirement, in order for the Fed to be able to at least monitor the narrow money supply, even if it does not choose to target its growth rate. With interest on required reserves, this would not be a burden on the banks offering them.

[12] See also McCulloch (2014b).

[13] Goodfriend (2000) considers a direct tax on demand deposits and currency, as had been proposed by Sylvio Gesell in the late 19th century. This could have a similar end effect, but would be far more intrusive than just a fee on excess reserves.

Four other important Taylor Rule issues do not relate directly to the ZLB. These are, first, the Fed's deliberate introduction of inertia into its Fed Funds target, second, how expected inflation should be proxied in the Rule, third, how the "output gap" should be proxied in the Rule, if indeed it is to be included at all, and fourth, in what maturity(ies) should the Fed conduct its Taylor Rule interventions and provide for long-run base growth?

5. Taylor Rule Inertia

In practice, the most important term in the empirical Taylor Rule has been one or more lags of the Federal Funds target itself. At a quarterly frequency, the sum of these lag coefficients can be 0.8 or even 0.9 (see, e.g., Clarida et al., 2000; McCulloch, 2007). This means that in fact the FOMC only reacts 10% or 20% to current conditions, and otherwise is just continuing whatever it was doing in the past. Even when it does finally decide that a big change in the target is long overdue, it timidly changes the target only in a series of small steps, typically only 25 basis points per meeting. As a result, it tends to keep interest rates too low for too long a time (as in 2001–2004) or too high for too long (as in 2005–2007), with the outcome that it ends up actually increasing their long-run variance and destabilizing the economy.

The FOMC should instead act at each meeting in response to its best estimate of current conditions, with no reference to its previous decisions. Of course, estimated current conditions ordinarily change only slowly, with the result that there will still be considerable serial correlation in the Fed's Fed Funds target.[14] Nevertheless, the lagged target itself should ideally have no explanatory power for the empirical Taylor Rule once the Fed's estimates of current conditions are taken into account.

The Fed does have a much-neglected mandate from Congress to "moderate long-term interest rates," in addition to its better-known goals of "price stability" and "maximizing employment."[15] However, as noted by Friedman (1968), the best way to stabilize long-term interest rates is to stabilize inflationary expectations. Under a Taylor Rule policy, this requires aggressively fighting high (or low) inflation with high (or low) short-term

[14] See, for example, McCulloch (2007).

[15] These three goals are popularly known as the Fed's "Dual Mandate." It is now generally recognized that the Fed cannot "maximize employment" through the Phillips Curve without runaway inflation. At best, price stability is only consistent with minimizing disturbances to employment.

interest rates as soon as high (or low) inflationary expectations materialize. This in turn will require rather volatile short-term interest rates.

6. Measuring Expected Inflation

In John Taylor's original (1993) exposition of the "Taylor Rule," he used the most recently realized year-over-year inflation as a proxy for expected future inflation. This would be an unbiased univariate time series forecast of inflation if inflation were a pure random walk.[16] However, before 1970 inflation experience was clearly mean-stationary, and since 1990 there is also evidence that it is again stationary, though less strongly so. A time series forecast using slowly time-varying coefficients as in McCulloch (2007) would therefore be an appropriate proxy for expected inflation.[17]

The lagged unemployment gap (unemployment relative to its "natural" rate) also has some explanatory power for inflation, though far less than lagged inflation itself, so that it would not be inappropriate to include this and/or other empirically relevant macroeconomic variables in the expected inflation proxy.[18]

If inflation empirically exhibits mean-reverting tendencies, as it has in recent decades, the best forecast of inflation will vary with horizon. However, inflation is highly seasonal, and its seasonality is continually changing, which makes monthly and quarterly inflation figures noisy and subject to varying interpretations. Year-over-year inflation has no seasonality, so that the relevant policy horizon should be at least one year. Horizons longer than one year start to be dependent on the mean reversion parameters, which themselves change gradually over time and so are

[16] In the absence of seasonality and measurement error, the optimal random walk forecast would in fact be the most recent realized month-over-month inflation rate. However, the CPI and PCE contain a large seasonal that changes over time, and also contain measurement error. Year-over-year inflation removes the seasonal without having to try to quantify it. A random walk with measurement error would make a simple exponentially weighted Kalman filter the optimal estimate.

[17] A distinction is often drawn in the literature between "backward-looking" inflation forecasts that just use the most recent inflation observation and "forward-looking" forecasts that optimally use all information. However, all real-time forecasts are entirely based on past data, so that the real distinction is how much past data is used, and how it is used, and not whether it is used.

[18] If the Taylor Rule really works to control inflation, the lagged nominal interest rate target itself (relative to inflation experience and other empirical predictors of inflation) should have some explanatory power. However, its direct short-run effect can be very subtle, as noted above, and hence it would make little difference simply to exclude it from the information set.

difficult to measure precisely. A one-year inflation forecast horizon is therefore a reasonable choice.

7. The Output Gap Term

Taylor (1993) originally defined the "output gap" term in the Taylor Rule as the deviation of GDP from its trend line. However, Nelson and Plosser (1982) had already shown that a unit root in the residuals of such a regression can typically not be rejected. Such a unit root implies that GDP has no tendency to return to its trend line, and hence that the "output gap" as originally measured by Taylor may be no more than a statistical illusion.

Unemployment, however, is more likely to be stationary, if only about a slowly time-varying "natural rate." An estimated "unemployment gap" is therefore a more meaningful proxy for what was intended by the "output gap" term in the Taylor equation, with its sign reversed and its magnitude adjusted for "Okun's Law." McCulloch (2007) finds that such a proxy does enter into the empirical Taylor Rule, over and above its contribution to expected inflation, with a time-varying coefficient averaging approximately −2.0 since 1980.[19]

Since 1968, however, there has been widespread agreement among economists that inflation can only affect unemployment and output to the extent it is unanticipated, and then only by tricking workers and vendors into accepting nominal wages or prices that have a lower real value than expected (Friedman, 1968). Therefore it is highly questionable whether even the unemployment gap should be in the Fed's interest rate rule, aside from its incorporation into the inflation forecast to the extent that it is empirically useful.[20]

Nevertheless, there is reason to believe that recessions, and therefore high unemployment rates, are associated with unanticipated declines in real interest rates, and therefore relatively low equilibrium real rates, through what I have elsewhere called the "Misintermediation" effect

---

[19] With an empirical "Okun's Law" coefficient of 2.0 relating the change in real income to the change in the unemployment rate, this would correspond to an output gap coefficient of approximately 1.0 rather than 0.5 as in the benchmark Taylor Rule above.

[20] The extraordinarily high average duration of unemployment during and following 2009 was, I have argued elsewhere, largely due to the extraordinarily generous 99 weeks of unemployment benefits enacted early in 2009 (see McCulloch, 2013). There is no point in using monetary policy to try to undo the effects of successful high unemployment policy.

(McCulloch, 1981). Indeed, Burns and Mitchell (1946) actually use bond yields as one indicator of the business cycle. Failure to take this into account could make a fixed-coefficient Taylor Rule with only an intercept and expected inflation term relatively contractionary and deflationary at times of high unemployment and relatively stimulative and inflationary at times of low unemployment, and thus be destabilizing to output and unemployment. If the estimated unemployment gap could serve as an indirect proxy for the unobserved equilibrium real interest rate, it might then be appropriate to include it in the Taylor Rule. However, it is unclear how large a coefficient on the unemployment gap would be appropriate to offset changes in the equilibrium real interest rate, or indeed if there might not be some other better indicator of equilibrium real rates.

8. The Fed's Maturity Choices

When the Fed buys or sells securities, it generates windfall profits or losses for holders of those securities. If the Fed is using a Taylor-like rule to directly influence interest rates, such windfalls are unavoidable. Since the inflationary or deflationary pressure called for by the Taylor Rule is by construction temporary, any intervention in the present will most likely be reduced in the future. If the Fed intervenes in maturities longer than the next FOMC meeting, this may require generating the opposite windfall profits or losses in the future. However, if it only intervenes in maturities shorter than the next meeting, the securities in which it has directly intervened will have all matured by then and there will be no question of reversing their price movement. Since longer-maturity yields contain within them short-term yields plus forward rates out to their maturity,[21] lowering or raising short-term yields will automatically generate capital gains or losses for holders of these longer-term securities. However, this will only be a one-time capital gain or loss, with no predictable echo in the opposite direction when the intervention is no longer called for. It is therefore appropriate that the Fed's temporary Taylor Rule interventions are restricted to maturities no longer than the next FOMC meeting, except in the unusual case when the ZLB is binding, as discussed above.

Since the Fed turns the bulk of its profits over to the Treasury, and since these profits arise primarily from interest on its portfolio of Treasury securities, the ultimate interest burden on taxpayers of the national debt is determined by the maturity composition of Treasury securities outstanding

[21] See footnote 3.

outside the Treasury and the Fed taken together. The maturity structure of this debt is an important decision, but one that should be up to the Treasury, within the parameters set by Congress. Year-to-year permanent growth in the Fed's portfolio of Treasury securities should therefore hold them approximately in proportion, by maturity, to their quantity outstanding outside the Treasury itself.[22]

If the Treasury is prudent, it will finance the long-term National Debt with long-term bonds, thereby locking in today whatever rates are now available, just as prudent homebuyers finance their homes with mortgages whose maturity is comparable to the longevity of their houses. Short-funding the National Debt with just short-term Treasury bills (or houses with one-year loans) would expose taxpayers (or homebuyers) to substantial unnecessary interest rate risk should rates rise in the future. In fact, since the Treasury acts as a financial intermediary between taxpayers and investors, and is big enough to move the market by itself, failure to match its funding structure to its repayment plans can distort the intertemporal structure of capital formation, and actually cause interest rates to move adversely to the strategy (see McCulloch, 1981).

Acknowledgment

The author is grateful to an anonymous referee for helpful comments and suggestions.

References

Anderson, R. G., & Rasche, R. H. (2001). Retail sweep programs and bank reserves, 1994–1999. *Federal Reserve Bank of St. Louis Review*, *83*(1), 51–72.

Baumol, W. J. (1952). The transactions demand for cash: An inventory theoretic approach. *Quarterly Journal of Economics*, *66*, 545–556.

Burns, A. F., & Mitchell, W. C. (1946). *Measuring business cycles*. New York, NY: National Bureau of Economic Research.

Clarida, R., Galí, J., & Gertler, M. (2000). Monetary policy rules and macroeconomic stability: Evidence and some theory. *Quarterly Journal of Economics*, *115*, 147–180.

Fisher, I. (1930/1974). *The Theory of Interest* (A. M. Kelley, Reprint ed., 1974).

[22] Historically, the Fed has periodically corrected an imbalance of short-term securities and/or loans to dealers accumulated through Taylor Rule intervention with a "coupon pass," that is, an intentional replacement of a portion of its short-term position with longer-term coupon bonds.

Friedman, M. (1960). A program for monetary stability. New York: Fordham University Press.

Friedman, M. (1968). The role of monetary policy. *American Economic Review*, *58*, 1–17.

Goodfriend, M. (2000). Overcoming the zero bound on interest rate policy. *Journal of Money, Credit and Banking*, *32*, 1007–1035.

Johnson, H. G. (1969). Inside money, outside money, income, wealth, and welfare in monetary theory. *Journal of Money, Credit and Banking*, *1*, 30–45.

McCulloch, J. H. (1975). An estimate of the liquidity premium. *Journal of Political Economy*, *83*, 95–119.

McCulloch, J. H. (1981). Misintermediation and macroeconomic fluctuations. *Journal of Monetary Economics*, *8*, 103–115.

McCulloch, J. H. (2007). *Adaptive least squares estimation of the time-varying Taylor rule*. Retrieved from http://www.econ.ohio-state.edu/jhm/papers/TaylorALS.pdf

McCulloch, J. H. (2013). A Chance to End the Great Recession. *The Beacon: The Blog of the Independent Institute*. Retrieved from http://blog.independent.org/2013/11/21/a-chance-to-end-the-great-recession/. Accessed on November 21, 2013.

McCulloch, J. H. (2014). Misesian insights for modern macroeconomics. *Quarterly Journal of Austrian Economics*, *17*(1), 3–18.

Miller, M., & Orr, D. (1966). A model of the demand for money by firms. *Quarterly Journal of Economics*, *80*, 413–435.

Nelson, C. R., & Plosser, C. I. (1982). Trends and random walks in macroeconomic time series. *Journal of Monetary Economics*, *10*, 139–162.

Serletis, A., & Barnett, W. A., (Eds.). (2000). The theory of monetary aggregation, *in* contributions to economic analysis (Vol. 245). Bingley, UK: Emerald Group Publishing Limited.

Taylor, J. (1993). Discretion versus Policy Rules in Practice. *Carnegie-Rochester Conference Series* 195–214.

Chapter 12

A Comparison of the Fed's and ECB's Strategies during the Subprime Crisis

Marcel Aloy[a] and Gilles Dufrénot[b]

[a] *Aix-Marseille Université and Aix-Marseille School of Economics (GREQAM & CNRS & EHESS), Château Lafarge, Route des Milles, 13290, Aix-en-Provence Les Milles, e-mail: marcel.aloy@univ-amu.fr*
[b] *Aix-Marseille Université and Aix-Marseille School of Economics (GREQAM & CNRS & EHESS), Banque de France, CEPII. Château Lafarge, Route des Milles, 13290, Aix-en-Provence Les Milles, e-mail: gilles.dufrenot@univ-amu.fr*

Abstract

This chapter proposes a comparative analysis of the monetary policies undertaken by the Federal Reserve Board and the European Central Bank after the 2008 subprime crisis. We point out the twin nature of the financial crises in Europe in comparison with the US crises: in addition to the role of bank funding, the euro area countries have also experienced a structural problem of balance of payment disequilibria. This explains why in the early stages of the subprime crisis, the Fed has succeeded in tackling the illiquidity problems facing the banking sector, while the ECB did not. The Fed could then focus on tackling the recession in the real sector by adopting quantitative easing policies to exert downward pressure on the long-term interest-rate. In the euro area quantitative easing policies came later, in 2013. Even the forward guidance policies have been different between the two central banks. Unlike the ECB, the Fed has gone through diverse forward guidance policies: qualitative, calendar-based, and state-contingent. The chapter proposes a new survey of the monetary policies after the subprime crisis by comparing two strategies in different contexts: the United States and the euro area.

Keywords: monetary policy, subprime crisis, ECB, Fed

JEL Classifications: C51, C52, E52, E58

International Symposia in Economic Theory and Econometrics, Vol. 24
William A. Barnett and Fredj Jawadi (Editors)

ISSN: 1571-0386/doi: 10.1108/S1571-038620150000024024

1. Introduction

This chapter proposes a comparative analysis of the unconventional monetary policies decided by the Federal Reserve (Fed) and the European Central Bank (ECB). They've had similar reactions during the early stages of the subprime crisis, by adopting measures to encourage banks with excess reserves to lend to those with short-term liquidity needs. These policies can be classified as "non-standard" or "unconventional conventional" policies, to say that they have remained initially within the operational monetary policy framework that prevails in normal times, but have been more flexible.

Once after 2009, the Fed had to support the economy at a time when the country was sinking into deep recession, and the interest rate had declined to a level close to zero. The question was: how could a monetary stimulus be done in a context of zero lower bound (ZLB)? This situation led to the adoption of the so-called quantitative easing policies. A bad economic juncture went hand in hand with a situation of low inflation. The relationship between the nominal policy rate and the market rates became tenuous and the monetary authorities needed to look for new instruments to cope with disinflation. The main concern was to choose the appropriate instrument that could influence market long-term real interest rates and to provide funds to the banking sector that could be channeled to the real sector. The Fed changed its operational framework by adopting "unconventional" monetary policies. It has gone through several rounds of quantitative and credit easing policies based on the expansion of the size of its balance sheet and changes in the composition of assets.

The ECB has also moved to unconventional policies, but for a different purpose. The ECB had to substitute for the core European banks as a lender of last resort, by refinancing the peripheral countries in order to dampen the contractionary effects of capital outflows in Greece, Italy, Portugal, Ireland, and Spain. Unconventional monetary policies retained by the ECB can be analyzed as a way of overcoming the problems caused by imbalances between "core" and "peripheral" countries.

This chapter is organized as follows. Section 2 recalls some sources of the recent crises (financial and debt crises). Section 3 presents some policies that are referred to as "unconventional conventional policies." Such policies have been temporary in the United States (and then the Fed rapidly turned to true unconventional policies), but last a longer time in the euro area where the adoption of the so-called quantitative easing policies took place lately. Section 4 compares the unconventional policies in the United States and in the euro area. Finally Section 5 concludes.

2. The Sources of Crises: Bank Funding and Current Account Disequilibria

2.1. The Role of Bank Funding of International Banks

Figure 1 shows that the activity of bank funding rests upon a wide range of financial instruments. Modern banks resources come from customer deposits (retail and secured deposits) and deposits collected from money market funds, corporations, non-residents. The funding model of an international bank is based on wholesale funding in credit markets. Before the subprime crisis, banks faced difficulty attracting stable deposits and had to rely on short-term wholesale finance (short-term unsecured funds like interbank loans, commercial paper, and wholesale certificates of deposit, and short-term secured funds like repurchase agreements, swaps, and asset-backed commercial paper). To avoid rolling debt over, banks issue bonds and various forms of securitization (including covered bonds and mortgage-backed securities). Finally, banks have access to central bank liquidity and can raise capital (common equity and certain types of subordinated debt).

The composition of bank funding has changed significantly since the past decades: the expansion of securitization has increased wholesale funding and financial globalization led to the expansion of international interbank US dollar markets.

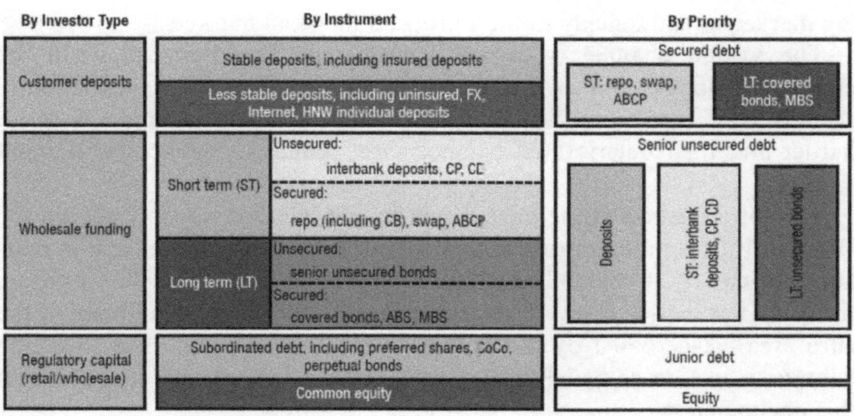

Figure 1: Typology of Bank Funding. Note: ABCP = asset-backed commercial paper; ABS = asset-backed securities; CB = central bank; CD = certificate of deposit; CoCo = contingent convertible; CP = commercial paper; FX = foreign exchange; HNW = high net worth; LT = long term; MBS = mortgage-backed security; ST = short term. Source: International Monetary Fund [IMF] (2013).

The onset of the subprime crisis caused a rise in home foreclosures and a bust of the housing bubble as the roots of the financial crisis. As a result, banks' reliance on wholesale markets fell and funding costs increased. This rise has been driven by two factors (see Committee on International Policy and Reform, 2012).

(i) The complex chain of securitization has involved higher financial risks and then a collapse of the securitized mortgage market. According to Benmelech and Dlugosz (2009), collateralized debt obligations backed by asset-back securities (ABS CDO) accounted for 42% of the total write-downs of financial institutions around the world. Using micro-level data, they document three features of ABS CDOs: high concentration in residential housing, high exposure to the most risky segment of residential housing, and low diversification (about 75% of ABS CDOs were composed of mortgages that originated in 2005 and 2006). The sharp decline in market prices of some AAA-rated securities reflects the mispricing of risk.

(ii) Cross-border banking brought benefits in terms of portfolio diversification, but it has also exacerbated the crisis through three channels.

The first channel was a contagion effect. Though cross-border banking helps insulating a bank from domestic shocks, it also increases its exposure to foreign shocks. The large exposure of the European banks to the US securitized asset markets until 2008 explains why the crisis in the US housing market spread quickly to the European financial markets.

The second channel is currency mismatch. This happens when the currency denomination of assets and liabilities differ and triggers balance sheet effects. Banks and financial institutions with foreign loans were hit harder and their deteriorated balance sheet reduced their access to credit markets.[1]

The third channel is the huge expansion of interbank flows between the Western European countries, which fueled bubbles in the real estate market, particularly in Ireland and Spain. The reversal of these flows during the crisis has caused a severe recession in the "peripheral" countries of the euro area, exacerbated by the slowdown in global growth. The sovereign debt crisis in Greece and Portugal was, at least in part, a consequence of this phenomenon.

To summarize, the reason why the mortgage crisis has escalated into a banking crisis was the disproportionally reliance of banks on non-deposit funding sources.

[1] For details the reader can refer to McGuire and Götz (2009).

2.2. Current Accounts Imbalances and Sudden Stops in the Euro Area

Many studies on the euro area crisis emphasize the role of the banking sector as a motor of the housing bubble (see, for instance, Merler & Pisani-Ferry, 2012). Cross-border banking within the euro area has grown rapidly since the introduction of the euro, fueling the real estate bubble in recipient countries such as Spain and Ireland. These flows allow rapid expansion of credits to households and corporates (see Figure 2).

However, as shown in Figure 3, the capital inflows were drained into the non-tradable sector (housing, tourism, and other services) where labor productivity is low. Rising wages in this sector spread to the whole economy, thereby implying a sharp deterioration in competitiveness. On the onset of

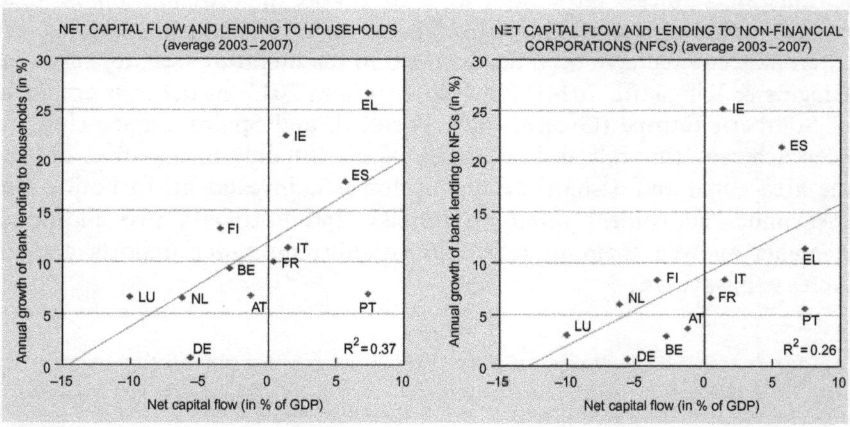

Figure 2: Net Capital Flow and Domestic Credit Growth. Source: de Sola Perea and Van Nieuwenhuyze (2014).

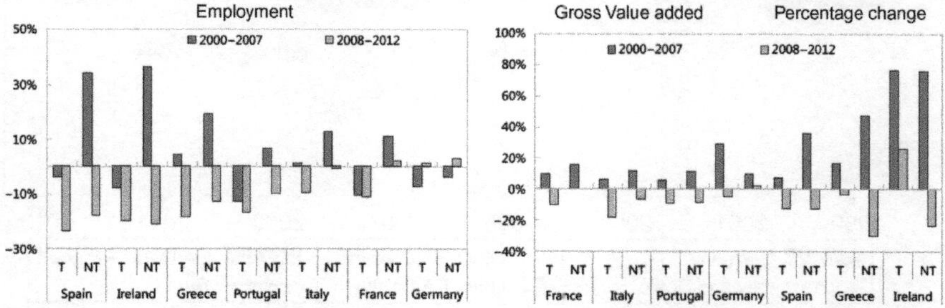

Figure 3: Changes in Tradable and Non-Tradable Sectors. Source: Tressel and Wang (2014).

the financial crisis, these countries' economic situation appeared fragile and private capital flowed back, not allowing the financing of external deficits other than by public capital (from governments and central bank). Since private capital flew back, investment decreased in the peripheral European countries.

Massive capital inflows have resulted into a sharp deterioration of these countries' current account balance, especially between 2004 and 2008 (see Figure 4): the sudden reversal of these flows has caused external financing issues.

Countries that had to cope with such a massive capital flight, as in Latin America and Asia, experienced a currency depreciation followed by a painful restoration of their current account balance. Although the channel of the devaluation could not work in the case of the euro area countries, the peripheral countries have been able to restore the equilibrium of their current account balance in 2013. The factors that helped restoring the external accounts have been documented in the literature (see, for instance, Higgins & Klitgaard, 2014). Between 2010 and 2013, in the four countries of Southern Europe (Greece, Italy, Portugal, and Spain), rebalancing has been achieved through an increase in exports (mainly to countries outside the area euro) and a sharp decline in domestic investment. In both countries under adjustment programs (Greece and Portugal), two additional elements allowed them to return to equilibrium: lower imports and an increase in savings.

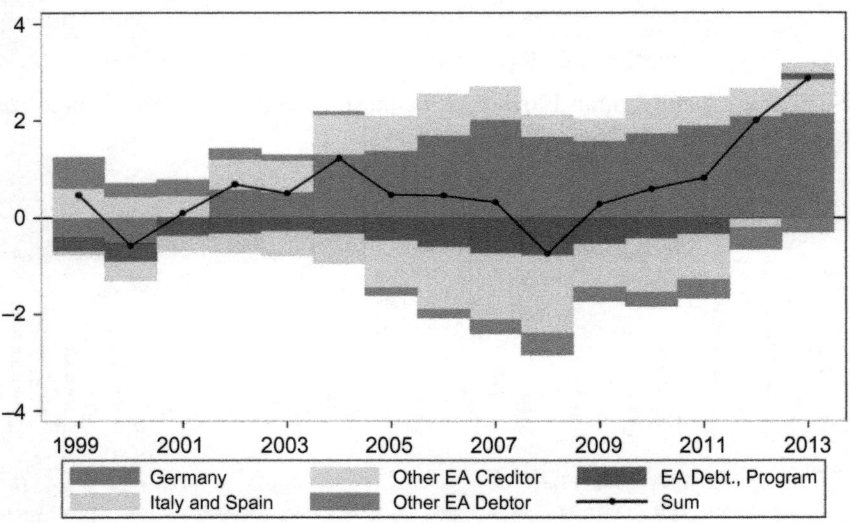

Figure 4: Euro Area Current Account Balances in % of Euro Area GDP. Source: Tressel and Wang (2014).

In addition to the current account imbalances, the euro area also experienced sovereign debt crises. The first debt crisis occurred in 2010, when the markets worried about a possible default of sovereign debts. Due to the economic recession and the restructuring of the banking sector, the peripheral countries' primary deficit exceeded 8% in Ireland, Portugal, and Spain and 10% in Greece and caused a rise in the debt over GDP ratio.

For the peripheral countries, which have faced both current account imbalances and private capital outflows, the TARGET2 (T2) settlement system emerged as a balance of payment equilibrating mechanism (Cecchetti, McCauley, & McGuire, 2012; Whelan, 2013). To explain how, let us consider a consolidated balance sheet of the banking system in Spain (Bank A) and in Germany (Bank B), and the balance sheet of their respective national central banks (NCB) and the ECB's (Figure 5).

In this example, a payment of imports or a capital outflow from Spain to Germany is materialized by a reduction in deposits (ΔD_0) and central bank reserves (ΔR_0) in the Spanish bank A, and by an increase of the same amount in deposits and reserves in the German bank B. As a result, the Spanish NCB has a T2 debtor position while the Bundesbank has T2 claims of the same amount.

In normal times, the T2 system imbalances remain low: in our example, the Spanish bank may borrow liquidity in the interbank market, probably from a German bank (Figure 6), in order to restore its central bank reserves account. The T2 balances are then reset to zero.

However, in times of financial stress, when the cross-border interbank market freezes, banks with excess liquidity prefer to hold deposit with their NCB rather than lending them to other banks. In this case, bank A has no

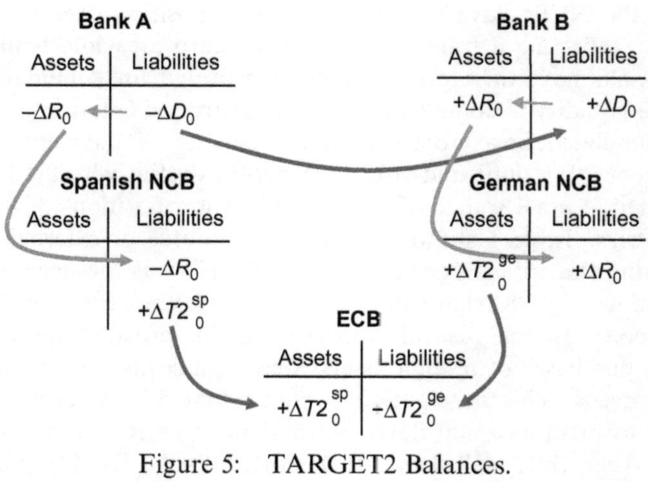

Figure 5: TARGET2 Balances.

Figure 6: Interbank Market Funding.

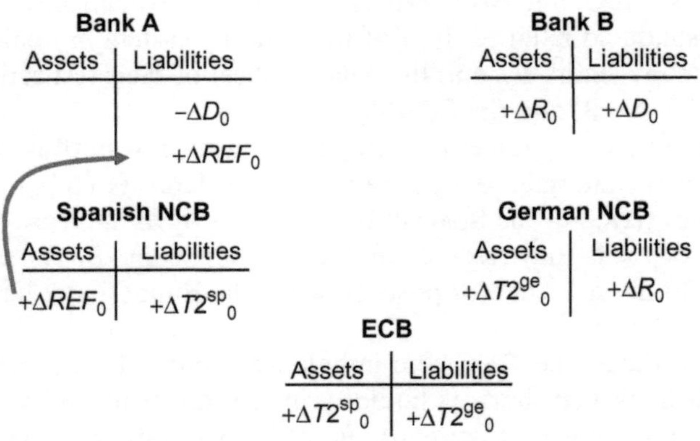

Figure 7: Central Bank Funding.

choice but to refinance with its NCB, which keeps the T2 accounts unchanged (see Figure 7).

Though at the aggregate level the sum of TARGET2 is null, the balance sheets of the NCBs have had an imbalanced position over long periods (Figure 8), reflecting a fragmentation of the euro area interbank market. Central banks have therefore gradually substituted for commercial banks to provide liquidity to commercial banks in distressed countries.

The cumulated flows recorded in the balance of payments from the beginning of 2011 until mid-2012 – a period during which T2 liabilities accumulated – are a source of a strong T2 debtor positions of the peripheral countries. Table 1 shows that the main source of external financing needs during the critical period of 2011–2012H1 was the negative private capital inflows (i.e., foreign sales of domestic assets), reflecting the capital flows reversal. In the case of Italy and Spain, private capital outflows (domestic purchases of foreign assets) were significant sources of external financing needs. This observation confirms that T2 balances owes their dynamics to private capital flows rather than to current account balances (see also Auer, 2012; Whelan, 2013). Portugal's T2 liability recorded its

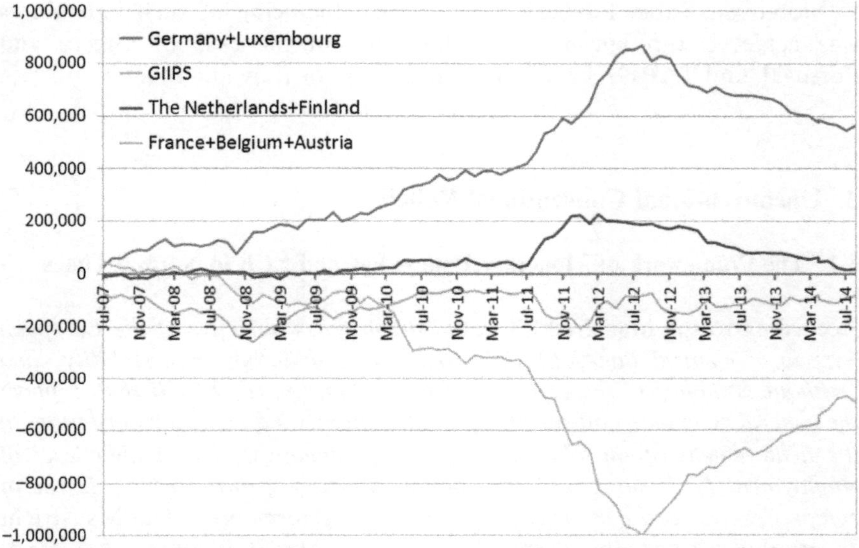

Figure 8: TARGET2 Balances (millions Euro). Source: Euro crisis Monitor.

Table 1: Balance of Payment Breakdown, Peripheral Countries (billion Euro)

Cumulated from 2011 to 2012 H1	Greece + Portugal	Italy + Spain
Current account	−36	−123
Private inflows	−167	−358
Private outflows	1	150
Program	170	0
TARGET2 credit	33	631

Source: Data from Higgins and Klitgaard (2014).

largest increase after April 2010 in a context in which the markets were anticipating that the Greek crisis could spread to other European countries. Ireland's T2 liabilities built up rapidly during late-summer of 2010 as international investors lost faith in the Irish government's abilities to rescue its banks, leading to deposit flight and a failure to roll over bond market funding. Spain and Italy's balances did not start to build up till the crisis intensified during the summer of 2011 amid widespread concerns that the Euro system would break up. The balances have declined in size since August 2012 as the introduction of the OMT program has calmed fears relating to a Euro breakup.

Moreover, Table 1 reveals that external financing of such imbalances was achieved through programs financing in the case of Greece and Portugal, and TARGET2 liabilities in the case of Italy and Spain.

3. Unconventional Conventional Policies

3.1. The Framework of Monetary Policy: Fed and ECB in Normal Times

According to the Maastricht Treaty "*the primary objective of the European System of Central Banks (ESCB) shall be to maintain price stability*" and "*without prejudice to the objective of price stability, the ESCB shall support the general economic policies of the Community with a view to contributing to the achievement of the objectives of the Community [...]: a high level of employment [...], sustainable and non-inflationary growth, a high degree of competitiveness and convergence of economic performance.*" The Maastricht Treaty thus assigns a hierarchy of objectives to the ECB, giving an overriding importance to price stability. Moreover, the ECB provides a precise quantitative definition of price stability: 2% in the long run.

Conversely, the Federal Reserve Act (section 2A.1) assigns to the Fed a multiple-objective mandate: "*the Board of Governors of the Federal Reserve System and the Federal Open Market Committee shall maintain long-run growth of the monetary and credit aggregates commensurate with the country's long-run potential to increase production, so as to promote effectively the goals of maximum employment, stable prices and moderate long-term interest rates.*" However, as underlined by Gerdesmeier, Mongelli, and Roffia (2007), in spite of these multiple objectives, the Fed's policymakers seem to have assigned an implicit ranking to these goals and they have traditionally placed more emphasis on achieving price stability.

Thus, in normal times, both the European Central Bank and the Federal Reserve share a similar monetary policy goal which consists in achieving price stability. However, until 2007, these institutions implemented monetary policy in different ways (see Table 2).

Until 2007, the US commercial banks hold virtually no reserves, unlike the European banks that hold minimum reserves required by the ECB.

In the United States, bank reserves were not paid, since the Fed had lowered in the early 1990s the volume of statutory reserves. This policy took place in a context wherein many banks had found ways of reducing their required reserves (for instance, reserve avoidance activities included sweeping checking account balances). Since the mid-1990s, the reserves of US banks thus declined steadily and at the beginning of the crisis, in 2007, they were low. In the euro area, the ECB remunerated required reserve balances

Table 2: Key Features of Central Banks Operating Procedures

	Federal reserve	ECB
Target rate	Federal funds	EONIA
Reserve requirements	0–10% of transactions accounts, 0 for non-transaction accounts	2% on deposits with term less than 2 years, 0 no longer-term deposits
Definition of reserve	Balance at the Fed + vault cash	Balance at the ECB, excluding deposited funds
Reserve maintenance period	Two weeks	One month
Reserve accounting	Lagged two weeks	Lagged one month
Standing facilities	Lending (as of January 2003) Interest on reserves (as of October 2008)	Both lending and deposit facilities
Open-market operations	Daily, at market rate	Weekly, at the higher of the main refinancing rate or the market rate

Source: Friedman and Kuttner (2010).
Note: The ECB lowered the reserve requirement ratio to 1% from January 18, 2012.

at the main operation rate and the excess reserves that were placed at the ECB's deposit facility (at a rate lower than the policy rate).

Since 2003, commercial banks have been able to borrow from the Fed's discount window rate (a penalty rate 100 basis point higher than the FOMC's target rate). Based on its expectations of the demand for reserves, the central bank set the supply of reserves via open-market operations.[2] In contrast, the ECB's situation is described by a symmetric channel system with the targeted rate evolving within a corridor. The key feature of such a system is the existence of a lending facility that permits banks in situation of shortfall to borrow from the ECB at an interest rate above the targeted rate and of a deposit facility that allows them to place their excess reserve holdings and to earn an interest rate below the targeted rate. Before the crisis the ECB operated relatively wide channel with a standing facility rate 100 basis points on either side of the target.

[2] The Fed has three credit facilities. Primary credit is extended to sound financial institutions with collateral at a rate above the market rate. A secondary credit facility allows lending funds to less-sound financial institutions at a higher rate. Finally a seasonal facility is designed to help small depository institutions. Only the primary credit rate matters for monetary policy.

3.2. Monetary Policies and the Rescue of the Banking Sector

During the early stages of the subprime crisis, both the Fed and the ECB were facing a financial crisis closely related to a banking crisis caused by a deterioration of banks' balance sheets. The huge losses caused by the falling prices of toxic assets resulted into a liquidity crisis in the interbank market and forced the two central banks to use unconventional tools. However, the latter initially conformed to the standard monetary policy framework. Sections 3.2.1 and 3.2.2 present different situations the two central banks faced and the way in which they chose to tackle the difficulties.

3.2.1. Insolvency, Credit Constraint, and Liquidity Shortage

We consider the following balance sheet describing a commercial bank's financial situation.

Assets		Liabilities	
Statutory reserves	Rm	Central bank refinancing	REF
Lending to non-financial sector	L	Non-financial sector deposits	D
Other assets	T^+	Other liabilities	T^-
		Equities	K

"Other assets" consist of excess reserves, securities holding, and interbank lending, while "Other liabilities" includes securities issued and interbank borrowing. Define B as the coins and notes. Deposit creation by lending operation implies that:

$$L = D + B.$$

The demand for coins and notes is given by $B = b.L$, then: $L(1 - b) = D$. Let r be the statutory reserves coefficient such that: $Rm = r.D$. Then, the balance sheet equilibrium can be expressed as:

$$L[r + b(1 - r)] + (T^+ - T^-) - REF = K. \tag{1}$$

3.2.1.1. Insolvency and the Drop of Assets Prices. Insolvency arises when $K < 0$, that is

$$L[r + b(1 - r)] + T^+ < REF + T^-. \tag{2}$$

In this case, the assets (LHS) do not allow to meet liabilities commitments (RHS). This situation is depicted in Figure 9.

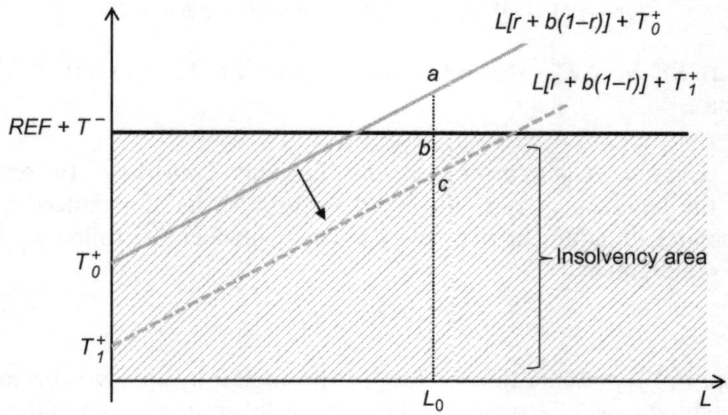

Figure 9: Drop of Asset Prices and Insolvency.

In the initial situation (point a), the bank meets its solvency requirement, since $a > b$. Let us consider the case of a drop in the market value of the "other assets" item (from T_0^+ to T_1^+): this was typically the banking system's situation during the subprime crisis in the United States and during the sovereign debt crises in Europe. For given levels of lending, central bank refinancing, and other liabilities item, the bank cannot meet its solvency requirement since $c < b$. Then, there are three options to avoid a bankruptcy (like Lehman Brothers) or takeover by another bank (like Bear Stearns, Merill Lynch, HBOS):

(1) the bank can increase its regulatory capital (K) by issuing common equity or junior debt. In this case, it will use this revenue to increase the "other assets" (for instance by increasing its liquidity position). However, this funding is likely to be very costly if the markets believe that the bank faces a risk of bankruptcy;
(2) the Government can nationalize the bank (e.g., Northern Rock, Bradford, and Bingley in the United Kingdom) or purchase preferred stock in the distressed bank (Citigroup);
(3) the central bank can buy the impaired assets in the "Other assets," in order to increase the market value and clean up the bank's balance sheet.

In the event of insolvency, an increase in central bank refinancing has no effect because the two lines in the figure move in the same proportion. Indeed, let ΔREF be the increase of central bank refinancing and ΔT^+ be the corresponding increase of other assets in the bank's balance sheet. Then Equation (2) becomes:

$$L[r+b(1-r)]+\Delta T^{+}+T^{+}<\Delta REF+REF+T^{-}.$$

Since $\Delta REF = \Delta T^{+}$, the refinancing operation has no effect on the imbalance.

3.2.1.2. Capital Requirement and the Lending Constraint. In order to reduce the bankruptcy risk, the Basel Committee has introduced a minimum capital requirement over risky assets. Consider the following simple capital requirement:

$$K>k_T T^{+}+k_L L.$$

k_T (resp. k_L) represents the product of the capital adequacy ratio and the risk-weighted assets T^{+} (resp. L). The aim of this minimum capital requirement is to reduce the risk of falling into a null or negative capital. The capital requirement formula is a constraint on the "other assets":

$$(K-k_L L)/k_T>T^{+}.$$

Substituting in the balance sheet (1) we have:

$$(K-k_L L)/k_T>K+REF+T^{-}-L[r+b(1-r)]. \quad (3)$$

The LHS term is the constraint introduced by the minimum capital requirement. This constraint is described by the (solid and dotted) black lines in Figure 10. The RHS term represents the amount of "other assets" in the bank balance sheet (liquidity and financial assets) and is represented by the gray line. Figure 10 describes the consequences of the capital adequacy requirement: the area under the constraint (solid black line), and above the amount of "other assets" (gray line) satisfies the capital adequacy

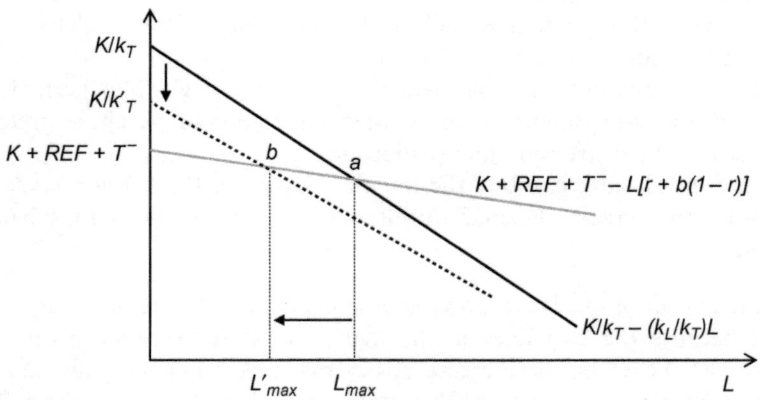

Figure 10: The Capital Adequacy Requirement Constraint.

requirement constraint. The intersection of these two lines determines the maximum supply of credit.

A downgrade in the rating of the "other assets" leads to an increase in k_T (from k_T to k'_T) and thus to a change of both the slope and the origin of the constraint (black dotted line). As a consequence, the bank must reduce its credit supply (from $L_{\max}$ to $L'_{\max}$). This case is interesting as it shows that a significant increase in the risk of financial assets leads to a drop in the credit supply, instead (or before) of a bankruptcy.

The remedies of such a downgrade in the rating of the "other assets" (for instance ABS or sovereign debt) are broadly in line with the case above: in order to restore its capacity to lend, the bank must increase capital (K). Indeed, such an increase will move the origin of the constraint (black line) more than proportionally than does the gray line.

An important conclusion can be drawn from this representation: an increase in the central bank refinancing does not ease the credit supply constraint. Instead, an increase in REF will shift the gray line upward: the amount of "other assets" will rise and, given the regulatory capital (K), the bank will need to reduce again the amount of its credit to meet the Basel standards. Finally, as in the preceding case, another solution for the Central Bank is to buy the impaired assets in the "Other assets" item, in order to clean up the bank's balance sheet.

3.2.1.3. Liquidity Shortage. Suppose now that the bank satisfies the minimum capital requirement. Equation (2) implies:

$$K = k_T T^+ + k_L L.$$

Inserting in the balance sheet Equation (1) leads:

$$L[r + b(1-r) - k_L] + T^+(1 - k_T) = REF + T^-.$$

Consider that the central bank's refinancing (REF) is collateralized with the bank's "Other assets" T^+. Denote γ such that:

$$REF = \gamma T^+ \quad 0 < \gamma < 1.$$

Thus $\gamma = 1$ is the upper limit of the amount of central bank's refinancing. The balance sheet equilibrium is therefore

$$L[r + b(1-r) - k_L] + T^+(1 - \gamma - k_T) = T^-. \tag{4}$$

Figure 11 portrays a situation of liquidity shortage. Consider the initial situation (point a) where the supply of credit is determined at the intersection point of the solid black (LHS of Equation (4)) and solid gray lines (RHS of Equation (4)).

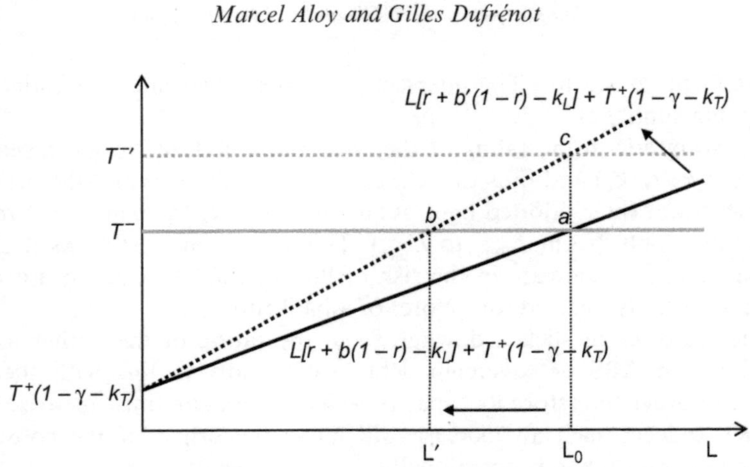

Figure 11: Liquidity Shortage: (a) Interbank Funding.

Now consider the parameter b, which represents the proportion of notes and coins and, in a more general case, the liquidity leaks out of the bank. For instance, to analyze a two-country situation where a fraction of deposits in bank A flows to bank B, because of cross-border commercial or financial transactions, the value of the parameter b can be increased to represent higher outflows. When the parameter b increases to b', this modifies the slope of the black solid line. The value of credit supply drops from L_0 to L', at the new equilibrium (point b) on the dotted black line. The liquidity leaks out is a common situation: when deposits flow from a given bank to another one, the liquidity shortage is usually compensated in the interbank market: banks in excess liquidity lend money to the others. This situation is depicted in the figure where the "Other liabilities" item increases from T^- to $T^{-'}$ leading to the point c in which the initial amount of lending is restored.

An additional way of funding liquidity is to use central bank refinancing. At the aggregated level, central bank refinancing is required when liquidity leaks out comes from cash withdrawal, because the central bank has a monopoly in issuing banknotes. In a stressful situation in the money markets (due to a higher counterparty risk), central banks need to substitute for the interbank market.

Figure 12 shows the funding in central bank liquidity: increasing γ to γ' (i.e., the fraction of assets collateralized in open-market transaction) leads to a translation toward the gray dashed line and the return to the original equilibrium (point a).

Nevertheless, it is noteworthy that the amount of central bank refinancing is restricted by the amount of assets eligible for open-market operations, which can be represented by the condition $\gamma < 1$. Thus, the supply of the central bank has a natural limit that is likely to prevent a return to the original balance (point a).

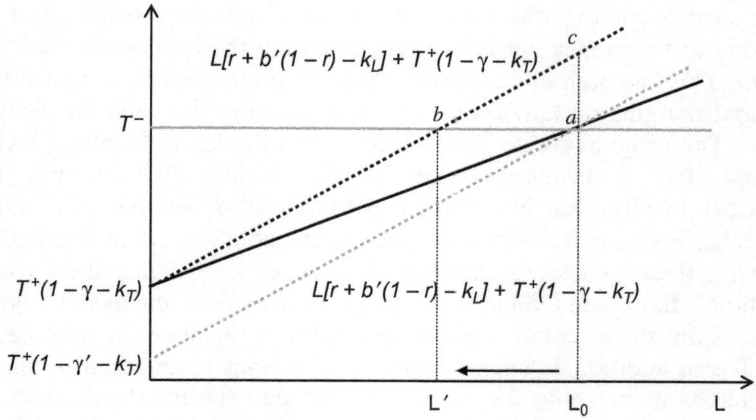

Figure 12: Liquidity Shortage: (b) Central Bank Refinancing.

3.2.2. The Operational Tools

Cutting the interest rate was the first response of the Fed when the subprime crisis erupted. The first goal was to provide liquidity to the money markets. Indeed, the commercial banks' and financial institutions' balance sheets had been exposed to the bust of the financial bubble, which induced mistrust in the markets for interbank lending. From August 2007 until April 2008, the Fed took the decision to simultaneously operate cuts in the target federal funds rate and in the primary lending rate. At the FOMC regular meetings the reduction in the target rate started from a 50 basis point cut in September 2007, to 4.75%, and was then further reduced nine times between August 2007 and April 2008 till it reaches 2%. The penalty rate was also reduced, a first time in August 2007, and then in March 2008.

The decrease in the interest rate was not enough to ease borrowing constraints in the interbank market. In contrast, the activity in the repo markets experienced a strong decline, thereby implying an increase in the haircuts for dealers. Also, the overnight repo spreads between asset-backed securities and Treasuries widened. This caused negative balance sheet effects and difficulties for borrowers to find lenders in the securitized loans markets. The decreases in the value of collaterals induced a rise in the margin calls.[3]

[3] The links between financial shocks and balance sheet effects have been examined in the literature, even before the subprime crisis. The reader can refer to Kiyotaki and Moore (1997), Shleifer and Vishny (1997), Greenwood and Vayanos (2008).

In such a context, the Fed had no choice but to provide short-term liquidity to the money market dealers by easing the borrower's credit constraint. This has been done through three programs aiming at reducing the required margins on new funds and by increasing the value of pledgable assets. The programs were respectively a Term Auction Facility (TAF) in August 2007, a Primary Dealer Credit Facility (PDCF), and Term Securities Lending Facility (TSLF) in March 2008. At this time, nobody was talking yet about « quantitative easing policy », since the Fed was pursuing these policies by keeping the size of its balance sheet roughly constant.[4] Banks and financial institutions were not inclined to borrow money from the discount window (even at a lower discount rate) because they feared additional "stigma" costs. The actions undertaken by the Fed thus aimed at boosting the refinancing through the interbank market by reducing the illiquidity risk. The policies were unconventional in the sense that the monetary authorities expanded the set collaterals that could be pledged, they extended the maturities of the securities sold by the depository institutions, and were proceeding to a "clean-up" of the balance sheets though the exchange of illiquid asset for liquid assets. Until April 2008, the Fed did not behave as a lender of last resort, but rather introduced innovations in such a way that the solvent institutions that were able to make loans could do it. Several empirical works show that these measures have put a downward pressure on the market interest rates.[5]

Similarly, the ECB wanted to provide liquidity to the interbank market to address the liquidity crisis. However, the "unconventional conventional" policies last a longer period in the euro area. The ECB has maintained its intermediation role between banks and the financial institutions (between the core and peripheral countries). The monetary authorities wanted to solve the liquidity crisis experienced by the euro area banking system, especially after the collapse of Lehman Brothers. The reaction was less drastic than in the United States, both in terms of the cut in the policy rate and in the volume of the injected liquidity in the interbank money market. Regarding the interest rates, the strategy was based on both tightening and then moving the corridor. Between October 2008 and May 2009 the policy rate has been cut from 4.25% to 1%.

To achieve its goal of lower target policy rate, the ECB initiated a facilitated access of banks to central bank liquidity through open-market operations. This was done primarily through Long-Term Refinancing Operations (LTROs) and the introduction of a Covered Bonds Purchase Program

---

[4] For a detailed description of the TAF, TSLF and PDCF, see Fleming, Hrung, and Keane (2009).

[5] See, for instance, Coffey, Hrung, and Sarkar (2009).

(CBPP). The share of eligible collateral assets for the LTROs was broadened (with a higher share of private securities) and the maturity was extended (from 6 to 12 months in June 2009 and then to 36 months). The cumulated amount of the extended LTRO programs introduced, respectively, in December 2011 and February 2012 has been greater than 1 trillion of euros and now accounts for almost 80% of the asset side of the ECB balance sheet. Besides, two programs of CBPP were introduced in 2009 and then in November 2011 to reduce the interest rate on a market which is central for banks' refinancing operations. Both the LTROs and the CBPP were components of a global program called "Enhanced Credit Support" (ECS). New LTRO and CBPP have been launched in 2014, but with a different purpose from the first round programs (discussed in the next section).

Just as in the case of the Fed, the ECB's policy goal was to secure the short-term refinancing of banks. However, the difference with the situation prevailing in the United States was that the need for refinancing was asymmetrical in light of the external account imbalances in the euro area. The ECB primarily wanted to deal with the problem of maturity mismatch of the banks in the peripheral countries of Europe (Greece, Ireland, Italy, Portugal, Spain). Like the Fed, the ECB's balance sheet did not change substantially during the adoption of the first non-standard measures.

4. Comparing Unconventional Monetary Policies

The peak of the financial turmoil can be dated to the months following the collapse of Lehman Brothers with crises hitting both the financial sector and the real economies. In October 2009, the unemployment rate in the United States surged to 10.2% reaching its highest peak in 25 years. The Fed thus turned to a more radical innovative monetary policy by implementing large-scale asset-purchase programs. This has been the beginning of the so-called quantitative easing policies. In Europe, during the years 2008 and 2009, the ECB still focused on maintaining the euro area banking system. However, failure to tighten fiscal policies and current account deficits led the euro area countries to enter a sovereign debt crisis with initial shocks originating in Greece, Portugal, and Ireland. The adverse developments on the sovereign debt markets exposed the banking sector to increased credit risk.[6] To avoid a bailout, the first responses came from

[6] For a description of the historical sequence from the financial to the sovereign debt crises in Europe, see Lane and Milesi-Ferretti (2012).

the Troika (IMF, ECB, and the European Commission) in the form of austerity and structural adjustment programs in exchange for funds provision to help recapitalize and deleverage the more fragile banks. However, the measures proved to be insufficient and this motivated the ECB to go beyond its initial non-standard conventional measures by buying large volume of sovereign debts in the secondary markets. The European quantitative easing policies were therefore different from those undertaken in the United States: the goals were different and the instruments used also differed. Moreover, one had to wait till 2014 before the ECB decides explicitly that its unconventional monetary policies was directed toward boosting the real economy.

The main problem facing the Fed at the time of Great economic recession was that it could not use its policy rate to put downward pressure on the market rates, especially on the long-term interest rates which are those influencing the cost of investment. The reason was the situation of zero lower bound of the Fed fund rate. Figure 13 shows a break in the level of the effective Fed fund rate from nearly 5.25% at the end of July 2007 to 0.11% in December 2008. Since then, the interest rate remained at very low levels near zero. This zero lower bound coincides with the regular increase in the size of the Fed's balance sheet from the end 2008 onward.

There are at least two explanations about the reasons why such a ZLB on the nominal rate was binding. One explanation is based on the Fisher relationship between nominal and real interest rates. In a time of Great recession the real interest rate (for instance a natural rate à la Wicksell) becomes very low. If the monetary strategy is such that agents have expectations of low level of short-term inflation, then it is likely that the nominal rate reaches a floor (zero in our case, since it can't be negative). A second explanation, based on the monetarist view, is that this arises because of monetary policy easing (in our case the non-standard conventional

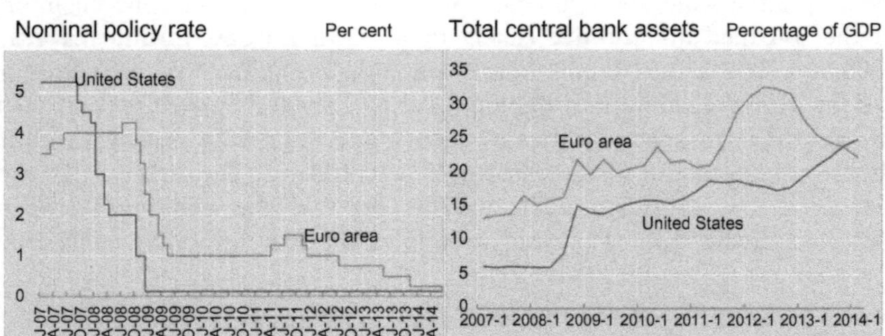

Figure 13: Policy Rates and Central Bank Assets. Source: BIS (2014).

policies).[7] These explanations opened several routes to the options that were at the central banks' disposal to stimulate aggregate demand after the nominal rate had reached a ZLB.

One way was to make an upward pressure on the long-term interest rate is through inflation expectations. As discussed in Section 4.3, this was the backbone of the so-called forward guidance policies. Another approach, that we discuss here, was based on quantitative measures. The idea was to activate the following different channels: credit, changes in the relative prices of assets, and tax on reserves.

Both the Fed and the ECB have adopted quantitative measures by increasing the monetary base. We first present the different programs and then discuss their implications on the liquidity and the real sector. The ECB also taxed money by introducing a negative deposit facility rate.

4.1. Quantitative Easing Policy in a Context of Zero Lower Bound in the United States

The important question was: how to get out of a recession when one could no longer use nominal interest rate to control monetary policy?

A first tool was the interest on excess reserves (IOER), introduced in October 2008, to drive the target fed fund rate to the target set by the FOMC. A prerequisite to retain control on the short-term rate was to have a control on the demand for reserves with banks receiving earnings on their balances. Initially offered at 75 basis points, the IOER has been cut to 25 basis points since December 2008. Accordingly, the amount of bank reserves in the Fed's balance sheet has remained high, meaning that they were keeping the reserves provided by the central bank on their balances at the Fed. A motivation for the introduction of IOER was that it helped implementing a floor for the market rates and to keep interest rates close to target rate.[8]

Two other tools were the Reverse Repo (RR) and the Term Deposit Facility (TDF). The first instrument was introduced in October 2008 and consists of loans made by many counterparties (not only primary dealers, but also institutions like MMFs and GSEs) to the Fed against an interest payment. TDF were adopted in April 2010 as loans made by financial institutions to the central banks of the US federal system against earning on

[7] For the different theoretical views of the ZLB, see Bullard (2010), Hamilton and Wu (2012).

[8] For the theoretical foundations, the reader may refer to Ennis and Keister (2008), Kashyap and Stein (2012), Martin, McAndrew, and Skeie (2013).

reserves for a length of time during which the loans are unusable. Both these tools have contributed to absorb bank reserves. But they have been done through small-scale operational exercises since 2009.

Since there was no room to further decrease the nominal policy interest rate, the Fed then turned to a policy that consisted in increasing base money through an expansion of the banks' reserves. An important difference with the standard open-market policy lies in the scale of the interventions and also in the composition of the asset side of its balance sheet. The demand for reserve became a target and was no longer a by-product of the Fed's open-market operations. The new policies have been defined as "quantitative" to mean that the Fed has been modifying the size of base money to reduce the long-term rate when there was no room to cut further the nominal Fed fund rates (because of the ZLB).

The Fed's balance sheet management policy has consisted in making a series of large-scale asset purchases of long-term securities (LSAP). A first asset-purchase program (LSAP I) was launched in November 2008 under which it bought large quantities of agency debt and agency-guaranteed MBS.[9] In March 2009, the Fed enlarged the pace of asset purchases to include Treasury coupon securities. It bought $300 billion in Treasury securities, $750 billion in MBS, and $200 billion in Government Sponsored Enterprises (GES). Later, under QEII, introduced in November 2010, the Fed purchased $600 billion of additional Treasury securities and adopted a Twist operation (for $400 billion). The principle was that the Fed was selling Treasury securities with a maturity of less than 3 months and buying Treasury securities with maturities from 6 to 30 years. In September 2011, it extended the maturity of its Treasury securities portfolio (this was the Maturity Extension Program, MEP, under which it sold shorter-term securities and used the proceeds to buy longer-term securities) and in September 2012, the Fed bought each month $40 billion of MBS and $45 billion of Treasury securities. Many other programs included credit easing (by direct loans to some segments of the private sector) or purchases of securities (Troubled Asset Relief Program, TARP; Commercial Paper Funding Facility, CPFF; Money Market Mutual Fund Liquidity Facility, MMMF; Money Market Investor Funding Facility, MMIFF).

The series of unprecedented unconventional policies have been known as QEI, QEII, and QEIII (QE for quantitative easing). These policies have substantially modified both the size and composition of its balance sheet, in spite of the sterilization policy that occurred occasionally during the period

9 Securities issued by Fannie Mae, Freddie Mac, the Federal Home Loan Banks and Ginnie Mae.

from September 2008 to August 2011 when the reserves created were reabsorbed under the Treasury Supplementary Financing Program (SFP). What was the Fed's goals through these QE policies? There seems to be evidence in the literature that LSAPs have reduced the slope of the term structure of the interest rates (see, D'Amico, English, Lopez-Salido, & Nelson, 2012; Gagnon, Raskin, Remache, & Sack, 2011; Krishnamurthy & Vissing-Jorgensen, 2011). Other papers adopt conclusions that are less optimistic, finding either that the positive effects of QE on market rates effect died out quickly or that the effect on the real economy has been weak (see, Chen, Cúrdia, & Ferrero, 2012; Wright, 2011). Whatever the appreciation of the impact of the quantitative easing policies, there is a consensus on the fact that they have contributed to increase in the size of the Fed's balance sheet as well as change in the composition of its asset.

4.2. Quantitative Easing Policies by the ECB

There was a difference in the timing of quantitative easing policies between the Fed and the ECB. The former has lent little money to banks. By contrast, the ECB has been providing funds to banks of the countries that faced constraints in the access to international capital markets (banks from the peripheral countries have been cut off from the interbank market). The main goal of monetary policy was not promoting growth, but first saving the banking system and solving the liquidity crisis caused by the sovereign debt crisis. To this end, the ECB introduced the SMP and then the OMT.

A Securities Market Program (SMP) has been initiated in May 2010 (and re-activated in August 2011) in response to enhanced tensions on certain segment of the European debt markets. The ECB purchased around €220 billion of Greek, Irish, Portuguese, and Spanish sovereign bonds in the secondary markets. The SMP terminated in September 2012 and was replaced by the Outright Monetary Operations (OMT). Under this program, the ECB purchases unlimited amount of short-term government bonds in the euro area markets. Banks are eligible to this program provided that their government agrees on a reform and fiscal adjustment program with the European Financial Stability Facility (EFSF) and with the European Stability Mechanism (ESM). The goal is to lower down the short-run market rates by cutting down the liquidity risk in the markets. The main beneficiaries of this program have been the peripheral countries of the euro zone: Greece, Portugal, and Spain (see Figure 14).

The ECB has been concerned with tackling the economic recession later than the Fed. The first measures to fight the decline of the GDP growth

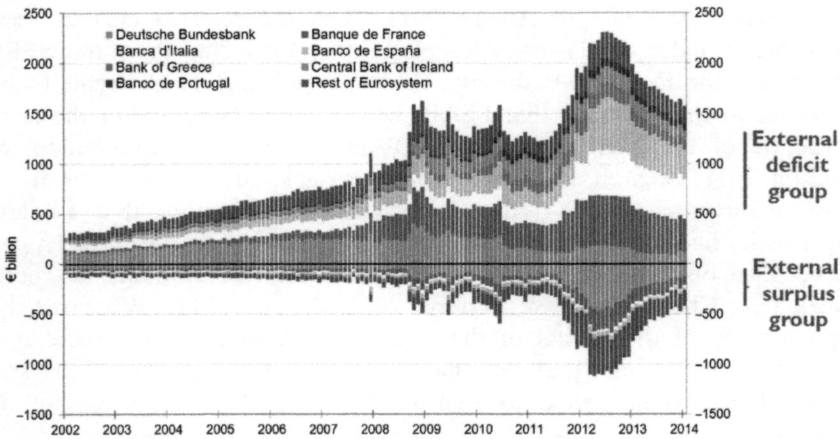

Figure 14: Liquidity Provision and Absorption throughout the Euro System. Source: Cour-Thimann and Winkler (2014).

dates back to 2013 when new LTROs programs were adopted and when the monetary authorities turned their attention to forward guidance (see the next section). Another difference with the Fed lies in the fact that interest-rates policies have been used simultaneously to the purchase of massive amount of securities. The marginal lending rate has been brought to 0.4% and the overnight rate on deposit facility is now negative at –0.10%. This negative rate aimed at forcing the banks in the core countries to lend their excess reserves to the banks in the periphery. Finally, the statutory reserves were decreased from 2% to 1%. As a consequence, the Eonia is now near zero and a substantial decrease in the 3-months and 12-months Euribor rates on futures has occurred. As a consequence of the interest rates decrease the corridor width has been reduced to 0.5%.

Moreover, the ECB has adopted six new LTRO programs ending in September 2018 for loan maturities between 2 years and 4 years. The aim is to provide incitation to banks so that they increase their loans to the private sector (households and corporates). The first new LTRO was adopted in September 2014, the second in December 2014 and four others will be introduced from March 2015 onward. The criteria to be eligible suggest that the goal is to raise the amount of bank credit to the real sector. For the two LTROs introduced in 2014, the amount allotted to banks by the ECB are conditioned by the stock of their current loans to the private non-financial sector. For the other four programs banks will be allowed to borrow an amount representing at most tree times the growth rate of their credit the private sector.

4.3. Forward Guidance Policy

Unconventional monetary policies, by both the Fed and the ECB, have been undertaken in a context of very low interest rates. In such a situation, one way of exerting a downward pressure on the long-term real interest rates was through the expectation channel.

By the Fisher relationship, the real short-term interest rate is defined as

$$r = (i - \pi^e) + \delta,$$

where r and i are, respectively, the real and nominal interest rates, π^e is an expected inflation, and δ is a constant. r is the interest rate in the financial markets (housing loans, corporate loans).

The equation of the yield curve gives a link between long-term and short-term rates

$$R_t^T = \sum_i^T r_{t+i}^e + \tau,$$

where r_{t+i}^e is the expected short-term rate, τ is a term premium, and R_t^T is a long-term rate.

Forward guidance means steering the short-term interest rate expectations. The long-term rate is determined through the likely future path of monetary policy. By undertaking massive asset purchases the Fed and the ECB demonstrates that they want to maintain the short-term rates at low levels. This is sometimes called a signaling effect. Central banks act in such a way to convince the public that they will pursue inflationary policies and that policy rates will not be raised earlier.[10] It is important to notice that forward guidance is expected to influence the long-term rate through the expectation of future path of monetary policy (this is referred as forward guidance on policy rates). Another form of forward guidance works through the purchase of assets. Indeed, in addition to the portfolio rebalancing effect mentioned above (which mainly influences the term premium in long-run interest rate), the purchase of massive amount of assets may signal the intention of the central bank to commit to low policy rates (this signal effect is called a balance sheet forward guidance policy[11]).

In the United States, the Fed's forward guidance strategy has evolved across time from general assessments to calendar-based and conditional forward guidance. The initial statements began in December 2008 and till

[10] For theoretical models of forward guidance policies, see Blinder, Ehrmann, Fratzscher, Dehann, and Jansen (2008).

[11] See Bauer and Rudebusch (2013), Woodford (2012).

February 2009, the FOMC was saying that the Fed fund rates would "exceptionally" be kept at low levels given the bad economic juncture (this is called qualitative forward guidance in the sense that no quantitative measure is associated with the announcement). And then, in March 2009, as the recession was deepening, the "exceptional" situation turned to and "extended period." But then, from August 2011 to December, the Fed began to provide the public with precise calendar dates with announcements like "keep the fed fund rate near zero, or warrant exceptionally low levels, at least through mid-2013, at least through late 2014, or through mid-2015." Then the calendar forward dependence was turned to a state-contingent forward guidance with the Fed conditioning its low interest rate policy according to some target values of the unemployment rate (below 6.5%) and of the inflation rate (below 2% long-run goal).

The ECB decided to turn to forward guidance policy later than the Fed, in July 2013, after the market rates had begun to raise when some banks were reimbursing their LTRO, and in a context in which the demand for liquidity in the interbank market was still high. One difference with the Fed is the following. In its public announcements, when talking about "an extended period," the ECB refers to the situation of inflation which is thought to remain subdued for an extended period of time (see Praet, 2013 for the explanation of the ECB viewpoint on forward guidance). The board of governors motivates this approach by the fact that their mandate is primarily to keep the inflation rate below 2% and want to commit to this objective. The promise to keep the ECB rate at low level for an extended period of time is motivated by the cross-checking of inflation through the monetary indicators. In spite of the increase in the money base, there has been slow growth in the monetary and credit aggregates so far.

The literature suggest expectations of future paths of short-term rates and long-term bond yields tended to decline on most announcements in both the United States and the euro area.[12] In the United States, the largest impact was seen for the qualitative forward guidance. The main differences between the Fed and ECB forward guidance policies are thus the following. First, the former has pursued forward guidance policy based on both its balance sheet and policy rates. The purchase of assets by the ECB was motivated to stabilize the banking sector in the euro zone, not to influence the market rates. Second, the ECB has used this kind of policy only recently. Thirdly, the Fed has been using diverse forward guidance policies: qualitative, calendar-based, and state-contingent. Is any of these strategies the best? Some author claims that stage-contingent forward policies

[12] See Campbell, Evans, Fisher, and Justiniano (2012), Filardo and Hofmann (2014).

increase financial stability because the recalibration of the guidance could lead to disruptive market reactions.[13]

5. Conclusion

To sum up, since the 2008 financial crisis, the Fed and ECB have adopted unconventional monetary policies with two goals: (i) to restore the functioning of the interbank money markets, (ii) to adapt an easy monetary policy in a context of zero lower bound. Several instruments were used to meet these targets: liquidity support to the markets, purchase of private assets and sovereign bonds for extended maturities, forward guidance.

In the early stage of the subprime crisis, preserving financial market stability has been the primary goal of monetary policies for both central banks. They accordingly adopted measures such as emergency liquidity programs and cuts in their short-term policy rates near zero. However, the Fed has been less "risk-adverse" than the ECB, by providing loans against mortgage-based securities (toxic assets) as collateral, while the ECB has been lending to banks against covered bonds through the LTROs. As explained in this chapter, the financial environments were different in the United States and in the euro area. Monetary policy during the early stages of the crisis helped stabilizing the banking sector in the United States, and the issue was then how to curb the economic recession. The euro area countries have experienced a second financial crisis, namely a sovereign debt crisis stemming from asymmetric external imbalances.

Asymmetric imbalances within the euro area is an integral part of the banking crisis in Europe. This is quite clear when one looks at TARGET2 imbalances. The fragmentation of the cross-border interbank market had become a central issue, as shown in several studies pointing to the presence of a break in different indicators of financial integration amongst the euro area countries between 2007 and 2012 (see, for instance, de Sola Perea & Van Nieuwenhuyze, 2014; Grande, 2014). Judging how much of the safeguard of the banking system can be attributable to the particular policies undertaken by the ECB is, however, not uncontroversial. Indeed, as capital flew from the peripheral countries of the euro zone, their central banks were receiving cross-border credits from the national banks of the core countries. Therefore, this financing through the balance of payment was concomitant with the supply of liquidity by the ECB (see Higgins & Klitgaard, 2014, for a detailed discussion on this point).

13 See Tucker (2013).

What next? A lot has been written on the exit strategies and this issue is still a matter of debate (see the collection of papers in European Parliament, 2014). On the one side, some advocates in favor of a return of monetary policy to its conventional form (monetary policy setting the interest rate to achieve price stability in the euro area and also the real activity in the United States). However, in practice, it is not clear to what extend such a policy would avoid a new financial crisis. Indeed, there are several issues that need to be understood more deeply.

First, the standard framework is based on several assumptions: the so-called "divine" coincidence, financial market efficiency and the stability of the macroeconomic equilibrium corresponding to the divine coincidence hypothesis. However, some recent papers points to the fact that, several years ahead the 2007, central banks have missed the building of financial imbalances because these assumptions do not hold in practice (see, for instance, Dufrénot, Jawadi, & Khayat, 2014). An interesting paper by Gagnon and Sack (2014) from the Peterson Institute for International Economics proposes an original new operating framework that would allow the Fed to conduct monetary policy while maintaining an elevated balance sheet with abundant liquidity in the financial system. Theoretically, the exit strategy does not necessarily implies to return to "pure" interest-rate-based rule but may be to adopt a mixture of quantity-base and interest-rate based rule.

Secondly, for the euro area an issue is back on the agenda, namely fiscal dominance. There is a growing agreement amongst the policymakers that in a context of sovereign over-indebtedness, the objectives of monetary and fiscal policies should be reversed: use expansive fiscal policy to anchor inflation expectations (through fiscal adjustment) and use monetary policy to avoid debt unsustainability. This should lead us to move away from the conventional approach of policy-mix.

To conclude, this chapter has identified a number of operational issues that differed in the design of monetary policy by the Fed and the ECB. This therefore enriches the panoply of potential different theoretical models that could be done for a better comprehension of what makes the monetary policies of the United States and euro area similar and what makes them different.

References

Auer, R. A. (2012). *What drives Target2 balances? Evidence from a panel analysis.* Swiss National Bank Working Paper 2012–15.

Bauer, M. D., & Rudebusch, G. D. (2013). *The signaling channel for Federal Reserve bond purchases.* Working Paper 2011–21, Federal Reserve Bank of San Francisco.

Benmelech, E., & Dlugosz, J. (2009). The credit rating crisis. *NBER Macroeconomics Annual*, *24*, 161–207.

BIS. (2014, June). 84th Annual Report, 2013–2014, Basel.

Blinder, A. M., Ehrmann, M., Fratzscher, M., Dehann, J., & Jansen, J. (2008). Central bank communication and monetary policy. *Journal of Economic Literature*, *46*(4), 910–945.

Bullard, J. (2010). Seven faces of the peril. Federal Reserve Bank of Saint-Louis Review, *92*(5), 339–352.

Campbell, J., Evans, C., Fisher, J., & Justiniano, A. (2012). Macroeconomic effects of Federal Reserve forward guidance. *Brookings Papers on Economic Activity*, (Spring), 1–80.

Cecchetti, S. G., McCauley, R. N., & McGuire, P. M. (2012, December). *Interpreting TARGET2 balances*. BIS Working Papers no.°393.

Chen, H., Cúrdia, V., & Ferrero, A. (2012). The macroeconomic effects of large-scale asset purchase programs. *The Economic Journal*, *122*(564), F289–315.

Coffey, N., Hrung, W. B., & Sarkar, A. (2009, October). Capital Constraints, Counterparty Risk, and Deviations from Covered Interest Rate Parity. Federal Reserve Bank of New York Staff Reports, no. 393.

Committee on International Economic Policy and Reform. (2012, September). Banks and Cross-Border Capital Flows: Policy Challenges and Regulatory Responses.

Cour-Thimann, P., & Winkler, B. (2014, April). A flow-of-funds perspective on non-standard monetary policy: The euro area in comparison with the US. Monetary analysis and monetary policy frameworks, Conference in Edinburgh.

D'Amico, S., English, W. B., Lopez-Salido, D., & Nelson, E. (2012). The Federal Reserve's large-scale asset purchase programs: Rationale and effects. *Economic Journal*, *122*(564), F415–F446.

de Sola Perea, M., & Van Nieuwenhuyze, C. (2014, June). Financial integration and fragmentation in the euro area. *NBB Economic Review*.

Dufrénot, G., Jawadi, F., & Khayat, A. (2014, August). Why did the central banks adopt the wrong policies by underestimating the financial cycle? *The society for Economic Measurement Conference*, Chicago, IL, USA.

Ennis, H. M., & Keister, T. (2008). Understanding monetary policy implementation. *Federal Reserve Bank of Richmond Economic Quarterly*, *94*(3), 235–263.

European Parliament. (2014). Exit strategies and the impact on the euro area. Compilation of Notes, Monetary Dialogue, Directorate General for Internal Policies, Policy Department, Economic and Scientific Policy.

Filardo, A., & Hofmann, B. (2014). Forward guidance at the zero lower bound. *BIS Quarterly Review*, (March), 37–53.

Fleming, M. J., Hrung, W. B., & Keane, F. H. (2009). The term securities lending facility: Origin, design, and effects. *Federal Reserve Bank of New York Current Issues in Economics and Finance*, *15*(2), 1–11.

Friedman, B. M., & Kuttner, K. N. (2010, July). *Implementation of monetary policy: How do central banks set interest rates?* NBER Working Paper no.°16165.

Gagnon, J., Raskin, M., Remache, J., & Sack, B. (2011). The financial market effects of the Federal Reserve's large-scale asset purchases. *International Journal of Central Banking*, *7*(1), 3–43.

Gagnon, J., & Sack, B. (2014, January). Monetary policy with abundant liquidity: A new operating framework for the Federal Reserve. Peterson Institute for International Economics, Policy Brief.

Gerdesmeier, D., Mongelli, F. P., & Roffia, B. (2007, March). *The Euro system, the US Federal Reserve and the bank of Japan: Similarities and differences*. ECB Working Paper no. 742.

Grande, M. (2014, April 28). Financial integration in Europe. ECB Report 2014, Joint ECB-EC Conference on Financial Integration, Frankfurt.

Greenwood, R., & Vayanos, D. (2008). *Bond supply and excess bond returns*. CEPR Discussion Paper 6694.

Hamilton, J. D., & Wu, J. C. (2012). The effectiveness of alternative monetary policy tools in a zero lower bound environment. *Journal of Money, Credit, and Banking*, *44*(s1), 3–46.

Higgins, M., & Klitgaard, T. (2014). The balance of payment crisis in the Euro area periphery. *Current Issues in Economics and Finance*, *20*(2), 1–8. Federal Reserve Bank of New York.

International Monetary Fund. (2013, October). Global Financial Stability Report.

Kashyap, A., & Stein, J. (2012). The optimal conduct of monetary policy with interest on reserves. American Economic Journal: Macroeconomics, *4*(1), 266–282.

Kiyotaki, N., & Moore, J. (1997). Credit cycles. *Journal of Political Economy*, *105*(2), 211–248.

Krishnamurthy, A., & Vissing-Jorgensen, A. (2011). The effects of quantitative easing on interest rates: Channels and implications for policy. *Brookings Papers on Economic Activity*, (Fall), 215–265.

Lane, P. R., & Milesi-Ferretti, G. M. (2012). External adjustment and the global crisis. *Journal of International Economics*, *88*(2), 252–265.

Martin, A., McAndrew, J., & Skeie, D. (2013). Bank lending in times of large bank reserves. Federal Reserve Bank of New-York, Staff Report.

McGuire, P., & Götz, P. (2009, October). The US dollar shortage in global banking and the international policy response. BIS Working Papers No. 291.

Merler, S., & Pisani-Ferry, J. (2012). Sudden stops in the Euro area. *Bruegel Policy Contribution*, *2012/6*(March), 1–16.

Praet, P. (2013). Forward Guidance and the ECB. Column by Peter Praet, Member of the Executive Board of the ECB, published on VoxEU.org on August 6, 2013.

Shleifer, A., & Vishny, R. W. (1997). The limits of arbitrage. *Journal of Finance*, *52*(1), 35–55.

Tressel, T., & Wang, S. (2014, July). *Rebalancing in the euro area and cyclicality of current account adjustments*. IMF Working Papers 14/130.

Tucker, P. (2013, September 29). Monetary strategy and prospects. Speech to the Association for Financial Markets in Europe, London.

Whelan, K. (2013, March). TARGET2 and Central Bank Balance Sheets. Draft, University College Dublin.

Woodford, M. (2012, August). Methods of policy accommodation at the interest rate lower bound. Federal Reserve Bank of Kansas City, Jackson Hole Symposium Conference Volume.

Wright, J. H. (2011). Term premia and inflation uncertainty: Empirical evidence from an international panel dataset. *American Economic Review*, *101*(4), 1514–1534.

Chapter 13

Was Bernanke Right? Targeting Asset Prices May *not* be a Good Idea After All

Tiziana Assenza[a,b], Michele Berardi[c] and Domenico Delli Gatti[a]

[a]*Department of Economics and Finance, CLE, Università Cattolica del Sacro Cuore, Largo Gemelli 1, 20123 Milano, Italy, e-mail: tiziana.assenza@unicatt.it*
[b]*Amsterdam School of Economics, CeNDEF, University of Amsterdam, Valckenierstraat 65-67, 1018 XE Amsterdam, The Netherlands, e-mail: michele.berardi@manchester.ac.uk*
[c]*School of Social Sciences, The University of Manchester, Oxford Road, Manchester M13 9PL, UK, e-mail: domenico.delligatti@unicatt.it*

Abstract

Should the central bank target asset price inflation? In their 1999 paper Bernanke and Gertler claimed that price stability and financial stability are "mutually consistent objectives" in a flexible inflation targeting regime which "dictates that central banks ... should not respond to changes in asset prices." This conclusion is straightforward within their framework in which asset price inflation shows up as a factor "augmenting" the IS curve. In this chapter, we pursue a different modeling strategy so that, in the end, asset price dynamics will be incorporated into the NK Phillips curve. We put ourselves, therefore, in the best position to obtain a significant stabilizing role for asset price targeting. It turns out, however, that inflation volatility is higher in the asset price targeting case. After all, therefore, targeting asset prices may not be a good idea.

Keywords: cost channel, asset prices, Taylor rules

JEL Classifications: E42, E52

International Symposia in Economic Theory and Econometrics, Vol. 24
William A. Barnett and Fredj Jawadi (Editors)

ISSN: 1571-0386/doi: 10.1108/S1571-038620150000024025

1. Introduction

The recent financial crisis has increased attention on financial stability and its connection to monetary policy. In a recent speech at the International Monetary Fund (Yellen, 2014), Janet Yellen, Chair of the Federal Reserve System, expressed the view that financial stability should be achieved mainly through macroprudential regulations, in order to leave monetary policy free to pursue its more traditional goals of price stability and full employment: "...it is critical for regulators to complete their efforts at implementing a macroprudential approach to enhance resilience within the financial system, which will minimize the likelihood that monetary policy will need to focus on financial stability issues rather than on price stability and full employment." She went on, though, to recognize that macroprudential policies are unlikely to solve all problems of financial instabilities, and that uncertainty still remains on the role of monetary policy in taming financial turmoil: "... there is no simple rule that can prescribe, even in a general sense, how monetary policy should adjust in response to shifts in the outlook for financial stability." At her confirmation hearing in front of the U.S. Senate she made her position on this issue even clearer: "I would not rule out using monetary policy as a tool to address asset price misalignments, but because it's a blunt tool and because Congress has asked us to use those tools to achieve the goals of maximum employment and price stability, I would like to see monetary policy directed toward achieving those goals Congress has given us."

The issue of the role of monetary policy in financial markets is not new and had been considered in the academic community long before recent events brought it to the attention of policymakers and the general public. In particular, academics had tried to understand whether conventional monetary policy, in the form of a change in interest rates, is an appropriate tool for stabilizing asset price dynamics.

The start of the debate over this crucial issue can be dated back to the Bernanke and Gertler (1999, 2001) (BG hereafter) versus Cecchetti, Genberg, Lipsky, and Wadhwani (2000) exchange – but it has not been settled yet. BG got a point at the time, with the authoritative (at the time) endorsement of Alan Greenspan. Their conclusion according to which central banks should not attempt to stabilize asset prices has been the consensus view in the first half of the decade. Following the 2007–2008 financial crisis, however, the conventional wisdom seemed to change, with more people – especially on the media and in policy circle – calling for a more active role of central banks in stabilizing asset prices, in order to avoid vicious booms and busts with remarkably negative real effects on the macroeconomy.

In this chapter we try to shed new light on this issue. In a sense, we put ourselves in the best (theoretical) position to find a role for monetary policy in stabilizing asset prices. It turns out, however – somewhat to our surprise – that also in this new framework targeting asset prices may be destabilizing. Asset prices booms and busts should be mitigated but a modified Taylor rule, augmented by asset price dynamics, may not be the best policy response.

In their 1999 paper BG made essentially the following point: "Central banks should view price stability and financial stability as highly complementary and mutually consistent objectives ... the best policy framework for attaining both objectives is a regime of flexible inflation targeting ... The inflation-targeting approach dictates that central banks should adjust monetary policy actively and pre-emptively to offset incipient inflationary or deflationary pressures" (Bernanke & Gertler, 1999, p. 18).

The main rationale for this claim is that "by focusing on the inflationary or deflationary pressures generated by asset price movements, a central bank effectively responds to the toxic side effects of asset booms and busts ... Inflation targeting ... implies that interest rates will tend to rise during (inflationary) asset price booms and fall during (deflationary) asset price busts" (ibid).

The debate over this crucial issue is at least a decade old – if we date it from the Bernanke and Gertler (1999, 2001) (BG hereafter) vs Cecchetti et al. (2000) exchange – but it has not been settled yet. BG got a point at the time, with the authoritative (at the time) endorsement of Alan Greenspan. Their conclusion according to which central banks should not attempt to stabilize asset prices has been the consensus view in the first half of the decade. Following the 2007–08 financial crisis, however, the conventional wisdom has changed dramatically. Nowadays – especially on the media and in policy circle – it seems to be that asset prices should indeed be stabilized by the central bank to avoid vicious booms and busts with remarkably negative real effects on the macroeconomy.

This conclusion is straightforward within the BG variant of the New Keynesian (NK) DSGE framework. In their model, asset price inflation shows up as a factor "augmenting" the IS curve: An asset price shock, in fact, yields a *net worth or balance sheet effect* on investment (the reference model is Bernanke, Gertler, & Gilchrist, 1999). Essentially the same approach has been adopted by Carlstrom and Fuerst (2007), Iacoviello (2005), and Monacelli (2008).[1] A different approach is followed by

[1] Iacoviello and Monacelli build rich models in which also the price of real assets (on the housing market) plays a role. In a sense they blend the BG approach to the Kiyotaki and Moore (1997) emphasis on endogenous borrowing constraints.

Airaudo, Nistico, and Zanna (2007) who stress the role of the *wealth effect* on consumption. Also in this case, however, asset prices affect aggregate demand and lead to an *"Augmented" (optimizing) IS curve*.

In the BG framework, therefore, a Stock market boom shows up as a demand shock so that asset prices and inflation move in the same direction. As a consequence, following the BG modeling strategy, one is led naturally to conclude that if the central bank follows an inflation targeting approach there is no need to specifically target asset prices above and beyond inflation. By stabilizing the latter, it will stabilize also the former.

In this chapter we follow a different route. In our model in fact, asset price dynamics will be eventually incorporated into the NK Phillips curve. In the simplified economy we consider, in fact, firms have to anticipate wages to workers before they can cash in sales proceeds. Assuming that firms do not accumulate internal finance, they need funds at the moment wages have to be paid. In other words, we explore the same environment as in Ravenna and Walsh's (2006) model of the *cost channel*. For simplicity, however, we assume that, in order to raise external finance, firms issue new equities ("equity only" financing) instead of asking for bank loans.

In our model the return on shares, which is determined by asset price dynamics, is in turn a determinant of the firms' marginal cost so that in the end we obtain an *"Augmented" NK Phillips curve*.

While in Ravenna–Walsh monetary policy impacts on inflation *directly* because the interest rate (on loans) is a determinant of the firm's cost, in our setting the cost channel is activated *indirectly* whenever monetary policy affects – through changes in the interest rate – asset price inflation.

As a consequence of this modeling strategy, in our framework a Stock market boom shows up as a positive supply shock – in fact, in a rational expectations equilibrium it yields a reduction of the return on shares – leading to lower inflation: asset prices and inflation move in opposite directions.[2] It is not true anymore, in this context, that by focusing on inflation the central bank is also checking an asset price boom. On the contrary, if the central bank adopts an inflation targeting approach, in the attempt to stabilize inflation it will boost Stock prices even further.

The empirical evidence on the correlation between inflation and asset price changes is mixed and certainly not overwhelmingly in favor of the BG

[2] Also De Grauwe (2008) implicitly assumes a negative correlation between asset price dynamics and inflation (along the NK Phillips curve). In his framework, the marginal cost is decreasing with the firms' net worth (because of the external finance premium). An increase of the asset price pushes up net worth and brings down the external finance premium, marginal cost, and inflation.

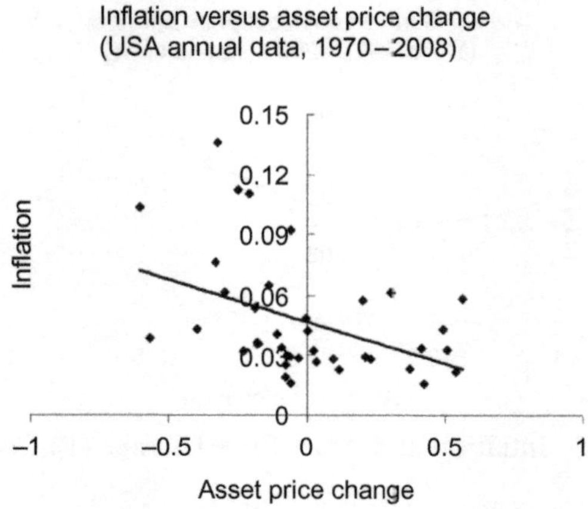

Figure 1: Inflation and Asset Price Change (USA).

approach. In Figure 1 we report the scatter diagram of inflation[3] and the change in real asset prices[4] in the United States from 1970 to 2008.

Linear interpolation returns a negatively sloped regression line. The correlation is −0.4, in line with the assumption proposed in this chapter.

In Figure 2 we focus on cross-sectional evidence summarized by the scatter diagram of the mean inflation rate and the mean asset price change[5] over the period 1957Q1–2003Q1 for 12 countries[6] as reported in Chih-Chuan Yeh and Ching-Fang Chi (2009).

Linear interpolation returns a positively sloped regression line (not shown in the figure). The linear correlation index is greater than 0.5 in line with BG. Notice, however, that a quadratic interpolation fits the data much better.[7] The relationship between inflation and asset price change over the long run, therefore, seems to be non-monotonic.

The toy economy we consider is of course a far cry from reality. For reasons of tractability and as a very preliminary step toward a more satisfactory – and necessarily more complicated – setting, in fact, we abstract

[3] Inflation is here defined as the rate of change of the Consumer Price Index.

[4] Asset price change is defined as the percent deviation of the real asset price (nominal asset price deflated by the Consumer Price Index) from a linear trend.

[5] The asset price change is defined as the natural logarithm of the nominal stock index divided by the consumer price index.

[6] Australia, Canada, Finland, France, Germany, Ireland, Italy, Japan, Netherlands, New Zealand, Spain, United States.

[7] R^2 is 0.26 in case of a linear interpolation while it is 0.55 in case of a quadratic interpolation.

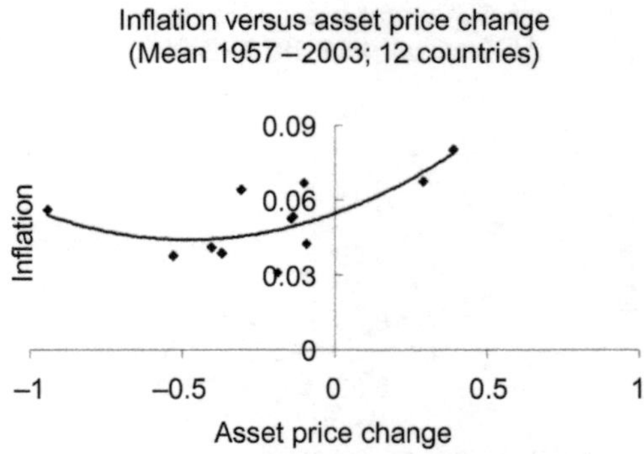

Figure 2: Inflation and Asset Price Change (12 Countries).

from a wide range of crucial imperfections of financial markets. The implications of the model, however, are surprisingly far reaching.

We analyze the design and the transmission mechanism of monetary policy in two regimes: (a) an instrument rule with no-reaction to asset prices (Strict Inflation Targeting, SIT), (b) an instrument rule with reaction to asset prices (Asset augmented Inflation Targeting, AIT).

In the case of a supply shock, the central bank reacts to inflation by raising the interest rate, asset prices fall, the output gap turns negative and dividends fall, the return on shares increases (even if dividends fall) to match the increase in the real interest rate. The central bank therefore faces a trade-off: An aggressive policy stance aiming at stabilizing inflation would make the asset price bust even worse. If it takes into account asset price changes – that is in the AIT case – the central bank will ease a bit and therefore in the end it will mitigate (with respect to the SIT case) the impact on output of its contractionary policy. On the other hand, however, it will exacerbate the impact of the shock on inflation. The AIT regime, therefore, is characterized by milder variations in output but larger changes in inflation.

Consider now a demand shock, which has a positive effect on inflation and the output gap (and dividends). As in the previous case, the central bank reacts to inflation by raising the interest rate. The asset price tends to increase because of the increase in dividends but the increase of the real interest rate prompts a flight from equities which depresses asset prices. In our model the second effect prevails over the first one so that in the end asset prices fall. If the central bank takes into account asset price changes – that is, in the AIT case – the fall in asset prices will induce a monetary easing so that the central bank will amplify the impact on output of the demand shock. On the other hand, it will exacerbate the impact of the shock on inflation. In the AIT regime, therefore, output grows more than in the SIT case but inflation will be higher.

In the AIT case, therefore, inflation volatility is always higher while output volatility is higher (lower) in case of a demand (supply) shock. After all, therefore, targeting asset prices may not be a good idea. At first sight, this is surprising because we put ourselves in the best position to obtain a significant stabilizing role for asset price targeting. Why is it so? In the end, as we will show in Section 4, in the AIT case the central bank is "too accommodating." Targeting asset prices makes the central bank particularly "wet." This may be welfare-reducing.

The chapter is organized as follows. Sections 2 and 3 describe households' and firms' decision rules. In Section 3.1 we derive the Augmented NK Phillips curve. In Section 4 we evaluate the impact of a Taylor-type instrument rule for monetary policy, with and without asset prices (i.e., in the AIT and SIT cases). In this section the comparison between the two regimes in case a demand or a supply shock occur is spelled out in detail. Section 5 is devoted to some welfare considerations. Finally, Section 6 concludes.

2. Households

The economy is populated by households and firms. The former decide on consumption, asset holdings (money, bonds, shares), and labor supply.

There is a continuum of unit mass of infinitely lived identical households which discount the future at the factor β. Period utility is represented by a standard CRRA function:

$$U(C_t, m_t, N_t) = \frac{C_t^{1-\sigma}}{1-\sigma} + \frac{\gamma}{1-\zeta} m_t^{1-\zeta} - \chi \frac{N_t^{1+\eta}}{1+\eta},$$

where $\sigma, \gamma, \zeta, \chi$, and η are positive parameters with the usual interpretation, C_t is a CES aggregator of consumption goods,[8] $m_t := M_t/P_t$ are real money balances[9] and N_t represents hours worked. Real money balances show up in the utility function because they provide liquidity services.

[8] C_t consists of differentiated consumption goods produced by monopolistically competitive firms and is defined as follows:

$$C_t = \left[\int_0^1 c_{jt}^{\frac{e-1}{e}} \mathrm{d}j\right]^{\frac{e}{e-1}}$$

where $e > 1$ turns out to be the price elasticity of demand of each good.

[9] The price level is a CES aggregator of the individual prices: $P_t = \left[\int_0^1 p_{jt}^{1-e} \mathrm{d}j\right]^{1/(e-1)}$.

The households' portfolio consists of money, bonds, and shares. The nominal value in t of money balances (resp. Government bonds) carried over from the past is denoted by M_{t-1} (B_{t-1}). Moreover the household owns A_{t-1} shares, whose price is Q_t. In period t the household receives a flow of interest payments on Government bonds $i_{t-1}B_{t-1}$ where i_{t-1} is the nominal interest rate in $t-1$. Moreover we assume that firms pay in t (nominal) dividends equal to D_t per share held in $t-1$.

The household employs "resources" consisting of wage income, interest payments, and dividends to consume and increase money, bond, and shareholdings according to the following budget constraint in real terms:

$$C_t + m_t + b_t + q_t A_t = w_t N_t + \frac{1}{1+\pi_t}[m_{t-1} + (1+i_{t-1})b_{t-1}] + (q_t + d_t)A_{t-1}, \tag{1}$$

where $b_t := B_t/P_t$ are real bond holdings; $q_t := Q_t/P_t$ is the real price of each share (asset price or Stock price for short in the following); $w_t := W_t/P_t$ is the real wage; $\pi_t := P_t/(P_{t-1} - 1)$ is the inflation rate and d_t are dividends per share.

Liquidity injections (withdrawals) are implemented (by the central bank) by means of open market purchases (sales) of bonds: $M_t - M_{t-1} = -[B_t - (1+i_{t-1})B_{t-1}]$.

Taking into account this procedure, the budget constraint of the representative household boils down to: $P_tC_t + Q_t(A_t - A_{t-1}) = W_tN_t + D_tA_{t-1}$. In the present context, the wage bill W_tN_t is financed by means of equity issues Q_tA_t (see next section). Hence $Q_tA_t = W_tN_t$. Using this equality, it turns out that

$$P_tC_t = (Q_t + D_t)A_{t-1}. \tag{2}$$

In period t, the representative household maximizes:

$$E_t \sum_{s=0}^{\infty} \beta^s \left[\frac{C_{t+s}^{1-\sigma}}{1-\sigma} + \frac{\gamma}{1-\zeta}(m_{t+s})^{1-\zeta} - \chi \frac{N_{t+s}^{1+\eta}}{1+\eta} \right], \tag{3}$$

subject to a sequence of budget constraints of the form (1). From the first-order conditions (see Appendix A for details) one can derive the usual optimal relations, that is, the Euler equations for consumption, money, and labor supply:

$$C_t^{-\sigma} = \beta(1+i_t)E_t\left(\frac{P_t}{P_{t+1}}\right)C_{t+1}^{-\sigma} \tag{4}$$

$$\frac{i_t}{1+i_t}=\gamma\frac{C_t^{\sigma}}{m_t^{\zeta}} \tag{5}$$

$$\chi C_t^{\sigma}N_t^{\eta}=w_t. \tag{6}$$

Moreover we get one additional optimal relation that we interpret as a *No-Arbitrage Condition*

$$\frac{1+i_t}{1+E_t\pi_{t+1}}=\frac{E_t(q_{t+1}+d_{t+1})}{q_t}. \tag{7}$$

Equation (7) establishes the equality between the return on bonds, that is, the real interest rate, and the return on equities, that is, the sum of the dividend yield and the capital gain (in real terms). By simple algebra, this condition can be turned into an *asset price equation*:[10]

$$q_t=\frac{E_t(q_{t+1}+d_{t+1})}{1+i_t}(1+E_t\pi_{t+1}). \tag{8}$$

From the consumption Euler Equation (4) through linearization around the steady state and taking into account the equilibrium condition $C_t=Y_t$ we get

$$x_t=E_tx_{t+1}-\frac{1}{\sigma}(i_t-E_t\pi_{t+1}), \tag{9}$$

where x_t denotes the output gap, that is, the difference between current output and flexible price equilibrium output (derived in Appendix B), while i_t denotes the deviation of the nominal interest rate from the steady state.[11]

From the asset price Equation (8) through linearization we get the Asset Price (AP) schedule:

[10] Consolidating the No-arbitrage condition and the Consumption Euler equation we get:

$$C_t^{-\sigma}q_t=\beta E_tC_{t+1}^{-\sigma}(q_{t+1}+d_{t+1}).$$

This optimality condition states the equality between the marginal utility the agent gives up by saving in order to purchase one share and the present value of the marginal utility the agent will gain one period ahead by transforming the dividend and the capital gain into consumption.

[11] In a zero-inflation steady state, the steady state nominal interest rate is equal to the real interest rate, which in turn is anchored to the rate of time preference (see again Appendix B).

$$\hat{q}_t = -(i_t - E_t\pi_{t+1}) + \left[\beta E_t\hat{q}_{t+1} + (1-\beta)E_t\hat{d}_{t+1}\right], \tag{10}$$

where hatted variables represent percent deviations from the steady state. In our framework, technology is linear (see next section): $Y_t = N_t$. Moreover, in equilibrium $C_t = Y_t$. Using these equalities to rewrite the optimality condition (6) and rearranging we get $w_t = \chi Y_t^{\eta+\sigma}$. Log-linearizing this expression around the steady state we get:

$$\hat{w}_t = (\eta + \sigma)x_t. \tag{11}$$

We assume that firms' real profits are paid out to households in the form of dividends: $d_t = Y_t - w_t Y_t$. Substituting the real wage w_t as defined above into this expression and log-linearizing around the s.s. we get:

$$\hat{d}_t = (1 + \delta)x_t, \tag{12}$$

where $\delta := (\beta/(\mu - \beta))(\eta + \sigma)$ where μ is the mark up.[12] Hence dividends are an increasing linear function of the output gap.

3. Firms

As in the standard New Keynesian model the corporate sector consists of J firms, indexed by j, which produce differentiated goods in a monopolistically competitive setting à la Dixit and Stiglitz using only labor. Therefore firms incur only the production cost represented by the wage bill.

We depart from the standard setting in assuming the following:

(a) *Financing gap:* Technology is represented by a one-to-one production function $Y_{jt} = N_{jt}$. Since firms hire workers at the beginning of period t and sell output at the end of the period, they cannot pay wages out of sales proceeds: at the beginning of each period they have to anticipate the wage bill to employees. This is the financing gap.

(b) *No internal funds*: firms do not accumulate internal finance so that the financing gap coincides with the wage bill. They have to raise external finance to fill the financing gap.

In order to concentrate on the role of asset prices in macroeconomic performance, we adopt the following simplifying shortcut:

[12] $\mu = e/(e-1)$; $e > 1$. Of course $\mu > \beta$. The ratio $\beta/(\mu - \beta)$ is the steady state ratio of wages to dividends.

(c) *"Equity only" financing:* there is only one source of external funds, the Stock market.

Assumptions (b) and (c) allow us to get rid, in the following, of the complications due to the accumulation of net worth and to ignore the credit market. This is patently unrealistic. We consider the present framework as only a first step toward a more satisfactory and realistic model.

From the *"equity only" financing* assumption follows that the *j*th firm raises funds issuing new shares and the amount of shares sold is equal to the wage bill:[13]

$$w_t N_{jt} = q_t A_{jt}. \tag{13}$$

(d) *Dividend and buy-back policy:* Shareholders are remunerated by means of dividends (distributed in $t+1$ on shares held in t), which represent the cost of external funds for the firms. Furthermore firms buy back all the shares outstanding in $t+1$.

The time schedule can be summarized as follows. At the beginning of period t, the firm issues equities and uses the proceeds to hire workers and start production. Since production takes an entire period, output will be available for sale in $t+1$. Sale proceeds are used in $t+1$ to pay dividends and buy back shares issued in t. In fact, as shown above – see Equation (2) – $P_{t+1}C_{t+1} = (Q_{t+1} + D_{t+1})A_t$. At the beginning of period $t+1$, the cycle starts again.

In the end, therefore, we are assuming that in the same period $(t+1)$ the firm is (i) paying dividends and reimbursing shareholders for the shares they bought in t and (ii) it is issuing new equities to finance production in $t+1$. This is clearly unrealistic but simplifies the analysis to a great extent.

From the standard microfoundations of the NK Phillips curve (see Section 3.1 for technical details), after linearization we get $\pi_t = k\hat{\phi}_t + \beta E_t \pi_{t+1}$ where $k = (1-\omega)(1-\beta\omega)/\omega$. Substituting Equation (17) and rearranging we get

$$\pi_t = \lambda x_t + k\left[\beta E_t \hat{q}_{t+1} + (1-\beta)E_t \hat{d}_{t+1} - \hat{q}_t\right] + \beta E_t \pi_{t+1}, \tag{14}$$

with $\lambda := k(\eta + \sigma)$. Equation (14) is the NK Phillips curve in the new setting.

[13] In principle, each firm issues its own shares so that there should be an entire range of heterogeneous asset prices, one for each firm. In order to simplify the argument, we will impose symmetry among firms so that *the asset price is uniform across equity-issuing firms*. Alternatively, one can think of q as the average Stock market index and assume that each individual share prices q_j is not too far from the average. In the end, however, firms will behave uniformly – they are essentially identical – so that the individual share price will coincide with the average.

The difference with respect to the canonical NKPC is the term in brackets, that is, $\widehat{\text{ROS}}$ (see Equation (16)). In fact, the cost channel and the equity-only financing assumptions imply that the cost of external finance, which coincides with the ROS, is affecting the firms' pricing decisions and therefore inflation. This is the reason why we will define the equation above the *Augmented* New Keynesian-Phillips Curve (A-NKPC).

3.1. The "Augmented" NK Phillips Curve

The firm's total disbursement occur in $t+1$ but are related to operating costs incurred in t. The firm's total cost in real terms, therefore, is $TC_{jt} = E_t(q_{t+1} + d_{t+1})A_{jt}$.[14] Substituting Equation (13) into this expression we obtain: $TC_j = E_t(q_{t+1} + d_{t+1})(w_t N_{jt})/(q_t)$. Hence the real marginal cost is:

$$\phi_t = \frac{E_t(q_{t+1} + d_{t+1})}{q_t} w_t. \tag{15}$$

The expression

$$\frac{E_t(q_{t+1} + d_{t+1})}{q_t} = \text{ROS},$$

is the novelty of this approach. With respect to the standard setting, whereby $\phi_t = w_t$, the marginal cost must be augmented by a term which represents the *cost of external finance* for the firm. This, in turn, coincides with the *Return On Shares (ROS)*, that is, the sum of the dividend yield $(E_t d_{t+1})/q_t$ and the capital gain $(E_t q_{t+1})/q_t$.

From the linearization of Equation (15) around the s.s. we get

$$\hat{\phi}_t = \hat{w}_t + \left[\beta E_t \hat{q}_{t+1} + (1-\beta) E_t \hat{d}_{t+1} - \hat{q}_t\right],$$

where the expression

$$\beta E_t \hat{q}_{t+1} + (1-\beta) E_t \hat{d}_{t+1} - \hat{q}_t = \widehat{ROS}, \tag{16}$$

[14] Since disbursement will occur one period ahead, in t the firm has to form expectations on the total gross return in $t+1$ of each share issued in t. This gross return in real terms is the sum of the asset price and dividends in $t+1$.

is the deviation of the ROS from the steady state.[15] In a *symmetric equilibrium with flexible prices* all the firms charge the same price P_t equal to a markup μ over nominal marginal cost $P_t\phi_t$. Therefore $\phi_t = 1/\mu$. Recalling Equation (15) we get $w_t = q_t/(\mu E_t(q_{t+1} + d_{t+1}))$. Plugging Equation (11) into the expression for $\hat{\phi}_t$ above and rearranging we get:

$$\hat{\phi}_t = (\eta + \sigma)\left\{x_t + \frac{1}{\eta + \sigma}\left[\beta E_t \hat{q}_{t+1} + (1-\beta)E_t \hat{d}_{t+1} - \hat{q}_t\right]\right\}. \tag{17}$$

In each period a fraction ω of firms is unable to adjust its price. As usual in a Calvo pricing context ω is a measure of the degree of *nominal rigidity*. The *j*th firm's pricing decision problem therefore is

$$\max_{p_{jt}} E_t \sum_{s=0}^{\infty} \omega^s \Delta_{s,t+s}\left[\left(\frac{p_{jt}}{P_{t+s}}\right)^{1-e} - \phi_{t+s}\left(\frac{p_{jt}}{P_{t+s}}\right)^{-e}\right]C_{t+s},$$

where $\Delta_{s,t+s} = \beta^s (C_{t+s}/C_t)^{-\sigma}$ is the consumption-based discount factor, $(p_{jt}/P_{t+s})^{-e} C_{t+s} = Y_{jt}$ is demand for the *j*th firm's product, and ϕ_t is the marginal (and average) cost.

The optimal relative price of the good produced by the adjusting firm in period *t*, therefore, takes into account the stream of future marginal costs, which, in our framework, depends on *current and future asset prices and dividends* (see Equation (15)).

4. Monetary Policy Rules

We will explore the transmission mechanism of monetary policy in the case in which the central bank adopts a simple Taylor-type *instrument rule*. In Section 4.1 we will assume that the central bank responds only to inflation (Strict Inflation Targeting, SIT). In Section 4.2 we will augment the instrument rule taking into account asset price dynamics (Asset augmented Inflation targeting, AIT).

[15] From the No-arbitrage condition it is immediate to infer that the steady state ROS ($ROS_s = (q_s + d_s)/q_s$) must be equal to the steady state real return on bonds β^{-1}. Hence $\beta = q_s/(q_s + d_s)$.

4.1. Strict Inflation Targeting (Model I-1)

For the sake of simplicity and without loss of generality, in this section we assume that the instrument rule is activated exclusively by the feedback from inflation (in other words, the central bank does not take into account the output gap in devising its policy). Hence, the rule specifies to:

$$i_t = \gamma_\pi \pi_t, \tag{18}$$

is of the *strict inflation targeting* (SIT) type.

The structural form of the macroeconomic model consists of the IS curve (9), No-Arbitrage Condition (10), dividend policy (12), Augmented NK Phillips curve (14), and Taylor rule (18) which we reproduce here for the reader's convenience.

$$\begin{aligned}
x_t &= E_t x_{t+1} - \frac{1}{\sigma}(i_t - E_t \pi_{t+1}) + g_t \\
\hat{q}_t &= -(i_t - E_t \pi_{t+1}) + \beta E_t \hat{q}_{t+1} + (1-\beta) E_t \hat{d}_{t+1} \\
\hat{d}_t &= (1+\delta) x_t \\
\pi_t &= \lambda x_t + k\left[\beta E_t \hat{q}_{t+1} + (1-\beta) E_t \hat{d}_{t+1}\right] + \beta E_t \pi_{t+1} + u_t \\
i_t &= \gamma_\pi \pi_t.
\end{aligned} \tag{M I-1}$$

Notice that we have appended a demand shock g_t to the IS curve and a supply shock u_t to the Phillips curve to avoid the "divine coincidence." As usual g_t and u_t follow an AR(1) process: $g_t = \psi g_{t-1} + \tilde{g}_t$ with $\tilde{g}_t \sim \text{i.i.d.}(0, \sigma_g^2)$; $u_t = \rho u_{t-1} + \tilde{u}_t$ with $\tilde{u}_t \sim \text{i.i.d.}(0, \sigma_u^2)$.

(M I-1) is a system of five linear difference equations in five state variables, $x_t, \hat{q}_t, \pi_t, i_t,$ and $\hat{d}_t$.

The model is *recursive*. Using the no-arbitrage condition, in fact, we obtain:

$$\begin{aligned}
\pi_t &= \lambda x_t + k(i_t - E_t \pi_{t+1}) + \beta E_t \pi_{t+1} + u_t \qquad \text{(M I-0)} \\
x_t &= E_t x_{t+1} - \frac{1}{\sigma}(i_t - E_t \pi_{t+1}) + g_t \\
i_t &= \gamma_\pi \pi_t.
\end{aligned}$$

These equations form "the core model" with SIT or model I-0, a system of three equations in $x_t, \pi_t,$ and i_t.

We can solve for these variables without any reference to $\widehat{ROS}$ and therefore to asset prices and dividends. In fact, we have replaced $\widehat{ROS}$ with the real interest rate $i_t - E_t\pi_{t+1}$, exploiting the no-arbitrage condition. In other words

Remark 1. If the economy is described by model I-1 the determination of the asset price and dividends can be separated from the determination of all the other state variables. The equilibrium values of x_t, π_t, i_t can be logically determined by solving model I-0 before determining asset prices and dividends.[16]

The Rational Expectations (RE) equilibrium of model I-0 and the conditions for determinacy are computed in Appendix C.

In order to solve the system by the method of undetermined coefficient, we guess $s_1 = s_1u_t + s_2g_t$ for each variable $s = \pi, x, i$. Therefore $E_ts_{t+1} = s_1\rho u_t + s_2\psi g_t$. For the sake of simplicity, we will adopt the following

Assumption 1. $\rho = \psi$.

This assumption is of course restrictive and may entail a modest loss of generality. It greatly simplifies the calculations, however, and yields very neat results since $E_ts_{t+1} = \rho(s_0u_t + s_1g_t) = \rho s_t$ for each and every variable.

Because of assumption 1, the model-consistent (i.e., rational) expectation of a variable taken in t for $t+1$ is a fraction of the current value of the variable.[17]

The RE solutions of the system can be represented as follows:

$$x_t = a_1u_t + a_2g_t$$

$$\pi_t = b_1u_t + b_2g_t$$

$$i_t = \gamma_\pi b_1u_t + \gamma_\pi b_2g_t,$$

where a_i and b_i; $i = 1, 2$ are polynomials of the "deep parameters" $\beta, \eta, \gamma_\pi, k, \rho, \sigma$. It turns out that $a_1 < 0, a_2 > 0, b_1 > 0, b_2 > 0$ (see Appendix C).

In the following we illustrate the transmission of shocks within model I-0 by means of simple diagrams.

From assumption 1 follows that $E_tx_{t+1} = \rho x_t, E_t\pi_{t+1} = \rho\pi_t$. Hence we can define the real interest rate as

---

[16] A similar dichotomy occurs also in Carlstrom and Fuerst (2007) albeit in a different context.

[17] The expected rate of change therefore is decreasing with the current value: $E_ts_{t+1} - s_t = -(1-\rho)s_t$. This implicitly determines a *mean reverting* behavior of that variable. If a shock hits a variable, causing a departure from the steady state, a negative (stabilizing) feedback is activated.

$$i_t - E_t\pi_{t+1} = (\gamma_\pi - \rho)\pi_t. \tag{19}$$

Using Equation (19), M I-0 boils down to:

$$x_t = -\frac{\gamma_\pi - \rho}{\sigma(1-\rho)}\pi_t + \frac{1}{1-\rho}g_t \tag{20}$$

$$\pi_t = \frac{\lambda}{1-\beta\rho - k(\gamma_\pi - \rho)}x_t + \frac{1}{1-\beta\rho - k(\gamma_\pi - \rho)}u_t. \tag{21}$$

Equation (20) can be conceived of as a policy-induced AD schedule in the present setting. Equation (21) represents therefore the AS schedule. Monetary policy affects the AS schedule through the cost channel.

Assumption 2. *We assume $\sigma < \eta$ and*

$$1 < \gamma_\pi < \hat{\gamma}_\pi \tag{22}$$

$$\hat{\gamma}_\pi := \rho + \frac{1-\beta\rho}{k}.$$

The inequality on the LHS of Equation (22) – that is, $\gamma_\pi > 1$ – is the *Taylor principle*. Thanks to this inequality the RE solution of model I-0 is determinate if $\sigma < \eta$ (see Appendix C for a discussion of determinacy) and the AD schedule is "well behaved," that is, downward sloping on the (x_t, π_t) plane.[18]

The inequality on the RHS of Equation (22) – that is, $\gamma_\pi < \hat{\gamma}_\pi$ – assures, on the other hand, that the AS schedule is "well behaved," that is, upward sloping. When the AD and the AS curves are both well behaved (i.e., they have the "appropriate slopes"), the solutions of (M I-0) are "realistic" in the precise sense that equilibrium inflation and the output gap respond to shocks in the usual way. In other words, the reaction of the central bank to current inflation must be neither too weak ($1 < \gamma_\pi$) *nor too strong* ($\gamma_\pi < \hat{\gamma}_\pi$) to assure well behaved (i.e., realistic) model solutions.

The RHS of Equation (22) is the truly novel feature of this setting. In the absence of the cost channel, in fact, model M I-0 would boil down to the following "canonical" model which we will label M I-0(c):

[18] Notice that $1 < \gamma_\pi$ is a *necessary* condition for determinacy (if $\sigma < \eta$) and a *sufficient* condition for a well behaved AD schedule. In fact, the slope of the AD curve is negative for $\rho < \gamma_\pi$.

$$\pi_t = \lambda x_t + \beta E_t \pi_{t+1} + u_t$$
$$x_t = E_t x_{t+1} - \frac{1}{\sigma}(i_t - E_t \pi_{t+1}) + g_t \qquad \text{(M I-0(c))}$$
$$i_t = \gamma_\pi \pi_t$$

which, after plugging the monetary policy rule into the IS curve and incorporating model-consistent expectations, becomes:

$$x_t = -\frac{\gamma_\pi - \rho}{\sigma(1-\rho)}\pi_t + \frac{1}{1-\rho}g_t \qquad (23)$$

$$\pi_t = \frac{\lambda}{1-\beta\rho}x_t + \frac{1}{1-\beta\rho}u_t. \qquad (24)$$

Hence only $1 < \gamma_\pi$ must be assumed to assure both determinacy and a downward sloping AD schedule. The AS curve in model M I-0(c), in fact, is upward sloping *for any* value of γ_π. Notice, moreover, that the AS schedule in the canonical case is flatter than in the presence of the cost channel.

4.1.1. The Effect of a Supply Shock

We are now ready to examine the transmission of shocks.

Suppose initially there are no shocks: $g_t = u_t = 0$. In Figure 3 we represent the AD and the AS schedules in the present setting (in bold) and in the canonical one.

Suppose a (temporary) *supply shock* hits the economy. In a canonical setting, inflation goes up by $(1/(1-\beta\rho))u_t$ on impact (see point B).

In the presence of the cost channel, the reaction of the central bank to the increase in inflation – that is, the increase of the interest rate – adds to inflation on impact. This is the reason why inflation goes up by $(1/(1-\beta\rho - k(\gamma_\pi - \rho)))u_t$ on impact (see point B′). In other words, the AS curve augmented with the cost channel shifts up more than in the canonical case.[19]

In equilibrium the economy will converge to C′. In the end, therefore, there will be more inflation and a more acute recession than in the

[19] It is easy to see, however, that the intercepts on the x-axis of the AS and AS(c) schedules after the shock coincide.

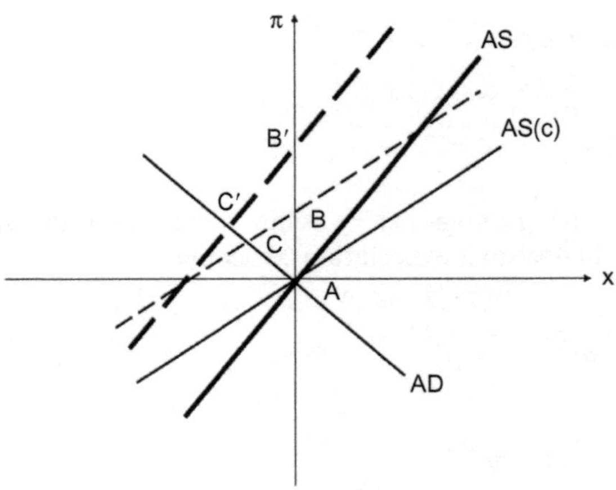

Figure 3: Effects of a Supply Shock in Model I-1.

canonical case (compare with C). In the case of a supply shock, the cost channel works therefore as an *amplification mechanism* of the shock.[20] Of course, since the shock is temporary, with the passing of time the economy will move back to point A.

4.1.2. The Effect of a Demand Shock

In the case of a *demand shock*, the new (short run) equilibrium will be B′ as shown in Figure 4. The output gap turns positive but, in the presence of the cost channel, the expansion is weaker and inflation is higher than in the canonical case (compare with B).

What happens to the stock price? Since the system is recursive we can solve for the asset price after having solved for the output gap, inflation and the interest rate. In order to do so, we have to start from dividends. Iterating Equation (12) one period ahead and taking the expected value we get

$$E_t\hat{d}_{t+1} = (1+\delta)E_t x_{t+1}. \tag{25}$$

[20] In fact, in the RE solution the coefficients of inflation and the output gap with respect to the supply shock are greater in absolute value in the presence of the cost channel. In symbols: $b_1 > b_1^c$, $|a_1| > |a_1^c|$ as shown in Appendix C where the superscript c refers to the canonical NK-DSGE model.

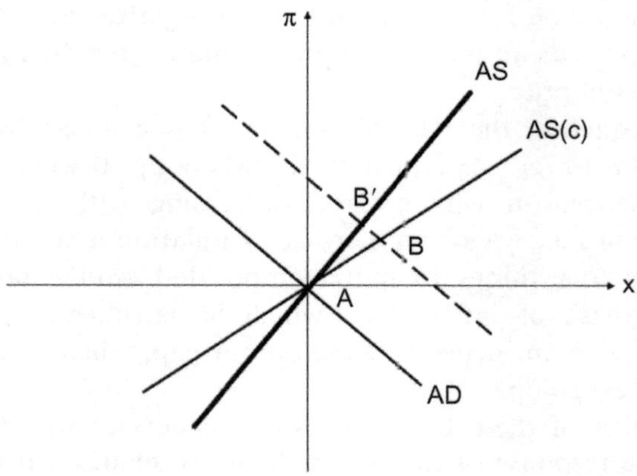

Figure 4: Effects of a Demand Shock in Model I-1.

When expected dividends are defined as in Equation (25), the no-arbitrage condition (10) becomes:[21]

$$\hat{q}_t = -(i_t - E_t\pi_{t+1}) + \beta E_t\hat{q}_{t+1} + (1-\beta)(1+\delta)E_t x_{t+1}. \tag{26}$$

Due to assumption 1, $E_t\hat{q}_{t+1} = \rho\hat{q}_t$ and $E_t x_{t+1} = \rho x_t$. Hence using Equation (19) the expression above boils down to:

$$\hat{q}_t = -\frac{\gamma_\pi - \rho}{1-\beta\rho}\pi_t + \frac{1-\beta}{1-\beta\rho}(1+\delta)\rho x_t. \tag{27}$$

Hence the asset price (i) falls when there is a burst of inflation and (ii) goes up in a boom, that is, when the output gap goes up. The reason for (i) is simple: When the economy is hit by an inflationary shock, the central bank raises the interest rate prompting a flight from equities; asset prices fall bringing about an increase of the return on shares such as to match the increase of the interest rate. This process re-establishes the no-arbitrage

---

[21] Taking Equation (25) into account, the $\widehat{ROS}$ becomes

$$\widehat{ROS} = \beta E_t\hat{q}_{t+1} + (1-\beta)(1+\delta)E_t x_{t+1} - \hat{q}_t$$

Taking model-consistent expectations into account we get:

$$\widehat{ROS} = (1-\beta)(1+\delta)\rho x_t - (1-\beta\rho)\hat{q}_t$$

Therefore $\widehat{ROS}$ is not only decreasing with $\hat{q}_t$ (because of the capital gain) but also increasing with x_t (because of the distribution of dividends).

condition. The reason for (ii) is even more straightforward: An increase of the output gap yields an increase in profits and dividends, which translates into a higher asset price.

As a consequence, the RE solution for $\hat{q}$ is a linear function of the shocks: $\hat{q}_t = c_1 u_t + c_2 g_t$ (see Appendix C) where $c_1 < 0$ while c_2 has uncertain sign. The reason why $\hat{q}_t$ is a decreasing with u is obvious: A supply shock, in fact, yields an increase of inflation and a decrease of the output gap. As to g, things are more complicated. A demand shock brings about an increase of inflation – which is detrimental for the Stock market – but also an increase of the output gap, which makes dividends (and asset prices) go up.

The net effect of these two contrasting tendencies will depend on the strength of the response of the central bank to inflation. It turns out (see Appendix C for details) that the net effect is negative – that is, asset prices fall in the presence of a demand shock – if

$$\gamma_\pi > \breve{\gamma}_\pi \tag{28}$$

$$\breve{\gamma}_\pi := \rho + \frac{1 - \beta\rho}{k + \frac{\lambda}{(1-\beta)(1+\delta)\rho}},$$

that is, if the response of the central bank is relatively "strong," greater than a threshold $\breve{\gamma}_\pi$. Notice that this threshold is smaller than the upper limit $\hat{\gamma}_\pi$ of condition (22).

4.2. Asset Augmented Inflation Targeting (Model I-2)

Let's consider now an *augmented* interest rate rule for monetary policy which takes into account not only inflation but also the asset price deviation from the steady state (asset inflation for short):

$$i_t = \gamma_\pi \pi_t + \gamma_q \hat{q}_t, \tag{29}$$

with $\gamma_q > 0$. We will characterize this rule as Asset augmented Inflation Targeting (AIT). In this case, the macroeconomic model in structural form consists of the IS curve (9), No-Arbitrage Condition (10), dividend policy (12), Augmented NK Phillips curve (14) and Taylor rule (29). In order to solve the model it is useful to incorporate dividend policy into the asset price equation, replacing Equation (10) with Equation (26). In the end we get:

$$
\begin{aligned}
x_t &= E_t x_{t+1} - \frac{1}{\sigma}(i_t - E_t\pi_{t+1}) + g_t \\
\hat{q}_t &= -(i_t - E_t\pi_{t+1}) + \beta E_t \hat{q}_{t+1} + (1-\beta)(1+\delta)E_t x_{t+1} \qquad \text{(M I-2)} \\
\pi_t &= \lambda x_t + k(i_t - E_t\pi_{t+1}) + \beta E_t \pi_{t+1} + u_t \\
i_t &= \gamma_\pi \pi_t + \gamma_q \hat{q}_t.
\end{aligned}
$$

This is "model I-2," a system of four linear difference equations in four variables, $x_t, \hat{q}_t, \pi_t$, and i_t.

This system is *not recursive*. In other words, when the central bank reacts to the asset price, the system does not dichotomize into two independent subsystems (one for x_t, π_t, i_t and the other for $\hat{q}_t$) as in model I-1.

The RE solutions of model I-2 can be represented as follows:

$$x_t = a_1^q u_t + a_2^q g_t$$

$$\pi_t = b_1^q u_t + b_2^q g_t$$

$$\hat{q}_t = c_1^q u_t + c_2^q g_t$$

$$i_t = (\gamma_\pi b_1^q + \gamma_q c_1^q)u_t + (\gamma_\pi b_2^q + \gamma_q c_2^q)g_t,$$

where $a_i^q, b_i^q, c_i^q;\ i=1,2$ are polynomials of the "deep parameters" (see Appendix D). It turns out that $a_1^q<0, a_2^q>0, b_1^q>0, b_2^q>0, c_1^q<0$. The sign of c_2^q is uncertain.[22]

In the following we will illustrate and discuss these results in a simple modified AD-AS framework in order to compare the transmission mechanism of the shocks and contrast it with the previous SIT case.

In the AIT setting, using assumption 1 (so that $Es_{t+1} = \rho s_t$, $s_t = x_t, \pi_t, \hat{q}_t, i_t$) we can write the ex-ante real interest rate as follows:

$$i_t - E_t\pi_{t+1} = (\gamma_\pi - \rho)\pi_t + \gamma_q \hat{q}_t. \qquad (30)$$

In order to solve this model, it is convenient to plug Equation (30) into Equation (26). Using model-consistent expectations one gets

$$\hat{q}_t = -\frac{\gamma_\pi - \rho}{1+\gamma_q - \beta\rho}\pi_t + \frac{1-\beta}{1+\gamma_q - \beta\rho}(1+\delta)\rho x_t. \qquad (31)$$

[22] For the configuration of numerical values of the parameters specified below (see Section 4.3), the Taylor principle $\gamma_\pi > 1$ is a sufficient condition for determinacy (assuming, of course, that $\gamma_q > 0$).

It is worth noting that plugging Equation (31) into Equation (29) one gets the following rule for monetary policy, which we label indirect instrument rule:

$$i_t = \gamma'_\pi \pi_t + \gamma'_x x_t \tag{32}$$

$$\gamma'_\pi = \gamma_\pi - \frac{\gamma_q(\gamma_\pi - \rho)}{1 + \gamma_q - \beta\rho}$$

$$\gamma'_x = \frac{\gamma_q(1-\beta)}{1 + \gamma_q - \beta\rho}(1+\delta)\rho.$$

The indirect rule (32) shows that adding asset inflation to a strict inflation targeting rule, in the end, is equivalent to targeting both inflation and the output gap, that is, to an instrument rule of the *flexible inflation targeting* type. It is worth noting that $\gamma'_\pi < \gamma_\pi$. Moreover $\gamma'_x > 0$.

Remark 2. In the AIT case, the response of the central bank to inflation is weaker than in the SIT case. Moreover, the central bank is indirectly targeting the output gap.

When the prices of goods and services go up, in fact, the price of assets goes down as shown by Equation (31). In the AIT case, the contraction of the asset price will induce a monetary easing, that is, a reduction of the interest rate with respect to the case in which the central bank is not concerned with asset inflation.

Using assumption 1 and substituting Equation (29), model M I-2 boils down to:

$$\pi_t = \frac{\lambda}{1 - \beta\rho - k(\gamma_\pi - \rho)} x_t + \frac{k\gamma_q}{1 - \beta\rho - k(\gamma_\pi - \rho)} \hat{q}_t + \frac{1}{1 - \beta\rho - k(\gamma_\pi - \rho)} u_t$$

$$x_t = -\frac{\gamma_\pi - \rho}{\sigma(1-\rho)} \pi_t - \frac{\gamma_q}{\sigma(1-\rho)} \hat{q}_t + \frac{g_t}{1-\rho}$$

$$\hat{q}_t = -\frac{\gamma_\pi - \rho}{1 + \gamma_q - \beta\rho} \pi_t + \frac{1-\beta}{1 + \gamma_q - \beta\rho}(1+\delta)\rho x_t.$$

(M I-2bis)

Substituting the third equation, that is, the asset price Equation (31), into the other equations we get:

$$x_t = -a\pi_t + cg_t \tag{33}$$

$$\pi_t = dx_t + fu_t \tag{34}$$

$$a = \frac{(1-\beta\rho)(\gamma_\pi - \rho)}{\sigma(1-\rho)(1+\gamma_q-\beta\rho)+\gamma_q(1-\beta)(1+\delta)\rho}$$

$$c = \frac{\sigma(1+\gamma_q-\beta\rho)}{\sigma(1-\rho)(1+\gamma_q-\beta\rho)+\gamma_q(1-\beta)(1+\delta)\rho}$$

$$d = \frac{\lambda(1+\gamma_q-\beta\rho)+k\gamma_q(1-\beta)(1+\delta)\rho}{(1-\beta\rho)\left[(1+\gamma_q-\beta\rho)-k(\gamma_\pi-\rho)\right]}$$

$$f = \frac{1+\gamma_q-\beta\rho}{(1-\beta\rho)\left[(1+\gamma_q-\beta\rho)-k(\gamma_\pi-\rho)\right]}.$$

Equation (33) represents the (policy induced) AD schedule in model I-2 (AD(q) for short). A sufficient condition for the AD(q) schedule to be downward sloping is $\gamma_\pi > 1$.

Equation (34) represents the (policy induced) AS schedule in model I-2 (AS(q) for short). The AS(q) schedule is upward sloping if $(1+\gamma_q-\beta\rho)-k(\gamma_\pi-\rho)>0$, that is, if

$$\gamma_\pi < \rho + \frac{1-\beta\rho}{k} + \frac{1}{k}\gamma_q. \qquad (35)$$

Notice that assumption 2 – that is, $\gamma_\pi < \hat{\gamma}_\pi$ where $\hat{\gamma}_\pi = \rho + ((1-\beta\rho)/k)$ – is a sufficient condition for Equation (35) to be satisfied. In other words, if we assume that the AD and AS schedules in the SIT case are well behaved, then the AD and AS schedules in the AIT case will always be well behaved.

It is important to compare the slope of the AS schedule in the SIT and AIT cases which will be labeled AS and AS(q), respectively. After some algebra we conclude that

Remark 3. The AS(q) schedule is flatter than the AS schedule if the response of the central bank to inflation is relatively "strong," that is, $\gamma_\pi > \breve{\gamma}_\pi$ where

$$\breve{\gamma}_\pi = \rho + \frac{1-\beta\rho}{k+\frac{\lambda}{(1-\beta)(1+\delta)\rho}}.$$

If, on the contrary, this response is relatively weak, that is, $\gamma_\pi < \breve{\gamma}_\pi$, then the AS($q$) schedule is steeper than the AS schedule.[23]

In order to understand the rationale behind this remark, recall first that, in the presence of the cost channel, the relationship between the increment of the output gap and the associated increase of inflation along the AS curve is

$$\left.\frac{\partial \pi_t}{\partial x_t}\right|_{AS} = \frac{\lambda}{1 - \beta\rho - k(\gamma_\pi - \rho)}.$$

Notice now that, according to Equation (31), the asset price is increasing with the output gap and decreasing with inflation.

- When the output gap turns positive, therefore, the asset price goes up. In the AIT case, the increase of the asset price will induce monetary tightening, that is, an increase of the interest rate, which translates into an increase of inflation due to the cost channel. Other things being equal, this effect would account for a slope of the AS(q) schedule greater than the slope of the AS schedule.
- On the other hand, induced inflation will bring down the asset price. The contraction of the asset price associated with inflation will induce monetary easing, that is, a reduction of the interest rate, which translates into a reduction of inflation due to the cost channel. This effect would account for a slope of the AS(q) schedule smaller than the slope of the AS schedule.

If the response of the central bank to inflation is relatively "weak" ("strong"), the first (second) effect will prevail and the AS(q) schedule will be steeper (flatter) than the AS schedule. In the following

Assumption 3. *We will assume that the response of the central bank to inflation is relatively "strong":* $\gamma_\pi > \breve{\gamma}_\pi$.

[23] The slope of the AS schedule, in fact, is

$$\left.\frac{\partial \pi_t}{\partial x_t}\right|_{\text{AS}} = \frac{\lambda}{(1 - \beta\rho) - k(\gamma_\pi - \rho)}$$

while that of the AS(q) schedule is

$$\left.\frac{\partial \pi_t}{\partial x_t}\right|_{\text{AS}(q)} = \frac{\lambda(1 + \gamma_q - \beta\rho) + k\gamma_q(1 - \beta)(1 + \delta)\rho}{(1 - \beta\rho)\left[(1 + \gamma_q - \beta\rho) - k(\gamma_\pi - \rho)\right]}.$$

Assumptions 2 and 3 together imply:

$$\check{\gamma}_\pi < \gamma_\pi < \hat{\gamma}_\pi,$$

and

$$k < \frac{(1-\beta\rho)(1-\beta)(1-\beta)\rho}{(1-\rho)[(1-\beta)(1+\delta)\rho + \eta + \sigma]}.$$

Notice moreover that when the central bank reacts to $\hat{q}_t$ also the slope of the AD curve changes with respect to the case of no reaction. In absolute value:

$$\left.\frac{\partial \pi_t}{\partial x_t}\right|_{\mathrm{AD}} = \frac{\sigma(1-\rho)}{\gamma_\pi - \rho} < \left.\frac{\partial \pi_t}{\partial x_t}\right|_{\mathrm{AD}(q)} = \frac{\sigma(1-\rho)\left(1+\gamma_q - \beta\rho\right) + \gamma_q(1-\beta)(1+\delta)\rho}{\left(\gamma_\pi - \rho\right)(1-\beta\rho)}.$$

In words, when $\gamma_q > 0$ the AD curve is steeper – on the (x_t, π_t) plane – than in the case $\gamma_q = 0$. In order to understand why, recall that, in the case $\gamma_q = 0$, an increase of inflation brings about a contraction of output whose magnitude is

$$\left.\frac{\partial x_t}{\partial \pi_t}\right|_{\mathrm{AD}} = \frac{\gamma_\pi - \rho}{\sigma(1-\rho)}.$$

This is due to the reaction of the central bank to inflation, that is, to the increase of the interest rate. Inflation, however, leads to a fall of asset prices. In the case $\gamma_q > 0$, the central bank contrasts this tendency by "easing," that is, reducing the interest rate with respect to the previous interest rate hike. This will make the contractionary impact of the increase of the interest rate smaller, as shown by

$$\left.\frac{\partial x_t}{\partial \pi_t}\right|_{\mathrm{AD}(q)} = \frac{\left(\gamma_\pi - \rho\right)(1-\beta\rho)}{\sigma(1-\rho)\left(1+\gamma_q - \beta\rho\right) + \gamma_q(1-\beta)(1+\delta)\rho}.$$

Solving Equations (33) and (34) gives x_t and π_t as linear functions of the shocks as shown above.

4.2.1. The Effect of a Supply Shock

We are now ready to examine the transmission of shocks.

Suppose initially there are no shocks: $g_t = u_t = 0$. In Figure 5 we represent the AD and the AS schedules in the case in which $\gamma_q > 0$ (AD(q) and AS(q) in bold). In the absence of shocks in both the SIT and AIT settings the AD and AS schedules intersect in the origin, point A.

Suppose a *supply shock* hits the economy. In the SIT case, inflation goes up by $(1/(1-\beta\rho - k(\gamma_\pi - \rho)))u_t$ (see point B′ in Figure 5, which corresponds

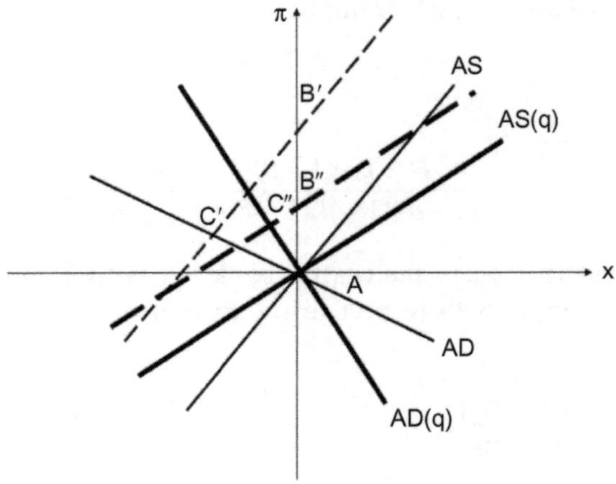

Figure 5: Effects of a Supply Shock in Model I-2.

to B′ in Figure 3). This burst of inflation incorporates the fact that the central bank reacts to the shock *raising* the interest rate, which adds to inflation on impact. The increase in inflation makes asset prices go down. When $\gamma_q > 0$, the central bank reacts to the fall of asset prices easing a bit so that the increase of the interest rate – and the additional inflation due to the cost channel – will be smaller than in the SIT case (see point B″). In other words, targeting asset prices will reduce the impact on inflation of a contractionary monetary policy in the presence of the cost channel.

The central bank then steers the economy to C″. Notice that the AD curve is now steeper than in the SIT case. In the end, therefore, there will be more inflation and a milder recession than in the case in which the central bank does not react to asset prices (compare with C′). When a supply shock hits the economy, therefore, the reaction of the central bank to asset prices has a *mitigating effect* on the change in output but a *magnifying effect* on inflation.[24] In the end, the central bank adopts a more accommodating stance than in the SIT case. In fact the indirect instrument rule (32) shows that by targeting asset prices the central bank is actually concerned indirectly with the output gap.

4.2.2. The Effect of a Demand Shock

In the case of a *demand shock*, in the AIT case the new short run equilibrium will be at the intersection B″ of the AS(q) curve and the new AD(q)

[24] In fact, it runs out that $|a_1^q| < |a_1|$ and $b_1^q > b_1$ (see Appendix D).

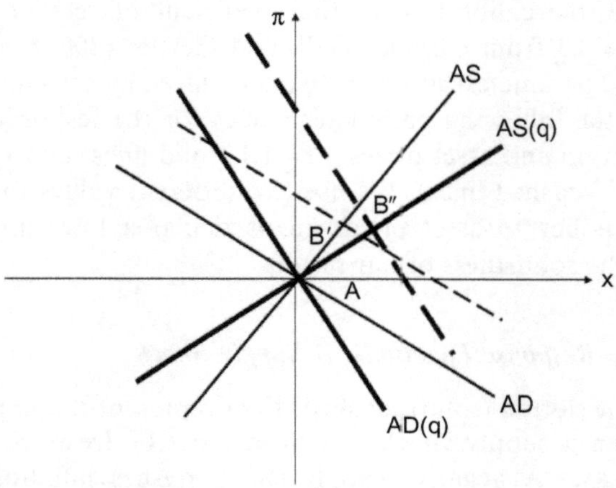

Figure 6: Effect of a Demand Shock in Model I-2.

curve as shown in Figure 6. The output gap turns positive and inflation goes up. In the AIT case, however, the expansion is stronger and inflation is higher than in the SIT case (compare with B′). When a demand shock hits the economy, therefore, the reaction of the central bank to asset prices has an effect of *amplification* on output and inflation with respect to SIT case.

What happens to the stock price? Recall that, as shown in Equation (31) the asset price (i) falls in response to a burst of inflation and (ii) goes up in the presence of an increase of the output gap. As a consequence, $\hat{q}$ is a linear decreasing function of u because a supply shock yields an increase of inflation and a decrease of the output gap. An increase of g, on the other hand, brings about an increase of inflation – which is detrimental for the Stock market – but also an increase of the output gap, which makes dividends go up (see Appendix D for details). The net effect of these two contrasting effects will depend on the strength of the response of the central bank to inflation. If the response is relatively strong – as we have assumed above (see assumption 3), the asset price will fall.

4.3. Impulse-Response Functions Analysis

In order to provide the usual "pictorial view" of the dynamic behavior of the model by means of impulse-response functions, we have simulated the model using the following parameterization: $\sigma=1$, $k=0.1$; $\eta=2$ (so that $\lambda=0.3$); $\beta=0.99$; $\rho=0.9$; $\mu=1.5$.

We borrow the calibration of the coefficient of relative risk aversion ($\sigma = 1$) and $\lambda = 0.3$ from Clarida, Gali, and Gertler (2000). Having chosen $\eta = 2$, with this parameterization, $\sigma < \eta$ (as required by assumption 2).

We adopt the following parameter values for the response of monetary policy to inflation and asset prices: $\gamma_\pi = 1.1$ (solid lines) and $\gamma_q = 0.1$ (dotted lines) or $\gamma_q = 1$ (dashed lines). We use two different values for the response of monetary policy to asset prices, in particular a low value and a high value to test the robustness of our results.

4.3.1. Impulse-Response Functions: A Supply Shock

In Figure 7 the dotted (solid) (dashed) lines represent the impulse-response functions when a supply shock occurs in the AIT (resp. SIT) (resp. AIT with $\gamma_q = 1$) case. A negative supply shock pushes inflation up and the

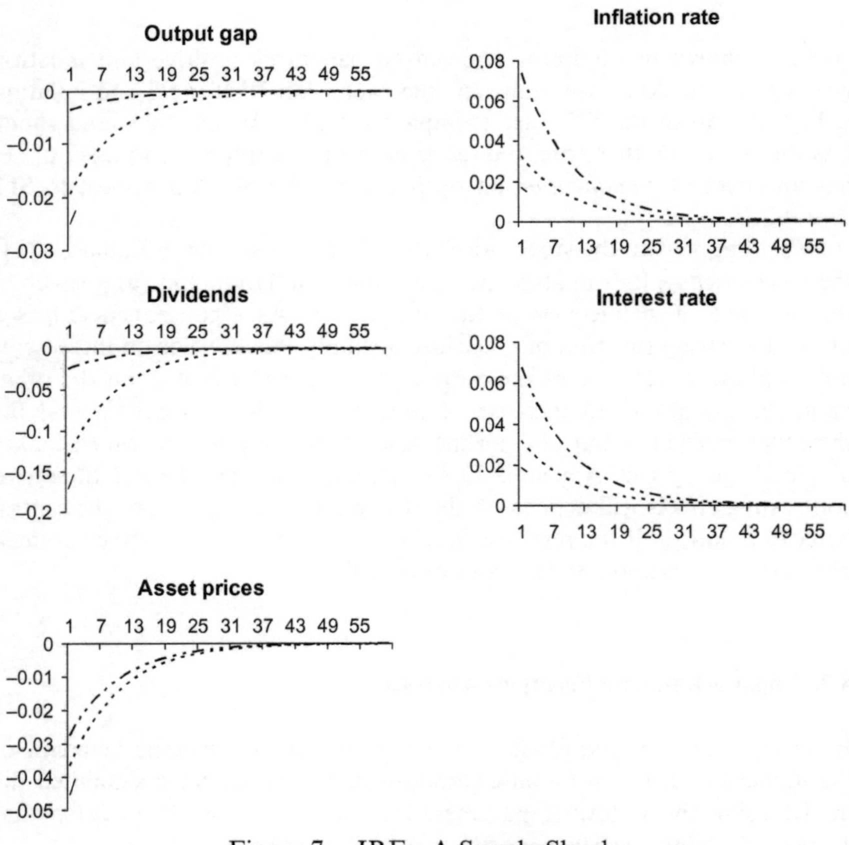

Figure 7: IRFs: A Supply Shock.

output gap down. Profits and dividends follow the dynamic behavior of the output gap. As expected (see the discussion above), targeting asset prices makes the recession milder (with respect to the SIT case) and inflation stronger. Asset prices fall because of the flight from equities and of the contraction of dividends but less than in the SIT case.

As to the interest rate, the reaction of the central bank to the supply shock makes the interest rate hike bigger in the AIT than in the SIT case. At first sight, this is strange. After all, targeting asset prices in a scenario in which they fall should lead to a monetary easing. The reason for this apparently odd result, however, is straightforward. As we noticed above, asset price targeting translates into an accommodating stance of monetary policy, leading to a big burst of inflation. The interest rate is driven up by this burst of inflation, the fall in asset prices notwithstanding. In other words the push of inflation on the interest rate prevails over the mitigating effect of the asset price bust. The stabilizing effect of the AIT rule on output, dividends and asset prices is offset by the destabilizing effect on inflation.

4.3.2. Impulse-Response Functions: A Demand Shock

In Figure 8 the dotted (solid) (dashed) lines represent the impulse-response functions when a demand shock occurs in the AIT (resp. SIT) (resp. AIT with $\gamma_q = 1$) case. A demand shock pushes inflation and the output gap up. Profits and dividends follow the dynamic behavior of the output gap. As expected (see the discussion above) targeting asset prices makes both inflation and the boom stronger (with respect to the SIT case). Asset prices fall because the flight from equities more than offset the expansion (due again to assumption 3).

As to the interest rate, the reaction of the central bank to the demand shock makes the interest rate hike bigger in the AIT than in the SIT case. The interest rate is driven up by inflation, the fall in asset prices notwithstanding. In other words the push of inflation on the interest rate prevails over the mitigating effect of the asset price fall (as in the case of a supply shock). The stabilizing effect of the AIT rule is only on asset prices while the effect is destabilizing on inflation, the output gap, and dividends.

5. Some Welfare Considerations

In order to sharpen our perception of the consequences of Asset Inflation Targeting on the part of the central bank, let's assume that society's preferences can be represented by a quadratic loss function whose arguments are

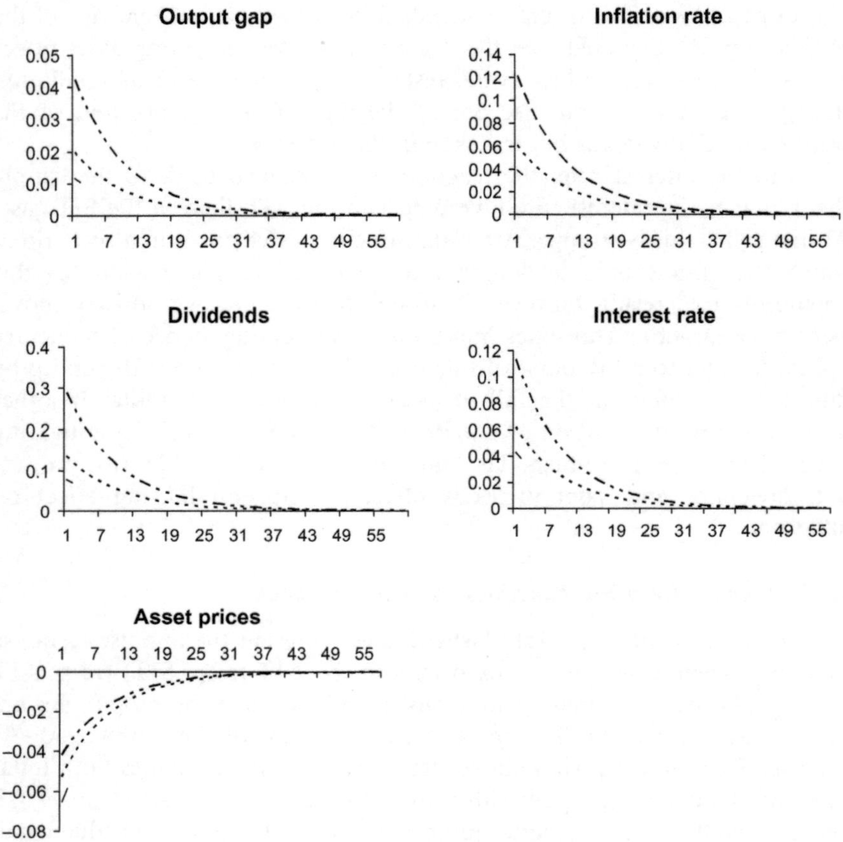

Figure 8: IRFs: A Demand Shock.

inflation and the output gap:[25] $L = \pi_t^2 + \alpha x_t^2$ where α is a measure of aversion to output volatility. Aversion to inflation therefore can be captured by $1/\alpha$.

In the SIT case, substituting the reduced form of model M I-0 into the above expression above one gets: $L = (b_1 u_t + b_2 g_t)^2 + \alpha(a_1 u_t + a_2 g_t)^2$. Rearranging and taking the expected value

$$E(L) = (\alpha a_1^2 + b_1^2)\sigma_u^2 + (\alpha a_2^2 + b_2^2)\sigma_g^2. \tag{36}$$

[25] Woodford (2003) provides a rationale for this loss function interpreting it as a second order approximation of the representative consumer's utility function.

Analogously, in the AIT case we have:

$$E(L^q) = \left(\alpha a_1^{q2} + b_1^{q2}\right)\sigma_u^2 + \left(\alpha a_2^{q2} + b_2^{q2}\right)\sigma_g^2, \tag{37}$$

with $|a_1^q| < |a_1|, b_1^q > b_1, a_2^q > a_2, b_2^q > b_2$. For the sake of comparison, and with a negligible loss of generality, let's assume $\sigma_u^2 = \sigma_g^2$.

AIT is better than SIT from society's point of view if $E(L) - E(L^q) > 0$, that is

$$\alpha\left[\left(a_1^2 - a_1^{q2}\right) + \left(a_2^2 - a_2^{q2}\right)\right] + \left(b_1^2 - b_1^{q2}\right) + \left(b_2^2 - b_2^{q2}\right) > 0. \tag{38}$$

All the differences in parentheses are negative with the exception of the first one.

There are two cases. If $a_1^2 - a_1^{q2} > a_2^{q2} - a_2^2$, that is

$$a_1^{q2} < \overline{a}_1^{q2} \tag{39}$$

$$\overline{a}_1^{q2} := a_1^2 + a_2^2 - a_2^{q2},$$

– so that the expression in brackets in Equation (38) is positive – the condition is satisfied if

$$\alpha > \overline{\alpha} \tag{40}$$

$$\overline{\alpha} := \frac{\left(b_1^{q2} - b_1^2\right) + \left(b_2^{q2} - b_2^2\right)}{\left(a_1^2 - a_1^{q2}\right) + \left(a_2^2 - a_2^{q2}\right)}.$$

If, on the contrary, the inequality Equation (39) is reversed so that the expression in brackets is negative, the condition (38) is never satisfied.

In words: AIT is preferable to SIT if:

- the reduction in output due to a supply shock in the AIT case a_1^{q2} is "small" enough, that is, smaller than a threshold $\overline{a}_1^{q2}$ defined in Equation (39),
- society's aversion to output volatility is "high" enough, that is, higher than a threshold $\overline{\alpha}$ defined in Equation (40).

This proposition can be illustrated graphically as follows. In Figure 9 we represent the difference $\Delta = E(L) - E(L^q)$ as a function of α.[26] When $\Delta > 0$ AIT is preferable to SIT and vice versa.

[26] $E(L)$ and $E(L^q)$ are defined in Equations (36) and (37), respectively. The difference Δ is normalized by the variance of the shock which we assume to be the same for both types of shocks for simplicity.

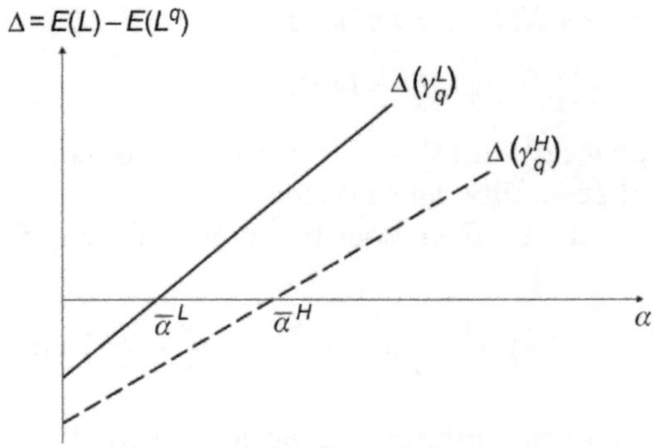

Figure 9: Difference in Loss from SIT and AIT.

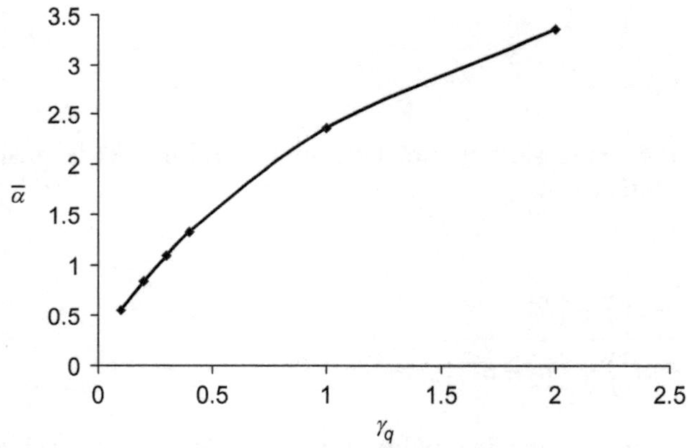

Figure 10: $\overline{\alpha}$ as a Function of γ_q.

The intercept on the *y*-axis is always negative. The slope is positive if condition (39) is satisfied, which is the case shown in the figure. In this case inequality (38) is satisfied if the aversion to output volatility is big enough, that is, higher than the intercept $\overline{\alpha}$ on the *x*-axis. If condition (39) is not satisfied, the slope of the line becomes negative so that inequality (38) is never satisfied.

Each line is parameterized to a certain level of γ_q. In the figure we represent two lines. The solid one is parameterized to a low level, which we label γ_q^L. An increase of γ_q from γ_q^L to γ_q^H yields a higher threshold $\overline{\alpha}^H$. In other words, if the central bank becomes more reactive to asset prices, it is more likely that society becomes worse off with AIT (unless it is extremely averse to output volatility).

The increasing concave curve in Figure 10 is obtained plotting the threshold $\overline{\alpha}$ which we obtain from the parameterization adopted to produce the impulse-response functions (see Section 4.3) for different values of γ_q.

Points above the curve represents combinations of γ_q and α such that society prefers AIT to SIT. It is clear that it takes an extremely high aversion to output volatility for society to prefer AIT even for relatively low values of γ_q.

It is clear therefore that it is highly unlikely that AIT would be preferred to SIT. Two conditions must be met: (i) the gain in output stabilization due to AIT in case of a supply shock should be non-negligible and (ii) society should be very averse to output volatility.

6. Conclusions

In this chapter we have presented an NK-DSGE model in which asset prices will be eventually incorporated into the NK Phillips curve. This is due to the assumption of a cost channel for monetary policy which is activated whenever monetary policy affects asset prices and therefore the return on shares. The latter in fact is the cost of external finance in our model. The novelty of the analysis consists in this peculiar treatment of financing decisions, which brings to the fore the relationship between pricing of goods and pricing of assets.

We analyze two monetary policy regimes: (a) an instrument rule with no-reaction to asset prices (Strict Inflation Targeting), (b) an instrument rule with reaction to asset prices (Asset augmented Inflation Targeting).

Inflation volatility is higher in the AIT scenario irrespective of the type of shock hitting the economy. As far as output volatility is concerned, in the case of a supply shock targeting asset prices may attenuate the contractionary impact of the shock on economic activity but at the cost: Higher inflation. It turns out, therefore that targeting asset prices may not be a good idea even if the framework used to explore this issue is much different from the BG one. In the end, in the AIT scenario the central bank adopts an accommodating policy stance which results in an unsatisfactory macroeconomic performance.

In our setting, the problem with asset price targeting is, in a nutshell, the violation of Tinbergen Law. By means of an asset augmented Taylor rule, in fact, the central bank is pursuing two different objectives (asset price stabilization and inflation stabilization) with only one policy instrument, the interest rate. In order to satisfy Tinbergen Law, a two-pillar approach is necessary. An interesting proposal in this direction has been put forward by De Grauwe and Gros (2009). The same point has been forcefully made by Bean (2010).

We consider these results encouraging even if this is a very preliminary exploration of the properties of the model. We want to pursue an appropriate generalization because the model has to be enriched to explore more realistic environments. The most straightforward extension will consist in incorporating credit markets and credit market imperfections because they have a major role to play in our "story." The list of possible extensions that one can imagine, however, is quite long and will figure on top of our research agenda in the near future.

Acknowledgments

We are grateful for comments and criticisms to A. Marcet, K. Lansing and participants to the CEF workshop, Sydney, July 2009; Guido Ascari, Andrea Colciago and participants to the Macroeconomic Dynamics workshop, Pavia, December 2009; Markus Knell and participants to the seminar at the Oesterreichische National bank, Wien, March 2010; J. Galì and participants to the Zeuthen workshop, Copenhagen, March 2010; participants to the 27th Symposium on Money, Banking and Finance, Bordeaux, June 2010; last but not least we thank M. Motolese and M. Lossani for insightful discussions. The usual disclaimer applies. The research leading to these results has received funding from the European Community's 7th Framework Programme (FP7/2007–2013) under Socio-economic Sciences and Humanities, grant agreement #225408 (POLHIA).

References

Airaudo, M., Nistico, S., & Zanna, L. (2007). Learning, monetary policy and asset prices. LLEE Working document no. 48.

Bean, C. (2010). The great moderation, the great panic, and the great contraction. *Journal of the European Economic Association, Proceedings of the Twenty-Fourth Annual Congress of the European Economic Association*, *8*(2–3), 289–325.

Bernanke, B., & Gertler, M. (1999). Monetary policy and asset market volatility. *Federal Reserve Bank of Kansas Economic Review*, *84*, 17–52.

Bernanke, B., & Gertler, M. (2001). Should central banks respond to movements in asset prices? *American Economic Review Papers and Proceedings*, *91*, 253–257.

Bernanke, B., Gertler, M., & Gilchrist, S. (1999). The financial accelerator in a quantitative business cycle framework. In J. Taylor & M. Woodford (Eds.), *Handbook of Macroeconomics* (Vol. 1C, pp. 1341–1393). The Netherlands: Elsevier.

Brooks, B. P. (2004). Linear stability conditions for a first-order three-dimensional discrete dynamic. *Applied Mathematics Letters*, *17*, 463–466.

Carlstrom, C. T., & Fuerst, T. S. (2007). Asset prices, nominal rigidities, and monetary policy. *Review of Economic Dynamics*, *10*, 256–275.

Cecchetti, S., Genberg, H., Lipsky, J., & Wadhwani, S. (2000). Asset prices and central bank policy. Report on the world economy, Geneva, CEPR and ICMB.

Chih-Chuan Yeh, & Ching-Fang Chi (2009). The co-movement and long-run relationship between inflation and stock returns: Evidence from 12 OECD countries. *Journal of Economics and Management*, *5*(2), 167–186.

Clarida, R., Gali, J., & Gertler, M. (2000). Monetary policy rules and macroeconomic stability: Evidence and some theory. *Quarterly Journal of Economics*, *115*, 147–180.

De Grauwe, P. (2008). Stock prices and monetary policy. CEPS Working document #304.

De Grauwe, P., & Gros, D. (2009). *A new two-pillar strategy for the ECB*. CESifo Working Paper #2818.

Iacoviello, M. (2005). House prices, borrowing constraints and monetary policy in the business cycle. *American Economic Review*, *95*, 739–764.

Kiyotaki, N., & Moore, J. (1997). Credit cycles. *Journal of Political Economy*, *105*, 211–248.

Monacelli, T. (2008). Optimal monetary policy with collateralized household debt and borrowing constraints. In J. Y. Campbell (Ed.), *Asset prices and monetary policy* (pp. 103–146). Chicago, IL: University of Chicago Press.

Ravenna, F., & Walsh, C. (2006). Optimal monetary policy with the cost channel. *Journal of Monetary Economics*, *53*, 199–216.

Woodford, M. (2003). *Interest and prices: Foundations of a theory of monetary policy*. Princeton, NJ: Princeton University Press.

Yellen, J. (2014). *Monetary policy and financial stability*. Speech at the 2014 Michel Camdessus Central Banking Lecture, International Monetary Fund, Washington, DC. Retrieved from http://www.federalreserve.gov/newsevents/speech/yellen20140702a.htm

Appendix A: The Household's Maximization Problem

The representative household's problem consists in:

$$\max_{C_t,m_t,N_t,A_t,b_t} E_t \sum_{s=0}^{\infty} \beta^s \left[\frac{C_{t+s}^{1-\sigma}}{1-\sigma} + \frac{\gamma}{1-\zeta}(m_{t+s})^{1-\zeta} - \chi \frac{N_{t+s}^{1+\eta}}{1+\eta} \right],$$

subject to a sequence of budget constraints of the form:

$$C_{t+s} + m_{t+s} + b_{t+s} + A_{t+s}q_{t+s} = w_{t+s}N_{t+s} + q_{t+s}A_{t-1+s} + m_{t-1+s}\frac{1}{1+\pi_{t+s}} + \frac{1+i_{t-1+s}}{1+\pi_{t+s}}b_{t-1+s} + d_{t+s}A_{t-1+s}.$$

The Lagrangian therefore is:

$$\begin{aligned} L = {} & E_t \sum_{s=0}^{\infty} \beta^s \left[\frac{C_{t+s}^{1-\sigma}}{1-\sigma} + \frac{\gamma}{1-\zeta}(m_{t+s})^{1-\zeta} - \chi \frac{N_{t+s}^{1+\eta}}{1+\eta} \right] \\ & - E_t \sum_{s=0}^{\infty} \beta^s \lambda_{t+s} \Big[C_{t+s} + m_{t+s} + b_{t+s} + A_{t+s}q_{t+s} \\ & - w_{t+s}N_{t+s} - m_{t-1+s}\frac{1}{1+\pi_{t+s}} - \frac{1+i_{t-1+s}}{1+\pi_{t+s}}b_{t-1+s} \\ & - q_{t+s}A_{t-1+s} - d_{t+s}A_{t-1+s} \Big]. \end{aligned}$$

Solving the problem above we get the following FOCs that hold $\forall t$:

$$\frac{\partial L}{\partial C_t} = 0 \Rightarrow \quad C_t^{-\sigma} - \lambda_t = 0$$

$$\frac{\partial L}{\partial m_t} = 0 \Rightarrow \quad \gamma(m_t)^{-\zeta} - \lambda_t + \beta\lambda_{t+1}\frac{1}{1+\pi_{t+1}} = 0$$

$$\frac{\partial L}{\partial N_t} = 0 \Rightarrow \quad -\chi N_t^{\eta} + \lambda_t w_t = 0$$

$$\frac{\partial L}{\partial A_t} = 0 \Rightarrow \quad -\lambda_t q_t + \beta E_t[\lambda_{t+1}(q_{t+1} + d_{t+1})] = 0$$

$$\frac{\partial L}{\partial b_t} = 0 \Rightarrow \quad -\lambda_t + \beta E_t \left[\lambda_{t+1}\frac{1+i_t}{1+\pi_{t+1}} \right] = 0.$$

From the above conditions we get the Euler equations (4)–(6) and the asset price Equation (7) as defined in Section 2.

Appendix B: Steady States and Log-Linearization

The economy consists of five markets: labor, goods, money, bonds, and shares.

The equilibrium condition on the goods market is $C_t = Y_t$. Moreover, $Y_t = N_t$.

In a *symmetric* flexible price equilibrium all the firms charge the same price P_t equal to the nominal marginal cost $P_t\phi_t$ augmented by the markup μ. Therefore, $\phi_t = 1/\mu$. Recalling Equation (15) we get the *price rule*:

$$w_t = \frac{1}{\mu}\frac{q_t}{E_t(q_{t+1} + d_{t+1})}.$$

Plugging $C_t = Y_t = N_t$ into Equation (6) and rearranging we get the *wage rule* $w_t = \chi Y_t^{\eta+\sigma}$. Equating these expressions and solving for output we obtain the *level* of the flexible price equilibrium:

$$Y_t^f = \left(\frac{1}{\chi\mu}\frac{q_t}{E_t(q_{t+1} + d_{t+1})}\right)^{1/(\eta+\sigma)}.$$

In the steady state this boils down to

$$Y_s^f = \left(\frac{\beta}{\chi\mu}\right)^{\frac{1}{\eta+\sigma}}. \tag{B.1}$$

Notice that in the canonical NK-DSGE model we have $Y_s^c = (1/(\chi\mu))^{1/(\eta+\sigma)}$. In the present setting, therefore, the steady state flexible price equilibrium output is a fraction $\beta^{1/\eta+\sigma}$ of the standard one. This is, in a sense, obvious since the marginal cost is augmented, in the present, context, by the cost of external finance, that is, the ROS, other things being equal.

Imposing the steady state condition in Equation (4), it turns out that

$$\frac{1 + i_t}{1 + E_t\pi_{t+1}} = \beta^{-1} = 1 + r, \tag{B.2}$$

that is, in the steady state the real interest rate is anchored to the rate of time preference r.

Using Equation (42) and imposing the steady state condition in the asset price Equation (8) we get

$$\frac{d_s}{q_s} = \beta^{-1} - 1 = r, \tag{B.3}$$

that is, in the steady state the dividend yield is constant and equal to the rate of time preference. From the above equation follows $q_s = d_s/r$, that is, a pure *dividend discount* model of asset price determination: in the steady state, the asset price is the discounted sum of an infinite stream of dividends. Therefore, the steady state ROS is:

$$ROS_s = \frac{q_s + d_s}{q_s} = 1 + r = \beta^{-1}.$$

This is obvious: Because of the no-arbitrage condition, the real interest rate should be equal to the ROS also in the steady state.

Appendix C: Model I-1

We proceed to the solution of model I-1 in two steps. First we solve model I-0, which yields the RE solutions for the output gap, inflation, and the interest rate. Then we find the solution for the asset price.

C.1 Model I-0

Model I-0 boils down to Equations (20) and (21). We solve by the method of undetermined coefficients. We "guess" the following:

$$x_t = a_1 u_t + a_2 g_t$$

$$\pi_t = b_1 u_t + b_2 g_t,$$

so that, under assumption 1,

$$E_t x_{t+1} = \rho(a_1 u_t + a_2 g_t)$$

$$E_t \pi_{t+1} = \rho(b_1 u_t + b_2 g_t).$$

After some algebra we verify that the conjecture is indeed correct and we get the following solutions:

$$a_1 = -\frac{\gamma_\pi - \rho}{\sigma K_0}$$

$$a_2 = \frac{1 - \beta\rho - k(\gamma_\pi - \rho)}{K_0}$$

$$b_1 = \frac{1 - \rho}{K_0}$$

$$b_2 = \frac{\lambda}{K_0},$$

where

$$K_0 := (1-\beta\rho)(1-\rho) + \frac{k}{\sigma}(\gamma_\pi - \rho)(\eta + \sigma\rho).$$

Under assumption 2 it turns out that $K_0 > 0$ so that $a_1 < 0$, $a_2 > 0$, $b_1 > 0$, $b_2 > 0$.

The coefficients for the fundamentals-based interest rate rule:

$$i_t = \gamma_u u_t + \gamma_u g_t,$$

can be computed as follows: $\gamma_u = \gamma_\pi b_1 > 0$; $\gamma_g = \gamma_\pi b_2 > 0$.

The canonical model (without the cost channel) M I-0(c) consists of Equations (23) and (24). The RE solution is:

$$a_1^c = -\frac{\gamma_\pi - \rho}{\sigma K_1}$$

$$a_2^c = \frac{1-\beta\rho}{K_1}$$

$$b_1^c = \frac{1-\rho}{K_1}$$

$$b_2^c = \frac{\lambda}{K_1},$$

where

$K_1 := (1-\beta\rho)(1-\rho) + \frac{k}{\sigma}(\gamma_\pi - \rho)(\eta + \sigma)$.

The coefficients have the same sign as the corresponding coefficients of the model with the cost channel. Moreover $K_1 > K_0$. Therefore $|a_1^c| < |a_1|$, $a_2^c > a_2$, $b_1^c < b_1$, $b_2^c < b_2$.

The coefficients for the fundamentals-based interest rate rule are: $\gamma_u = \gamma_\pi b_1^c > 0$; $\gamma_g = \gamma_\pi b_2^c > 0$.

C.2 Asset Prices

From Equation (27) follows that the solution for $\hat{q}_t$ is $\hat{q}_t = c_1 u_t + c_2 g_t$ where

$$c_1 = -\frac{\gamma_\pi - \rho}{1-\beta\rho} b_1 + \frac{1-\beta}{1-\beta\rho}(1+\delta)\rho a_1$$

$$c_2 = -\frac{\gamma_\pi - \rho}{1-\beta\rho} b_2 + \frac{1-\beta}{1-\beta\rho}(1+\delta)\rho a_2.$$

Therefore $c_1 < 0$. c_2 has uncertain sign. It turns out that $c_2 < 0$ if

$$\gamma_\pi > \rho + \frac{(1-\beta\rho)}{k + \dfrac{\lambda}{(1-\beta)(1+\delta)\rho}}.$$

This completes the solution of model I-1.

C.3 Determinacy

Substituting the monetary policy rule (18) into the IS schedule and the NK Phillips curve of model I-0 and rearranging, we can write the model in matrix format:

$$Z_t = A E_t Z_{t+1} + B W_t,$$

where Z_t is the column vector of endogenous variables, $E_t Z_{t+1}$ is the column vector of the expectations taken in t of the endogenous variables in $t+1$, W_t is the column vector of the shocks:

$$Z_t = \begin{bmatrix} \pi_t \\ x_t \end{bmatrix}; E_t Z_{t+1} = \begin{bmatrix} E_t \pi_{t+1} \\ E_t x_{t+1} \end{bmatrix}$$

$$A = \frac{1}{1-\gamma_\pi\left(k - \dfrac{\lambda}{\sigma}\right)} \begin{bmatrix} \beta - k + \dfrac{\lambda}{\sigma} & \lambda \\ \dfrac{1-\gamma_\pi \beta}{\sigma} & 1 - k\gamma_\pi \end{bmatrix}$$

$$B = \begin{bmatrix} 1 & \lambda \\ -\dfrac{\gamma_\pi}{\sigma} & 1 - \dfrac{\lambda \gamma_\pi}{\sigma} \end{bmatrix}$$

$$W_t = \begin{bmatrix} u_t \\ g_t \end{bmatrix}.$$

The RE solution is determinate if the Blanchard–Kahn conditions are satisfied.

Determinacy requires all the eigenvalues of A to lie inside the unit circle. Necessary and sufficient conditions for this to happen are

$$D < 1$$

$$T - D < 1$$

$$T + D > -1,$$

where D and T denote, respectively, the determinant and the trace of matrix A.

After some tedious algebra we reach the following conclusions:

- If $\sigma < \eta$, determinacy requires $\gamma_\pi > 1$
- If $\sigma > \eta$, determinacy occurs if and only if $1 < \gamma_\pi < (2\sigma(1 - \beta\rho))/(k(\sigma - \eta)) - 1 := \overline{\gamma}_\pi$.

Let's assume $\sigma < \eta$. From Section 4.1 we know that a well-behaved AD curve requires $\gamma_\pi > \rho$. Hence in order to have both determinacy and well-behaved solutions we have to impose

$$1 < \gamma_\pi < \rho + \frac{1 - \beta\rho}{k} := \hat{\gamma}_\pi, \tag{C.1}$$

and assume that $k < (1 - \beta\rho)/(1 - \rho)$.

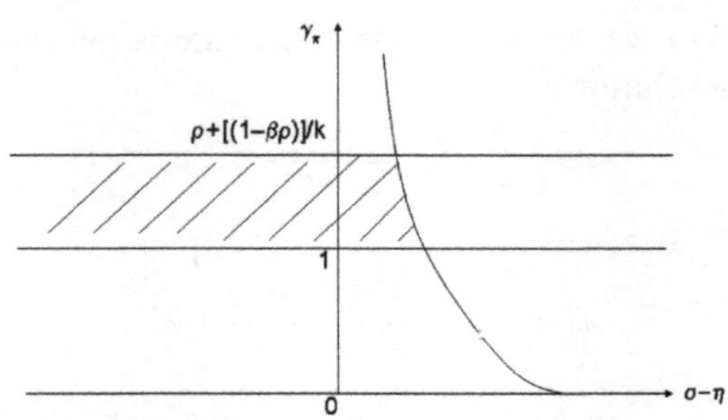

Figure C.1: Determinacy of RE Solution in M I-0.

In case $\sigma > \eta$, in order to have both determinacy and well-behaved solutions we have to impose

$$1 < \gamma_\pi < \min\left(\hat{\gamma}_\pi, \overline{\gamma}_\pi\right). \tag{C.2}$$

In Figure C1 the downward sloping curve represents the threshold $\overline{\gamma}_\pi$ as a function of the difference $\sigma - \eta$ (when $\sigma > \eta$). The dashed area represents the locus of $\left(\gamma_\pi, \sigma - \eta\right)$ points such that both determinacy and well-behaved curves are guaranteed.

Appendix D: Model I-2

In order to find the RE solution of model I-2 we "guess" the following:

$$x_t = a_1^q u_t + a_2^q g_t$$

$$\pi_t = b_1^q u_t + b_2^q g_t$$

$$\hat{q}_t = c_1^q u_t + c_2^q g_t,$$

so that, under assumption 1,

$$E_t x_{t+1} = \rho\left(a_1^q u_t + a_2^q g_t\right)$$

$$E_t \pi_{t+1} = \rho\left(b_1^q u_t + b_2^q g_t\right)$$

$$E_t \hat{q}_{t+1} = \rho\left(c_1^q u_t + c_2^q g_t\right).$$

After some algebra we verify that the conjecture is indeed correct and we get the following solutions:

$$a_1^q = -\frac{\gamma_\pi - \rho}{\sigma K_2}$$

$$a_2^q = \frac{\left(1 + \gamma_q - \beta\rho\right) - k\left(\gamma_\pi - \rho\right)}{K_2}$$

$$b_1^q = \frac{\sigma(1-\rho)\left(1 + \gamma_q - \beta\rho\right) + \gamma_q(1-\theta)(1+\delta)\rho}{\sigma(1-\beta\rho)K_2}$$

$$b_2^q = \frac{\lambda(1+\gamma_q-\beta\rho)+k\gamma_q(1-\beta)(1+\delta)\rho}{(1-\beta\rho)K_2}$$

$$c_1^q = \frac{(1-\beta)(1+\delta)\rho a_1^q - (\gamma_\pi - \rho)b_1^q}{1+\gamma_q-\beta\rho}$$

$$c_2^q = \frac{(1-\beta)(1+\delta)\rho a_2^q - (\gamma_\pi - \rho)b_2^q}{1+\gamma_q-\beta\rho},$$

where

$$K_2 := (1-\rho)\left[(1+\gamma_q-\beta\rho)-k(\gamma_\pi-\rho)\right]+\frac{1}{\sigma}\left[\lambda(\gamma_\pi-\rho)+\gamma_q(1-\theta)(1+\delta)\rho\right].$$

Under assumption 2 it turns out that $K_2>0$. Notice moreover that $(\lambda/\sigma)-k(1-\rho)=k((\eta/\sigma)+\rho)>0$. Therefore, $a_1^q<0, a_2^q>0, b_1^q>0, b_2^q>0, c_1^q<0$. The sign of c_2^q is uncertain.

We can determine the coefficients for the interest rate in the fundamentals-based rule:

$$i_t = \gamma_u u_t + \gamma_u g_t,$$

as follows: $\gamma_u=\gamma_\pi b_1^q+\gamma_q c_1^q$; $\gamma_g=\gamma_\pi b_2^q+\gamma_q c_2^q$.

This completes the solution of model I-2.

Comparing the RE solutions in the SIT and AIT case, it turns out that:

$$|a_1^q|<|a_1|, b_1^q>b_1.$$

If

$$\gamma_\pi>\rho+\frac{(1-\beta\rho)}{k+\dfrac{\lambda}{(1-\beta)(1+\delta)\rho}}$$

then

$$a_2^q>a_2, b_2^q>b_2.$$

D.1 Determinacy

Substituting the monetary policy rule (29) into the Asset price equation, the NK Phillips curve and the IS schedule of model I-2 – that is. Equations (26), (14), and (9) – and rearranging, we can write the model in matrix format:

$$Z_t = AE_tZ_{t+1} + BW_t,$$

where Z_t is the column vector of endogenous variables (π_t, x_t, q_t), E_tZ_{t+1} is the column vector of the expectations taken in t of the endogenous variables in $t+1$, W_t is the column vector of the shocks (u_t, g_t). Matrix A reads as follows: $A = \Lambda\ \overline{A}$ where $\Lambda = 1/(1-\gamma_\pi(k-(\lambda/\sigma)) + \gamma_q - \lambda\gamma_q\gamma_\pi\ (1-(1/\sigma)))$ and the entries of matrix $\overline{A}$ are

$$\overline{a}_{11} = \beta(1+\gamma_q) - \left(k - \frac{\lambda}{\sigma}\right) - \lambda\gamma_q\left(1 - \frac{1}{\sigma}\right)$$

$$\overline{a}_{12} = \lambda(1+\gamma_q) + (1+\delta)(1-\beta)(k-\lambda)\gamma_q$$

$$\overline{a}_{13} = \beta(k-\lambda)\gamma_q$$

$$\overline{a}_{21} = (1-\beta\gamma_\pi)\left[\frac{1}{\sigma} - \left(1 - \frac{1}{\sigma}\right)\gamma_q\right]$$

$$\overline{a}_{22} = 1 - k\gamma_\pi + \gamma_q - (1+\delta)(1-\beta)\left[\gamma_q(1-k\gamma_\pi) + \frac{1}{\sigma}k\gamma_q\gamma_\pi\right]$$

$$\overline{a}_{23} = -\beta\left[\gamma_q(1-k\gamma_\pi) + k\frac{1}{\sigma}\gamma_q\gamma_\pi\right]$$

$$\overline{a}_{31} = 1 - \beta\gamma_\pi$$

$$\overline{a}_{32} = -\lambda\gamma_\pi + (1+\delta)(1-\beta)\left[1 - \gamma_\pi\left(k - \frac{\lambda}{\sigma}\right)\right]$$

$$\overline{a}_{33} = \beta\left[1 - \gamma_\pi\left(k - \frac{\lambda}{\sigma}\right)\right].$$

As shown by Brooks (2004) determinacy of the RE solution requires all the eigenvalues of A to lie inside the unit circle. Necessary and sufficient conditions for the eigenvalues of A to lie inside the unit circle are:

$$D - 1 < 0$$
$$T + D - M - 1 < 0$$
$$D^2 - TD + M - 1 < 0,$$

where D, T, and M denote, respectively, the determinant, the trace and the sum of leading minors of order two of matrix A.

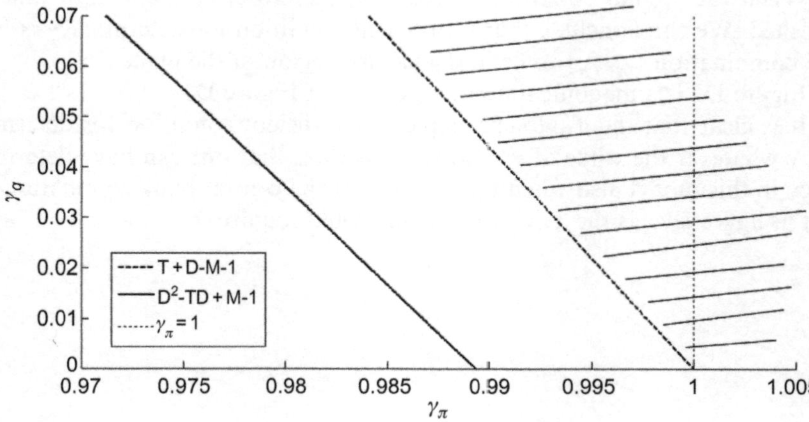

Figure D.1: Determinacy of RE Solutions in M I-2.

We assume the following parameter values (see Section 4.3): $\sigma=1$, $k=0.1$; $\eta=2$ (so that $\lambda=0.3$); $\beta=0.99$, $\mu=1.5$. With this parameterization, the LHS of each of the above three conditionsbecomes a function of γ_q and γ_π only. Therefore the determinacy region can be represented on the (γ_q, γ_π) plane (see Figure D1).

It turns out that:

- the first condition $(D-1<0)$ is always satisfied for positive γ_q and γ_π;
- the second condition $(T+D-M-1<0)$ is satisfied for points lying above the steep downward sloping curve;
- the third condition $(D^2-TD+M-1<0)$ is satisfied for points lying above the flat downward sloping line.

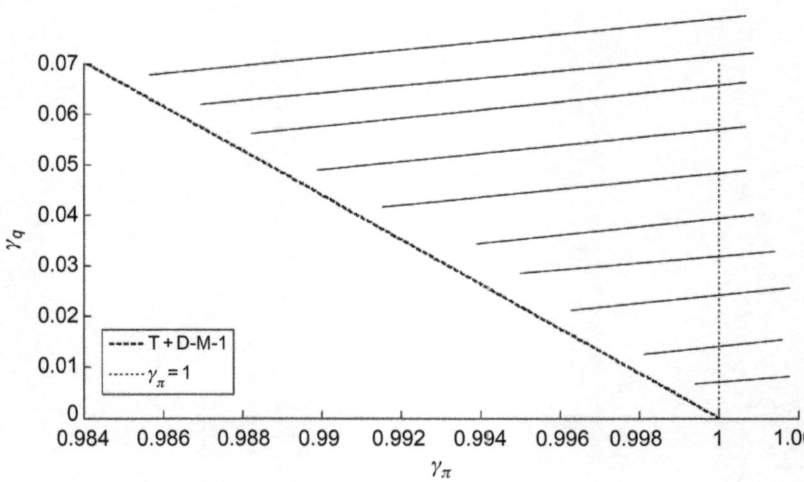

Figure D.2: Magnification of the Determinacy Area.

When the second condition is satisfied, therefore, also the third one is satisfied. We can conclude that a sufficient condition for determinacy is for the combination (γ_q, γ_π) to lie in the dashed region of the plane.

Figure D2 is a magnification of a portion of Figure D1.

It is clear that the Taylor principle is a sufficient condition for determinacy whatever the value of γ_q. Notice, however, that one can have determinacy in this model also when the reaction of the central bank to inflation is not as aggressive as the Taylor principle would require.

Chapter 14
Shareholding Relationships and Financial Crisis: A Network Analysis

Nicolò Pecora[a] and Alessandro Spelta[b]

[a]*Department of Economics and Social Science, Catholic University, Via Emilia Parmense 84, 29100, Piacenza, Italy, e-mail: nicolo.pecora@unicatt.it*
[b]*Department of Economics and Finance, Catholic University, Largo Gemelli 1, 20100, Milano, Italy, e-mail: alessandro.spelta@unicatt.it*

Abstract

One of the main lessons of the recent financial crisis is that the network structure of the banking system has to be taken into account to assess systemic risk.

In this chapter, we analyze the topological properties of the network of the Euro Area banking sector with the primary aim of assessing the importance of a bank in the financial system with respect to ownership and control of other credit institutions.

The network displays power law distributions in both binary and weighted degree metrics indicating a *robust yet fragile* structure and a direct nexus between an increase of control diversification and a rise in the market power. Therefore, while in good time the network is seemingly robust, in bad times many banks can go into distress simultaneously. This behavior opens a narrow for Central bank's actions. In particular, we investigate whether the Single Supervisory Mechanism introduced by the European Central Banks and based on banks' total asset is a good proxy to quantify their systemic importance. Results indicate that not all the financial institutions with high value of total asset are systemically important but only few of them.

Keywords: shareholding network, European banking system, weighted graphs, power law

JEL Classifications: D85, E58, L14

International Symposia in Economic Theory and Econometrics, Vol. 24
William A. Barnett and Fredj Jawadi (Editors)

ISSN: 1571-0386/doi: 10.1108/S1571-038620150000024026

1. Introduction

Over the last decades, a different approach to economics has been slowly birthing and growing – *complexity economics*. As the complexity and interactions increased worldwide, man-made systems can become unstable, creating uncontrollable situations even when decision-makers are well-skilled, have all data, information, and technology at their disposal. Systemic failures and extreme events are consequences of the highly interconnected systems and networked risks humans have created. Initially, beneficial trends such as globalization, sparse use of resources, higher complexity, and an acceleration of institutional decision processes may ultimately push the economic environment toward systemic instability.

Just to mention few examples, the letter of the British Academy to Her Majesty The Queen, dated July 22, 2009, stresses the importance of looking at the economy as a complex system, in order to trace the risk associated with the entire economic environment.

Nobody noticed that the credit crunch was on its way, everyone seemed to be doing their own job properly on its own merit. The failure was to see how collectively this added up to a series of interconnected imbalances over which no single authority had jurisdiction. Individual risks may rightly have been viewed as small, but the risk to the system as a whole was vast.[1]

And the Governor Jean-Claude Trichet opened the ECBs 2010 flagship annual Central Banking Conference reiterating that

> *when the crisis came, the serious limitations of existing economic and financial models immediately became apparent. Macro models failed to predict the crisis and seemed incapable of explaining what was happening to the economy in a convincing manner.*[2]

Network analysis is increasingly recognized as a powerful methodological tool for modeling interactions between economic agents, companies, and financial institutions. Network techniques have been used, among others, to describe the global architecture of cross-border financial flows, to analyze financial contagion, and to examine the dynamics of interbank markets. Renewed interest in the application of network analysis tools to analyze economic interconnectedness was spurred by the 2008–2009 global financial crisis, which has revealed the networked nature of banking systems as a set of companies acting in close connection with each other. Indeed, as the events unfolded, it became clear that the consequences of

[1] http://www.britac.ac.uk/news/newsrelease-economy.cfm
[2] http://www.ecb.europa.eu/press/key/date/2010/html/sp101118.en.html

such an interconnected system are difficult to predict. Differently from early theoretical research about financial contagion (see Allen & Gale, 2000; Freixas, Parigi, & Rochet, 2000 among others), which states that a high degree of interconnectedness in financial markets is in general beneficial for the economy, in recent years a growing literature has emphasized the role of financial networks as amplifiers of shocks and how these can increase the overall fragility of the system (see Acemoglu, Ozdaglar, & Tahbaz-Salehi, 2013; among others).

As a matter of facts, it is almost natural coming up with the following question: *Why does the network of banking relationships among countries matter above and beyond cross-country bilateral flows?*

In the wake of the recent crisis, it has been argued that network theories can enrich our understanding of the functioning of financial systems by helping model complexity, systemic risk, and the factors that cause failures in financial markets. A thorough knowledge of topological structures of real-world financial markets could therefore be useful in developing models that can predict the observed patterns and forecast the reaction of the financial system to shocks.

The research in the field of network theory evolved so that different levels of analysis are nowadays possible and several approaches to measure financial linkages have been proposed. A growing interest in applying methods from complex networks in financial research has recently been developed.

On the theoretical side, one branch of the literature draws elements from the literature on contagious diseases in networks and simulate default cascades under different network setups (see Gai & Kapadia, 2010; Haldane & May, 2011; Nier, Yang, Yorulmazer, & Alentorn, 2007 among others).

Another field of studies has approached financial systems through the study of linkages among banks, exploring the international banking system through the analysis of the time series of interbank liabilities and claims. The main findings uncovered by this branch of literature can be shortly summarized in four points: (i) the interbank market displays a community structure and disassortative mixing based on the banks' degree[3] (see Craig & Von Peter, 2014; Fricke, 2012; Fricke & Lux, 2014; Iori, De Masi, Precup, Gabbi, & Caldarelli, 2008; Iori, Reno, De Masi, & Caldarelli,

[3] The degree of a bank is the number of partners that every bank has. See Section 2 below for further details. Assortative mixing refers to the property by which nodes in a network establish a relationship with similar nodes, according to a certain characteristic (size, degree, geographical location, etc.). Disassortative mixing refers to the opposite situation, that is, nodes connecting to nodes belonging to different groups.

2007; Soramäki, Bech, Arnold, Glass, & Beyeler, 2007); (ii) the banks' degree is heavy tailed distributed (see Bech & Atalay, 2010; Boss, Elsinger, Summer, & Thurner, 2004; De Masi, Iori, & Caldarelli, 2006; Fricke et al., 2013; Hatzopoulos & Iori, 2012; Inaoka, Ninomiya, Taniguchi, Shimizu, & Takayasu, 2004; Iori et al., 2008; Soramäki et al., 2007); (iii) the network topology of many interbank markets is highly sparse (Bech & Atalay, 2010; Soramäki et al., 2007); and (iv) interbank networks shows a small-world characteristic[4] (see Boss et al., 2004; Soramäki et al., 2007). By and large this literature shows that financial networks are *robust yet fragile*.

Furthermore, researchers also focused on interconnections among credit institutions through direct interaction networks (or control networks), which are useful tools to detect chains of control (e.g., stock ownership networks or board of directors networks), as in Battiston, Glattfelder, Garlaschelli, Lillo, and Caldarelli (2010) and in Davis, Yoo, and Baker (2003). The topics addressed by this literature can be grouped into three major categories: (i) analyzing the dispersion or concentration of control (see Eisenhardt, 1989; Shleifer & Vishny, 1997); (ii) empirically investigating how the patterns of control vary across countries and what determines them (see Porta, Lopez de Silanes, & Shleifer, 1999); (iii) studying the impact of frequently observed complex ownership patterns (see Brioschi, Buzzacchi, & Colombo, 1989; Chapelle, 2004; Flath, 1992) such as the so-called pyramids (Almeida & Wolfenzon, 2006) and cross-shareholding (also known as business groups) (Granovetter, 1995). Remarkably, the investigation of the financial architecture of corporations in national or global economies taken as a whole is just at the beginning (see Battiston & Glattfelder, 2009; Capocci, Servedio, Caldarelli, & Colaiori, 2005; Corrado & Zollo, 2006; Kogut & Walker, 2001; Vitali, Glattfelder, & Battiston, 2011 among others).

The complexity of the interbank system has been analyzed mainly through the study of financial flows but, to the best of our knowledge, the literature has not deeply focused on the study of the shareholding relationships among banks. Few works about ownership networks in the literature have focused essentially on the analysis of their small-world properties (see Kogut & Walker, 2001; Vedres, 2000).

Despite the fact that the topology of a network is known to play a major role in robustness against shocks, no systematic statistical investigation of the topological properties of the shareholding networks in the banking market, especially the Euro Area, has yet been carried out.

[4] The small-world effect refers to the property observed in a large number of social networks by which the distance between any two nodes (n) grows at a speed $\log(n)$ as $n \to \infty$, where n is the number of nodes.

In this work, we analyze the topological properties of the shareholding network of Euro Area banks. We carry on the aim to analyze systematically the complex structure of the banks' network in the Euro Area by a network approach, with a special attention to edge weights reflecting how ownership is distributed among banks. Moreover in the hypothesis that the structure of the ownership network constitutes the backbone of the interbank market on which it is likely that the interbank flows are transmitted, this analysis is relevant to quantify systemic risk as well.

Collected data from Bankscope Ownership Database allows us to analyze the behavior of 1534 banks during the year 2012. The 2298 links establish ownership relationships between the entities, namely a bank and the corresponding controlled. We employ the technique presented in Battiston and Glattfelder (2009) and in Garlaschelli, Battiston, Castri, Servedio, and Caldarelli (2005) but we deviate from this approach in two aspects: firstly, we focus only on the banking sector of the Euro Area and secondly we enlarge the analysis using also non-listed banks. We adopt these overtures to understand to which extent the diversification of shareholding in banks' portfolios gives a good estimate of the relevance of a bank in the market, with respect to ownership and control of other banks. This, in turn, enables to establish the way in which banks can acquire control and to understand their weight in the banking market.

We find that the degree distribution of the European banking network displays power laws in both the binary and the weighted case. Thus, the network displays robust-yet-fragile behavior, meaning that, while in good times the network is seemingly robust, in bad times nodes can go into distress simultaneously. We also uncover that the exponents are linked by a scaling relation, revealing a direct relationship between an increase of portfolio diversification and an increase of market power.

Furthermore, since European financial and sovereign debt crises have become increasingly interconnected, the EU has decided to create a common supervisory framework for the banking sector. The Single Supervisory Mechanism (SSM) aims to monitor the financial stability of banks based on participating countries (Eurozone countries are obliged to participate). We estimate whether SSM, which is based on banks' total assets, could be a considered a good proxy for the assessment of systemic risk associated to a particular financial institution. Results indicate that, beside the positive relationship between the value of the total assets and the probability of connection to partners, not all the financial institutions with an high value of total asset are systemically important but only a few of them.

The remaining of the work is organized as follows: Section 2 briefly presents the network structure and the methodology we work with, Section 3 illustrates the existence of a power law distribution for the linkages in the network, showing the relationship between power law coefficients in the binary and in the weighted networks. Beside these results, the same model is employed to emphasize how the SSM deals with systemic risk. Section 4 discusses the economic implications of the main results and concludes.

2. Network Structure

2.1. Dataset

We collect the ownership data of the 1534 Euro Area banks from Bankscope database. The Bureau van Dijk (BvD) Ownership Database is a complete source for owners and subsidiary links worldwide, with over 30 million active and 245 million archived links, providing information on over 30 million companies. The shareholder information is gathered from several possible sources, including Annual Reports or privately written communications addressed by the company to BvD. The Ownership Database intends to track control relationships rather than patrimonial relationships. This is why, when there are two categories of shares split into Voting/Non voting shares, the percentages that are recorded are those attached to the category Voting shares.

2.2. The Network

A graph $G=(V;E)$ consists of a set V of n vertices and a set E of m edges. A weight w_{ij}, $i,j=1,\ldots,n$, is possibly associated to each edge $(i;j)$ and, if this is the case, a weighted (or valued) graph is defined. In our network, vertices are all the European banks and links are represented by the proportion of banks' total asset controlled by another financial institution via shareholding relationships (see below for a formal definition).

One of the problems that has received most attention in the study of complex networks has been to look for ways to determine the relative importance, or centrality, of a node in a network. The simplest way of measuring the centrality of a bank, is by counting the number of partners that each bank has or, in the weighted case, the proportion of all market total assets that a bank control via shareholding relationships.

The degree k_i of a vertex i $(i=1,\ldots,n)$ is the number of edges incident to it. A directed graph (digraph) is a graph in which all the edges are directed from one vertex to another. In a directed graph the in-degree k_i^{in} of a vertex i is the number of arcs directed from other vertices to i and the out-degree k_i^{out} of a vertex i is the number of arcs directed from i to other vertices.

In our network construction, the out-degree k_i^{out} of a vertex can be considered as the number of owners of the corresponding bank, whereas the in-degree k_i^{in} shows the number of different banks controlled by bank i (for this reason, it can be seen as the portfolio diversification for bank i). Since we are interested in the shareholding relationships between banks, the data necessarily report, for each bank, only a limited number of investors (excluding all the other non-financial companies). While this biases the estimate of k_i^{out} – the number of investors in each bank – (which can in principle be very large), it does not affect qualitatively the statistical properties of the number of assets in the portfolio of each reported investor.

The quantities k_i^{in} and k_i^{out} do not consider non-topological state variables assigned to the nodes themselves. A natural choice may be using the total assets value of banks in million US dollars ν_j, as a proxy for their size. As a consequence, a weight (Φ_{ij}) proportional to the economic value (total asset) that a bank has in other banks via its percentages of voting shares (w_{ij}) can be associated to each node:

$$k_i^{in,w} = \sum_j \Phi_{ij} = \sum_j w_{ij}\nu_j. \qquad (1)$$

In this way, $k_i^{in,w}$ represents a proxy for the market power of bank i. It can be the case that a bank has large total asset but no voting shares in other banks and thus its network control is zero. On the other hand, a small bank can acquire enormous network control via shares in institutions with large total asset. The weighed out-degree $k_i^{out,w}$ of a vertex is the percentage of shareholders of the corresponding bank, but as discussed above, this is a biased quantity and we cannot deal with its statistical descriptions.

Even if many other accurate centrality measures exists to determine the relative importance of network nodes, the Basel Committee, in determining the interconnectedness of individual financial institutions, is proposing to measure the in- and out-degree and in- and out-weighted degree.

According to one of the reforms proposed by the Basel III regulatory framework, namely the adoption of a Liquidity Cover Ratio (LCR), banks should have an adequate amount of high-quality assets reflecting their systemic importance. Such an amount is determined according to five categories,[5] one of which is *interconnectedness*, whose aim is to capture impact that an institution's bilateral exposure can have on other institutions in the network. Interconnectedness, as defined by the Basel Committee, is given

[5] The five categories are *size, cross-jurisdictional activity, interconnectedness, substitutability/financial institution infrastructure*, and *complexity*.

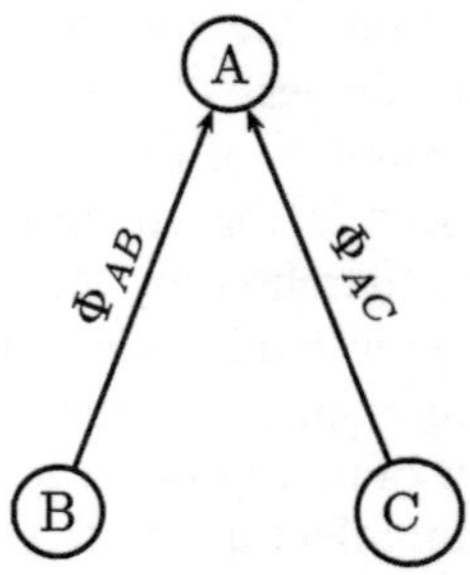

Figure 1: Example of the Network Structure with Three Banks and Weighted Links: $\Phi_{AB} = w_{AB}v_B = 5$, $\Phi_{AC} = w_{AC}v_C = 100$, $k_A^{in} = 2$, $k_A^{in,w} = 105$.

by the weighted sum of intra-financial system assets, intra-financial system liabilities, and securities outstanding. Intra-financial assets and liabilities are aggregate interbank exposures and provide information regarding the exposures that individual institutions face vis-à-vis other banks in the system.

Although we do not consider intra-financial assets and liabilities in constructing the shareholding network, we provided an alternative way to estimate those quantities through the amount of voting shares a bank owns in another institution.

In order to clarify how the European network has been created, in Figure 1 we display an example of the network structure in the case with only three banks. Suppose that bank A owns 5% of the shares issued by bank B and 50% by bank C. Suppose also that the total assets of B and C are \$100 and \$200, respectively; thus, according to Equation (1) we can state that bank A has $k_A^{in} = 2$ and $k_A^{in,w} = \$105$.

Figure 2 shows the resulting network of Euro Area banks: it reveals the existence of some giant components and other weakly connected entities (here the size of the nodes are proportional to $k_i^{in,w}$). There are some bigger nodes with a higher value of the weighted in-degree (see Section 3) and a large portfolio diversification, reported from the values of the in-degree. Three French banks stand out with respect to this feature (Crèdit Agricole S.A., BPCE S.A., BNP Paribas) but also banks from other countries, such as Deutsche Bank AG, ABN Amro Group N.V., KBC Groep NV, and Intesa Sanpaolo.

Besides that, we report the study of other topological features of the shareholding banking network allowing to characterize the market under study.

In graph theory, the clustering coefficient CC is a measure of the probability to which nodes in a graph tend to cluster together. In our case, this is the probability that two banks in the portfolio of a holder are institutions, one of which owns shares of the other. Evidence suggests that in

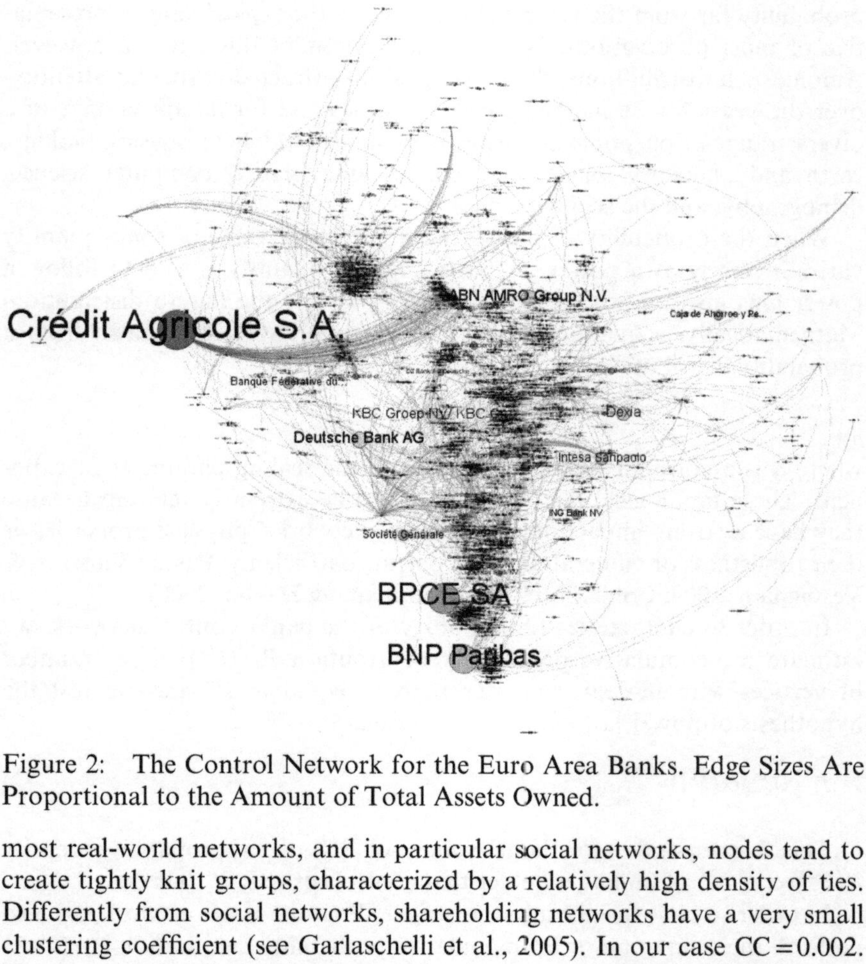

Figure 2: The Control Network for the Euro Area Banks. Edge Sizes Are Proportional to the Amount of Total Assets Owned.

most real-world networks, and in particular social networks, nodes tend to create tightly knit groups, characterized by a relatively high density of ties. Differently from social networks, shareholding networks have a very small clustering coefficient (see Garlaschelli et al., 2005). In our case CC = 0.002. We can explain this feature considering banks making large and long-term investments. In this case, institutions might prefer to avoid having stocks of interconnected banks in their portfolios because of the fear of contagion. Similar results are found in Caldarelli, Capocci, De Los Rios, and Muñoz (2002) regarding the shareholder networks in the NYSE, Nasdaq, and MIB.

3. Measuring Power Laws in the Euro Area Ownership Network

Many empirical quantities group around a typical value. These quantities may vary somewhat but their distributions place a negligible amount of probability far from the typical value, making the typical value representative of most observations. Not all distributions fit this pattern, however. Among such distributions, the power law has attracted particular attention over the years for its mathematical properties and for its appearance in a diverse range of phenomena. Power laws appear widely in physics, biology, earth and planetary sciences, economics and finance, computer science, demography, and the social sciences.

When the probability of measuring a particular value of some quantity varies inversely as a power of that value, the quantity is said to follow a power law, also known variously as Zipf's law or the Pareto distribution. Mathematically, a quantity x obeys to a power law if it is drawn from a probability distribution

$$p(x) \propto x^{-\alpha},$$

where α is a constant parameter known as the scaling parameter or exponent. These topological features turn out to be extremely relevant because they have a strong impact on assessing the networks' physical properties as their robustness or vulnerability (see Barrat, Barthelemy, Pastor-Satorras, & Vespignani, 2004; Cohen, Erez, Ben-Avraham, & Havlin, 2000).

In order to characterize the topology of the banks control network, we estimate the cumulative probability distribution $P>\left(k^{in}\right)$ of the number of vertices with in-degree greater than or equal to k^{in} and we test the hypothesis of power law curve, which means

$$P>\left(k^{in}\right)\propto\left(k^{in}\right)^{1-\gamma}. \tag{2}$$

This corresponds (for large values of k^{in}) to a probability density $P\left(k^{in}\right)\propto\left(k^{in}\right)^{-\gamma}$ of finding a holder that controls exactly k^{in} banks.

In order to have insight into the weighted nature of the network, we also perform the estimation of the cumulative probability distribution $P>\left(k^{in,w}\right)$ of the weighted in-degree $k^{in,w}$, testing

$$P>\left(k^{in,w}\right)\propto\left(k^{in,w}\right)^{1-\delta}. \tag{3}$$

Namely, we find the probability density function $P\left(k^{in,w}\right)\propto\left(k^{in,w}\right)^{-\delta}$ that a bank owns $k^{in,w}$ US millions of dollars of the other banks.

Since the detection and characterization of power laws is complicated by large fluctuations that occur in the tail of the distribution – the part of the distribution representing large but rare events – and by the difficulty of identifying the range over which power law behavior holds, our estimation strategy follows Clauset, Shalizi, and Newman (2009).

Figure 3 represents the cumulative distribution functions and the best fit for the in-degree k^{in} (top panel) and for the weighted in-degree $k^{in,w}$

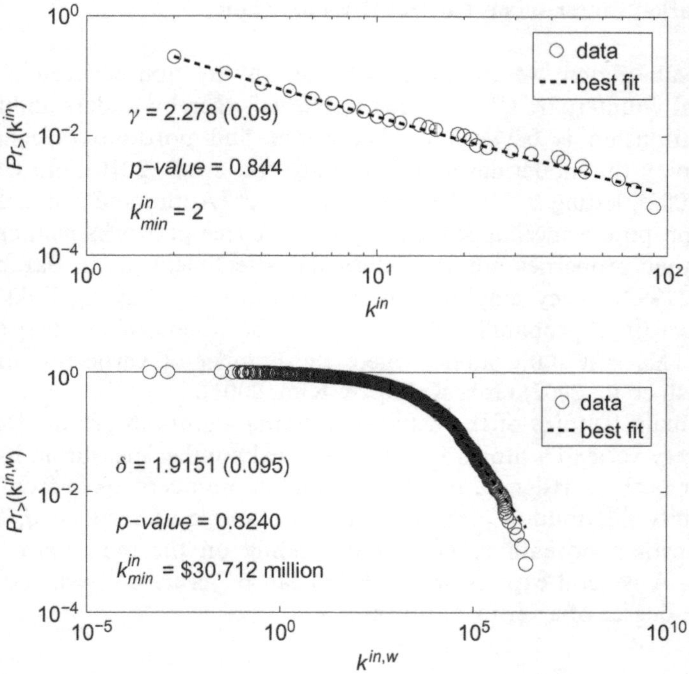

Figure 3: Cumulative Distribution Functions and Their Maximum Likelihood Power Law Fits for: k^{in} (Top Panel) and $k^{in,w}$ (Bottom Panel).

(bottom panel). Results suggest that the values of the exponent differ across the type of networks. Indeed we find $\gamma = 2.278$ and $\delta = 1.9151$. It has also to be noticed that few empirical phenomena obey power laws for all values of a generic variable x. More often the power law applies only for values greater than some minimum x_{min}. In such cases, we say that the tail of the distribution follows a power law. We find that $k_{min}^{in} = 2$ while $k_{min}^{in,w} = 30,712$ US million dollars meaning that, in the binary case, banks that have more than two links follow a power law whereas, in the weighted case, this behavior is observed for banks that own, on average, more than 30,712 US million dollars.

Consistently with Garlaschelli et al. (2005), it has to be noted that the small $k^{in,w}$ range of $P > (k^{in,w})$ does not mimic the typical form displayed by power law distributions. Since in the following we are interested in $k^{in,w} > k_{min}^{in,w}$, the characterization of the left part of the distributions is however irrelevant, and we shall only consider the Pareto tails and the corresponding exponents.

3.1. Market Power versus Control Diversification

In this sub-section, we investigate whether any relation between k_i^{in} and its weighted counterpart $k_i^{in,w}$ can be established, thereby understanding what the relationship is between market power and portfolio diversification. We employ the model developed by Battiston et al. (2010) and Caldarelli et al. (2002), letting $k_i^{in,w}$ to be dependent on k_i^{in}. Authors in Caldarelli et al. (2002) propose a mechanism leading to scale-free networks neither related to dynamic properties nor to preferential attachment, as in Barabási and Albert (1999). They employ a fitness measure x_i, drawing links among vertices, with a probability depending on the fitness of the two involved nodes. This is a static model where the number of vertices is fixed (see Caldarelli et al., 2002; Goh, Kahng, & Kim, 2001).

The main features of the network building algorithm are the following: (i) at every vertex i a fitness x_i, which is a real number measuring its importance or rank, is assigned. Fitness are random numbers taken from a given probability distribution $\rho(x)$. (ii) For every couple of vertices, ij, a link is drawn with a probability $f(x_i, x_j)$ depending on the *importance* of both vertices. A general expression for $P(k^{in})$ can be easily derived. Indeed, the mean in-degree of a vertex of fitness x is

$$k(x) = N \int_0^{+\infty} f(x, y)\rho(y)\ \mathrm{d}y = Ng(x),$$

with $x_i \in (0, +\infty)$.

The simplest choice for the fitness function is the factorable form $f(x_i, x_j) = g(x_i)h(x_j)$. However, since our information regarding k^{out} is incomplete, we cannot test the model with respect to the function $h(x_j)$, and in the following we consider the quantities derived from $g(x_i)$. For large web sizes, the expected in-degree of a node with fitness x_i is given by

$$k^{in}(x) = g(x)h_T, \tag{4}$$

where g_T is the total value of $g(x)$ summed overall N nodes.

Assuming $g(x)$ to be a monotonous function of x, we can calculate, for large enough number of nodes N, the in-degree distribution as

$$P\left(k^{in}\right) = \rho\left[g^{-1}\left(\frac{k^{in}}{N}\right)\right] \frac{\mathrm{d}}{\mathrm{d}k^{in}} g^{-1}\left(\frac{k^{in}}{N}\right), \tag{5}$$

given that the connection probability is $g(x) = cx^{\alpha}$ $(\alpha > 0,\ c = 1)$ and $x = k^{in,w}/max\left(k^{in,w}\right)$.

Since we know that the statistical distributions of x is $\rho(x) \propto x^{-\delta}$ for x large, expression (5) now reads as

$$P(k^{in}) \propto (k^{in})^{(1-\delta-\alpha)/\alpha}. \tag{6}$$

Therefore, using Equations (2) and (6), we are able to find the following relation between the exponents:

$$\alpha = \frac{1-\delta}{1-\gamma}, \tag{7}$$

so obtaining the coefficient α corresponding to $k^{in,w}(k^{in}) \propto (k^{in})^{1/\alpha}$.

Figure 4 shows the behavior of $k^{in,w}$ and k^{in}, where the straight line is the curve $k^{in,w}(k^{in}) \propto (k^{in})^{1/\alpha}$ with α predicted by Equation (7). As Figure 4 suggests, $k^{in,w}$ is an increasing function of the corresponding k^{in}, following approximately a straight line in double-logarithmic scale. Points that obey to this law (near or on the curve $k^{in,w}(k^{in}) \propto (k^{in})^{1/\alpha}$) denote a direct relationship between an increase of portfolio diversification and an increase of market power. These points represent banks with many partners and wide ownership of other banks' asset. In particular, the most important hubs Crédit Agricole S.A., BPCE S.A., BNP Paribas, Deutsche Bank AG, and Intesa Sanpaolo are found to have many links and high market power.

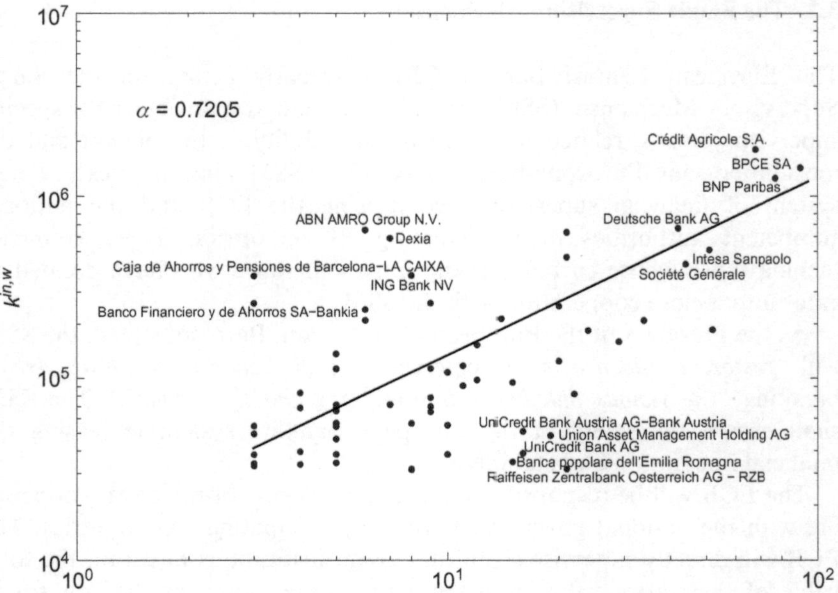

Figure 4: k^{in} versus $k^{in,w}$. The Straight Line is the Curve $k^{in,w}(k^{in}) \propto (k^{in})^{1/\alpha}$ with α Predicted by Equation (7).

Points below the straight line, correspond to banks holding high portfolio diversification but small market control power, informing that these banks have many small connections with many other banks. Therefore, they are not the effective controllers of the corresponding banks. This is the case of two Austrian banks (RZB and UniCredit Bank Austria AG), two German banks (Union Asset Management Holding AG and UniCredit Bank AG), and one Italian bank, namely Banca popolare dell'Emilia Romagna.

On the contrary, points above the straight line correspond to banks whose portfolio has a large volume even if their diversification is small, for example, Caja de Ahorros y Pensiones de Barcelona-LA CAIXA, Banco Financiero y de Ahorros SA-Bankia. This group encompasses also banks like ABN Amro Group N.V., ING bank NV, and Dexia that are among the biggest nodes with a high value of the weighted in-degree. These banks have few but big connected partners.

As stated by Garlaschelli et al. (2005), previous results support the hypothesis that the presence of non-topological quantities associated to the vertices (e.g., total asset) may be at the basis of the emergence of complex scale-free topologies in a large number of real networks.

3.2. The Single Supervisory Mechanism

The European Central Bank (ECB) is recently acting on the Single Supervisory Mechanism (SSM) assuming ultimate responsibility for specific supervisory tasks, related to the financial stability of the biggest and the most important Eurozone-based banks. The SSM aims to create a new system of financial supervision, comprising the ECB and the national competent authorities of participating EU countries. These countries include those whose currency is the Euro and those who have decided to enter into a close cooperation with the SSM.

As the President of the European Commission, Barroso, stated, the SSM will "*restore confidence in the supervision of all banks in the Euro Area*," breaking "*the vicious link between sovereigns and their banks*." The SSM shall ensure the safety of the European banking system increasing the financial integration and stability in Europe.

The ECB will be responsible for the effectiveness of the SSM, cooperating with the national governments of the participating EU countries. The ECB will directly supervise significant credit institutions based on the total value of their assets, the importance for the economy of the country in which they are located or the EU as a whole, the significance of their cross-border activities and whether they have requested or received public financial assistance from the European Stability Mechanism (ESM) or the European Financial Stability Facility (EFSF). In this framework, the ECB will directly oversee almost 130 credit institutions, representing around 85% of total banking assets in the Euro Area.

Considering the total assets as the main ingredient to select the significant credit institutions, could be only a raw proxy to identify the systemic risk associated to a particular bank. Indeed, having a large value of total asset is more likely to be associated with many connections to other banks but it cannot be always the case. To shed some insight about this eventuality, we repeat the previous exercise (see Sub-section 3.1) associating the total assets with the probability of possible connections a bank has. In particular, once we have proved that total asset follows a power law with exponent $\beta = 1.7285$, as the inset of Figure 5 shows, we can employ the model described by Equations (5)–(7) to find the relationship between the value of the total asset and the probability of the number of partners connected to a bank. We discover that the two quantities are linked by a scaling coefficient $\alpha_{ta} = 0.57$ denoting a direct relationship between the size of total assets and the number of connections. Moreover, results indicate that, beside the positive relationship between the value of the total assets and the probability of connection to partners, not all the financial

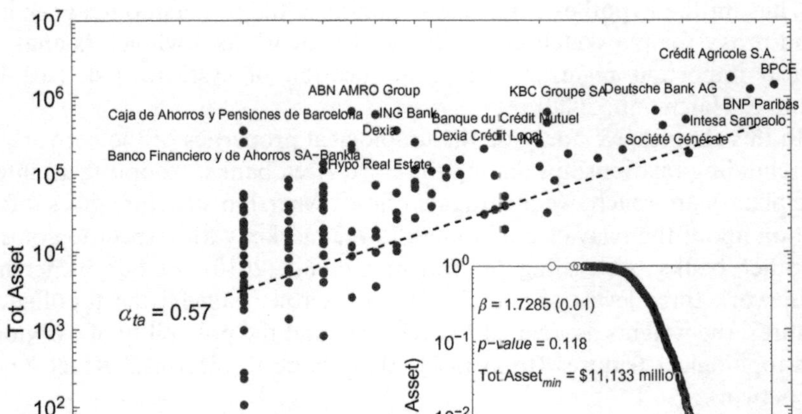

Figure 5: k^{in} versus Total Asset for the 130 Banks under SSM.

institutions with an high value of total asset are systemically important but only few of them.

Indeed notice from Figure 4 that the same group that owns high portfolio diversification and market power, also has a large value of total assets. We point out that the 130 institutions under SSM are characterized by different connectivity behavior. Therefore, only the banks located in the top right corner of Figure 5 display an high degree of systemic risk, while the remaining although displaying a high value of total asset, having lower connections, are less prone to spread contagion.

4. Discussion and Concluding Remarks

It is known that financial institutions establish financial contracts, such as lending or credit derivatives, with several other institutions. This allows them to diversify risk but, at the same time, it also exposes them to financial contagion (see Allen & Song, 2005). Unfortunately, information on these contracts is usually not disclosed due to strategic reasons. However, in various countries, the existence of such financial ties is correlated with the existence of ownership relationships (see Iannotta, Nocera, & Sironi, 2007).

Thus, in the hypothesis that the structure of the ownership network is a good proxy for the sketch of the financial network as a whole, its analysis is also important regarding the quantification of systemic risk (see De Bandt & Hartmann, 2000).

In this chapter, we analyzed the topological properties of the network of shareholding relationships among the Euro Area banks. Adopting an interdisciplinary approach, we investigated how ownership structure gives information about the relevance of a bank in the market with respect to control of other banks. According to Battiston et al. (2010), in our ownership framework three levels of complexity play a role, namely, the topological features, the weights associated to each link, and the possibility of assigning non-topological features (total asset) that shape the intrinsic structure of the network.

Our results revealed that the European banking network displays power laws in both the binary and the weighted case with exponents γ and δ; moreover, we find a direct nexus between the exponents: an increase of control diversification is positively linked with a rise in the market power. Scale-free networks are typically robust with respect to random breakdown of nodes and fragile with respect to intentional attack against the hubs. Indeed, while in good times the network is seemingly robust, in bad times firms go into distress simultaneously.

In the light of these considerations, the Single Supervisory Mechanism implemented by the ECB is related to the financial stability of the biggest and most important Eurozone-based banks. The SSM shall ensure the safety of the European banking system increasing the financial integration and stability in Europe. We find out that, although there exists a positive correlation between the value of the total asset and the weighted in-degree, representing market power, results indicate that not all the financial institutions with high value of total asset are systemically important but also few of them. The 130 institutions under SSM are characterized by different connectivity behavior. Only banks with a very high value of total asset display a relevant degree of systemic risk, while the remaining, having lower connections, are less prone to spread contagion.

This work emphasizes how a network framework can provide a possible reform of the current global financial architecture, in order to make the interbank market less prone to contagion. Indeed a systemwide approach yields a deeper understanding of risk concentration among financial institutions. Given the inherent existence of power laws in the Euro Area banking system, we recognize that financial companies are not all equal in terms of possible risk spreading and that increasing concentration through *too big to fail* or *too interconnected to fail* are real risks.

Hence, a network approach to financial reform offers the potential to suggest reforms that can improve the financial systems' robustness, resilience, and resistance to contagion.

References

Acemoglu, D., Ozdaglar, A., & Tahbaz-Salehi, A. (2013). *Systemic risk and stability in financial networks*. Working Paper No. w18727. National Bureau of Economic Research.

Allen, F., & Gale, D. (2000). Financial contagion. *Journal of Political Economy*, *108*(1), 1–33.

Allen, F., & Song, W. L. (2005). Financial integration and EMU. *European Financial Management*, *11*(1), 7–24.

Almeida, H. V., & Wolfenzon, D. (2006). A theory of pyramidal ownership and family business groups. *The Journal of Finance*, *61*(6), 2637–2680.

Barabási, A. L., & Albert, R. (1999). Emergence of scaling in random networks. *Science*, *286*(5439), 509–512.

Barabási, A. L., & Albert, R. (2002). Statistical mechanics of complex networks. *Reviews of Modern Physics*, *74*(1), 47.

Barrat, A., Barthelemy, M., Pastor-Satorras, R., & Vespignani, A. (2004). The architecture of complex weighted networks. *Proceedings of the National Academy of Sciences of the United States of America*, *101*(11), 3747–3752.

Battiston, S., & Glattfelder, J. B. (2009). Backbone of complex networks of corporations: The flow of control. *Physical Review E*, *80*(3), 036104.

Battiston, S., Glattfelder, J. B., Garlaschelli, D., Lillo, F., & Caldarelli, G. (2010). The structure of financial networks. In *Network science* (pp. 131–163). London: Springer.

Bech, M. L., & Atalay, E. (2010). The topology of the federal funds market. *Physica A: Statistical Mechanics and its Applications*, *389*(22), 5223–5246.

Boss, M., Elsinger, H., Summer, M., & Thurner, S. (2004). An empirical analysis of the network structure of the Austrian interbank market. *Oesterreichesche Nationalbank Financial stability Report*, *7*, 77–87.

Brioschi, F., Buzzacchi, L., & Colombo, M. G. (1989). Risk capital financing and the separation of ownership and control in business groups. *Journal of Banking & Finance*, *13*(4), 747–772.

Caldarelli, G., Capocci, A., De Los Rios, P., & Muñoz, M. A. (2002). Scale-free networks from varying vertex intrinsic fitness. *Physical Review Letters*, *89*(25), 258702.

Capocci, A., Servedio, V. D., Caldarelli, G., & Colaiori, F. (2005). Detecting communities in large networks. *Physica A: Statistical Mechanics and its Applications*, *352*(2), 669–676.

Chapelle, A. (2004). *Separation between ownership and control: Where do we stand?* Brussels: Université Libre de Bruxelles. Mimeographed document.

Clauset, A., Shalizi, C. R., & Newman, M. E. (2009). Power-law distributions in empirical data. *SIAM Review*, *51*(4), 661–703.

Cohen, R., Erez, K., Ben-Avraham, D., & Havlin, S. (2000). Resilience of the Internet to random breakdowns. *Physical Review Letters*, *85*(21), 4626.

Corrado, R., & Zollo, M. (2006). Small worlds evolving: governance reforms, privatizations, and ownership networks in Italy. *Industrial and Corporate Change*, *15*(2), 319–352.

Craig, B., & Von Peter, G. (2014). Interbank tiering and money center banks. *Journal of Financial Intermediation*, *23*(3), 322–347.

Davis, G. F., Yoo, M., & Baker, W. E. (2003). The small world of the American corporate elite, 1982–2001. *Strategic Organization*, *1*(3), 301–326.

De Bandt, O., & Hartmann, P. (2000). *Systemic risk: A survey*. Discussion Paper No. 2634. CEPR.

De Masi, G., Iori, G., & Caldarelli, G. (2006). Fitness model for the Italian interbank money market. *Physical Review E*, *74*(6), 066112.

Eisenhardt, K. M. (1989). Agency theory: An assessment and review. *Academy of Management Review*, *14*(1), 57–74.

Flath, D. (1992). Indirect shareholding within Japan's business groups. *Economics Letters*, *38*(2), 223–227.

Freixas, X., Parigi, B. M., & Rochet, J. C. (2000). Systemic risk, interbank relations, and liquidity provision by the central bank. *Journal of Money, Credit and Banking*, *32*(3), 611–638.

Fricke, D. (2012). Trading strategies in the overnight money market: Correlations and clustering on the e-MID trading platform. *Physica A: Statistical Mechanics and its Applications*, *391*(24), 6528–6542.

Fricke, D., & Lux, T. (2013). *On the distribution of links in the interbank network: Evidence from the e-mid overnight money market*. Working Paper No. 1819. Kiel Working Paper.

Fricke, D., & Lux, T. (2014). Core–periphery structure in the overnight money market: Evidence from the e-mid trading platform. *Computational Economics*, *10*(2), 187–211.

Gai, P., & Kapadia, S. (2010). Contagion in financial networks. *Proceedings of the royal society A: Mathematical, physical and engineering science, rspa20090410*.

Garlaschelli, D., Battiston, S., Castri, M., Servedio, V. D., & Caldarelli, G. (2005). The scale-free topology of market investments. *Physica A: Statistical Mechanics and its Applications*, *350*(2), 491–499.

Goh, K. I., Kahng, B., & Kim, D. (2001). Universal behavior of load distribution in scale-free networks. *Physical Review Letters*, *87*(27), 278701.

Granovetter, M. (1995). Coase revisited: Business groups in the modern economy. *Industrial and Corporate Change*, *4*(1), 93–130.

Haldane, A. G., & May, R. M. (2011). Systemic risk in banking ecosystems. *Nature*, *469*(7330), 351–355.

Hatzopoulos, V., & Iori, G. (2012). *Information theoretic description of the e-Mid interbank market: implications for systemic risk*. Working Paper. Department of Economics, City University, London.

Iannotta, G., Nocera, G., & Sironi, A. (2007). Ownership structure, risk and performance in the European banking industry. *Journal of Banking & Finance*, *31*(7), 2127–2149.

Inaoka, H., Ninomiya, T., Taniguchi, K., Shimizu, T., & Takayasu, H. (2004). *Fractal network derived from banking transaction – An analysis of network structures formed by financial institutions*. Working Paper No. 4. Bank of Japan Working Papers.

Iori, G., De Masi, G., Precup, O. V., Gabbi, G., & Caldarelli, G. (2008). A network analysis of the Italian overnight money market. *Journal of Economic Dynamics and Control*, *32*(1), 259–278.

Iori, G., Reno, R., De Masi, G., & Caldarelli, G. (2007). Trading strategies in the Italian interbank market. *Physica A: Statistical Mechanics and its Applications*, *376*, 467–479.

Kogut, B., & Walker, G. (2001). The small world of Germany and the durability of national networks. *American Sociological Review*, *66*(3), 317–335.

Nier, E., Yang, J., Yorulmazer, T., & Alentorn, A. (2007). Network models and financial stability. *Journal of Economic Dynamics and Control*, *31*(6), 2033–2060.

Porta, R., Lopez de Silanes, F., & Shleifer, A. (1999). Corporate ownership around the world. *The Journal of Finance*, *54*(2), 471–517.

Shleifer, A., & Vishny, R. W. (1997). A survey of corporate governance. *The Journal of Finance*, *52*(2), 737–783.

Soramäki, K., Bech, M. L., Arnold, J., Glass, R. J., & Beyeler, W. E. (2007). The topology of interbank payment flows. *Physica A: Statistical Mechanics and its Applications*, *379*(1), 317–333.

Vedres, B. (2000). The constellations of economic power: The position of political actors, banks and large corporations in the network of directorate interlocks in Hungary, 1997. *Journal Title Connections: Journal of the International Network of Social Network Analysis*, *23*(1), 44–59.
Vitali, S., Glattfelder, J. B., & Battiston, S. (2011). The network of global corporate control. *PloS One*, *6*(10), e25995.

Chapter 15
Finance Otherwise: The End of Banks?

Michel Roux

Honorary Dean of the Faculty of Economic and Management Sciences, Université Paris 13 – Sorbonne Paris Cité, Paris, France, email: michel.roux@univ-paris13.fr

Abstract

Contrary to what its title might suggest, this chapter does not develop an alternative vision of finance. On the basis of the financial world as it currently operates, we propose to identify the paradoxes and the likely evolution of a banking and financial system evolving. Based on the facts, this chapter seeks to extend the discussions initiated in the last chapter, entitled "Socially responsible banks?" of our book "The management of the bank," published by Vuibert editions. The frantic pace of innovation and the requirements of regulators encourage banks to review their organization and their governance. This chapter attempts to position the bank between two paradoxes: on one side, the crises have not made more responsible banks. The facts remain: rates and currency manipulation, embezzlement rules on bonuses, even if some are still under financial assistance of the United States. On the other hand, the "finance otherwise" innovates, disturbs, and upsets. Creative players such as collaborative funding or virtual currencies are not really threatening to the big banks. But in the past, marked by their personnel costs and infrastructure cannot meet the agility of these new entrants "crowdfunding," and other online payment methods have backed the Web. These innovations really threaten banks that do not lack the resources to adapt. And if tomorrow, the banks no longer existed? Behavior changes and already a growing number of clients save, borrow, and lend the use of means of payment to settle their online purchases without using the services of traditional financial institutions! A certainty,

International Symposia in Economic Theory and Econometrics, Vol. 24
William A. Barnett and Fredj Jawadi (Editors)

ISSN: 1571-0386/doi: 10.1108/S1571-038620150000024027

"finance otherwise," will play a stimulatory role. The speed and magnitude of change is such that it becomes necessary for banks and financial institutions to adapt to these new technologies to increase or simply maintain their business. Based on the facts, the chapter explores and analyzes the developments that may become sustainable for a banking system reluctant to lose the monopoly of the distribution of credit and means of payment. The "end of the banks," is a "provocative" subject but insufficiently addressed in the economic literature.

Keywords: banking strategy, despairs, facts, governance, finance otherwise

JEL Classifications: G21, G28, P34

1. Introduction

We are in a phase of acceleration of time: social time, political time, and technological time with public debate focused on the distribution of wealth, taken for granted, rather than on their production. The illusions of inflation and debt have disappeared. Growth will not return before long. Before, we had nothing and we do not know; now there is a shortage of everything and we know. This is not because France loves much its companies. The French must first understand that before distribution, you must first create value. A context in which everyone loses its bearings and loses confidence! European countries do not invest enough and businesses are too indebted companies would have cash are not investing more because of the instability of the rules. Financial markets doubt in the ability of politicians to deal with globalization, only by debt. In 2008, we prevented the transfer of a financial crash in recession due to the partial substitution of private for public debt. Prudential rules are gradually capital and liquidity in short supply and we do not measure all the effects that may reduce eventual financing of the real economy. In this time of crisis, the central issue for the bank remains that of its usefulness to the community, that is to say, the need to recover the sense of reality. If the profession has continued with intensity changes involved for many years. Today, in an international context of innovations, all sectors combined, the successive crises and their consequences amplify the change process: changes in markers, behaviors, economic paradigms to face stiffer competition and a crisis of confidence and image. With social networking, digital, the pace of change continues to accelerate and could jeopardize a good number of strategies, tools, and trades. Are we not already beyond prophecy over 30 years of "The bank could be the steel of tomorrow."[1] Without dispel threats to the bank, the main question is can be different? From the late 1980s, the French banks, like all their competitors, have engaged in a policy: diversification trades practiced and proposed offer to customers increasingly segmented products, unprecedented development of market activities and internationalization increasingly thrust. Until the mid-2000s, the bank seemed to continually push the boundaries of its activities. Initially the crisis was financial. Then the sovereign debt before becoming the US subprime future crisis in the automobile? This changing and uncertain environment should be viewed through the consequences of the above uncertainties and the players' strategies to deploy in response to changes in the new regulatory requirements and customer expectations. But already, some profound changes looming: Basel III, Asian competition, separation of retail banking, and market, and this in a context of stigma of the banking profession. The debate about the role and advisability of market activities of banks are no end to lead the economic and political sphere. Faced with a multitude of preconceived ideas, we would modestly help rebalance the debate. If modern finance was sometimes an aggravating crisis, some dream of a finance differently! They would like finance where the profit motive is not the only objective, a finance which would leave room for altruism, a finance work for the common good! The small number of actors, their weight, ambient mimicry management techniques to reduce risks, all adds up to increased financial market fluctuations. So they are calling for the emergence of new forms of management. In finance, more social responsibility would, may make it less predatory and more efficient. New technologies raise some questions regarding the bank strategies. There was a time when Google was a search engine, a partner comparator trips. That time has passed. There was a time when Google was the affiliation with insurance comparators. It became their main competitor. Nothing ever really stopped Google, which sees in the financial services what could become its biggest market. A similar point can be made for Apple. Moreover, the reforms since 2009 under the leadership of the G20 and the Financial Stability Board (FSB), as a result of the financial and economic crisis on the one hand and the redesign of the architecture of European financial regulation with the creation of three independent authorities on the other hand, have significantly changed the situation. On banking strategy, today it is permissible to consider the impact of all these factors on future models of banks. This chapter

[1] Paper title, Michel Godet and Jean-Pierre Plas, published in "Le Monde" dated February 22, 1979.

strives to continue discussions initiated by us in a collective book, "The year in finance" and in an article in "The letter no. 38 of the French Association on corporate governance."[2] As a first point, we recall the facts of uncertainty for the banking industry. Then, in a second step, we consider the hopes and despairs for our banking system.

2. Facts

This first party claims no completeness examples. It presents facts that are likely to hinder the development of the banking business: the changing economic and regulatory environment, new technologies, and new players. The scope of the "other" is to find the freedom to decide in conscience with all the discernment with regard to the complexity of our environment, step back and propagate the views to open the field of possibilities that is the meaning of our approach through the new landmarks: the collaborative consumption complementary currencies; responsible finance savings solidarity, and participatory finance. The second part will highlight the capacity to react in the profession.

2.1. Economic and Regulatory Context

After a rash of development finance market which constituted an aggravating factor in recent crises today, some would imagine an otherwise where financial, beyond appearing as predators that rather play the role of efficient players. Gradually and in parallel, the commercial bank debt rose from an economy characterized by a balance sheet intermediation in a market economy governed by market intermediation. So with globalization and deregulation, there, since the late 1980s, witnessed what is called "*financialization*" of markets, concomitant regression of indirect finance the balance sheet of a bank. With this in mind, can we therefore see that the next disappearance of disintermediation of the banking function? We are entering a world of economic ends. We are moving from an approach based on the distribution of wealth and the value added by labor in an economy of human intelligence and technology economy. However, this

[2] Collective book: "Comment la finance peut-elle contribuer à la reprise": Chapter: "La finance autrement: mythe réalité et interrogations pour les professions financières," Revue Banque Edition/Centre des Professions Financières, November 2014. Paper: La Lettre de l'AFGE n° 38; "Banque: Fin d'un monopole, fin d'un modèle…?" pp. 8–12, October 2014.

transition takes place in the world at different degrees, which explains the difficulty of diagnosis. This world does not end all at the same time and same place. For Europe, force-fed equipment that is not yet the case of China, India, or Africa, heritage enhancement is realized by more debt and wages. Our problem is not the distribution of wealth, but wealth creation. Successive IMF reports constantly focus our attention on the paradox that we are trapped between two risks: the presence of excess liquidity on the one hand and cash on the other hand. The more we are indebted and interest rates are low. To overcome the crisis, how to react, by austerity or inflation? Not the gloomy growth that seems to characterize our economies is due, according to the latest report of the Economic Analysis Council of September 2014 entitled "Potential growth," a lack of innovation. Innovation like greenwashing[3] (in French: blanchire, dissimuler), finance manager … would not be an argument of communication. Too often overworked and ignored in times of hardship, innovation is not the cause of dismal growth but the scapegoat for some pessimists has ceased to observe it. This is somewhat the same pessimistic discourse that affects capitalism in the early 21st century. After a reign unchallenged for over 25 years, researchers like Thomas Piketty (economist, "*The capital in the twenty-first century*," 2013), David Graeber (anthropologist, "*5,000 years of history, with debt*," 2014), Jerome BASCHET (historian, "*Farewell capitalism*," 2014), and Jeremy Rifkin ("*New society with zero marginal cost*," 2014), are its contradictions and dysfunctions (spiral of debt, end of fossil resources, tensions on the labor market, etc). Beyond announcing his sentence, the experts prefer more of a decline in the model face a new world centered on sharing and the emergence of collaborative. After the enlargement of modern finance after hypertrophy of the market where the logic of buying and selling no longer applies only to material goods, but increasingly affects our lives, we'll let grow this "*commodification*" of society, behaviors, and services that formerly fell civic or altruism.

On banking reform and regulation of financial activities, it is necessary to examine this complex and widely discussed strong subjects for many years. It projects that many laws have become more or less, inadequate or applied too late. One has the feeling that what happened could happen again. Too many laws kill the law. Many of these measures are inconsistent in their subject. The subprime financial crisis and sovereign risks have been

[3] A compound word modeled on "whitewash" or "green sheen" is a form of spin in which green PR or green marketing is deceptively used to promote the perception that an organization's products, aims, or policies are environmentally friendly. Process of marketing or public relations used by an organization (company, government) in order to give a green image.

followed by a dizzying regulatory effervescence if it creates more than a doubt about the consistency and even the purpose of the reform. Major global banks, major players in the system have been implicated in triggering or worsening of these successive crises. Sometimes, with reason for their active role in the production or release of toxic substances, swelling their balance sheets without relation to their core business, the financing of real-estate bubbles. Sometimes, the responsibility of banks was sought wrongly. In this regard, we agree, totally, the words of Dominique Garabiol at the symposium: "*Banking reform: apple of discord*" *June 23, 2014.*[4] It stated: "*Banks are intermediaries financing of the economy. When an economy collapses, as in Greece and Spain, private losses are mechanically carried over banks that are only one link circuit socialization. This socialization of losses is necessary for the capitalist system to become solvable private agents and avoid depressive spiral. But in these cases, the actual responsibilities rather macro-economic order.*" The purpose of banking regulation is to ensure that banks, financial institutions, and businesses pay the consequences of the risks they take. Banks, for their role is important, are only actresses system. Is banking reform meets the objectives of political power? It is difficult to envisage that a systemic crisis cannot engage the responsibility of the builders of the system in crisis. After very open discussions, monetary policies have failed to renew, such as finding only answer to the crisis the direct and massive intervention by central banks in money creation. Similarly, Dominique Garabiol continued: "It is difficult to believe that the prudential rules made from 1998 to 2004, which we call" Basel II "and which are set by the European Union, have not played a role in the less permissive destabilization of the system: the rules have strongly encouraged banks to favor assets reduced ..." risk. If the goal of the banking reform to separate activities in order to save the taxpayer of all errors of system seems laudable, the reality is much more complex than it seems. This is a large text, which aims to regulate more closely the banking business in France, which does not exist anywhere else. Projects under discussion in other countries (the United States, the United Kingdom, etc.) or at the European level will not be ready before long. The discussions that led to the development of Vickers (the United Kingdom) or Volcker (the United States) reports are based on a specific context that has no exclusive link with crises. In the United Kingdom, the questioning is directly related to the Northern Rock case (conventional commercial bank that needed help from the British government due to the granting of mortgages of poor quality). The debate is not only of isolation of retail banking but also of a substantial increase

[4] Symposia Res Publica Foundation, Paris, June 2014.

in capital requirements and that, beyond the requirements envisaged by Basel III.

The first difficulty lies in defining and securing the perimeter useful to the real economy activities. What is useful? Where is the line between useful and useless? This is a real issue; when banks develop speculative activities, it is often driven by a shareholder which requires that returns on investment are not always consistent with the activity expected by the proximity of the customer retail banking. This bill gives some the impression of a response to citizens' expectations. Should it be the first in healthy control face instead of London? There is probably no absolute answer. Where to position the cursor? Between back to basics to protect the taxpayer and the applicant and preserve the economic sovereignty of France, which has prevailed? Was there not more pressing issues that banking reform? Reform for whom? Enshrined in the French law of July 2013 on the separation of banking activities, the universal banking model was based on an implicit form of solidarity among all creditors and the state. The bailout passed by the shareholders, holders of debt ranking last and external funds, guarantee funds fed by banks deposits or subordinated creditors of public funds. With the EU Directive, it is expected, on the contrary, the involvement of ordinary bond and large depositors, above 100,000 euros, before external bailouts. As part of the banking union, the same logic applies. A "resolution fund crisis" fueled by the banks and added to the panel comes before public funds. The highly speculative activity, it is less than 2% of the overall activity of French banks as defined in the definition of the state bill. The Liikanen Report or "Report of the European Commission's High-level Expert Group on Bank Structural Reform" (known as the "Liikanen Group") is a set of recommendations published in October 2012 by a group of experts led by Erkki Liikanen, governor of the Bank of Finland and ECB council member. The Liikanen Report shows: 13% for BNP Paribas, 14% for Credit Agricole, and 16% for Societe Générale. Fréderic Oudéa caused a sensation, January 30, 2013, when he was interviewed by the National Assembly, stating how the project would impact 0.75% of the banking group he leads activities, including Sociéte Generale. Amendments specify, presumably, from the "market making" (market making) to be a subsidiary under the arbitration of the Ministry of Finance. Before 1984, French banks lived well under the supervision of the state and trapped in the credit crunch. In continental Europe, funding is predominantly bank, then our bill, how will it fit into the draft European Directive? As for shareholders, opinions are all too divergent. At a time of increasing disintermediation, it would be damaging to break this increased synergy between commercial activities within retail banking on the one hand and bank financing and investment on the other hand. Banks are required to provide both bond arrangements as to place their clients' securities markets. In the event of a separation of the two activities after which the holder of a share of a universal bank become a shareholder of the two structures, then the question will arise of recovery, particularly in Banking and investment, the more destabilized due to regulatory uncertainties surrounding it, and also because, likely, a contributing factor to its benefit costs related to its relative "independence." The intention to separate the activities of speculative activities market is commendable. It is due to hypertrophy of our banking system in which the assets of the four largest banks account for nearly 400% of GDP (against 85% for the US). French banks are too big to fail, according to the formula, but it is also too big to be rescued.

2.2. Complementary Currencies, Inclusive and Participatory Finance

Faced with the rise of productivism and greed, we are more likely to want to reduce inequalities. We are also likely to become more numerous wanting to resist excesses while being confident in one's ability to grow; to seek fairer balance between the social, economic, and environmental and be demanding consistency between what is said and promised to see what is actually achieved. At the margin, attempts to grow to fill reaction to lack of confidence. Some seem to have understood that we were in a transition phase between a world that never ceases to decline and another world that remains largely to invent and build. It is in this context that we see in lifestyles and consumption, resulting, no doubt, not only for a share of the crisis and the constraints on income but also the changing values and benchmarks the rise of so-called "collaborative" consumption. Collaborative consumption (car sharing, co-work, private hire, local trading system or SEL = form of exchange of goods or services, usually in associative networks, etc.) increased as a result of innovations social and new uses of the Internet. Some recent examples to illustrate this trend are the following:

- *The bitcoin* (from the English "corner" coin and "bit" binary unit of information) refers to both a payment system through the Internet and a unit of account used by the payment system. According to the Financial Glossary, Bitcoin is an electronic currency designed by Satoshi Nakamoto in 2009 and created outside of any state field; however, it has only one of the attributes of a classic money if it is a currency and a payment instrument for those who accept it, has no statutory liberating effect because it is not possible to require payment in bitcoin outside the community. The problem of bitcoin is its volatility (40 times more volatile than the euro/dollar exchange rate). With tensions are in the stock market in mid-October 2014, its valuation, up, reached 400 dollars! Is this a currency without a legal tender, a raw material, and a technology offer? Action of a start-up, an option that would qualify for a share of potential development?

- *Case of "low cost"* distributed tobacconist and named the account as *"account Nickel."* Account that does not impose income requirements, deposits, or assets has also found adherents beyond its initial target: banking banned and vulnerable populations. Apart from the project account opening associations and very small businesses, start-up manager of Nickel account "the French Electronic Payments" intends, also, to expand its services installed in office tobacco. This would include authenticating documents for insurance companies or telecom operators.
- Even more inclusive and based on logic sharing, proximity, a new form of exchange, *collaborative consumption* means, generally, an economic model where the predominant use on the property, the use of goods, services, privilege, may be increased by the sharing, exchange, barter, sale, or lease thereof. While economists observe the evolution of GDP, people increasingly use the exchange, sharing, donation. In support of these behavioral changes, other financing is set up under the aegis of complementary currencies.

A complementary currency is a currency that does not parallel that of a national government[5] that is to be exchanged only in a limited geographical area. It works as a complement to the national currency with local characteristics (e.g., promote another form of consumption), and its objectives are usually to defend the principles of social economy and to promote social link between people in proximity. Without legal tender, it cannot be the subject of speculation. Complementary currencies have a long history; for example, there is a trace in ancient Egypt with the "ostracon" debt recorded by a scribe on a shard of pottery, Languedoc in the middle of the Middle Ages. More recently, following the 1929 crisis, complementary currencies were allowed to maintain a satisfactory level of employment in local economies (for Austria against the rise of Nazism). Today, the French cities equip themselves, it is the case to: Brest, Bayonne, Bordeaux, Nantes, Saint-Die, Toulouse …Nantes … .

Cities that have one thing in common is that they have developed their local currency. Ile de France proposed the creation of a Cooperative

[5] Methods of payment are formed by fiat currency (banknotes and coins) and bank money (deposits, electronic purse); payment instruments are not of money but allow circulating it widely (checks, credit cards, transfers …).

Society[6] (CICS): "SYMBA IDF" is a symbiotic money for organizations (companies, associations, etc.). Ile de France to relocate the economy, create virtuous trade, and develop economic wealth, social, environmental, and cultural territory. Participants will be able to get credit within the network in the currency called the Symba[7] (one euro equals a Symba, the Symba is not convertible) through a clearing and thus expand their trade without paying interest banks to have access to money. To date, it is more than 5000 local currency or complementary that exists in the world. Include: the "Wir"[8] Switzerland, Belgium and RES systems that represent the US barter alone 14 billion per year trade. Except Argentina and Switzerland, the weight of additional local currencies has been quite marginal in the global economy. They meet a success especially in times of crisis by allowing the local economy to continue to operate and individuals to meet their most basic needs.

- *From finance charge savings solidarity and participa7tory finance ....*[9] Favored by globalization in raising the question of duty of care to civil society, the definition and dimensions of the social responsibility of companies and organizations are far from a consensus. In finance, it is reasonable to differentiate responsible solidarity savings and participatory finance investment Socially. We try to decipher these three areas.

---

[6] The Cooperative Society of Collective Interest (SCIC), created by the law 2001-624 of July 17, 2001, is a cooperative venture as SARL, SA ... which associates around the same project multiple stakeholders: employees, volunteers, users, public authorities, enterprises, associations, individuals ... all types of beneficiaries and interested persons in various capacities? SCIC is supposed to produce goods or services that meet the collective needs of a territory by the best possible mobilization of its economic and social resources. Respecting the principles of cooperative governance (one man, one vote), decision (collective) and reinvestment optimum results. It is part of a logic of local development and sustainable dear to the Social and Solidarity Economy (SSE).

[7] www.symba-idf.org

[8] Wir bank, Switzerland, is a cooperative non-profit corporation that issues its own currency, the WIR ("we" in German, as opposed to "Ich," the "I" French). The aim of the initiators of the project, dice, 1934, was to create an organization to support and supplement the shortage of cash. Beyond trade in goods and services, Knowledge Exchange Network (RES) offer intercultural or inter lessons and sharing of knowledge exchange; they have spread in Europe. The Barter system is an intermediate form that provides a platform for business exchange, usually for the SOHO or SME.

[9] For comments and more accurate statistical data, the reader may refer to the subsection "B) Finance and ethical relationship with money" in our book "Management of the bank: new risks for new forms of governance," pp. 240–244, Vuibert Edition, Paris, September 2013.

- *SRI* (*socially responsible investment*) is an investment that seeks to reconcile economic performance and social and environmental impact by supporting businesses and public entities that contribute to sustainable development regardless of their industry. Influencing governance and the behavior of actors, SRI promotes a responsible economy. In Europe and in the world, there are different approaches, often linked to local culture. In Europe and in the world, there are different approaches, often linked to local culture. For example, in France, the emphasis is on social aspect, Switzerland and Germany on environment, in Britain on governance, and in the Scandinavian countries and the United States, ethical values. The contemporary roots of SRI can be found in the United States in the 1920s at the initiative of religious congregations who refused to invest in "values of sin": alcohol, pornography, gambling, tobacco, etc. This form then took a more secular and militant approach to targeting the 70 cases such as apartheid, the war in Vietnam, human rights, nuclear, etc. This trend still exists today. A second form of SRI appeared from the 80s, taking into account the fact that good social practices, environmental, and governance could have a positive impact on the financial results of a company and its market value. Extra credit rating agencies then appeared to provide investors with information that allows them to select the best companies. In France, according to Novethic (SRI observatory within the group of the Caisse des Dépôts et Consignations), the SRI market has increased between 2003 and 2013, from 3.9 billion euros to 169.7 billion, but it takes forms more complex to build portfolios differentiated and attract issuers. In an attempt to better understand these diverse approaches and the lack of a common definition of investors, Novethic tries to propose a new classification distinguishing four categories of SRI: SRI fund (above our 169.7 billion euros for 2013, with a selection of titles on financial and non-financial criteria, see a label ...); ESG integration fund (integrating environmental, social and governance) to 440 billion euros or 15% of 3000 billion euros in asset management in France; exclusion normative (management excluded companies that do not meet the standards or international conventions portfolios), weighs 1.445 trillion euros, nearly half of the French asset management; commitment usually shareholder, it requires companies' improvements in environmental, social, and governance matters through direct dialogue, the exercise of voting rights in general meetings or filing resolutions when the dialogue is unsuccessful, its outstanding would cover about forty billion. On our planet, SRI and responsible finance are largely shaped by the cultures and history. SRI estimated at 2500 billion for 12 European countries in 2012, is dominated by the British for nearly 1000 billion of which 97% is held by institutional investors. In North America, the "classic" SRI market benefits from the prior (1971) with $3744 billion in late 2012, 11.3% of asset management. This is because of the selection criteria of the fund where the sectoral exclusion and shareholder engagement are dominant for US SRI funds. Therefore, these data are in perspective and comparisons of a country to another. Asia, although small, the amounts are experiencing growth variables (with $4 billion in China, SRI represents 1% of managed assets in Japan in 2011, they advanced an outstanding €8 billion, essentially, invested in the environment.

- *The solidarity savings* to be split between: *sharing and solidarity savings investments*. The first is the taxation of gifts and is to return a portion of the income of an investment for charity (e.g., a passbook or 50% interest is donated to charities selected) solidarity investments are, in turn, assigned to corporate finance integration, social housing, microcredit, life insurance solidarity, etc. "The barometer of social finance in 2013 said over six Billion Euros (+ 28% compared to 2012 despite the crisis)."[10] These cover the whole six billion of savings in solidarity with 12% for shared savings, 32% for secured funding, and 55% invested in employee savings.
- *Participatory Finance or crowdfunding*. This is a new funding model in short circuit, which allows to project, often innovative in artistic and cultural, technical and scientific, political, but also entrepreneurial, social, or charity to raise funds directly to the general public. Worn by web platforms (according to the World Bank the number of 700 in 2013) which replace the traditional intermediaries – banks, venture capital funds, business angels – playing a role linking. It offers individuals the ability to mobilize funding for projects they choose themselves, according to several formulas – gift, loan, equity – and for amounts ranging from tens to tens of thousands euros. France appeared not there five years ago, participatory finance is still in its infancy. In 2012, the area that would have raised 24.5 million euros, according to Finance Association participatory or 40 million according to Afip (French Association of Investment Participatory). According to a study Massolution.com the system crowdfunding helped raise $2.7 billion worldwide in 2012, 60% of the United States ($1.6 billion). In Europe, France ranks second, but far behind the United Kingdom €609 million was collected in 2012. The collection at world level is estimated at more than $5 billion in 2013. Another study prepared by SME Finance[11] for the Department of the digital economy

[10] According to the survey published by "Finansol" and the newspaper "La Croix," Sample barometer of social finance 2014–2015.

[11] Monitor Report Entrepreneurs – Equity Corporate Finance – The establishment of an appropriate regulatory framework, February 14, 2014, www.PMEFINANCE.org, reading, special: pp. 26–29, regulation of funding participatory companies in the world.

provided an overview of the regulations governing this new phenomenon in different countries. It appears that the main obstacle to the development of crowdfunding is the emission prospectus exemption threshold (in the United States, this threshold is €735,000 and €5 million for Italy and Great Britain). In France before the publication of Order No. 2014-559 of May 30, 2014 on the participatory financing, it was 100,000 euros. According to Forbes magazine, the growth forecasts funding crowdfunding would be in the world in 2020, estimated at 1000 billion!

3. Hopes and Despairs!

This second part of the chapter attempts to cast a critical eye on the importance and impact of innovations on previous developments in the financial sector. The new entrants can be a source of uncertainty for banks in place. In the meantime, innovations can lead to increased competitive pressure. In recent years, Internet use has grown to upset certain segments of industrial and commercial activities. The magnitude of change is such that it becomes necessary for banks and financial institutions to adapt to these new technologies to increase or simply maintain their business. These developments are promising benefits for both customers and to financial intermediaries, but they are also uncertainties for the latter. Risks brought by these new technologies are primarily strategic, legal (licensing, protection of clients, etc.), financial (automation of stock trading, credits, equity injunction to exercise, etc.), and operational (security of information systems and transactions). In addition to this brief review of the evolution of risks, "hopes and despairs," will be treated in three ways: the development of distribution networks; new means of payment; and the sharing economy.

3.1. Evolution of Economic Models of Distribution

In France, long time, the network of bank branches remained close to 38,000 agents following the arrival, on January 1, 2006, 12,000 branches of Banque Postale (an average of 600 branches per million in France inhabitants to a European average of 450 per million inhabitants). It is often described as "multi-channel" where new technologies are estimated to be complementary to the branch network. Very quickly, fearing commoditization of their products and image, some banks have preferred to create their own portal and add other products (insurance, travel, etc.) to the banking and financial loss products. Meanwhile, insurance companies are getting their turn in online banking, relying on their network of general agents to provide banking products. In 2012, times are changing. The study published in December 2012 by Equinox Consulting EFMA highlights the demographic trends, the digitalization of society, regulatory pressure, and consumer behavioral changes profoundly changing the balance of local distribution. Three additional studies (Capgemini, Score Advisor, and the European Central Bank), published in 2013, clearly reinforce a concern: 15% of traditional bank branches are not profitable and Europe, the number rose from 237,000 in 2008 to 217,000 in five years. Holland and the Nordic countries are the most affected, with France losing only 3% of its network. That calls and reveals the need to reinvent the distribution models. The branch retail banking networks in Europe will face major changes in format, layout, and missions, as well as increased pressure on their business model and selective closures.

There are three major challenges: having to arbitrate between local channels and direct channels; reinventing the social contract with commercial agencies; and rethinking the training of employees.

The above study, published in December 2012, Equinox Consulting EFMA cost beyond savings solutions or selective closures; it becomes essential for managers in retail banking to make more drastic offs allocation of resources, highlighting two recommendations:

- "The reformatting" the workstation and posture commercial. Thus, the role of Branch Manager should facilitate the implementation of the collective expertise of point of sale (emphasizing the how more than the what). Regarding the commercial counselor, accountability sales (incarnation of listening diagnosis and counseling) will be focused on the essential range with a gradual assimilation by the agency digital channels He will have to learn to break his timely (commercial) between different channels: meet the customer face-to-face (less often, but better) and also, increasingly, restart the phone, grab a quick feedback via SMS, respond to emails within 24 hours, participate a chat with the client user, etc.
- New requirements, subject to give decision-making authority to the agency, and to train employees cope with these transitions. The big challenge is the consolidation of management and training so that every employee is multi-player and progress in the quality of advice provided. Regarding training, "ready-to-wear" uniform respond less to adapt to the local context and needs of the territory. If regulatory requirements remain the same, the future of networks through "intrapreneurship."

3.2. New Payment Methods, New Players!

According to the 10th World payment deferral, published in 2014 by Capgemini, in partnership with the Royal Bank of Scotland (RBS), the cash settlement still yields some ground. In 2012, non-cash transactions have in fact increased by 7.7% worldwide to $334.3 billion of transactions and are expected to grow 8.6% in 2013. Is this a good or bad news for banks?

What is the strategy to deploy the fast pace of innovation and standardization of means of payment? It becomes very difficult for all stakeholders, including banks, to be competitive on both services treatments of transactions that require very large industrial logistics and services that require a detailed analysis of consumer needs. Will we see a specialization of the actors of the chain of means of payment? Behind these many questions, in addition to substantial costs for updates to their information flow and processing systems aspect, there are the question banks for their ability to respond quickly to innovations nonbank players (Apple, Google, and other Twitter). Are they able to choose, so they come out, barely, the site of the standardization of payment standards, particularly with the implementation of the Single Euro Payments Area[12] (Sepa = Single Euro Payments Area) in Europe, which still grows in this specialization of actors?

Prior to the exercise of a choice, if necessary, retrace rapidly, the course of the evolution of trends that are emerging. Confrontation with financial services technology is a real challenge. By nature, we presented the banks as intermediaries between savers and borrowers, individuals or businesses. During the first era of the Web, as meilleurtaux.com models have facilitated the search and comparison of the best deals. Then, the new generations have relied on the power of the web tool par excellence of disintermediation in the form of trade "peer to peer." And the Big Data has arrived in the heart of the financial world. Thus, in the face of increasing digital capabilities of data processing, new players have emerged, often in the form of start-ups. We distinguish two kinds. Those that cater to customers with competing offers or alternatives to banks (crowdfunding, mobile payment, bitcoin) and those that seek to improve the infrastructure of banks and insurance management information or risk analysis.

In these circumstances, banks would they failed, in part, this turn of digital technology? The answer must be qualified. First, banks are far from absent from these technological developments. And in early October 2014,

[12] SEPA is an area payment-unified euro set up by members of the European Payments Council (EPC) banks in response to the request of the European Commission. This initiative aims to harmonize the means of payment in euro (currency of expression) among member countries (transfers, direct debits, credit card). All countries of the European Union, even those not having the euro as their currency, plus Monaco, Switzerland, Liechtenstein, Norway, Iceland, and St. Marinol are members of SEPA.

the cooperative French banking group "BPCE"[13] launched a payment solution, "S-Money" that allowed any holder of a credit card and a Twitter user in France to transfer money from a simple tweet, whatever be the bank and bank details of the recipient. Second, for regulatory reasons, any creative process in terms of payment must have a status (payment institution, electronic money, credit institution, fund manager, etc.). He leans back, usually a bank. Nothing prevents begin as independent technology provider, but it will take him quickly acquire one of these statuses. A good example is here now the PayPal payment institution, then bank in Luxembourg. If this revolution worried central bankers, it is amusing to note the competition between European regulators because getting a license from one of them allows you to enjoy throughout the euro zone status. Candidates begin to select the place where it is easier to get the necessary status! For central bankers operational or legal risks posed by these new actors in the chain of payments (risk of bankruptcy fraud, data security … technical problems) is measured. On an international level, the strategic interests between "bank" and "non-bank" agents in the management of flows vary widely.

Toward global regulation goes on! Faced with PayPal and Square (founded by Jack Dorsey, co-founder of Twitter), Amazon, is the giant online distribution markets since July 2014, a bank card reader for smartphones (Amazon Local Register). We must remain cautious in deploying an all-out strategy. This is expensive sometimes! Amazon has just announced one of the greatest losses in its history ($437 million in the third quarter of 2014 after 126 million in the second quarter already), reflecting a surge of investments in strong areas distant from the heart of business that represents the online business. The international competition is increasing, including in emerging markets to rivals such as Chinese Alibaba. Phone the Fire, Amazon's first phone, launched in last summer does not seem to find its audience!

In the list of innovations, Twitter aims to install all applications and wants to disrupt the online identification systems. Under the name of "Fabric" Twitter offers a battery of tools for the general public (a visualization system bugs in real-time audience measurement consultations at a given time, the monetization tweet, etc.). The idea is to have an entry in

[13] BPCE acronym to describe Banques Populaires Caisses d'Epargne from the merger of Banque Fédérale des Banques and NCCC (Caisse Nationale des Caisses d'Epargne) was officially created on August 3, 2009. 2nd French banking group that is backed by two banking networks of autonomous and complementary retail, those 17 Caisses d'Epargne and Banques Populaires 20. At its inception, the new group had approximately 34 million customers a dense mesh of hexagonal territory with 8000 branches, 110,000 employees, and more than seven million members.

each mobile and be able to evolve its advertising revenues estimated at 2.6% of the global market (against more than 20% for Facebook) door. Another bet, Twitter is to provide a new method of identification on internet services. Identification by e-mail and password is over, it is automatically generated and verified by the call number. Originality for the emerging countries where some users do not have e-mail address.

Similarly, Apple with its latest phone called "Apple 6" will replace the bank payment card to pay for purchases at merchants. A simple process as a Navigo pass with near-field communication (NFC) fingerprints to identify the payer in total anonymity for the seller instead of the card also beginning to be questioned. Bitcoin decentralizing perfectly illustrates the power of digital. Built on a model of "currency" decentralized cryptographic even maligned, it is an alternative to large networks of acceptance as PayPal, Visa, Mastercard or Swift. Traditional networks are affected by a high rate of attrition due dates validity of their cards.

What about Google spent a search engine function comparators (travel, insurance, etc.) and direct competitor to them. Google is experimenting a lot (investment in a credit rating with the Credit Karma, investment in real estate in line with Auction.com, etc.) and research the financial sector that will bring him the best added value. Traditional banks, insurance companies, credit institutions, payment institutions, money transfer business all have reason to worry about Google's investment capabilities. Don't we say that the firm would have more than 150 billion US dollars cash?

3.3. The Economy of Sharing

If the initial goal was to share, pay less, pollute less in services, this has been made possible by the existence of the Internet and the development of social networks in the form of forums. These models have jostling behavior and are being criticized by the destabilization of traditional markets they induce. The informal and generous offer of origin eventually compete with the regulated offer. This goes well, recent criticisms of US models as AIRBNB (vacation rentals in real estate) or UBER specializes in the rental of private property (car rental services and non-professional drivers). They are accused of inflationary practices and sometimes outside the legal framework. It is the same for taxis with new entrants that are not subject to the same constraints and regulatory obligations. The legislator sometimes is very difficult to discern what a regular activity of an occasional activity is (e.g., in France the marauding is reserved for official taxis and online booking for VTC or touring car with driver). These new players contribute to growth and innovation because of the benefits and algorithms developed, but these advances do not they have only been out a lucrative demand control?

What about participatory finance, effective phenomenon in drastic reduction of transaction costs for some, for others and social myth to some. On the sidelines of the media buzz associated with its vertiginous growth, the "crowdfunding" he is an exceptional and innovative way of financing business? A form of digitization activity "business angels,"[14] the question remains as to what "ROI" (Return On Equity) investors will expect to receive in the event of significant funding needs for firms engaged in innovation breaks. That is to say, an expectation of recovery and/or capital gains more consistent than in the case of conventional loans. The future earnings dimension of risk cannot be underestimated, and that the comparison with the angels in their "partner-entrepreneur" and contribution of competence and expertise role. The rise of participatory finance in financing innovative company requires the support of a referent for each project.

Favored by globalization in raising the question of duty of care to civil society, definitions and dimensions of ethical finance and the social responsibility of companies or organizations are far from a consensus. Fashionable world, these concepts are still unclear and contested despite the work carried out in the framework of the United Nations Environment Program (UNEP) to state the Principles for Responsible Investment. They translate into finance in the form of socially responsible investment that is experiencing strong growth relative (less than 7% of managed assets in France) with innovative initiatives in the areas of savings products "sustainable" and the extra-financial analysis. However, to date, as Gaetan Mortier points out in his book "Finance ethics: the big misunderstanding,"[15] ethical finance "*failed to offer credible alternatives to the excesses of speculation and greed of banking systems … victim of its own success with banks and rating agencies, the project has been gutted. Worse, it was sometimes used by large investors to legitimate speculation, uncertainty, indecent salaries and pollutants investments.*" We could add in a world where financial innovation is determined to create differentiation to create better margin, Professor Olivier Pastré in the preface of our book: "The ethics finance, structures, actors and perspectives in France,"[16] explained: "*When I hear about ethical finance, I take out my Return On Equity … ethical finance is fashionable to volatile and fleeting sense that this word can have. Gargle some of that term in good faith and in total solitude, even though the vast majority of those who*

[14] Literally "business angel," also called "angel" – an individual who invests in innovative business potential and, in addition to its investment, accompanies and provides contractor, skills, experience, its relational networks, and part of his time ….
[15] Fyp editions STIMULO Collection, April 2013.
[16] Review Bank Edition, Paris, November 2005, work having obtained an honorable mention in the Turgot Prize 2005 for the best book of Financial Economics.

have the power to invest considers c type of investment falls at best alms ...." He wondered, too, about "*ethicality of certain financial products ... and the gap between the desire of ethics, best shared aspiration of the world, and the scarcity of capital are diverted to this type of investment.*" In 10 years, things have not fundamentally changed. Socially Responsible Investment (SRI) remains largely the result of institutional investors and managers of employee participation, the individual remains under-informed and weak actor. The proliferation and variety of definitions of concepts and agencies of extra-financial analysis does not facilitate the dissemination of ISR to the general public. Too often still, analysts of this ethical finance have not received dedicated training and remain under the control of conventional approaches of modern finance. There is a need for training and information to fill.

4. Conclusion: Between Disintermediation, Restoring Faith and New Players

Faced with these attempts to explain, in this period of transition, we are still in the early stages of what psychologists call the curve of change in which individuals and institutions will experience successive states of denial, loss of benchmarks, and see anger before admitting their usefulness. How to respond to these new players we have presented briefly and those who have failed? They are based on the "peer-to-peer" (translation anglicism peer-to-peer, often abbreviated as "P2P") and operate in networks. They fit all, in logic of proximity, disintermediation trade, and the search for meaning fueled by the growing mistrust of financial markets, amid connectivity. They upset our economic paradigms, our ability to resource allocation, and governance within traditional systems of financing. These new tools be complementary or an alternative to traditional financing? Even retail banking, including our earnings and the relative constancy of its activity is affected and no longer the "all risks" to the vagaries of bank financing and investment guarantee. Resilience is linked to the erosion of profitability; it does not find its limits, to a term up, face the creeping forms of disintermediation above, facing the electronic banking increasingly provided by telecommunications operators or the Internet. It is necessary to rethink quickly, the reorganization of its distribution, its offerings, and its back-office, without omitting the fields of banking inclusion and social responsibility.

But the crisis has not healed the banks of their demons For more than six months a dozen regulators are investigating all nationalities in the world to identify the responsibility of 15 banks accused of agreement on rates exchange. All belong to the group called "systemic" banks for their global reach. Targeted by the IMF in its latest financial stability report, the latter estimated at about $600 billion the amount of aid received in 2012 implied by these large institutions considered "too big to fail." The support that the government has made during the crisis in different forms: loan guarantees to the direct injection of public funds, has allowed banks to borrow at lower rates. Governments are caught in their own trap because they cannot completely eliminate their competition. The three pillars of the banking union (mechanism of single management, recovery and crisis resolution, the guarantee fund) have probably calmed some concerns systemic. But if the test parameters continue to debate because of the construction of contested scenarios, the assessment exercise sheets ("asset quality review") should, however, facilitate comparisons of banks and can set limits on remuneration of shareholders and managers. Verdict, October 26, 2014! This review of current assets in Europe is probably in the right direction, but still insufficient to stem the above mistakes and restore confidence. This is also why financial innovations continue to escalate: to escape controls to restore profit levels before the crisis for the big banks who feel "supported." These behaviors do not encourage the wisdom and confidence building. In this modest and partial census, many gambles committed and uncertainty is required. The central issue is the following fact: "*Should we maintain Wild West sheriffs without*?"

Further Reading

Year 2014 Financial Professions (collective work). *How finance can contribute to the recovery*. Work under the direction of Denise Flouzat Osmont Amilly and Pierre-Henri Cassou. M. Roux, *The finance otherwise: myth, reality and questions for financial professionals*, forthcoming. Revue Banque Edition, France.

French Association of Corporate Governance (AFGE), Letter No. 38, 3rd Quarter 2014. M. Roux, *Bank: End of a monopoly, Ending a model ...?* (pp. 8–12). AFGE.

Roux, M. *Finance ethics: Structures, actors and perspectives in France*, Editions Revue Bank. Books nominated Turgot Prize for the best book of Financial Economics, honorable mention in 2005. Revue Banque Edition, France.

Roux Collection. Master. Directed by Jacques Igallens. *Retail banking*. Eska editions. Books nominated Turgot Prize for the best book of Financial Economics, honorable mention 2010 class collective work in October 2010. ESKA Edition, France.

Roux, M. (2013, September). *Management of the bank: new risks for new forms of governance*. Vuibert Edition, France.